Edexcel

Advanced Economics

Peter Smith

Philip Allan Updates
Market Place
Deddington
Oxfordshire
OX15 0SE

tel: 01869 338652
fax: 01869 337590
e-mail: sales@philipallan.co.uk
www.philipallan.co.uk

ISBN-13: 978-1-84489-209-9
ISBN-10: 1-84489-209-3

This textbook has been written specifically to support students studying Edexcel Advanced Economics. The content has been neither approved nor endorsed by London Qualifications and remains the sole responsibility of the author.

All website addresses included in this book are correct at the time of going to press but may subsequently change.

All photographs are reproduced by permission of Topfoto, except where otherwise specified.

Design and artwork by Juha Sorsa and Dianne Shaw
Printed by Ian Allan Printing Ltd, Hersham

Environmental information
The paper on which this title is printed is sourced from managed, sustainable forests.

P00730

Contents

Introduction vii

Part 1 Markets: how they work

Chapter 1 Introducing economics 2
Chapter 2 Specialisation and international trade 12
Chapter 3 Demand, supply and equilibrium 20
Chapter 4 Applying demand and supply analysis 39
Chapter 5 Prices and resource allocation 50
Review section 64

Part 2 Markets: why they fail

Chapter 6 Introducing market failure 70
Chapter 7 Monopoly and market dominance 78
Chapter 8 Externalities 90
Chapter 9 Public goods, information problems and equity 102
Chapter 10 Government intervention and government failure 113
Review section 131

Part 3 Managing the economy

Chapter 11 Measuring economic performance 138
Chapter 12 Aggregate demand, aggregate supply and equilibrium output 155
Chapter 13 Macroeconomic policy objectives 168
Chapter 14 Economic growth 180
Chapter 15 Policy: supply or demand? 193
Review section 205

Part 4 Industrial economics

Chapter 16 Firms and their motivations 212
Chapter 17 Market structure: perfect competition and monopoly 230
Chapter 18 Market structure: monopolistic competition and oligopoly 245
Chapter 19 Pricing strategies and contestable markets 264
Chapter 20 Competition policy and regulation 273
Review section 291

Part 5 Labour markets

Chapter 21 The demand and supply of labour and market equilibrium 300
Chapter 22 Wage differentials, discrimination and the trade unions 312
Chapter 23 Labour market imperfections 324
Chapter 24 Labour markets in the UK and EU 336
Chapter 25 Poverty and inequality 350
Review section 363

Part 6 Economic development

Chapter 26 What is development? 370
Chapter 27 Economic growth in less-developed countries 387
Chapter 28 Obstacles to growth and development 401
Chapter 29 Structural change 418
Chapter 30 Mobilising external resources for development 431
Review section 446

Part 7 The UK in the global economy

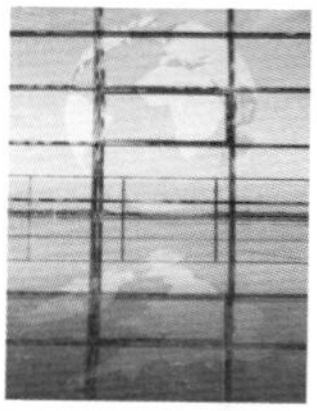

Chapter 31 Globalisation and the world economy 454
Chapter 32 The balance of payments and competitiveness 472
Chapter 33 Exchange rate systems 489
Chapter 34 European monetary union 502
Chapter 35 Economic policy 517
Review section 536

Glossary of key terms 543

Index 554

Introduction

This textbook provides an introduction to economics. It has been tailored explicitly to cover the content of the Edexcel specification for AS and A-level economics, module by module. The text provides the foundation for studying Edexcel economics, but you will no doubt wish to keep up to date by referring to additional topical sources of information about economic events. You can do this by reading the serious newspapers, visiting key sites on the internet, and by reading such magazines as *Economic Review*.

The core content of the text is as follows:

Edexcel module	Text
AS Unit 1 Markets: how they work	**Part 1:** Markets: how they work Chapters 1–5
AS Unit 2 Markets: why they fail	**Part 2:** Markets: why they fail Chapters 6–10
AS Unit 3 Managing the economy	**Part 3:** Managing the economy Chapters 11–15
Advanced Unit 4 Industrial economics	**Part 4:** Industrial economics Chapters 16–20
Advanced Unit 5 Option A Labour markets	**Part 5:** Labour markets Chapters 21–25
Advanced Unit 5 Option B Economic development	**Part 6:** Economic development Chapters 26–30
Advanced Unit 6 The UK in the global economy	**Part 7:** The UK in the global economy Chapters 31–35

The text features the following:

- a statement of the intended learning outcomes for each chapter
- clear and concise but comprehensive explanation and analysis of economic terms and concepts
- definitions of key terms
- examples to show these concepts applied to real-world situations
- exercises to provide active engagement with economic analysis
- sample examination questions at the end of each of the seven parts of the book, i.e. for each module of the specification

A separate Teacher Answer Guide is available that provides complete answers to all exercises, plus answers and some commentary on the sample exam questions.

Assessment objectives

In common with other economics specifications, Edexcel economics entails four assessment objectives. Candidates will therefore be expected to:

- demonstrate knowledge and understanding of the specified content
- apply knowledge and critical understanding to problems and issues arising from both familiar and unfamiliar situations
- analyse economic problems and issues
- evaluate economic arguments and evidence, making informed judgements

In the overall assessment of the A-level, the four assessment objectives count equally. However, there is a greater weighting given to the first two objectives in AS, and a greater weighting to the final two objectives in A2.

In addition, the final Unit 6 is a *synoptic* unit, which tests understanding of the connections between different elements of the subject, and which relates to all of the assessment objectives. This will test the ability to:

- understand the interrelatedness of many economic issues, problems and institutions
- understand how certain economic concepts, theories and techniques may be relevant to a range of different contexts
- apply such concepts, theories and techniques in analysing economic issues and problems and in evaluating arguments and evidence

(See the Edexcel AS/A GCE in Economics Specification at **http://www.edexcel.org.uk**.)

The subject

Economics is different from some other A-level subjects in that relatively few students will have studied it before embarking on the AS course. The text therefore begins from the beginning, and provides a thorough foundation in the subject and its applications. By studying this book, you should develop an awareness of the economist's approach to issues and problems, and the economist's way of thinking about the world.

The study of economics also requires a familiarity with recent economic events in the UK and elsewhere, and candidates will be expected to show familiarity with 'recent historical data' — broadly defined as covering the last 7–10 years. The following websites will help you to keep up to date with recent trends and events:

- Recent and historical data about the UK economy can be found at the website of the Office for National Statistics (ONS) at: **http://www.statistics.gov.uk/**
- Also helpful is the site of HM Treasury at: **http://www.hm-treasury.gov.uk/**
- The Bank of England site is well worth a visit, especially the *Inflation Report* and the Minutes of the Monetary Policy Committee: **http://www.bankofengland.co.uk/**

- The Institute for Fiscal Studies offers an independent view of a range of economic topics: **http://www.ifs.org.uk**

For information about other countries, visit the following:

- **http://www.oecd.org/home/**
- **http://europa.eu.int/**
- **http://www.worldbank.org/**
- **http://www.undp.org/**

Another way of keeping up to date with economic topics and events is to read *Economic Review*, a magazine specifically written for A-level economics students which comes out four times during the academic year (also published by Philip Allan Updates).

How to study economics

There are two crucial aspects of studying economics. The first stage is to study the theory, which helps us to explain economic behaviour. However, in studying AS and A2 economics it is equally important to be able to *apply* the theories and concepts that you meet, and to see just how these relate to the real world.

If you are to become competent at this, it is vital that you get plenty of practice. In part, this means doing the exercises included in this book. However, it also means thinking about how economics helps us to explain news items and data that appear in the newspapers and on the television. Make sure that you practise as much as you can.

In economics, it is important to be able to produce examples of economic phenomena. You will find some examples in this book that help to illustrate ideas and concepts. Do not rely solely on the examples provided here, but be aware of what is going on in the world and find your own examples. Keep a note of these ready for use in essays and exams. This will help to convince the examiners that you have understood economics. It will also help you to understand the theories.

Enjoy economics

Most important of all, I hope that you will enjoy your study of economics. I have always been fascinated by the subject and hope that you will capture something of the excitement and challenge of learning about how markets and the economy operate. I wish you every success with your AS/A-level studies.

Acknowledgements

I would like to express my deep gratitude to Russell Dudley-Smith, whose careful reading of the first draft of the book and thoughtful and helpful comments were invaluable in improving the scope and focus of the book. I would also like to thank everyone at Philip Allan Updates, especially Penny Fisher and David Cross, for their efficiency in the production of this book, and also for their support and encouragement.

I am grateful to London Qualifications Ltd (trading as Edexcel) for permission to reproduce past examination questions.

Many of the data series shown in figures in this book were drawn from the National Statistics website: **www.statistics.gov.uk**. Crown copyright material is reproduced with the permission of the Controller of HMSO.

Other data were from various sources, including OECD, World Bank, United Nations Development Programme and elsewhere as specified.

Whilst every effort has been made to trace the owners of copyright material, I would like to apologise to any copyright holders whose rights may have unwittingly been infringed.

Peter Smith

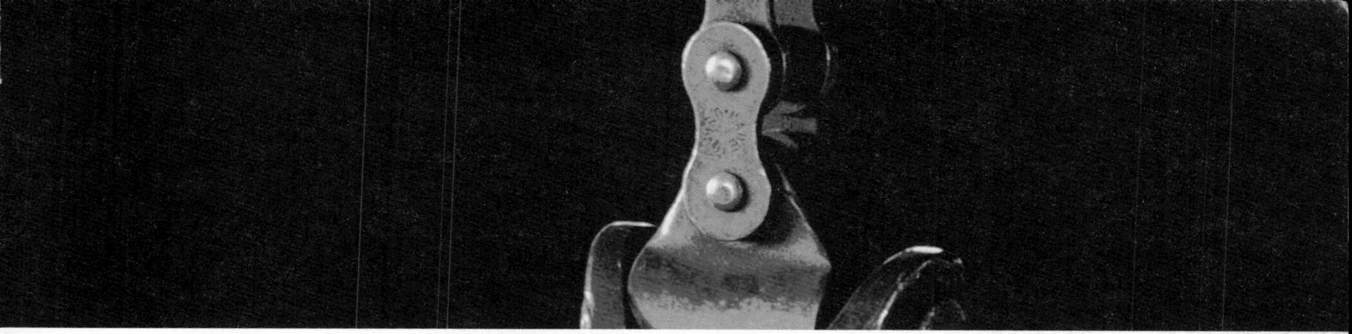

Markets: how they work

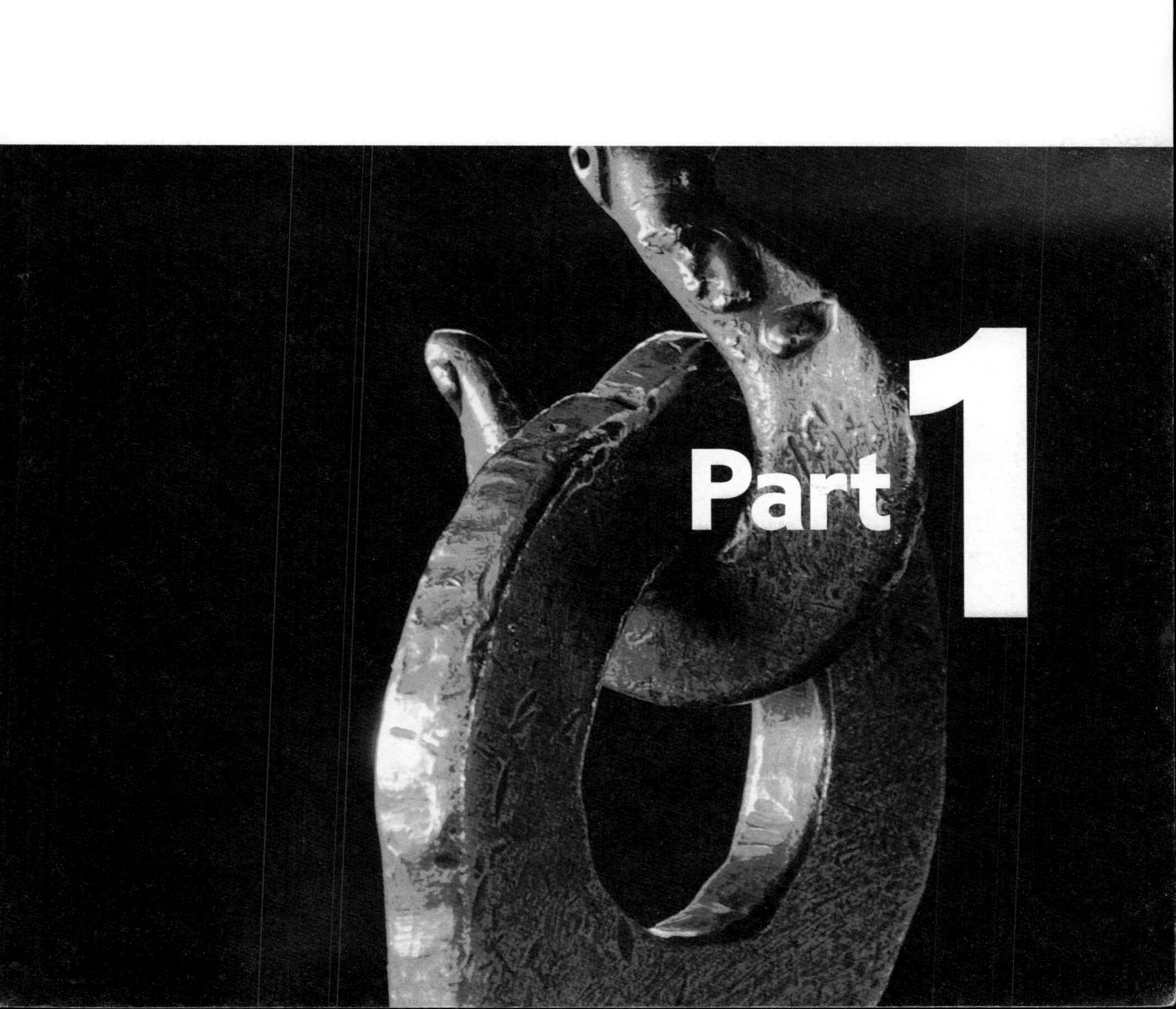

Part 1

part 1

Chapter 1

Introducing economics

Welcome to economics. Many of you opening this book will be meeting economics for the first time, and you will want to know what is in store for you as you set out to study the subject. This opening chapter sets the scene by introducing you to some key ideas and identifying the scope of economic analysis. As you learn more of the subject, you will find that economics is a way of thinking that will broaden your perspective on the world around you.

Learning outcomes

This chapter will introduce you to:

- the nature and scope of economic analysis
- the distinction between microeconomics and macroeconomics
- the notion of factors of production
- the role of models and assumptions in economics
- the production possibility frontier
- positive and normative statements

The fundamental economic problem

For any society in the world, the fundamental economic problem faced is that of **scarcity**. You might think that this is obvious for some societies in the less-developed world, where poverty and hunger are rife. But it is also true for relatively prosperous economies such as those of Switzerland, the USA or the UK.

Key term

scarcity: a situation that arises when people have unlimited wants in the face of limited resources

It is true in the sense that all societies have *finite resources*, but people have *unlimited wants.* A big claim? Not really. There is no country in the world in which all wants can be met, and this is clearly true at the global level.

Talking about *scarcity* in this sense is not the same as talking about *poverty*. Poverty might be seen as an extreme form of scarcity, in which individuals lack the basic necessities of life; whereas even relatively prosperous people face scarcity, because resources are limited.

Scarcity and choice

The key issue that arises from the existence of scarcity is that it forces people to make choices. Each individual must choose which goods and services to consume. In other words, everyone needs to prioritise the consumption of whatever commodities they need or would like to have, as they cannot satisfy all their wants. Similarly, at the national level governments have to make choices between alternative uses of resources.

It is this need to choose that underlies the subject matter of economics. Economic analysis is all about analysing those choices made by individual people, firms or governments.

Opportunity cost

This raises one of the most important concepts in all of economic analysis — the notion of **opportunity cost**. When an individual chooses to consume one good, she does so at the cost of the item that would have been next in her list of priorities. For example, suppose you are on a strict diet, and at the end of the day you can 'afford' either one chocolate or a piece of cheese. If you choose the cheese, the opportunity cost of the cheese is the chocolate that you could have had instead.

> ***Key term***
>
> **opportunity cost:** in decision-making, the value of the next best alternative that could have been chosen

This important notion can be applied in many different contexts, because whenever you make a decision you reject an alternative in favour of your chosen option. You have chosen to read this book — when instead you could be watching TV or meeting friends.

Exercise 1.1

Andrew has just started his AS, and has chosen to take economics, mathematics, geography and French. Although he was certain about the first three, it was a close call between French and English. What is Andrew's opportunity cost of choosing French?

As you move further into studying economics, you will encounter this notion of opportunity cost again and again. For example, firms take decisions about the sort of economic activity in which to engage. Or a market gardener has to decide whether to plant onions or potatoes; if he decides to grow onions, he has to forgo the opportunity to grow potatoes. From the government's point of view, if it decides to devote more resources to the National Health Service, then it will have fewer resources available for, say, defence.

The coordination problem

With so many different individuals and organisations (consumers, firms, governments) all taking decisions, a major question is how it all comes together. How are

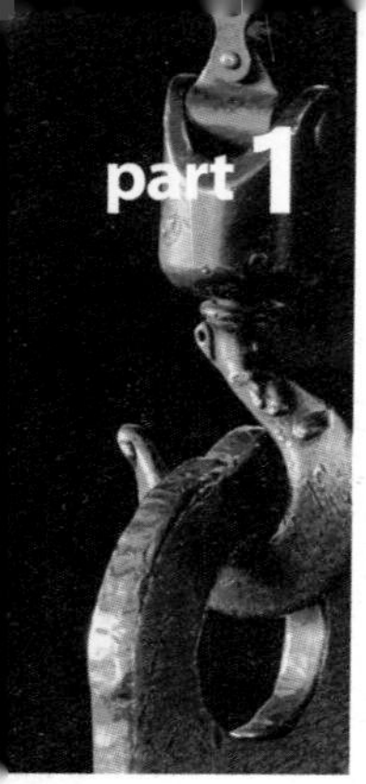

all these separate decisions coordinated so that the overall allocation of resources in a society is coherent? In other words, how can it be ensured that firms produce the commodities that consumers wish to consume? And how can the distribution of these products be organised? These are some of the basic questions that economics sets out to answer.

A *market economy* is one in which market forces are allowed to guide the allocation of resources within a society. Prices play a key role in this sort of system.

In contrast, a *centrally planned economy* is one in which the government undertakes the coordination role, planning and directing the allocation of resources. The collapse of the Soviet bloc in the 1990s largely discredited this approach, although a small number of countries (North Korea, Cuba) continue to stick with central planning.

Most economies operate a *mixed economy* system, in which market forces are complemented by some state intervention. It has been argued that any such state intervention should be *market-friendly*; in other words, when governments do intervene in the economy, they should do so in a way that helps markets to work, rather than trying to have the government replace market forces.

Factors of production

People in a society play two quite different roles. On the one hand, they are the consumers, the ultimate beneficiaries of the process of production. On the other, they are a key part of the production process in that they are instrumental in producing goods and services.

More generally, it is clear that both *human resources* and *physical resources* are required as part of the production process. These productive resources are known as the **factors of production**.

> ***Key term***
>
> **factors of production:** resources used in the production process; *inputs* into production, in particular including labour, capital, land and entrepreneurship

The most obvious human resource is *labour*. Labour is a key input into production. Of course, there are many different types of labour, encompassing different skill levels and working in different ways. *Entrepreneurship* is another key human resource. An entrepreneur is someone who organises production and identifies projects to be undertaken, often bearing the risk of the activity. *Management* might also be classified as a key human resource. *Natural resources* are also inputs into the production process. In particular, all economic activities require some use of *land*, and most use some raw materials. An important distinction here is between *renewable resources* such as forests, and *non-renewable resources* such as oil or coal.

There are also *produced resources*, inputs that are the product of a manufacturing process. For example, machines are used in the production process; they are resources manufactured for the purpose of producing other goods. These inputs are referred to as *capital*, which may include things like factory buildings and transport equipment as well as plant and machinery.

Factors of production — labour (workers), capital (buildings) and land.

The way in which these inputs are combined in order to produce output is another key part of the allocation of resources. Firms need to take decisions about the mix of inputs used in order to produce their output. Such decisions are required in whatever form of economic activity a firm is engaged.

Exercise 1.2

Classify each of the following as human, natural (renewable or non-renewable) or produced resources:

a timber
b services of a window cleaner
c natural gas
d solar energy
e a combine harvester
f a computer programmer who sets up a company to market his software
g a computer

By now you should be getting some idea of the subject matter of economics. The American economist Paul Samuelson (who won the Nobel Prize for Economic Sciences in 1970) identified three key questions that economics sets out to investigate:

1. *What?* What goods and services should be produced in a society from its scarce resources? In other words, how should resources be allocated among producing DVD players, potatoes, banking services and so on?
2. *How?* How should the productive resources of the economy be used to produce these various goods and services?
3. *For whom?* Having produced a range of goods and services, how should be these allocated among the population for consumption?

Summary

- The fundamental problem faced by any society is scarcity, because resources are finite but wants are unlimited. As a result, choices need to be made.
- Each choice has an opportunity cost — the value of the next-best alternative.
- Decisions need to be coordinated within a society, either by market forces or by state intervention, or a mixture of the two.
- The amount of output produced in a period depends upon the inputs of factors of production.
- Economics deals with the questions of what should be produced, how it should be produced, and for whom.

Models and assumptions

Economics sets out to tackle some complex issues concerning what is a very complex real world. This complexity is such that it is essential to simplify reality in some way; otherwise the task would be overwhelming. Economists thus work with **models**. These are simplified versions of reality that are more tractable for analysis, allowing economists to focus on some key aspects of the world.

Often this works by allowing them to focus on one thing at a time. A model almost always begins with assumptions that help economists to simplify their questions. These assumptions can then be gradually relaxed so that the effect of each one of them can be observed. In this way economists can gradually move towards a more complicated version of reality.

To evaluate a model, it is not necessary that it be totally realistic. The model's desired objectives may help in predicting future behaviour, or in testing empirical evidence collected from the real world. If a model provides insights into how individuals take decisions, or helps to explain economic events, then it has some value, even if it seems remote from reality.

However, it is always important to examine the assumptions that are made, and to ask what happens if these assumptions do not hold.

> ***Key terms***
>
> **model:** a simplified representation of reality used to provide insight into economic decisions and events
>
> **production possibility frontier (PPF):** curve showing the maximum combinations of goods or services that can be produced in a given period with available resources

The production possibility frontier

Economists rely heavily on diagrams to help in their analysis. In exploring the notion of opportunity cost, a helpful diagram is the **production possibility frontier (PPF)**. This shows the maximum combinations of goods that can be produced with a given set of resources.

First consider a simple example. In an earlier exercise Andrew was studying for his AS. Suppose now that he has got behind with his homework. He has limited time available, and has five economics questions to answer and five maths exercises. An economics question takes the same time to answer as a maths exercise.

What are the options? Suppose he knows that in the time available he can either tackle all the maths and none of the economics, or all of the economics and none of the maths. Alternatively, he can try to keep both teachers happy by doing some of each. Figure 1.1 shows his options. He can devote all of his efforts to maths, and leave the economics for another day. He will then be at point *A* on in the figure. Alternatively, he can do all the economics exercises and no maths, and be at point *B*. The line joining these two extreme points shows the intermediate possibilities. For example, at *C* he does 2 economics exercises and 3 maths problems.

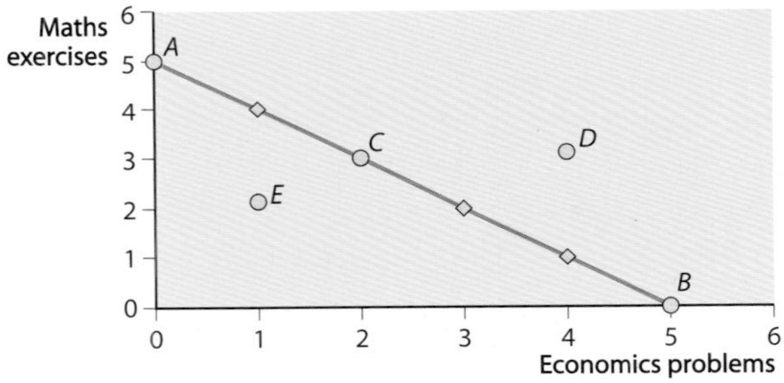

Figure 1.1
The production possibility frontier

The line shows the maximum combinations that Andrew can tackle – which is why it is called a 'frontier'. There is no way he can manage to be beyond the frontier (for example at point *D*), as he does not have the time (i.e. resources) to do so. However, he could end up *inside* the frontier, at a point such as *E*. This could happen if he gives up, and squanders his time by watching television; that would be an inefficient use of his resources – at least in terms of tackling his homework.

As Andrew moves down the line from left to right, he is spending more time on economics and less on maths. The opportunity cost of tackling an additional economics question is an additional maths exercise forgone.

Consumption and investment

To move from thinking about an individual to thinking about an economy as a whole, it is first necessary to simplify reality. Assume an economy that produces just two types of good: capital goods and consumer goods. Consumer goods are for present use, whereas the capital goods are to be used to increase the future capacity of the economy – in other words, for investment.

Figure 1.2 illustrates society's options in a particular period. Given the resources available, society can produce any combination of capital and consumer goods along the *PPF* line. Thus, point *A* represents one possible combination of outputs, in which

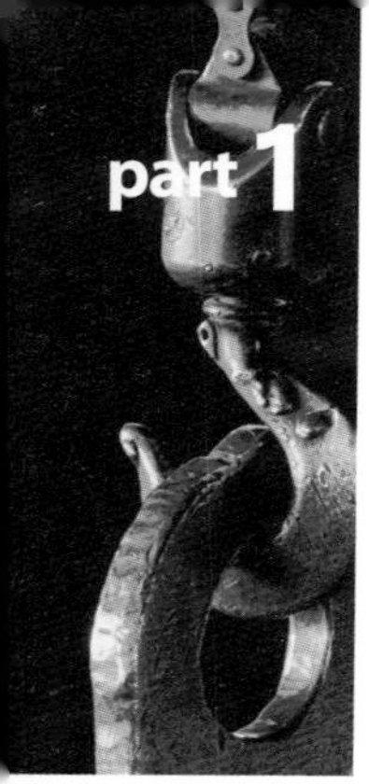

the economy produces C_1 consumer goods and K_1 capital goods. (Economists often use K to denote capital – because they normally use C to denote costs.)

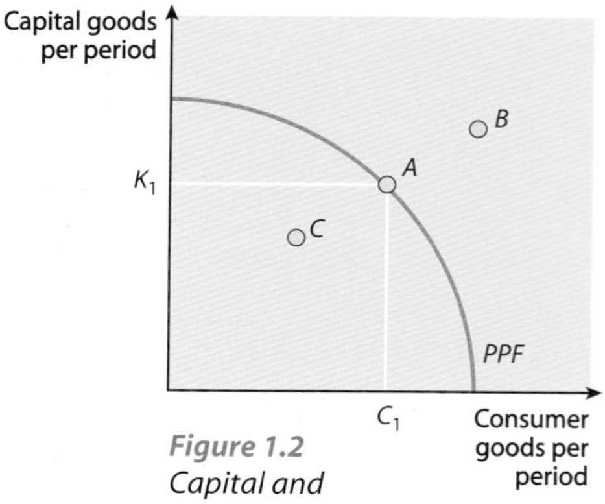

Figure 1.2
Capital and consumer goods

As with the simpler example, if society were to move to the right along the *PPF* it would produce more consumer goods – but at the expense of capital goods. Thus, it can be seen that the opportunity cost of producing consumer goods is in terms of forgone opportunities to produce capital goods. Notice that this time the *PPF* has been drawn as a curve instead of a straight line. This is because not all factors of production are equally suited to the production of both sorts of good. When the economy is well balanced, as at *A*, the factors can be allocated to the uses to which they are best equipped. However, as the economy moves towards complete specialisation in one of the types of goods, factors are no longer being best used, and the opportunity cost changes. For example, if nearly all of the workers are engaged in producing consumer goods, it becomes more difficult to produce still more of these, whereas those workers producing machinery find they have too few resources with which to work. In other words, the more consumer goods are being produced, the higher is their opportunity cost.

It is now possible to interpret points *B* and *C*. Point *B* is unreachable given present resources, so the economy cannot produce that combination of goods. This applies to any point outside the *PPF*. On the other hand, at point *C* society is not using its resources efficiently. In this position there is *unemployment* of some resources in the economy. By making better use of the resources available, the economy can move towards the frontier, reducing unemployment in the process.

Economic growth

Figure 1.2 focused on a single period. However, if the economy is producing capital goods, then in the following period its capacity to produce should increase, as it will have more resources available for production. How can this be shown on the diagram? An expansion in the available inputs suggests that in the next period the economy should be able to produce more of both goods. This is shown in Figure 1.3.

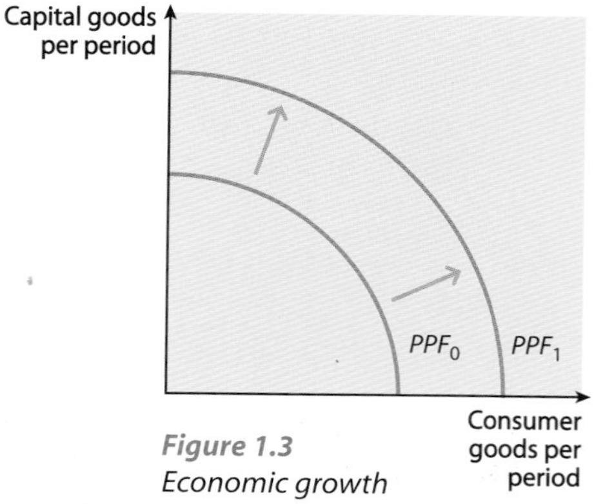

Figure 1.3
Economic growth

In the initial period the production possibility frontier is at PPF_0. However, in the following period the increased availability of resources enables greater production, and the frontier moves to PPF_1. This is a process of **economic growth**, an expansion of the economy's productive capacity through the increased availability of inputs.

Notice that the decision to produce more capital goods today means that fewer consumer goods will be produced today. People must choose between 'more jam today' or 'more jam tomorrow'.

Key terms

economic growth: an expansion in the productive capacity of the economy

gross domestic product (GDP): a measure of the economic activity carried out in an economy over a period

Total output in an economy

Remember that the PPF is a model: a much simplified version of reality. In a real economy there are many different goods and services produced by a wide range of different factors of production – but it is not possible to draw diagrams to show all of them.

The total output of an economy like the UK is measured by its **gross domestic product (GDP)**.

By calculating the *average* level of GDP per person in a country, it is possible to derive a measure of the average amount of resources per person – or average income per head.

Exercise 1.3

Beverly has been cast away on a desert island, and has to survive by spending her time either fishing or climbing trees to get coconuts. The *PPF* in Figure 1.4 shows the maximum combinations of fish and coconuts that she can gather during a day. Which of the points *A* to *E* represent each of the following?

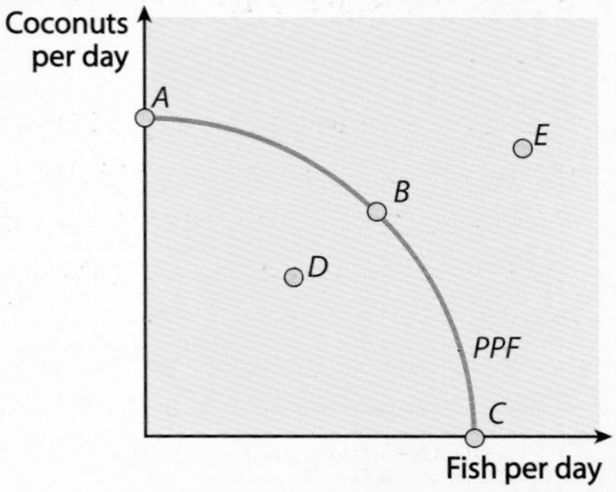

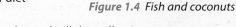

Figure 1.4 Fish and coconuts

a a situation where Beverly spends all her time fishing

b an unreachable position

c a day when Beverly goes for a balanced diet — a mixture of coconuts and fish

d a day when Beverly does not fancy fish, and spends all day collecting coconuts

e a day when Beverly spends some of the time trying to attract the attention of a passing ship

Microeconomics and macroeconomics

The discussion so far has focused sometimes on individual decisions, and sometimes on the decisions of governments, or of 'society' as a whole. Economic thinking is applied in different ways, depending on whether the focus is on the decisions taken by individual agents in the economy or on the interaction between economic variables at the level of the whole economy:

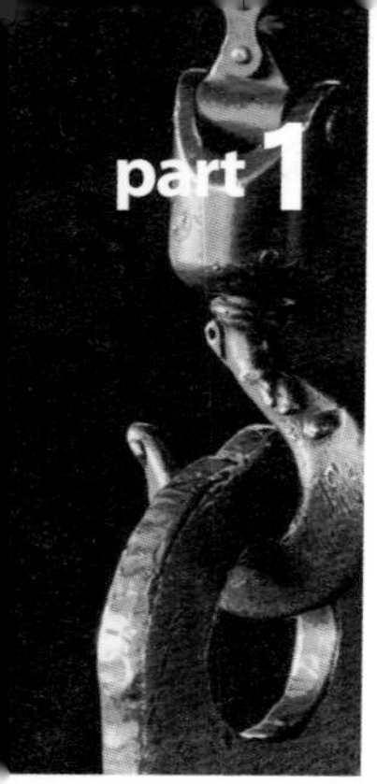

➤ **Microeconomics** deals with individual decisions taken by households or firms, or in particular markets.

➤ **Macroeconomics** examines the interactions between economic variables at the level of the aggregate economy.

In some ways the division between the two types of analysis is artificial. The same sort of economic reasoning is applied in both types, but the focus is different.

Key terms

macroeconomics: the study of the interrelationships between economic variables at an aggregate (economy-wide) level

microeconomics: the study of economic decisions taken by individual economic agents, including households and firms

positive statement: a statement about what *is*, i.e. about facts

normative statement: a statement about what *ought to be*

Positive and normative statements

Economics tries to be objective in analysis. However, some of its subject matter requires careful attention in order to retain an objective distance. In this connection, it is important to be clear about the difference between **positive** and **normative** statements.

In short, a positive statement is about *facts*. In contrast, a normative statement is about *what ought to be*. Another way of looking at this is that a statement becomes normative when it involves a *value judgement*.

Suppose the government is considering raising the tax on cigarettes. It may legitimately consult economists to discover what effect a higher tobacco tax will have on the consumption of cigarettes and on government revenues. This would be a *positive* investigation, in that the economists are being asked to use economic analysis to forecast what will happen when the tax is increased.

A very different situation will arise if the government asked whether it *should* raise the tax on cigarettes. This moves the economists beyond positive analysis, because it entails a value judgement — so it is now a *normative* analysis. There are some words that betray normative statements, such as 'should' or 'ought to' — watch for these.

Most of this book is about positive economics. However, you should be aware that positive analysis is often called upon to inform normative judgements. If the aim of a policy is to stop people from smoking (which reflects a normative judgement about what *ought* to happen), then economic analysis may be used to highlight the strengths and weaknesses of those alternatives in a purely positive fashion.

Critics of economics often joke that economists always disagree with one another; for example, it has been said that if you put five economists in a room together they will come up with at least six conflicting opinions. However, although economists may arrive at different value judgements, and thus have differences when it comes to normative issues, there is much greater agreement when it comes to positive analysis.

Summary

- The production possibility frontier shows the maximum combinations of goods or services that can be produced in a period by a given set of resources.
- At any point on the frontier, society is making full use of all resources.
- At any point inside the frontier, there is unemployment of some resources.
- Points beyond the frontier are unattainable.
- In a simple society producing two goods (consumer goods and capital goods), the choice is between consumption, and investment for the future.
- As society increases its stock of capital goods, the productive capacity of the economy increases, and the production possibility frontier moves outwards: this may be termed 'economic growth'.
- Microeconomics deals with individual decisions made by consumers and producers, whereas macroeconomics analyses the interactions between economic variables in the aggregate — but both use similar ways of thinking.
- Positive statements are about *what is*, whereas normative statements are about *what ought to be*.

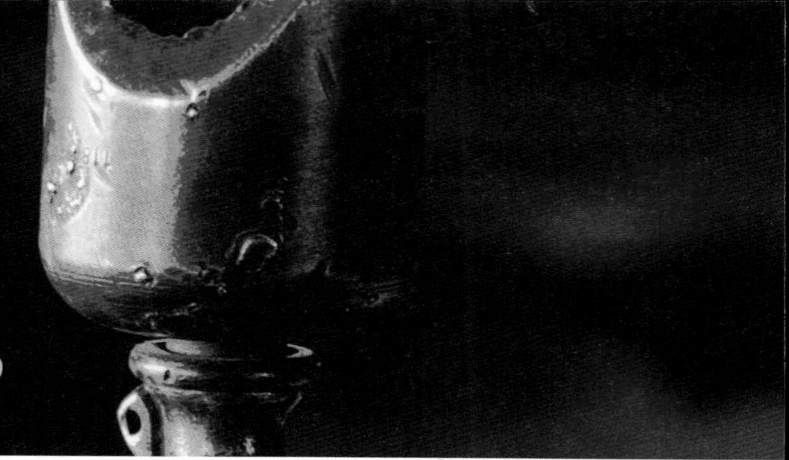

Chapter 2

Specialisation and international trade

This chapter introduces some economic ideas that have been well known for centuries, but still have great relevance today. Adam Smith wrote about the division of labour in his famous book An Inquiry into the Nature and Causes of the Wealth of Nations *in 1776. A few years later, in 1817, David Ricardo discussed the principle of comparative advantage. Nearly 300 years on, governments are still reluctant to take on board the full implications of the law of comparative advantage, as can be seen by the many bitter disputes between nations over the tricky matter of restrictions on international trade. However, some ideas must be understood before you can move on to these issues.*

Learning outcomes

After studying this chapter, you should:

- understand the concept of the division of labour
- see how specialisation can improve productivity
- be familiar with notions of absolute and comparative advantage
- realise how countries may be able to gain from engaging in international trade
- be aware of the risks that come from over-specialisation
- become aware of the patterns in world trade, in particular between the UK, the EU and the rest of the world

Specialisation

How many workers does it take to make a pin? Adam Smith figured that 10 was about the right number. He argued that when a worker was producing pins on his own, carrying out all the various stages involved in the production process, the maximum number of pins that could be produced in one day was 20 — given the technology of his day, of course. This would imply that 10 workers could produce about 200 pins if they worked in the same way as the lone worker. However, if the pin production process were broken into 10 separate stages, with one worker specialising in each stage, the maximum production for a day's work would be a staggering 48 000. This is known as **division of labour**.

Key term

division of labour: a process whereby the production procedure is broken down into a sequence of stages, and workers are assigned to particular stages

The division of labour is effective because individual workers become skilled at performing specialised tasks. By focusing on a particular stage, they can become highly adept, and thus more efficient, at carrying out that task. In any case, people are not all the same, so some are better at different activities. Furthermore, this specialisation is more efficient because workers do not spend time moving from one activity to another. Specialisation may also enable firms to operate on a larger scale of production. You will see later that this may be advantageous.

This can be seen in practice in many businesses today, where there is much specialisation of functions. Workers are hired for particular tasks and activities. You do not see Wayne Rooney pulling on the goalkeeper's jersey at half time because he fancies a change. In Chapter 1 it was argued that 'labour' is considered a factor of production. This idea will now be developed further by arguing that there are different types of labour, having different skills and functions.

At another level, firms and even nations specialise in particular kinds of activities. This leads to the theory of comparative advantage.

Absolute and comparative advantage

Everyone is different. Individuals have different natural talents and abilities that make them good at different things. Indeed, there are some lucky people who seem to be better at everything.

Consider this example. Colin and Debbie try to supplement their incomes by working at weekends. They have both been to evening classes and have attended pottery and jewellery-making classes. At weekends they make pots and bracelets. Depending on how they divide their time, they can make differing combinations of these goods; some of the possibilities are shown in Table 2.1.

Colin		Debbie	
Pots	Bracelets	Pots	Bracelets
12	0	18	0
9	3	12	12
6	6	6	24
3	9	3	30
0	12	0	36

Table 2.1 Colin and Debbie's production

The first point to notice is that Debbie is much better at both activities than Colin. If they each devote all their time to producing pots, Colin produces only 12 to Debbie's 18. If they each produce only bracelets, Colin produces 12 and Debbie, 36.

This illustrates **absolute advantage**. Debbie is simply better than Colin at both activities. Another way of looking at this is that, in order to produce a given quantity of a good, Debbie needs less labour time than Colin.

There is another significant feature of this table. Although Debbie is better at producing both goods, the difference is much more marked in the case of bracelet production than for pot production. So Debbie is relatively more proficient in bracelet production; in other words, she has a **comparative advantage** in making bracelets. This can be illustrated in terms of opportunity cost. If Debbie switches from producing pots to producing bracelets, she gives up 6 pots for every 12 additional bracelets that she makes. The opportunity cost of an additional bracelet is thus 6/12 = 0.5 pot. For Colin, there is a one-to-one trade-off between the two, so his opportunity cost of a bracelet is 1 pot.

More interesting is what happens if the same calculation is made for Colin and pot-making. Although Debbie is absolutely better at making pots, if Colin increases his production of pots, his opportunity cost in terms of bracelets is still 1. But for Debbie the opportunity cost of making pots in terms of bracelets is 12/6 = 2, so Colin has the lower opportunity cost. Although Debbie has an *absolute* advantage in pot-making, Colin has a *comparative* advantage.

Why does comparative advantage matter? It illustrates the potential benefits to be gained from specialisation. Suppose that both Colin and Debbie divide their time between the two activities in such a way that Colin produces 6 pots and 6 bracelets, and Debbie produces 6 pots and 24 bracelets. Between them, they will have produced 12 pots and 30 bracelets. However, if they each specialise in the product in which they have a comparative advantage, their joint production will increase. If Colin devotes all his time to pottery, he produces 12 pots, while Debbie, focusing only on bracelets, produces 36. So between them they will have produced the same number of pots as before — but 6 extra bracelets.

Key terms

absolute advantage: the ability to produce a good more efficiently (e.g. with less labour)

comparative advantage: the ability to produce a good *relatively* more efficiently, i.e. at a lower opportunity cost

law of comparative advantage: a theory arguing that there may be gains from trade arising when countries (or individuals) specialise in the production of goods or services in which they have a comparative advantage

The **law of comparative advantage** states that overall output can be increased if all individuals specialise in producing the goods in which they have a comparative advantage.

One final point before leaving Colin and Debbie. Figure 2.1 shows their respective production possibility frontiers (*PPFs*). You can check this by graphing the points in Table 2.1 and joining them up. In this case the *PPFs* are straight lines. You can see that Debbie has an absolute advantage because her *PPF* lies entirely above Colin's. The differences

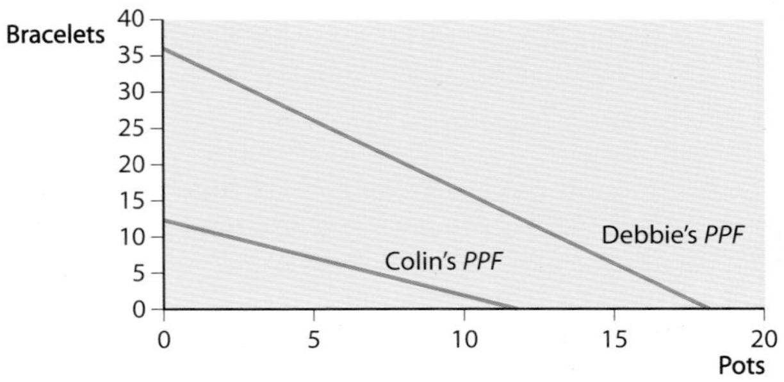

Figure 2.1 Colin and Debbie's production possibilities

in comparative advantage are shown by the fact that the two *PPF*s have different slopes, as the opportunity cost element is related to the slope of the *PPF* — the rate at which one good is sacrificed for more of the other.

Gains from international trade

This same principle can be applied in the context of international trade. Suppose there are two countries — call them Anywhere and Somewhere. Each country can produce combinations of agricultural goods and manufactures. However, Anywhere has a comparative advantage in producing manufactured goods, and Somewhere has comparative advantage in agricultural goods. Their respective *PPF*s are shown in Figure 2.2.

International trade can bring economic benefits to all.

You can see the pattern of comparative advantage reflected in the different slopes of the countries' *PPF*s. If the countries each produce some of each of the goods, one possibility (chosen for simplicity) is that they produce at point *A*, which is the intersection of the two *PPF*s. At this point each country produces 20 units of manufactures and 20 units of agricultural goods. Total world output is thus 40 units of manufactures and 40 units of agricultural goods — this point is marked on the figure.

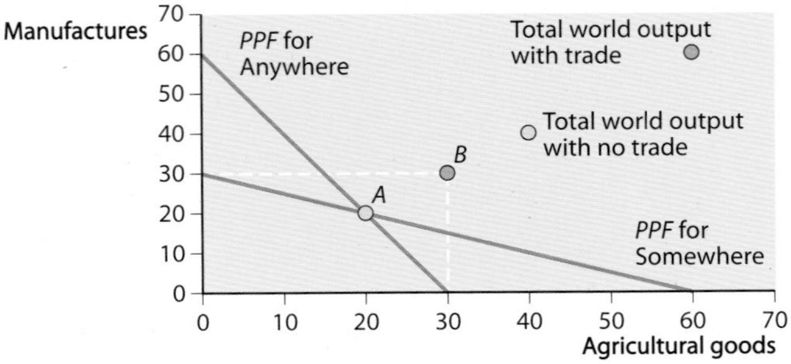

Figure 2.2 PPFs for Anywhere and Somewhere

However, suppose each country were to specialise in the product in which it has a comparative advantage. Anywhere could produce 60 units of manufactured products, and Somewhere could produce 60 units of agricultural goods. Then if they were to engage in trade, one possible outcome is point *B*, where they would

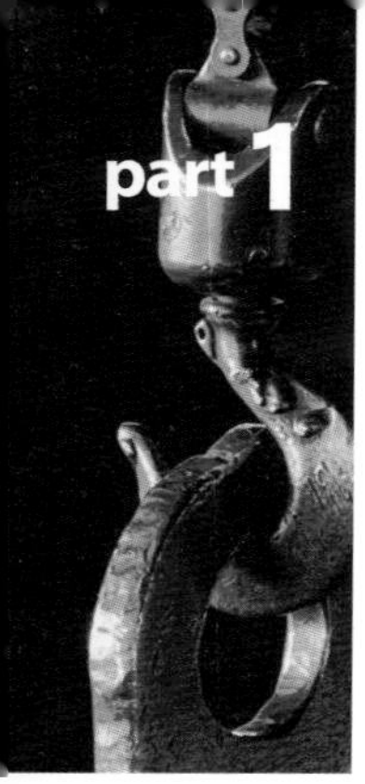

each now have 30 units of each good, leaving them both unequivocally better off: they would each have more of both commodities. The figure shows that total world output of each type of good has increased by 20 units.

It can be seen that in this situation trade may be mutually beneficial. Notice that this particular result of trading has assumed that the countries exchange the goods on a one-to-one basis. Although this exchange rate makes both better off, it is not the only possibility. It is possible that exchange will take place at different prices for the goods, and clearly, the prices at which exchange takes place will determine which of the countries will gain most from the trade that occurs.

Exercise 2.1

Figure 2.3 shows production possibility frontiers for two countries, each of which produces both coats and scooters. The countries are called 'Here' and 'There'.

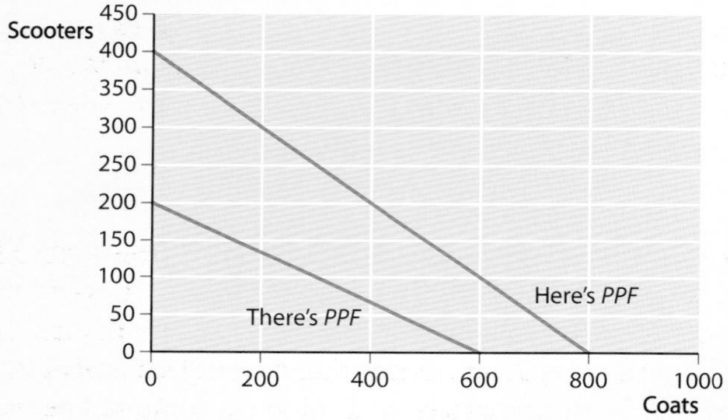

Figure 2.3 Coats and scooters

a Which country has an absolute advantage in the production of both commodities?

b Which country has a comparative advantage in the production of coats?

c Which country has a comparative advantage in the production of scooters?

d Suppose that Here produces 200 scooters and There produces 100: how many coats are produced in each country?

e Now suppose that 300 scooters and 200 coats are produced by Here, and that There produces only coats. What has happened to total production of coats and scooters?

In the above examples and exercises, specialisation and trade are seen to lead to higher overall production of goods. Although the examples have related to goods, you should be equally aware that services too may be a source of specialisation and trade. This is potentially important for an economy like the UK, where there is a comparative advantage in the provision of financial services.

Who gains from international trade?

Specialisation can result in an overall increase in total production. However, one of the fundamental questions of economics in Chapter 1 was 'for whom?' So far nothing has been said about which of the countries will gain from trade. It is possible that exchange can take place between countries in such a way that both countries are better off. But whether this will actually happen in practice depends on the prices at which exchange takes place. After analysing the way in which prices come to be determined in various markets, this question will be revisited, as the rate at which commodities are exchanged between nations will have important implications for determining who gains from trade.

In particular, specialisation may bring dangers and risks, as well as benefits. One obvious way in which this may be relevant is that, by specialising, a country allows some sectors to run down. For example, suppose a country came to rely on imported food, and allowed its agricultural sector to waste away. If the country then became involved in a war, or for some other reason was unable to import its food, there would clearly be serious consequences if it could no longer grow its own foodstuffs. For this reason, many countries have in place measures designed to protect their agricultural sectors — or other sectors that are seen to be strategic in nature.

Over-reliance on some commodities may also be risky. For example, the development of artificial substitutes for rubber had an enormous impact on the demand for natural rubber; this was reflected in falls in its price and caused difficulties for countries that had specialised in producing rubber.

Trade between nations

Countries all around the world engage in international trade. This is partly for obvious reasons; for example, the UK is not a sensible place to grow bananas on a commercial scale, but people living in Britain like to eat bananas. International trade enables individuals to consume goods that cannot be easily produced domestically. It makes sense for countries that have a comparative advantage in producing bananas to do so.

The extent to which countries engage in international trade varies enormously, as can be seen in Figure 2.4, which shows total trade (exports plus imports) as a percentage of GDP (a measure of the total output produced in an economy in a period of time). In some cases, the extent of dependence on trade reflects the availability of natural resources in a country, but it may also reflect political attitudes towards trade.

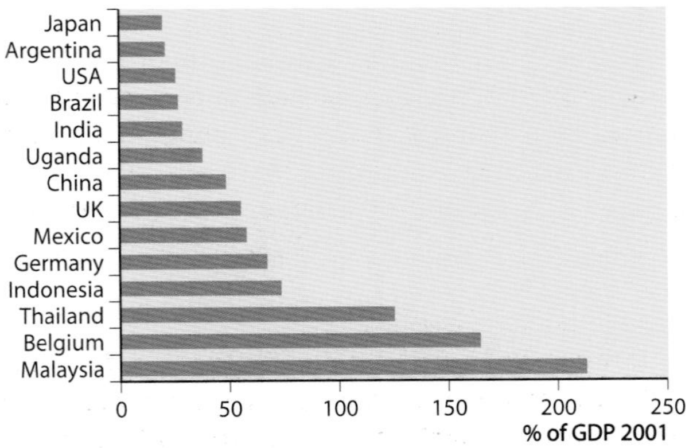

Figure 2.4 *Trade as a percentage of GDP*

Source: *Human Development Report* 2003.

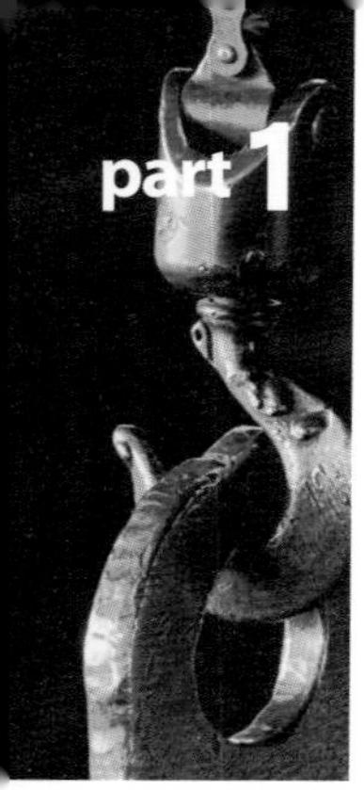

The USA has a large economy, with a wealth of natural resources, and does not depend so heavily on trade. Argentina, Brazil and India have a similar level of dependence, but this partly reflects a conscious policy over many years to limit the extent to which their economies have to rely on external trade. At the other extreme, countries like Malaysia and Thailand have followed policies that promote exports, believing that this will allow more rapid economic growth.

Moves towards closer integration between countries have strongly affected the pattern of world trade. For example, the moves towards European integration have made western Europe a major player in world trade. Something of this can be seen in Figure 2.5, which shows the destination of world exports in 2002. You can see that 40% of the world's exports head for Western Europe and 22% to North America. Asia has also become an important part of the world trade scene, with China expanding its trading at an unprecedented rate in recent years.

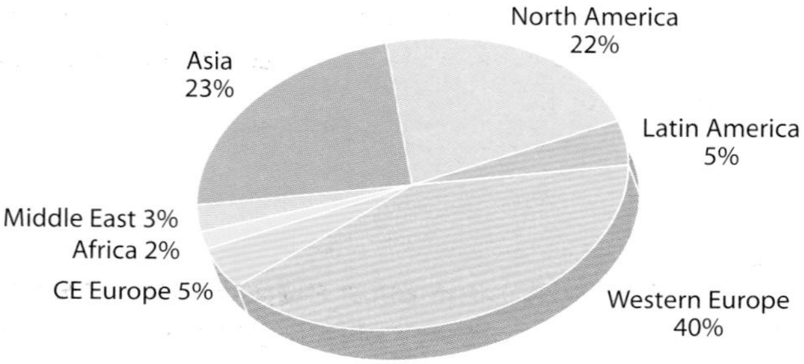

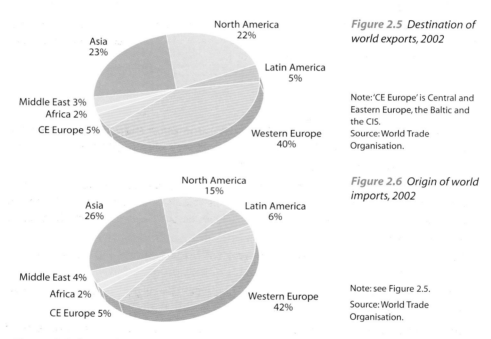

Figure 2.5 Destination of world exports, 2002

Note: 'CE Europe' is Central and Eastern Europe, the Baltic and the CIS.
Source: World Trade Organisation.

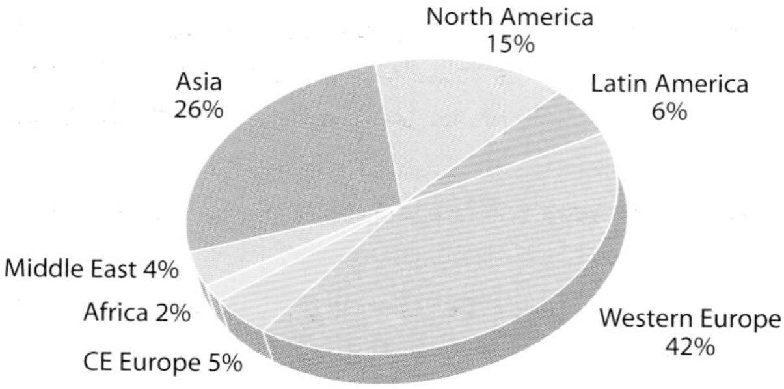

Figure 2.6 Origin of world imports, 2002

Note: see Figure 2.5.
Source: World Trade Organisation.

Figure 2.6 shows the origin of those exports. Notice that North America has a much smaller share in this diagram, indicating that it is importing far more than it is exporting. On the other hand, Asia and Western Europe were exporting more than they were importing in 2002. Given the size of its population, Africa contributes very little to world trade.

From a British perspective, there has been a move towards greater dependence on Europe for both imports and exports, although the USA remains an important trading partner. The increased share of UK exports going to the 15 members of the European Union is shown in Figure 2.7. Although the share has eased a bit since the mid-1990s, Europe remains a much more important trading partner for the UK than it was back in 1960.

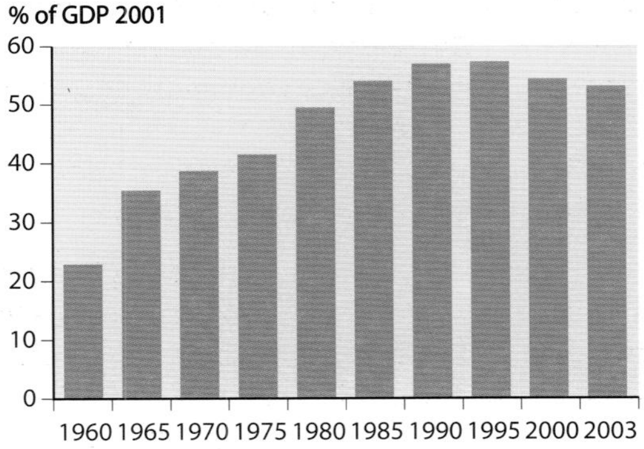

Figure 2.7 *Percentage of UK exports of goods going to the EU 15*

'EU 15' refers to the 15 countries that were members of the European Union prior to the expansion in May 2004.

Source: calculated from data in *Europa: EU Economy Annual Review 2004.*

Exercise 2.2

Next time you go shopping, make a list of the goods that you see on offer that have been imported from elsewhere in the world. See if you can detect any patterns in the sorts of goods that come from different parts of the world.

Summary

- Adam Smith introduced the notion of division of labour, which suggests that workers can become more productive by specialising in stages of the production process.
- Specialisation opens up the possibility of trade.
- The theory of comparative advantage shows that, even if one country has an absolute advantage in the production of goods and services, trade may still increase total output if each country specialises in the production of goods and services in which it has a comparative advantage.
- Who gains from specialisation and trade depends crucially on the prices at which an exchange takes place.
- Countries all around the world engage in international trade, partly in order to take advantage of the pattern of comparative advantage.
- Some countries are much more open to international trade than others, partly because of natural resource endowments but also because of political decisions.
- The UK depends heavily on trade with the USA and with countries within Europe. This has changed considerably over the past 40 years, with closer integration with Europe.

part 1

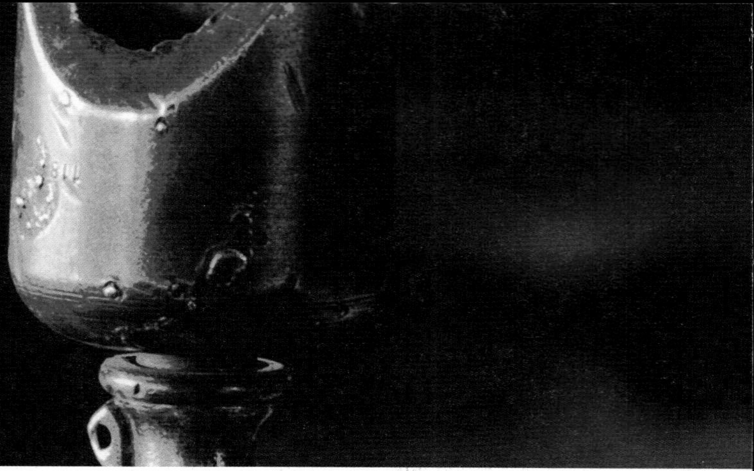

Chapter 3

Demand, supply and equilibrium

The demand and supply model is perhaps the most famous of all pieces of economic analysis, but it is also one of the most useful. It has many applications that help explain the way markets work in the real world, It is thus central to understanding economics. This chapter introduces the model. Some applications will be investigated in Chapter 4.

Learning outcomes

After studying this chapter, you should:

- be familiar with the demand curve and the factors that influence its shape and position
- be familiar with the supply curve and the factors that influence its shape and position
- be able to distinguish between movements *of* and *along* the demand and supply curves
- be familiar with the notion of equilibrium and its relevance in the demand and supply model
- be familiar with normal and inferior goods
- understand the concept of elasticity measures and appreciate their importance and applications

Demand

Consider an individual consumer. Think of yourself, and a product that you consume regularly. What factors influence your **demand** for that product? Put another way, what factors influence how much of the product you choose to buy?

When thinking about the factors that influence your demand for your chosen product, common sense will probably get you to focus on a range of different points.

> ***Key term***
>
> **demand:** the quantity of a good or service that a consumer would choose to buy at any possible price in a given period

You may think about why you enjoy consuming the product. You may focus on how much it will cost to buy the product, and whether you can afford it. You may decide that you have consumed a product so regularly that you are ready for a change; or perhaps you will see something advertised on TV, or being bought by a friend.

Whatever the influences you come up with, they can probably be categorised under four headings that ultimately determine your demand for a good. First, the *price* of the good is an important influence on your demand for it, and will affect the quantity of it that you choose to buy. Second, the *price of other goods* may be significant. Third, *your income* will determine how much of the good you can afford to purchase. Finally, almost any other factors that you may have thought of can be listed as part of your *preferences*. After a few preliminaries, each of these factors will be considered in turn.

Markets

In developing the theory of demand and supply the term **market** is frequently used, so it is important to be absolutely clear about what is meant by it.

Key term

market: a set of arrangements that allows transactions to take place

A market need not be a physical location (although it could be – you might regard the local farmers' market as an example of 'a set of arrangements that allows transactions to take place'). With the growth of the internet everyone is becoming accustomed to ways of buying and selling that do not involve direct physical contact between buyer and seller, so the notion of an abstract market should not be too alien a concept.

To focus on a particular product, a market brings together potential buyers and sellers. One can then talk of market demand in terms of the factors that influence all potential buyers of that good or service. The same four factors will be relevant in influencing market demand that influence your own decision to buy. In addition, the number of potential buyers in the market also influences the size of total demand at any price.

Demand and the price of a good

Assume for the moment that the influences mentioned other than the price of the good are held constant, so that the focus is only on the extent to which the price of a good influences your consumption of it. This is a common assumption in economics, which is sometimes expressed by the Latin phrase *ceteris paribus*, meaning 'other things being equal'. Given the complexity of the real world, it is often helpful to focus on one thing at a time.

So how is the demand for, say, DVDs, influenced by their price? Other things being equal, you would expect the demand for DVDs to be higher when the price is low and lower when the price is high. In other words, you would expect an inverse relationship between the price and the quantity demanded. This is such a strong phenomenon that it is referred to as the **law of demand**.

Key term

law of demand: a law that states that there is an inverse relationship between quantity demanded and the price of a good or service, *ceteris paribus*

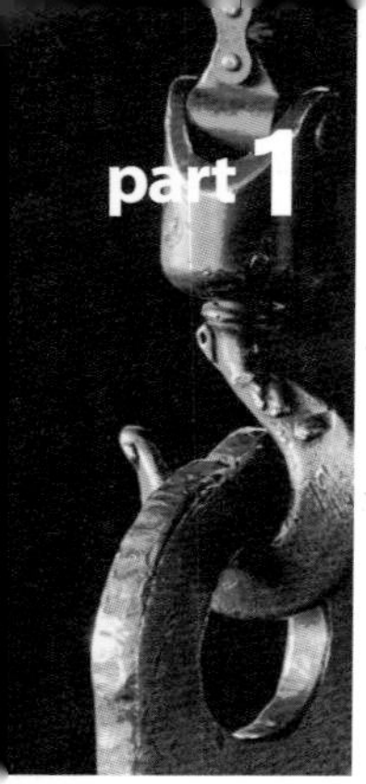

If you were to compile a list that showed how many DVDs would be bought at any possible price and plot these on a diagram, this would be called the **demand curve**. Figure 3.1 shows what this might look like. As it is an inverse relationship, the demand curve slopes downwards. Notice that this need not be a straight line: its shape depends upon how consumers react at different prices. According to this curve, if price were to be set at £40, then the quantity demanded would be 20,000 per period. However, if the price were only £20 the demand would be higher, at 60,000.

Key term

demand curve: a graph showing how much of a good will be demanded by consumers at any given price

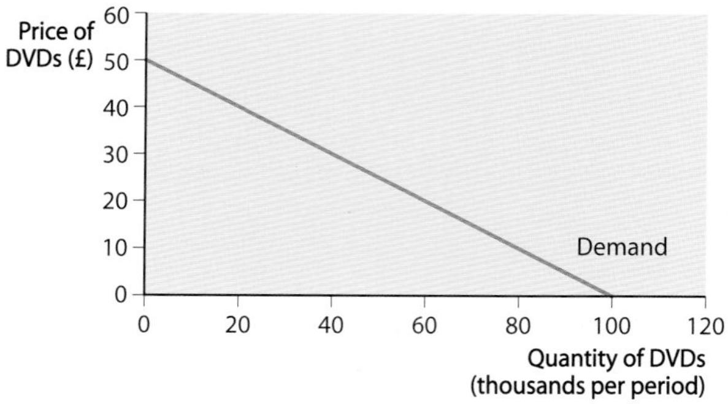

Figure 3.1
A demand curve for DVDs

Extension point

An analysis of why the demand curve should be downward-sloping would reveal that there are two important forces at work. At a higher price, a consumer buying a DVD has less income left over. This is referred to as the *real income effect* of a price increase. In addition, if the price of DVDs goes up, consumers may find other goods more attractive and choose to buy something else instead of DVDs. This is referred to as the *substitution effect* of a price increase.

As the price of a good changes, a movement along the demand curve can be observed as consumers adjust their buying pattern in response to the price change.

Notice that the demand curve has been drawn under the *ceteris paribus* assumption. In other words, it was assumed that all other influences on demand were held constant in order to focus on the relationship between demand and price. There are two important implications of this procedure.

First, the price drawn on the vertical axis of a diagram such as Figure 3.1 is the relative price – it is the price of DVDs under the assumption that all other prices are constant.

Second, if any of the other influences on demand change, you would expect to see a movement of the whole demand curve. It is very important to distinguish between factors that induce a movement *along* a curve, and factors that induce a movement *of* a curve. This applies not only in the case of the demand curve – there are many other instances where this is important.

Snob effects

It is sometimes argued that for some goods a 'snob effect' may lead to the demand curve sloping upwards. The argument is that some people may value certain goods more highly simply because their price is high, especially if they know that other people will observe them consuming these goods; an example might be Rolex watches. In other words, people gain value from having other people notice that they are rich enough to afford to consume a particular good. There is thus a *conspicuous consumption* effect, which was first pointed out by Thorstein Veblen at the end of the nineteenth century.

The 'snob effect' may encourage the 'conspicuous consumption' of certain goods.

However, although there may be individual consumers who react to price in this way, there is no evidence to suggest that there are whole markets that display an upward-sloping demand curve for this reason. In other words, most consumers would react normally to the price of such goods.

Demand and consumer incomes

The second influence on demand is consumer incomes. For a **normal good**, an increase in consumer incomes will, *ceteris paribus*, lead to an increase in the quantity demanded at any given price.

Figure 3.2 illustrates this. D_0 here represents the initial demand curve. An increase in consumers' incomes causes demand to be higher at any given price, and the demand curve shifts to the right – to D_1.

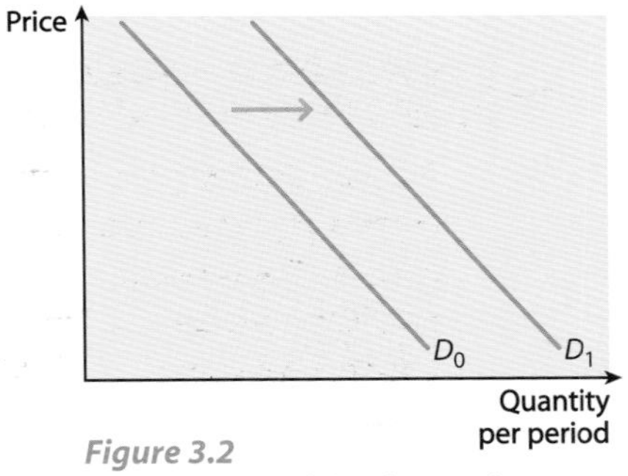

Figure 3.2
A movement of the demand curve following an increase in consumer incomes (a normal good)

However, demand does not always respond in this way. For example, think about bus journeys. As incomes rise in a society, more people can afford to have a car, or to use taxis. This means that, as incomes rise, the demand for bus journeys may tend to fall. Such goods are known as **inferior goods**.

This time an increase in consumers' incomes in Figure 3.3 causes the demand curve to shift to the left, from its initial position at D_0 to D_1, where less is demanded at any given price.

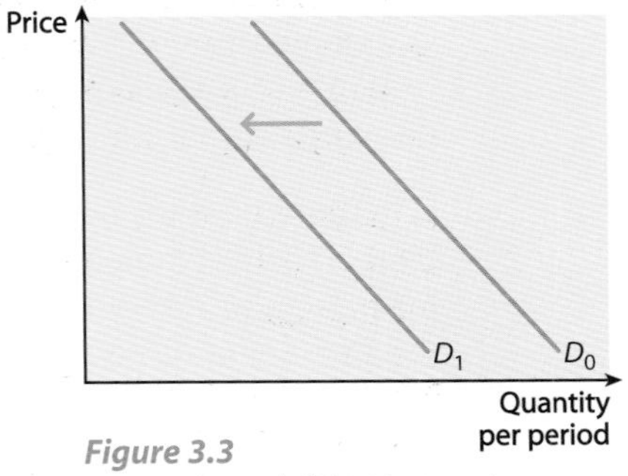

Figure 3.3
A movement of the demand curve following an increase in consumer incomes (an inferior good)

Key terms

normal good: one for which the quantity demanded increases in response to an increase in consumer incomes

inferior good: one for which the quantity demanded decreases in response to an increase in consumer incomes

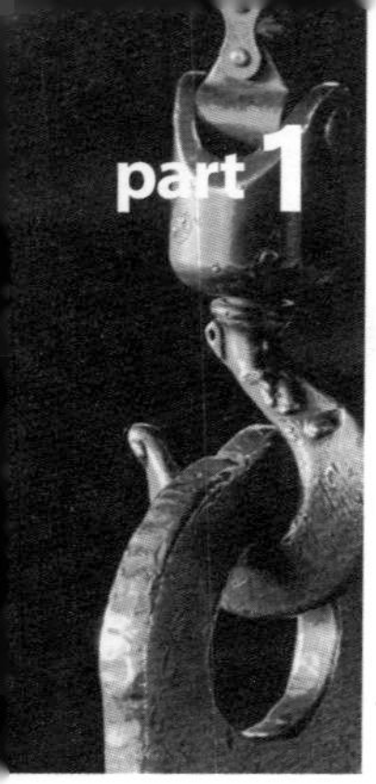

Extension material: a Giffen good

Remember that a consumer's response to a price change of a good is made up of a substitution effect and a real income effect. The substitution effect always acts in the opposite direction to the price change; in other words, an increase in the price of a good always induces a switch *away* from the good towards other goods. However, it can now be seen that the real income effect may operate in either direction, depending on whether it is a normal good or an inferior good that is being considered.

Suppose there is a good that is *very* inferior. A fall in the price of a good induces a substitution effect towards the good, but the real income effect works in the opposite direction. The fall in price is equivalent to a rise in real income, so consumers will consume less of the good. If this effect is really strong, it could overwhelm the substitution effect, and the fall in price could induce a *fall* in the quantity demanded; in other words, for such a good the demand curve could be upward-sloping.

Such goods are known as *Giffen goods*, after Sir Robert Giffen, who pointed out that this could happen. However, in spite of stories about the reaction of demand to a rise in the price of potatoes during the great Irish potato famine, there have been no authenticated sightings of Giffen goods. The notion remains a theoretical curiosity.

Demand and the price of other goods

The demand for a good may respond to changes in the price of other related goods, of which there are two main types. On the one hand, two goods may be **substitutes** for each other. For example, consider two different (but similar) breakfast cereals. If there is an increase in the price of one of the cereals, consumers may switch their consumption to the other, as the two are likely to be close substitutes for each other. Not all consumers will switch, of course — some may be deeply committed to one particular brand — but some of them are certainly likely to change over.

Key terms

substitutes: goods for which the demand is likely to rise if the price of a similar good increases

complements: goods for which the demand is likely to fall if the price of a related good rises

There may also be goods that are **complements** — for example products that are consumed jointly, such as breakfast cereals and milk.

Whether goods are substitutes or complements determines how the demand for one good responds to a change in the price of another. Figure 3.4 shows the situation for two goods that are substitutes. If there is an increase in the price of a substitute commodity, more consumers will switch to the first

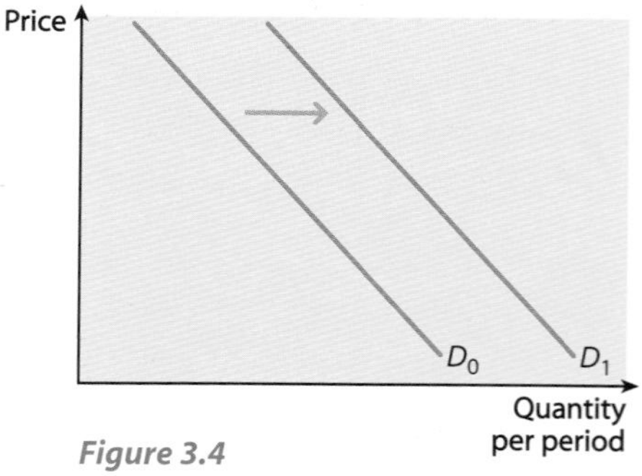

Figure 3.4
A movement of the demand curve following an increase in the price of a substitute good

good and the demand curve will move to the right – say, from D_0 to D_1.

For complements the situation is the reverse: in Figure 3.5 an increase in the price of a complementary good causes the demand curve to move leftwards, from D_0 to D_1.

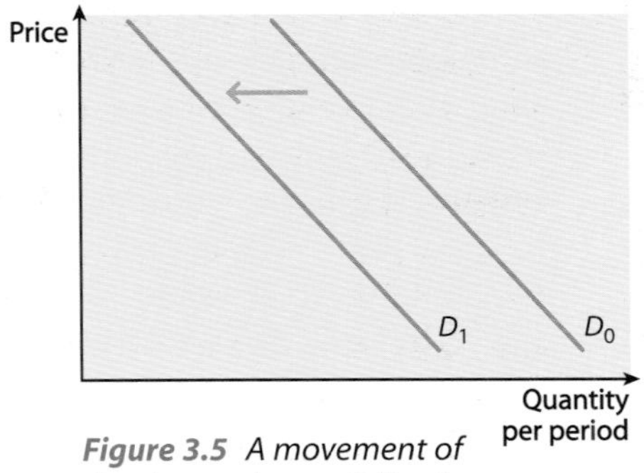

Figure 3.5 A movement of the demand curve following an increase in the price of a complementary good

Demand, consumer preferences and other influences

It was stated above that almost everything else that determines demand for a good can be represented as 'consumer preferences'. In particular, this refers to whether you like or dislike a good. There may be many things that influence whether you like or dislike a product. In part it simply depends upon your own personal inclinations – some people like dark chocolate, others prefer milk chocolate. However, firms may try to influence your preferences through advertising, and sometimes they succeed. Or you might be one of those people who get so irritated by television advertising that you compile a black list of products that you will never buy! Even this is an influence on your demand.

In some cases your preferences may be swayed by other people's demand – again, this may be positive or negative. Fashions may influence demand, but some people like to buck (or lead) the trend.

You may also see a movement of the demand curve if there is a sudden surge in the popularity of a good – or, indeed, a sudden collapse in demand.

Exercise 3.1

Sketch some demand curves for the following situations, and think about how you expect the demand curve to change (if at all):

a the demand for chocolate following a campaign highlighting the dangers of obesity

b the demand for oranges following an increase in the price of apples

c the demand for oranges following a decrease in the price of oranges

d the demand for DVDs following a decrease in the price of DVD players

e the demand for VCRs following a decrease in the price of DVD recorders

f the demand for private transport following an increase in consumer incomes

g the demand for public transport following an increase in consumer incomes

The above discussion has covered most of the factors that influence the demand for a good. However, in some cases it is necessary to take a time element into account. Not all of the goods bought are consumed instantly. In some cases consumption is spread over long periods of time. Indeed, there may be instances

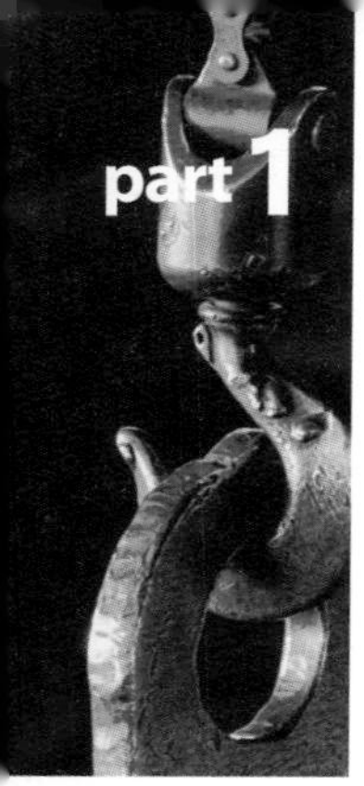

where goods are not bought for consumption at all, but are seen by the buyer as an investment, perhaps for resale at a later date. In these circumstances expectations about future price changes may be relevant. For example, people may buy fine wine or works of art in the expectation that prices will rise in the future. There may also be goods whose prices are expected to fall in the future. This has been common with many hi-tech products; initially a newly launched product may sell at a high price, but as production levels rise costs may fall, and prices also. People may therefore delay purchase in the expectation of future price reductions.

Summary

- A market is a set of arrangements that enables transactions to take place.
- The market demand for a good depends upon the price of the good, the price of other goods, consumers' incomes and preferences and the number of potential consumers.
- The relationship between demand for a product and its price is known as the demand schedule.
- The demand curve shows this relationship graphically, and is downward sloping, as the relationship between demand and price is an inverse one.
- A change in price induces a movement *along* the demand curve, whereas a change in the other determinants of demand induces a movement *of* the demand curve.
- When the demand for a good rises as consumer incomes rise that good is referred to as a *normal good*; when demand falls as income rises the good is referred to as an *inferior good*.
- A good or service may be related to other goods by being either a *substitute* or a *complement*.
- For some products, demand may be related to expected future prices.

Supply

On the basis of how consumers respond to different price levels for goods, a demand curve can be drawn to represent their behaviour. A similar relationship can be examined in relation to the behaviour of firms in a competitive market — that is, a market in which individual firms cannot influence the price of the good or service that they are selling, because of competition from other firms.

In order to analyse how firms decide how much of a product to supply, it is necessary to make an assumption about what it is that firms are trying to achieve. Assume that they aim to maximise their profits, where 'profits' are defined as the difference between a firm's total revenue and its total costs.

Key term

supply curve: shows the quantity supplied at any given price

In such a market it may well be supposed that firms will be prepared to supply more goods at a high price than at a lower one (other things being equal), as this will increase their profits. The **supply curve** traces out how much the firms in a market will supply at any given price on a diagram, as shown in Figure 3.6. As firms are expected to supply more goods at a high price than at a lower price, the supply curve will be upward-sloping, reflecting this positive relationship between quantity and price.

Notice that, again, focus is on the relationship between quantity supplied and the price of a good, *holding other things constant*. As with the demand curve, there are other factors affecting the quantity supplied. These other influences on supply will determine the position of the supply curve: if any of them change, the supply curve can be expected to move.

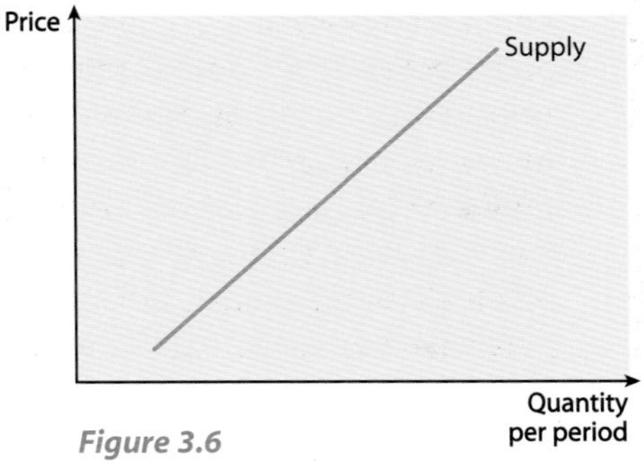

Figure 3.6
A supply curve

What influences supply?

We can identify five important influences on the quantity that firms will be prepared to supply to the market at any given price: (i) production costs, (ii) the technology of production, (iii) taxes and subsidies, (iv) the price of related goods and (v) firms' expectations about future prices.

Costs and technology

If firms are aiming to maximise profits, an important influence on their supply decision will be the costs of production that they face. Chapter 1 explained that in order to produce output firms need to use inputs of the factors of production – labour, capital, land etc. If the cost of those inputs increases, firms will in general be expected to supply less output at any given price. The effect of this is shown in Figure 3.7, where an increase in production costs induces firms to supply less output at each price. The curve shifts from its initial position at S_0 to a new position at S_1.

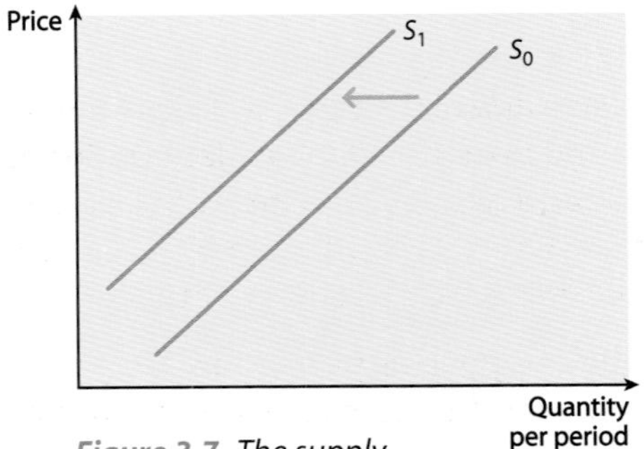

Figure 3.7 The supply curve shifts to the left if production costs increase

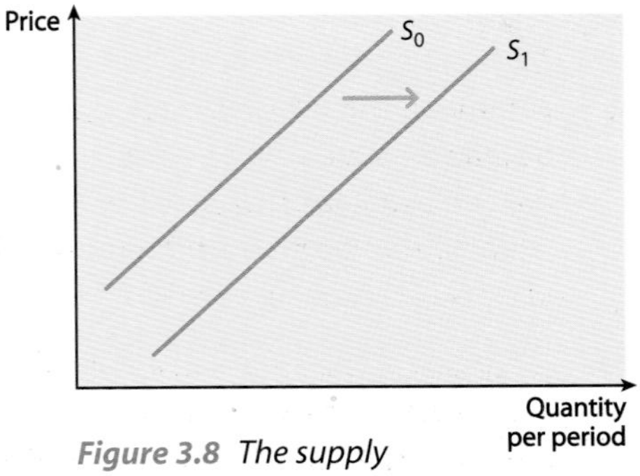

Figure 3.8 The supply curve shifts to the right if production costs fall

In contrast, if a new technology of production is introduced that means that firms can produce more cost-effectively, this could have the opposite effect, moving the supply curve to the right. This is shown in Figure 3.8, where improved technology induces firms to supply more output at any given price, and the supply curve moves from its initial position at S_0 to a new position at S_1.

Taxes and subsidies

Suppose the government imposes a sales tax such as VAT on a good or service. The price paid by consumers will be higher than the revenue received by firms, as the tax has to be paid to the government. This means that firms will (*ceteris paribus*) be prepared to supply less output at any given market price. Again, the supply curve shifts to the left. This will be analysed more carefully in the next chapter. On the other hand, if the government pays firms a subsidy to produce a particular good, this will reduce their costs, and induce them to supply more output at any given price. The supply curve will then shift to the right.

Prices of other goods

It can be seen that, from the consumers' perspective, two goods may be substitutes for each other in that, if the price of one good increases, consumers may be induced to switch their consumption to substitute goods. Similarly, there may be substitution on the supply side. A firm may face a situation in which there are alternative uses to which its factors of production may be put; in other words, it may be able to choose between producing a range of different products. A rise in the price of a good raises its profitability, and therefore may encourage a firm to switch production from other goods. This may happen even if there are high switching costs, provided the increase in price is sufficiently large. For example, a change in relative prices of potatoes and organic swedes might encourage a farmer to stop planting potatoes and grow organic swedes instead.

In other circumstances, a firm may produce a range of products jointly. Perhaps one good is a byproduct of the production process of another. An increase in the price of one of the goods may mean that the firm will produce more of both goods. This notion of joint supply is similar to the situation on the demand side where consumers regard two goods as complements.

Expected prices

Because production takes time, firms often take decisions about how much to supply on the basis of expected future prices. Indeed, if their product is one that can be stored, there may be times when a firm will decide to allow stocks of a product to build up in anticipation of a higher price in the future, perhaps by holding back some of its production from current sales.

Movements along and movements of the supply curve

As with the demand curve, it is very important to remember that there is a distinction between movements *along* the supply curve, and movements *of* the supply curve. If there is a change in the market price, this induces a movement along the supply curve. After all, the supply curve is designed to reveal how firms will react to a change in the price of the good.

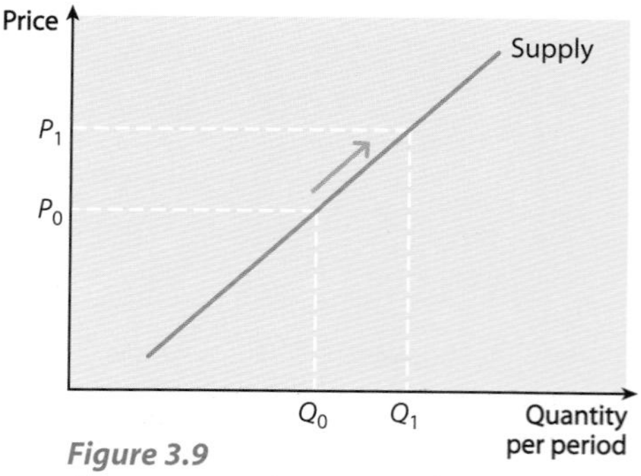

Figure 3.9
A movement along a supply curve in response to a price change

For example, in Figure 3.9, if the price is initially at P_0 firms will be prepared to supply the quantity Q_0, but if the price then increases to P_1 this will induce a movement along the supply curve as firms increase supply to Q_1.

In contrast, as seen in the previous section, a change in any of the other influences on supply will induce a movement of the whole supply curve, as this affects the firms' willingness to supply at any given price.

Exercise 3.2

For each of the following, decide whether the demand curve or the supply curve will move, and in which direction:

a Consumers are convinced by arguments about the benefits of organic vegetables.

b A new process is developed that reduces the amount of inputs that firms need in order to produce bicycles.

c There is a severe frost in Brazil that affects the coffee crop.

d The government increases the rate of value added tax.

e Real incomes rise.

f The price of tea falls: what happens in the market for coffee?

g The price of sugar falls: what happens in the market for coffee?

Summary

- Other things being equal, firms in a competitive market can be expected to supply more output at a higher price.
- The supply curve traces out this positive relationship between price and quantity supplied.
- Changes in the costs of production, technology, taxes and subsidies or the prices of related goods may induce movements of the supply curve, with firms being prepared to sell more (or less) output at any given price.
- Expectations about future prices may affect current supply decisions.

Market equilibrium

The previous sections in this chapter have described the components of the demand and supply model. It only remains to bring them together, for this is how the power of the model can be appreciated. Figure 3.10 shows the demand for and supply of butter.

Suppose that the price were to be set at a relatively high price (above P^*). At such a price firms wish to supply lots of butter to the market. However, consumers are not very keen on butter at such a high price, so demand is not strong. Firms now have a problem: they find that their stocks of butter are building up. What has happened is that the price has been set at a level that exceeds the value that

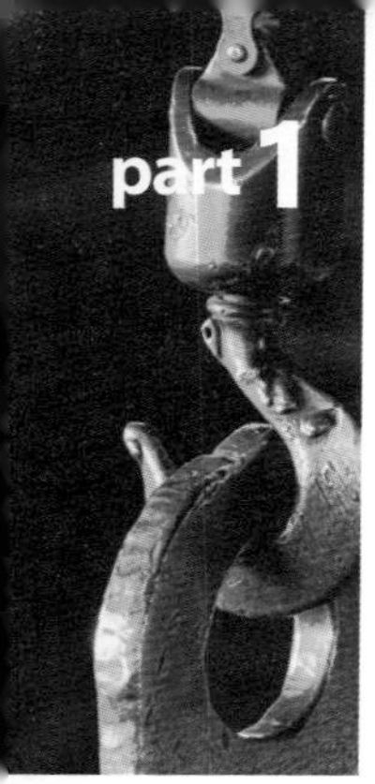

most consumers place on butter, so they will not buy. There is *excess supply*. The only thing that the firms can do is to reduce the price in order to clear their stocks.

Suppose they now set their price relatively low (below P^*). Now it is the consumers who have a problem, because they would like to buy more butter at the low price that firms are prepared to supply. There is *excess demand*. Some consumers may offer to pay more than the going price in order to obtain their butter supplies, and firms realise that they can raise the price.

How will it all end? When the price settles at P^*, there is a balance in the market between the quantity that consumers wish to demand and the quantity that firms wish to supply, i.e. namely Q^*. This is the *market equilibrium*. In a free market the price can be expected to converge on this equilibrium level, through movements along both demand and supply curves.

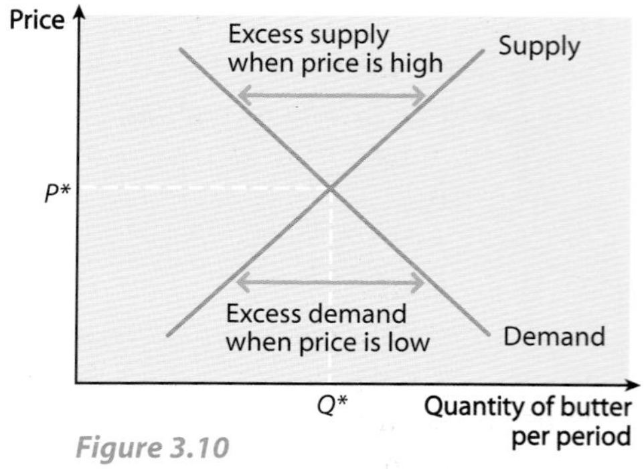

Figure 3.10
Bringing demand and supply together

Exercise 3.3

Identify the equilibrium market price if demand and supply are as in Figure 3.11.

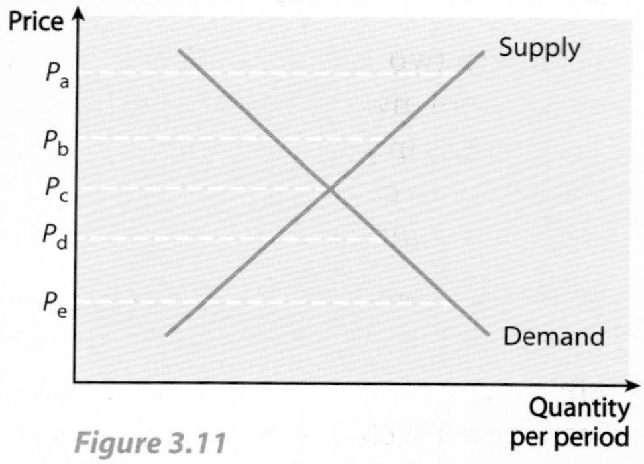

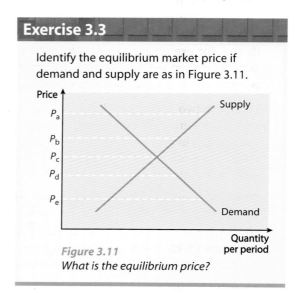

Figure 3.11
What is the equilibrium price?

Summary

- Bringing demand and supply together, you can identify the market equilibrium.
- The equilibrium price is the unique point at which the quantity demanded by consumers is just balanced by the quantity that firms wish to supply.
- In a free market, natural forces can be expected to encourage prices to adjust to the equilibrium level.

Elasticity: the sensitivity of demand and supply

Both the demand for and the supply of a good or service can be expected to depend upon its price as well as other factors. It is often interesting to know just how sensitive demand and/or supply will be to a change in either price or one of the other determinants – for example in predicting how market equilibrium will change in response to a change in the market environment. (This is an important issue which will be taken up again in the next chapter.) The sensitivity of demand or supply to a change in one of its determining factors can be measured by its **elasticity**.

> **Key terms**
>
> **elasticity:** a measure of the sensitivity of one variable to changes in another variable
>
> **price elasticity of demand:** a measure of the sensitivity of quantity demanded to a change in the price of a good or service; measured as:
>
> $$\frac{\%\ \text{change in quantity demanded}}{\%\ \text{change in price}}$$

The price elasticity of demand

The most common elasticity measure is the **price elasticity of demand**. When the demand is highly price sensitive, the percentage change in quantity demanded following a price change will be large relative to the percentage change in price. In this case elasticity of demand (E_d) will take on a value that is numerically greater than 1. For example, suppose that a 2% change in price leads to a 5% change in quantity demanded; the elasticity is then –5 divided by 2 = –2.5. When the elasticity is numerically greater than 1, demand is referred to as being *price-elastic*.

There are two important things to notice about this. First, because the demand curve is downward sloping, the elasticity will always be negative. This is because the changes in price and quantity are always in the opposite direction. Second, you should try to calculate the elasticity only for a relatively small change in price, as it becomes unreliable for very large changes.

When demand is not very sensitive to price, the percentage change in quantity demanded will be smaller than the original percentage change in price, and the elasticity will then be numerically less than 1. For example, if a 2% change in price leads to a 1% change in quantity demanded, then the value of the elasticity will be –1 divided by 2 = –0.5. In this case, demand is referred to as being *price-inelastic*.

Calculating the price elasticity of demand

Define the percentage change in price as $100 \times \Delta P/P$ (where the Δ means 'change in' and P stands for price). Similarly, the percentage change in quantity demanded is $100 \times \Delta Q/Q$. Then the formula for the elasticity is:

$$E_d = \frac{100 \times \Delta Q/Q}{100 \times \Delta P/P}$$

If you look at this expression, you will see that it can be simplified. First, the 100s top and bottom cancel out:

$$E_d = \frac{\Delta Q/Q}{\Delta P/P}$$

This can be written as:

$$E_d = \frac{\Delta Q}{\Delta P} \times \frac{P}{Q}$$

Figure 3.12 shows a demand curve for pencils. When the price of a pencil is 40p, the quantity demanded will be 20. If the price falls to 35p, the quantity demanded will rise to 30. The change in quantity (ΔQ) is 10 and the change in price (ΔP) is –5. Thus the elasticity can be calculated as (10/–5) × (40/20) = –4. At this price,

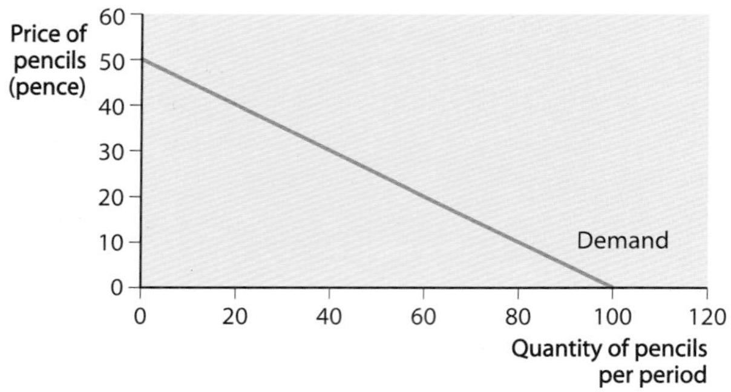

Figure 3.12
A demand curve for pencils

demand is highly price elastic. However, at a lower price the result is quite different. Suppose that price is initially 10p, at which price the quantity demanded is 80. If the price falls to 9p, demand increases to 82. Again, elasticity can be calculated as (2/−1) × (10/80) = −0.25, so demand is now price inelastic. This phenomenon is true for any straight-line demand curve; in other words, demand is price-elastic at high prices and inelastic at low prices. At the halfway point the elasticity is exactly −1, which is referred to as *unit elasticity*.

Why should this happen? The key is to remember that elasticity is defined in terms of the percentage changes in price and quantity. Thus, when price is high a 1p change in price is a small percentage change, and the percentage change in quantity is relatively large — because when price is relatively high, the initial quantity is relatively low. The reverse is the case when price is relatively low.

Figure 3.13 shows how the elasticity of demand varies along a straight-line demand curve.

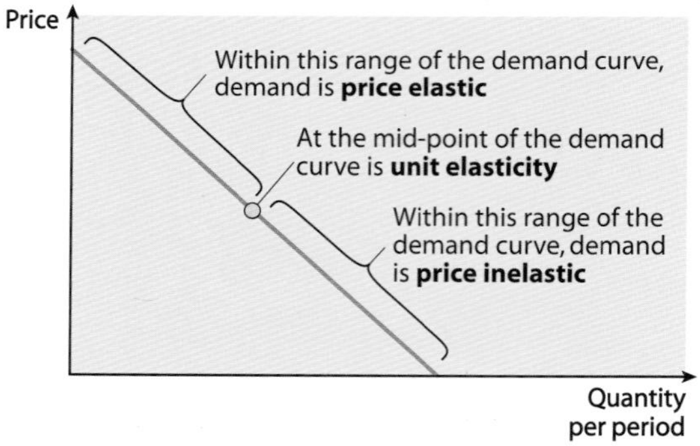

Figure 3.13
The price elasticity of demand varies along a straight line

Extension material

An alternative way of looking at this is to notice that, because the demand curve is drawn as a straight line, the ratio of the change in quantity to the change in price ($\Delta Q/\Delta P$) is always the same. (In fact, this is the slope of the demand curve.) However, the ratio of the level of quantity to price varies along the demand curve. When price is relatively high, quantity is relatively low, so P/Q is high and elasticity is high. Conversely, when price is low, quantity is high and P/Q is low.

The price elasticity of demand and total revenue

One reason why firms may have an interest in the price elasticity of demand is that, if they are considering changing their prices, they will be eager to know the extent to which demand will be affected. For example, they may want to know how a change in price will affect their total revenue. It turns out that there is a consistent relationship between the price elasticity of demand and total revenue.

Total revenue is given by price multiplied by quantity. In Figure 3.14, if price is at P_0, quantity demanded is at Q_0 and total revenue is given by the area of the rectangle OP_0AQ_0. If price falls to P_1 the quantity demanded rises to Q_1, and you can see that total revenue has increased, as it is now given by the area OP_1BQ_1. This is larger than at price P_1, because in moving from P_0 to P_1 the area P_1P_0AC is lost, but the area Q_0CBQ_1 is gained, and the latter is the larger. As you move down the demand curve, total revenue at first increases like this, but then decreases – try sketching this for yourself to check that it is so.

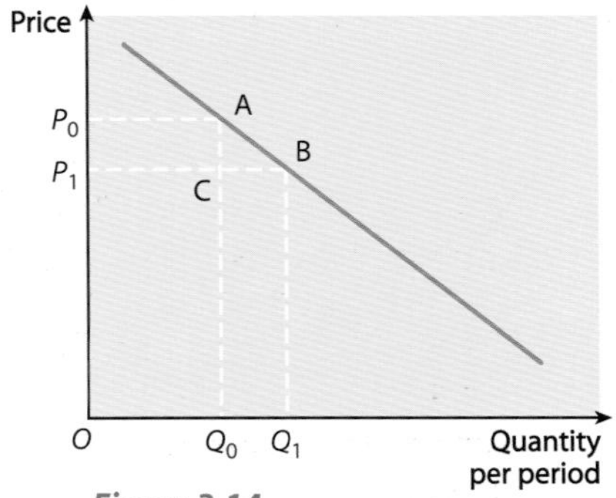

Figure 3.14
Demand and total revenue

The relationship is illustrated in Figure 3.15 for the case of a straight-line demand curve. Remember that demand is price-elastic when price is relatively high. This is the range of the demand curve in which total revenue rises as price falls. This makes sense, as in this range the quantity demanded is sensitive to a change in price and increases by more (in percentage terms) than the price falls. This implies that, as you move to the right in this segment, total revenue rises. The increase in quantity sold more than compensates for the fall in price. However, when the mid-point is reached and demand becomes unit elastic, total revenue stops rising – it is at its maximum at this point. The remaining part of the curve is inelastic; that is, the increase in quantity demanded is no longer sufficient to compensate for the decrease in price, and total revenue falls. Table 3.1 summarises the situation.

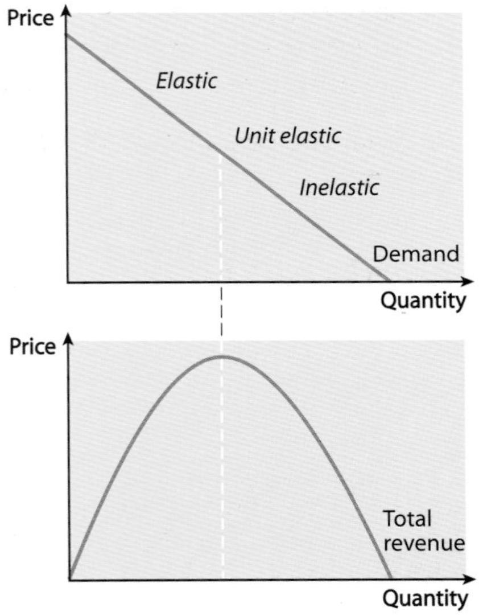

Figure 3.15
Elasticity and total revenue

Table 3.1
Total revenue, elasticity and a price change

Price elasticity of demand	For a price increase, total revenue...	For a price decrease, total revenue ...
Elastic	falls	rises
Unit elastic	does not change	does not change
Inelastic	rises	falls

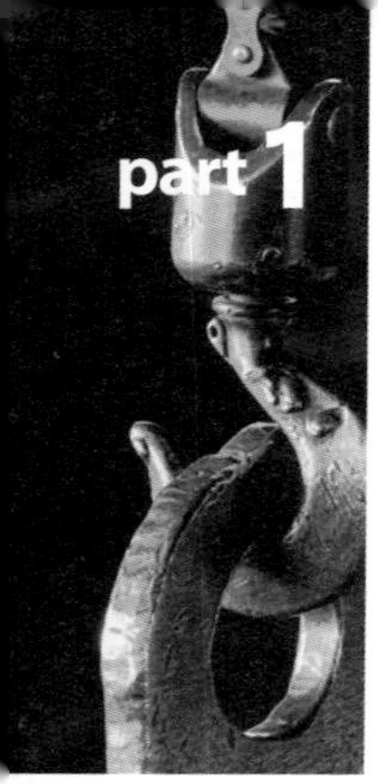

Thus, if a firm is aware of the price elasticity of demand for its product, it can anticipate consumer response to its price changes, which may be a powerful strategic tool.

One very important point must be made here. If the price elasticity of demand varies along a straight-line demand curve, such a curve cannot be referred to as either elastic or inelastic. To do so is to confuse the elasticity with the *slope* of the demand curve. It is not only the steepness of the demand curve that determines the elasticity, but also the point on the curve at which the elasticity is measured.

Two extreme cases of the price elasticity of demand should also be mentioned. Demand may sometimes be totally insensitive to price, so that the same quantity will be demanded whatever price is set for it. In such a situation demand is said to be *perfectly inelastic*. The demand curve in this case is vertical — like D_i in Figure 3.16. In this situation the numerical value of the price elasticity is zero, as quantity demanded does not change in response to a change in the price of the good.

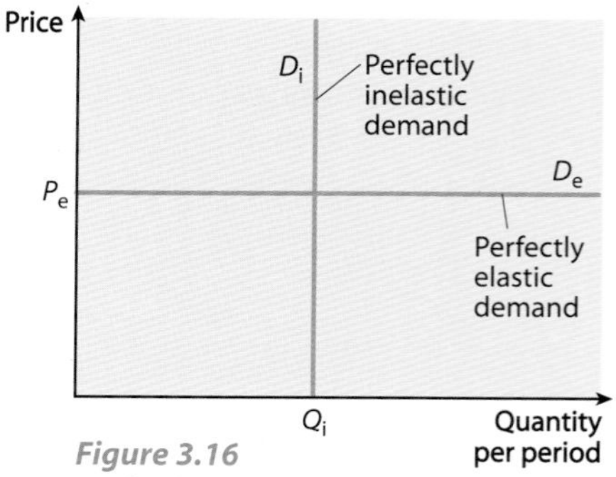

Figure 3.16
Perfectly elastic and inelastic demand

The other extreme is shown on the same figure, where D_e is a horizontal demand curve and demand is *perfectly elastic*. The numerical value of the elasticity here is infinity. Consumers demand an unlimited quantity of the good at price P_e. No firm has any incentive to lower price below this level, but if price were to rise above P_e, demand would fall to zero.

Influences on the price elasticity of demand

A number of important influences on the size of the price elasticity of demand can now be identified. The most important is the availability of substitutes for the good or service under consideration. For example, think about the demand for cauliflower. Cauliflower and broccoli are often seen as being very similar, so if the price of cauliflower is high one week people might quite readily switch to broccoli. The demand for cauliflower can be said to be price sensitive (elastic), as consumers can readily substitute an alternative product. On the other hand, if the price of all vegetables rises demand will not change very much, as there are no substitutes for vegetables in the diet. Thus, goods that have close substitutes available will tend to exhibit elastic demand, whereas the demand for goods for which there are no substitutes will tend to be more inelastic.

Many vegetables have close substitutes, leading to their high price elasticity of demand.

Associated with this is the question of whether an individual regards a good or service as a necessity or as a luxury item. If a good is a necessity, then demand for it will tend to be inelastic, whereas if a good is regarded as a luxury consumers will tend to be more price-sensitive. This is closely related to the question of substitutes, as by labelling a good as a necessity one is essentially saying that there are no substitutes for it.

A second influence on the price elasticity of demand is the relative share of the good or service in overall expenditure. You may tend not to notice small changes in the price of an inexpensive item that is a small part of overall expenditure – such as salt, or sugar. This tends to mean that demand for that good will be relatively inelastic. On the other hand, an item that figures large in the household budget will be seen very differently, and consumers will tend to be much more sensitive to price when a significant proportion of their income is involved.

Finally, the time period under consideration may be important. Consumers may respond more strongly to a price change in the long run than to one in the short run. An increase in the price of petrol may have limited effects in the short run; however, in the long run consumers may buy smaller cars or switch to diesel. Thus, the elasticity of demand tends to be more elastic in the long run than in the short run. Habit or commitment to a certain pattern of consumption may dictate the short-run pattern of consumption, but people do eventually adjust to price changes.

Summary

- The price elasticity of demand measures the sensitivity of the quantity of a good demanded to a change in its price.
- As there is an inverse relationship between quantity demanded and price, the price elasticity of demand is always negative.
- Where consumers are sensitive to a change in price, the percentage change in quantity demanded will exceed the percentage change in price. Demand then takes on a value that is numerically greater than 1, and demand is said to be elastic.
- Where consumers are not very sensitive to a change in price, the percentage change in quantity demanded will be smaller than the percentage change in price. Demand then takes on a value that is numerically smaller than 1, and demand is said to be inelastic.
- When demand is elastic, a fall (rise) in price leads to a rise (fall) in total revenue.
- When demand is inelastic, a fall (rise) in price leads to a fall (rise) in total revenue.
- The size of the price elasticity of demand is influenced by the availability of substitutes for a good, the relative share of expenditure on the good in the consumer's budget and the time that consumers have to adjust.

The income elasticity of demand

Elasticity is a measure of the sensitivity of a variable to changes in another variable. In the same way as the price elasticity of demand is determined, an elasticity measure can similarly be calculated for any other influence on demand or supply.

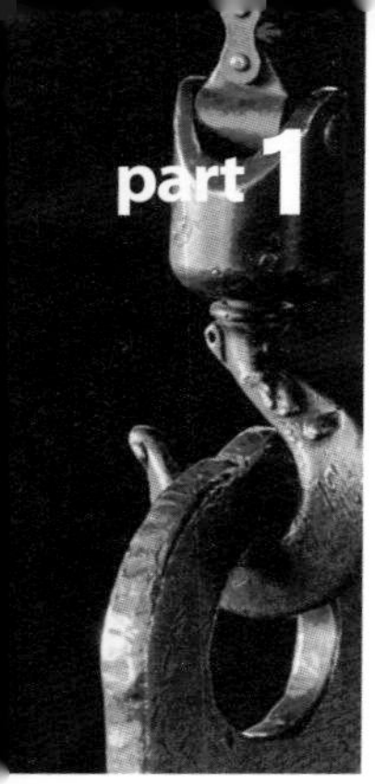

Unlike the price elasticity of demand, the **income elasticity of demand** may be either positive or negative. Remember the distinction between normal and inferior goods? For normal goods the quantity demanded will increase as consumer income rises, whereas for inferior goods the quantity demanded will tend to fall as income rises. Thus, for normal goods the income elasticity of demand will be positive, whereas for inferior goods it will be negative.

Suppose you discover that the income elasticity of demand for wine is 0.7. How do you interpret this number? If consumer incomes were to increase by 10%, the demand for wine would increase by $10 \times 0.7 = 7\%$. This example of a normal good may be helpful information for wine merchants, if they know that consumer incomes are rising over time.

On the other hand, if the income elasticity of demand for coach travel is –0.3, that means that a 10% increase in consumer incomes will lead to a 3% fall in the demand for coach travel — perhaps because more people are travelling by car. In this instance coach travel would be regarded as an inferior good.

In some cases the income elasticity of demand may be very strongly positive. For example, suppose that the income elasticity for digital cameras is +2. This implies that the quantity demanded of such cameras will increase by 20% for every 10% increase in incomes, which suggests that an increase in income is encouraging people to devote more of their incomes to this product, which increases its share in total expenditure. Such goods are referred to as **luxury goods**.

Key terms

income elasticity of demand: a measure of the sensitivity of the quantity demanded of a good or service to a change in consumer income, measured as:

$$\frac{\text{\% change in quantity demanded}}{\text{\% change in consumer income}}$$

luxury good: one for which the income elasticity of demand is positive and greater than 1, so that as income rises consumers spend proportionally more on the good

cross-price elasticity of demand: a measure of the sensitivity of quantity demanded of one good or service to a change in the price of some other good or service, measured as:

$$\frac{\text{\% change in quantity demanded of good X}}{\text{\% change in price of good Y}}$$

Cross-price elasticity of demand

Another useful measure is the **cross-price elasticity of demand**. This is helpful in revealing the interrelationships between goods.

Again, this measure may be either positive or negative, depending on the relationship between the goods.

If the cross-price elasticity of demand is seen to be positive, it means that an increase in the price of good Y leads to an increase in the quantity demanded of good X. For example, an increase in the price of apples may lead to an increase in the demand for pears. Here apples and pears are regarded as substitutes for each other; if one becomes relatively more expensive, consumers will switch to the other. A high value for the cross-price elasticity indicates that two goods are very close substitutes. This information may be useful for a firm in helping it to identify its close competitors.

On the other hand, if an increase in the price of one good leads to a fall in the price of another good, this suggests that they are likely to be complements. The cross-price elasticity in this case will be negative. An example of such a relationship would be that between coffee and sugar, which tend to be consumed together.

Price elasticity of supply

As elasticity is a measure of sensitivity, its use need not be confined to influences on demand, but can also be turned to evaluating the sensitivity of quantity supplied to a change in its determinant — price in particular.

> **Key term**
>
> **price elasticity of supply:** a measure of the sensitivity of quantity supplied to a change in the price of a good or service, measured as:
>
> $$\frac{\text{\% change in quantity supplied}}{\text{\% change in price}}$$

It was argued above that the supply curve is likely to be upward sloping, the price elasticity of supply can be expected to be positive. In other words, an increase in the market price will induce firms to supply more output to the market. If the price elasticity of supply is 0.8, then an increase in price of 10% will encourage firms to supply 8% more. As with the price elasticity of demand, if the elasticity is greater than 1 supply is referred to as being elastic, whereas if the value is between 0 and 1 supply is considered inelastic. *Unit elasticity* occurs when the price elasticity of supply is exactly 1, so that a 10% increase in price induces a 10% increase in quantity supplied.

The value of the elasticity will depend on how willing and able firms are to increase their supply. For example, if firms are operating close to the capacity of their existing plant and machinery, they may be unable to respond to an increase in price, at least in the short run. So here again, supply can be expected to be more elastic in the long run than in the short run. Figure 3.17 illustrates this. In the short run firms may be able to respond to an increase in price only in a limited way, and so supply may be relatively inelastic, as shown by S_s in the figure. However, firms can become more flexible in the long run by installing new machinery or building new factories, so supply can then become more elastic, moving to S_l.

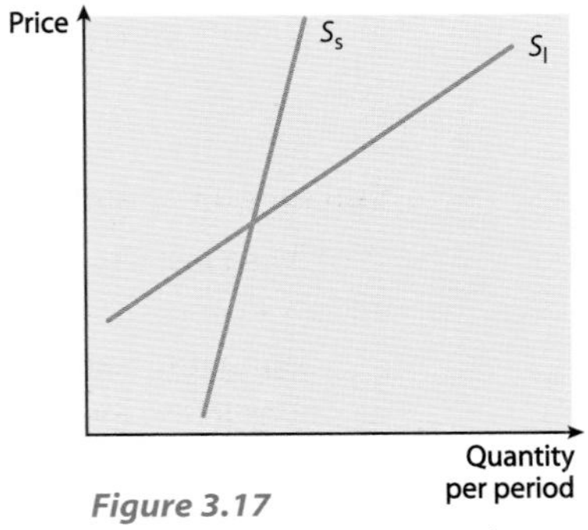

Figure 3.17
Short- and long-run supply

There are two limiting cases of supply elasticity. For some reason supply may be fixed, such that, no matter how much price increases, firms will not be able to supply any more. For example, it could be that a certain fixed amount of fish is available in a market, and however high the price goes no more can be obtained. Equally, if the fishermen know that the fish they do not sell today cannot be stored for another day, then they have an incentive to sell however low the price goes. In these cases supply is perfectly inelastic. At the other extreme is perfectly elastic supply, where firms would be prepared to supply any amount of the good at the going price.

These two possibilities are shown in Figure 3.18. Here S_i represents a perfectly inelastic supply curve: firms will supply Q_i whatever the price, perhaps because that is the amount available for sale. Supply here is vertical. At the opposite extreme, if supply is perfectly elastic then firms are prepared to supply any amount at the price P_e, and the supply curve is given by the horizontal line S_e.

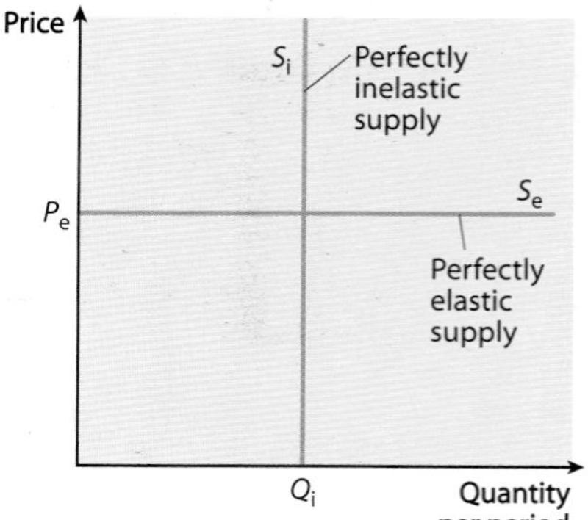

Figure 3.18
Perfectly elastic and inelastic supply

Exercise 3.4

Imagine the following scenario. You are considering a pricing strategy for a bus company. The economy is heading into recession, and the company is running at a loss. Your local rail service provider has announced an increase in rail fares. How (if at all) do you use the following information concerning the elasticity of bus travel with respect to various variables to inform your decision on price? Do you raise or lower price?

- Price elasticity of demand −1.58
- Income elasticity of demand −2.43
- Cross-price elasticity of demand with respect to rail fares +3.21
- Your price elasticity of supply +1.15

Summary

- The income elasticity of demand measures the sensitivity of quantity demanded to a change in consumer incomes. It serves to distinguish between normal, luxury and inferior goods.
- The cross-price elasticity of demand measures the sensitivity of the quantity demanded of one good or service to a change in the price of some other good or service. It can serve to distinguish between substitutes and complements.
- The price elasticity of supply measures the sensitivity of the quantity supplied to a change in the price of a good or service. The price elasticity of supply can be expected to be greater in the long run than in the short run, as firms have more flexibility to adjust their production decisions in the long run.

Chapter 4

Applying demand and supply analysis

The previous chapter introduced the notions of demand and supply, together with the key concepts of market equilibrium and elasticity. It is now time to begin to apply this model to see how it provides insights about how markets operate. You will encounter demand and supply in a wide variety of contexts, and begin to glimpse some of the ways in which the model can help to explain how the economic world works.

Learning outcomes

After studying this chapter, you should be able to:

- understand what is meant by comparative static analysis
- apply demand and supply analysis in a variety of different market situations
- analyse the effect of taxes and subsidies in a market, using demand and supply analysis
- evaluate the extent to which a sales tax is borne by buyers and sellers
- use demand and supply analysis to interpret economic events in the real world

All the examples of demand and supply covered in the previous chapter were consumer goods of some sort – DVDs, butter, pencils and so on. However, it would be wrong to think that demand and supply analysis is of relevance only in that sort of market. So this chapter broadens the horizons, looking beyond consumer goods markets to markets for housing, labour and exchange rates.

Comparative statics

First, however, it is necessary to introduce another of the economist's key tools – comparative static analysis. Chapter 3 described the way in which a market moves towards an equilibrium between demand and supply through price adjustments and movements along the demand and supply curves. This is called static analysis,

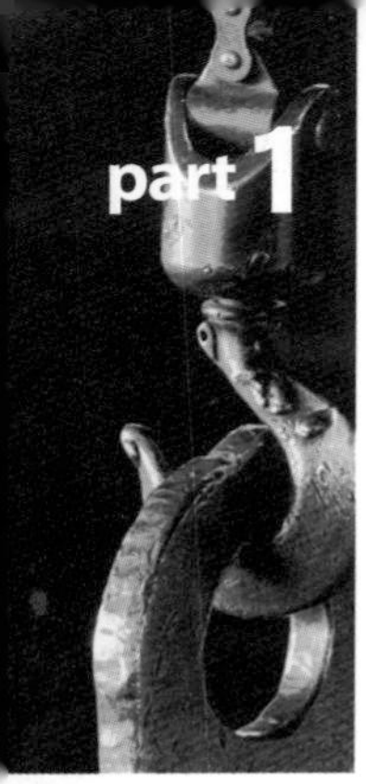

in the sense that a *ceteris paribus* assumption is imposed by holding constant the factors that influence demand and supply and focusing on the way in which the market reached equilibrium.

In the next stage one of these background factors is changed, and the effect of this change on the market equilibrium is then analysed. In other words, beginning with a market in equilibrium, one of the factors affecting either demand or supply is altered, and the new market equilibrium is then studied. In this way, two static equilibrium positions — before and after — will be compared. This approach is known as **comparative static analysis.**

Key term

comparative static analysis: examines the effect on equilibrium of a change in the external conditions affecting a market

A market for dried pasta

Begin with a simple market for dried pasta, a basic staple foodstuff obtainable in any supermarket. Figure 4.1 shows the market in equilibrium. D_0 represents the demand curve in this initial situation, and S_0 is the supply curve. The market is in equilibrium with the price at P_0, and the quantity being traded is Q_0. It is equilibrium in the sense that pasta producers are supplying just the amount of pasta that consumers wish to buy at that price. This is the 'before' position. Some experiments will now be carried out with this market by disturbing the equilibrium.

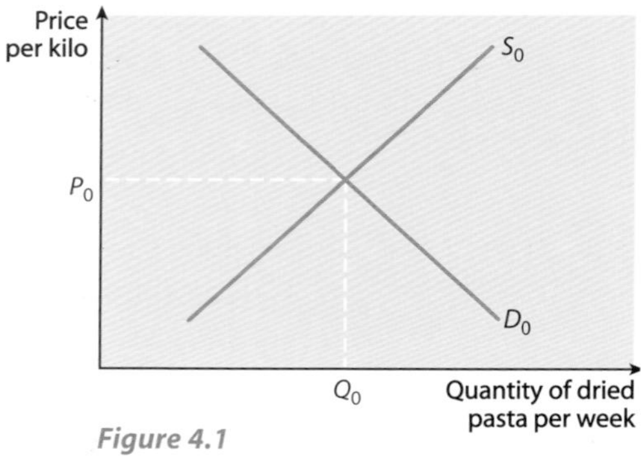

Figure 4.1
A market for dried pasta

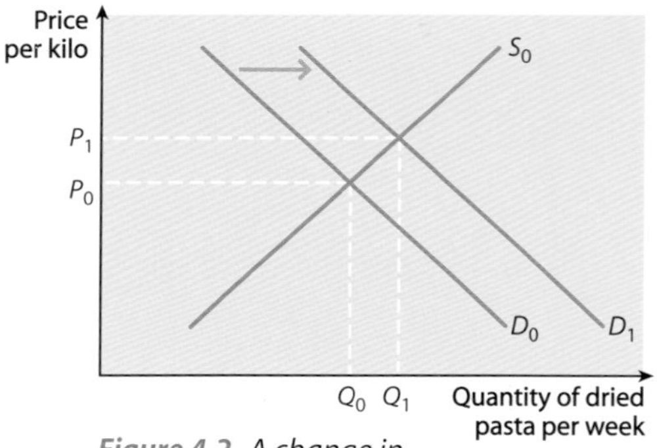

Figure 4.2 A change in consumer preferences for dried pasta

A change in consumer preferences

Suppose that a study is published highlighting the health benefits of eating pasta, backed up with an advertising campaign. The effect of this is likely to be an increase in the demand for pasta at any given price. In other words, a change in consumer preferences will shift the demand curve to the right, as shown in Figure 4.2.

The market now adjusts to a new equilibrium, with a new price P_1, and a new quantity traded at Q_1. In this case both price and quantity have increased as a result of the change in preferences.

A change in the price of a substitute

A second possibility is that there is a fall in the price of fresh pasta. This is likely to be a close substitute for dried pasta, so the probable result is that some former consumers of dried pasta will switch their allegiance to the fresh variety. This time the demand curve for dried pasta moves in the opposite direction, as can be seen in Figure 4.3. Here the starting point is the original position, with market equilibrium at price P_0 and quantity traded Q_0. After the shift in the demand curve from D_0 to D_2, the market settles again with a price of P_2 and quantity traded of Q_2. Both price and quantity traded are now lower than in the original position.

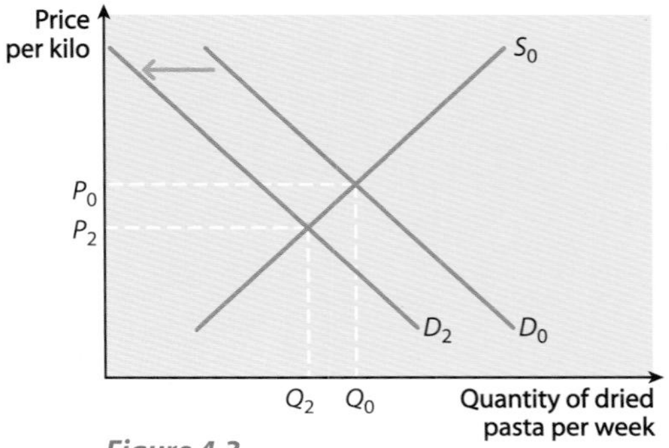

Figure 4.3
A fall in demand for dried pasta

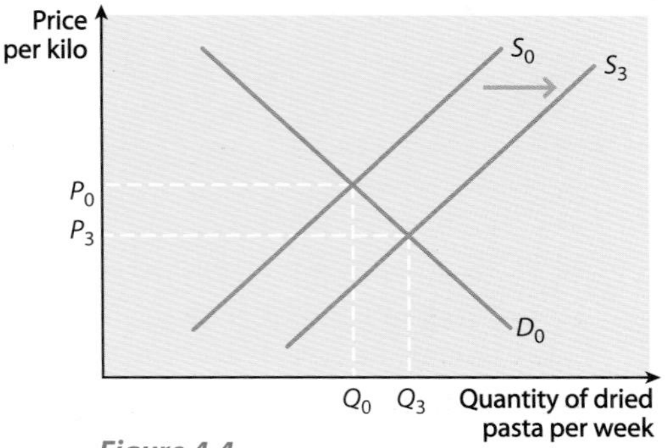

Figure 4.4
New pasta-making technology

An improvement in pasta technology

Next, suppose that a new pasta-making machine is produced enabling dried pasta makers to produce at lower cost than before. This advancement reduces firms' costs, and consequently they are prepared to supply more dried pasta at any given price. The starting point is the same initial position, but now it is the supply curve that moves – to the right. This is shown in Figure 4.4.

Again, comparative static analysis can be undertaken. The new market equilibrium is at price P_3, which is lower than the original equilibrium, but the quantity traded is higher at Q_3.

An increase in labour costs

Finally, suppose that pasta producers face an increase in their labour costs. Perhaps the Pasta Workers' Union has negotiated higher wages, or the pasta producers have become subject to stricter health and safety legislation which raises their production costs. Figure 4.5 starts as usual with equilibrium at price P_0 and quantity Q_0.

The increase in production costs means that pasta producers are prepared to supply less dried pasta at any given price, so the supply curve shifts to the left – to S_4. This takes the market to a new equilibrium at a higher price than before (P_4), but with a lower quantity traded (Q_4).

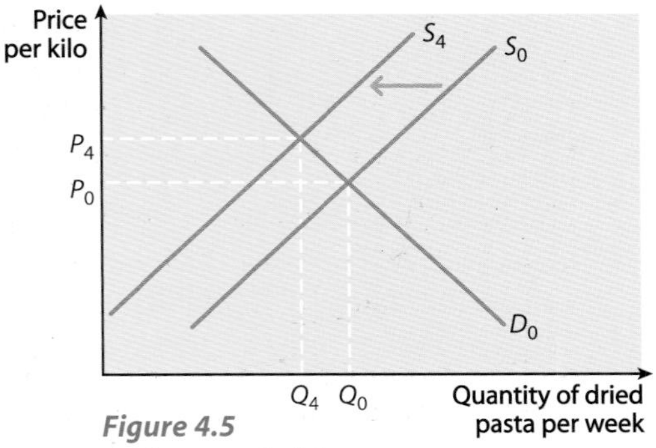

Figure 4.5
An increase in labour costs

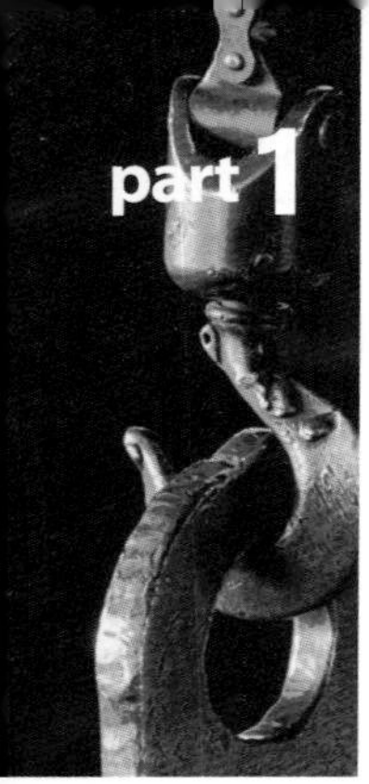

Summary

- Comparative static analysis enables you to analyse the way in which markets respond to external shocks, by comparing market equilibrium before and after a shock.
- All you need to do is to figure out whether the shock affects demand or supply, and in which direction.
- The size and direction of the movements of the demand and supply curves determine the overall effect on equilibrium price and quantity traded.

Exercise 4.1

For each of the following market situations, sketch a demand and supply diagram, and undertake a comparative static analysis to see what happens to equilibrium price and quantity. Explain your answers.

a An increase in consumer incomes affects the demand for bus travel.

b New regulations on environmental pollution force a firm making paint to increase outlay on reducing its emission of toxic fumes.

c A firm of accountants brings in new faster computers which have the effect of reducing the firm's costs.

d An outbreak of chicken flu causes consumers of chicken to buy burgers instead. (What is the effect on both markets?)

Agricultural markets

The markets for agricultural produce have some interesting characteristics that can be analysed with the demand and supply model. One particular characteristic of many such markets is that the supply side of the market can be strongly affected by weather and climate. This can create conditions in which it is difficult to predict market outcomes in advance.

Suppose that weather conditions one season are especially unfavourable, and that the onion crop is ruined. Such a poor harvest means that the supply curve is well to the left of its normal position. Consider Figure 4.6. Suppose that in an average year the harvest produces a supply curve such as S_{av}. Notice that it is relatively steep, reflecting the fact that there are limits to how long the onion sellers can store onions for later sale, or how many more onions they can produce for sale if the price is favourable. In other words, the quantity of onions available at any point in time is constrained by previous decisions about how many onions to plant. This sort of market will be considered again in Chapter 10.

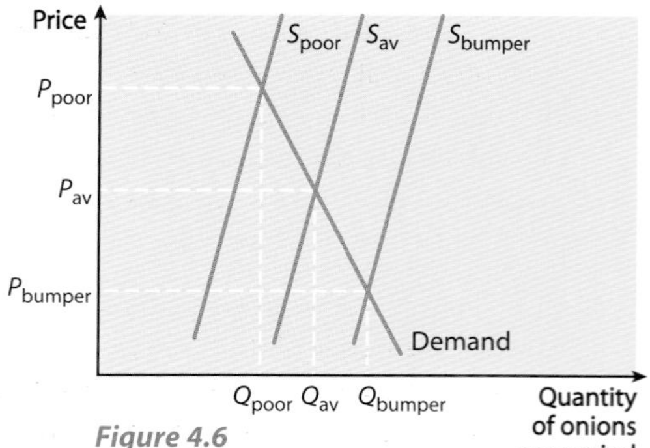

Figure 4.6
The market for onions

Furthermore, notice that the demand curve is relatively price-inelastic ('*relatively*', because elasticity varies along a straight-line demand curve, so is not inelastic throughout its length). It could be expected that the demand for onions would be relatively price-inelastic partly because there are no close substitutes for onions and they are an essential ingredient for many dishes. Furthermore, onions comprise a relatively minor part of a household's spending.

Figure 4.6 can now be used to analyse the market situation. If the harvest is poor, supply will be at S_{poor} instead of at S_{av}, and the equilibrium price will rise to P_{poor} with the quantity traded falling to Q_{poor}. It can be seen that the shortage of onions in the market pushes up the equilibrium price. Furthermore, notice that the inelasticity of both supply and demand in this market means that the price effect is stronger than the quantity effect. You can see this for yourself by sketching a diagram in which the curves are relatively more elastic.

Figure 4.6 also shows what happens in a bumper year, when the harvest is especially good. The supply curve S_{bumper} is now to the right of its normal position at S_{av}. Price falls to P_{bumper}, and quantity traded rises to Q_{bumper}. Again, the price effect is stronger than the quantity effect because of the relatively inelastic supply and demand.

One of the important aspects of this discussion is that weather conditions can vary substantially from one harvest to the next. This means that prices can vary quite widely from year to year, making conditions in agricultural markets difficult to predict. For some commodities attempts can be made to stabilise prices by storing surplus produce in good years to sell in bad years. These will be explored in Chapter 10.

The supply side of a market can be strongly affected by weather and climate.

Exercise 4.2

In April 2003 South East Asia was suffering from an outbreak of the SARS virus which had spread around the region. On 20 April one of the main wholesale fruit and vegetable markets in Singapore, at Pasir Panjang, had to be closed when workers were found to have been infected. Sketch a demand and supply diagram to predict how the retail market for vegetables was affected.

Commodity markets

Another category of market that is of particular interest is the one for commodities. This encompasses markets for various types of raw material used in the production process of many manufacturing industries. Prices in these markets too can be volatile, but this time the volatility arises from the demand side of the market.

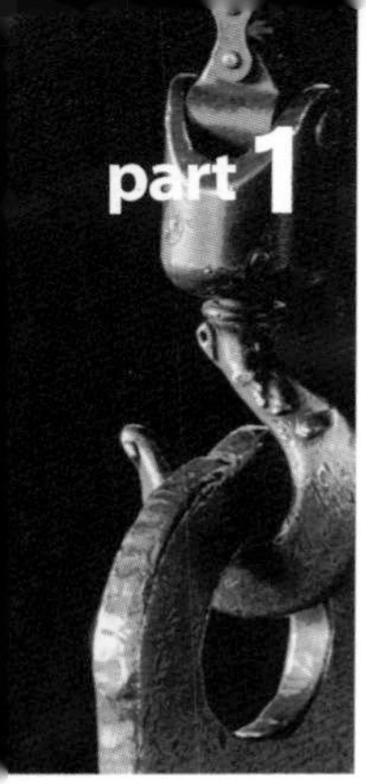

Figure 4.7 shows the market for bauxite, a commodity used as a raw material in the production of aluminium. Many countries experience fluctuations in the overall level of economic activity over time. There are periods of boom and periods of recession. The demand for aluminium (and hence for bauxite) tends to vary with these cycles of activity. D_{av} here represents the average position of the demand curve for bauxite. At the peak of the cycle demand is high and the price rises to P_{peak}, but at the trough of the cycle prices fall to P_{trough}. The quantity traded does not vary very much. This is because the figure has been drawn showing supply to be relatively inelastic, so the main burden of adjustment to market equilibrium takes place through the price level.

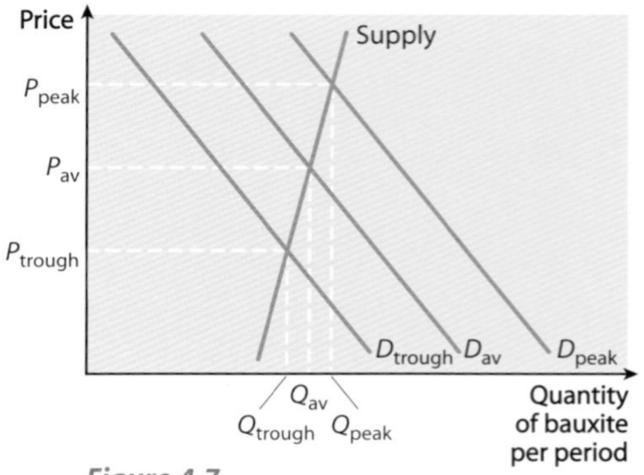

Figure 4.7
The market for bauxite

Such markets are sometimes complicated by the existence of *futures markets*, in which commodities can be bought in the present period for delivery at a future date at prices agreed now. This adds a speculative element to the demand.

Exercise 4.3

The Financial Times in March 1998 reported that the Jamaican bauxite industry was experiencing a combination of record output and falling revenues. It seems that capacity in the industry was rising, and improved labour relations were increasing productivity. However, there was considerable uncertainty in the market, with weak demand for aluminium, following the Asian financial crisis. On the basis of this information, sketch a demand and supply diagram to show the market situation. From your diagram, would you expect price to increase or decrease? How about quantity?

The housing market

Everyone needs somewhere to live, and housing makes up a large part of the household budget. This makes the housing market particularly important in any economy. Here too, demand and supply can be used to explain how the market operates.

The housing market is not in fact a single market, as there are different segments that may operate in quite different ways. There is the owner–occupier market and the private and public rental sectors. Of course these segments interact in some ways, but they may be influenced by different factors.

The owner–occupier housing market often features in the news. The purchase of a house is the largest single transaction that most people will make in their lifetimes, and is normally funded through borrowing (apart from the occasional lottery win). The demand for houses to buy is thus influenced partly by the cost of borrowing – in other words, the interest rate. Later chapters of this book will cover the way in which interest rates are used as a policy instrument to stabilise the overall economy. In the early part of the twenty-first century interest rates have been relatively low by historical standards, and this has encouraged borrowing, which has fed into the demand for houses, pushing the demand curve to the right.

At the same time, the supply of houses has been expanding only slowly – at least in some regions. Building takes time, of course, but also there have been environmental concerns, and the resulting regulation has limited the growth of the housing stock by restricting the amount of new stock to be built.

Figure 4.8 sketches how this might be seen in terms of demand and supply. Demand increases rapidly, but supply expands relatively slowly. The result is an increase in the equilibrium price, from P_0 to P_1, with only a modest expansion of supply, from Q_0 to Q_1. The late 1990s and the early part of this century did indeed see a rapid increase in house prices, and there has been much speculation that they were rising too rapidly to be sustainable. The importance of housing in everyone's lives makes this an important issue.

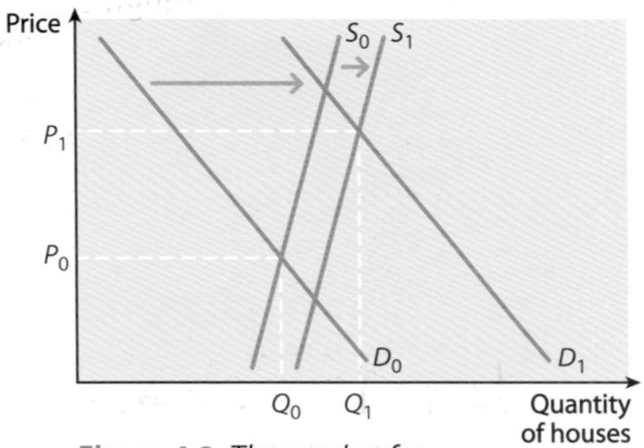

Figure 4.8 The market for houses for owner occupation

Demand and supply may help to explain why house prices have been rising. However, there are other factors to be considered before arriving at a complete explanation of the market. Some of these other aspects of the housing market will be considered in Chapter 10.

The labour market

Within the economy, firms demand labour and employees supply labour – so why not use demand and supply to analyse the market? This can indeed be done.

From the firms' point of view, the demand for labour is a *derived demand*. In other words, firms want labour not for its own sake, but for the output that it produces. This will be explored more carefully in Chapter 21. For now, note that when the 'price' of labour is low firms will tend to demand more of it than when the 'price' of labour is high. The wage rate can be regarded as this 'price' of labour. On the employee side, it is argued that more people tend to offer themselves for work when the wage is relatively high.

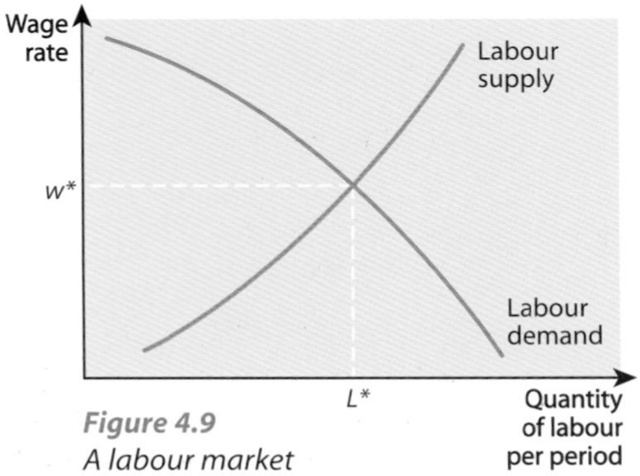

Figure 4.9
A labour market

On this basis, the demand for labour is expected to be downward sloping and the supply of labour upward sloping, as in Figure 4.9. As usual, the equilibrium in a free market will be at the intersection of demand and supply, so firms will hire L^* labour at a wage rate of w^*.

Key term

unemployment: results when people seeking work at the going wage cannot find a job

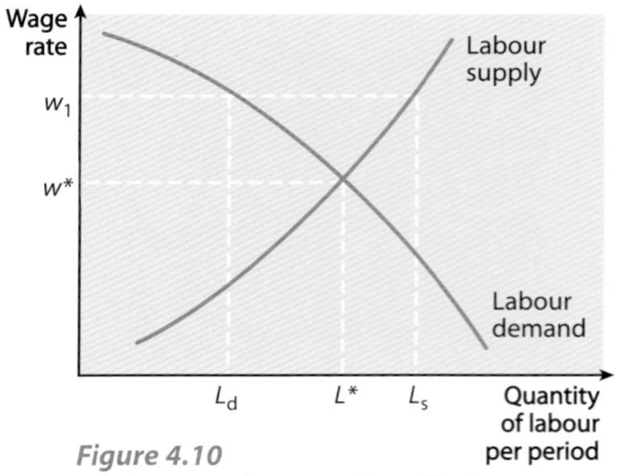

Figure 4.10
A labour market out of equilibrium

The consequences of such a market being away from equilibrium are important. Consider Figure 4.10. Suppose the wage rate is set above the equilibrium level at w_1. The high wage rate encourages more people to offer themselves for work – up to the amount of labour L_s. However, at this wage rate employers are prepared to hire only up to L_d labour. Think about what is happening here. There are people offering themselves for work who cannot find employment; in other words, there is **unemployment**. Thus, one possible cause of unemployment is a wage rate that is set above the equilibrium level.

The foreign exchange market

When you take your holidays in Spain you need to buy euros. Equally, when German tourists come to visit London they need to buy pounds. If there is buying going on, then there must be a market – remember from Chapter 1 that a market is a set of arrangements that enable transactions to be undertaken. So here is another sort of market to be considered. The exchange rate is the price at which two currencies exchange, and it can be analysed using demand and supply.

Consider the market for pounds, and focus on the exchange rate between pounds and euros, as shown in Figure 4.11. Think first of all about what gives rise to a demand for pounds. It is not just German tourists who need pounds to spend on holiday: anyone holding euros who wants to buy British goods needs pounds in order to pay for them. So the demand for pounds comes from people in the euro area who want to buy British goods or services – or assets. When the exchange rate for the pound in euros is high, potential buyers of British goods get relatively few pounds per euro so the demand will be relatively low, whereas if the euro per pound rate is relatively low, they get more for their money. Hence the demand curve is expected to be downward sloping.

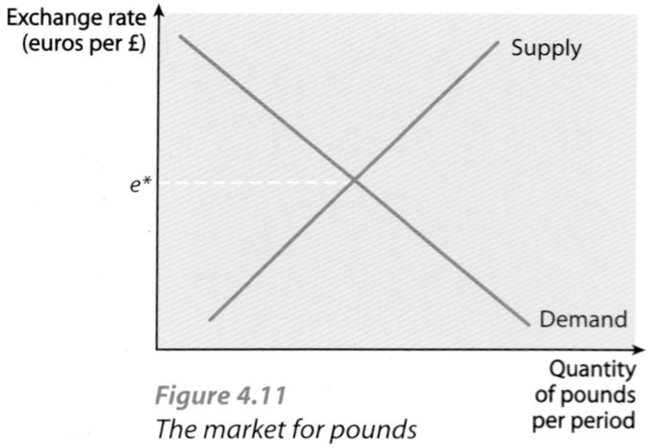

Figure 4.11
The market for pounds

One point to notice from this is that the foreign exchange is another example of a derived demand, in the sense that people want pounds not for their own sake, but for the goods or services that they can buy. One way of viewing the exchange rate is as a means by which to learn about the international competitiveness of British exports. When the exchange rate is high British goods are less competitive in Europe, *ceteris paribus*. Notice the *ceteris paribus* assumption there. This is important, because the exchange rate is not the only determinant of the competitiveness of British goods: they also depend on the relative price levels in the UK and Europe.

How about the supply of pounds? Pounds are supplied by UK residents wanting euros to buy goods or services from Europe. From this angle, when the euro/pound rate is high UK residents get more euros for their pounds, and therefore will tend to supply more pounds.

If the exchange market is in equilibrium, the exchange rate will tend to e^*, where the demand for pounds is matched by the supply.

Indirect taxes and subsidies

One final application of the demand and supply model is to analyse the effect on a market of the imposition of **indirect taxes** and subsidies.

In the UK, value added tax (VAT) is the most prominent example of an indirect tax, although other levies, such as excise duties on alcohol and tobacco, are also indirect taxes. An indirect tax is paid by the seller, so affects the supply curve for a product.

Key term

indirect tax: a tax levied on expenditure on goods or services (as opposed to a direct tax, which is a tax charged directly to an individual based on a component of income)

Figure 4.12 illustrates the case of a fixed rate, or specific tax – a tax that is set at a constant amount per pack of cigarettes. Without the tax, the market equilibrium is at the intersection of demand and supply, with price P_0, and quantity traded Q_0. The effect of the tax is to reduce the quantity that firms are prepared to supply at any given price; to put it another way, for any given quantity of cigarettes, firms need to receive the amount of the tax over and above the price at which they would have been prepared to supply that quantity. The effect is thus to move the supply curve upwards by the amount of the tax, as shown in the figure. A new equilibrium is reached with a higher price at P_1 and a lower quantity traded at Q_1.

An important question is: who bears the burden of the tax? If you look at the diagram, you will see that the price difference between the with- and without-tax situations (i.e. $P_1 - P_0$) is less than the amount of the tax, which is the vertical distance between the with and without supply curves. So, although the seller may be responsible for the mechanics of paying the tax, part of the tax is effectively passed on to the buyer in

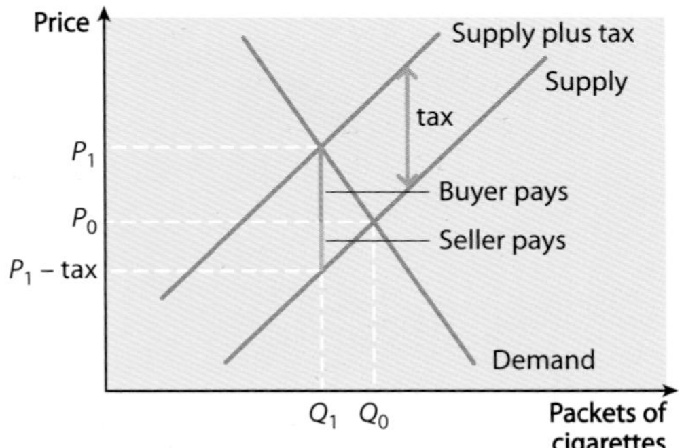

Figure 4.12 The effects of an indirect tax on cigarettes

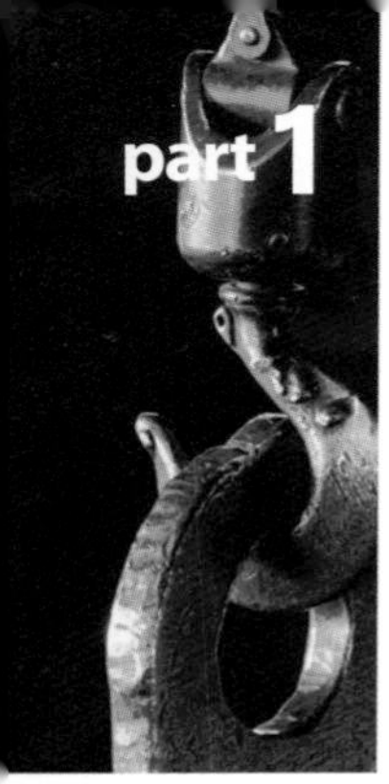

the form of the higher price. So the **incidence of the tax** falls partly upon the seller, but in Figure 4.12 most of the tax is borne by the buyer.

The price elasticity of demand determines the incidence of the tax. If demand were perfectly inelastic, sellers would be able to pass the whole burden of the tax on to buyers through an increase in price equal to the value of the tax, knowing that this would not affect demand. However, if demand were perfectly elastic sellers would not be able to raise the price at all, so they would have to bear the entire burden of the tax. The effects of a sales tax will be discussed further in Chapter 10.

Key terms

incidence of a tax: the way in which the burden of paying a sales tax is divided between buyers and sellers

subsidy: a grant given by the government to producers to encourage production of a good or service

If the tax is not a constant amount, but a percentage of the price (known as an *ad valorem* tax), the supply curve is still affected; but now it steepens, as shown in Figure 4.13.

In some situations the government may wish to encourage production of a particular good or service, perhaps because it views the good as having strategic significance to the country. One way it can do this is by giving **subsidies**.

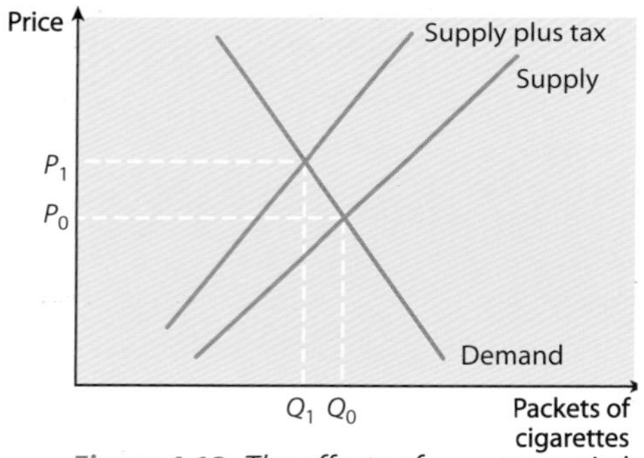

Figure 4.13 The effects of an ad valorem *tax on cigarettes*

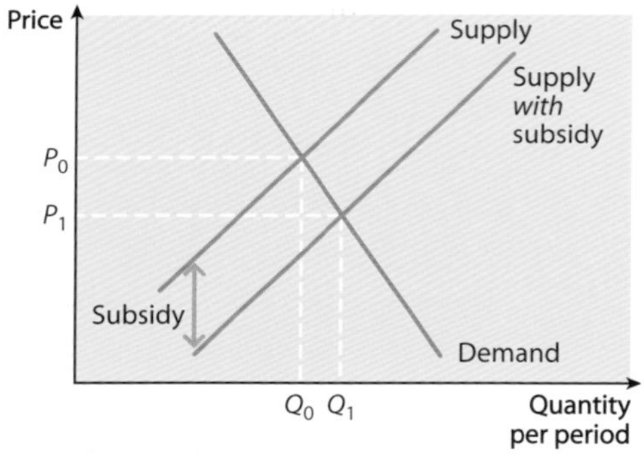

Figure 4.14 The effects of a subsidy

Such subsidies have been especially common in agriculture, which is often seen as being of strategic significance. In the early years of this century the USA has come under pressure to reduce the subsidies that it grants to cotton producers. Analytically, a subsidy can be regarded as a sort of negative indirect tax that shifts the supply curve down, as shown in Figure 4.14. Without the subsidy, market equilibrium is at price P_0 and quantity traded Q_0. With the subsidy in place, the equilibrium price falls to P_1 and the quantity traded increases to Q_1.

Again, notice that, because the price falls by less than the amount of the subsidy, the benefits of the subsidy are shared between buyers and sellers, depending on the elasticity of demand. If the aim of the subsidy is to increase production, it is only partially successful — the degree of success also depends upon the elasticity of demand.

Summary

- In agricultural markets supply can fluctuate between seasons because of weather conditions. This causes volatility in prices.
- In commodity markets demand may fluctuate across the business cycle, again causing volatility in prices.
- The housing market can be analysed using demand and supply analysis. The level of demand may be influenced by government policy on interest rates.
- In the labour market equilibrium is achieved through the wage rate. If the wage rate is set too high, it leads to unemployment.
- Demand and supply enable you to examine how the foreign exchange rate is determined.
- An indirect tax levied on a good or service will be seen as a shift in the supply curve. The incidence of the tax (whether the burden is borne by buyers or sellers) is determined by the elasticity of demand.

Exercise 4.4 Profits and superships

In August 2001 *The Financial Times* reported that ship-owners were facing serious problems. Shipping rates (the prices that ship-owners charge for carrying freight) had fallen drastically in the second quarter of 2001. For example, on the Europe–Asia route rates fell by 8% eastbound and 6% westbound, causing the ship-owners' profits to be squeezed. Here are some relevant facts and issues:

a New 'superships', having been ordered a few years earlier, were coming into service with enhanced capacity for transporting freight.

b A worldwide economic slowdown was taking place; Japan was in lengthy recession, and the US economy was also slowing, affecting the growth of world trade.

c Fuel prices were falling.

d The structure of the industry is fragmented, with ship-owners watching each other's orders for new ships.

e New ships take a long time to build.

f Shipping lines face high fixed costs with slender margins.

Assume that the market is competitive. (This will allow you to draw supply and demand curves for the market.) There is some evidence for this, as shipping lines face 'slender margins' (see f). This suggests that the firms face competition from each other, and are unable to use market power to increase profit margins.

How would you expect the demand and supply curves to move in response to the first three factors mentioned (i.e. a, b and c)? Sketch a diagram for yourself.

Why should the shipping lines undertake a large-scale expansion at a time of falling or stagnant demand?

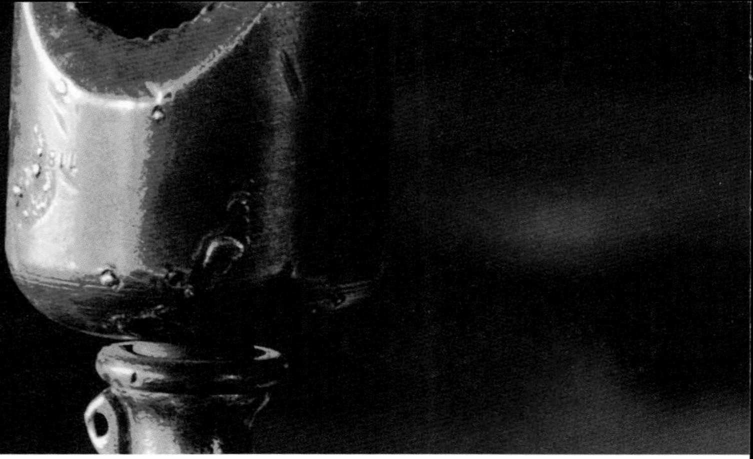

Chapter 5

Prices and resource allocation

The previous four chapters have introduced a range of crucial tools of the economist. This chapter returns to the fundamental economic problem of scarcity, and uses the tools of analysis described previously to investigate the way in which resources are allocated in society. Some of the limitations of the free market economy will also be considered.

Learning outcomes

After studying this chapter, you should:

- have an overview of how the price mechanism works to allocate resources
- see how prices respond to changing preferences
- understand the meaning and significance of consumer surplus
- see how prices provide incentives to producers
- understand the meaning and significance of producer surplus
- understand the effects of the entry and exit of firms into and out of a market
- be able to review the advantages and disadvantages of a free market economy
- be aware of the meaning and relevance of a mixed economy
- appreciate the importance of the public sector in the UK economy
- have on overview of resource allocation under central planning and the problems faced by the transition economies

The coordination problem

As Chapter 1 indicated, all societies face the fundamental economic problem of scarcity. Because there are unlimited wants but finite resources, it is necessary to take decisions on which goods and services should be produced, how they should be produced and for whom they should be produced. For an economy the size of the UK, there is thus an immense coordination problem. Another way of looking at this is to ask how consumers can express their preferences between alternative goods so that producers can produce the best mix of goods and services.

Some alternative possibilities for handling this problem will now be considered. In a **free market economy**, market forces are allowed to allocate resources. At the other extreme, in a centrally planned economy the state plans and directs resources into a range of uses. In between there is the mixed economy. In order to evaluate these alternatives, it is necessary to explore how each of them operates.

In a free market economy prices play the key role; this is sometimes referred to as the *laissez-faire* approach to resource allocation.

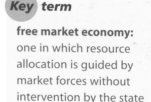

Key term

free market economy: one in which resource allocation is guided by market forces without intervention by the state

Prices and preferences

How can consumers signal their preferences to producers? Demand and supply analysis provides the clue. Figure 5.1 shows the demand and supply for laptop computers. These have become popular goods in recent years. That is to say, over time there has been a rightward shift in the demand curve – in the figure, from D_0 to D_1. This simply means that consumers are placing a higher value on these goods; they are prepared to demand more at any given price.

The result, as you know from comparative static analysis, is that the market will move to a new equilibrium, with price rising from P_0 to P_1 and quantity traded from Q_0 to Q_1: there is a movement along the supply curve.

The movement of the demand curve is an expression of consumers' preferences; it embodies the fact that they value laptop computers more highly now than before. The price that consumers are willing to pay represents their valuation of laptop computers.

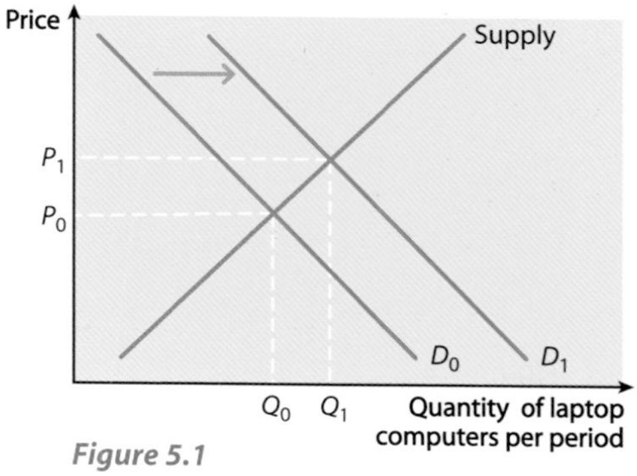

Figure 5.1
The market for laptop computers

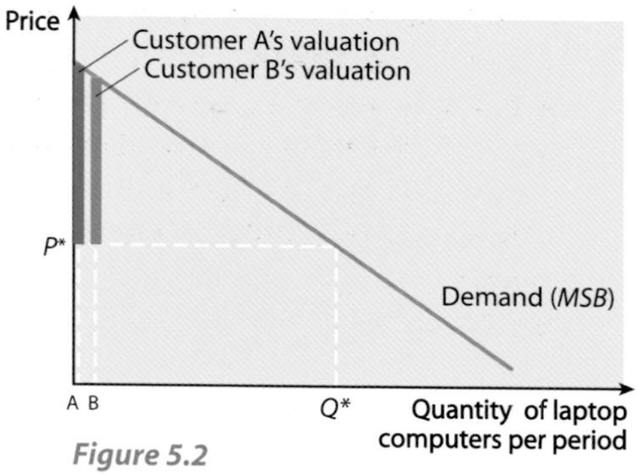

Figure 5.2
Price as marginal benefit

Consumer surplus

Think a little more carefully about what the demand curve represents. Figure 5.2 again shows the demand curve for laptop computers. Suppose that the price is

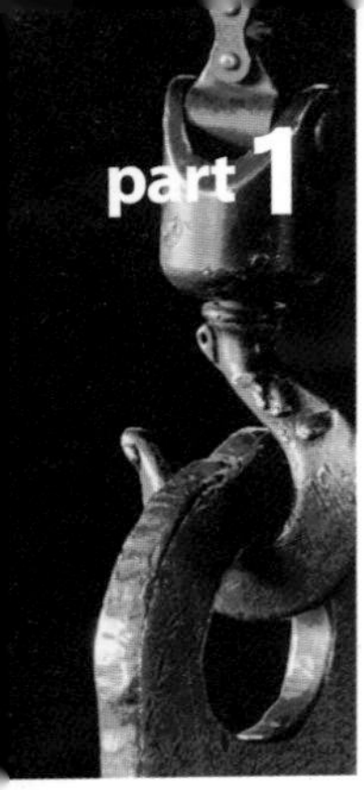

set at P^* and quantity demanded is thus Q^*. P^* can be seen as the value that the last customer places on a laptop. In other words, if the price were even slightly above P^*, there would be one consumer who would choose not to buy: this individual will be referred to as the *marginal consumer.*

To that marginal consumer, P^* represents the marginal benefit derived from consuming this good – it is the price that just reflects the consumer's benefit from a laptop, as it is the price that just induces her to buy. Thinking of the society as a whole (which is made up of all the consumers within it), P^* can be regarded as the **marginal social benefit** derived from consuming this good.

> ***Key term***
>
> **marginal social benefit:** the additional benefit from a good that society gains from consuming an additional unit of a good or service

The same argument could be made about any point along the demand curve, so the demand curve can be interpreted as the marginal social benefit (MSB) to be derived from consuming laptop computers.

In most markets, all consumers face the same prices for goods and services. This leads to an important concept in economic analysis. P^* may represent the value of laptops to the *marginal* consumer, but what about all the other consumers who are also buying laptops at P^*? They would all be willing to pay a higher price for a laptop. Indeed, consumer A in Figure 5.2 would pay a very high price indeed, and thus values a laptop much more highly than P^*. When consumer A pays P^* for a laptop he gets a great deal, as he values the good so much more highly – as represented by the vertical green line on Figure 5.2. Consumer B also gains a surplus above her willingness to pay (the blue line).

> ***Key term***
>
> **consumer surplus:** the value that consumers gain from consuming a good or service over and above the price paid; represented by the area under the demand curve above the market price

If all these surplus values are added up, they sum to the total surplus that society gains from consuming laptops. This is known as the **consumer surplus**, represented by the shaded triangle in Figure 5.3. It can be interpreted as the welfare that society gains from consuming the good.

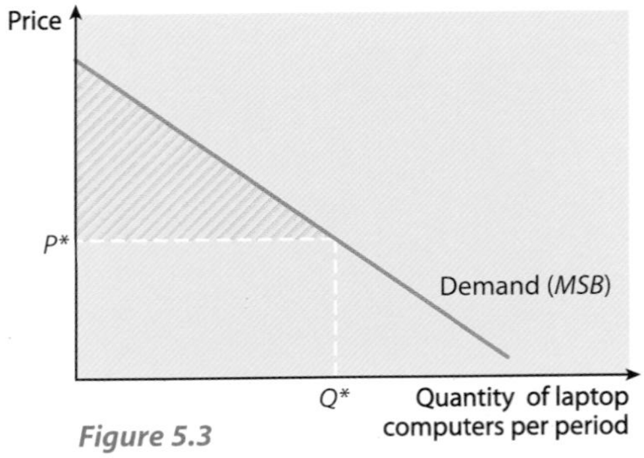

Figure 5.3
Consumer surplus

Prices as signals and incentives

From the producers' perspective, the question is how they receive signals from consumers about their changing preferences. Price is the key. Figure 5.1 shows how an increase in demand for laptop computers leads to an increase in the equilibrium market price. That increase in price encourages producers to supply more computers – there is a movement *along* the supply curve. This is really saying that producers find it profitable to increase their output of laptop computers at that higher price. The price level is thus a signal to producers about consumer preferences.

Notice that the price signal works equally well when there is a *decrease* in the demand for a good or service. Figure 5.4, for example, shows the market for video recordings. With the advent of DVDs, there has been a large fall in the demand for video recordings, so the demand for them has shifted to the left – consumers are demanding fewer videos at any price. Thus, the demand curve shifts from D_0 to D_1. Producers of video recordings are beginning to find that they cannot sell as many videos at the original price as before, so they have to reduce their price to avoid an increase in their unsold stocks. They have less incentive to produce videos, and will supply less. There is a movement *along* the supply curve to a lower equilibrium price at P_1, and a lower quantity traded at Q_1. You may like to think of this as a movement along the firm's production possibility frontier for DVDs and videos.

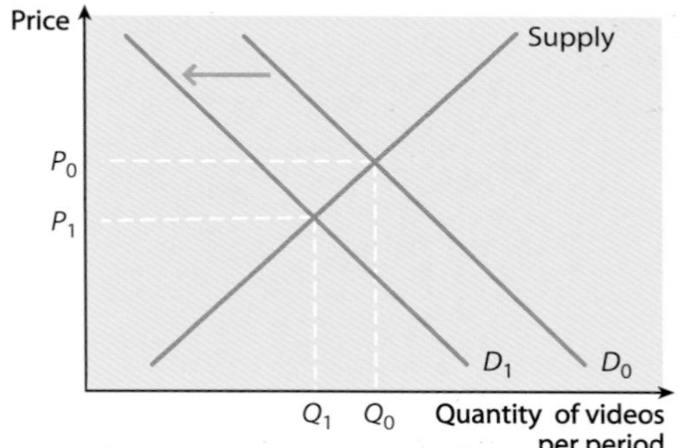

Figure 5.4
The market for video recordings

Thus, you can see how existing producers in a market receive signals from consumers in the form of changes in the equilibrium price, and respond to these signals by adjusting their output levels.

> ***Key term***
>
> **producer surplus:** the difference between the price received by firms for a good or service and the price at which they would have been prepared to supply that good or service

Producer surplus

Parallel to the notion of consumer surplus is the concept of producer surplus. Think about the nature of the supply curve: it reveals how much output firms are prepared to supply at any given price in a competitive market. Figure 5.5 depicts a supply curve. Assume the price is at P^*, and that all units are sold at that price. P^* represents the value to firms of the marginal unit sold. In other words, if the price had been set slightly below P^*, the last unit would not have been supplied, as firms would not have found this profitable.

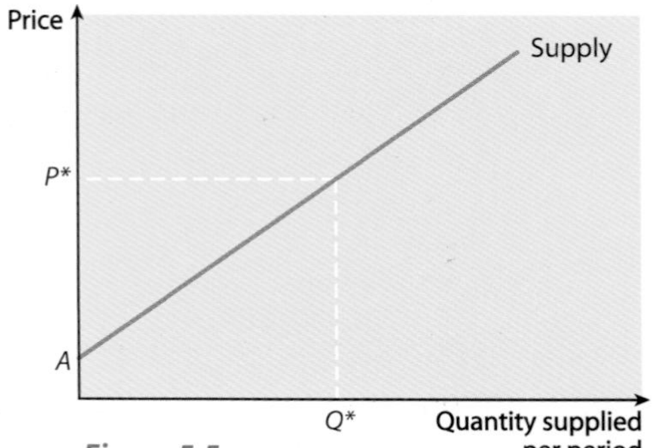

Figure 5.5
A supply curve

Notice that the threshold at which a firm will decide it is not profitable to supply will be the point at which the price received by the firm reaches the cost to the firm of producing the last unit of the good. Thus, in a competitive market the supply curve reflects marginal cost. This will be discussed in more detail in Chapter 16.

The supply curve shows that, in the range of prices between point A and P^*, firms would have been willing to supply positive amounts of this good or service. So at P^*, they would gain a surplus value on all units of the good supplied below Q^*. The total area is shown in Figure 5.6 – it is the area above the supply curve below P^*, shown as the shaded triangle.

One way of defining this producer surplus is as the surplus earned by firms over and above the minimum that would have kept them in the market. It is the *raison d'être* of firms.

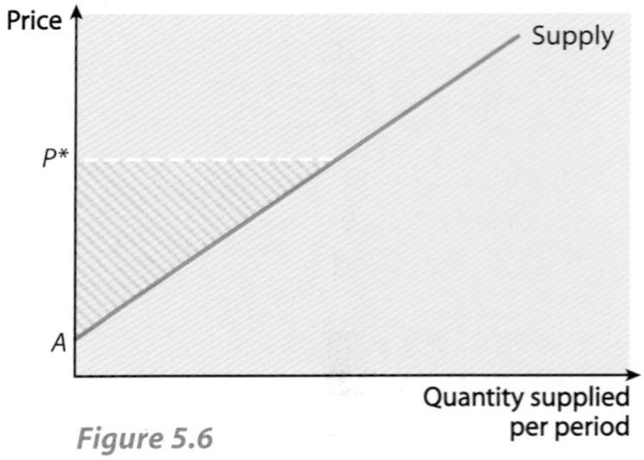

Figure 5.6 Producer surplus

Entry and exit of firms

The discussion so far has focused on the reactions of existing firms in a market to changes in consumer preferences. However, this is only part of the picture. Think back to Figure 5.1, where there was an increase in demand for laptop computers following a change in consumer preferences. The equilibrium price rose, and existing firms expanded the quantity supplied in response. Those firms are now earning a higher producer surplus than before. Other firms not currently in the market will be attracted by these surpluses, perceiving this to be a profitable market in which to operate.

If there are no barriers to entry, more firms will join the market. This in turn will tend to move the supply curve to the right, as there will then be more firms prepared to supply. As a result, the equilibrium market price will tend to drift down again, until the market reaches a position in which there is no further incentive for new firms to enter the market. This will occur when the rate of return for firms in the laptop market is no better than in other markets.

Figure 5.7 illustrates this situation. The original increase in demand leads, as before, to a new equilibrium with a higher price P_1. As new firms join the market in quest of producer surplus, the supply curve shifts to the right to S_2, pushing the price back down to P_0, but with the quantity traded now up at Q_2.

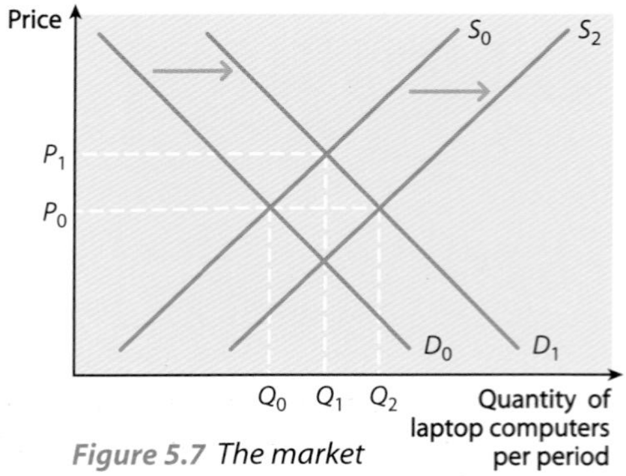

Figure 5.7 The market for laptop computers revisited

If the original movement in demand is in the opposite direction, as it was in

Figure 5.4, a similar long-run adjustment takes place. As the market price falls, some firms in the market may decide that they no longer wish to remain in production, and will exit from the market altogether. This will move the supply curve to the left in Figure 5.8 (to S_2) until only firms that continue to find it profitable will remain in the market. In the final position price is back to P_0, and quantity traded has fallen to Q_2.

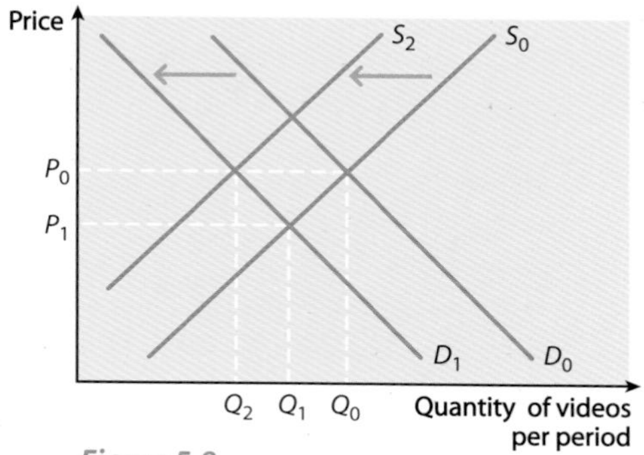

Figure 5.8
The market for video recordings

Exercise 5.1

a Sketch a demand and supply diagram and mark on it the areas that represent consumer and producer surplus.

b Using a demand and supply diagram, explain the process that provides incentives for firms to adjust to a decrease in the demand for fountain pens in a competitive market.

Summary

- If market forces are to allocate resources effectively, consumers need to be able to express their preferences for goods and services in such a way that producers can respond.
- Consumers express their preferences through prices, as prices will adjust to equilibrium levels following a change in consumer demand.
- Consumer surplus represents the benefit that consumers gain from consuming a product over and above the price they pay for that product.
- Producer surplus represents the benefit gained by firms over and above the price at which they would have been prepared to supply a product.
- Producers have an incentive to respond to changes in prices. In the short run this occurs through output adjustments of existing firms (movements along the supply curve), but in the long run firms will enter the market (or exit from it) until there are no further incentives for entry or exit.

The working of a market economy

You have seen that the price mechanism allows a society to allocate its resources effectively if firms respond to changes in prices. Consumers express changes in their preferences by their decisions to buy (or not to buy) at the going price, which leads to a change in the equilibrium price. Firms thus respond to changes in consumer demand, given the incentives of profitability, which is related to price. In the short run, existing firms adjust their output levels along the supply curve.

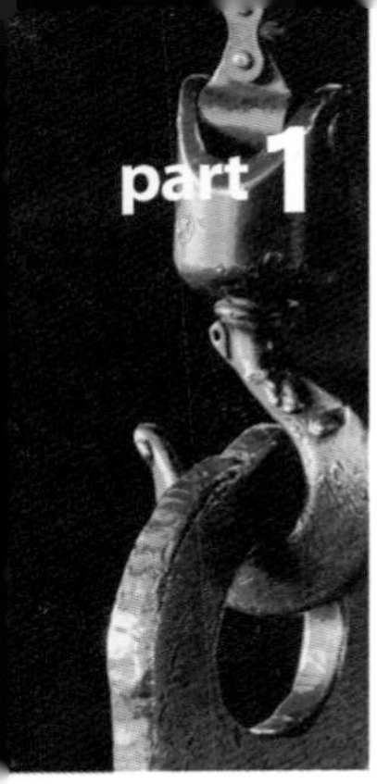

In the long run firms enter into markets (or exit from them) in response to the relative profitability of the various economic activities that take place in the economy.

One way of viewing this system is through the notion of opportunity cost, introduced in Chapter 1. For example, in choosing to be active in the market for video recordings, a firm faces an opportunity cost. If it uses its resources to produce video recordings, it is *not* using those resources to produce DVDs. There may come a point at which the cost of producing video recordings becomes too high, if the profitability of DVDs is so much higher than that for video recordings, because of changes in the pattern of consumer demand. When the firm finds that it is not covering its opportunity costs, it will transfer production from the video market to the DVD market.

This sort of system of resource allocation is often referred to as **capitalism**. The key characteristic of capitalism is that individuals own the means of production, and can pursue whatever activities they choose – subject, of course, to the legal framework within which they operate.

The government's role in a free capitalist economy is relatively limited, but nonetheless important. A basic framework of *property rights* is essential, together with a basic legal framework. However, the state does not intervene in the production process directly. Secure property rights are significant, as this assures the incentives for the owners of capital.

Within such a system, consumers try to maximise the satisfaction they gain from consuming a range of products, and firms seek to maximise their profits by responding to consumer demand through the medium of price signals.

As has been shown, this is a potentially effective way of allocating resources. In the eighteenth century Adam Smith discussed this mechanism, arguing that when consumers and firms respond to incentives in this way resources are allocated effectively through the operation of an **invisible hand,** which guides firms to produce the goods and services that consumers wish to consume. Although individuals pursue their self-interest, the market mechanism ensures that their actions will bring about a good result for society overall. A solution to the coordination problem is thus found through the free operation of markets. Such market adjustments provide a solution to Samuelson's three fundamental economic questions of what? how? and for whom?

However, Adam Smith also sounded a word of warning. He felt that there were too many factors that interfered with the free market system, such as over-protectionism and restrictions on trade. At the same time, he was not utterly convinced that a free market economy would be wholly effective, noting also that firms might at times collude to prevent the free operation of the market mechanism:

Key terms

capitalism: a system of production in which there is private ownership of productive resources, and individuals are free to pursue their objectives with minimal interference from government

invisible hand: term used by Adam Smith to describe the way in which resources are allocated in a market economy

> People of the same trade seldom meet together, even for merriment and diversion, but the conversation ends in a conspiracy against the public, or in some contrivance to raise prices... (Adam Smith, *The Wealth of Nations*, Vol. I)

So there may be situations in which consumer interests need to be protected. This issue will be revisited in Chapter 7.

Centrally planned economies

In contrast to the free market economy, a number of economies in the past have used the much more interventionist style of resource allocation known as central planning.

Key term

centrally planned economy: one in which decisions on resource allocation are guided by the state

The most obvious examples of this were seen in the economies of the Soviet bloc (the Soviet Union and much of Eastern Europe), China and one or two other countries that followed their lead, such as Cuba and North Korea. The breakdown of the Soviet bloc after the Berlin Wall was demolished in 1989 seem to have discredited this form of resource allocation, and almost no example of a pure centrally planned economy now exists. In the Russian Federation, the countries of Eastern Europe and China, market-oriented reforms have been introduced allowing market forces to have much more influence on the way in which resources are allocated.

Karl Marx is often cited as the inspiration for the centrally planned ideology. Marx believed that capitalism was destined to fail, because allowing private ownership of the means of production would lead to exploitation of the working class, which would culminate in revolution. A sequence of inevitable stages would eventually lead to an idealistic communist state, in which individuals would be rewarded according to their contribution to the economy (i.e. their productivity), and no state would be needed.

Central planning would seem as far away from this as from the free market economy, although it may be seen as an intermediate stage. The 1917 revolution in Russia was not the sort of revolution that Marx had predicted, however, as capitalism had not yet reached maturity in the country, which was still primarily an agrarian-based society. Nonetheless, after the revolution the state took control of resource allocation and dictated the way in which the economy was to develop.

Marx's theory of the exploitation of the working class was the inspiration for most centrally planned economies.

Central planning faces some complex issues. The question of what is to be produced has to be resolved, and for a large and complex society it is no easy matter to do that through a central dictatorship without any guidance provided by price signals. Many mistakes were made after the 1917 revolution, with substantial resources being directed into heavy industry at the expense of consumer goods, leading to severe shortages and much poverty.

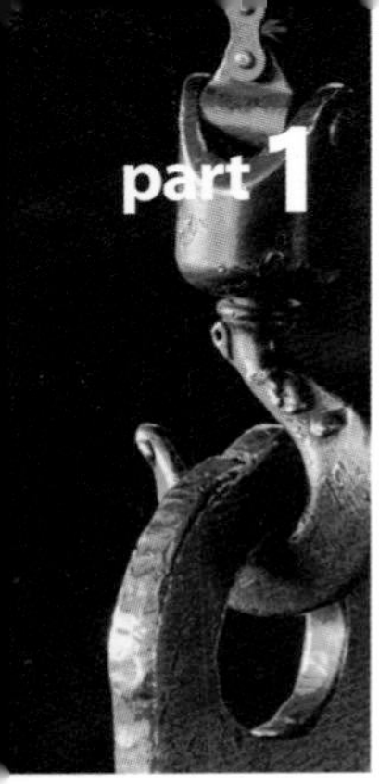

In addition, if prices are not acting as signals, some alternative method of providing incentives to firms has to be found. In particular, the question of *how* output should be produced proved difficult in Russia. Without prices that reflect the relative scarcity of factors of production, inefficiencies crept in to the choice of techniques of production. When East and West Germany were reunified, and East German steel plants began facing market prices for labour, capital and other inputs, it was found that many had been producing *negative* value added; in other words, inputs were being used so inefficiently that the value of the output was less than the value of the inputs being used in its production.

It is now widely accepted that central planning cannot cope with the complexities of a modern economy. But can a totally free market be allowed to allocate resources without some form of state influence?

The mixed economy

In 1991 the World Bank offered the following advice to developing countries:

> Put simply, governments need to do less in those areas where markets work, or can be made to work reasonably well ... at the same time, governments need to do more where markets alone cannot be relied upon. (World Bank, *World Development Report*, 1991)

This argues for a **mixed economy**, i.e. an economy in which market forces guide resource allocation wherever possible, but in which it is recognised that there are areas in the economy where some government intervention is needed to safeguard the allocation of resources. Part 2 of this book explores some of the ways in which markets may fail to operate effectively.

Key term

mixed economy: one in which resources are allocated partly through price signals and partly on the basis of direction by government

In practice, most economies have operated as mixed economies. Even in Hong Kong, which was often held up as the ultimate example of a free market economy, there was state intervention in the housing market and in guiding land use, in particular. Other democracies have shown varying degrees of government intervention in resource allocation, but market forces have always played some role.

Summary

- A free market economy is one in which market forces guide the allocation of resources within an economy — but in most societies there is some form of state intervention.
- A centrally planned economy is one in which the state takes responsibility for resource allocation — but centralisation has been largely discredited as a sustainable system.
- A mixed economy is one in which resource allocation reflects the results of a mix of private and public sector decisions.

The mixed economy in practice

How can the relative importance of government in the overall economy be measured? One way is by looking at the share of the public sector in total expenditure. Figure 5.9 shows one measure of the importance of the public sector in the UK economy since 1963/64. 'Total managed expenditure' is the government's preferred measure of total public expenditure. This covers expenditure by local and central government and by public corporations, and includes both current and capital expenditure. You can see from the graph that the public sector's overall share in total expenditure was not very different in 2003/04 from what it was back in 1963/64, but it has fluctuated somewhat in the intervening years. On average, public expenditure was just over 40% throughout this period.

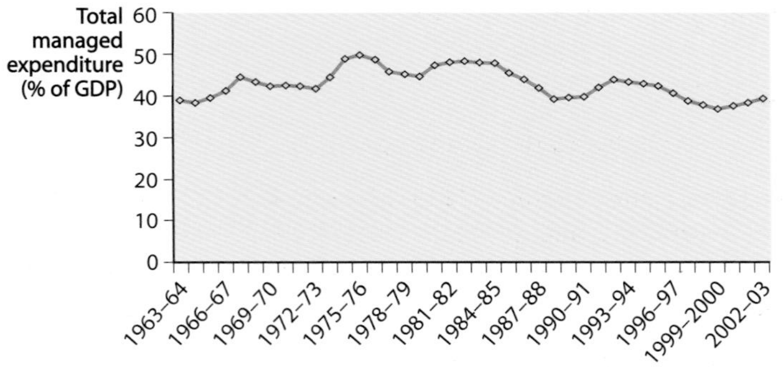

Figure 5.9 *The public sector in the UK*

Source: ONS.

Another overall measure is the so-called 'National Debt'. This is a measure of the stock of outstanding government debt, which reflects past decisions about borrowing. Data since 1858 are shown in Figure 5.10, expressed as a percentage of GDP.

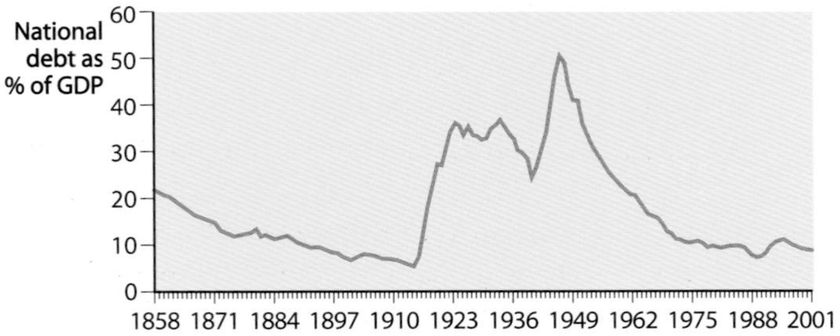

Figure 5.10 *The 'National Debt'*

Source: HM Treasury.

The large expansions in the 1920s and late 1940s are partly associated with the two world wars, which left a legacy of increased debt. Remember that one component of public expenditure is national defence, so a major war tends to push up the share of public sector expenditure relative to that of the private sector. Figure 5.10 also reveals that current levels of outstanding debt are low by historic standards.

In judging the relative size of the public sector, it is useful to compare the UK with other economies. Figure 5.11 presents total government outlays (again relative to GDP) in selected OECD countries. This shows that the share of public sector in total expenditure in the UK is slightly higher than the average across OECD countries, but rather lower than the average for the European Union.

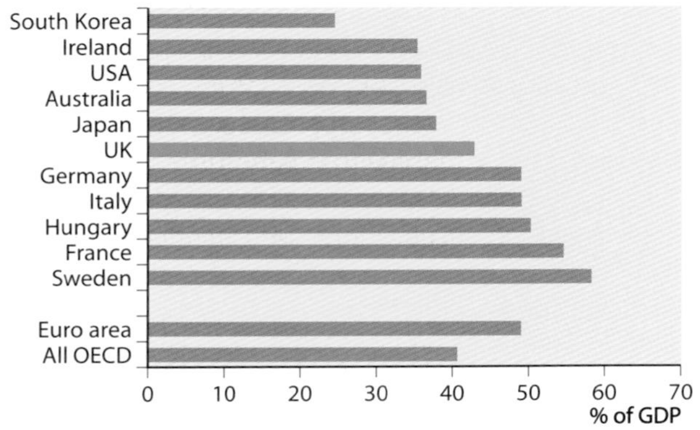

Figure 5.11 *Total government outlays in selected OECD countries*

Source: OECD.

In interpreting these data, it is important to be aware that the importance of the public sector cannot be judged purely on the basis of spending figures. This is in part because the data include 'social protection', which is made up partly of transfers between groups in society – for example payments of unemployment and other benefits. This is to do with redistribution of income. Figure 5.12 shows how the Treasury expects government spending in 2004/05 to be divided up by function. Notice the importance of social protection, which is the largest single category shown, followed by health and education.

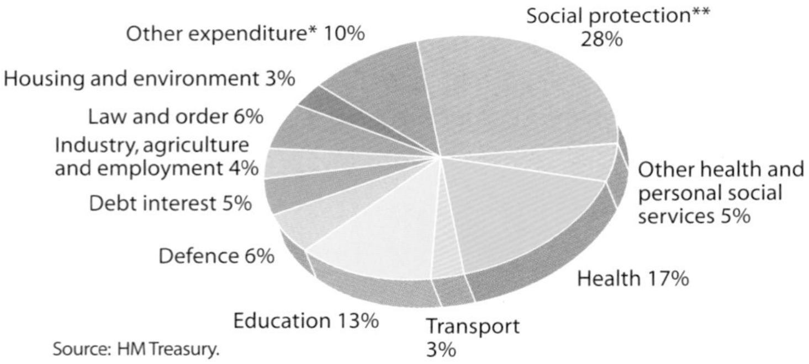

Source: HM Treasury.

* Includes spending on general public services; recreation, culture and religion; international cooperation and development; public service pensions; plus spending yet to be allocated and some accounting adjustments.

** Includes tax credit payments in excess of an individual's tax liability.

Figure 5.12 Government spending by function: 2004/05 projection

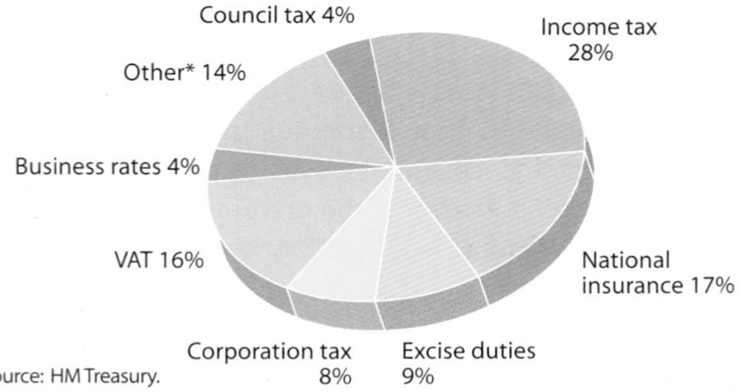

Source: HM Treasury.

*Other receipts include capital taxes, stamp duties, vehicle excise duties and some other tax and non-tax receipts, e.g. interests and dividends.

Figure 5.13 Government receipts, 2004/05 projection

Figure 5.13 shows the other side of the coin, i.e. the way in which the government raises its revenues. One significant aspect of this is the division between direct taxes such as income tax and corporation tax, and indirect taxes such as VAT and excise duties.

Figure 5.14 shows the balance between the government's total receipts and total outlays since 1986. Notice that if outlays exceed receipts the difference has to be funded in some way. This will be explored in Chapter 35.

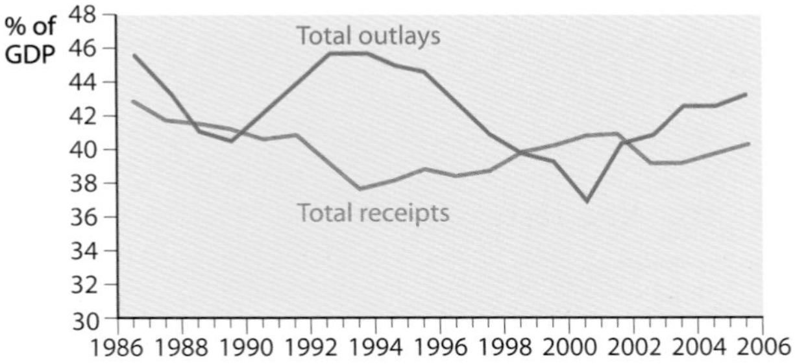

Figure 5.14 *UK public sector receipts and outlays*

Source: OECD.

The transition economies

Making the transition from a centrally planned economy to one in which market forces play a significant role in allocating resources has been a painful process for the countries of the former Soviet bloc. Most went through a period of falling average incomes during the transition phase, as can be seen in Figure 5.15, which shows average growth rates of per capita incomes during the 1990s.

Key term

transition economies: a set of economies that are in the process of transition from central planning to being mixed economies

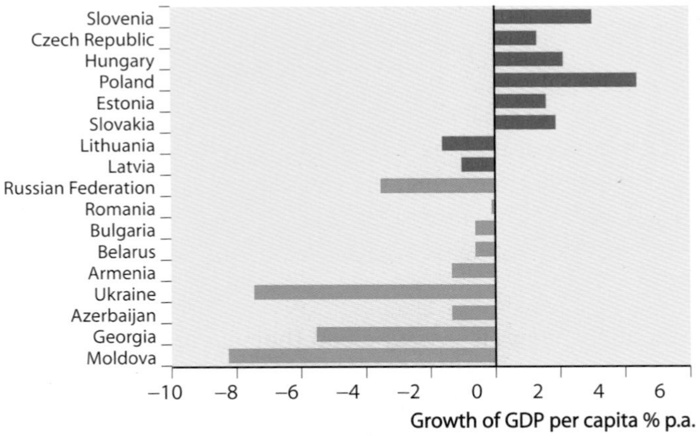

Figure 5.15 *Growth in transition economies, 1990–2001*

Source: *Human Development Report 2003.*

Notice that the countries in this diagram are in descending order of per capita income from top to bottom, so it seems that the lowest-income countries suffered the most during this period. For some of these countries this was a period of severe political upheaval as well as economic disruption. From an economic perspective,

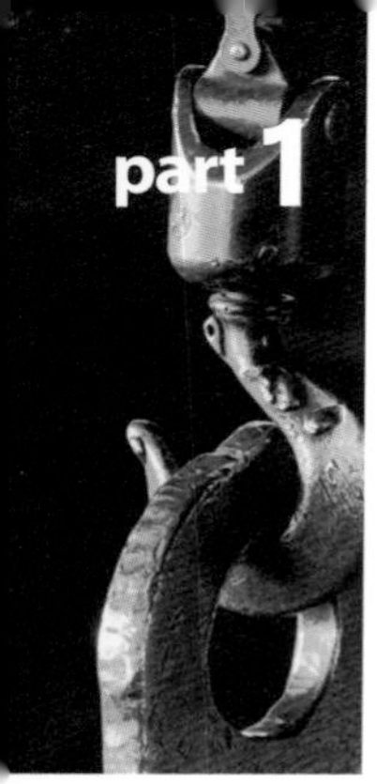

it takes time to learn to respond to economic incentives when decision-makers have become accustomed to responding to state directives.

Nonetheless, significant progress has been made, and on 1 May 2004 some of these countries had progressed to the point where they could become part of the European Union. These are the ones coloured green in the figure. Figure 5.16 gives growth rates in 2001-02, which shows a much more optimistic picture, with all countries now displaying positive growth – in some cases, very rapid growth.

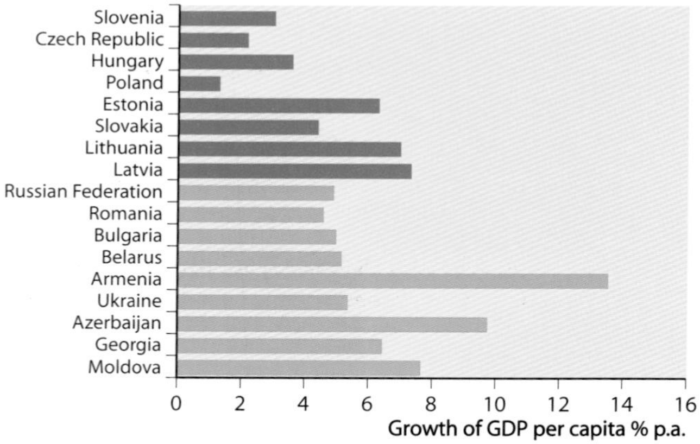

Figure 5.16
Growth in transition economies, 2001–02

Source: World Bank: *World Development Report 2004.*

China is a different case again. China too went through a period of strong central control, coupled with being closed to international trade. However, market reforms have been gradually brought in, and the country has been increasingly active in the international trade arena. China's growth has been impressive since market reforms began, averaging above 8% per year since 1975. In this instance, market reforms were phased in gradually, beginning with Deng Xiaoping in 1978.

The global economy

In the early part of the twenty-first century, there has been much talk about globalisation, and moves towards a global economy. In part, this has reflected the growth of large corporations that operate in the global market, and it has not been universally welcomed. Protesters have argued that globalisation is destroying the environment and perpetuating poverty. Supporters point to the opportunities offered by globalisation.

From an economic point of view, it seems clear that advances in technology, especially communications, have fuelled the process of globalisation. The ease with which information can be transmitted around the world through the world-wide web and the improved efficiency of financial markets have also contributed to globalisation by making it so much easier (and quicker) to gather information and undertake transactions. However, there has also been a political element, with moves towards the establishment of trading areas – not just the European Union, but elsewhere in the world – and a general reduction in barriers to international trade.

This still has a long way to go, however, and many contentious issues need to be resolved before a truly global economy can emerge. Apart from anything else, substantial global inequality remains, with the sub-Saharan African region still excluded from development and struggling to escape poverty. These issues will be revisited later in the book. Meanwhile, Part 2 begins to address the question of how markets may sometimes fail to produce the best possible response to fundamental economic questions.

Summary

- In the UK, public sector expenditure accounts for around 40% of total expenditure in the economy, and raises revenue at a similar level.
- The Chancellor of the Exchequer follows a Golden Rule that, on average over the economic cycle, borrowing should be undertaken by the government only for investment purposes, and not for current spending.
- The transition economies went through a painful decade of adjustment to allow market forces to influence resource allocation. Some of them are now members of the European Union.

part 1

Review section

This section will remind you of the material that has been covered in Part 1, and provides some sample examination questions from past papers for you to try out. It should help you to consolidate the ideas that you have met so far.

It begins with a brief summary of the contents of the first five chapters. You should make sure that you are familiar with all the key terms that have been introduced in the chapters — they also appear in the Glossary at the end of the book.

Chapter 1 Introducing economics

The opening chapter described the key subject matter of economics and identified some basic concepts. In particular, it emphasised that economics is about how society deals with the problem of *scarcity*. This leads to the very important notion of *opportunity cost*, the idea that every choice involves the sacrifice of an alternative option. This is illustrated by the *production possibility frontier*, the first of many diagrams that are crucial in economic analysis. The chapter also introduced the *factors of production* used by firms in the production process, and drew a distinction between *positive* and *normative* analysis.

Chapter 2 Specialisation and international trade

Specialisation through the *division of labour* leads to improved productivity in production. If nations choose to engage in international trade, and to specialise in the production of goods and services in which they have a *comparative advantage*, then trade can be mutually beneficial for the countries engaging in it. However, there may be dangers in becoming over-specialised, as dependence on a narrow range of commodities can create a certain amount of vulnerability. Chapter 2 introduced these ideas, and also set out some data about the extent to which the UK and other countries rely on international trade. The direction of UK trade was also mentioned, in particular the growing share of exports to and imports from the European Union.

Chapter 3 Demand, supply and equilibrium

The *demand* and *supply* model is almost certainly the most famous model used in economics, partly because it is one of the most useful and widely applicable. Chapter 3 introduced the basics of the model, looking at the factors that influence the shape and position of demand and supply curves, and the way these can be used to investigate market equilibrium. It also introduced the notion of *elasticity*, which is important because it allows economists to measure the sensitivity of demand or supply to changes in any of the factors that affect them.

Chapter 4 Applying demand and supply analysis

Following on from the introduction of the demand and supply model, this chapter described a range of applications of the analysis by looking at different sorts of market, including markets for housing, labour and foreign exchange. It also explored the effects of a *sales tax*, and explained how to use *comparative static analysis* to investigate changes in the *market equilibrium*.

Chapter 5 Prices and resource allocation

The final chapter of Part 1 drew on the analysis of the previous chapter by considering the way in which prices in a *market economy* guide the *allocation of resources*. The notions of *consumer surplus* and *producer surplus* were introduced, along with the effects of free *entry* into and exit from markets, which explain how *prices act as signals* to producers about the preferences of consumers. Alternative forms of resource allocation, such as *central planning*, were also discussed, and the UK *public sector* was introduced in describing the way in which the UK government intervenes to influence the course of the economy.

Preparing for the examination

Economics is a subject that needs to be *used*. It is crucial that you get plenty of practice at applying economic models and economic thinking to practical situations. It is by thinking about how (for example) demand and supply analysis can be used to interpret economic events that you will learn to become an economist. The examination reflects this: you will need to be able to handle 'supported multiple-choice questions', and to tackle data-response questions.

Supported multiple-choice questions require you not only to pick the right answer (as in *Who Wants to be a Millionaire?*) — the correct answer nets you only 1 mark. You also need to be able to explain your answer. Indeed, most of the marks come from the explanation rather than from choosing the right answer. Remember this when you practise the following questions. Remember also that the question paper encourages you to use diagrams in your explanations where this is appropriate — and you should do this if you want to get good marks.

In the data-response, you are provided with some information about a market situation, and will need to answer a sequence of questions that will test your understanding of the information provided — and, of course, your knowledge of economics.

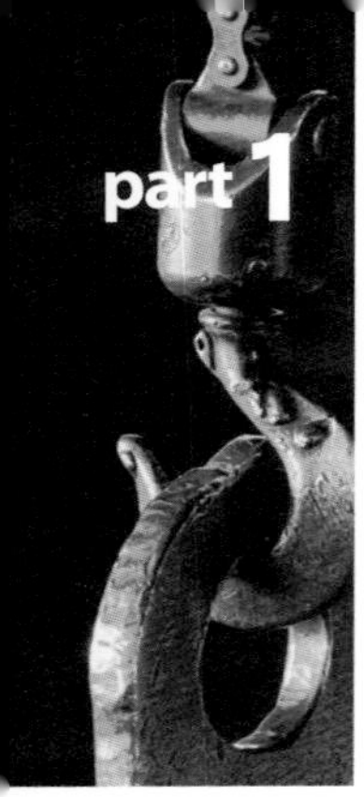

Supported multiple-choice questions

P1.1 A production possibility frontier can be used to illustrate the concept of:

A opportunity cost
B equilibrium price
C consumer surplus
D producer surplus

P1.2 Which of the following is the most likely consequence of an increase in the division of labour in the production of motor vehicles?

A increased cost of producing each car
B a decrease in the market size
C less use of specialised production equipment
D reduced cost of producing each car

P1.3 The market for a luxury good shown in Figure P1.1 is in equilibrium at point *X*, where S_1S_1 is the supply of the good and D_1D_1 is the demand for the good. Following a decrease in real incomes and the exit of some firms from the industry, what will be the new long-run equilibrium: *A*, *B*, *C* or *D*?

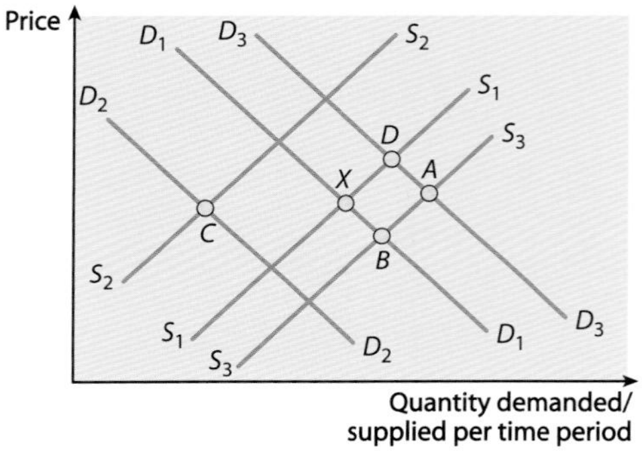

Figure P1.1 The market for a luxury good

P1.4 Which of the following factors is likely to cause the price of tea to rise without a shift in the demand curve?

A an increase in the productivity of tea pickers
B an increase in real incomes of consumers
C an increase in the wages of tea pickers
D an increase in the total population that drinks tea

P1.5 If spending on foreign holidays rises faster than spending on bread when income rises, this suggests that:

A the cross elasticity of demand for foreign holidays with regard to bread is negative
B income elasticity of demand is greater for foreign holidays than for bread
C price elasticity of demand is greater for foreign holidays than for bread
D bread can be described as an inferior good

P1.6 Figure P1.2 shows the demand for bus travel. The figure suggests that bus travel is:

A an inferior good
B a necessity
C a free good
D a normal good

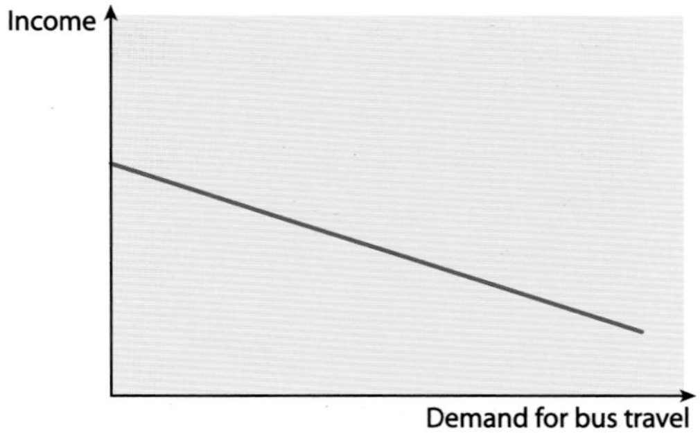

Figure P1.2 *The demand for bus travel*

P1.7 In Figure P1.3, the imposition of a tax shifts the supply curve of a good from S_1 to S_2. What is the incidence of the tax on producers?

A *UVW*
B *UPZ*
C *VPXW*
D *OQYM*

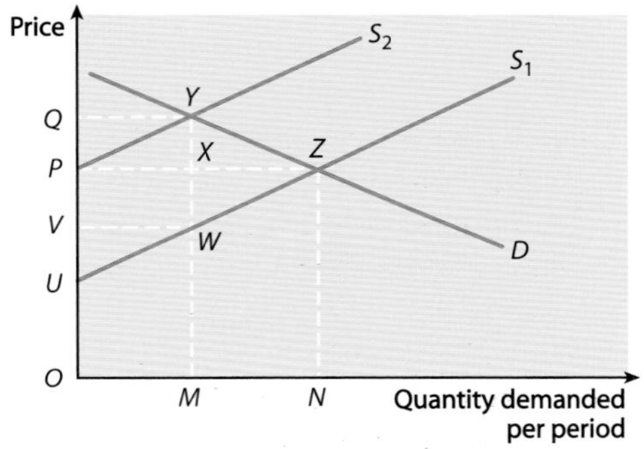

Figure P1.3 *The incidence of a sales tax*

P1.8 In Figure P1.4, *DD* is a consumer's demand curve for a good and *OM* is the quantity demanded.

If the consumer faces a price of *OP* for all units consumed, then consumer surplus is represented by the area:

A *X*
B *Y*
C *Z*
D *Y* + *Z*

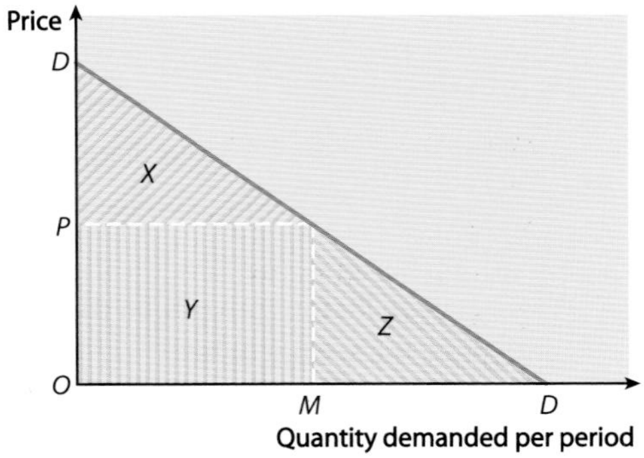

Figure P1.4 *A demand curve for a good*

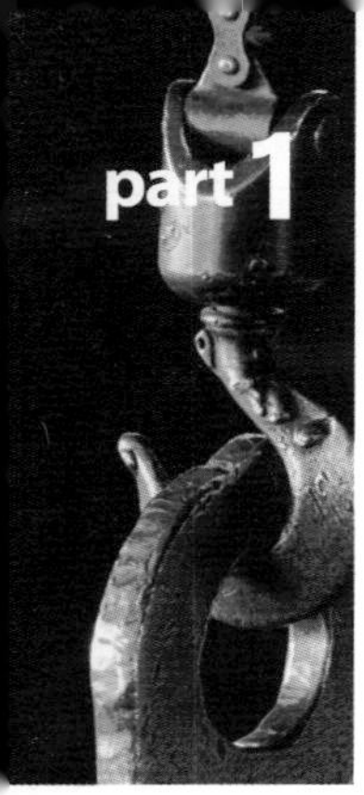

Data-response question P1.9

The question paper recommends spending 30 minutes on this section.

Falling tea prices

Tea prices have fallen dramatically over recent years as new and established producers flood the market with cheap, mass-produced leaves. Vietnam, for example, has joined the ranks of major tea producers, while the more established suppliers have embarked upon large expansion programmes — Uganda has increased its supply by 20% since 1995, while India has recorded a sharp jump in output. Stocks of tea are at record levels. The fall in the price of tea is bad news for producers, particularly since demand for tea is price inelastic.

To make matters worse, sales of tea have steadily declined as many consumers switch to soft drinks and coffee. Tea suffers from an image problem, particularly with the young generation who regard it as dull and old fashioned. There is also concern over the quality of tea, which varies enormously among producers. In Sri Lanka tea is produced by expensive traditional methods, where the machines gently rub the tea leaves to release the full flavour. However, in some countries the tea leaves are crushed and ground, leaving a harsher flavour.

The tea industry is fighting back and has begun to modernise its advertising campaign, promoting the product as a natural, authentic and healthy drink. Some commentators believe the solution rests in opening up 'tea shops' on High Streets — something already common with coffee. Work also needs to be done on ensuring that the quality of tea reaches a minimum standard throughout the industry. Other issues are concerned with ways of developing new markets and uses for tea.

Adapted from 'How to make tea', Fran Abrams, *Guardian*, 25 June 2002

a Using a supply and demand diagram, analyse the causes of falling tea prices. *(5 marks)*

b Examine the impact on the revenue of tea producers of 'the fall in the price of tea' (line 6). *(5 marks)*

c Analyse two factors, other than those referred to in the passage, that could influence the supply of tea. *(4 marks)*

d Examine the likely impact on the demand for tea of a change in the price of:

(i) a substitute good

(ii) a complementary good *(6 marks)*

These questions were taken from examinations set for the Edexcel AS Economics examination for Unit 1 — Markets: how they work. We are grateful to London Qualifications for permission to reproduce them here.

Markets: why they fail

Part 2

Introducing market failure

Part 1 described how markets work to reconcile producers' decisions about what to produce with consumers' preferences about the goods and services that they want to consume. In this discussion it was hinted that there would be circumstances in which governments might need to intervene to make sure that markets work effectively. Part 2 begins to explore some of the reasons why markets may fail to produce the best possible outcome for resource allocation in a society.

Learning outcomes

After studying this chapter, you should:

- understand the concepts of productive and allocative efficiency
- have an awareness of the concepts of average and marginal cost
- appreciate the situations in which markets may fail to allocate resources effectively

Aspects of efficiency

In tackling the fundamental economic problem of scarcity, a society needs to find a way of using its limited resources as effectively as possible. In normal parlance it might be natural to refer to this as a quest for *efficiency*. From an economist's point of view there are two key aspects of efficiency, both of which are important in evaluating whether markets in an economy are working effectively.

Chapter 1 introduced one of these aspects in relation to the production possibility frontier (PPF). Figure 6.1 shows a country's production possibility frontier. One of the choices to be made in allocating resources in this country is between producing agricultural and manufactured goods.

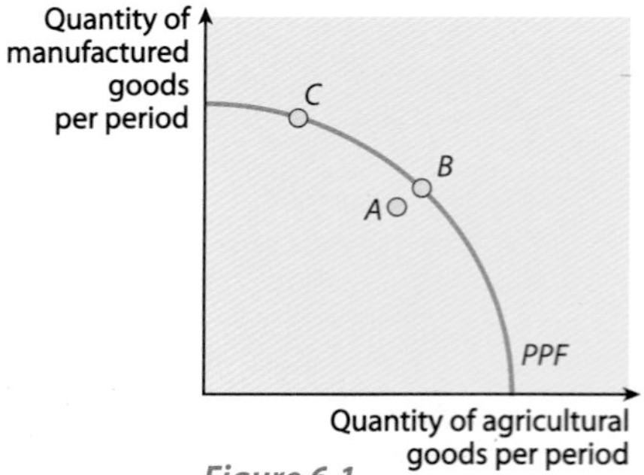

Figure 6.1
Productive efficiency

In Chapter 1 it was seen that at a production point such as *A* the economy would not be using its resources fully, since by moving to a point *on* the PPF it would be possible to produce more of both types of good. For example, if production took place at the point *B*, then more of both agricultural and manufactured goods could be produced, so that the society would be better off than at *A*.

A similar claim could be made for any point along the PPF: it is more efficient to be at a point *on* the frontier than at some points *within* it. However, if you compare point *C* with point *B* you will notice that the economy produces more manufactured goods at *C* than at *B* – but only at the expense of producing fewer agricultural goods.

This draws attention to the trade-off between the production of the two sorts of goods. It is difficult to judge whether society is better off at *B* or at *C* without knowing more about the preferences of consumers.

This discussion highlights the two aspects of efficiency. On the one hand, there is the question of whether society is operating on the PPF, and thus using its resources effectively. On the other hand, there is the question of whether society is producing the balance of goods that consumers wish to consume. These two aspects of efficiency are known as **productive efficiency** and **allocative efficiency**.

In terms of Figure 6.1, both *B* and *C* are productively efficient points, but it is not possible to judge which of the two is the better without knowing consumers' preferences.

An efficient point for a society would be one in which no redistribution of resources could make any individual better off without making some other individual worse off. This is known as the *Pareto criterion*, after the nineteenth-century economist Vilfredo Pareto, who first introduced the concept.

Notice, however, that *any* point along the frontier is a **Pareto optimum**: with a different distribution of income among individuals in a society, a different overall equilibrium will be reached.

Key terms

productive efficiency: achieved when a firm is operating at minimum average total cost

allocative efficiency: achieved when society is producing an appropriate bundle of goods relative to consumer preferences

Pareto optimum: an allocation of resources such that no reallocation of them can make any individual better off without making some other individual worse off

Efficiency in a market

Aspects of efficiency can be explored further by considering an individual market. First, however, it is necessary to identify the conditions under which productive and allocative efficiency can be attained.

Productive efficiency

The production process entails combining a range of inputs of factors of production in order to produce output. One way of measuring productive efficiency would be to calculate the average total cost of production. This is simply the total cost of production divided by the quantity of output produced. Productive efficiency can then be

defined in terms of the minimum average cost at which output can be produced, noting that average cost is likely to vary at different scales of output.

There are two aspects to productive efficiency. One entails making the best possible use of the inputs of factors of production; in other words, it is about producing as much output as possible from a given set of inputs. This is known as **technical efficiency**.

However, there is also the question of whether the *best* set of inputs has been chosen. For example, there may be techniques of production that use mainly capital and not much labour, and alternative techniques that are more labour intensive. The choice between these techniques will depend crucially on the relative costs of capital and labour, which will determine a firm's choice of technique. This is known as **cost efficiency**.

Key terms

technical efficiency: attaining the maximum possible output from a given set of inputs

cost efficiency: the appropriate combination of inputs of factors of production, given the relative price of those factors

marginal cost: the cost of producing an additional unit of output

To attain productive efficiency, both technical efficiency and cost efficiency need to be achieved. In other words, productive efficiency is attained when a firm chooses the appropriate combination of inputs (cost efficiency) and produces the maximum output possible from those inputs (technical efficiency).

It is worth noting that the choice of technique of production may depend crucially upon the level of output that the firm wishes to produce. The balance of factors of production may well change according to the scale of activity. If the firm is producing very small amounts of output, it may well choose a different combination of capital and labour than if it were planning mass production on a large scale.

Thus, the firm's decision process is a three-stage procedure. First, the firm needs to decide how much output it wants to produce. Second, it has to choose an appropriate combination of factors of production, given that intended scale of production. Third, it needs to produce as much output as possible, given those inputs. Once the intended scale of output has been decided, the firm has to minimise its costs of production. These decisions are part of the response to the question of *how* output should be produced.

Another important concept is that of **marginal cost**, which refers to the cost faced by a firm in changing the output level by a small amount.

Exercise 6.1

A firm producing chilli sauce faces the following total cost conditions:

Output per hundred bottles	Total cost (£)
0	0
1	60
2	80
3	81
4	140
5	275
6	480

Calculate average cost at each level of output. Plot your results on a graph, and identify the point of minimum average total cost.

Allocative efficiency

Allocative efficiency is about whether an economy allocates its resources in such a way as to produce a balance of goods and services that matches consumer preferences. In a complex modern economy, it is clearly difficult to identify such an ideal result. How can an appropriate balance of goods and services be identified?

Take the market for an individual product. Chapter 5 considered the market for laptop computers and argued that, in the long run, the market could be expected to arrive at an equilibrium in which price reached a level at which there was no incentive for firms either to enter the market or to exit from it. Figure 6.2 will remind you of the market situation.

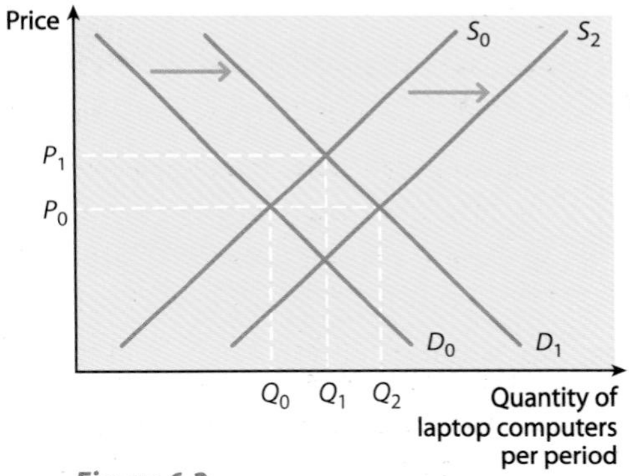

Figure 6.2
The market for laptop computers again

The sequence of events in the diagram showed that, from an initial equilibrium with price at P_0 and quantity traded at Q_0, there was an increase in demand, with the demand curve moving to D_1. In response, existing firms expanded their supply, moving up the supply curve. However, the lure of the producer surplus that was being made by these firms then attracted more firms into the market, such that the supply curve moved to S_2, a process that brought the price back down to the original level of P_0.

Now think about that price from the point of view of a firm. P_0 is at a level where there is no further incentive to attract new firms, but no firm wishes to leave the market. In other words, no surplus is being made on that marginal unit, and the marginal firm is just breaking even on it. The price in this context would seem to be just covering the marginal cost of production.

However, it was also argued that from the consumers' point of view any point along the demand curve could be regarded as the marginal benefit received from consuming a good or service.

Where is all this leading? Putting together the arguments, it would seem that market forces can carry a market to a position in which, from the firms' point of view, the price is equal to marginal cost, and from the consumers' point of view the price is set equal to marginal benefit.

This is an important result. Suppose that the marginal benefit from consuming a good were higher than the marginal cost to society of producing it. It could then be argued that society would be better off producing more of the good, because by increasing production more could be added to benefits than to costs. Equally, if the marginal cost were above the marginal benefit from consuming a good, society would be producing too much of the good and would benefit from producing less. The best possible position is thus where marginal cost is equal to marginal benefit.

If all markets in an economy operated in this way, resources would be used so effectively that no reallocation of resources could generate an overall improvement. Allocative efficiency would be attained. The key question is whether the market mechanism will work sufficiently well to ensure that this happens — or whether it will fail.

Summary

- A society needs to find a way of using its limited resources as efficiently as possible.
- Productive efficiency occurs when firms have chosen appropriate combinations of factors of production and produce the maximum output possible from those inputs.
- Allocative efficiency occurs when firms produce an appropriate bundle of goods and services, given consumer preferences.
- An allocation of resources is said to be Pareto efficient if no reallocation of resources can make an individual better off without making some other individual worse off.
- An individual market exhibits aspects of allocative efficiency when the marginal benefit received by society from consuming a good or service matches the marginal cost of producing it.

Exercise 6.2

Consider Figure 6.3, which shows a production possibility frontier (PPF) for an economy that produces consumer goods and investment goods.

Identify each of the following (*Hint*: in some cases more than one answer is possible):

a a point of productive inefficiency
b a point that is Pareto-superior to *B*
c a point of productive efficiency
d a point of allocative efficiency
e an unattainable point (*Hint*: think about what would need to happen for society to reach such a point)

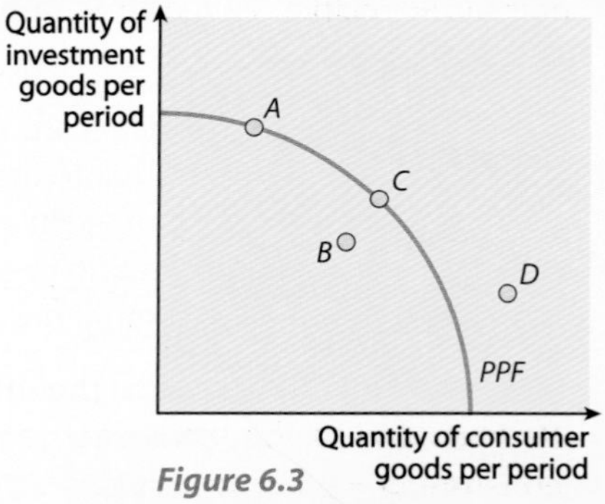

Figure 6.3
A production possibility frontier

Causes of market failure

The following chapters explore a number of ways in which markets may fail to bring the best result for society as a whole. In each case the failure will arise because a market settles in a position in which marginal social cost diverges from marginal social benefit. The remainder of this chapter introduces the most important reasons for **market failure**.

Key term

market failure: a situation in which the free market mechanism does not lead to an optimal allocation of resources — for example where there is a divergence between marginal social benefit and marginal social cost

Imperfect competition

The discussion so far has rested on the assumption that markets are competitive. Firms have been fairly passive actors in these markets, responding perhaps rather tamely to changes in consumer preferences. The real world is not necessarily like that, and in many markets firms have more power over their actions than has so far been suggested.

In the extreme, there are markets in which production is dominated by a single firm. At the time of the US trial in 1998, Microsoft was said to control 95% of the market for operating systems for PC computers — and not just in the USA: this was 95% of the *world* market. When a firm achieves such dominance, there is no guarantee that it will not try to exploit its position at the expense of consumers.

The very fact that there was a trial in which Microsoft was accused of abusing its dominant position bears witness to the need to protect consumers against dominant firms. In the UK, the Office of Fair Trading (OFT) and the Competition Commission have a brief to monitor the way in which markets operate and to guard against anti-competitive acts by firms.

Bill Gates, founder of Microsoft. Was the company anti-competitive in dominating the market for computer operating systems?

This is one example of how imperfect competition can lead to a distortion in the allocation of resources. Firms with a dominant position in a market may be able to drive prices to a level that is above marginal cost; consumers then lose out in terms of allocative efficiency. Chapter 7 explores these issues more carefully.

Externalities

If market forces are to guide the allocation of resources, it is crucial that the costs that firms face and the prices to which they respond fully reflect the actual costs and benefits associated with the production and consumption of goods. However, there are a number of situations and markets in which this does not happen because of **externalities**. These cause a divergence between marginal social cost and marginal social benefit in a market equilibrium situation.

> ***Key term***
>
> **externality:** a cost or a benefit that is external to a transaction, and thus is not reflected in market prices

There are many examples of such externalities. An obvious one is pollution. A firm that causes pollution in the course of its production process imposes costs on others that are not reflected in market prices unless the firm is forced to face the full cost of its activities. This causes a distortion in the allocation of resources.

Not all externalities are negative. There may be situations in which a firm takes an action that benefits others. For example, if it chose to upgrade the road that ran past its factory, this would benefit other users of the road, even though they did not have to contribute to the cost of the upgraded road.

Not all externalities are on the supply side of the market. There may also be externalities in consumption, which may be positive or negative. If your neighbours mount an excellent firework display on 5 November, you can benefit without having to pay.

These causes of a breakdown in allocative efficiency will be discussed in Chapter 8.

Information failure

If markets are to perform a role in allocating resources, it is extremely important that all relevant economic agents (buyers and sellers) have good information about market conditions; otherwise they may not be able to take rational decisions.

For example, it is important that consumers can clearly perceive the benefits to be gained by their consuming particular goods or services, in order to determine their own willingness to pay. Such benefits may not always be clear. For example, people may not fully perceive the benefits to be gained from education — or they may fail to appreciate the harmfulness of smoking tobacco.

In other market situations, economic agents on one side of the market may have different information from those on the other side; for example, sellers may have information about the goods that they are providing that buyers cannot discern. Chapter 9 explains that such information failure can also lead to a suboptimal allocation of resources.

Public goods

There is a category of goods known as public goods, which because of their characteristics cannot be provided by a purely free market. Street lighting is one such example: there is no obvious way in which a private firm could charge all the users of street lighting for the benefits that they receive from it. Such goods are discussed in Chapter 9.

Income distribution

Chapter 9 will also discuss equity. It is commonly accepted that there need to be safeguards in any economy to ensure that the distribution of income does not become so skewed that poverty escalates. If there is substantial poverty in a society, the allocation of resources is unlikely to be optimal. Chapter 9 examines the extent to which inequality in the distribution of income can be considered a form of market failure that requires some intervention by government.

Dealing with market failure

If unregulated free markets fail to produce good outcomes for society, the obvious next question to address is how to deal with the situation.

Over the years, economic analysis has been used to devise a range of policies at the microeconomic level that are intended to correct market failures, or at least to enable markets to work more effectively. Chapter 10 draws together analyses of alternative policies that have been proposed for this purpose.

Finally, it turns out that some forms of government intervention can themselves lead to a market failure – even when the intervention was intended to correct another form of market failure. Chapter 10 also examines some of the unintended outcomes that well-meaning policies can have.

Summary

- Free markets do not always lead to the best possible allocation of resources: there may be market failure.
- Markets may fail when there is imperfect competition, so that firms are able to utilise market power to disadvantage consumers.
- When there are costs or benefits that are external to the price mechanism, the economy will not reach allocative efficiency.
- Markets can operate effectively only when participants in the market have full information about market conditions.
- Public goods have characteristics that prevent markets from supplying the appropriate quantity.
- Most societies are concerned to some extent with notions of equity.

Monopoly and market dominance

By historic standards, some of the firms operating in the world today are giants, often operating on a global scale. This chapter examines some of the factors that can encourage the development of large firms, and discusses how this may affect whether markets can operate effectively for society's best interests. It also looks at how firms may attain and sustain a dominant position in markets, and at how a market works if there are limits on competition.

Learning outcomes

After studying this chapter, you should:

- understand the concepts of economies of scale and economies of scope
- be able to identify causes of economies of scale
- be familiar with the general form of the long-run average cost curve
- be aware of the relationship between firm size and market concentration
- understand what is meant by market dominance
- be familiar with factors that may give rise to natural and strategic barriers to entry
- be aware of some of the effects on a market if competition is limited

Economies of scale

One of the reasons why firms find it beneficial to be large is the existence of **economies of scale**. These occur when a firm finds that it is more efficient in cost terms to produce on a larger scale.

It is not difficult to think of a number of industries in which there are likely to be some economies of

Key term

economies of scale: economies arising if an increase in the scale of production leads to production at a lower long-run average cost

scale. Indeed, Chapter 2 introduced the notion of the *division of labour*. When a firm is expanding, it eventually reaches a scale of production at which it is worthwhile for workers to begin to specialise in certain stages of the production process, and as a result their productivity increases. This is possible only for relatively large-scale production; in other words, it is the size of the firm (in terms of its output level) that enables it to produce more efficiently, i.e. at lower average cost.

Although the division of labour is one source of economies of scale, it is by no means the only one. There are several conditions under which cost benefits can be expected from large-scale production, some of them industry specific. It is in those sectors of the economy that exhibit more significant economies of scale that the larger firms tend to be found. For example, there are no hairdressing salons that come into the top 10 largest firms, but there are plenty of oil companies.

Technology

One source of economies of scale lies in the technology of production. There are many procedures entailing a degree of technology such that large-scale production is more efficient.

One source of technical economies of scale arises from the physical properties of the universe. There is a physical relationship between the volume and the surface area of an object, whereby the storage capacity of an object increases proportionately more than its surface area. Consider the volume of a cube. If the cube is 2 metres each way, its volume is $2 \times 2 \times 2 = 8$ cubic metres, whereas its surface area is $6 \times 2 \times 2 = 24$ square metres. If the dimension of the cube is 3 metres, its volume is 27 cubic metres – but the surface area is 54 square metres. Thus, the larger the cube, the lower the average cost of storage. A similar relationship applies to other shapes of storage containers, whether they be barrels or ships.

What this means in practice is that a large ship can transport proportionally more than a small ship; or that large barrels hold more wine relative to the surface area of the barrel than small barrels. Hence there may be benefits in operating on a large scale.

Furthermore, some capital equipment is designed for large-scale production, and would be viable only for a firm operating at a high volume of production. Combine harvesters cannot be used in small fields, and a production line for car production would not be viable for small levels of output.

An important distinction in analysing costs is that between fixed and variable costs. **Variable costs** are costs such as labour input which vary with the scale of production – in order to increase output, a firm has to employ more labour. On the other hand, some costs are **fixed costs** in the sense that they do not vary with the scale of production – having built a factory, the cost of that factory is the same regardless of the amount of output that is produced in it.

Why is this relevant to the discussion of economies of scale?

Key terms

variable cost: a component of a firm's costs that varies with the level of output

fixed cost: a component of a firm's costs that does not vary with the quantity of output

Consider a simple arithmetic example. A firm faces fixed costs of production of £5000, and variable costs of £100 per unit. If the firm produces 10 units in a week, the total cost is £5000 + 10 × 100 = £6000. Average cost is thus £6000/10 = £600. If the firm expands the scale of production to 20 units, total cost is then £5000 + 20 × 100 = £7000, and average cost is £7000/20 = £350. What is happening here is that the fixed costs are being spread out over more units of output as the firm expands, thereby lowering average costs.

Notice that there are some economic activities in which these fixed costs are highly significant. Take the Channel Tunnel. The construction (fixed) costs were enormous compared with the (variable) costs of running trains through the Tunnel. Thus, the fixed cost element is substantial — and so the economies of scale will be significant for such an industry.

Initial construction costs of the Channel Tunnel were enormous compared with the costs of running trains through it.

There are other examples of this sort of cost structure — railway networks, electricity supply and so on. The largest firm in such a market will always be able to produce at a lower average cost than smaller firms in that market. This could prove such a competitive advantage that no other firms will be able to become established in that market, leading to a **natural monopoly**.

Intuitively, this makes sense. Imagine having several underground railway systems operating in a single city, all competing against each other!

Management and marketing

A second source of scale economies pertains to the management of firms. One of the key factors of production is managerial input. A certain number of managers is required to oversee the production process. As the firm expands, however, the management team does not need to grow as rapidly, because a large firm can be managed more efficiently. However, there are likely to be limits to this process. At some point the organisation will begin to get so large and complex that management will find it more difficult to manage. At this point **diseconomies of scale** are likely to cut in; in other words, average costs may begin to rise with an increase in output at some volume of production.

Similarly, the cost of marketing a product may not rise as rapidly as the volume of production, leading to further scale economies. One interpretation of this is that marketing expenses might be seen as a component of fixed costs — or at least as having a substantial fixed cost element.

Key terms

natural monopoly: an industry in which there are such substantial economies of scale that only one firm is viable

diseconomies of scale: a situation in which an increase in the scale of production leads to production at higher average cost for a firm

Finance and procurement

Large firms may have advantages in a number of other areas. For example, a large firm with a strong reputation may be able to raise finance for further expansion on more favourable terms than a small firm. This, of course, reinforces the market position of the largest firms in a sector and makes it more difficult for relative newcomers to become established.

Once a firm has grown to the point where it is operating on a relatively large scale, it will be purchasing its inputs in relatively large volumes, particularly raw materials, energy or transport services. When buying in bulk in this way, a firm may be able to negotiate good deals with its suppliers, and thus again reduce average cost as output increases.

It may even be that some of the firm's suppliers will find it beneficial to locate in proximity to the firm's factory, which would reduce costs still further.

External economies of scale

The factors listed so far that may lead to economies of scale arise from the **internal** expansion of a firm. If the firm is in an industry that is itself expanding, there may also be **external economies of scale**.

Some of the most successful firms of recent years have been in activities requiring high levels of technology and skills. The computer industry is one example of an economic activity that has expanded rapidly. As this sector has expanded, a pool of skilled labour has built up from which all the firms can draw. The very success of the sector encourages people to acquire the skills needed to enter it; colleges may provide courses, and so on. Each individual firm benefits in this way from the overall expansion of the sector.

Computer engineering is by no means the only example of this. Formula 1 development teams, pharmaceutical companies and others enjoy similar external economies of scale. A comparable argument has been used to help understand the rapid growth of the East Asian region, so it can be seen that these effects are not confined to particular sectors.

Key terms

internal economies of scale: cost savings arising if average costs fall as a firm increases its scale of production as a result of advantages internal to the firm

external economies of scale: cost savings arising if average costs for a firm fall as the output of its industry as a whole expands

Economies of scope

Firms can expand their scale of operations in various ways. Some do so within a relatively focused market, but others are multi-product firms producing a range of different products, sometimes in quite different markets.

For example, look at Nestlé. You may immediately think of instant coffee, and indeed, Nestlé produces 200 different brands of instant coffee worldwide. However, it also produces baby milk powder, mineral water, ice cream and pet food, and has diversified into hotels and restaurants — not to mention locally popular items such as lemon cheesecake flavoured KitKats (a strong seller in Japan).

Such conglomerate companies can benefit from **economies of scope**, whereby there may be benefits from size across a range of different products.

These economies may arise because there are activities that can be shared across the product range. For example, a company may not need a finance or accounting section for each product, or separate human resource or marketing departments. There is thus scope for economies to be made as the firm expands.

> **Key term**
>
> **economies of scope:** economies arising when average cost falls as a firm increases output across a range of different products
>
> **short run:** a period in which a firm is free to vary only some of its inputs of factors of production
>
> **long run:** the period over which a firm can vary inputs of all its factors of production

The long run and the short run

So far this chapter has focused on the efficiency of firms as their volume of output is increased. There is an implicit assumption underlying this analysis: namely, that a firm is free to vary its factors of production in order to produce at minimum cost for any given level of output. In other words, as a firm expands it can hire new labour, commission new capital equipment and buildings as necessary to accommodate the higher scale of output.

This assumption seems valid, provided that the firm has a sufficiently long period in which to accumulate all the new factors of production that it needs for the larger scale of production. However, it should be clear that some factors of production can be varied more readily than others. It may be relatively straightforward to hire some unskilled labour, but may take some time to build a Channel Tunnel!

Economists use this notion to define the **short run** and the **long run** in the context of costs.

To simplify the discussion, economists often assume that labour is the flexible factor of production, and that capital is fixed in the short run. This may not always be the case — there may be occasions in which it is easier for a firm to obtain some new faster computers than to train its labour to use them. However, it is a convenient simplification.

Viewed in this way, it should be clear that economies of scale apply to the long-run position faced by the firm, and when considering the effect on costs it is the effect on *long-run average cost* that is significant. The question of short-run and long-run costs will be explored in more detail in Chapter 16 in the course of an analysis of industrial economics.

Long-run average costs

The discussion so far establishes many reasons to expect that as a firm expands its scale of production it becomes more efficient, in the sense that the long-run average cost of production per unit of output can be expected to fall.

A relationship can be drawn between long-run average costs and the level of output to show the effect of economies of scale, as in Figure 7.1. Here, as output expands the average cost per unit of output falls. This is one way in which the efficiency of a firm can be evaluated. Again, Chapter 16 will explore the make-up of the long-run average cost curve more carefully.

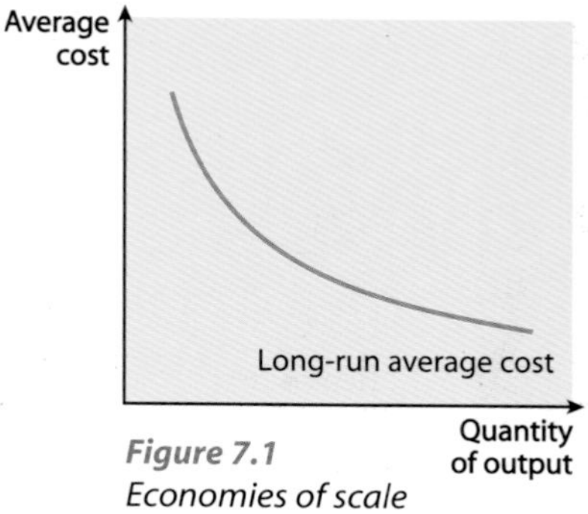

Figure 7.1
Economies of scale and average cost

A very important question is whether these economies of scale effects go on for ever, or whether there is a limit to which output can expand before long-run average costs cease to fall. It could be that at some level of output costs will begin to level out.

Consider Figure 7.2. When output is relatively low there are economies of scale to be reaped, but at some point all these economies will have been exhausted, and the long-run average cost will stabilise such that the curve becomes flat. The level of output Q_{mes} is known as the **minimum efficient scale**. Beyond this point, in the flat range of the curve, there will be **constant returns to scale**.

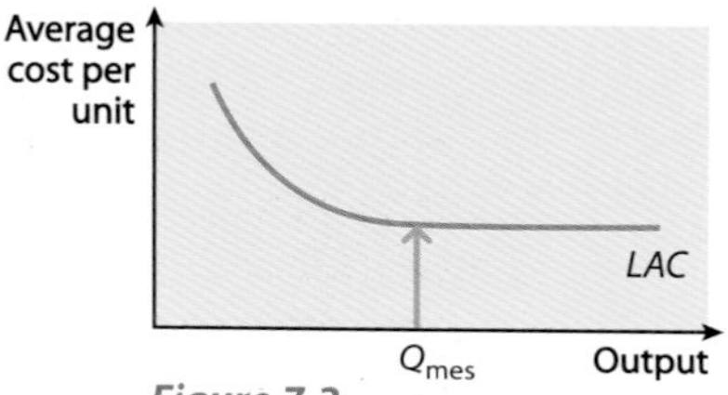

Figure 7.2
An L-shaped average cost curve

It may even be that a point is reached at which the organisation of the firm becomes so complex that diseconomies of scale begin to set in; in other words, the long-run average cost will begin to *rise* as output continues to expand. This could happen as soon as the firm reaches the minimum efficient scale, in which case the long-run average cost curve will have a U-shape, as in Figure 7.3. This shape of cost curve will be considered further in Chapter 16, as it is a common form and one that economists work with a lot.

For a U-shaped average cost curve like the one in Figure 7.3, the firm experiences economies of scale (sometimes known as *increasing returns to scale*) up to the minimum efficient scale (Q_{mes}), and diseconomies of scale (*decreasing returns to scale*) beyond that level. At the point Q_{mes}, the firm faces constant returns to scale.

Key terms

minimum efficient scale: the lowest scale of output at which a firm reaches the minimum long-run average cost: the level of output at which long-run average cost stops falling

constant returns to scale: that part of the long-run average cost curve where average costs remain constant as the level of output increases

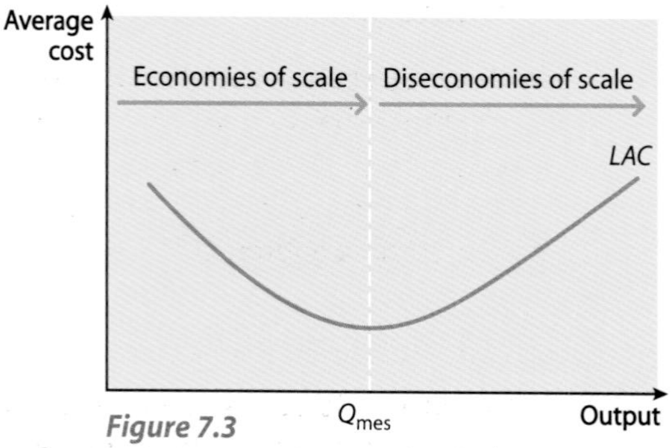

Figure 7.3
A U-shaped average cost curve

Learning by doing

As time goes by and a firm becomes established in a market, it tends to become more efficient through a process of 'learning by doing'. Workers become more proficient, managers find good ways of organising production, and in general the firm learns the tricks of the trade.

Think for a moment about how this should be interpreted. In effect, a firm that has been well established in a market will be able to produce more efficiently than a newly established firm. In other words, for any given scale of output, average costs will tend to be lower for the longer-established firm. Graphically, this is shown as a downward shift of the long-run average cost curve – say, from LAC_0 to LAC_1 in Figure 7.4.

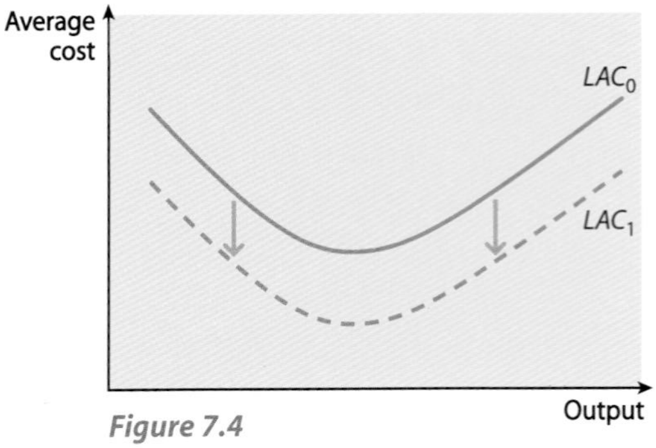

Figure 7.4
Learning by doing

Summary

- Economies of scale arise when a firm faces falling long-run average costs per unit as the scale of output increases.
- This can occur for a variety of reasons, including technology, the spreading of fixed costs, management, marketing, finance and procurement.
- External economies of scale may arise when a particular industry expands.
- Some conglomerate firms may also be able to tap economies of scope by sharing some common management functions across the organisation.
- In the short run the input of some factors of production may be fixed, but in the long run all inputs can be varied.
- The long-run average cost curve represents the relationship between average costs and the level of output as the firm varies its inputs and therefore its scale of production.
- There may be limits to economies of scale, and at some output level average costs may begin to rise if the firm further increases its scale of production.
- The level of output at which long-run average costs ceases to fall is known as the 'minimum efficient scale'.

Exercise 7.1

Which of the following reflects a movement *along* a long-run average cost curve, and which would cause a movement *of* a long-run average cost curve?

a A firm becomes established in a market, learning the best ways of utilising its factors of production.

b A firm observes that average cost falls as it expands its scale of production.

c The larger a firm becomes, the more difficult it becomes to manage, causing average cost to rise.

d A firm operating in the financial sector installs new, faster computers, enabling its average cost to fall for any given level of service that it provides.

Scale and market concentration

An important issue that arises as firms become larger concerns the number of firms that a market can support. Suppose the minimum efficient scale is large relative to the size of market demand, as in Figure 7.5. If more than one firm were to try to supply this market, each producing at the minimum efficient scale, there would be substantial excess supply, and the situation would not be viable.

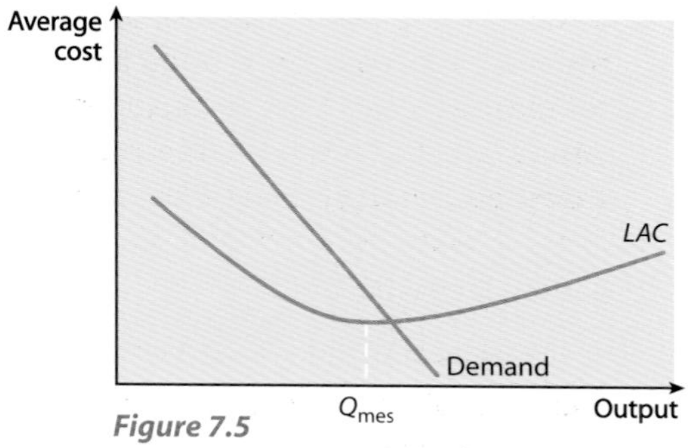

Figure 7.5
How many firms can a market support?

When long-run average costs decrease right up to the limit of market demand, the largest firm in the market will come to dominate the market, as it will be able to produce at lower average costs than any potential competitor. This will be reinforced if there are significant learning-by-doing effects which will further embed the largest firm as the market leader. As mentioned earlier in the chapter, such a market is likely to become a **natural monopoly**.

Such substantial economies of scale are not available in all sectors. It will depend upon the nature of technology and all the other factors that can give rise to economies of scale. In some activities there may be little scope at all for economies of scale. For example, there are no great fixed costs in setting up a restaurant, a hairdressing salon or a dental surgery — at least, compared with those involved in setting up a steel plant or an underground railway. The minimum efficient scale for such activities may thus be relatively small compared with market demand, so there may be room for many firms in the market. This helps to explain the proliferation of bars and take-away restaurants.

There may also be an intermediate position, where the economies of scale are not sufficient to bring about a monopoly situation, but only relatively few firms can operate efficiently. Such markets are known as **oligopolies**, and will be investigated in Chapter 16.

Key terms

natural monopoly: a market in which a single seller of a good or service would emerge through market forces

oligopoly: a market in which there are just a few sellers

How does this affect the way in which a market works? Is there any reason to believe that a monopoly or oligopoly will work against society's best interests? If market share is concentrated among a small number of firms, does this *inevitably* mean that consumers will suffer?

The answer to these questions depends upon the behaviour of firms within the market. There may be an incentive for a monopoly firm to use its market power to increase its profits. It can do this by restricting the amount of output that it releases on to the market, and by raising the price to consumers. In Chapter 16 you will see that a monopoly has the incentive to act in this way, since by lowering output and raising price it can increase its overall profits. From the consumer's point of view, the result is a loss of consumer surplus.

If there is an incentive for a single firm to act in this way, there is a similar incentive for firms in an oligopoly to do the same, as they can increase their joint profits — with the same effects on consumers. However, the oligopoly case is more complicated, as there is always the possibility that individual firms will try to increase their own share of the market at the expense of others in the oligopoly.

Market dominance

A key issue is whether firms actually have the market power to exploit consumers in this way. Do firms have market dominance which can be exploited to bring higher profits? In other words, to what extent do firms have the freedom to set prices at their preferred levels, and to what extent do they have to take into account the actions of other firms or face other constraints?

Even monopoly firms have to accept the constraint of the demand curve. They are not free to set a price at any level they choose, otherwise consumers would simply not buy the product. The question is more one of whether firms are free to choose where to position themselves on their demand curve, rather than having to accept the market equilibrium price.

The fact that most countries have legislation in place to protect consumers from this sort of exploitation by firms recognises that firms might have market power and also have an incentive to use it. In the UK this monitoring is in the hands of the Office of Fair Trading and the Competition Commission. For these purposes, a firm is said to have a dominant position if its market share exceeds 40%. The existence of such bodies helps to act as a restraint on anti-competitive practices by firms.

There may also be natural constraints that limit the extent to which a firm is able to achieve a position of dominance in a market. An important consideration is whether a firm (or firms) in a market need to be made aware of the possibility of new firms joining the market. Remember that in Chapter 5 a market was seen to tend towards a long-run equilibrium. In response to an increase in consumer demand, a key part of the adjustment involved the entry of new firms, which would be attracted into the market when the incumbent firms were seen to be making high profits. This had the effect of competing away those profits until the incentive for entry was removed. Can firms in a market prevent this from happening?

Barriers to entry

Another way of thinking about this is to examine what might constitute a **barrier to the entry** of new firms into a market. If such barriers exist, the existing firm or firms may be able to continue to make higher profits.

Key term

barrier to entry: a characteristic of a market that prevents new firms from readily joining the market

Economies of scale

One source of entry barriers is the existence of economies of scale, as was already discussed. If the largest firm has a significant cost advantage over later entrants, it can adopt a pricing strategy that makes it very difficult for new firms to become established.

This advantage of the existing firm is likely to be reinforced by the learning-by-doing effect; this could produce an even stronger cost advantage that would need to be overcome by new entrants.

Ownership of raw materials

Suppose that the production of a commodity requires the input of a certain raw material, and that a firm in the market controls the supply of that raw material. You can readily see that this would be a substantial barrier to the entry of new firms. Until very recently, DeBeers controlled the world's supply of uncut diamonds, and there was no way that new firms could enter the market because of the agreements that DeBeers had with mining companies and governments in those parts of the world where diamonds are mined. This monopoly has lasted for many years, and is only now beginning to break down.

The patent system

The patent system exists to provide protection for firms developing new products or processes. The rationale for this is that unless firms know that they will have ownership over innovative ideas, they will have no incentive to be innovative. The patent system ensures that, at least for a time, firms can be assured of gaining some benefit from their innovations. For the duration of the patent, they will be protected from competition. This therefore constitutes a legal barrier to the entry of new firms.

Strategic and innocent barriers to entry

In the case of economies of scale, it could be argued that the advantage of the largest firm in the industry is a purely natural barrier to entry that arises from the market position of the firm.

In other cases, it may be that firms can consciously erect barriers to entry in order to make entry into the market more difficult for potential new firms. In other words, firms may make strategic moves to protect their market position behind entry barriers.

One example of this might be the advertising undertaken by firms. Some firms have become (and remain) well known by dint of heavy advertising expenditures. In some cases these expenditures have very little impact on market shares, and merely serve to maintain the status quo. However, for potential entrants they make life very difficult. Any new firm coming into the market has to try to match the advertising levels of existing firms in order to gain a viable market share. Effectively, existing firms have increased the fixed costs of being in the market, making entry more difficult to achieve. For example, when the soft drink 'Sunny Delight' was launched, it had to undertake a large-scale TV advertising campaign to try to break into a market dominated by Coca-Cola and PepsiCo.

An alternative method is for an existing firm to operate with spare capacity, making it clear to potential entrants that entry will trigger a price war. The surplus capacity adds credibility to this threat, as the existing firm is seen to be able to increase output — and thus force down price — very quickly.

'Sunny Delight' required heavy advertising expenditure to compete with Coca-Cola and Pepsi.

Market failure

How is the market affected if there are limits to the extent of competition in it?

By restricting output and raising price, firms are able to increase their profits, effectively increasing the market price to a level above the marginal cost of production. This implies that there is a loss of allocative efficiency in this situation. From society's point of view, too little of the product is being produced.

To the extent that the monopolist is a member of society, the increase in producer surplus might be regarded as a redistribution from consumers to producers. However, more crucial is the fact that there is a loss of consumer surplus that is not recoverable.

Figure 7.6 shows a market in which a monopoly firm has raised price from P_0 to P_1. With the price at the original level of P_0, consumer surplus is the area of the triangle AP_0D. However, if the monopoly firm raises its price to P_1, the consumer surplus falls to AP_1B. Some of the former consumer surplus becomes profits for the firm (the area P_0P_1BC) and the remaining area (the triangle BCD) is a net loss to society. This is known as the **deadweight loss** that society incurs as a result of the restriction to competition.

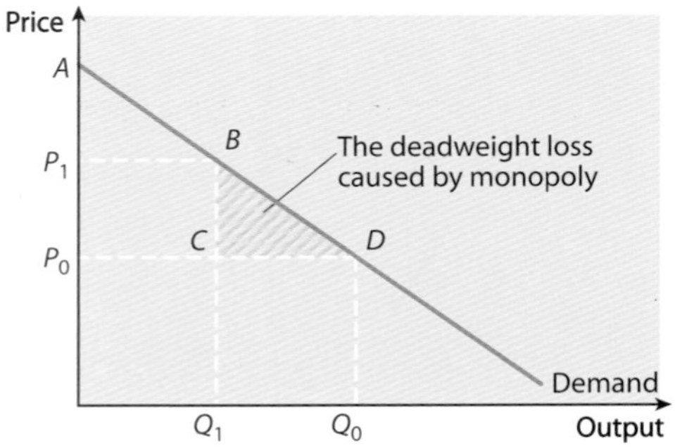

Figure 7.6
The deadweight loss of monopoly

This deadweight loss is a measure of the welfare loss imposed on society in a

Key term

deadweight loss: loss of consumer surplus that arises when a monopoly raises price and restricts output

monopoly situation. However, there are two key aspects of efficiency, as was shown in Chapter 6, and it is also important to take account of *productive efficiency*. The loss in allocative efficiency may be partly offset by improved productive efficiency, for example because a monopoly is able to take advantage of economies of scale that would be sacrificed if it were to be split into many small firms, none of which would be able to reach the minimum efficient scale. This will be examined more carefully in Part 4 of the book, which deals with industrial economics.

Summary

- Cost conditions in a market may affect the number of firms that can be viable.
- Firms that attain market dominance may be able to harness market power at the expense of consumers, reducing output and raising price.
- This is especially the case where the existing firm(s) is (are) protected by barriers to entry.
- When firms do use such market power, there is a deadweight loss to society that reflects allocative inefficiency.
- However, this may in part be balanced by a gain in productive efficiency.

Exercise 7.2

Figure 7.7 shows a market in which there are only two firms operating.

a The two firms competing in the market produce at constant marginal cost *OD*, which means that average cost is also constant and equal to marginal cost. Competing intensively, the price is driven down to a level at which no surplus above marginal cost is made. Identify the price charged, the quantity traded and consumer surplus.

b Suppose the two firms decide to collude to raise price to a level *OB*. Identify the quantity traded and the consumer surplus.

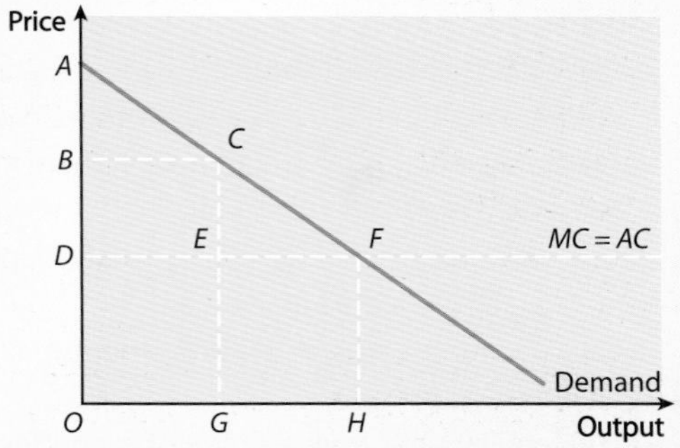

Figure 7.7
Anti-competitive behaviour

c You should have found that consumer surplus is much smaller in the second situation than in the first. What has happened to the areas that were formerly part of consumer surplus?

Externalities

If markets are to be effective in guiding the allocation of resources in society, a precondition is that market prices are able to reflect the full costs and benefits associated with market transactions. However, there are many situations in which this is not so, and there are costs or benefits that are external to the workings of the market mechanism. This chapter examines the circumstances in which this may happen, and provides a justification for government intervention to improve the workings of the market.

Learning outcomes

After studying this chapter, you should:

- recognise situations in which the free market mechanism may fail to take account of costs or benefits that are associated with market transactions
- be familiar with situations in which there may be a divergence between private and social costs or benefits
- be able to use diagrams to analyse positive and negative externalities in either production or consumption
- appreciate reasons why government may need to intervene in markets in which externalities are present
- be familiar with a wide range of examples of externalities
- recognise ways in which external costs or benefits may be valued

What is an externality?

'Externality' is one of those ugly words invented by economists that says exactly what it means. It simply describes a cost or a benefit that is external to the market mechanism.

> ***Key term***
>
> **externality:** a cost or a benefit arising from an economic activity or transaction that is not reflected in market prices

An externality will lead to a form of market failure, because if the cost or benefit is not reflected in market prices it cannot be taken into consideration by all parties to a transaction. This in turn implies that decisions will not be aligned with the best interests of society.

For example, if there is an element of costs that is not borne by producers, it is likely that 'too much' of the good will be produced. Where there are benefits that are not included, it is likely that too little will be produced. Later in the chapter, it will be shown that this is exactly what does happen. Externalities can affect either demand or supply in a market; that is to say, they may arise either in consumption or in production.

In approaching this topic, begin by tackling Exercise 8.1, which offers an example of two types of externality.

Exercise 8.1

Each of the following situations describes a type of externality. Do they affect production or consumption?

a A factory situated in the centre of a town, and close to a residential district, emits toxic fumes through a chimney during its production process. As a result, residents living nearby have to wash their clothes more frequently, and incur higher medical bills as a byproduct of breathing in the fumes.

b Residents living along a main road festoon their houses with lavish Christmas lights and decorations during the month of December, helping passers-by to capture the festive spirit.

Toxic fumes

Example (a) is a negative **production externality**. The factory emits toxic fumes that impose costs on the residents living nearby, who face high washing and medical bills. The households face costs as a result of the production activities of the firm, so the firm does not face the full costs of its activity.

Thus, the private costs faced by the producer are lower than the social costs, i.e. the costs faced by society as a whole. The producer will take decisions based only on its private costs.

Key term

production externality: an externality that impacts on the production side of a market, which may be either positive or negative

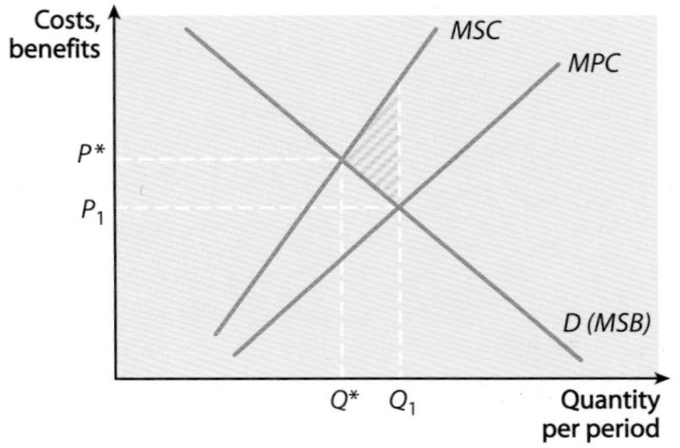

Figure 8.1
A negative production externality

Figure 8.1 illustrates this situation under the assumption that this firm operates in a competitive market (i.e. is not a monopoly). Here, D (MSB) represents the demand curve, which was characterised in Chapter 5 as representing the marginal social benefit derived from consuming a good. In other words, the

demand curve represents consumers' willingness to pay for the good, and thus reflects their marginal valuation of the product.

Producers face marginal private costs given by the line *MPC*, but in fact impose higher costs than this on society, such that marginal social cost is represented by *MSC*.

If the market is unregulated by the government, the firms will choose how much to supply on the basis of the marginal cost they face. The market equilibrium will thus be at quantity traded Q_1, where firms just break even on the marginal unit sold; price will be set at P_1.

This is not a good outcome for society, as it is clear that there is a divergence between marginal social benefit and marginal social cost. It is this divergence that is at the heart of the market failure. The last unit of this good sold imposes higher costs on society than the marginal benefit derived from consuming it. Too much is being produced.

In fact, the optimum position is at Q^*, where marginal social benefit is equal to marginal social cost. This will be reached if the price is set at P^*. Less of the good will be consumed, but also less pollution will be created, and society will be better off than at Q_1.

The extent of the welfare loss that society suffers can be identified: it is shown by the shaded triangle in the figure. Each unit of output that is produced above Q^* imposes a cost equal to the vertical distance between *MSC* and *MPC*. The shaded area thus represents the difference between marginal social cost and marginal benefit over the range of output between the optimum output and the market outcome level of output. This is another example of the notion of deadweight loss that was introduced in the previous chapter.

Key term

consumption externality: an externality that impacts on the consumption side of a market, which may be either positive or negative

Christmas lights

Example (b) above is an example of a positive **consumption externality**. Residents of this street decorate their homes in order to share the Christmas spirit with passers-by. The benefit they gain from the decorations spills over and adds to the enjoyment of others. In other words, the social benefits from the residents' decision to provide Christmas decorations go beyond the private enjoyment that they receive.

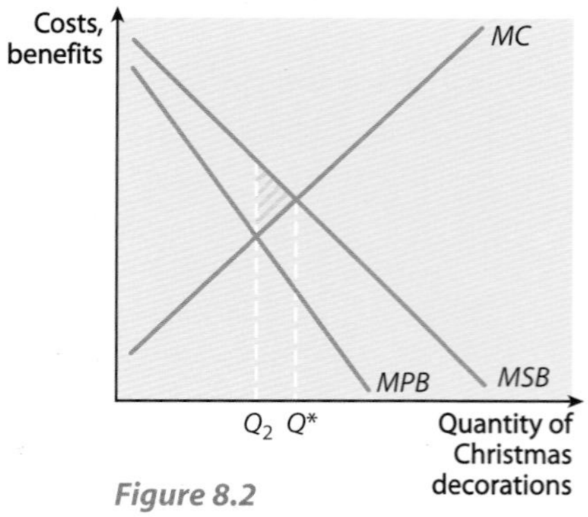

Figure 8.2
A positive consumption externality

Figure 8.2 illustrates this situation. *MPB* represents the marginal private benefits gained by residents from the Christmas lights; but *MSB* represents the full marginal social benefit that the community gains, which is higher than the *MPB*. Residents will provide decorations up to the point Q_2, where their marginal private benefit is just balanced by the marginal cost of the lights. However, if the full social benefits received are taken into account, Q^* would be the optimum choice point: the residents do not provide enough décor for the community to reach the optimum.

Positive and normative revisited

Example (b) is a reminder of the distinction between positive and normative analysis, which was introduced in Chapter 1. Economists would agree that the diagram shows the effects of a beneficial consumption externality. However, probably not everyone would agree about whether the lavish Christmas decorations are providing such benefits. This is where a *normative judgement* comes into play. It could equally be argued that the lavish Christmas decorations are unsightly and inappropriate, or that they constitute a distraction for drivers and are therefore likely to cause accidents. After all, not everyone enjoys the garish.

Extension material

Discussion has centred around two examples of externalities: a production externality that had negative effects, and a *consumption externality* that was beneficial to society. In fact, there are two other possibilities.

c A factory located on the banks of a river that produces chemicals installs a new water purification plant which improves the quality of water discharged into the river. A trout farm located downstream finds that its productivity increases, and that it has to spend less on filtering the water.

d Liz, a jazz enthusiast, enjoys playing her music at high volume late at night, in spite of the fact that she lives in a flat with inadequate sound insulation. The neighbours prefer Mozart, but cannot escape the jazz.

Water purification

Example (c) is a production externality that has *positive* effects. The action taken by the chemical firm to purify its waste water has beneficial effects on the trout farm, which finds that its costs have been reduced without its having taken any action whatsoever. Indeed, it finds that it has to spend less on filtering the water.

Figure 8.3 shows the position facing the chemicals firm. It faces relatively high marginal private costs given by *MPC*. However, its actions have reduced the costs faced by the trout farm, so the 'social' cost of the firm's production activities is lower than its private cost. Thus, in this case marginal social cost is lower than marginal private cost, shown by *MSC* in the figure. The firm will produce up to the point where *MPC* equals marginal social benefit, i.e. at Q_A.

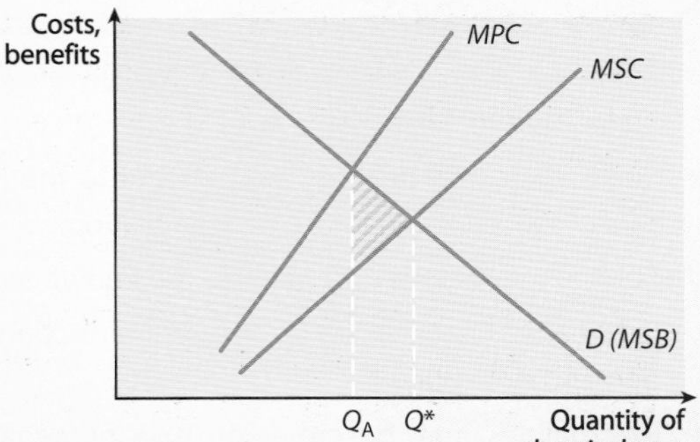

Figure 8.3
A positive production externality

In this market position, notice that the marginal benefit that society receives from consuming the product is higher than the marginal social cost of producing it, so too little of the product is being consumed for society's good. Society would be better off at Q^*, where marginal social benefit is equal to marginal social cost.

Again, the shaded triangle in Figure 8.3 represents the extent of the inefficiency: it is given by the excess of marginal social benefit over marginal social cost over the range of output between the market outcome and society's optimum position.

All that jazz

Example (d) is a negative consumption externality. Liz, the jazz fan, gains benefit from listening to her music at high volume, but the neighbours also hear her music and suffer as a result. Indeed, it may be that when they try to listen to Mozart, the jazz interferes with their enjoyment — especially in the quiet passages of the Mozart. Their benefit is reduced by having to hear the jazz.

Figure 8.4 illustrates this. The situation can be interpreted in terms of the benefits that accrue as a result of Liz's consumption of loud jazz music. Liz gains benefit as shown by the line *MPB*, which represents marginal private benefit. However, the social benefit is lower than this if the vexation suffered by the neighbours is taken into account, so *MSB* in Figure 8.4 represents the marginal social benefits from Liz's jazz.

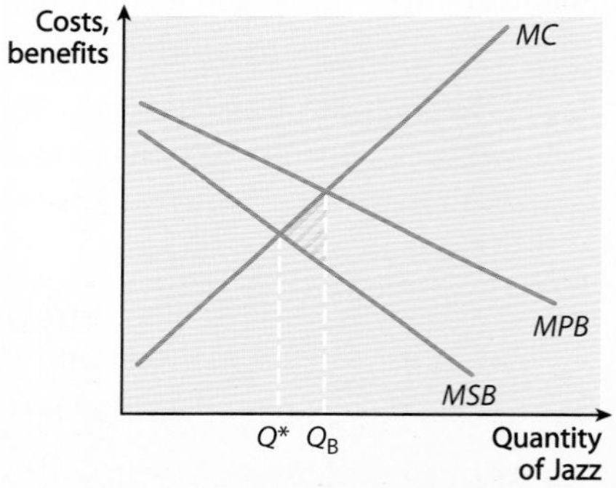

Figure 8.4 A negative consumption externality

Liz will listen to jazz up to the point where her marginal private benefit is just equal to the marginal cost of playing it, at Q_B. However, the optimal position that takes the neighbours into consideration is where marginal social benefit is equal to marginal cost — at Q^*. Thus, Liz plays too much jazz for the good of society.

Summary

- Markets can operate effectively only if all relevant costs and benefits are taken into account in decision making.
- Some costs and benefits are external to the market mechanism, and are thus neglected, causing a distortion in resource allocation.
- Such external costs and benefits are known as 'externalities'.
- Externalities may occur in either production or consumption, thereby affecting either demand or supply.
- Externalities may be either positive or negative, but either way resources will not be optimally allocated if they are present.

Exercise 8.2

Discuss examples of some externalities that you meet in everyday situations, and classify them as affecting either production or consumption.

Externalities occur in a wide variety of market situations, and constitute an important source of market failure. This means that externalities may hinder the achievement of good resource allocation from society's perspective. The final section of this chapter explores some ways in which attempts have been made to measure the social costs imposed by externalities. First, however, a number of other externalities that appear in various parts of the economy will be examined.

Externalities and the environment

Concern for the environment has been growing in recent years, with 'green' lobbyist groups demanding attention, sometimes through demonstrations and protests. There are so many different facets to this question that it is sometimes difficult to isolate the core issues. Externalities lie at the heart of much of the debate.

Some of the issues are international in nature, such as the debate over global warming. At the heart of this concern is the way in which emissions of greenhouse gases are said to be warming up the planet, so that sea levels are rising and major climate change seems imminent.

One reason why this question is especially difficult to tackle is that actions taken by one country can have effects on other countries. Scientists argue that the problem is caused mainly by pollution created by transport and industry, especially in the richer countries of the world. However, poorer countries suffer the consequences as well, especially countries such as Bangladesh, where much of the land is low lying and prone to severe flooding – indeed, two-thirds of the country was under water during the floods of 2004.

In principle, this is very similar to the example (a) in Exercise 8.1 above: it is an example of a negative production externality, in which the nations causing most of the damage face only part of the costs caused by their lifestyles and production processes. The inevitable result in an unregulated market is that too much pollution is produced.

When externalities cross international borders in this way, the problem can be tackled only through international cooperation. For example, at the Kyoto World Climate Summit held in Japan in 1997 almost every developed nation agreed to cut greenhouse gas emissions by 6% by 2010. (The USA, the largest emitter of carbon dioxide, withdrew from the agreement in early 2001, fearing the consequences of such a restriction on the US economy.)

Global warming is not the only example of international externality effects. Scandinavian countries have suffered from acid rain caused by pollution in other

European countries (including the UK). Forest fires left to burn in Indonesia have caused air pollution in neighbouring Singapore.

Another environmental issue concerns rivers. Some of the big rivers of the world, such as the Nile in Africa, pass through several different countries on their way to the sea. For Egypt, coming at the end of the chain, the Nile is crucial for the livelihood of the economy. If countries further upstream were to increase their usage of the river, perhaps through new irrigation projects, this could have disastrous effects on Egypt. Again, the actions of one set of economic agents would be having damaging effects on others, and these effects would not be reflected in market prices, in the sense that the upstream countries would not have to face the full cost of their actions.

Egypt depends on irrigation from the Nile and could be critically affected by the actions of other countries closer to its source.

Part of the problem here can be traced back to the difficulty of enforcing property rights. If the countries imposing the costs could be forced to make appropriate payment for their actions, this would help to bring the costs back within the market mechanism. Such a process is known in economics as 'internalising the externality', and will be examined in Chapter 10, which looks at the measures a government could undertake to tackle the problem of externalities. For now, note simply that such action may well be needed.

Concern has also been expressed about the loss of *biodiversity*, a word that is shorthand for 'biological diversity'. The issue here is that when a section of rainforest is cleared to plant soya, or for timber, it is possible that species of plants, insects or even animals whose existence is not even known at present may be wiped out. Many modern medicines are based on chemicals that occur naturally in the wild. By eradicating species before they have been discovered, possible scientific advances will be forgone. Notice that, when it comes to measuring the value of what is being destroyed, biodiversity offers particular challenges — namely, the problem of putting a value on something that might not even be there!

Externalities and transport

With the introduction of the congestion charge in parts of central London, the London authorities have been attempting to tackle congestion. When traffic on the roads reaches a certain volume, congestion imposes heavy costs on road users. This is another example of an externality.

Figure 8.5 illustrates the situation. Suppose that *D* (*MSB*) represents the demand curve for car journeys along a particular stretch of road. When deciding whether or not to undertake a journey, drivers will balance the marginal benefit gained from making the journey against the marginal cost that they face. This is given by *MPC* – the marginal private cost of undertaking journeys. When the road is congested, a motorist who decides to undertake the journey adds to the congestion, and slows the traffic. The *MPC* curve incorporates the cost to the motorist of joining a congested road, and the chosen number of journeys will be at Q_1.

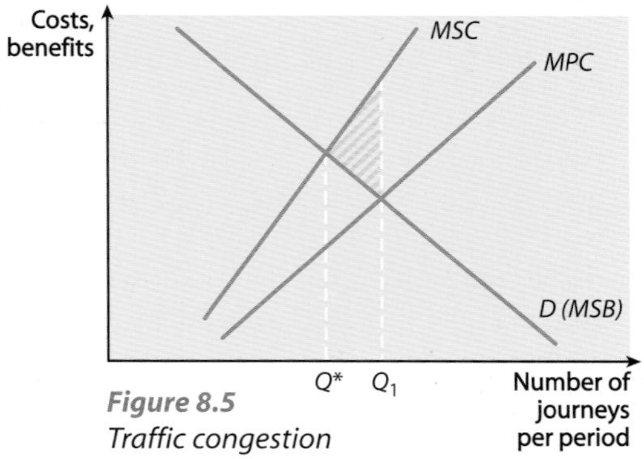

Figure 8.5
Traffic congestion

However, in adding to the congestion the motorist not only suffers the costs of congestion, but also imposes some marginal increase in costs on all other users of the road, as everyone suffers from the slower journeys resulting from the extra congestion. Thus, the marginal social costs (*MSC*) of undertaking journeys are higher than the cost faced by any individual motorist. *MSC* is therefore higher than *MPC*. Society would be better off with lower congestion, i.e. with the number of journeys undertaken being limited to *Q**, where marginal social benefits equals marginal social cost.

Externalities and health

Health care is a sector in which there is often public provision, or at least some state intervention in support of the health services. In the UK the National Health Service is the prime provider of health care, but private health care is also available, and the use of private health insurance schemes is on the increase. Again, externalities can help to explain why there should be a need for government to intervene.

Consider the case of vaccination against a disease such as measles. Suppose an individual is considering whether or not to be vaccinated. Being vaccinated reduces the probability of that individual contracting the disease, so there are palpable potential benefits. However, these benefits must be balanced against the costs. There may be a direct charge for the vaccine; some individuals may have a phobia against needles; or they may be concerned about possible side-effects. Individuals will opt to be vaccinated only if the marginal expected benefit to them is at least as large as the marginal cost.

From society's point of view, however, there are potential benefits that individuals will not take into account. After all, if they do contract measles there is a chance of their passing it on to others. Indeed, if lots of people decide not to be vaccinated, there is the possibility of a widespread epidemic, which would be costly and damaging to many.

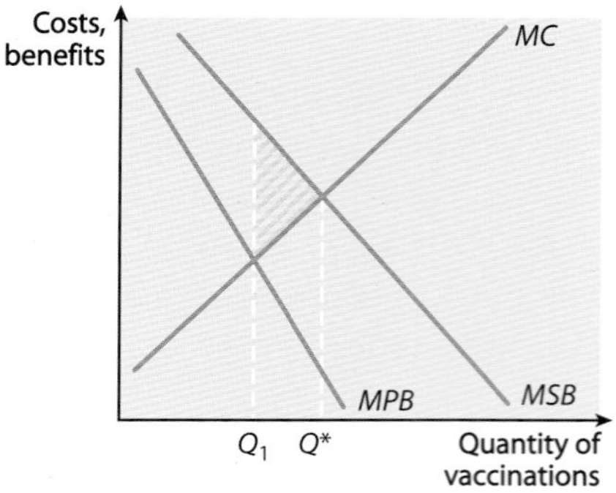

Figure 8.6 *Vaccination*

Figure 8.6 illustrates this point. The previous paragraph argues that the social benefits to society of having people vaccinated against measles exceed the private benefits that will be perceived by individuals, so that marginal social benefits exceed marginal private benefits. Private individuals will choose to balance marginal private benefit against marginal private cost at Q_1, whereas society would prefer more people to be vaccinated at Q^*. This parallels the discussion of a positive consumption externality. Chapter 9 returns to consider another aspect of health care provision.

Externalities and education

As you are reading this textbook, it is reasonably safe to assume that you are following a course in AS/A-level economics. You have decided to demand education. This is yet another area in which externalities may be important.

When you decided to take A-levels (including economics), there were probably a number of factors that influenced your decision. Perhaps you intend to demand even more education in the future, by proceeding to study at university. Part of your decision process probably takes into account the fact that education improves your future earnings potential. Your expected lifetime earnings depend in part upon the level of educational qualifications that you attain. Research has shown that, on average, graduates earn more during their lifetimes than non-graduates. This is partly because there is a productivity effect: by becoming educated, you cultivate a range of skills that in later life will make you more productive, and this helps to

Your education benefits society as a whole, in addition to the benefits you yourself derive.

explain why you can expect higher lifetime earnings than someone who chooses not to demand education.

What does society get out of this? Evidence suggests that, not only does education improve productivity, but a *group* of educated workers cooperating with each other become even more productive. This is an externality effect, as it depends upon interaction between educated workers – but each individual perceives only the individual benefit, and not the benefits of cooperation.

In other words, when you decide to undertake education, you do so on the basis of the expected private benefits that you hope to gain from education. However, you do not take into account the additional cooperation benefits that society will reap. So here is another example of a positive consumption externality. As with health care, some other aspects of education will be discussed in Chapter 9.

Externalities and tourism

As international transport has become easier and cheaper, more people are wanting to travel to new and different destinations. For less-developed countries, this offers an opportunity to earn much-needed foreign exchange.

There has been some criticism of this. The building of luxury hotels in the midst of the poverty that characterises many less-developed countries is said to have damaging effects on the local population by emphasising differences in living standards.

However, constructing the infrastructure that tourists need may have beneficial effects on the domestic economy. Improved roads and communication systems can benefit local businesses. This effect can be interpreted as an externality, in the sense that the local firms will face lower costs as a result of the facilities provided for the tourist sector.

Valuing externalities

It is all very well drawing demand and supply diagrams and identifying triangles of deadweight loss, but can a value be put on these social costs that arise from the presence of externalities?

If there are no externalities in a market, it is possible to interpret the market price as the marginal consumer's valuation of a good or service. However, if there are externalities this approach cannot be adopted.

Take the example of an environmental good – a clean beach, or a landscape. One alternative approach is to ask people about their willingness to pay for an environmental good. This is known as the *stated preference*, or *contingent-valuation*, approach. This could then provide an estimate of how much a particular item is valued by members of a society.

However, there are problems with this method of trying to value goods, as it is not possible to ensure that people will reveal their true willingness to pay. If you went

around your college and asked people how much they would give in order to save the whale, or preserve a landscape that they might never see, there is no guarantee that they would, or could, give a very accurate response.

There may also be a **NIMBY** (Not In My Back Yard) syndrome, whereby people are quite happy to support the construction of unsightly facilities — so long as they are somewhere other than near where they live.

An alternative is to use a **revealed preference** approach. For example, anyone wanting to put a value on preserving a particular environmental feature such as an area of outstanding natural beauty could undertake a survey of people who actually visit the area, and find out how much they had paid in terms of travel costs in order to get there. This would then reveal something about how much they value the amenity.

> ***Key terms***
>
> **NIMBY:** a syndrome under which people are happy to support the construction of an unsightly or unsocial facility, so long as it is 'Not In My Back Yard'
>
> **revealed preference:** an approach to valuing an environmental good that entails surveying people who visit an environmental facility to see how much they spent to get there

Alternatively, it has been suggested that *defensive expenditures* or *averting expenditures* could be used to place a value on some dis-amenities. For example, in considering the negative effects of noise pollution caused by traffic on a busy road, residents could be asked how much they would be prepared to pay to deal with the problem, perhaps by installing replacement windows; or inferences could be made from relative house prices in different areas that were more or less affected by the problem under investigation.

Social cost–benefit analysis

The importance of externalities in regard to environmental issues means that it is especially important to be aware of externalities when taking decisions that are likely to affect the environment. One area in which this has been especially contentious in recent years has been in connection with road-building programmes. If decisions to build new roads, or to expand existing ones such as the M25, are taken only by reference to commercial considerations, there could be serious implications for resource allocation.

In taking such decisions, it is desirable to weigh up the costs and benefits of a scheme. If it turns out that the benefits exceed the costs, it might be thought appropriate to go ahead. However, in valuing the costs and the benefits, it is clearly important to include some estimate for the externalities involved in order that the decision can be based on all relevant factors.

A further complication is that with many such schemes the costs and benefits will be spread out over a long period of time, and it is important to come to a reasonable balance between the interests of present and future generations.

Summary

- Externalities arise in many aspects of economic life.
- Environmental issues are especially prone to externality effects, as market prices do not always incorporate environmental issues, especially where property rights are not assigned.
- Congestion on the roads can also be seen as a form of externality.
- Externalities also arise in the areas of healthcare provision and education, where individuals do not always perceive the full social benefits that arise.
- A number of approaches have been proposed to measuring externalities. Measurement may enable a **social cost–benefit analysis** to be made of projects involving a substantial externality element.

Key term

social cost–benefit analysis: a process of evaluating the worth of a project by comparing both direct and social costs and benefits, including externality effects

Exercise 8.3

Suppose it is proposed to construct a new stretch of motorway close to where you live. Identify the costs and benefits of the scheme, including direct costs and benefits and not forgetting externalities.

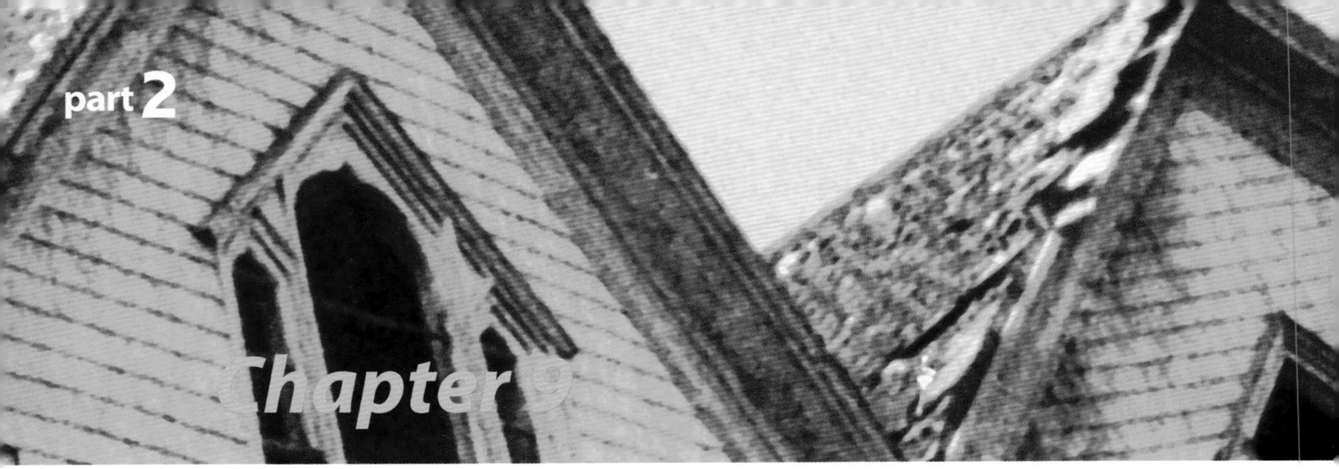

part 2

Chapter 9

Public goods, information problems and equity

This chapter considers some goods with unusual economic characteristics and some markets that may fail because of problems with information. It also investigates questions of equity, and discusses whether inequality in the distribution of income requires intervention by government.

Learning outcomes

After studying this chapter, you should:

- understand the nature of public goods and problems that arise in their provision
- be able to identify examples of public goods
- be aware of the characteristics of merit and demerit goods
- be able to give examples of possible merit and demerit goods
- appreciate the significance of asymmetric information as a source of market failure
- be aware of inequality in the distribution of income and how to evaluate it

Private goods

Most of the goods that individuals consume are private goods. You buy a can of Diet Coke, you drink it, and it's gone. You may choose to share it with a friend, but you do not have to: by drinking it you can prevent anyone else from doing so. Furthermore, once it is gone, it's gone: nobody else can subsequently consume that Coke.

Key term

private good: one that, once consumed by one person, cannot be consumed by somebody else

The two features that characterise a private good are that (1) other people can be excluded from consuming it, and (2) once consumed by one person it cannot be consumed by another. This second feature might be described by saying that consumption of a private good is *rivalrous*: the act of consumption uses up the good.

Public goods

Not all goods and services have these two characteristics. There are goods that, once provided, are available to all. In other words, people cannot be excluded from consuming such goods. There are other goods that do not diminish through consumption, so that they are non-rivalrous in consumption. Goods that have both of these characteristics are known as public goods.

Key term

public good: one that is non-exclusive and non-rivalrous: consumers cannot be excluded from consuming such a good, and consumption by one person does not affect the amount of the good available for others to consume

The examples of public goods that are often cited include street lighting, a lighthouse or a nuclear deterrent. For example, once street lighting has been provided in a particular street, anyone who walks along that street at night benefits from the lighting — no one can be excluded from consuming it. So street lighting is non-exclusive. In addition, the fact that one person has walked along the street does not mean that there is less street lighting left for later walkers. So street lighting is also non-rivalrous.

Street lighting is a public good — non-exclusive and non-rivalrous

A key question is how well the market for such a good is likely to operate. In particular, will a free market reach a position where there is allocative efficiency, with marginal social benefit equal to marginal social cost?

Think about the supply and demand curves for a public good such as a lighthouse. To simplify matters, suppose there are just two potential demanders of the good, *a* and *b*. Consider Figure 9.1. If it is assumed that the supply is provided in a competitive market, *S* represents the supply curve, reflecting the marginal cost of providing lighthouse services. The curves d_a and d_b represent the demand curves of the two potential demanders. For a given quantity Q_1, *a* would be prepared to pay P_a and *b* would pay P_b. If these prices are taken to be the value that each individual places on this amount of the good, then $P_a + P_b = P_T$ represents the social benefit derived from consuming Q_1 units of lighthouse services. Similarly, for any given quantity of lighthouse services, the marginal social benefit derived from

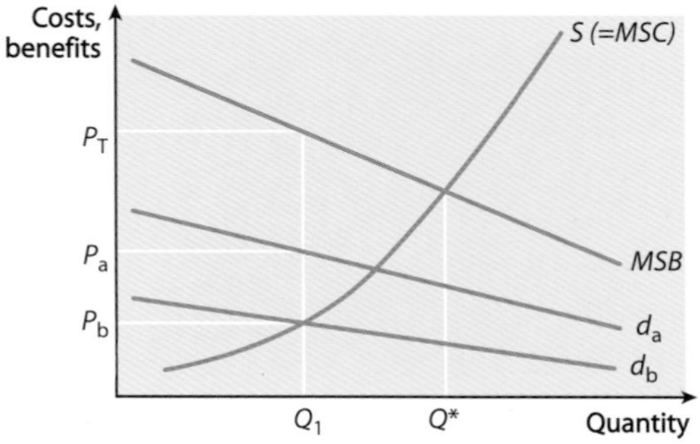

Figure 9.1 *Demand and supply of a public good*

consumption can be calculated as the vertical sum of the two demand curves. This is shown by the curve *MSB*. So the optimal provision of lighthouse services is given by Q^*, at which point the marginal social benefit is equated with the marginal cost of supplying the good.

However, if person *a* were to agree to pay P_a for the good, person *b* could then consume Q_1 of the good free of charge, but would not be prepared to pay in order for the supply to be expanded beyond this point – as person *b*'s willingness to pay is below the marginal cost of provision beyond this point. So the social optimum at Q^* cannot be reached. Indeed, when there are many potential consumers, the likely outcome is that *none* of this good will be produced: why should any individual agree to pay if he/she can free-ride on others?

The **free-rider problem** helps to explain why these sorts of goods have typically been provided through state intervention. This begs the question of how the state can identify the optimal quantity of the good to be provided – in other words, how the government determines Q^*. The extent to which individuals value a particular good cannot be directly observed. However, by including statements about the provision of public goods in their election manifestos, politicians can collect views about public goods provision via the medium of the ballot box. This is an indirect method, but it provides some mandate for the government to take decisions.

Key term

free-rider problem: when an individual cannot be excluded from consuming a good, and thus has no incentive to pay for its provision

Note that public goods are called 'public goods' not because they are publicly provided, but because of their characteristics.

It can be seen that the free-rider problem makes it difficult to charge for a public good, so the private sector will be reluctant to supply such goods. In fact, pure public goods are relatively rare, but there are many goods that have some but not all of the required characteristics. On the face of it, the lighthouse service seems to be a good example of a public good. Once the lighthouse has been constructed and is sending out its signal, all boats and ships that pass within the range of its light can benefit from the service; i.e., it is non-excludable. Moreover, the fact that one ship has seen the lighthouse signal does not reduce the amount of light available to the next ship, so it is also non-rivalrous.

However, this does not mean that ships cannot be charged for their use of lighthouse services. In 2002 an article in the *Guardian* reported that ships were complaining about the high charges to which they were subjected for lighthouse services. Ships of a certain size must pay 'light dues' every time they enter or leave British ports, and the fees collected are used to fund lighthouses, buoys and beacons around the coast. In principle, it could be argued that this renders lighthouses excludable, as ships can be prevented from sailing if they have not paid their dues, and so could not consume the lighthouse services. At the heart of the complaints from the shipping companies was the fact that leisure craft below a certain threshold did not have to pay the charges, and they made more use of the lighthouses than the larger vessels.

In fact, there are many goods that are either non-rivalrous or non-excludable, but not both. One example of this is a football match. If I go to watch a premiership football match, my 'consumption' of the match does not prevent the person sitting next to me from also consuming it, so it is non-rivalrous. However, if I go along without my season ticket (or do not have a ticket), I can clearly be excluded from consuming the match, so it is *not* non-exclusive.

A stretch of road may be considered non-exclusive, as road users are free to drive along it. However, it is not non-rivalrous, in the sense that as congestion builds up consumption is affected. This example is also imperfect as a public good, because by installing toll barriers users can be excluded from consuming it.

Where goods have some features of a public good, the free market may fail to produce an ideal outcome for society. Exercise 9.1 provides some examples of goods: to what extent may each of these be considered to be non-rivalrous or non-excludable?

Exercise 9.1

For each of the following goods, think about whether they have elements of non-excludability, non-rivalry, both, or neither:

a a national park
b a playground
c a theatre performance
d an apple
e a TV programme
f a firework display
g police protection
h a lecture
i a DVD recording of a film
j the national defence

Summary

- A private good is one that, once consumed by one person, cannot be consumed by anyone else — it has characteristics of excludability and rivalry.
- A public good is non-exclusive and non-rivalrous.
- Because of these characteristics, public goods tend to be under-provided by a free market.
- One reason for this is the free-rider problem, whereby an individual cannot be excluded from consuming a public good, and thus has no incentive to pay for it.

Merit goods

There are some goods that the government believes everyone should consume, whether or not they wish to, and whether or not they have the means to do so. The key argument is that individuals do not fully perceive the benefits that they will gain from consuming such goods. These are known as merit goods.

Key term

merit good: a good that society believes brings unanticipated benefits to the individual consumer

Clearly, there is a strong political element involved in identifying the goods that should be regarded as merit goods: indeed, there is a subjective or normative judgement involved, since declaring a good to be a merit good requires the decision maker to make a paternalistic choice on behalf of the population.

One way of viewing merit goods is that they reflect a divergence between the value that individual members of society place on goods and the decision maker's views about their value to society as a whole. There is clearly a danger here that the decision makers will force their views on the rest of society, and again, the ballot box may be the ultimate way of preventing this.

Another aspect of the merit good phenomenon is that the government may be in a better position than individuals to take a long-term view of what is good for society. In particular, governments may need to take decisions on behalf of future generations as well as the present. Resources need to be used wisely in the present in order to protect the interests of tomorrow's citizens. Again, this may require decision makers to make normative judgements about the appropriate weighting to be given to the present as opposed to the future.

At the heart of the notion of a merit good, therefore, is the decision maker's perception that there is a divergence between the marginal benefit that individuals perceive to arise from consuming a good, and the social benefit that actually accrues from its consumption. This is reminiscent of the arguments in Chapter 8 about consumption externalities, where a positive consumption externality arises when the marginal social benefit from consuming a good is greater than the marginal private benefit.

Figure 9.2 shows how this situation can be analysed. The example used here is education. In the UK everyone is required to attend school at least up to age 16. Part of this requirement may be attributed to a merit good argument. It can be argued that education provides benefits to society in excess of those that are perceived by individuals. In other words, society believes that individuals will derive a benefit from education that they will not realise until after they have acquired that education. Thus, the government decrees that everyone must consume education up to age 16, whether they want to or not and whether they have the means to do so or not. This is a merit good argument. In Figure 9.2 marginal social benefit (*MSB*) is shown as being higher than marginal private benefit (*MPB*). Thus, society would like to provide Q^* education, where $MSB = MC$ (marginal social cost), but individuals would choose to consume only Q_1 education, where $MPB = MC$, because they do not expect the future benefits to be as high as the government does. The shaded triangle shows the extent of the distortion in resource allocation that would be present in a free market.

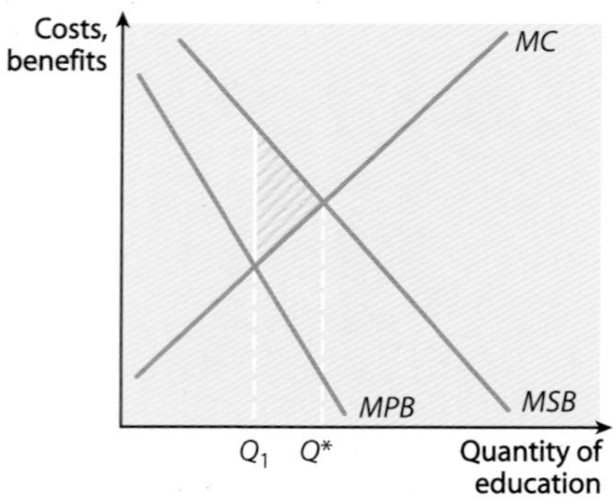

Figure 9.2 A merit good

In this case there may be other issues affecting the market for education. Chapter 8 argued that there would also be positive externality effects from it if educated workers were better able to cooperate with each other. There may be a further argument that individuals may fail to demand sufficient education because of information failure; in other words, they may not perceive the full benefits that will arise from education. The situation may be aggravated if parents have the responsibility of financing their children's education, because they are taking decisions *on behalf of* their children. In the case of tertiary education, there is no guarantee that parents will agree with their children about the benefits of a university education — it could go either way.

Other examples of merit goods include museums and libraries or the arts. These are goods that are provided or subsidised because someone somewhere thinks that communities should have more of them. Economists are wary of playing the merit good card too often, as it entails such a high normative element. It is also difficult sometimes to disentangle merit good arguments from externality effects.

Demerit goods

In contrast, there is a category of goods that government thinks should not be consumed even if individuals want to do so. These are known as **demerit goods** — or sometimes as merit bads. Obvious examples are hard drugs and tobacco. Here the argument is that individual consumers over-value the benefits from consuming such a good.

Key term

demerit good: a good that society believes will bring lower-than-expected benefits to consumers

Figure 9.3 shows the market for cocaine. Marginal private benefits (*MPB*) are shown as being much higher than marginal social benefits (*MSB*), so that in a free market too much cocaine is consumed. Society would like to be at Q^*, but ends up at Q_1. In this particular market, the government may see the marginal social benefit from consuming cocaine to be so low (e.g. at *MSB** in the figure) that consumption should be driven to zero.

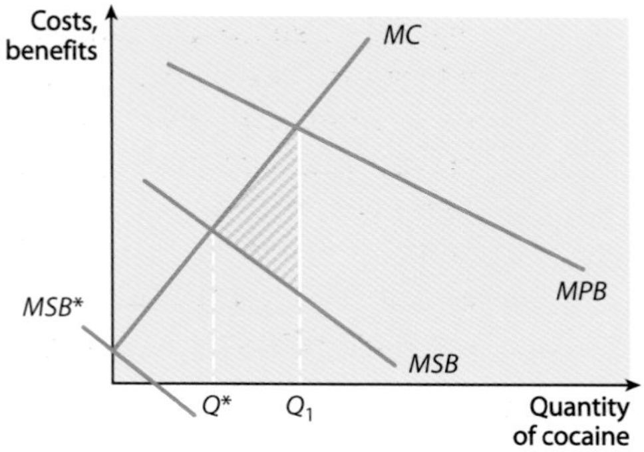

Figure 9.3 A demerit good

Again, this could be interpreted as partly an information problem, in the sense that individual consumers may not perceive the dangers of addiction and thus may overvalue cocaine. In addition, addiction would have the effect of making an individual's demand for the good highly inelastic in the long run. However, it is paternalistic of the government to intervene directly for this reason, although it might wish to correct other externalities — for instance those imposed on others when addicts steal to fund their habit. An alternative approach is to try to remove the information failure; clearly, the government has adopted this approach in seeking to educate people about the dangers of tobacco smoking.

Information failures

> **Key term**
>
> **asymmetric information:** a situation in which some participants in a market have better information about market conditions than others

If markets are to be effective in guiding resource allocation, it is important that economic decision makers receive full and accurate information about market conditions. Consumers need information about the prices at which they can buy and the quality of the products for sale. Producers need to be able to observe how consumers react to prices. Information is thus of crucial significance if markets are to work. However, there are some markets in which not all traders have access to good information, or in which some traders have more or better access to it than others. This is known as a situation of **asymmetric information**, and can be a source of market failure.

Health care

One example of asymmetric information is in health care. Suppose you go to your dentist for a checkup. He tells you that you have a filling that needs to be replaced, although you have had no pain or problems with it. In this situation the seller in a market has much better information about the product than the buyer. You as the buyer have no idea whether or not the recommended treatment is needed, and without going to another dentist for a second opinion you have no way of finding out. You might think this is an unsatisfactory situation, as it seems to give a lot of power to the seller relative to the consumer. The situation is even worse where the dentist does not even publish the prices for treatment until after it has been carried out! The Office of Fair Trading criticised private dentists for exactly this sort of practice when they reported on this market in March 2003. Indeed, dentists are now required by law to publish prices for treatment.

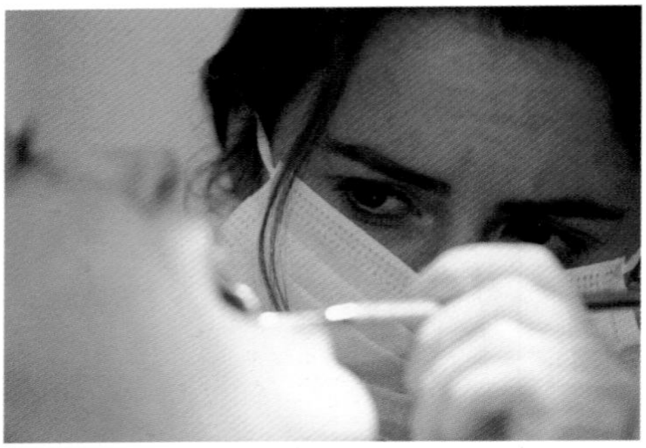

How much dental treatment do you need? A problem of asymmetric information.

The same argument applies in the case of other areas of health care, where doctors have better information than their patients about the sort of treatment that is needed.

Exercise 9.2

Ethel, an old-age pensioner, is sitting quietly at home when the doorbell rings. At the door is a stranger called Frank, who tells her that he has noticed that her roof is in desperate need of repair, and if she does not get something done about it very soon, there will be problems in the next rainstorm. Fortunately, he can help — for a price. Discuss whether there is a market failure in this situation, and what Ethel (or others) can do about it.

Education

The market for education is similar. Teachers or government inspectors may know more about the subjects and topics that students need to study than the students do themselves. This is partly because teachers are able to take a longer view and can see education provision in a broader perspective. Students taking economics at university may have to take a course in mathematics and statistics in their first year, and some will always complain that they have come to study economics, not maths. It is only later that they come to realise that competence in maths is crucial these days for the economics that they will study later in their course.

Second-hand cars

One of the most famous examples of asymmetric information relates to the second-hand (or 'pre-owned', by the latest terminology) car market. This is because the first paper that drew attention to the problem of asymmetric information, by Nobel laureate George Akerlof, focused on this market.

Akerlof argued that there are two types of car. Some cars are good runners and are totally reliable, whereas some are continually breaking down and needing parts and servicing; the latter are known as 'lemons' in the USA (allegedly from fruit machines, where lemons offer the lowest prize). The problem in the second-hand car market arises because the owners of cars (potential sellers) have better information about their cars than the potential buyers. In other words, when a car owner decides to sell a car, he/she knows whether it is a lemon or a good-quality car — but a buyer cannot tell.

In this sort of market car dealers can adopt one of two possible strategies. One is to offer a high price and buy up all the cars in the market, knowing that the lemons will be sold on at a loss. The problem is that, if the lemons make up a large proportion of the cars in the market, this could generate overall losses for the dealers. The alternative is to offer a low price, and just buy up all the lemons to sell for scrap. In this situation, the market for good-quality used cars is effectively destroyed — an extreme form of market failure!

Summary

- A merit good is one that society believes should be consumed by individuals whether or not they have the means or the willingness to do so.
- There is a strong normative element in the identification of merit goods.
- Demerit goods (or merit bads) are goods that society believes should not be consumed by individuals even if they wish to do so.
- In the case of merit and demerit goods, 'society' (as represented by government) believes that it has better information than consumers about these goods, and about what is good (or bad) for consumers.
- Information deficiency can lead to market failure in other situations, for example where some participants in a market have better information about some aspect/s of the market than others.
- Examples of this include health care, education and second-hand cars.

Exercise 9.3

The *Guardian* reported on 27 August 2004 that the pharmaceutical company Glaxo/Smith/Kline had been forced to publish details of a clinical trial of one of its leading antidepressant drugs, following a lawsuit that had accused the company of concealing evidence that the drug could be harmful to children. Discuss the extent to which this situation may have led to a market failure because of information problems.

Equity

In discussing ways in which markets may fail to lead to an optimal allocation of resources, the focus has been primarily on questions of efficiency. In particular, it has been noted that allocative efficiency will not be attained in circumstances in which there is a divergence between private and social costs or benefits. However, it was noted in Chapter 6 that there is no unique overall equilibrium for a society, and that a different distribution of income between individuals will lead to a different Pareto optimum position.

This highlights the potential importance of issues of *equity*. One aspect of this is whether individuals face equal opportunities, and whether identical people receive identical treatment in economic terms. However, there is also the fact that people are not identical, and that different innate abilities and talents command different rewards. This then raises the question of whether society needs to provide some protection for any of its members who find themselves disadvantaged by the way in which resources are allocated. In other words, do communities need a system whereby resources are transferred from some members of society to others?

This is another area in which normative judgements arise. The government may take the view that everybody in society has the right to some minimum standard of living. This may reflect the government's view of the collective desires of the population. In order to alleviate poverty, therefore, some income may need to be transferred from the relatively rich in society to the relatively poor. The normative judgement arises because of the need to define what constitutes a minimum standard of living, and to determine the extent to which such transfers should be undertaken.

This argument is effectively saying that a free market allocation of resources may produce a distribution of income among individuals that is not acceptable in terms of society's objectives.

The question of income distribution can be explored at a number of levels. You could look at the global distribution — the way in which incomes are distributed between countries. You could also examine income distribution *within* countries — that is, between different groups in society.

Global inequality

It is well known that there is substantial inequality in the distribution of incomes worldwide. Figure 9.4 gives some indication of how unequal it is. The World Bank

Over 30% of the world's population live in low-income countries, but they receive only 3% of world GDP.

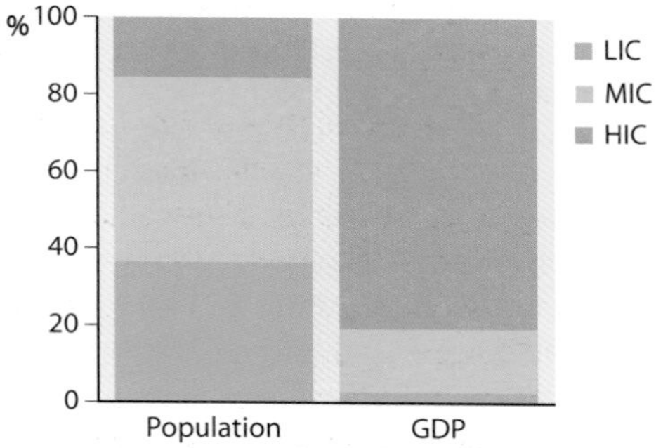

Figure 9.4 Distribution of the world population and GDP, 2003
Source: World Bank 2004.

classifies countries according to income. Low-income countries (LICs) are those in which average annual income is less than \$735, middle-income countries (MICs) have an average income between \$736 and \$9075; high-income countries (HICs) have average incomes above \$9075. Figure 9.4 shows the distribution of income and people between these broad groups of countries. In 2003 about 37% of the world's population lived in low-income countries, but they received only 3% of the world's GDP. In contrast, the 15.5% of people living in the high-income countries received more than 80% of the world's GDP.

There is also substantial inequality *within* many societies. Some inequality is to be expected, as people differ in their innate ability, talents and training. However, it is clear that the degree of inequality varies between countries. In order to examine this more carefully, it is necessary to have a way of measuring inequality.

Measuring income inequality

Table 9.1 (overleaf) presents data for some selected countries. Such data are not collected every year, as it is quite expensive to gather the statistics needed to describe the distribution of income; hence the variety of survey years for the data. As the pattern of income distribution tends not to change dramatically from one year to the next, there is still some justification in comparing across countries.

These data come from surveys conducted on the income levels of individual households. Households are then ranked in ascending order of income levels, and the shares of total income going to groups of households are calculated.

For example, for Ethiopia, the first country listed in the table, it can be seen that the poorest 10% of households receive 3.0% of total household income, and the poorest 20% receive just 7.1%. At the top end of the distribution, the richest 10% receive 33.7% of the total income. This contrasts quite markedly with the second country listed (Sierra Leone), where the data suggest greater inequality in distribution, with the poorest 10% receiving only 0.5% of total household income and the richest 10% getting as much as 43.6%.

	GNI per capita		Percentage share of income or consumption						
	US$ 2002	Survey year	Lowest 10%	Lowest 20%	Second 20%	Third 20%	Fourth 20%	Highest 20%	Highest 10%
Ethiopia	100	1995	3.0	7.1	10.9	14.5	19.8	47.7	33.7
Sierra Leone	140	1983–5	0.5	1.1	2.0	9.8	23.7	63.4	43.6
Bangladesh	360	1995–6	3.9	8.7	12.0	15.7	20.8	42.8	28.6
Pakistan	410	1996–7	4.1	9.5	12.9	16.0	20.5	41.4	27.6
India	480	1997	3.5	8.1	11.6	15.0	19.3	46.1	33.5
Zimbabwe	706	1990–1	1.8	4.0	6.3	10.0	17.4	62.3	46.9
Indonesia	710	1996	3.6	8.0	11.3	15.1	20.8	44.9	30.3
Sri Lanka	840	1995	3.5	8.0	11.8	15.8	21.5	42.8	28.0
Bolivia	900	1990	2.3	5.6	9.7	14.5	22.0	48.2	31.7
China	940	1998	2.4	5.9	10.2	15.1	22.2	46.6	30.4
Belarus	1 360	1998	5.1	11.4	15.2	18.2	21.9	33.3	20.0
South Africa	2 600	1993–4	1.1	2.9	5.5	9.2	17.7	64.8	45.9
Brazil	2 850	1996	0.9	2.5	5.5	10.0	18.3	63.8	47.6
Malaysia	3 540	1995	1.8	4.5	8.3	13.0	20.4	53.8	37.9
Hungary	5 280	1996	3.9	8.8	12.5	16.6	22.3	39.9	24.8
South Korea	9 930	1993	2.9	7.5	12.9	17.4	22.9	39.3	24.3
UK	25 250	1991	2.6	6.6	11.5	16.3	22.7	43.0	27.3
USA	34 870	1997	1.8	5.2	10.5	15.6	22.4	46.4	30.5
Japan	35 990	1993	4.8	10.6	14.2	17.6	22.0	35.7	21.7

Note: Countries are listed in ascending order of average incomes.
Source: *World Development Report*.

***Table 9.1** Income distribution in selected countries*

Income distribution in the UK

Table 9.1 shows that the UK is neither the most equal nor the most unequal of societies as far as post-tax income is concerned. Inequality in the UK increased between the mid-1970s and the mid-1990s, but has stabilised since then. The trends in income distribution, and the causes of inequality, will be explored in Chapter 25.

Summary

- Allocative efficiency can be achieved in a range of alternative situations, some of which may be more 'equitable' than others.
- There may be situations in which the government finds it appropriate to intervene to influence the income distribution within a society.
- There is substantial global disparity in the distribution of resources, and significant inequality within countries.

Government intervention and government failure

Previous chapters have identified various ways in which markets can fail to bring about an efficient allocation of resources in a society. This chapter investigates measures that a government may take in order to improve matters. It also explores how such well-intentioned intervention can sometimes produce unintended results.

Learning outcomes

After studying this chapter, you should:

- be aware of schemes devised to stabilise prices in a volatile market
- be familiar with features of agricultural markets and measures that have been adopted to stabilise farm incomes
- be aware of legislation introduced to monitor monopolies, mergers and market concentration
- understand policies designed to correct for the effects of externalities
- be able to identify areas in which government actions may have unintended distortionary effects

Commodity markets

Chapter 4 explored the demand and supply model. In the case of agricultural markets, it was apparent that vagaries of the weather could affect the size of the harvest and lead to instability in prices from one season to the next.

This is not, strictly speaking, a market failure, but it may nonetheless be seen as undesirable, as uncertainty about the harvest makes it difficult for farmers to plan ahead and hence may have damaging effects on supply.

Buffer stock schemes

If the commodity concerned can be stored, a **buffer stock** can be used to try to stabilise prices over time.

> **Key term**
>
> **buffer stock:** surplus stock that is bought up when the harvest is good with a view to selling when it is poor, in an attempt to stabilise commodity prices

Figure 10.1 illustrates how such a scheme could work for a grain market. Suppose that demand for grain is relatively stable from year to year, but supply varies between S_{poor}, when the weather is unfavourable, and S_{glut}, when conditions are good for agriculture and there is a bumper harvest. This means that the free market price will vary between P_p when the harvest is poor and P_g when the harvest is strong.

Suppose a buffer stock scheme is set up with the aim of stabilising price at a medium level between the two extremes that occur — say, at P^*. In order to achieve this, grain is bought up as a buffer stock when there is a glut. Notice that, if the scheme buys up the quantity *BC*, then the remaining quantity is bought by consumers at price P^*. The buffer stock scheme has to pay out the area *BCFE* as expenditure.

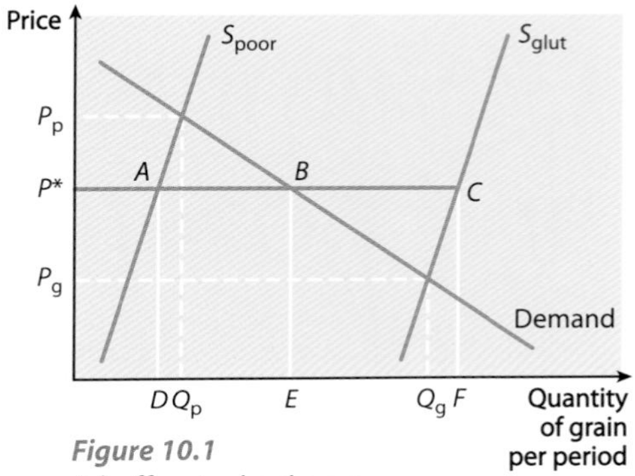

Figure 10.1
A buffer stock scheme

In a poor harvest year, grain is sold via this scheme to prevent the price from rising too high. Thus, if the harvest is at S_{poor} the buffer stock will sell the amount *AB*. Again, P^* is the price at which the quantity supplied by farmers plus the amount released on to the market from the buffer stock just meets the amount demanded by the market. This time the buffer stock scheme benefits from revenue generated from the sale of past stocks, to the tune of area *ABED*.

This scheme can be effective in stabilising prices; indeed, it can also stabilise the quantity traded through time. The difficulty with such a scheme comes in identifying the level at which prices should be set. If the price is set too high, the buffer scheme will find itself buying up more grain than it sells, and so grain will accumulate as time goes by. Thus, its expenditure in bumper years could (on average) exceed its revenues in poorer years. This would also become very costly in terms of storage. On the other hand, if the price is set at too low a level, the scheme will not have sufficient stocks to be able to prevent prices rising in times of poor harvests.

The cobweb model

Instability in prices has arisen not only as a result of volatility in supply or demand. One of the characteristics of agricultural goods is that there are *inflexibilities* in supply. Farmers take decisions on how much of each crop to plant in advance of knowledge about demand conditions. Once the crop is in the ground, the quantity cannot be varied until the following year. Price signals to producers thus operate with a time lag.

Consider Figure 10.2, which shows a market for an agricultural commodity. Suppose this market first has the price set relatively high at P_1. Farmers react by planting enough of the crop to supply Q_2 in the next period. However, given the demand curve, market price then falls to P_3; so farmers in the *next* period plant less of the crop. Quantity in the following period thus falls to Q_4, which leads to a price rise to P_5. This then encourages farmers to expand production; and so the process goes on. In this case the market price spirals in towards the equilibrium (forming a kind of cobweb shape), which comes at the intersection of demand and supply. Once the equilibrium is reached, the market will settle down.

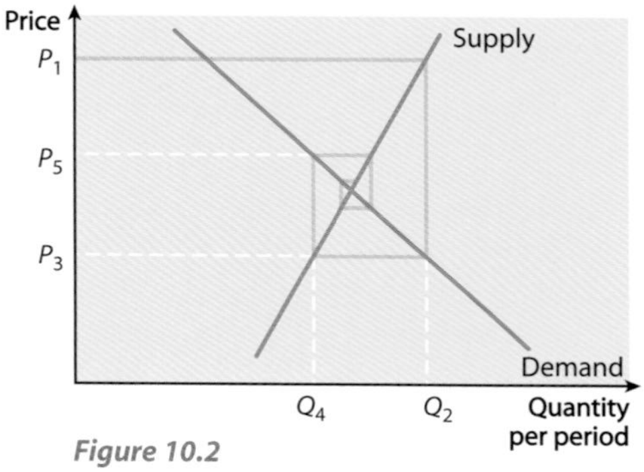

Figure 10.2
A stable cobweb

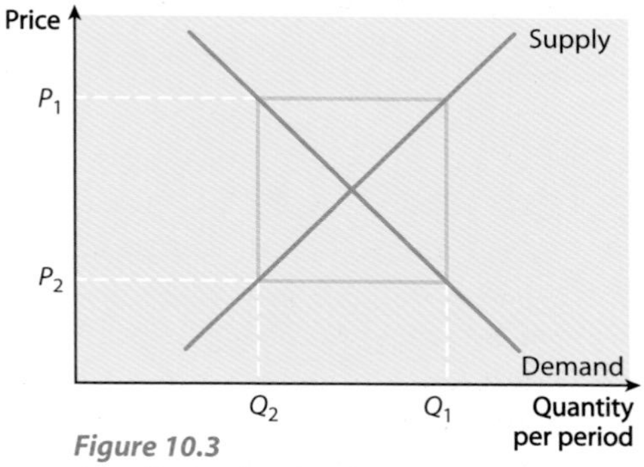

Figure 10.3
A cyclical cobweb

This does not seem too bad, as the instability in prices is just a short-term phenomenon. However, such stability of the market cannot be guaranteed. Consider Figure 10.3. If to begin with the market price is at P_1, it is clear that farmers will react by supplying Q_1 in the next period; this will cause price to fall to P_2, which will induce a supply response to Q_2, and in the next period price will return to P_1. In this situation prices alternate between P_1 and P_2, and the equilibrium is never reached.

Indeed, matters could be even worse, as you can see in Figure 10.4. If the price is first observed to be at P_0, you might think that this market is safe, as P_0 is not too far away from the potential equilibrium price. However, if you follow the lines of the 'cobweb', you will find that the market becomes increasingly unstable, fluctuating violently and moving further and further away from the equilibrium.

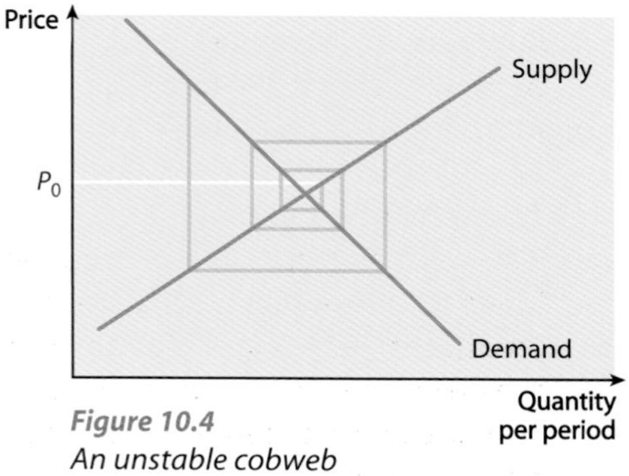

Figure 10.4
An unstable cobweb

What determines the stability of the cobweb model is the elasticity of supply and demand. Figures 10.3 and 10.4 have been drawn with the demand curve in common, and only the elasticity of supply varying. Intuitively, this makes sense, as the more flexible is supply, the more unstable is the market.

The Common Agricultural Policy (CAP)

In the past, many governments have regarded agricultural markets as in need of particular attention, partly because of their strategic significance. For example, in times of war it is important to be able to feed the population, so governments have been reluctant to be dependent on imported food supplies. Within the European Economic Community (EEC), which has now been superseded by the European Union (EU), there was an additional concern to avoid too much migration from the rural areas into the towns.

The Common Agricultural Policy (CAP) was devised to stabilise the incomes of farmers in the EEC/EU. There were two key components of the policy. The first was to provide guaranteed prices to farmers for their crops. However, as the guaranteed prices were typically above the prices that prevailed in world markets, the second element was a variable tariff designed to prevent Europe from being flooded by cheaper imports.

Figure 10.5 describes this graphically. It represents the market for wheat in the EU. As agricultural producers in the EU may be seen as relatively high cost by world standards, suppose that the world price is below the equilibrium price that would obtain in the EU (which would, of course, be at the intersection of demand and supply). P_w represents the world price and, if this price were also to be set within the EU, demand in the market would be given by D_0, of which only a small quantity (S_0) would be produced by EU wheat producers; the remainder ($D_0 - S_0$) would be imported.

Such a situation shows why there might be concern, as wheat production within the EU is on a limited scale and imports seem to make up most of the market. Furthermore, if farmers desert the rural areas for better-paid jobs in the cities, the long-term prospects for agriculture will be even worse, as once people leave the rural areas, it will be difficult to sustain the agricultural sector. In terms of Figure 10.5, the supply curve will drift to the left as more farmers withdraw from the sector – and probably the demand curve will drift to the right as incomes rise, and the dependence on imports will therefore escalate.

The CAP thus set guaranteed prices for key agricultural commodities, so that farmers could be assured of a certain income. Suppose the guaranteed price for wheat were set at P_g in Figure 10.5. In current market conditions supply would increase to S_1, and demand would fall to D_1. This would maintain the viability of the agricultural sector and eliminate the need for imports. Indeed, at P_g farmers would produce more than consumers would demand at that price, and the EU would have to purchase the excess supply ($S_1 - D_1$).

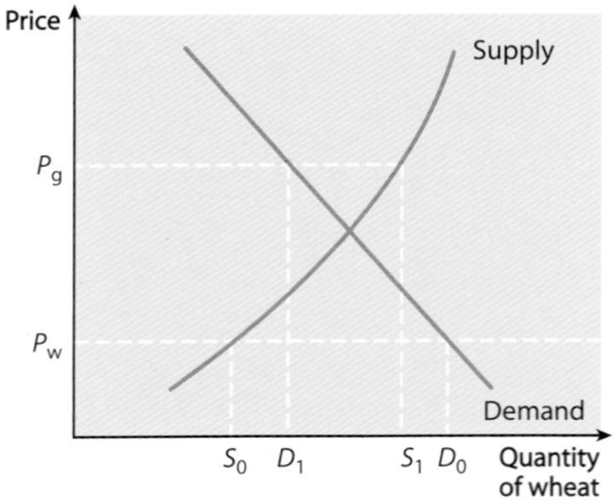

Figure 10.5 The CAP

The second component of the CAP then cuts in, in that a variable levy is imposed on the price of non-European wheat, set at a level that covers the difference between the guaranteed price and the world price. This ensures that foreign producers are not able to undercut prices within the European area. The levy is variable in order to maintain the guaranteed price in the face of varying world prices.

The CAP has come under increasing criticism, especially from producers in less-developed countries, who are desperate to find markets for their produce and feel that it is unfair that European producers should be so heavily subsidised.

Selling surpluses cheaply overseas leads to unfair competition and often attracts allegations of 'dumping'.

In addition, as the EU bought up more and more wheat and other commodities, the costs of storage escalated. This led to the build-up of the now infamous wine 'lakes' and butter 'mountains'. Selling the surplus cheaply elsewhere in the world brought allegations of dumping from governments that did not want their own agricultural sectors to be faced with unfair competition.

The CAP has been going through a process of reform in response to these pressures. Milk quotas were introduced in 1984 to limit excess production, and the McSharry reforms of 1992 brought beef quotas and the notion of 'set-aside', under which farmers were paid for setting some of their land aside, i.e. not using it. Guaranteed prices began to be reduced, so that the variable levy could also be reduced — as was required under international agreements on tariff reduction. Additional reforms under Agenda 2000 brought more cuts to guaranteed prices, and rural development schemes were introduced to encourage farmers to engage in other activities within rural areas. In 2003 further measures forced farmers to plan supply in relation to market prices rather than the guaranteed prices. Instead, subsidies are now being provided for a range of environmental and rural development schemes.

Reform has been slow, because there has been much lobbying and political pressure from farmers who felt their interests were being threatened. This is a reminder that economic analysis has to be set into the political context in which it operates.

Subsidies and efficiency

One problem that arises with the use of subsidies to encourage higher production of a commodity relates to the incentives given to producers. If producers are cushioned from having to compete at world prices, there is little incentive for them to achieve cost efficiency. Thus, an indirect effect of a system of subsidies may be a reduction in the efficiency with which production is carried out.

Summary

- Volatility in supply and demand conditions can result in instability in prices in commodity markets.
- Buffer stock schemes offer one way of trying to stabilise prices through buying when supply is high (and price is low), and selling when supply is low (and price is high).
- In agricultural markets, instability may also come where supply reacts to price with a time lag.
- Governments have often regarded it as desirable to intervene in agricultural markets to sustain food production.
- In the EU, the Common Agricultural Policy (CAP) involved intervention buying to maintain prices and sustain agriculture.
- Over time this proved costly, in view of the need to store commodities; there was also political pressure from the rest of the world.
- Recent reforms to the CAP have lowered guaranteed prices and redirected subsidies towards environmental goals and the encouragement of rural development.

Exercise 10.1

Examine why prices in some markets may be unstable from year to year, and evaluate ways in which more stability might be achieved. How effective would you expect such measures to be?

Regulation of monopoly and mergers

The effectiveness of the market system in allocating resources requires prices to act as signals to producers about consumer demand. Firms will be attracted into activities where consumer demand is buoyant and profitability is high, and will tend to exit from activities in which demand is falling and profitability is low.

This process relies on the existence of healthy competition between firms, and on freedom of entry to and exit from markets. In the absence of these conditions, resources may not be best allocated according to the pattern of consumer demand. For example, if there are barriers to entering a market, the existing firms in the market may have the power to restrict output and raise the price, producing less of the product than is desirable for society. As explained in Chapter 7, such barriers to entry may arise from features such as economies of scale or the patent system. In some situations, existing firms may take strategic action to deter entry.

Key term

competition policy: an area of economic policy designed to promote competition within markets to encourage efficiency and safeguard consumer interests

This is one area of the economy in which governments often choose to intervene to protect consumers. In the UK the Office of Fair Trading and the Competition Commission are responsible for this part of government policy. These bodies have the power to investigate markets that appear to be overly concentrated or in which competition appears weak. They can also take action to encourage competition in markets. This is known as **competition policy**.

One of the knotty problems that arises here is that, if firms benefit from economies of scale, it may be more productively efficient to allow large firms to develop than to fragment the industry into lots of small firms in the name of encouraging competition. Thus, the authorities have to find a way of balancing the potential costs of losing allocative efficiency against the potential benefits of productive efficiency.

Merger and acquisition activity has led to the creation of some giant firms in recent years, and one responsibility of the competition authorities is to monitor such activity, which may be seen to have an effect on concentration in markets. These issues will be investigated more thoroughly in Chapter 20.

Dealing with externalities

As seen in Chapter 8, externalities arise in situations where there are items of cost or benefit associated with transactions that are not reflected in market prices. In these circumstances a free market will not lead to an optimum allocation of resources. One approach to dealing with such market situations is to bring those externalities into the market mechanism, a process known as **internalising an externality**. For example, in the case of pollution this principle would entail forcing the polluting firms to face the full social cost of their production activities. This is sometimes known as the polluter pays principle.

Key term

internalising an externality: an attempt to deal with an externality by bringing an external cost or benefit into the price system

Pollution

Figure 10.6 illustrates a negative production externality, i.e. pollution. Suppose that firms in the market for chemicals use a production process that emits toxic fumes, thereby imposing costs on society that the firms themselves do not face. In other words, the marginal private costs faced by these firms are less than

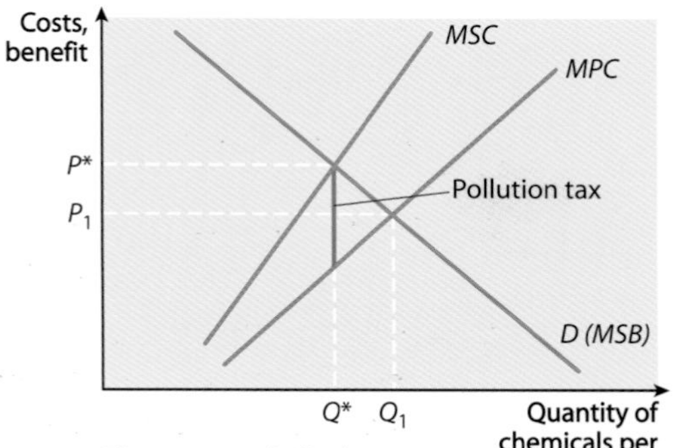

Figure 10.6 Pollution

the marginal social costs that are inflicted on society. As explained in Chapter 8, firms in this market will choose to produce up to the point Q_1 and charge a price of P_1 to consumers. At this point marginal social benefit is below the marginal cost of producing the chemicals, so it can be claimed that 'too much' of the product is being produced – that society would be better off if production were at Q^*, with a price charged at P^*.

Note that this optimum position is not characterised by *zero* pollution. In other words, from society's point of view it pays to abate pollution only *up to* the level where the marginal benefit of reducing pollution is matched by the marginal cost of doing so. Reducing pollution to zero would be too costly.

How can society reach the optimum output of chemicals at Q^*? In line with the principle that the polluter should pay, one approach would be to impose a tax on firms such that polluters face the full cost of their actions. In Figure 10.6, if firms were required to pay a tax equivalent to the vertical distance between marginal private cost (*MPC*) and marginal social cost (*MSC*), they would choose to produce at Q^*, paying a tax equal to the green line on the figure.

An alternative way of looking at this question is via a diagram showing the marginal benefit and marginal cost of emissions reduction. In Figure 10.7, *MB* represents the marginal social benefits from reducing emissions of some pollutant and *MC* is the marginal costs of reducing emissions. The optimum amount of reduction is found where marginal benefit equals marginal cost, at e^*. Up to this point, the marginal benefit to society of reducing emissions exceeds the marginal cost of the reduction, so it is in the interest of society to reduce pollution. However, beyond that point the marginal cost of reducing the amount of pollution exceeds the benefits that accrue, so society will be worse off. Setting a tax equal to t^* in Figure 10.7 will induce firms to undertake the appropriate amount of emission reduction.

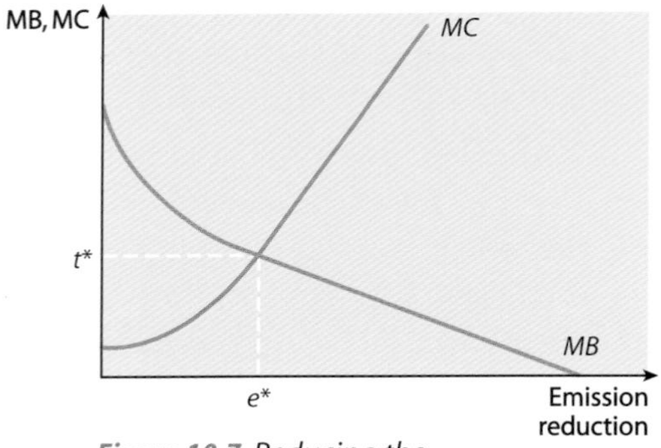

Figure 10.7 Reducing the emission of toxic fumes

This is not the only way of reaching the objective, however. Figure 10.7 suggests that there is another possibility – namely, to impose environmental standards, and to prohibit emissions beyond e^*. This amounts to controlling quantity rather than price; and, if the government has full information about marginal costs and marginal benefits, the two policies will produce the equivalent result.

Either of the approaches outlined above will be effective – *if* the authorities have full information about the marginal costs and benefits. But how likely is this? There are many problems with this proviso. The measurement of both marginal benefits and marginal costs is fraught with difficulties.

The marginal social benefits of reducing pollution cannot be measured with great precision, for many reasons. It may be argued that there are significant gains to be made in terms of improved health and lower death rates if pollution can be reduced, but quantifying this is not straightforward. Even if it were possible to evaluate the saving in resources that would need to be devoted to future medical care resulting from the pollution, there are other considerations – quantification of the direct improvements to quality of life, whether or not to take international effects into account when formulating domestic policy, and the appropriate discount rate for evaluating benefits that will be received in the future. Moreover, the environmentalist and the industrialist may well arrive at different evaluations of the benefits of pollution control.

The measurement of costs may also be problematic. For example, it is likely that there will be differences in efficiency between firms. Those using modern technology may face lower costs than those using relatively old capital equipment. Do the authorities try to set a tax that is specific to each firm to take such differences into account? If they do not, but instead set a flat-rate tax, then the incentives may be inappropriate. This would mean that a firm using modern technology would face the same tax as one using old capital. The firm using new capital would then tend to produce too little output relative to those using older, less efficient capital.

Pollution permits

Another approach is to use a *pollution permit system*, under which the government issues or sells permits to firms allowing them to pollute up to a certain limit. These permits are then tradable, so that firms that are relatively 'clean' in their production methods and do not need to use their full allocation of permits can sell their polluting rights to other firms whose production methods produce greater levels of pollution.

One important advantage of such a scheme lies in the incentives for firms. Firms that pollute because of their relatively inefficient production methods will find they are at a disadvantage because they face higher costs. Rather than continuing to purchase permits, they will find that they have an incentive to produce less pollution

With tradable permits, polluters are encouraged by market forces to clean up their act.

— which, of course, is what the policy is intended to achieve. In this way, the permit system uses the market to address the externality problem — in contrast to direct regulation of environmental standards, which tries to solve pollution by overriding the market.

A second advantage is that the overall level of pollution can be controlled by this system, as the authorities control the total amount of permits that are issued. After all, the objective of the policy is to control the overall level of pollution, and a mixture of 'clean' and 'dirty' firms may produce the same amount of total emissions as uniformly 'slightly unclean' firms.

However, the permit system may not be without its problems. In particular, there is the question of enforcement. For the system to be effective, sanctions must be in place for firms that pollute beyond the permitted level, and there must be an operational and cost-effective method for the authorities to check the level of emissions.

Furthermore, it may not be a straightforward exercise for the authorities to decide upon the appropriate number of permits to issue in order to produce the desired reduction in emission levels. Some alternative regulatory systems share this problem, as it is not easy to measure the extent to which marginal private and social costs diverge.

One possible criticism that is unique to a permit form of regulation is that the very different levels of pollution produced by different firms may seem inequitable — as if those firms that can afford to buy permits can pollute as much as they like. On the other hand, it might be argued that those most likely to suffer from this are the polluting firms, whose public image is likely to be tarnished if they acquire a reputation as heavy polluters. This possibility might strengthen the incentives of such firms to clean up their production. Taking the strengths and weaknesses of this approach together, it seems that on balance such a system could be effective in regulating pollution.

Global warming

Global warming is widely seen to require urgent and concerted action at a worldwide level. The Kyoto summit of 1997 laid the foundations for action, with many of the developed nations agreeing to take action to reduce emissions of carbon dioxide and other so-called 'greenhouse' gases that are seen to be causing climate change. Although the USA withdrew from the agreement in early 2001, apparently concerned that the US economy might be harmed, in November of that year 178 other countries did reach agreement on how to enforce the Kyoto Accord. The absence of US cooperation is potentially significant, as the USA is the world's largest emitter of carbon dioxide, responsible for about a quarter of the world's greenhouse gas emissions.

At the heart of the Kyoto Accord is the decision of countries to reduce their greenhouse gas emissions by an agreed percentage by 2010. The method chosen to achieve these targets was based on a tradable pollution permit system. This was seen to be especially demanding for countries like Japan, whose industry is already relatively energy-efficient. Japan was thus concerned that there should be sufficient permits available for purchase. More explicitly, it was concerned that sloppy compliance by Russia would limit the amount of permits on offer. The issue of monitoring and compliance is thus seen as critical.

Road pricing

Chapter 8 showed how the economic analysis of externalities could be used to examine the question of traffic congestion. This was portrayed as another example of a negative production externality. In Figure 10.8, the marginal motorist choosing to use a road suffers from congestion to an extent that is reflected in marginal private costs. However, further costs are imposed on other road users, as the congestion affects all drivers on the road. Thus, marginal social costs exceed marginal private costs, and too many journeys will be undertaken for society's good.

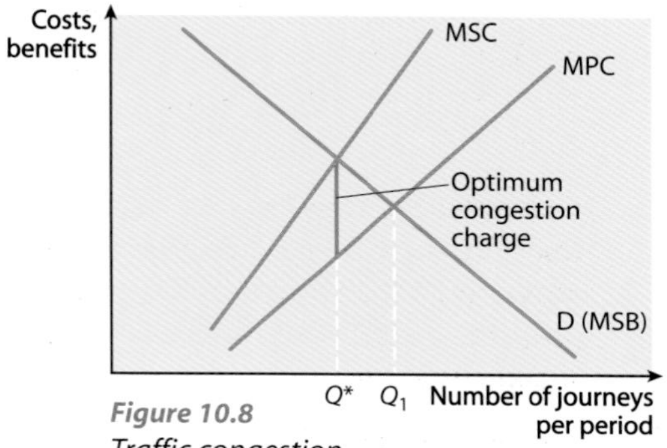

Figure 10.8
Traffic congestion

Road pricing acts as a tax to help internalise the externality by forcing individual drivers to face the full social cost of their motoring. The congestion charge introduced in London in 2003 tries to exploit this analysis by charging drivers for entering the central district during peak hours. Singapore has had similar charges in place for many years, and they have been very successful in controlling congestion.

However, there can be side-effects of such a policy. Singapore first introduced a form of road pricing in 1974, by which cars entering the central business district (CBD) during certain hours had to pay a charge. One effect of the policy was that traffic within the CBD moved smoothly and there was virtually no congestion, even in peak periods. However, roads just outside the controlled area became subject to congestion, with vehicles queuing up as the time approached for free entry in the evenings. In other words, to some extent the pricing simply diverted traffic on to other roads.

One debate of recent years has been whether the solution to congestion is to widen roads or to build new ones. For example, the M6 toll road opened in 2004 to try to relieve congestion on the notorious M6. This is another way of charging for road usage. Indeed, toll systems are common in some countries such as France.

However, it has been argued that road-widening schemes are ineffective; as motorists realise that road capacity has increased, they expect their journeys to be quicker, and this raises their expected marginal private benefit from undertaking journeys, thereby increasing traffic. By this argument, extending road capacity merely encourages more traffic on to the roads, with no relief to congestion after all.

Extension material: taxing tobacco

Chapter 9 analysed the case of merit and demerit goods, where the key feature was that the government perceived that the marginal private benefits from consuming a good or service diverged from the marginal social benefits. In the case of merit goods, this meant that the government would be keen to encourage their greater consumption, e.g. of education. For demerit goods the reverse would be the case, with the government trying to find a way of discouraging such consumption.

Consider the case of smoking tobacco, which might be seen as an example of a demerit good. This market is characterised in Figure 10.9. *MPB* represents the marginal private benefit that consumers gain from smoking tobacco. However, the government believes that consumers underestimate the damaging effects of smoking, so that the true benefits are given by *MSB* (marginal social benefit). Given the marginal cost (supply) curve, in an unregulated market consumers will choose to smoke up to Q_1 tobacco. The optimum for society, however, is at Q^*.

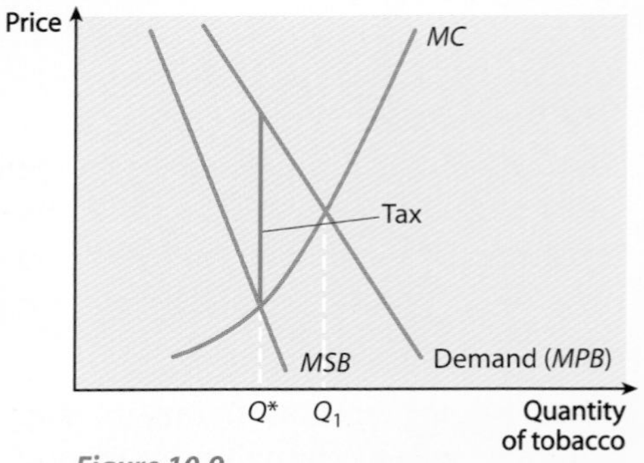

Figure 10.9
Taxing tobacco

One way of tackling this problem is again through taxation. If the government imposes a tax shown by the red line in Figure 10.9, consumers can be persuaded to reduce their consumption to the optimal level at Q^*. However, because the demand curve (*MPB*) is so steep (relatively inelastic), a substantial tax is needed in order to reach Q^*. Empirical evidence suggests that the demand for tobacco is relatively inelastic — and therefore tobacco taxes have risen to comprise a large portion of the price of a packet of cigarettes.

Conversely, if the government wishes to encourage the consumption of a merit good, it may do so through subsidies. Thus, the museum service is subsidised, and the ballet and opera have enjoyed subsidies in the past.

The NIMBY syndrome

One problem that arises in trying to deal with externalities is that you cannot please all of the people all of the time. For example, it may well be that it is in society's overall interests to relocate unsightly facilities – it may even be that everyone would agree about this; but such facilities have to be located somewhere, and someone is almost bound to object because they are the ones to suffer. This is the NIMBY (Not In My Back Yard) syndrome.

For example, many people would agree that it is desirable for the long-run sustainability of the economy that cleaner forms of energy are developed. One possibility is to build wind farms. People may well be happy for these to be constructed – *as long as* they do not happen to be living near them.

This is perhaps not the best example, however, as the evidence on the effectiveness of wind farms is by no means proven, and there is a strong movement against their use on these grounds.

Exercise 10.2

You discover that your local authority has chosen to locate a new landfill site for waste disposal close to your home. What costs and benefits for society would result? Would these differ from your private costs and benefits? Would you object?

Property rights

The existence of a system of secure property rights is essential as an underpinning for the economy. The legal system exists in part to enforce property rights, and to provide the set of rules under which markets operate. When property rights fail, there is a failure of markets.

One of the reasons underlying the existence of some externalities is that there is a failing in the system of property rights. For example, think about the situation in which a factory is emitting toxic fumes into a residential district. One way of viewing this is that the firm is interfering with local residents' clean air. If those residents could be given property rights over clean air, they could require the firm to compensate them for the costs it was inflicting. However, the problem is that, with such a wide range of people being affected to varying degrees (according to prevailing winds and how close they live to the factory), it is impossible in practical terms to use the assignment of property rights to internalise the pollution externality. This is because the coordination problem requires high transaction costs in order for property rights to be individually enforced. Therefore, the government effectively takes over the property rights on behalf of the residents, and acts as a collective enforcer.

Nobel prize winner Ronald Coase argued that externality effects could be internalised in conditions where property rights could be enforced, and where the transaction costs of doing so were not too large.

Summary

- Competition policy is an area of economic policy whereby governments seek to protect consumers and to promote healthy competition between firms.
- A balance needs to be maintained between preserving allocative efficiency through competition and allowing large firms to reap economies of scale and scope, thus improving productive efficiency.
- In seeking to counter the harmful effects of externalities, governments look for ways of internalising the externality, by bringing external costs and benefits within the market mechanism.
- For example, the 'polluter pays' principle argues that the best way of dealing with a pollution externality is to force the polluter to face the full costs of its actions.

- Attempts have been made to tackle pollution through taxation, the regulation of environmental standards and the use of pollution permits.
- Road pricing is seen as one way of internalising the externality caused by traffic congestion.
- Taxation and other measures such as limits on advertising have been used to tackle the problem of demerit goods such as tobacco consumption.
- In some cases the allocation of property rights can be effective in curbing the effects of externalities — so long as the transaction costs of implementing it are not too high.

Government failure

Most governments see it as their responsibility to try to correct some of the failures of markets to allocate resources efficiently. This has led to a wide variety of policies being devised to address issues of market failure. Some of these have been discussed already. However, some policies have unintended effects that may not culminate in successful elimination of market failure. Indeed, in some cases government intervention may introduce new market distortions, leading to a phenomenon known as government failure.

The remainder of this chapter examines some examples of government failure.

Key terms

government failure: a misallocation of resources arising from government intervention

minimum wage: a system designed to protect the low paid by setting a minimum on the wage rate that employers are permitted to offer workers

The minimum wage

In 1999 the UK National Minimum Wage came into force, designed to protect workers on low pay. To illustrate how this works, Figure 10.10 represents the labour market for office cleaners. Employers demand labour according to the wage rate – the lower the wage, the higher the demand for the labour of office cleaners. On the supply side, more workers will offer themselves for work when the wage rate is relatively high. If the market is unregulated, it will reach equilibrium with a wage rate W^* and labour L^*.

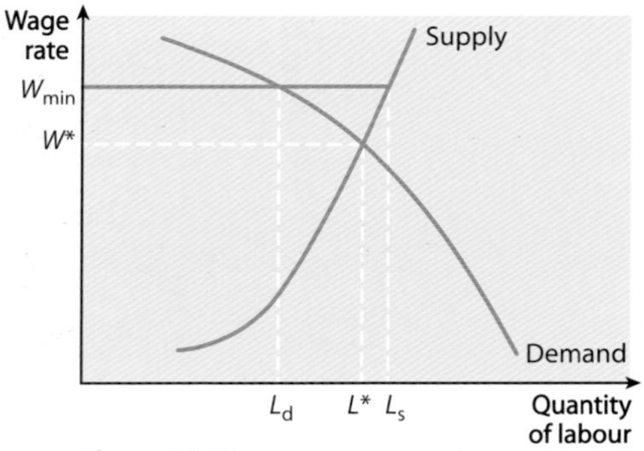

Figure 10.10
A minimum wage

Suppose now that the government comes to the view that W^* is not sufficiently high to provide a reasonable wage for cleaners. One response is to impose a minimum wage, below which employers are not permitted to offer employment – say W_{min} on the figure. This will have two effects on the market situation. First, employers will demand less labour at this higher wage, so employment will fall to L_d. Second, more workers will be prepared to offer themselves for employment at the higher wage, so labour supply will rise to L_S. However, the net effect of this is that there is an excess supply of labour at this wage and hence unemployment, with more workers offering themselves for work than there are jobs available in the market.

What is happening here is that, with the minimum wage in effect, *some* workers (those who manage to remain in employment) are better off, and now receive a better wage. However, those who are now unemployed are worse off. It is not then clear whether the effect of the minimum wage is to make society as a whole better off — some people will be better off, but others will be worse off.

Notice that this analysis rests on some assumptions that have not been made explicit. In particular, it rests on the assumption that the labour market is competitive. Where there are labour markets in which the employers have some market power, and are able to offer lower wages to workers than would obtain in a free market equilibrium situation, it is possible that the imposition of a minimum wage will increase employment. This possibility will be explored in Chapter 23.

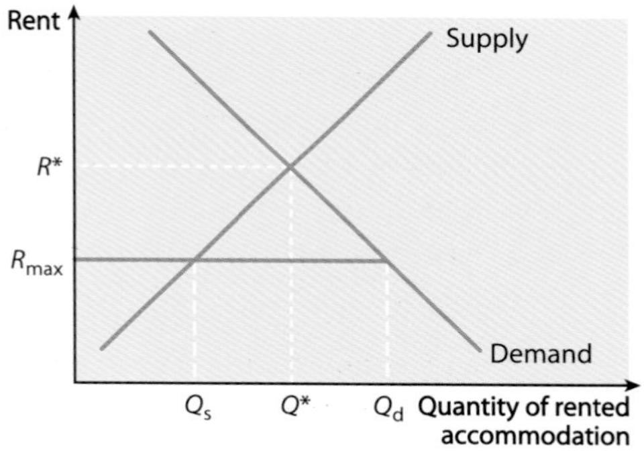

Figure 10.11 Rent controls

Rent controls

Another market in which governments have been tempted to intervene is the housing market. Figure 10.11 represents the market for rented accommodation. The free market equilibrium would be where demand and supply intersect, with the equilibrium rent being R^* and the quantity of accommodation traded being Q^*.

If the government regards the level of rent as excessive, to the point where households on low incomes may be unable to afford rented accommodation, then, given that housing is one of life's necessities, it may regard this as unacceptable.

The temptation for the government is to move this market away from its equilibrium by imposing a maximum level of rent that landlords are allowed to charge their tenants. Suppose that this level of rent is denoted by R_{max} in Figure 10.11. Again, there are two effects that follow. First, landlords

Rent controls distort the market for housing and lead to shortages of supply.

will no longer find it profitable to supply as much rental accommodation, and so will reduce supply to Q_S. Second, at this lower rent there will be more people looking for accommodation, so that demand for rented accommodation will move to Q_d. The upshot of the rent controls, therefore, is that there is less accommodation available, and more homeless people.

It can be seen that the well-meaning rent control policy, intended to protect low-income households from being exploited by landlords, merely has the effect of reducing the amount of accommodation available. This was not what was supposed to happen.

Sales tax

Chapter 4 analysed the effects of a sales tax imposed on a good. The burden of a tax is thereby shared between buyers and sellers of the good, depending on the elasticity of demand. This analysis can now be taken a bit further.

It is recognised that governments need to raise funds to finance the expenditure that they undertake. One way of doing this is through expenditure taxes such as the value added tax (VAT). You might think that raising money in this way to provide goods and services that would otherwise not be provided would be a benefit to society. But there is a downside to this action, even if all the funds raised by a sales tax are spent wisely.

Consider Figure 10.12, which shows the markets for DVDs. Suppose that the government imposes a specific tax on DVDs. Chapter 4 explained that this would have the effect of taking market equilibrium from the free market position at P^* with quantity traded at Q^* to a new position, with price now at P_t and quantity traded at Q_t. Remember that the price rises by less than the amount of the tax, implying that the incidence of the tax falls partly on buyers and partly on sellers. In Figure 10.12 consumers pay more of the tax (the area P^*P_tBE) than the producers (who pay FP^*EG). The effect on society's overall welfare will now be examined.

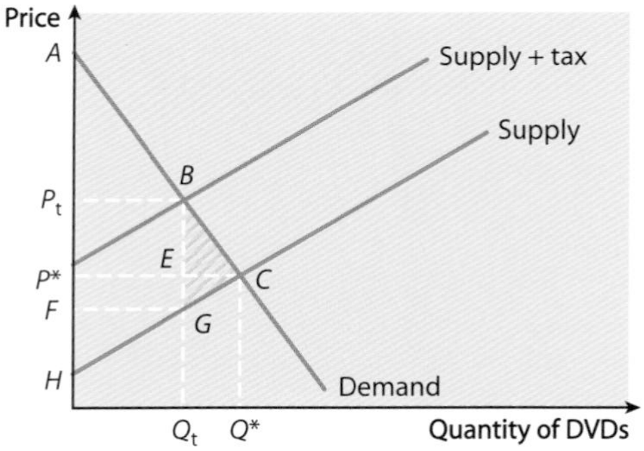

Figure 10.12 A sales tax

Remember that the total welfare that society receives from consuming a product is the sum of consumer and producer surplus. (Check Chapter 5 if you need to remind yourself of this.)

The situation before and after the sales tax is as follows. Before the tax, consumer surplus is given by the area AP^*C and producer surplus is given by the triangle P^*CH. How about afterwards? Consumer surplus is now the smaller triangle AP_tB, and producer surplus is FGH. The area P_tBGF is the revenue raised by the government from the tax, which should be included in total welfare on the assumption that the government uses this wisely. The total amount of welfare is now *ABGH*. If you compare these total welfare areas before and after the tax, you will realise that they differ by the area *BCG*. This triangle represents a deadweight loss that arises from the imposition of the tax. It is sometimes referred to as the **excess burden** of the tax.

So, even where the government intervenes to raise funding for its expenditure – and spends wisely, a distortion is introduced to resource allocation, and society must bear a deadweight loss.

Key terms

excess burden of a sales tax: the deadweight loss suffered by society following the imposition of a sales tax

prohibition: an attempt to prevent the consumption of a demerit good by declaring it illegal

Prohibition

Another example of a demerit good cited in Chapter 9 was that of hard drugs such as cocaine. The argument was that there were substantial social disbenefits arising from the consumption of hard drugs, and that addicts and potential addicts were in no position to make informed decisions about their consumption of them. One response to such a situation is to consider making the drug illegal – that is, to impose **prohibition**.

Figure 10.13 shows how the market for cocaine might look. You may wonder why the demand curve takes on this shape. The argument is that there are two types of cocaine users. There are the recreational users, who will take cocaine if it is available at a reasonable price but who are not addicts. In addition, there is a hard core of habitual users who are addicts, and whose demand for cocaine is highly inelastic. Thus, at low prices demand is relatively elastic because of the presence of the recreational users, who are relatively price-sensitive. At higher prices the recreational users drop away, and demand from the addicts is highly price-inelastic. Suppose that the supply in free market equilibrium is given by S_0; the equilibrium will be with price P_0 and quantity traded Q_0. If the drug is made illegal, this will affect supply. Some dealers will leave the market to trade in something else, and the police will succeed in confiscating a certain proportion of the drugs in the market. However, they are unlikely to be totally successful, so supply could move to, say S_1.

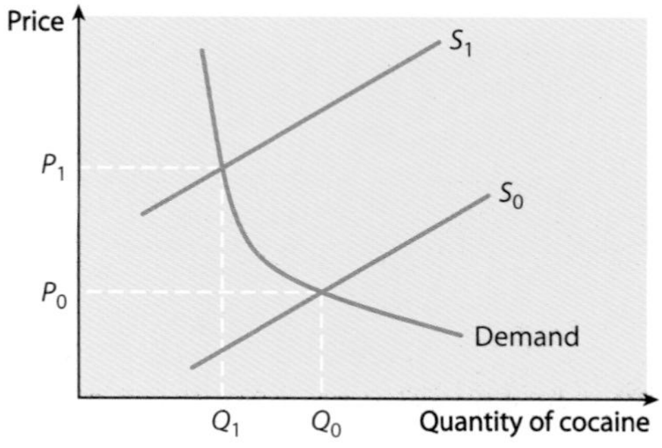

Figure 10.13 Prohibition

In the new market situation, price rises substantially to P_1, and quantity traded falls to Q_1. However, what has happened is that the recreational users have dropped out of the market, leaving a hard core of addicts who will pay any price for the drug, and who may resort to muggings and robberies in order to finance their habit. This behaviour clearly imposes a new sort of externality on society. And the more successful are the police in confiscating

supplies, the higher will the price be driven. There may thus be disadvantages in using prohibition as a way of discouraging consumption of a demerit good.

Costs of intervention

Some roles are critical for a government to perform if a mixed economy is to function effectively.

A vital role is the provision by the government of an environment in which markets can operate effectively. There must be stability in the political system if firms and consumers are to take decisions with confidence about the future. And there must be a secure system of property rights, without which markets could not be expected to work.

In addition, there are sources of market failure that require intervention. This does not necessarily mean that governments need to substitute direct action for markets. However, it does mean that they need to be more active in markets that cannot operate effectively, while at the same time performing an enabling role to encourage markets to work well whenever this is feasible.

Such intervention entails costs. There are costs of administering, and costs of monitoring the policy to ensure that it is working as intended. This includes the need to look out for the unintended distortionary effects that some policies can have on resource allocation in a society. It is therefore important to check that the marginal costs of implementing and monitoring policies do not exceed their marginal benefits.

Summary

- Government failure can occur when well-meaning intervention by governments has unintended effects.
- In some circumstances a minimum wage intended to protect the low paid may aggravate their situation by increasing unemployment.
- Rent controls may have the effect of reducing the amount of accommodation available.
- A sales tax imposes an excess burden on society.
- Prohibition may also have unintended effects.

part 2

Review section

Part 2 has investigated a range of situations that arise in a modern economy in which markets may fail to allocate society's resources in the best possible way. This review section summarises the main findings of the last five chapters, and presents some sample past examination questions that offer you the chance to see how this material may be presented to you under exam conditions. Before you tackle these, it would be helpful to remind yourselves of the key terms and issues that have been raised.

Chapter 6 Introducing market failure

The opening chapter of Part 2 provided a brief overview of the sources of *market failure* and introduced some important concepts. In analysing market failure, it is crucial to establish some criteria by which you can judge whether a particular market situation is imposing costs on society. In this context, the notions of *productive efficiency* and *allocative efficiency* are both important. It turns out that there are situations in which the ideals of efficiency cannot be reached because of the way that markets operate — these are situations of *market failure*. The concepts of *average* and *marginal costs* were also introduced. The key sources of market failure were identified as:

- imperfect competition
- externalities
- information failure
- public goods
- income distribution

Chapter 7 Monopoly and market dominance

In some industries the nature of the production process gives rise to *economies of scale* and *economies of scope*. The presence of these features of production means that large firms have an advantage in terms of the efficiency of production, and face a downward-sloping *long-run average cost curve*, at least over some range of output. This may mean that an industry can support only a limited number

of efficient firms, so there is a relationship between firm size and *market concentration*. In such markets it is possible for firms to gain a position of *market dominance* and, by choosing to maximise profits, to create a situation of market failure. This state of affairs arises in particular where there is some form of *barrier to entry* that makes it difficult for new firms to join the market. Such barriers may arise from either natural or strategic factors. Markets in which competition is limited are thus susceptible to market failure.

Chapter 8 Externalities

There are many market situations that arise where there is some element of costs or benefits that is not reflected in market prices. Such items are known as *externalities*. Where such externalities exist, decisions made by participants in the market will not lead to allocative efficiency in the distribution of resources. Put another way, this is another example of market failure, which the government may wish to try to correct. Externalities can be positive or negative, and can affect either production or consumption.

Chapter 9 Public goods, information problems and equity

This chapter deals with three important aspects of market failure. First, *public goods* pose particular problems for a market system. Such goods are non-exclusive and non-rivalrous, and in the absence of some form of intervention will be under-provided by the market because of the *free-rider problem*. This led on to a discussion of *merit* and *demerit goods*, i.e. goods that the government might consider *ought* to be consumed (in the case of merit goods, or ought *not* to be consumed in the case of demerit goods) by members of society even if they do not (or do) choose to do so. This may reflect the fact that the government has better information about the characteristics of such goods than do consumers. Finally, information failure can cause market failure in a number of areas, especially where there is *asymmetric information* — in other words, where some participants in a market have more information than others and can exploit this to their advantage. Governments may also choose to protect certain groups in society in order to affect the overall distribution of income within a society in the interests of *equity*.

Chapter 10 Government intervention and government failure

Having identified a number of possible types of market failure, Chapter 10 described various ways in which governments have intervened in order to try to deal with these failures. Some governments have tried to stabilise prices in some markets characterised by volatility, such as agricultural markets. Legislation has also been put in place to monitor monopolies, mergers and market concentration, in order to limit the effects of market dominance by firms. In addition, policies have been designed to deal with externalities, to correct information failures and to influence the distribution of income. However, a cautionary note has also to be sounded, as there are situations in which well-meaning government actions have unintended distortionary effects, resulting in *government failure*.

Preparing for the examination

For Unit 2 the focus is on data-response questions. You may think that these are tough to prepare for, given that you cannot know in advance which topics are likely to face you when you open the paper. However, remember that the examination is on *economics*, and that you do not need to know in detail about the topic that appears, as long as you have the economic analysis ready to apply to whatever the topic turns out to be. So do not waste time trying to out-guess the examiners about what questions will be on the paper, but concentrate instead on becoming familiar with the sorts of economic techniques and theories that you may have to explain and apply.

Below you will find two data-response questions, although in the examination you would only be required to tackle one of them.

Data-response question P2.1

EU intervention in agricultural markets

Year	Farm incomes (£bn)
1992	3.0
1993	4.2
1994	4.5
1995	5.3
1996	4.9
1997	3.0
1998	2.2
1999	2.3
2000	1.5
2001	1.7

Table P2.1
UK farm incomes

Source:
www.defra.gov.uklesg/summary.htm

Extract 1: The Common Agricultural Policy

The European Union's Common Agricultural Policy (CAP) was intended to increase agricultural production, stabilise markets and provide farmers with a fair standard of living.

The CAP was based on guaranteed prices for individual items and a form of buffer stock system that bought up surplus production. It imposed duties on imports to encourage the purchase of home-grown food, and provided export subsidies to enable EU produce to compete in the lower-priced world markets. The policy achieved its aims of making the original six member states self-sufficient in food and of raising farm incomes. But open-ended subsidies and technological progress encouraged excess production, resulting in wine and milk 'lakes' and butter 'mountains'.

Taxpayers were paying twice over: first in higher food prices, and then by subsidising the storage or export of the unwanted food. Nor was the policy helping small

producers, since more than 80% of the subsidies went to just 20% of the farmers. From 1979, attempts at reform have been made by introducing quotas and 'set aside' schemes (which paid farmers for not using land to produce crops).

The most recent proposals for reform are to 'decouple' subsidies and production and to redirect a lot more CAP spending towards environmental and rural development projects. Under a reformed CAP, farmers will be encouraged to be greener.

Sources: adapted from *The Times*, 28 June 2002, and *The Economist*, 13 July 2002.

Extract 2: The threatened countryside

Since the Second World War nearly half of UK ancient woodland has been lost. Farmland bird populations have crashed. Rural life is also suffering: 23 000 farmers and workers lost their jobs in the year 2000 alone. Friends of the Earth believes that modern farming techniques, promoted by the EU and the UK government, are to blame. For example:

- **pesticide usage:** poisoning insects and destroying farmland food chains by reducing weed populations
- **heavy machinery:** damaging soil structure and causing erosion
- **larger farms:** removing hedgerows to create larger fields
- **emphasis on productivity:** farmers receiving subsidies based on production and not on protecting the environment

Source: **www.foe.co.uk/campaigns/real_food/issues/countryside/**

a With reference to Table P2.1, how might the fluctuations in farm incomes be explained? *(6 marks)*

b Assess the case for government intervention in agriculture. *(10 marks)*

c **(i)** Examine the factors that led to the development of 'wine and milk "lakes" and butter "mountains"' (Extract 1, lines 10–11). Illustrate your answer with a diagram. *(8 marks)*

(ii) Assess **two** methods that might be used to reduce these surpluses. *(8 marks)*

d Giving examples, distinguish between the private and external costs associated with modern farming methods. *(8 marks)*

Data-response question P2.2

Waste: problems, disposal and remedies

Extract 1: The problem of waste

The UK Government's Strategy Unit produced a report on waste (*Waste: An Interim Discussion Paper*) in which the following points were made:

- Each year households, commerce and industry in the UK produce over 100 million tonnes of waste.

- The amount of waste collected by UK local authorities is growing at around 3% per year. This is faster than the growth in GDP and is one of the fastest growth rates in Europe. By 2020 the amount of waste is set to double.
- Each tonne of paper recycled saves 15 trees, as well as their surrounding habitat and wildlife.
- Waste growth is fuelled by a range of economic and social factors linked to prosperity, including rising household income, increasing number of households and changing household sizes, changing lifestyles, influential advertising and the growth in sales of pre-packed goods.

Figure P2.1 shows how different countries dispose of waste.

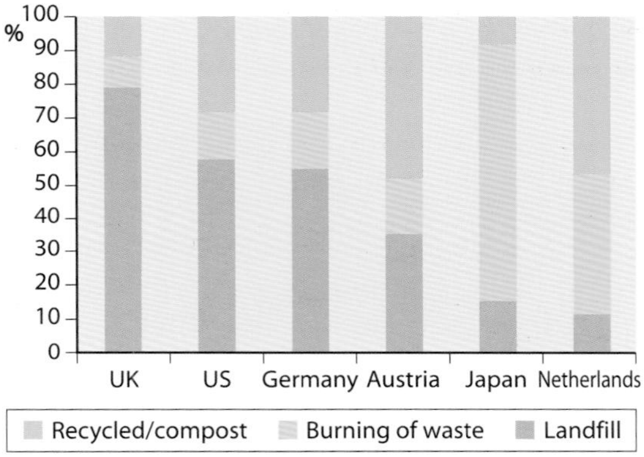

Figure P2.1 *Methods of waste management by country*

There are good reasons for reducing the volume of waste sent to landfill. First, landfilling biodegradable waste produces 25% of the UK's methane, a powerful greenhouse gas. Second, landfilling means that resources that could otherwise be recycled or reused with associated benefits to the environment are lost. Finally, the UK is currently running out of landfill sites especially in South East England.

Source: **www.strategy.gov.uk**

Extract 2: Landfill tax

In the 2002 pre-Budget report, the Government announced that the landfill tax on waste will nearly treble from £13 to £35 per tonne.

In a separate report, the government reiterated its determination to use the tax system to achieve environmental goals. Mr Brown, the Chancellor, said: 'Well-designed environmental taxes and other economic instruments can play an important role in ensuring that price reflects environmental cost – in line with the "polluter pays" principle – and discouraging behaviour that damages the environment.'

The Treasury's analysis of environmental taxes reinforced its 1997 statement of intent on environmental taxation, which promised to shift the burden from 'goods' to 'bads'.

Source: *The Financial Times*, 28 November 2002.

a **(i)** Define the term 'external costs'. *(2 marks)*

(ii) How do the external costs of waste disposal differ from the private costs? Illustrate your answer with a diagram. *(8 marks)*

b Analyse **two** factors which might explain the increase in UK waste levels. *(6 marks)*

c **(i)** With reference to Figure P2.1, outline **two** factors which might explain the differences in methods of waste management between the UK and **one** other country shown. *(6 marks)*

(ii) Examine the likely economic effects of a landfill tax. *(8 marks)*

d A government agency offers to buy waste paper at a minimum guaranteed price. Evaluate the implications of such a scheme, assuming that it leads to a significant increase in the quantity of waste paper supplied for recycling. *(10 marks)*

These questions were taken from examinations set for the Edexcel AS Economics examination for Unit 2 – Markets: why they fail. We are grateful to London Qualifications for permission to reproduce them here.

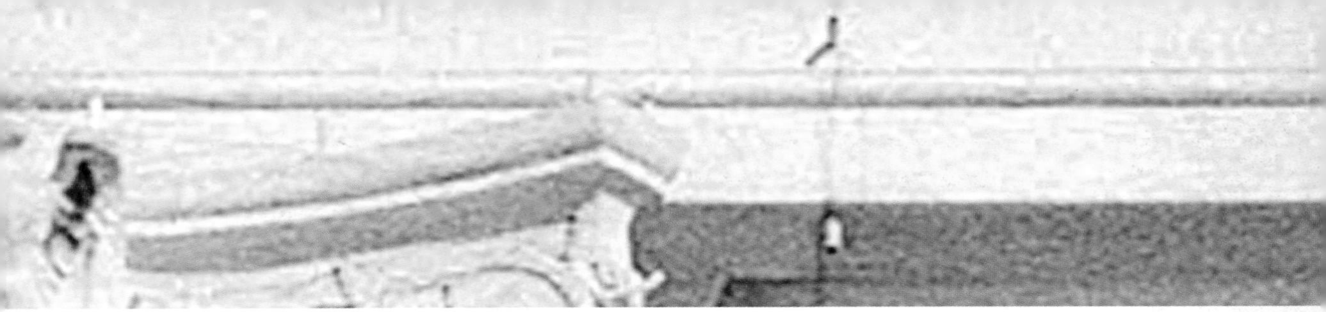

Managing the economy

Part 3

part 3

Chapter 11

Measuring economic performance

This part of the book switches attention to macroeconomics. Macroeconomics has much in common with microeconomics, but focuses on the whole economy, rather than on individual markets and how they operate. Although the way of thinking about issues is similar, and although similar tools are used, now it is interactions between economic variables at the level of the whole economy that is studied. This process will introduce some of the major concerns of the media, such as unemployment, inflation and economic growth.

Learning outcomes

After studying this chapter, you should:

- be aware of the main economic aggregates in a modern economy
- understand the distinction between real and nominal variables
- be familiar with the use of index numbers and the calculation of growth rates
- appreciate the significance of alternative measurements of inflation and unemployment in the context of the UK economy
- be familiar with the role and importance of the balance of payments
- be aware of the circular flow of income, output and expenditure
- understand the meaning of GDP and its use as an indicator in international comparisons

Economic performance

Previous chapters have emphasised the importance of individual markets in achieving allocative and productive efficiency. In a modern economy, there are so many separate markets that it is difficult to get an overall picture of how well the economy is working. When it comes to monitoring its overall performance, the focus thus tends to be on the **macroeconomic** aggregates. 'Aggregate' here means 'totals' — e.g. total unemployment in an economy, or total spending on goods and services — rather than, say, unemployed workers in a particular occupation, or spending on a particular good.

Key term

macroeconomics: the study of the inter-relationships between economic variables at an aggregate (macro-economic) level

There are a number of dimensions in which the economy as a whole can be monitored. One prime focus of economic policy in recent years has been the inflation rate, as it has been argued that maintaining a stable economic environment is crucial to enabling markets to operate effectively. A second focus has been unemployment, which has been seen as an indicator of whether the economy is using its resources to the full — in other words, whether there are factors of production that are not being fully utilised. In addition, of course, there may be concern that the people who are unemployed are being disadvantaged.

Perhaps more fundamentally, there is an interest in economic growth; in other words, is the economy expanding its potential capacity as time goes by, thereby making more resources available for members of the society? In fact, it might be argued that this is the most fundamental objective for the economy, and the most important indicator of the economy's performance. Indeed, Chapter 14 will be wholly devoted to this topic.

Other concerns may also need to be kept in mind. In particular, there is the question of how the economy interacts with the rest of the world. The UK is an 'open' economy, i.e. one that actively engages in international trade, and this aspect of UK economic performance needs to be monitored too. This is done through the balance of payments accounts.

The importance of data

To monitor the performance of the economy, it is crucial to be able to observe how the economy is functioning, and for this you need data. Remember that economics, especially macroeconomics, is a non-experimental discipline. It is not possible to conduct experiments to see how the economy reacts to various stimuli in order to learn how it works. Instead, it is necessary to observe the economy, and come to a judgement about whether or not its performance is satisfactory, and whether macro-economic theories about how the economy works are supported by the evidence.

So, for each of the variables mentioned above a reliable measure is needed for tracking it, in order to observe how the economy is evolving through time. The key indicators of the economy's performance will be introduced as this chapter unfolds.

Most of the economic statistics used by economists are collected and published by various government agencies. Such data are published mainly by the Office of National Statistics (ONS). Data on other countries are published by the International Monetary Fund (IMF), the World Bank and the United Nations, as well as national sources. There is little alternative to relying on such sources, because the accurate collection of data is an expensive and time-consuming business.

Care needs to be taken in the interpretation of economic data. It is important to be aware of how the data are compiled, and the extent to which they are indicators

The Executive Board of the International Monetary Fund, Washington, DC, April 1999.

of what economists are trying to measure. It is also important to remember that the economic environment is ever changing, and that single causes can rarely be attributed to the economic events that are observed. This is because the *ceteris paribus* condition that underlies so much economic analysis is rarely fulfilled in reality. In other words, you cannot rely on 'other things remaining constant' when using data about the real world.

It is also important to realise that even the ONS cannot observe with absolute accuracy. Indeed, some data take so long to be assembled that early estimates are provisional in nature and subject to later revision as more information becomes available. Data used in international comparisons must be treated with even greater caution.

Real and nominal measurements

The measurement of economic variables poses many dilemmas for statisticians. Not least is the fundamental problem of what to use as units of measurement. Suppose economists wish to measure total output produced in an economy during successive years. In the first place, they cannot use volume measures. They may be able to count how many computers, passenger cars, tins of paint and cauliflowers the economy produces — but how do they add all these different items together to produce a total?

An obvious solution is to use the money values. Given prices for all the items, it is possible to calculate the money values of all these goods and thus produce a measurement of the total output produced in an economy during a year in terms of pounds sterling. However, this is just the beginning of the problem, because, in order to monitor changes in total output between two years, it is important to be aware that not only do the volumes of goods produced change, but so too do their prices. In effect, this means that, if pounds sterling are used as the unit of measurement, the unit of measurement will change from one year to the next as prices change.

This is a problem that is not faced by most of the physical sciences. After all, the length of a metre does not alter from one year to the next, so if the length of something is being measured the unit is fixed. Economists, however, have to make allowance for changing prices when measuring in pounds sterling.

Measurements made using prices that are current at the time a transaction takes place are known as measurements of **nominal values**. When prices are rising, these nominal measurements will always overstate the extent to which an economic variable is growing through time. Clearly, to analyse performance economists will be more interested in **'real' values** — that is, the quantities produced after having removed the effects of price changes. One way in which these real measures can be obtained is by taking the volumes produced in each year but valuing these quantities at the prices that prevailed in some base year. This then enables allowance to be made for the changes in prices that take place, permitting a focus on the real values. These can be thought of as being measured at *constant prices*.

For example, suppose that last year you bought a tub of ice cream for £2, but that inflation has been 10%, so that this year you had to pay £2.20 for the same tub. Your *real* consumption of the item has not changed, but your spending has increased. If you were to use the value of your spending to measure changes in consumption through time, it would be misleading, as you know that your *real* consumption has not changed at all (so is still £2), although its *nominal* value has increased to £2.20.

Key terms

nominal value: value of an economic variable based on current prices

real value: value of an economic variable taking account of changing prices over time

index number: a device for comparing the value of a variable with a base point

Index numbers

In some cases there is no apparent unit of measurement that is meaningful. For example, if you wished to measure the general level of prices in an economy, there is no meaningful unit of measurement that could be used. In such cases the solution is to use index numbers, which is a form of ratio that compares the value of a variable with some base point.

For example, suppose the price of a 250 g pack of butter last year was 80 p, and this year it is 84 p. How can the price between the two periods be compared? One way of doing it is to calculate the percentage change:

$$100 \times (84 - 80) \div 80 = 5\%$$

(Note that this is the formula for calculating any growth rate in percentage terms. The change in the variable is always expressed as a percentage of the initial value, not the final value.)

An alternative way of doing this is to calculate an index number. In the above example, the current value of the index could be calculated as $100 \times 84 \div 80 = 105$. In other words, the current value is divided by the base value and multiplied by 100. The resulting number gives the current value relative to the base value. This turns out to be a useful way of expressing a range of economic variables where you want to show the value relative to a base period.

One particular use for this technique is when you want to show the average level of prices at different points in time. For such a general price index, one procedure is to define a typical basket of commodities that reflects the spending pattern of a representative household. The cost of that bundle can be calculated in a base year, and then in subsequent years. The cost in the base year is set to equal 100, and in subsequent years the index is measured relative to that base date, thereby reflecting the change in prices since that base date. For example, if in the second year the weighted average increase in prices were 2.5%, then the index in year 2 would take on the value 102.5 (based on year 1 = 100). Such a general index of prices could be seen as an index of the *cost of living* for the representative household, as it would give the level of prices faced by the average household relative to the base year.

Summary

- Macroeconomics is the study of the interrelationships between economic variables at the level of the whole economy.
- There are some variables that are of particular interest when monitoring the performance of an economy — for example inflation, unemployment and economic growth.
- As economists cannot easily conduct experiments in order to test economic theory, they rely on the use of economic data, i.e. observations of the world around them.
- Data measured in money terms need to be carefully handled, as prices change over time, thereby affecting the units in which many economic variables are measured.
- Index numbers are helpful in comparing the value of a variable with a base date or unit.

The consumer price index

The most important general price index in the UK is the **consumer price index** (CPI), which has been used by the government in setting its inflation target since the beginning of 2004. This index is based on the prices of a bundle of about 650 goods and services measured at different points in time. The information is compiled through the Family Expenditure Survey, in which data about the prices of goods and services in the bundle are collected on a monthly basis from a sample of 7000 households across the country. Some prices are observed directly in randomly selected shops; these are then used to create an index based on 1996 = 100. The weights for the items included in the index are set to reflect the typical spending habits of consumers in the economy, based on the share of each component in their total expenditure. These weights are updated each year, as changes in the consumption patterns of households need to be accommodated if the index is to remain representative.

It is important to remember that the CPI provides a measurement of the *level* of prices in the economy. This is not inflation: **inflation** is the *rate of change* of prices, and the percentage change in the CPI provides one estimate of the inflation rate.

Key terms

consumer price index (CPI): a measure of the average level of prices in the UK

inflation: the percentage rate of change of the consumer price index

Being able to calculate percentage changes is a useful skill. Going back to the example of the ice cream from page 141, remember that you had bought a tub of ice cream for £2 last year, but now have to pay £2.20.

The percentage change in the price is obtained by dividing the *change* in price by the original price and multiplying by 100. Thus, the percentage change is $0.20/2.00 \times 100 = 10\%$.

Alternative measurements of inflation

Key term

retail price index (RPI): a measure of the average level of prices in the UK

The traditional measure of inflation in the UK for many years was the **retail price index** (RPI), which was first calculated in the early twentieth century to evaluate the extent to which workers were affected by price changes during the First World War. When the Blair government first set an explicit inflation target, it chose the RPIX, which is the RPI calculated excluding mortgage interest payments. This was felt to be a better measure of the effectiveness of macroeconomic policy. It was argued that if interest rates are used to curb inflation, then including mortgage interest payments in the inflation measure would be misleading.

The CPI replaced RPIX partly because it is believed to be a more appropriate indicator for evaluating policy effectiveness. In addition, it has the advantage of being calculated using the same methodology as is used in other countries within the European Union, so that it is more useful than the RPIX as a measure for making international comparisons of inflation.

Figure 11.1 shows data for the rates of change of the RPI and the CPI since March 1997. These rates have been calculated on a monthly basis, computing the percentage rate of change of each index relative to the value 12 months previously.

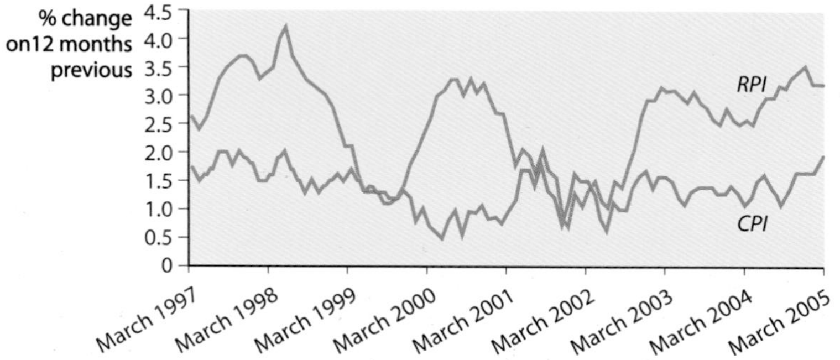

Figure 11.1 *Alternative inflation measures in the UK*

Source: ONS.

A noticeable characteristic of Figure 11.1 is that for much of the period the CPI has shown a lower rate of change than the RPI. In part this reflects the way in which the prices are combined, but it also reflects the fact that different items and households are covered. The National Statistician, Len Cook, said:

> The CPI's fairly recent development as a macroeconomic indicator of inflation means that it has some distinct advantages over RPIX.... Its coverage of spending and households better matches other economic data. The way it combines individual prices also has some clear statistical benefits, and helps us to compare UK inflation with inflation in other countries.

For RPIX the government's target rate for inflation was set at 2.5%. For CPI inflation the government has set the target at 2%.

Inflation in the UK and throughout the world

Figure 11.2 shows a time path for the rate of change of the RPI since 1949. RPI has been used for this purpose, as the CPI was introduced only in 1997, so there is no consistent long-run series for it. The figure provides the backdrop to understanding the way the UK economy evolved during this period. Apart from the period of the Korean War, which generated inflation in 1951–52, the 1950s and early 1960s were typified by a low rate of inflation, with some acceleration becoming apparent in the early 1970s. The instability of the 1970s was due to a combination of factors. Oil prices rose dramatically in 1973–74 and again in 1979–80, which certainly contributed to rising prices, not only in the UK but worldwide. However, inflation was further fuelled by the abandonment of the fixed exchange rate system under which sterling had been tied to the US dollar until 1972. Chapter 33 explains the effect on the economy of having a floating exchange rate, but in essence it freed up monetary policy in a way that was perhaps not fully understood by the government of the day. As you can see in Figure 11.2, prices were allowed to rise rapidly – by nearly 25% in 1974–75. The figure also shows how inflation was gradually reined in during the 1980s, and underlines the relative stability that has now been achieved, with inflation keeping well within the target range that has been set by the Blair government.

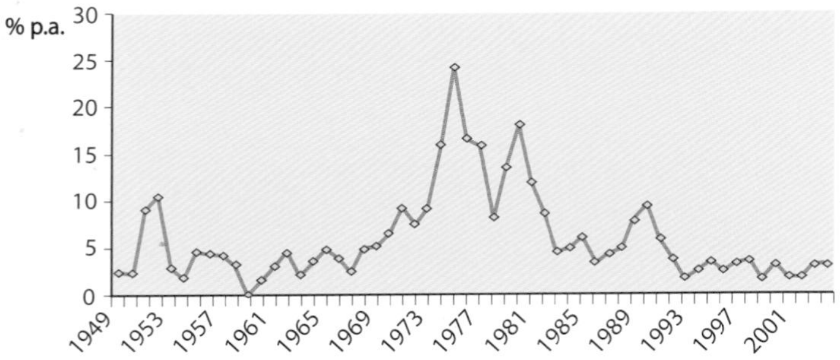

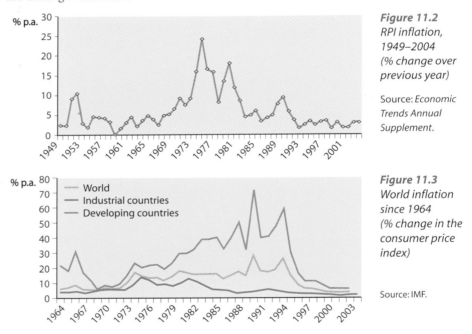

Figure 11.2
RPI inflation, 1949–2004 (% change over previous year)

Source: *Economic Trends Annual Supplement.*

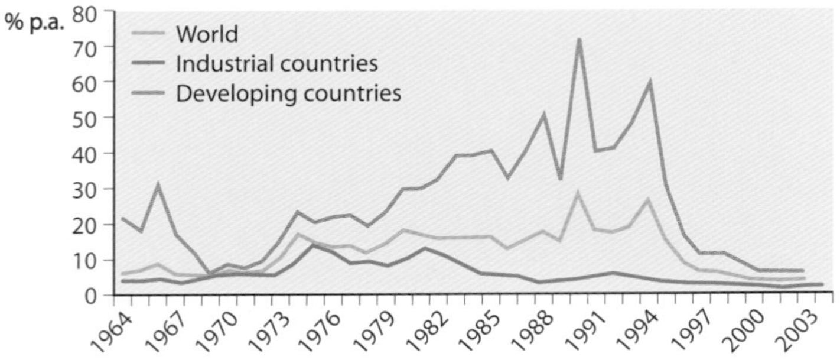

Figure 11.3
World inflation since 1964 (% change in the consumer price index)

Source: IMF.

Figure 11.3 shows something of the extent to which the UK's experience is typical of the pattern of inflation worldwide. You can see from this how inflation in the industrial countries followed a similar general pattern, with a common acceleration in the early 1970s, and a period of gradual control after 1980. However, you can also see that the developing countries in the world experienced inflation at a much higher average level after 1974, because they proved to be less able to bring prices under control after the oil price shocks. Much of this reflects events in Latin America, which suffered especially high rates of inflation in the 1980s and 1990s. This instability in the macroeconomic environment has almost certainly hindered development in the countries affected, and makes it important to understand how inflation is generated and how to curb it. This topic will be revisited later.

Unemployment

The measurement of unemployment in the UK has also been contentious over the years, and the standard definition used to monitor performance has altered several times, especially during the 1980s, when a number of rationalisations were introduced.

Key term

claimant count of unemployment: measure by which the number of people claiming the Jobseeker's Allowance is calculated

Historically, unemployment was measured as the number of people registered as unemployed and claiming unemployment benefit (the Jobseeker's Allowance (JSA)). This measure of employment is known as the **claimant count of unemployment**. People claiming the JSA must declare that they are out of work, capable of, available for and actively seeking work, during the week in which their claim is made.

The 'claimant count' of unemployment is the number of people claiming the Jobseeker's Allowance.

Figure 11.4 shows monthly data on the claimant count since 1971, expressed as a percentage of the workforce. The surge in unemployment in the early 1980s stands out on the graph, when the percentage of the workforce registered as unemployed more than doubled in a relatively short period. Although this seemed to be coming under control towards the end of the 1980s, unemployment rose again in the early 1990s before a steady decline into the new millennium.

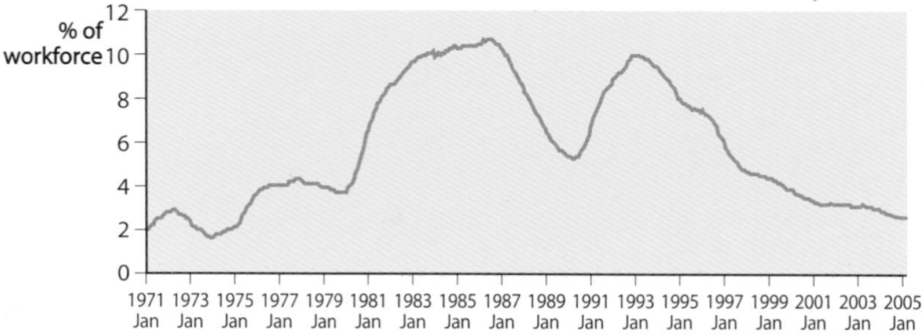

Figure 11.4 *Claimant count (%)*

Source: ONS.

One of the problems with the claimant count is that it includes some people who are claiming benefit but are not actually available or prepared for work. It also excludes some people who would like to work, and are looking for work, but are not eligible for unemployment benefit, such as women returning to the labour force after child birth.

Because of these problems, the claimant count has been superseded for official purposes by the so-called **ILO unemployment rate**, a measure based on the *Labour Force Survey*. This identifies the number of people available for work, and seeking work, but without a job. This definition corresponds to that used by the International Labour Organisation (ILO), and is closer to what economists would like unemployment to measure. It defines as being unemployed those people who are:

> **Key term**
>
> **ILO unemployment rate:** measure of the percentage of the workforce who are without jobs but are available for work, willing to work and looking for work

- without a job, want a job, have actively sought work in the last four weeks and are available to start work in the next two weeks; or
- out of work, have found a job and are waiting to start it in the next two weeks

(*Labour Market Statistics*, September 2004)

Figure 11.5 shows both the claimant and ILO measures for the period since 1984. You can see that the difference between the two measures is narrower when unemployment is relatively high, and wider when unemployment is falling. This may be partly because low unemployment encourages more people who are not eligible for unemployment benefit to look for jobs, whereas they withdraw from the workforce when unemployment rises and they perceive that finding a job will be difficult. This is said to affect women in particular, who may not be eligible for the Jobseeker's Allowance because of their partners' earnings.

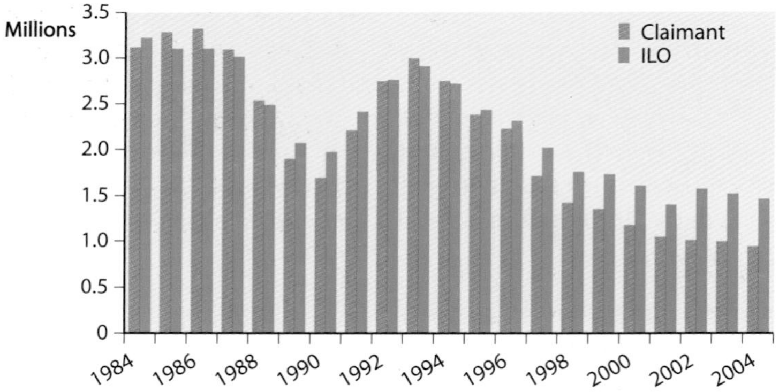

Figure 11.5 Alternative measures of unemployment in the UK

Note: millions unemployed in March–May each year (average).

Source: ONS.

Summary

- The retail price index (RPI) is the best known measure of the average price level in the UK.
- In December 2003 the government adopted the consumer price index (CPI) as its preferred measure of the price level, and inflation is now monitored through the rate of change of CPI.
- Unemployment is measured in two ways. The claimant count is based on the number of people claiming Jobseeker's Allowance. However, the ILO measure, based on the *Labour Force Survey*, is more accurate.

The circular flow of income, expenditure and output

Chapter 1 introduced the notion of **gross domestic product (GDP)**, which was described as the total output of an economy. It is now time to examine this concept more closely, and to see how it may be measured.

Consider a simplified model of an economy. Assume for the moment that there are just two types of economic agent in an economy: households and firms. In other words, ignore the government and assume there is no international trade. (These agents will be brought back into the picture soon.)

Key term

gross domestic product (GDP): a measure of the total amount of goods and services produced in an economy over a period by residents living on its territory

In this simple world, assume that firms produce goods and hire labour and other factor inputs from households. Also assume that they buy investment goods from other firms, for which purpose they need to borrow in a financial market. Households supply their labour (and other factor inputs) and buy consumer goods. In return for supplying factor inputs, households receive income, part of which they spend on consumer goods and part of which they save in the financial market.

If you examine the monetary flows in this economy, you can see how the economy operates. In Figure 11.6 the blue arrow shows the flow of income that goes from firms to households as payment for their factor services (labour, land and capital). The red arrows show what happens to the output produced by firms: part of it goes to households in the form of consumer goods (*C*); the rest flows back to other firms as investment goods (*I*). The green arrows show the expenditure flows back to firms, part of which is for consumer goods (*C*) from households, and part for investment goods (*I*) from firms. The circle is closed by households' savings, by which part of their income is invested in the financial market; this is then borrowed by firms to finance their purchases of investment goods. These flows are shown by the orange arrows.

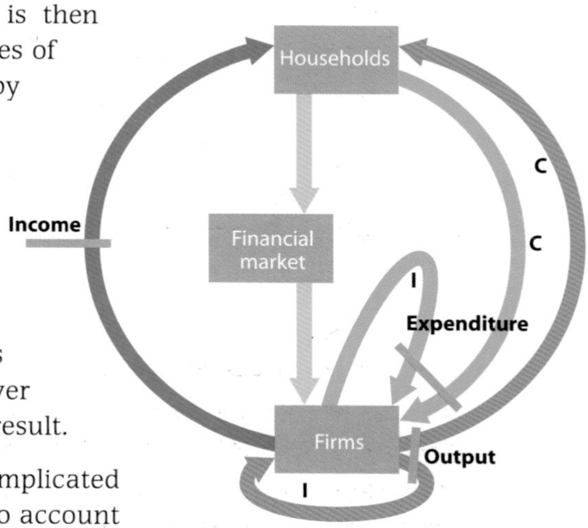

Figure 11.6 The circular flow of income, expenditure and output

As this is a closed system, these flows must balance. This means that there are three ways in which the total amount of economic activity in this economy can be measured: by the incomes that firms pay out, by the total amount of output that is produced, or by total expenditure. Whichever method is chosen, it should give the same result.

An economy such as the UK's is more complicated than this, so it is also necessary to take into account the economic activities of government, and the fact that the UK engages in international trade, so that some of the output produced is sold abroad and some of the expenditure goes on foreign goods and services. However, the principle of measuring total economic activity is the same: GDP can be measured in three ways. In practice, when the ONS carries out the measurements the three answers are never quite the same, as it is impossible to measure with complete accuracy. The published data for GDP are therefore calculated as the average of these three measures, each of which gives information about different aspects of a society's total resources.

The expenditure-side estimate describes how those resources are being used, so that it can be seen what proportion of society's resources is being used for consumption and what for investment etc.

The income-side estimate reports on the way in which households earn their income. In other words, it tells something about the balance between rewards to labour (e.g. wages and salaries), capital (profits), land (rents), enterprise (self-employment) and so on.

The output-side estimate focuses on the economic structure of the economy. One way in which countries differ is in the balance between primary production such as agriculture, secondary activity such as manufacturing, and tertiary activity such as services. Service activity has increased in importance in the UK in recent years, with financial services in particular emerging as a strong part of the UK's comparative advantage.

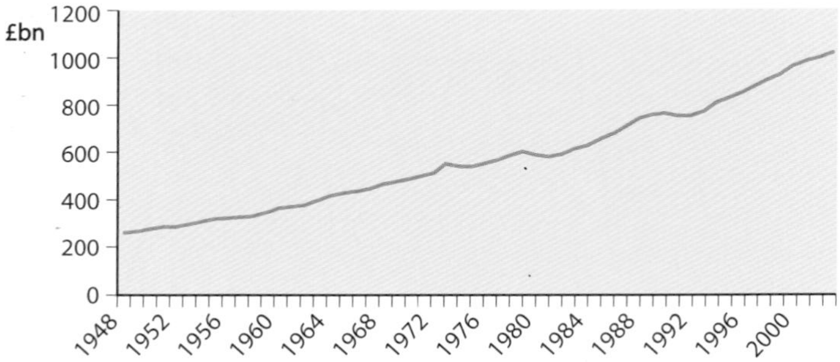

***Figure 11.7** Real GDP, 1948–2003 (£ billion)*

Source: *Economic Trends Annual Supplement.*

Note: reference year is 2000.

Figure 11.7 traces real GDP in the UK since 1948. In some ways this is an unhelpful way of presenting the data, as the trend component of the series is so strong. In other words, real GDP has been increasing steadily throughout the period. There are one or two periods in which there was a movement away from the trend, but these are relatively rare, and not easy to analyse. This reflects the nature of economic variables such as GDP, where the fluctuations around trend are small relative to the trend, but can seem substantial when the economy is experiencing them.

> **Key term**
>
> **GDP deflator:** an implicit price index showing the relationship between real and nominal measures of GDP, providing an alternative measure of the general level of prices in the economy

The ratio of nominal to real GDP is a price index, known as the **GDP deflator**. This is defined as:

$$\text{price index} = 100 \times \frac{\text{GDP at current prices}}{\text{GDP at constant prices}}$$

This provides another measure of the average level of prices in the economy.

It is also sometimes useful to be able to convert nominal measurements into real terms. This can be done by dividing the nominal measurement by the price index, a process known as *deflating* the nominal measure.

Figure 11.8 converts the data into annual growth rates, which in some ways are more revealing. This certainly makes it more straightforward to identify the main periods of fluctuation, in particular periods of negative growth, i.e. when the economy contracted. Also apparent in this figure is the relative stability of the economy since 1995.

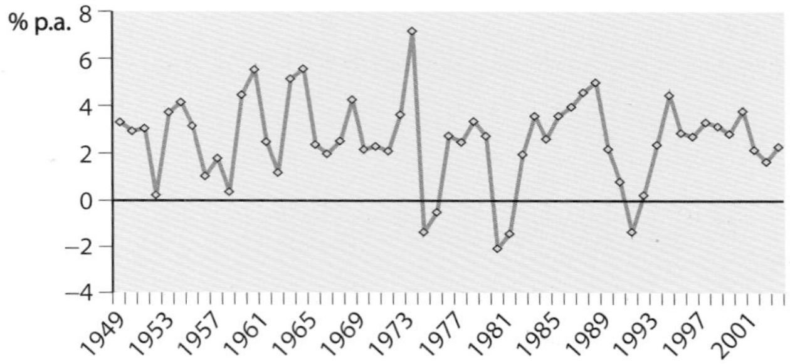

Figure 11.8
Growth of real GDP, 1949–2003 (% change over previous year)

Source: *Economic Trends Annual Supplement.*

It should be noted that the measure of GDP has not been without its critics. In particular, economists have questioned whether this provides a reasonable measure of the standard of living enjoyed by the residents of a country, and whether its rate of change is therefore informative about economic growth. Chapter 14 will revisit GDP, and evaluate its strengths and weaknesses in this context.

The business cycle

In the past it has not been uncommon for economies to go through a regular **business cycle**, where the level of economic activity has varied around an underlying trend. Figure 11.9 shows an economy in which real GDP is trending upwards over time but fluctuating around the trend, so that actual GDP follows a regular cycle around the trend. The point of maximum growth is often referred to as the *peak* of the cycle – or a *boom* period, whereas the low point is known as the *trough* of the cycle. If the growth rate is negative for two consecutive quarters, the economy is considered to be officially in *recession.*

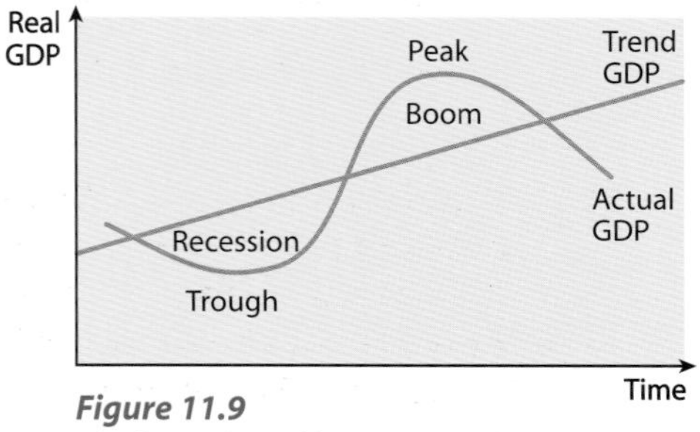

Figure 11.9
The business cycle

Key term

business cycle: a phenomenon whereby GDP fluctuates around its underlying trend, following a regular pattern

Figure 11.10 illustrates this in a different way, by showing the growth rates of real GDP in the

UK over a cycle from 1984 to 1994. There was some evidence in Figure 11.8 that the fluctuations have been less marked in the later years shown.

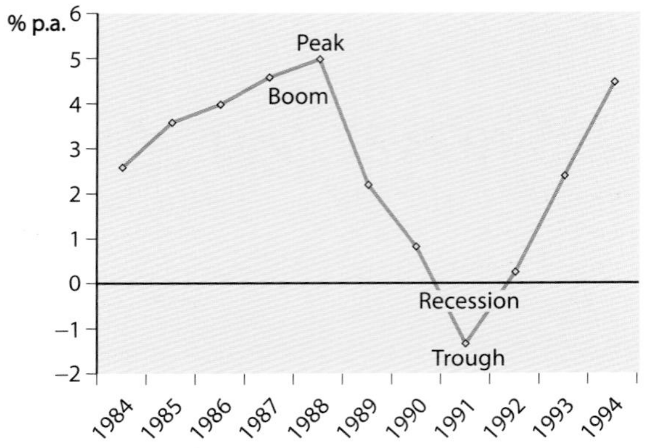

Figure 11.10 Profile of a cycle: growth of real GDP, 1984–94 (% change over previous year)

Source: *Economic Trends Annual Supplement.*

A number of explanations have been advanced to explain the business cycle. One suggestion is that some governments engineer the cycle, taking the economy into a boom in the lead-up to an election only to slow it down again once elected. This has become known as the *political business cycle.* Another suggestion is that cycles arise because of the lagged impact of policy measures on the economy; in other words, it takes time for policies to take effect — sometimes so long that they can destabilise the economy by having unintended effects.

In the past, much effort has gone into trying to predict the turning points of the business cycle by looking for *leading indicators* that turn in advance of the cycle — for example the CBI quarterly survey of business optimism, which is designed to gather firms' views about the cycle. Changes in the number of new dwellings started and changes in consumer borrowing are also seen as leading indicators. In contrast, *coincident indicators* move in step with the current state of the business cycle — for example real GDP or the volume of retail sales. On the other hand, unemployment tends to be a *lagging indicator*, as firms may not reduce their labour force right at the start of a recession, preferring first to ensure that it is not a temporary blip. In Chapter 15 it will be seen that there are some responses within the economy that tend to dampen the business cycle automatically; these are known as *automatic stabilisers.*

Summary

- The circular flow of income, expenditure and output describes the relationship between these three key variables.
- The model suggests that there are three ways in which the total level of economic activity in an economy during a period of time can be measured: by total income, by total expenditure, and by total output produced.
- In principle, these should give the same answers, but in practice data measurements are not so accurate.

- GDP is a measure of the total economic activity carried out in an economy during a period by residents living on its territory.
- Economies tend not to grow according to a constant trend, but to fluctuate around the underlying trend, creating the business cycle.

Exercise 11.1

Table 11.1 provides data on real GDP for the period from 1998–2004. Convert the series to an index based on 1998 = 100. Calculate the growth rate of GDP for each year from 1999/2000 to 2003/4. In which year was growth at its highest and in which year was it the slowest?

Table 11.1 Real GDP in the UK (£ billion)

1998	892
1999	917
2000	951
2001	972
2002	987
2003	1009
2004 (est.)	1044

The balance of payments

Another important dimension over which the macro-economy needs to be monitored is in relation to a country's transactions with the rest of the world. Such transactions involve exports and imports of goods and services, but also assets, not to mention the flow of factor incomes. All of these transactions are monitored through the balance of payments, which is a set of accounts designed to identify international transactions between the UK economy and the rest of the world.

Key term

balance of payments: a set of accounts showing the transactions conducted between residents of a country and the rest of the world

The transactions in the balance of payments are separated into three categories. Transactions in goods and services, together with income payments and transfers, comprise the *current account*. The *capital account* reflects transactions in fixed assets, and is relatively small; it refers mainly to transactions involving migrants. The *financial account* (which confusingly used to be called the 'capital account') records transactions in financial assets.

Commentators often focus on the current account. Three main items appear on this account. First, there is the balance of trade in goods and services — in other words, the balance between UK exports and imports of such goods and services. If UK residents buy German cars, this is an import and counts as a negative entry on the current account; on the other hand, if a German resident buys a British car, this is an export and constitutes a positive entry. The trade in goods is normally negative overall. However, this is partly balanced by a normally positive flow in trade in services, where the UK earns strong credits from its financial services.

The second item in the current account is income. Part of this represents employment income from abroad, but the major item of income is made up of profits, dividends and interest receipts arising from UK ownership of overseas assets.

Finally, there are international transfers – either transfers through central government or transfers made or received by private individuals. This includes transactions and grants with international organisations or with the EU. The current balance combines these items together into an overall balance.

Overall, the balance of payments must always be zero, as in some way or other we have to pay for all we consume, and receive payment for all we sell. However, because data can never be entirely accurate, the accounts also incorporate a 'net errors and omissions' item, which ensures that everything balances at the end of the day.

What this really means is that any deficit in the current and capital accounts will always be balanced by a surplus on the financial account. Notice that the financial account incorporates official foreign exchange transactions undertaken by the government. In other words, if British residents buy more goods and services than they sell (i.e. if there is a current account deficit), then they must pay for them by selling financial assets or foreign exchange (i.e., there must be a financial account surplus).

There are a number of ways in which the overall balance can be achieved. 'Balance' could mean that both current and financial accounts are small, or it could mean that a deficit on one is balanced by a surplus on the other. The media tend to focus on the current balance, and a deficit on current account is sometimes seen as a matter of concern. Perhaps this harks back to the fixed exchange rate days, when a current deficit would require authorities to sell foreign exchange reserves in order to balance the accounts. This is no longer the case, as there are other ways of balancing the books. Nonetheless, a persistent deficit on the current account may pose long-term problems that need to be addressed, as it may not be desirable to continue selling UK assets indefinitely.

Trade in goods and services	–32 402
Income	23 385
Current transfers	–9 743
Current balance	–18 760
Capital account	**1 204**
Financial account	**15 825**
Net errors and omissions	1 731
Overall balance of payments	**0**

Table 11.2 *The UK balance of payments 2003 (£ million at current prices)*

Table 11.2 presents the components of the balance of payments accounts for 2003. This was a year in which the current account was in deficit, in particular because of a negative balance on trade in goods and services. The financial account was in surplus.

Suppose the Bank of England holds interest rates high compared with other countries, in order to try to control inflation. High UK interest rates will tend to attract financial inflows from abroad, as investors find the UK attractive as a home for their funds. This implies a surplus on the financial account – and hence a deficit on current account. The downside of such a structure is that UK assets are being sold abroad, which might not be in the best interest of the economy in the long run.

It is this potential long-run difficulty that makes it important to monitor the current balance over time. Figure 11.11 shows the main components of the balance of payments since 1980, in current price terms, which is the form in which the data are published by ONS. This is in the form of a stacked bar chart, and the nature of the balance of payments is that the positive and negative components exactly balance each year. The clear picture that emerges is that the current account has been negative (in deficit) for most of the period since 1980, and that this has been balanced by a positive balance (surplus) on the financial account. In other words, the UK has been importing more goods and services than it has been exporting; but this has been counterbalanced by the surplus on the financial account, i.e. of UK assets sold abroad.

The data in Figure 11.11 are measured in current prices, which means that they are *nominal* measurements, which make no attempt to allow for the effects of inflation. It would thus be misleading to infer too much about the magnitude of the quantities shown. A better perspective on this is provided by Figure 11.12, which shows the current account balance expressed as a percentage of nominal GDP. This helps to put the more recent data into perspective.

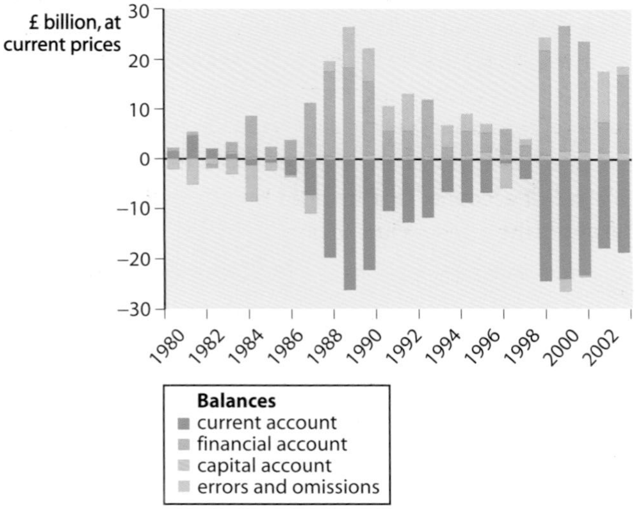

Figure 11.11 *UK balance of payments, 1980–2003*

Source: ONS.

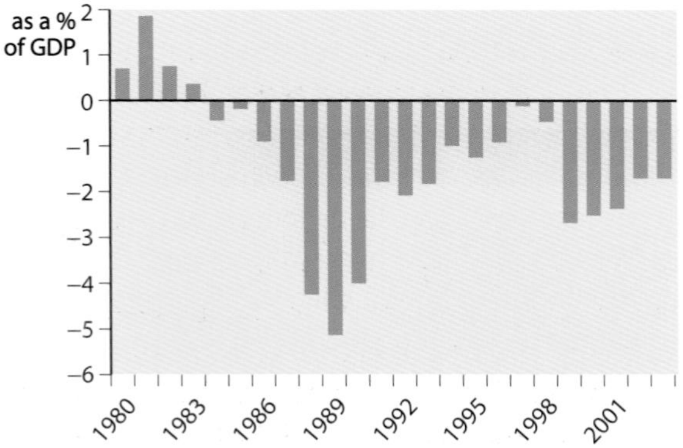

Figure 11.12 *The current account of the UK balance of payments*

Source: ONS.

Closely associated with the balance of payments is the **exchange rate** – the price of domestic goods in terms of foreign currency. Chapter 4 introduced the notion of the demand and supply of foreign currency, shown in Figure 11.13. The demand for pounds arises from overseas residents (e.g. in the euro area) wanting to purchase UK goods, services or assets, whereas the supply of pounds emanates from domestic residents wanting to purchase overseas goods, services or assets. The connection is that the balance of payments accounts itemise these transactions, which entail the demand for and supply of pounds.

Key term

exchange rate: the price of one currency in the terms of another

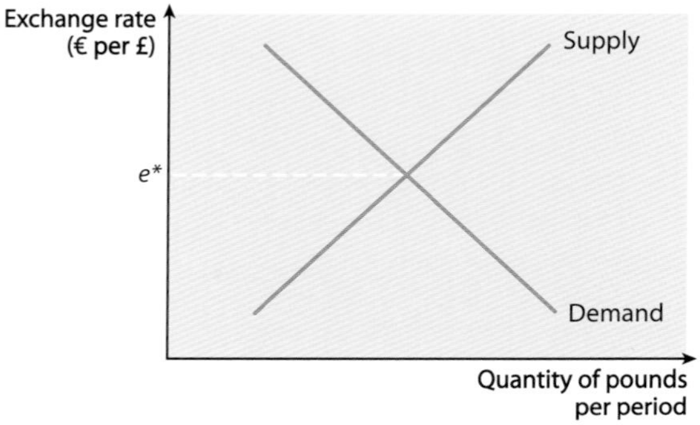

Figure 11.13
The market for pounds sterling

Summary

- The balance of payments is a set of accounts that itemises transactions that take place between an economy and the rest of the world, including goods, services, income and assets.
- The current account sets out transactions in goods, services, investment income and transfers.
- The capital account itemises transactions in fixed assets, and is relatively small.
- The financial account covers transactions in financial assets, and includes direct investment and official intervention in the foreign exchange market ('official financing').
- The overall balance of payments is always zero.
- However, this overall balance has often been achieved in the UK through a persistent deficit on the current account, balanced by a corresponding surplus on the financial account.
- This may be a matter for concern in the long run.

Exercise 11.2

Use the data presented in this chapter to evaluate the performance of the UK economy since 1997. If you were the chancellor of the exchequer, which aspects of the economy's performance would you be pleased with, and which ones would concern you?

part 3

Chapter 12

Aggregate demand, aggregate supply and equilibrium output

Now that you are familiar with the main macroeconomic aggregates, it is time to start thinking about how economic analysis can be used to explore the way in which these variables interact. This chapter also investigates the notion of macroeconomic equilibrium. As in microeconomics, this relates to the process by which balance can be achieved between the opposing forces of demand and supply. However, there are some important differences in these concepts when applied at the macroeconomic level.

Learning outcomes

After studying this chapter, you should:

- understand what is meant by aggregate demand and aggregate supply
- be able to identify the components of aggregate demand, and their determinants
- be aware of the possibility of multiplier effects
- be familiar with the notion of the aggregate demand curve
- identify the factors that influence aggregate supply
- be familiar with the notion of the aggregate supply curve
- understand the nature of equilibrium in the macroeconomy
- be able to undertake comparative static analysis of external shocks affecting aggregate demand and aggregate supply

The components of aggregate demand

Chapter 11 introduced the notion of the circular flow of income, expenditure and output. If aggregate demand were considered in that model, it would comprise the combined spending of households (on consumer goods) and firms (on investment goods). It was noted that in the real world it is also necessary to include international trade (exports and imports) and spending by government in this measure. The full version of aggregate expenditure can be written as:

$$AD = C + I + G + X - M$$

where *AD* denotes aggregate demand, *C* is consumption, *I* is investment, *G* is government spending, *X* is exports and *M* is imports.

Figure 12.1 shows the expenditure-side breakdown of real GDP in the UK in 2003. This highlights the relative size of the components of aggregate demand. Consumption is by far the largest component, amounting to more than 60% of real GDP in 2003. Government current expenditure accounted for more than a quarter (26.1%), but notice that this somewhat understates the importance of government in overall spending, as it excludes public spending on investment, which is treated together with private sector investment in the data. Combined public and private sector investment made up about 16% of total GDP; this includes changes in the inventory holdings of firms. Notice that imports were rather higher than exports, indicating a negative balance of trade in goods and services.

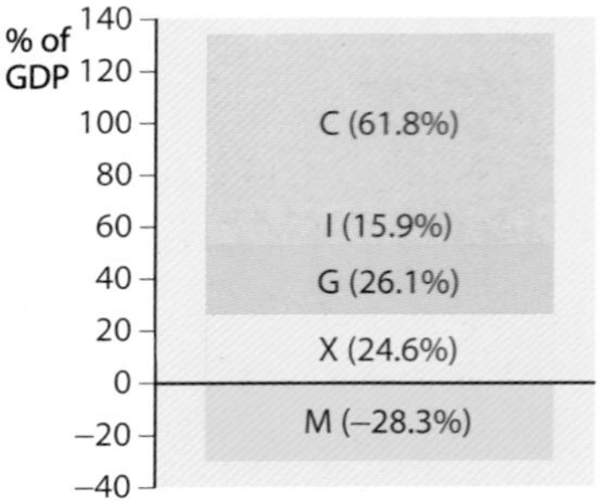

***Figure 12.1** The breakdown of real GDP in 2003*

Note: C includes spending by non-profit institutions serving households; I includes changes in inventory holdings; the statistical discrepancy is not shown.

Source: ONS.

In the circular flow model it was noted that total expenditure should be the same as total income and total output if all were measured fully. This seems to suggest that the macroeconomy is always in a sort of equilibrium, in the sense that expenditure and output are always the same. However, this is misleading. Although when you observe the economy you should find that expenditure and output are the same *after* the event, this does not mean that equilibrium holds in the sense that all economic agents will have found that their plans were fulfilled. In other words, it is not necessarily the case that planned expenditure equals planned output.

This is the significance of the inclusion of inventory changes as part of investment. If firms find that they have produced more output than is subsequently purchased, their inventory holdings increase. Thus, although after the event expenditure always equals output, this is because any disequilibrium is reflected in unplanned inventory changes.

When you come to consider the conditions under which a macroeconomy will be in equilibrium, you will need to think in terms of the factors that will influence *ex ante* (planned) aggregate demand. The first step is to consider each component in turn.

Consumption

Consumption is the largest single component of aggregate demand. What factors could be expected to influence the size of total spending by households? John

Maynard Keynes, in his influential book *The General Theory of Employment, Interest and Money*, published in 1936, suggested that the most important determinant is **disposable income**. In other words, as real incomes rise households will tend to spend more. However, he also pointed out that they would not spend all of an increase in income, but would save some of it. Remember that this was important in the circular flow model.

J. M. Keynes's hugely influential book The General Theory of Employment, Interest and Money *was published in 1936.*

Keynes defined the *average propensity to consume* as the *ratio* of consumption to income, and the *marginal propensity to consume* as the proportion of an *increase* in disposable income that households would devote to consumption. He argued that the average propensity to consume falls as income rises, and that the marginal propensity to consume is lower than the average propensity to consume.

Key term

disposable income: the income that households have to devote to consumption and saving, taking into account payments of direct taxes and transfer payments such as social security benefits

Extension material

Later writers argued that consumption does not necessarily depend upon current income alone. For example, Milton Friedman put forward the *permanent income hypothesis*, which suggested that consumers take decisions about consumption based on a notion of their permanent, or normal, income levels — that is, the income that they expect to receive over a 5- or 10-year time horizon. This suggests that households do not necessarily vary their consumption patterns in response to changes in income that they perceive to be only transitory. An associated theory is the *life-cycle hypothesis*, developed by Ando Modigliani, who suggested that households smooth their consumption over their lifetimes, on the basis of their expected lifetime incomes. Thus, people tend to borrow in their youth against future income; then in middle age, when earning more strongly, they pay off their debts and save in preparation to fund their consumption in retirement. Consumption thus varies by much less than income, and is based on expected lifetime earnings rather than on current income.

However, income will not be the only influence on consumption. Consumption may also depend partly on the *wealth* of a household. Notice that income and wealth are not the same. Income accrues during a period as a reward for the supply of factor services such as labour. Wealth, on the other hand, can be thought of as representing the stock of accumulated past savings. If you like, wealth can be thought of in terms of the asset holdings of households. If households experience an increase in their asset holdings, this may influence their spending decisions.

Furthermore, if part of household spending is financed by borrowing, the rate of interest may be significant in influencing the total amount of consumption spending. An increase in the rate of interest that raises the cost of borrowing may deter consumption. The rate of interest may also have an indirect effect on consumption through its effect on the value of asset holdings. In addition, households may be influenced in their consumption decisions by their expectations about future inflation. Notice that some of these effects may not be instantaneous; that is, consumption may adjust to changes in its determinants only after a time lag.

This **consumption function** can be portrayed as a relationship between consumption and income. This is shown in Figure 12.2, which focuses on the relationship between consumption and household income, *ceteris paribus*; in other words, in drawing the relationship between consumption and income, it is assumed that the other determinants of consumption, such as wealth and the interest rate, remain constant. A change in any of these other influences will affect the *position* of the line. Notice that the marginal propensity to consume is the slope of this line.

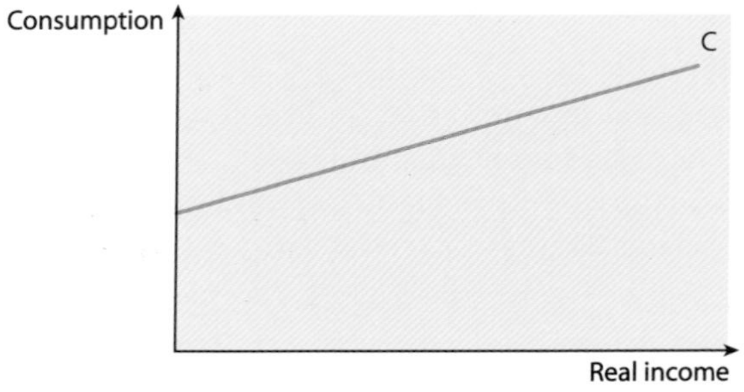

Figure 12.2 The consumption function

Key term

consumption function: function showing the relationship between consumption and disposable income, which also depends upon the other factors that affect how much households spend on consumption

In practice, it is not expected that the empirical relationship between consumption and income will reveal an exact straight line, if only because over a long time period there will be changes in the other influences on consumption, such as interest rates and expected inflation. However, Figure 12.3 shows that the hypothesis is not totally implausible.

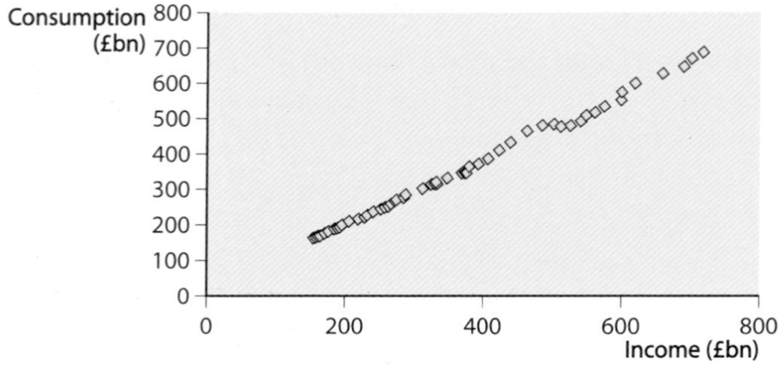

Figure 12.3 Real consumption and income in the UK, 1948–2003

Source: ETAS, ET.

Investment

The rate of interest is also likely to be influential in affecting firms' decisions about investment spending. Again, this is because the interest rate represents the cost of borrowing; so, if firms need to borrow in order to undertake **investment**, they may be discouraged from spending on investment goods when the rate of interest is relatively high.

Key term

investment: expenditure undertaken by firms to add to the capital stock

Investment leads to an increase in the productive capacity of the economy, by increasing the stock of capital available for production. This capital stock comprises plant and machinery, vehicles and other transport equipment and buildings, including new dwellings, which provide a supply of housing services over a long period.

Although important, the rate of interest is not likely to be the only factor that determines how much investment firms choose to undertake. First, not all investment has to be funded from borrowing — firms may be able to use past profits for this purpose. However, if firms choose to do this they face an opportunity cost. In other words, profits can be used to buy financial assets that will provide a rate of return dependent on the rate of interest. The rate of interest is thus still important, as it represents the opportunity cost of an investment project.

In considering an investment project, firms will need to form expectations about the future stream of earnings that will flow from the investment. Their expectations about the future state of the economy (and of the demand for their products) will thus be an important influence on current investment. This is one reason why it is argued that inflation is damaging for an economy, as a high rate of inflation increases uncertainty about the future and may dampen firms' expectations about future demand, thereby discouraging investment.

Government expenditure

By and large, you might expect government expenditure to be decided by different criteria from those influencing private sector expenditures. Indeed, some aspects of government expenditure might be regarded as part of macroeconomic policy, as will be seen in Chapter 15. Some other aspects of government expenditure may vary automatically with variations in the overall level of economic activity over time. For example, unemployment benefit payments are likely to increase during recessionary periods. The effects of this will be examined in Chapter 15.

From the point of view of investigating macroeconomic equilibrium, however, government expenditure can be regarded as mainly *autonomous*, i.e. independent of the variables in the model that will be constructed in this chapter.

Trade in goods and services

Finally, there are the factors that may influence the level of exports and imports. One factor that will affect both of these is the exchange rate between sterling and other currencies. This affects the relative prices of UK goods and those produced overseas. Other things being equal, an increase in the sterling exchange rate makes UK exports less competitive and imports into the UK more competitive.

However, the demand for exports and imports will also depend upon the relative prices of goods produced in the UK and the rest of the world. If UK inflation is high relative to elsewhere, again, this will tend to make UK exports less competitive and imports more competitive. These effects will be examined more carefully in Chapters 15 and 32, when it will be shown that movements in the exchange rate tend to counteract changes in relative prices between countries.

In addition, the demand for imports into the UK will depend partly upon the level of domestic aggregate income, and the demand for UK exports will depend partly upon the level of incomes in the rest of the world. Thus, a recession in the European Union will affect the demand for UK exports.

The multiplier

In his *General Theory*, Keynes pointed out that there may be multiplier effects in response to certain types of expenditure. Suppose that the government increases its expenditure by £1 billion, perhaps by increasing its road-building programme. The effect of this is to generate incomes for households – for example those of the contractors hired to build the road. Those contractors then spend part of the additional income (and save part of it). By spending part of the extra money earned, an additional income stream is generated for shopkeepers and café owners, who in turn spend part of *their* additional income, and so on. Thus, the original increase in government spending sparks off further income generation and spending, causing the multiplier effect. In effect, equilibrium output may change by more than the original increase in expenditure.

Key term

multiplier: the ratio of a change in equilibrium real income to the autonomous change that brought it about

The size of this multiplier effect depends on a number of factors. Most importantly, it depends upon the size of *withdrawals* or *leakages* from the system. In particular, it depends upon how much of the additional income is saved by households, how much is spent on imported goods, and how much is returned to the government in the form of direct taxes. These items constitute withdrawals from the system, in the sense that they detract from the multiplier effect. However, there are also *injections* into the system in the form of autonomous government expenditure, investment and exports. One condition of macroeconomic equilibrium is that total withdrawals equal total injections.

Extension material

A numerical value for the multiplier can be calculated with reference to the withdrawals from the circular flow. First, define the *marginal propensity to withdraw (MPW)* as the sum of the marginal propensities to save, tax and import. The multiplier formula is then 1 divided by the marginal propensity to withdraw (1/*MPW*). If the value of the multiplier is 2, then for every £100 million injection into the circular flow, there will be a £200 million increase in equilibrium output.

It is worth noting that the size of the leakages may depend in part upon the domestic elasticity of supply. If domestic supply is inflexible, and therefore unable to meet an increase in demand, more of the increase in income will spill over into purchasing imports, and this will dilute the multiplier effect.

Summary

- Aggregate demand is the total demand in an economy, made up of consumption, investment, government spending and net exports.
- Consumption is the largest of these components, and is determined by income and other influences such as interest rates, wealth and expectations about the future.
- Investment leads to increases in the capital stock, and is influenced by interest rates, past profits and expectations about future demand.
- Government expenditure may be regarded as largely autonomous.
- Trade in goods and services (exports and imports) is determined by the competitiveness of domestic goods and services compared with the rest of the world, which in turn is determined by relative inflation rates and the exchange rate. Imports are also affected by domestic income, and exports are affected by incomes in the rest of the world.
- Autonomous spending, such as government expenditure, may give rise to a magnified impact on equilibrium output through the multiplier effect.

Exercise 12.1

Identify each of the following as an injection or a leakage, and state whether it increases or decreases the impact of the multiplier:

a savings by households

b expenditure by central government

c spending by UK residents on imported goods and services

d expenditure by firms on investment

e spending by overseas residents on UK goods and services

f income tax payments

The aggregate demand curve

The key relationship to carry forward is the **aggregate demand curve**, which shows the relationship between aggregate demand and the overall price level. Formally, this curve shows the total amount of goods and services demanded in an economy at any given overall level of prices.

It is important to realise that this is a very different sort of demand curve from the microeconomic demand curves that were introduced in Chapter 3, where the focus was on an individual product and its relationship

Key term

aggregate demand curve (AD): a curve showing the relationship between the level of aggregate demand and the overall price level; it shows planned expenditure, at any given possible overall price level

with its own price. Here the relationship is between the *total* demand for goods and services relative to the overall price level. Thus, aggregate demand is made up of all the components discussed above, and price is an average of all prices of goods and services in the economy.

Figure 12.4 shows an aggregate demand curve. The key question is why it slopes downwards. To answer this, it is necessary to determine the likely influence of the price level on the various components of aggregate demand that have been discussed in this chapter, as prices have not been mentioned explicitly (except for how expectations about inflation might influence consumer spending). First, however, the discussion needs to be cast in terms of the price *level*.

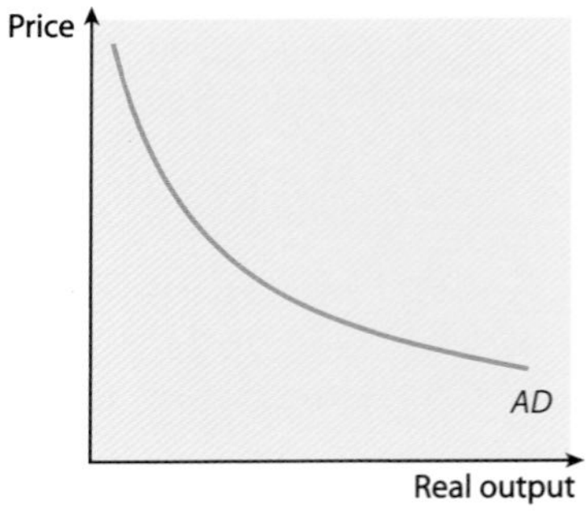

Figure 12.4 *An aggregate demand curve*

When the overall level of prices is relatively low, the purchasing power of income is relatively high. In other words, low overall prices can be thought of as indicating relatively high real income. Low prices also impact on the value of household assets; that is, a low price implies a high value of wealth. From the above discussion, this suggests that, *ceteris paribus*, a low overall price level means relatively high consumption.

A second argument relates to interest rates. When prices are relatively low, interest rates also tend to be relatively low, which, it was argued, would encourage both investment and consumption expenditure, as interest rates can be seen as representing the cost of borrowing.

A third argument concerns exports and imports. It has been argued that, *ceteris paribus,* when UK prices are relatively low compared with the rest of the world, this will increase the competitiveness of UK goods, leading to an increase in foreign demand for UK exports, and a fall in the demand for imports into the UK as people switch to buying British goods and services.

All of these arguments support the idea that the aggregate demand curve should be downward sloping. In other words, when the overall price level is relatively low aggregate demand will be relatively high, and when prices are relatively high aggregate demand will be relatively low.

Other factors discussed above will affect the *position* of the *AD* curve. This point will be explored after the introduction of the other side of the coin – the aggregate supply curve.

The aggregate supply curve

In order to analyse the overall macroeconomic equilibrium, it is necessary to derive a second relationship: that between aggregate supply and the price level. Again, remember that the level of aggregate supply covers the output of all sorts of goods and services that are produced within an economy during a period of time.

However, it is not simply a question of adding up all the individual supply curves from individual markets. Within an individual market, an increase in price may induce higher supply of a good because firms will switch from other markets in search of higher profits. What you now need to be looking for is a relationship between the *overall* price level and the total amount supplied, which is a different kettle of fish.

The total quantity of output supplied in an economy over a period of time depends upon the quantities of inputs of factors of production employed, i.e. the total amounts of labour, capital and other factors used. The ability of firms to vary output in the short run will be influenced by the degree of flexibility the firms have in varying inputs. This suggests that it is necessary to distinguish between short-run and long-run aggregate supply.

In the short run, firms may have relatively little flexibility to vary their inputs. Money wages are likely to be fixed, and if firms wish to vary output they may need to do so by varying the intensity of utilisation of existing inputs. For example, if a firm wishes to expand output, the only way of doing so in the short run may be by paying its existing workers overtime, and it will be prepared to do this only in response to higher prices. This suggests that in the short run aggregate supply may be upward sloping, as shown in Figure 12.5, where *SAS* represents **short-run aggregate supply**.

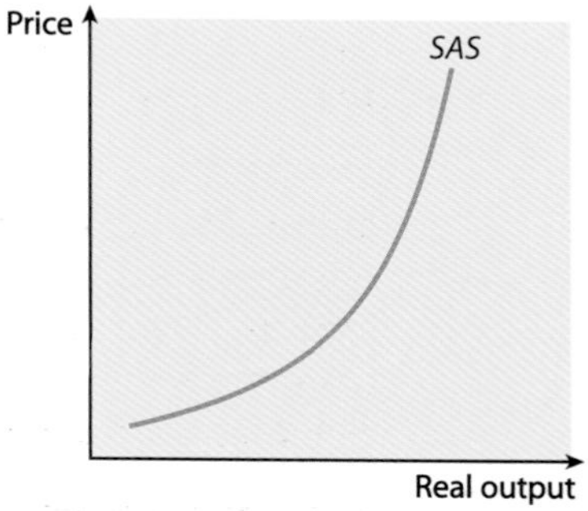

Figure 12.5 *Aggregate supply in the short run*

Firms will not want to operate in this way in the long run. It is not good practice to be permanently paying workers overtime. In the long run, therefore, firms will adjust their working practices and hire additional workers to avoid this situation.

Key term

short-run aggregate supply curve: a curve showing how much output firms are prepared to supply in the short run at any given overall price level

A crucial question is whether the macroeconomy will always be flexible enough to adjust to a long-run equilibrium with full employment. In other words, will the ultimate equilibrium be a situation in which factors of production are fully employed? And how long will it take to reach that position? This issue will be examined later in the book.

What factors influence the position of aggregate supply? Given that aggregate supply arises from the use of inputs of factors of production, one important influence is the availability and effectiveness of factor inputs.

As far as labour is concerned, an increase in the *size* of the workforce will affect the position of aggregate supply. In practice, the size of the labour force tends to change relatively slowly unless substantial international migration is taking place. However, another important factor is the *level of skills* in the workforce. An increase in the skills that workers have will increase the amount of aggregate output that can be produced and lead to a shift in the aggregate supply curve.

For example, in Figure 12.6 aggregate supply was originally at SAS_0. An increase in the skills of the workforce means that firms are prepared to supply more output at any given overall price level, so the aggregate supply curve moves to SAS_1.

An increase in the efficiency of capital, perhaps arising from improvements in technology, would have a similar effect, enabling greater aggregate supply at any given overall price level, and raising the productive capacity of the economy.

An increase in the quantity of capital will also have this effect, by increasing the capacity of the economy to produce. However, such an increase requires firms to have undertaken investment activity. In other words, the balance of spending between consumption and investment may affect the position of the aggregate supply curve in future periods.

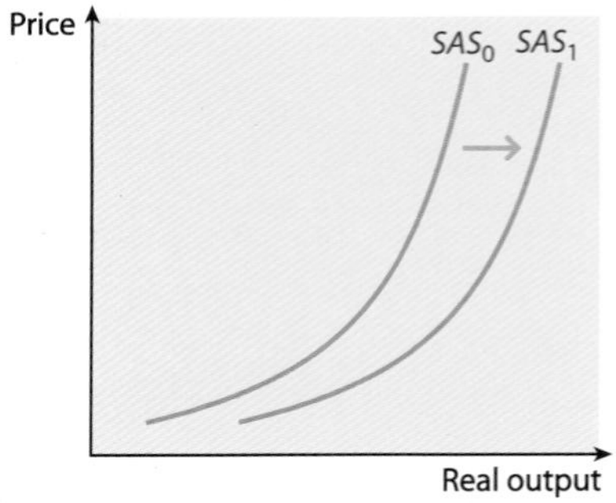

Figure 12.6
A shift in aggregate supply

Macroeconomic equilibrium

Bringing aggregate demand and aggregate supply together, the overall equilibrium position for the macroeconomy can be identified. In Figure 12.7, with aggregate supply given by *SAS* and aggregate demand by *AD*, equilibrium is reached at the real output level *Y*, with the price level at *P*.

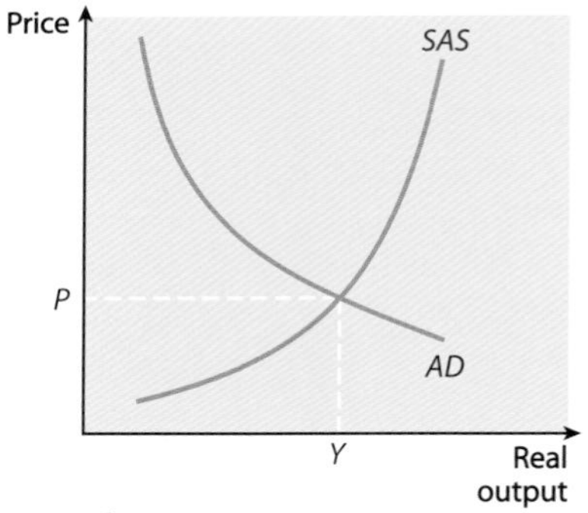

Figure 12.7
Macroeconomic equilibrium

This is an equilibrium, in the sense that if nothing changes then firms and households will have no reason to alter their behaviour in the next period. At the price *P*, aggregate supply is matched by aggregate demand.

Can it be guaranteed that the macroeconomic equilibrium will occur at the full employment level of output? For example, suppose that in Figure 12.8 the output level *Y** corresponds to the full employment level of output – that is, the level of output that represents productive capacity when all factors of production are fully employed. It may be possible to produce more than this in the short run, but only on a temporary basis, perhaps by the use of overtime. If aggregate demand is at *AD**, the macroeconomic equilibrium is at this full employment output *Y**. However, if the aggregate demand curve is located at AD_1 the equilibrium will occur at Y_1, which is below the full employment level, so there is surplus capacity in the economy.

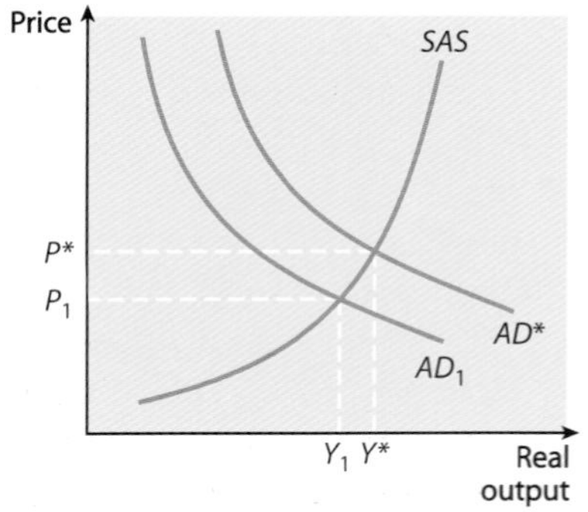

Figure 12.8 *Macroeconomic equilibrium at full employment*

Summary

- The aggregate demand curve (*AD*) shows the relationship between aggregate demand in the economy and the overall price level.
- *AD* is downward sloping because of the effect of the price level on real incomes and wealth, because of interest rate effects, and because of the effect of the price level on the competitiveness of domestic goods in international markets.
- The position of the *AD* curve depends upon the components of aggregate demand.
- The aggregate supply curve (*SAS*) shows the relationship between aggregate supply and the overall price level.
- Macroeconomic equilibrium is reached at the intersection of *AD* and *AS*.

An increase in aggregate demand

Having identified macroeconomic equilibrium, it is possible to undertake some comparative static analysis. The position of the aggregate demand curve depends on the components of aggregate demand: consumption, investment, government spending and net exports. Factors that affect these components will affect the position of aggregate demand.

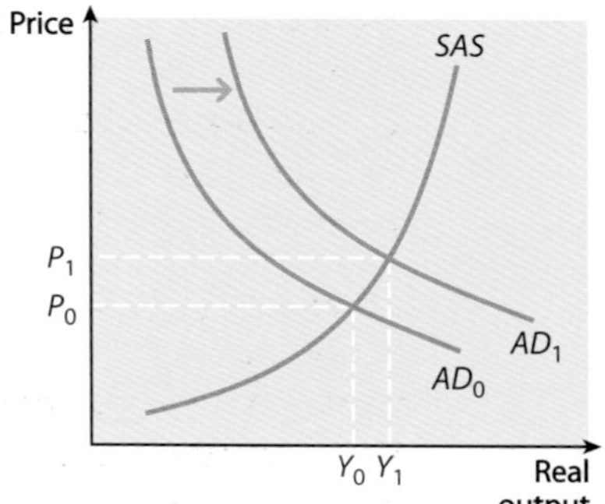

Figure 12.9
A shift in aggregate demand

Consider Figure 12.9. Suppose that the economy begins in equilibrium with aggregate demand at AD_0. The equilibrium output level is Y_0, and the price level is at P_0. An increase in government expenditure will affect the position of the aggregate demand curve, shifting it to AD_1. The economy will move to a new equilibrium position, with higher output level Y_1 and a higher price level P_1.

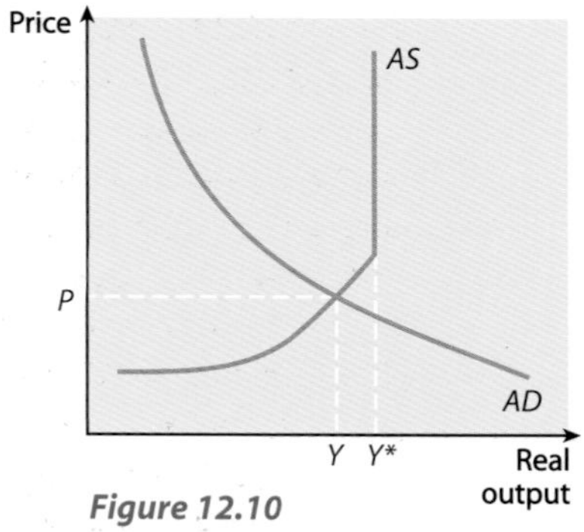

Figure 12.10
Macroeconomic equilibrium explained

This seems to suggest that the government can always reach full employment, simply by increasing its expenditure. However, you should be a little cautious in reaching such a conclusion, as the effect on equilibrium output and the price level will depend upon how close the economy is to the full employment level. Notice that the aggregate supply curve becomes steeper as output and price increase. In other words, the closer is the economy to the full employment level, the smaller is the elasticity of supply, so an increase in aggregate demand close to full employment will have more of an effect on the price level than on the level of real output. Indeed, it might be argued that the aggregate supply curve becomes vertical at some point, as there is a maximum level of output that can be produced given the availability of factors of production. Such a curve is shown in Figure 12.10, where Y^* represents the full employment level of real output. In this case, the economy has settled into an equilibrium that is below potential capacity output. We may regard this as a longer-run aggregate supply curve (*AS*), as the only way that real output can be beyond Y^* is through the temporary use of overtime, which could not be sustained in the long run.

The effect of a supply shock

The *AD/AS* model can also be used to analyse the effects of an external shock that affects aggregate supply. For example, suppose there is an increase in oil prices arising from a disruption to supplies in the Middle East. This raises firms' costs, and leads to a reduction in aggregate supply. Comparative static analysis can again be employed to examine the likely effects on equilibrium.

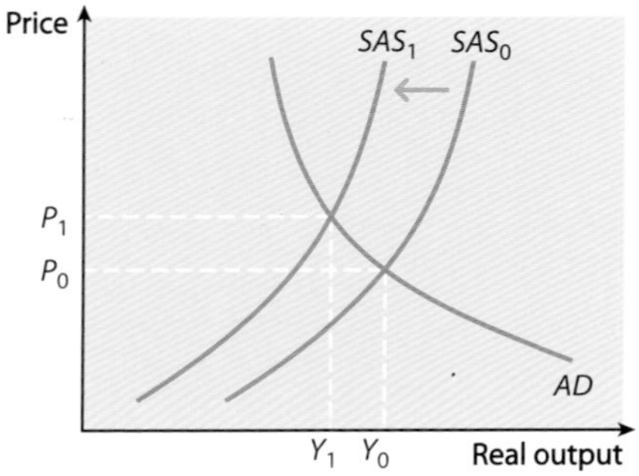

***Figure 12.11** A supply shock*

Figure 12.11 analyses the situation. The economy begins in equilibrium with output at Y_0 and the overall level of prices at P_0. The increase in oil prices causes a movement of the aggregate supply curve from SAS_0 to SAS_1, with aggregate demand unchanged at *AD*. After the economy returns to equilibrium, the new output level is now at Y_1 and the overall price level has increased to P_1.

At the time of the first oil price crisis back in 1973/4, the UK government of the day tried to maintain the previous level of real output by stimulating aggregate demand. This had the effect of pushing up the price level, but did not have any noticeable effect on real output. Such a result is not unexpected, given the steepness of the aggregate supply curve. Indeed, in Figure 12.11 the previous output level Y_0 cannot be reached with aggregate supply in its new position. You can see the effects of the oil shock on the UK economy by looking back at Figures 11.2 and 11.8.

Exercise 12.2

For each of the following, decide whether the change affects aggregate demand or aggregate supply, and sketch a diagram to illustrate the effects on equilibrium real output and overall price level. Undertake this exercise first for a starting position in the steep part of the *SAS* curve, and then repeat the exercise for an initial position further to the left, where *SAS* is more elastic:

a an advancement in technology that improves the efficiency of capital

b a financial crisis in Asia that reduces the demand for UK exports

c an improvement in firms' expectations about future demand, such that investment expenditure increases

d the introduction of new health and safety legislation that raises firms' costs

Movements of and along *AD* and *AS*

It is important to be aware of the distinction between movements *of* the *AD* and *AS* curves, and movements *along* them. Typically, if a shock affects one of the curves, it will lead to a movement *along* the other. For example, if the *AS* curve moves as a result of a supply shock, the response is a movement *along* the *AD* curve, and vice versa. Thus, in trying to analyse the effects of a shock, the first step is to think about whether the shock affects *AD* or *AS*, and the second is to analyse whether the shock is positive or negative — that is, which way the relevant curve will move. The move towards a new equilibrium can then be investigated.

Summary

- Comparative static analysis can be used to analyse the effects of changes in the factors that influence aggregate demand and aggregate supply.
- Changes in the components of aggregate demand shift the aggregate demand curve. Within the vertical segment of *AD*, changes in *AD* affect only the overall price level, but below full employment both price and real output will be affected.
- Changes in the factors affecting aggregate supply alter the long-run potential productive capacity of the economy.

part 3

Chapter 13

Macroeconomic policy objectives

Inevitably, there is a policy dimension to the study of the performance of the macroeconomy. Indeed, in evaluating such performance, it is the success of macroeconomic policy that is under scrutiny. However, the success of macroeconomic policy can be judged only if you are aware of what it is that the policy is trying to achieve. This chapter introduces and analyses the main objectives of policy at the macroeconomic level.

Learning outcomes

After studying this chapter, you should:

- be familiar with the principal objectives of macroeconomic policy
- understand the reasons for setting these policy objectives
- be aware of some potential obstacles that may inhibit the achievement of the targets
- appreciate that the targets may sometimes conflict with each other
- see UK policy objectives in a European context

Targets of policy

Chapter 11 introduced a number of ways in which economists try to monitor and evaluate the performance of the economy at the macroeconomic level. If the macroeconomic performance is found to be wanting in some way, then it is reasonable to ask whether some policy intervention might improve the situation. This chapter considers aspects of the macroeconomy that might be regarded as legitimate targets for policy action. Chapter 15 analyses the policy actions that might be introduced, and evaluates their possible effectiveness.

Chapter 11 discussed some key measures of an economy's performance, in particular inflation, unemployment, the balance of payments and GDP. In addition, in Chapter 9 questions were raised about whether governments should be concerned about inequality of income distribution within a society. These areas all raise policy questions that need to be addressed. In addition, there is a growing concern about the need to preserve the environment in which we live; Chapter 8 pointed out that an externality element in connection with the environment may be a cause of market failure, and commented that there may be international externalities that need to be considered. As this issue has a macroeconomic dimension to it, it will also need to be analysed in conjunction with the discussion of macroeconomic policy. Each of these objectives will now be considered in turn.

Price stability

One of the most prominent objectives of macroeconomic policy in recent years has been the need to control **inflation**. Indeed, this has been at the heart of governments' stated policy objectives since 1976.

Key terms

inflation: a rise in the overall price level

cost-push inflation: inflation initiated by an increase in the costs faced by firms, arising on the supply side of the economy

Causes of inflation

Inflation occurs when there is a rise in the general price level. However, it is important to distinguish between a one-off increase in the price level and a sustained rise over a long period of time. For example, a one-off rise in the price of oil may have an effect on the price level by shifting aggregate supply, thus affecting the equilibrium price level — as shown in Figure 13.1 (reproducing Figure 12.11 from the previous chapter). However, this takes the economy to a new equilibrium price level, and if nothing else were to change there would be no reason for prices to continue to rise beyond P_1.

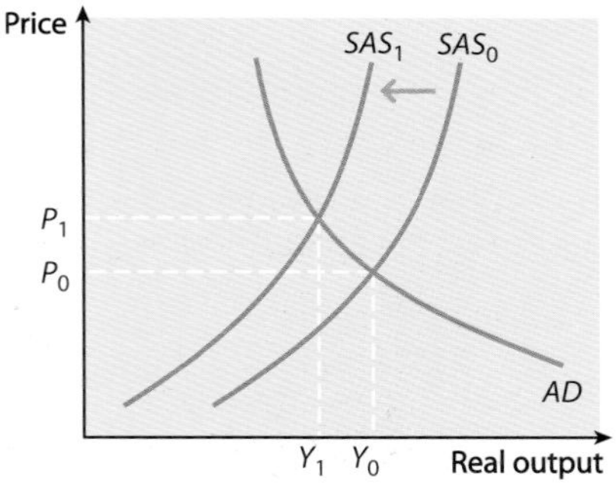

Figure 13.1 A supply shock

Nonetheless, this is one reason why prices may begin to increase. Inflation thus may be initiated on the supply side of the macroeconomy, arising from an increase in the costs faced by firms. This is sometimes referred to as **cost-push inflation**, as the increase in the overall level of prices is cost-driven.

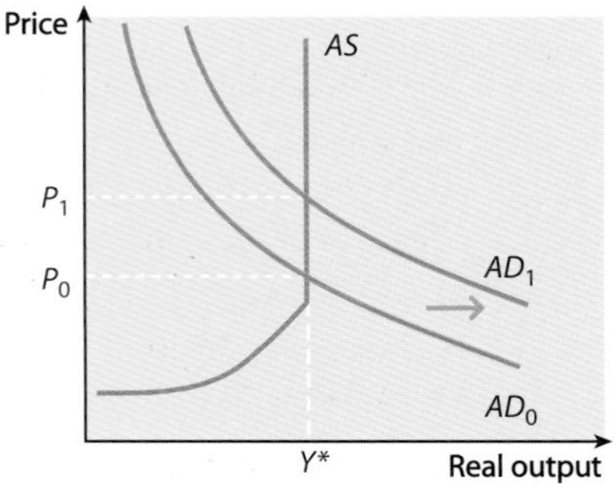

Figure 13.2
An increase in aggregate demand

In terms of the AD/AS model, it is clear that an alternative explanation of a rise in the general price level could come from the demand side, where an increase in aggregate demand leads to a rise in prices, especially if the AS curve becomes so steep in the long run as to become vertical (as some macroeconomists believe) as in Figure 13.2, where the increase in aggregate demand from AD_0 to AD_1

leads to a rise in the overall price level from P_0 to P_1 with no change at all in real output. An increase in the price level emanating from the demand side of the macroeconomy is sometimes referred to as **demand-pull inflation**.

But why should there be *persistent* increases in prices over time? One-off movements in either aggregate demand or aggregate supply may lead to one-off changes in the overall price level, but unless the movements continue in subsequent periods there is no reason to suppose that inflation will continue. One explanation is provided in terms of changes in the supply of money in circulation in an economy.

Key terms

demand-pull inflation: inflation initiated by an increase in aggregate demand

money stock: the quantity of money in circulation in the economy

Persistent inflation can take place only when the **money stock** grows more rapidly than real output. This can be shown in terms of aggregate demand and aggregate supply. If the money supply increases, firms and households in the economy find they have excess cash balances; that is, for a given price level they have more purchasing power than they had expected to have. Their impulse will thus be to increase their spending, which will cause the aggregate demand curve to move to the right. They will probably also save some of the excess, which will tend to result in lower interest rates — which will then reinforce the increase in aggregate demand. However, as the *AD* curve moves to the right, the equilibrium price level will rise, returning the economy to equilibrium.

If the money supply continues to increase, the process repeats itself, with prices then rising persistently. One danger of this is that people will get so accustomed to the process that they speed up their spending decisions, which simply accelerates the whole process.

To summarise, the analysis suggests that, although a price rise can be triggered on either the supply side or the demand side of the macroeconomy, persistent inflation can arise only through persistent excessive growth in the money stock, which can be seen in terms of persistent movements of the aggregate demand curve.

Costs of inflation

A crucial question is why it matters if an economy experiences inflation. The answer is that very high inflation gives rise to a number of costs.

The fact that firms have to keep amending their price lists raises the costs of undertaking transactions. These costs are often known as the *menu costs* of inflation; however, this should not be expected to be significant unless inflation really is very high. A second cost of very high inflation is that it discourages people from holding money, because at the very high nominal interest rates that occur when inflation is high the opportunity cost of holding money becomes great, and people try to keep their money in interest-bearing accounts for as long as possible, even if it means making frequent trips to the bank — for which reason these are known as the *shoe leather costs* of inflation.

This reluctance to use money for transactions may inhibit the effectiveness of markets. For example, there was a period in the early 1980s when inflation in Argentina was so high that some city parking fines had to be paid in litres of petrol rather than in cash. Markets will not work effectively when people do not use money and the economy begins to slip back towards a barter economy. The situation may be worsened if taxes or pensions are not properly indexed so that they do not keep up with inflation.

However, these costs are felt mainly when inflation reaches the *hyperinflation* stage. This has been rare in developed countries in recent years, although Latin America was prone to hyperinflation for a period in the 1980s, and some of the transition economies also went through very high inflation periods as they began to introduce market reforms; one example of this was the Ukraine, where inflation reached 10 000% per year in the early 1990s.

Inflation imposes costs such as the frequent re-pricing of items for sale (menu costs).

However, there may be costs associated with inflation even when it does not reach these heights, especially if inflation is volatile. If the rate of change of prices cannot be confidently predicted by firms, the increase in uncertainty may be damaging, and firms may become reluctant to undertake the investment that would expand the economy's productive capacity.

Furthermore, as Part 1 of this book emphasised, prices are very important in allocating resources in a market economy. Inflation may consequently inhibit the ability of prices to act as reliable signals in this process, leading to a wastage of resources and lost business opportunities.

It is these last reasons that have elevated the control of inflation to one of the central planks of UK government macroeconomic policy. However, it should be noticed that the target for inflation has not been set at zero. During the period when the inflation target was set in terms of RPIX (as explained in Chapter 11) the inflation target was 2.5%; the new target for CPI inflation is 2%. The reasoning here is two-fold. One argument is that it has to be accepted that measured inflation will overstate actual inflation, partly because it is so difficult to take account of quality changes in products such as PCs, where it is impossible to distinguish accurately between a price change and a quality change. Second, wages and prices tend to be sticky in a downward direction; in other words, firms may be reluctant to lower prices and wages. A modest rate of inflation (e.g. 2%) thus allows relative prices to change more readily, with prices in some sectors rising by more than in others. This may help price signals to be more effective in guiding resource allocation.

Summary

- The control of inflation has been the major focus of macroeconomic policy in the UK since about 1976.
- Inflation can be initiated on either the supply side of an economy or the demand side.
- However, sustained inflation can take place only if there is also a sustained increase in money supply.
- High inflation imposes costs on society and reduces the effectiveness with which markets can work.
- Low inflation reduces uncertainty, and may encourage investment by firms.

Exercise 13.1

Suppose that next year inflation in the British economy suddenly takes off, reaching 60% per annum. In other words, prices rise by 60% — but so do incomes. Discuss how this would affect your daily life. Why would this be damaging for the economy in the future?

Full employment

For an economy to be operating on the production possibility frontier, the factors of production need to be fully employed. From society's point of view, surplus capacity in the economy represents waste. In the macroeconomic policy arena, attention in this context focuses on unemployment. For example, Figure 13.3 shows that it is possible for the economy to be in macroeconomic equilibrium at a level of output Y_1 that is below the potential full employment level at Y^*. This may be seen as an unnecessary waste of potential output. In addition, there may be a cost suffered by the people who are unemployed in this situation and could have been productively employed.

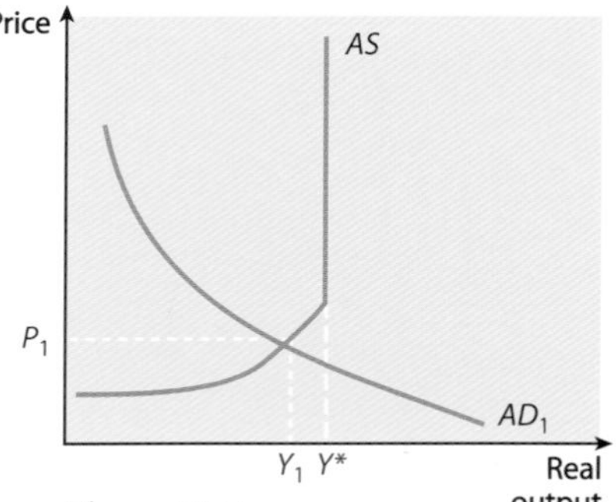

Figure 13.3
Macroeconomic equilibrium below full employment

Causes of unemployment

There will always be some unemployment in a dynamic economy. At any point in time, there will be workers transferring between jobs. Indeed, this needs to happen if the pattern of production is to keep up with changing patterns of consumer demand and comparative advantage. In other words, in a typical period of time there will be some sectors of an economy that are expanding and others that are in decline. It is crucial that workers are able to transfer from those activities that are in decline to those that are booming. Accordingly, there will be some unemployment while this transfer takes place, and this is known as **frictional unemployment**.

In some cases this transfer of workers between sectors may be quite difficult to accomplish. For example, coal mining may be on the decline in an economy, but international banking may be booming. It is clearly unreasonable to expect coal miners to turn themselves into international bankers overnight. In this sort of situation there may be some longer-term unemployment while workers retrain for new occupations and new sectors of activity. Indeed, there may be workers who find themselves redundant at a relatively late stage in their career and for whom the retraining is not worthwhile, or who cannot find firms that will be prepared to train them for a relatively short payback time. Such unemployment is known as **structural unemployment**. It arises because of the mismatch between the skills of workers leaving contracting sectors and the skills required by expanding sectors in the economy.

Key terms

frictional unemployment: unemployment associated with job search, i.e. with people who are between jobs

structural unemployment: unemployment arising because of changes in the pattern of economic activity within an economy

demand-deficient unemployment: unemployment that arises because of a deficiency of aggregate demand in the economy, so that the equilibrium level of output is below full employment

Figure 13.3 showed a different form of unemployment, one that arises because the economy is trapped in an equilibrium position that is below full employment. This is sometimes referred to as **demand-deficient unemployment** — and a solution to it might be to boost aggregate demand. This possibility will be discussed in Chapter 15.

A further reason for unemployment concerns the level of wages. Figure 13.4 shows a labour market in which a free market equilibrium would have wage W^* and quantity of labour L^*. If for some reason wages were set at W_0, there would be a disequilibrium between labour supply (at L_s) and labour demand (at L_d). Expressing this in a different way, here is a situation in which there are more workers seeking employment at the going wage (L_s) than there are firms prepared to hire at that wage (L_d). The difference is unemployment.

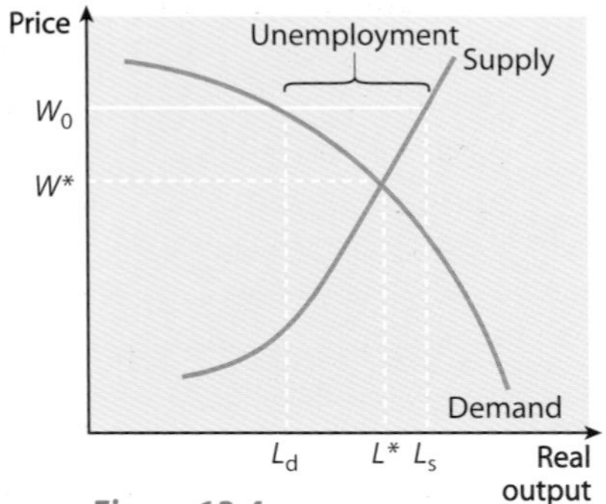

Figure 13.4
Unemployment in a labour market

There are a number of reasons why this situation might arise. Trade unions may have been able to use their power and influence to raise wages above the equilibrium level, thereby ensuring higher wages for their members who remain in employment but denying jobs to others. Alternatively, it could be argued that wages will be inflexible downwards. Thus, a supply shock that reduced firms' demand for labour could leave wages above the equilibrium, and they may adjust downwards only slowly. Chapter 10 mentioned that in some situations the imposition of a minimum wage in a low-wage competitive labour market could also have the effect of institutionally setting the wage rate above its equilibrium level.

Finally, if unemployment benefits are set at a relatively high level compared with wages in low-paid occupations, some people may choose not to work, thereby creating some **voluntary unemployment**. From the point of view of those individuals, they are making a rational choice on the basis of the options open to them. From society's point of view, however, there needs to be a balance between providing appropriate social protection for those unable to obtain jobs and trying to make the best use of available resources for the benefit of society as a whole.

Costs of unemployment

The costs of unemployment were mentioned earlier. From society's perspective, if the economy is operating below full capacity, then it is operating within the production possibility frontier, and therefore is not making the best possible use of society's resources. From the perspective of prospective workers, **involuntary unemployment** carries a cost to each such individual in terms of forgone earnings, personal worth and dignity.

Key terms

voluntary unemployment: situation arising when an individual chooses not to accept a job at the going wage rate

involuntary unemployment: situation arising when an individual who would like to accept a job at the going wage rate is unable to find employment

Summary

- Full employment occurs when an economy is operating on the production possibility frontier, with full utilisation of factors of production.
- An economy operating below full capacity is characterised by unemployment.
- Some unemployment in a dynamic economy is inevitable, as people may have to undergo short spells of unemployment while between jobs — this is known as frictional unemployment.
- Structural unemployment occurs when there is a mismatch between the skills that workers have to offer and the skills that employers want. This occurs when the economy is undergoing structural change, with some sectors expanding and some contracting.
- Demand-deficient unemployment may occur if the macroeconomy is in equilibrium below full employment.
- If wages are held above the equilibrium level, for example by minimum wage legislation or trade union action, then unemployment may occur.
- High levels of unemployment benefit may encourage some workers not to accept jobs as the opportunity cost of not working is low.

Exercise 13.2

Classify each of the following types of unemployment as arising from frictional, structural, demand-deficient or other causes, and decide whether they are voluntary or involuntary:

a unemployment arising from a decline of the coal mining sector, and the expansion of financial services

b a worker leaving one job to search for a better one

c unemployment that arises because the real wage rate is held above the labour market equilibrium

d unemployment arising from slow adjustment to a fall in aggregate demand

e unemployment arising because workers find that low-paid jobs are paying less than can be obtained in unemployment benefit

The balance of payments

Lists of macroeconomic policy objectives invariably include equilibrium on the balance of payments as a key item. Unlike inflation and unemployment, it is not so obvious why disequilibrium in the balance of payments is a problem that warrants policy action.

Figure 13.5 shows the market for pounds relative to euros. Here the demand for pounds arises from residents in the euro area wanting to buy British goods, services and assets, whereas the supply arises from British residents wanting to buy goods, services and assets from the euro area. If the exchange rate is at its equilibrium level, this implies that the demand for pounds (i.e. the foreign demand for UK goods, services and assets) is equal to the supply of pounds (i.e. the domestic demand for goods, services and assets from the euro area).

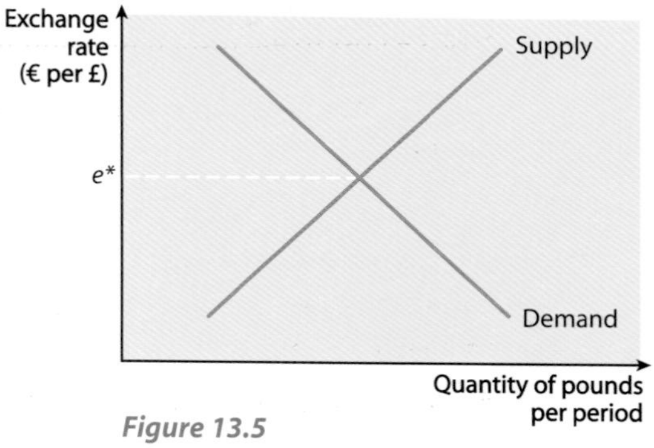

Figure 13.5
The market for pounds sterling

In a free exchange market, the exchange rate can be expected to adjust in order to bring about this equilibrium position. Even under a fixed exchange rate system in which the government pledges to hold the exchange rate at a particular level, any discrepancy between the demand and supply of pounds would have to be met by the monetary authorities buying or selling foreign exchange reserves. Thus, the overall balance of payments is always in equilibrium. So why might there be a problem?

The problem arises not with the *overall* balance of payments, but with an imbalance between components of the balance of payments. In particular, attention focuses on the balance of the current account of the balance of payments, which shows the balance in the trade in goods and services together with investment income flows and current transfers.

If the current account is in deficit, UK residents are purchasing more in imports of goods and services than the economy is exporting. In other words, UK earnings from exports are not sufficient to pay for UK imports. This is a bit like a household spending beyond its income, which could be sustained only by selling assets or by borrowing.

The concern for the economy is that a large and sustained deficit on the current account implies that the financial account must be in large and sustained surplus. This in turn means that the UK is effectively exporting assets. And this means that overseas residents are buying up UK assets, which in turn may mean a leakage of investment income in the future. Alternatively, overall balance could be achieved through the sale of foreign exchange reserves in order to soak up the excess supply of pounds that arises because UK residents are supplying more pounds in order to buy imports than overseas residents are demanding in order to buy UK exports.

However the current account deficit is financed, a large deficit cannot be sustained indefinitely. This begs the question of what is meant by a 'large' deficit. Figure 11.12 showed the current account balance as a percentage of GDP, which gives some idea of the relative magnitude of the deficit. This shows that, although the current account has been in deficit every year since 1984, the deficit has been less than 3% of GDP since 1990 and less than 2% in 2002 and 2003. This might be regarded as tolerable.

A critical issue is whether UK assets remain attractive to foreign buyers. Running a sustained deficit on current account requires running a surplus on financial account. If foreign buyers of UK assets become reluctant to buy, UK interest rates might have to rise in order to make UK assets more attractive. A byproduct of this would be a curb in spending by British firms and consumers. Given that part of this reduction in spending would impact on imports, this would begin to reduce the current account deficit.

A major concern during the early years of the twenty-first century has been the large and persistent current account deficit being run by the US economy. This has been associated in part with the sizeable government spending of the Bush administration, which was forecast to reach a level that could have global repercussions.

Causes of a deficit on current account

In Chapter 12 it was argued that the quantity of exports of goods and services from the UK would depend partly on income levels in the rest of the world and partly upon the competitiveness of UK goods and services, which in turn depends partly on the sterling exchange rate and partly on relative price levels in the UK and elsewhere. Similarly, the level of imports depends partly on domestic income and partly on the international competitiveness of UK and foreign goods and services.

This suggests that a fundamental cause of a deficit on the current account is a lack of competitiveness of UK goods and services, arising from an overvalued exchange rate or from high relative prices of UK goods and services. Alternatively, UK incomes may be rising more rapidly than those in the rest of the world.

Summary

- If the exchange rate is free to reach its equilibrium value, the overall balance of payments will always be zero.
- However, a deficit on the current account of the balance of payments must always be balanced by a corresponding surplus on the financial account.
- A persistent deficit on current account means that in the long run domestic assets are being sold to overseas buyers, or that foreign exchange reserves are being run down. Neither situation can be sustained in the long run.
- A key cause of a deficit on the current account is the lack of competitiveness of domestic goods and services.

Economic growth

If you accept that the ultimate aim of a society is to improve the wellbeing of its citizens, then in economic terms this means that the resources available within the economy need to expand through time, in order to widen people's choices and provide the increased resources that are required to make this happen.

This is such an important policy objective for an economy that the whole of Chapter 14 is devoted to it. For now, note that the nearest measure that economists have of the resources available to members of a society is GDP; so in looking for economic growth, they are looking for growth in GDP over time.

In many ways, economic growth may be regarded as the most fundamental of all macroeconomic policy objectives, with all other objectives being subsidiary to it. For example, one of the key reasons for maintaining low inflation is to encourage investment – which enables economic growth. Maintaining full employment ensures the best possible use of a society's resources, enabling it to reach the production possibility frontier – failure to do this may have indirect consequences for economic growth. Running a sustained current account deficit that requires the sale of UK assets may limit future growth prospects of the economy.

Concern for the environment

International externalities pose problems for policy design, because they require coordination across countries. If pollution caused by the British manufacturing sector causes acid rain elsewhere in Europe, Britain is imposing costs on other countries that are not fully reflected in market prices. Furthermore, there may be effects that cross generations. If the environment today is damaged, it may not be enjoyed by future generations – in other words, there may be intergenerational externality effects.

There is a macroeconomic dimension to these issues. If policy were only designed to achieve economic growth, regardless of the consequences for the environment, these externality effects could be severe, and for this reason they cannot be tackled solely at the microeconomic level of individual markets. Chapter 14 further develops this theme as part of the discussion of economic growth.

Income redistribution

The final macroeconomic policy objective to be considered concerns attempts to influence the distribution of income within a society. This may entail transfers of income between groups in society – i.e. from richer to poorer – in order to protect the latter. Income redistribution may work through progressive taxation (whereby those on high incomes pay a higher proportion of their income in tax) or through a system of social security benefits such as the Jobseekers' Allowance or Income Support.

Causes of inequality

Some degree of inequality in the income distribution within a society is inevitable. People have different innate talents and abilities, and choose to undergo different types and levels of education and training, such that they acquire different sets of skills. Market forces imply that different payments will be made to people in different sectors of economic activity and different occupations. Income inequality also arises because of inequality in the ownership of assets. Nonetheless, people in identical circumstances and with identical skills and abilities *may* receive identical income. This notion is sometimes known as *horizontal equity*, which most people would agree is desirable.

Equal Opportunities legislation seeks to ensure equal pay for equal work.

One category of policy measures is designed to encourage horizontal equity. Equal Opportunities legislation tries to ensure that members of society do not suffer discrimination that might deny them equal pay for equal work, or equal access to employment. Nonetheless, there remain significant differences in earnings and employment between ethnic groups and between men and women. These issues are explored more fully in Chapter 22.

Setting this aside, the key question remaining is the extent to which the government needs to intervene at the macroeconomic level in order to influence the distribution of income and protect vulnerable groups by redistributing from richer to poorer. Indeed, are there economic effects of inequality suggesting that redistribution of income is needed for reasons other than the purely humanitarian objective of alleviating poverty and protecting the vulnerable?

The costs of inequality

In a society where there is substantial inequality in the distribution of income, there are likely to be groups of people who are disadvantaged in various ways: for example, they may find it more difficult to obtain education for themselves or for their children – in the UK it remains the case that a lower proportion of students from low-income families go to university. It may also be that some potential entrepreneurs find it more difficult to obtain the credit needed to launch their business ideas.

If this is so, it suggests that there are people in society who are inhibited from developing their productive potential – which in turn implies that economic growth in the future will be lower than it might be. This could provide a justification for redistributing income – or at least for trying to ensure that there is equality of opportunity for all members of society. However, it might be argued that redistribution can be taken too far. If the higher-income groups in society face too high a marginal tax rate on their income – in other words, if additions to income are very heavily taxed for the rich – this could remove their incentive to exploit income-earning opportunities, which could have a damaging impact on economic growth.

Too much inequality may also lead to high crime rates and social discontent, which in turn may lead to political instability in a society. This could affect the security of property rights and inhibit economic growth.

There is some evidence that inequality has been widening in many countries in recent years. In particular, the way that technology has been progressing places a higher premium on skills, so that the gap between the earnings of skilled and unskilled workers has been widening.

Summary

- Economic growth is the most important long-run macroeconomic policy objective for an economy, as this enables improvements in the wellbeing of the society's citizens.
- However, there may be a need to moderate the pursuit of economic growth in order to protect the environment.
- Macroeconomic policy may also encompass the redistribution of income within society, on grounds of equity and also because extreme inequality may inhibit economic growth.

part 3

Chapter 14

Economic growth

One of society's prime responsibilities is to provide a reasonable standard of living for its citizens and to promote their wellbeing. Hence one of the major objectives for economic policy in the long run is to enable improvements in wellbeing, and in order to do this it is first necessary to expand the resources available within society. A key element in this process is to achieve economic growth, which is the subject of this chapter. However, there may be more to wellbeing than just growth, and the chapter also explores some of the limitations of a strategy that aims to maximise GDP growth.

Learning outcomes

After studying this chapter, you should:

- be able to understand the meaning of economic growth and productivity
- be familiar with factors that can affect the rate of economic growth, in particular the role of investment
- appreciate the strengths and weaknesses of GDP as a measure of the standard of living in comparisons across time and between countries
- be aware of differences in growth rates between countries and of the explanations that have been advanced to explain them
- evaluate the importance to a society of economic growth and the costs that such growth may impose
- understand the meaning and significance of sustainable growth

Defining economic growth

From a theoretical point of view, **economic growth** can be thought of as an expansion of the productive capacity of an economy. If you like, it is an expansion of the potential output of the economy.

There are two ways in which this has been presented in earlier chapters. The first is in terms of the production possibility frontier (PPP), which was introduced in

> **Key term**
>
> **economic growth:** the expansion of the productive capacity of an economy

Chapter 1. Figure 14.1 is a reminder, and reproduces Figure 1.3, where economic growth was characterised as an outward movement of the production possibility frontier from PPF_0 to PPF_1. In other words, economic growth enables a society to produce more goods and services in any given period as a result of an expansion in its resources.

A second way of thinking about economic growth is to use the AD/AS model introduced in Chapter 12. In Figure 14.2, an increase in the skills of the workforce will enable firms to produce more output at any given price, so that the aggregate supply curve will shift outwards from AS_0 to AS_1. This entails an increase in full employment output (or capacity output) from Y^* to Y^{**}. This again can be characterised as economic growth. Chapter 15 investigates policies that might be introduced to affect aggregate supply. In this chapter the focus is on a broader perspective within which long-run growth can be achieved.

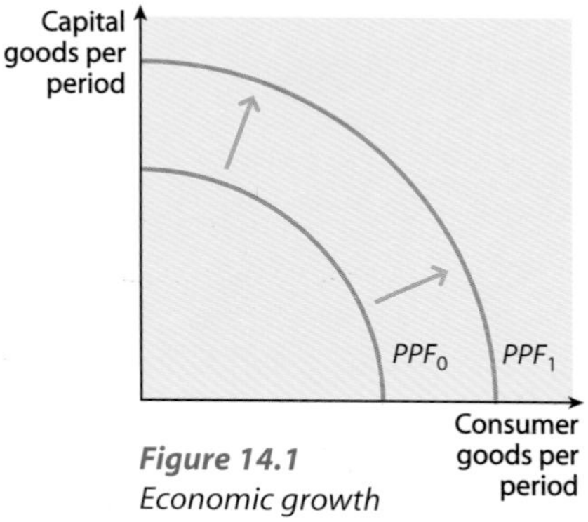

Figure 14.1
Economic growth

If economists try to measure economic growth using the rate of change of GDP as an indicator, they are not necessarily measuring what they want to. GDP growth measures the *actual* rate of change of output rather than the growth of the *potential* output capacity of the economy.

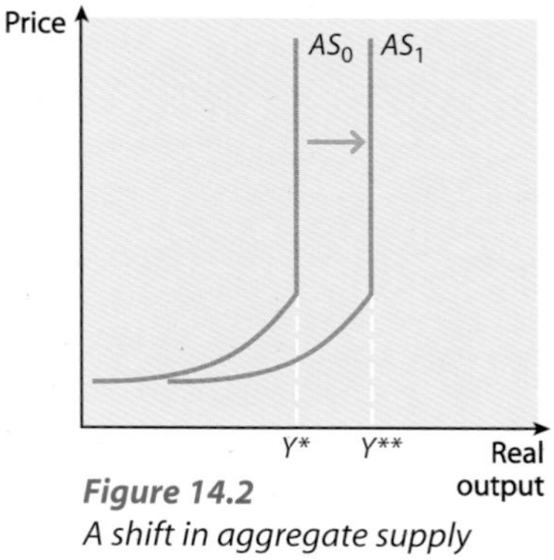

Figure 14.2
A shift in aggregate supply

In Figure 14.3, a movement from *A* to *B* represents a move to the frontier. This is an increase in actual output resulting from using up surplus capacity in the economy, but it is *not* economic growth in our theoretical sense, as moving from *A* to *B* does not entail an increase in productive capacity. On the other hand, a movement of the frontier itself, enabling the move from *B* to *C*, *does* represent economic growth. However, when economists observe a change in GDP they cannot easily distinguish between the two sorts of effect, especially if the economy is subject to a business cycle. It is therefore better to think of economic growth in terms of the underlying trend rate of growth of real GDP.

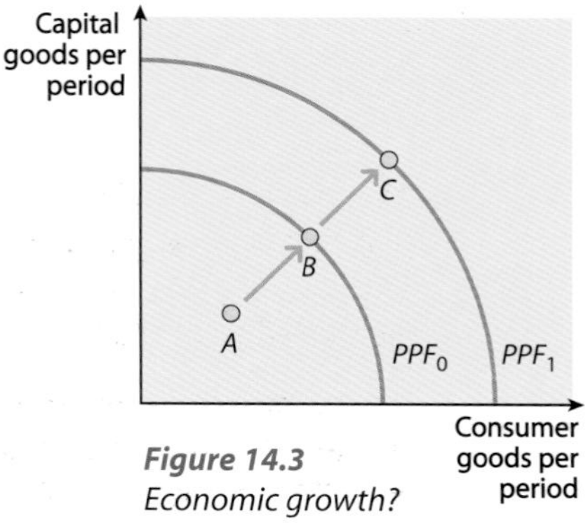

Figure 14.3
Economic growth?

Figure 14.4 helps to illustrate this. It shows the annual growth rate of real GDP in the UK since 1949. You can see that it is quite difficult to determine the underlying trend because the year-to-year movements are so volatile. Figure 14.5 takes 5-yearly average growth rates over the same period, with the horizontal red line showing the underlying trend rate of growth.

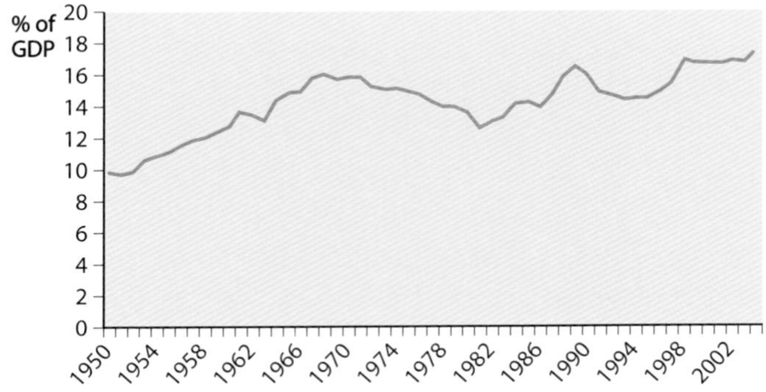

Figure 14.4
Gross fixed capital formation in the UK, 1950–2004

Source: ONS.

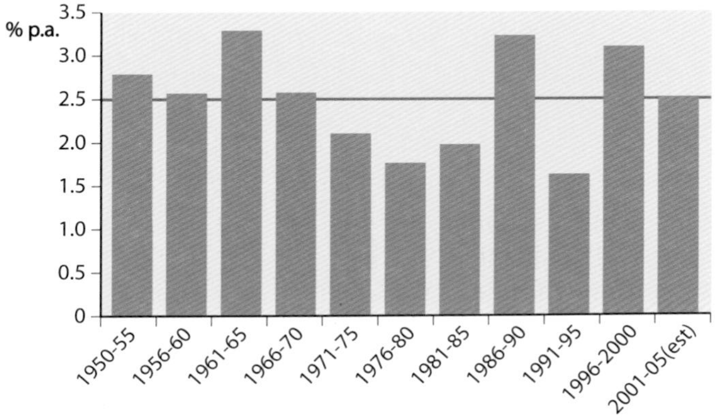

Figure 14.5
Average annual growth rates in the UK since 1950

Sources of economic growth

At a basic level, production arises from the use of factors of production — capital, labour, entrepreneurship and so on. Capacity output is reached when all factors of production are fully and efficiently utilised. From this perspective, an increase in capacity output can come either from an increase in the quantity of the factors of production, or from an improvement in their efficiency or productivity. **Productivity** is a measure of the efficiency of a factor of production. For example, **labour productivity** measures output per worker, or output per hour worked. The latter is the more helpful measure, as clearly total output is affected by the number of hours worked, which does vary somewhat across countries. **Capital productivity** measures output per unit of capital. **Total factor productivity** refers to the average productivity of all factors, measured as the total output divided by the total amount of inputs used.

An increase in productivity raises aggregate supply and the potential capacity output of an economy, and thus contributes to economic growth.

Key terms

productivity: measure of the efficiency of a factor of production

labour productivity: measure of output per worker, or output per hour worked

capital productivity: measure of output per unit of capital

total factor productivity: the average productivity of all factors, measured as the total output divided by the total amount of inputs used

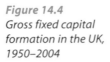

Capital

Capital is a critical factor in the production process. An increase in capital input is thus one source of economic growth. In order for capital to accumulate and increase the capacity of the economy to produce, **investment** needs to take place.

Notice that in economics 'investment' is used in this specific way. In common parlance the term is sometimes used to refer to investing in shares or putting money into a deposit account at the bank. Do not confuse these different concepts. In economics 'investment' relates to a firm buying new capital, such as machinery or factory buildings. If you put money into a bank account, that is an act of saving, not investment.

Key terms

investment: an increase in the capital stock

depreciation: the fall in value of physical capital equipment over time as it is subject to wear and tear

net investment: gross investment *minus* depreciation

In the national accounts, the closest measurement that economists have to investment is 'Gross Fixed Capital Formation'. This covers net additions to the capital stock, but it also includes **depreciation**. Some of the machinery and other capital purchased by firms is to replace old, worn-out capital, i.e. to offset depreciation. It does not therefore represent an addition to capital stock. As depreciation cannot be observed easily, the convention in the accounts is to measure gross investment (i.e. including depreciation) and then make an adjustment for depreciation to arrive at **net investment**.

Figure 14.6 shows the time path for gross investment in the UK since 1950, expressed as a percentage of GDP. You can see that the share of investment in GDP has fluctuated a little over the years, but it has settled at about 17% in recent years, which is relatively high by historical standards.

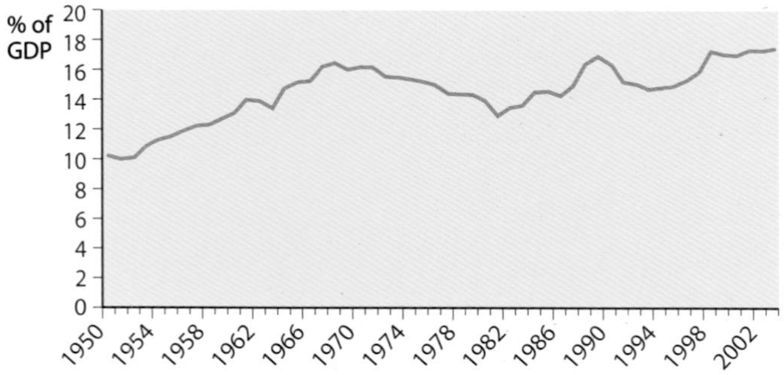

Figure 14.6 Gross fixed capital formation in the UK, 1950–2003

The choice that any society makes here is between using resources for current consumption and using resources for investment. Investment thus entails sacrificing present consumption in order to have more resources available in the future.

Different countries give investment very different priorities. Something of this can be seen in Figure 14.7, which shows gross capital formation in a selection of countries around the world. The diversity is substantial, ranging from just 7% in Burundi to 39% in China. It is perhaps not surprising to discover that China is among the fastest growing economies in the world in the early twenty-first century — but it must also be remembered that this means sacrificing present consumption in China.

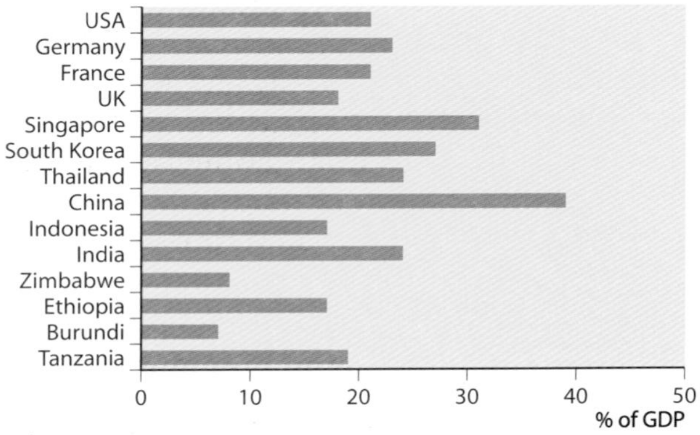

Figure 14.7 *Gross capital formation, selected countries, 2001 (% of GDP)*

Source: *WDR 2003*.

Note: countries are in descending order of GNI per capita.

The contribution of capital to growth is reinforced by technological progress, as the productivity of new capital is greater than that of old capital that is being phased out. For example, the speed and power of computers has increased enormously over recent years, which has had a great impact on productivity. Effectively, this means that technology is increasing the contribution that investment can make towards enlarging capacity output in an economy.

Innovation can also contribute, through the invention of new forms of capital and new ways of using existing capital, both of which can aid economic growth.

Labour

Capital has sometimes been seen as the main driver of growth, but labour too has a key contribution to make. There is little point in installing a lot of hi-tech equipment unless there is the skilled labour to operate it.

There is relatively little scope for increasing the size of the labour force in a country, except through international migration. (Encouraging population growth is a rather long-term policy!) Nonetheless, the size of the workforce does contribute to the size of capacity output. A number of sub-Saharan African countries have seen this effect in reverse in recent years, with the impact of HIV/AIDS. The spread of this epidemic has had a devastating impact in a number of countries in the region; in some countries the percentage of adults affected is over 30% — nearly 40% in Botswana. This has a serious impact on capacity output, because the disease affects people of working age disproportionately, diminishing the size of the workforce and the productivity of workers.

Key term

human capital: the stock of skills and expertise that contribute to a worker's productivity; can be increased through education and training

The quality of labour input is more amenable to policy action. Education and training can improve the productivity of workers, and can be regarded as a form of investment in **human capital**.

Chapter 8 discussed how education and health care may have associated externalities. In particular, individuals may not perceive the full social benefits associated with education, training and certain kinds of health care, and thus may choose to invest less in these forms of human capital than is desirable from the perspective of society as a whole. Another such externality is the impact of human capital formation on economic growth as a justification for viewing education and health care as being merit goods — which were discussed in Chapter 9.

For many developing countries, the provision of healthcare and improved nutrition can be seen as additional forms of investment in human capital, since such investment can lead to future improvements in productivity.

Summary

- Economic growth is the expansion of an economy's productive capacity.
- This can be envisaged as a movement outwards of the production possibility frontier, or as a rightward shift of the aggregate supply curve.
- Economic growth can be seen as the underlying trend rate of growth in real GDP.
- Economic growth can stem from an increase in the inputs of factors of production, or from an improvement in their productivity, i.e. the efficiency with which factors of production are utilised.
- Investment contributes to growth by increasing the capital stock of an economy, although some investment is to compensate for depreciation.
- The contribution of capital is reinforced by the effects of technological progress.
- Labour is another critical factor of production that can contribute to economic growth; for instance, education and training can improve labour productivity. This is a form of human capital formation.

Exercise 14.1

Which of the following represent genuine economic growth, and which may just mean a move to the PPF?

a an increase in the rate of change of potential output

b a fall in the unemployment rate

c improved work practices that increase labour productivity

d an increase in the proportion of the population joining the labour force

e an increase in the utilisation of capital

f a rightward shift in the aggregate supply curve

GDP and growth

Chapter 11 introduced GDP as a way of measuring the total output of an economy over a period of time. Although this measure can provide an indicator of the quantity of resources available to citizens of a country in a given period, as an assessment of the standard of living it has its critics.

GDP does have some things going for it. First, it is relatively straightforward and thus is widely understood. Second, it is a well-established indicator and one that is available for almost every country in the world, so that it can be used to compare income levels across countries. For this purpose, it naturally helps to adjust for population size by calculating GDP per person (GDP *per capita*, as it is known). This then provides a measure of average income per head.

Figure 14.8 provides data on GDP per capita for the same countries that appeared in Figure 14.7. The extreme differences that exist around the globe are immediately apparent from the data. GDP per capita in Ethiopia is just $90, whereas in the USA the figure is $36 006. Luxembourg heads this particular league table, with average income of $47 354 in 2002.

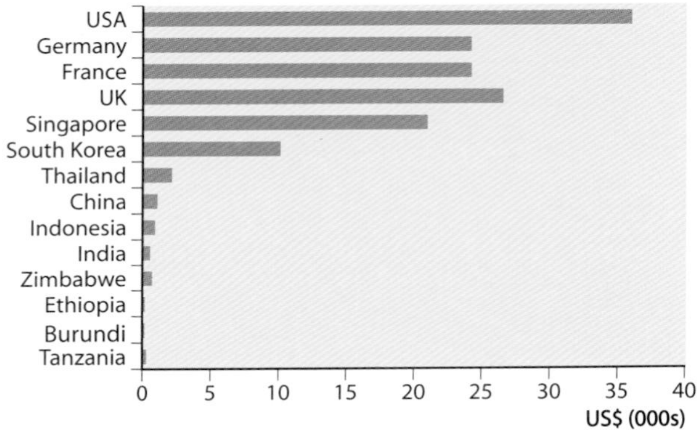

Figure 14.8
GDP per capita, selected countries, 2002, in US$

Source: *HDR 2004*.

In trying to interpret these data, there are a number of issues that need to be borne in mind, as the comparison is not as straightforward as it looks.

Inequality in income distribution

One important point to notice is that looking at the average level of income per person may be misleading if there are wide differences in the way in which income is distributed within countries. In other words, it cannot be assumed that every Ethiopian receives $90, or that every Luxembourgian receives $47 354. If income is more unequally distributed in some countries, this will affect one's perception of what the term 'average' means. For example, India and Zimbabwe had similar GDP per capita levels in 2002, but the income distribution in India was far more equitable than in Zimbabwe.

The informal sector and the accuracy of data

A further problem with undertaking international comparisons is that it is never absolutely certain that the accuracy with which data are collected is consistent across countries. Definitions of GDP and other variables are now set out in a clear, internationally agreed form, but even when countries are working to the same definitions, some data collection agencies may be more reliable than others.

One particular area in which this is pertinent relates to the informal sector. In every economy there are some transactions that go unrecorded. In most economies, there are economic activities that take place that cannot be closely monitored because of their informal nature. This is especially prevalent in many developing countries, where often substantial amounts of economic activity take place without an exchange of money. For example, in many countries subsistence agriculture remains an important facet of economic life. If households are producing food simply for their own consumption, there is no reason for a money transaction to take place with regard to its production, and thus such activity will not be recorded as a part of GDP. Equally, much economic activity within the urban areas of less-developed countries comes under the category of the 'informal sector'.

In many developing countries, substantial economic activity may take place without an exchange of money.

Where such activity varies in importance between countries, comparing incomes on the basis of measured GDP may be misleading, as GDP will be a closer indicator of the amount of real economic activity in some countries than in others.

Exchange rate problems

The data presented in Figure 14.8 were expressed in terms of US dollars. This allows economists to compare average incomes using a common unit of measurement. At the same time, however, it may create some problems.

Economists want to compare average income levels so that they can evaluate the standard of living, and compare standards across countries. In other words, it is important to be able to assess people's command over resources in different societies, and to be able to compare the purchasing power of income in different countries.

GDP is calculated initially in terms of local currencies, and subsequently converted into US dollars using official exchange rates. Will this provide information about the relative local purchasing power of incomes? Not necessarily.

One reason for this is that official exchange rates are sometimes affected by government intervention. Indeed, in many of the less-developed countries exchange rates are pegged to an international currency – usually the US dollar. In these circumstances exchange rates are more likely to reflect the government's policy and actions than the relative purchasing power of incomes in the countries under scrutiny.

Where exchange rates are free to find their own equilibrium level, exchange rates are likely to be influenced strongly by the price of internationally traded goods – which is likely to be a very different combination of goods than that typically consumed by residents in these countries. Again, it can be argued that the official exchange rates may not be a good reflection of the relative purchasing power of incomes across countries.

The United Nations International Comparison Project has been working on this problem for many years. It now produces an alternative set of international estimates of GDP based on purchasing power parity (PPP) exchange rates, which are designed to reflect the relative purchasing power of incomes in different societies more accurately. Figure 14.9 shows estimates for the same set of countries.

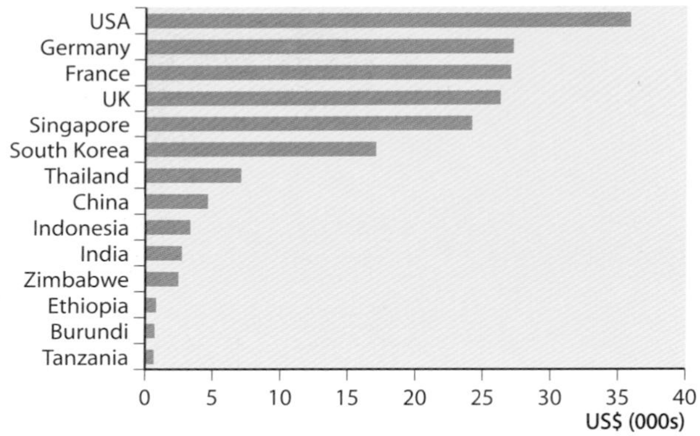

Figure 14.9
GDP per capita, selected countries, 2002, in PPP$

Source: *HDR* 2004.

Comparing this with Figure 14.8, you will notice that the gap between the low-income and high-income countries seems less marked when PPP dollars are used as the unit of measurement. In other words, the US dollar estimates exaggerate the gap in living standards between rich and poor countries. This is a general feature of these measurements – that measurements in US dollars tend to understate real incomes for low-income countries and overstate them for high-income countries compared with PPP-dollar data. Put another way, people in the lower-income countries have a stronger command over goods and services than is suggested by US-dollar comparisons of GDP per capita.

Social indicators

A final question that arises is whether GDP can be regarded as a reasonable indicator of a country's standard of living. You have seen that GDP provides an indicator of the total resources available within an economy in a given period, calculated from data about total output, total incomes or total expenditure. This focus on summing the transactions that take place in an economy over a period can be seen as a rather narrow view of what constitutes the 'standard of living'. After all, it may be argued that the quality of people's lives depends on more things than simply the material resources that are available.

For one thing, people need to have knowledge if they are to make good use of the resources that are available. Two societies with similar income levels may nonetheless provide very different quality of life for their inhabitants, depending on the education levels of the population. Furthermore, if people are to benefit from consuming or using the available resources, they need a reasonable lifespan coupled with good health. So, good standards of health are also crucial to a good quality of life.

It is important to remember that different societies tend to set different priorities on the pursuit of growth and the promotion of education and health. This needs to be taken into account when judging relative living standards through a comparison of GDP per capita, as some countries have higher-than-average levels of health and education as compared with other countries with similar levels of GDP per capita.

A reasonable environment in which to live may be seen as another important factor in one's quality of life; indeed, Chapter 13 has already pointed out the possible trade-off that may exist between economic growth and environmental standards.

There are some environmental issues that can distort the GDP measure of resources. Suppose there is an environmental disaster – perhaps an oil tanker breaks up close to a beautiful beach. This reduces the overall quality of life by degrading the landscape and preventing enjoyment of the beach. However, it does not have a negative effect on GDP; on the contrary, the money spent on clearing up the damage actually adds to GDP, so that the net effect of an environmental disaster may be to *increase* the measured level of GDP!

Summary

- GDP is a widely used measure of the total amount of economic activity in an economy over a period of time.
- The trend rate of change of GDP may thus be an indicator of economic growth.
- GDP is a widely understood and widely available measure, but it does have some drawbacks.
- Average GDP per person neglects the important issue of income distribution.
- There may be variation in the effectiveness of data collection agencies in different countries, and variation in the size of the informal sector.
- Converting from a local currency into US dollars may distort the use of GDP as a measure of the purchasing power of local incomes.
- GDP may neglect some important aspects of the quality of life.

Exercise 14.2

Below are some indicators for two countries, A and B. Discuss the extent to which GDP (here measured in PPP$) provides a good indication of relative living standards in the two countries. (All data are for 2001 unless otherwise stated. Data are taken from *Human Development Report 2003*.)

	Country A	Country B
GDP per capita (PPP$)	11 320	11 290
Life expectancy (in years at birth)	73.9	50.9
Adult literacy rate (%)	96.9	85.6
People living with HIV/AIDS (% of adults aged 15–49)	0.69	20.1
Infant mortality rate (per 1000 live births)	16	56

Discuss what other indicators might be useful in this evaluation.

Economic growth: international experience

The growth performance of different regions around the world has shown contrasting patterns in recent years. As early as the 1950s, a gap had opened up between the early developing countries in North America, Western Europe and Japan and the late developers in sub-Saharan Africa and Latin America.

Between 1960 and 1980 this gap began to widen, except for a small group of countries, mainly in East Asia, that had begun to close it. Figure 14.10 gives some data for countries in different regions. Tanzania and Ethiopia (in sub-Saharan Africa), together with Sri Lanka and India (in South Asia) grew relatively slowly in this period, with only Sri Lanka achieving an average growth rate above 2% per annum. Latin America showed a diverse experience: the examples shown in the figure are Colombia, which grew at about 3% per annum, and Brazil, which achieved growth of above 5% per annum. However, East Asia (represented here by South Korea and Singapore) took off during this period, growing at an average rate of 7% per year and more. Japan also grew rapidly at this time, while the UK and the USA grew at a more sedate pace of just above 2% per annum.

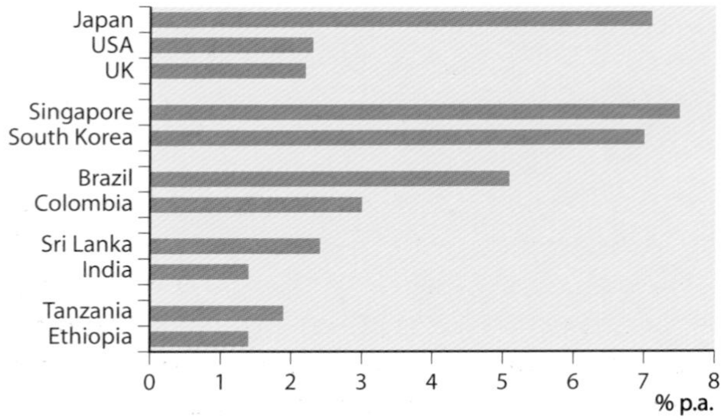

***Figure 14.10** Growth of GNP* per capita, selected countries, 1960–1980*

Source: World Bank, *World Development Report*, 1982.

*GNP is GDP plus net factor income from abroad: the difference between GNP and GDP is slight for most countries.

Figure 14.11 presents some more recent data, this time by region, for the period 1975–2000 (and for 1990–2000). This reveals some important patterns. The high-income OECD member countries continued to grow at a rather sedate rate of around 2% per annum, and less in the 1990s. Countries in East Asia and the Pacific maintained their impressive high growth of nearly 6% per annum, but again slowed a bit in the 1990s. South Asia showed some improvement, and even accelerated in the 1990s, as indeed did Latin America and the Caribbean. However, sub-Saharan African countries went through a dismal period in which their GDP per capita growth was negative – in other words, GDP per capita was lower in 2000 than it had been in 1975. This is serious indeed. The transition economies of central and eastern Europe offer data only for the 1990s. This was the decade in which they went through a painful process of transition, with negative growth rates.

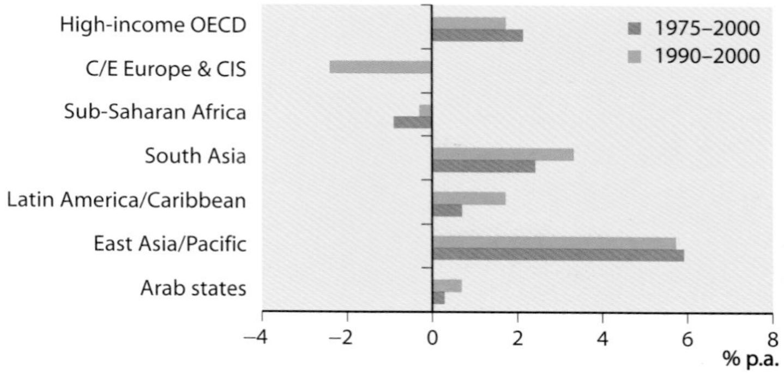

Figure 14.11 Growth of GDP per capita

Note: data represent growth rates of real GDP per capita measured in local currency.

Source: *UNDP*.

The importance of economic growth

Expanding the availability of resources in an economy enables the standard of living of the country to increase. For developing countries this may facilitate the easing of poverty, and may allow investment in human capital that will improve standards of living further in the future. In the industrial economies, populations have come to expect steady improvements in incomes and resources.

Thus for any society economic growth is likely to be seen as a fundamental objective – perhaps even the most important one. As was argued in Chapter 13, other policy objectives may be regarded as subsidiary to the growth target. In other words, the control of inflation, the maintenance of full employment and the achievement of stability in the current account of the balance of payments are all seen as important short-run objectives, because their achievement facilitates long-run economic growth.

In some less-developed countries the perspective may be different, and there has been a long-running debate about whether a society in its early stages of development should devote its resources to achieving the growth objective or to catering for basic needs. By making economic growth the prime target of policy, it may be necessary in the short run to allow inequality of incomes to continue, in order to provide the incentives for entrepreneurs to pursue growth. With such a 'growth-

first' approach, it is argued that eventually, as growth takes place, the benefits will trickle down; in other words, growth is necessary in order to tackle poverty and provide for basic needs. However, others have argued that the first priority should be to deal with basic needs, so that people gain in human capital and become better able to contribute to the growth process.

For the industrial countries, growth has become embedded as the main long-run objective of the economy, although the short-run objective of inflation control sometimes dominates media discussion. Nonetheless, the long-run growth rate of GDP is monitored on a regular basis, to assess how the UK is performing relative to other countries. If you would like to see how the UK is doing, Figure 14.12 shows some growth rates for 2002–03 for a selected group of OECD countries. However, remember that these are observations for just one year, so do not necessarily reflect long-term trends.

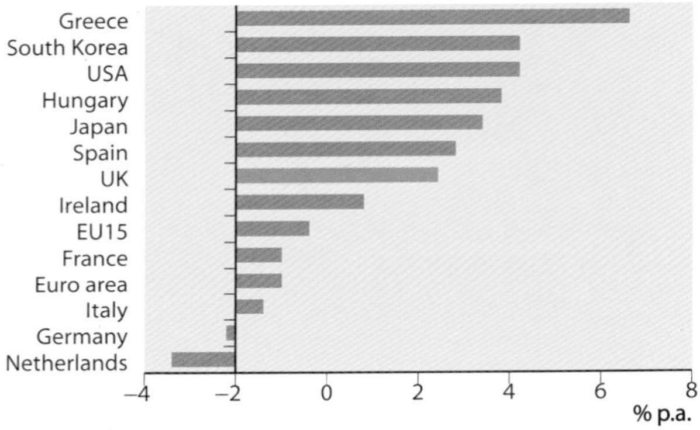

Figure 14.12 *Growth of real GDP, selected countries, 2002–03*

Source: OECD.

Costs of economic growth

Economic growth does bring some costs, perhaps most obviously in terms of pollution and degradation of the environment. Detailed discussion of these issues is postponed until Chapter 27.

Summary

- The experience of economic growth has varied substantially in different regions of the world.
- There is a gap in living standards between countries that industrialised early and countries that are now classified as being less developed.
- A few countries, mainly in East Asia, went through a period of rapid growth from the 1960s that has allowed them to close the gap. This was achieved partly through export-led growth, although other factors were also important.
- However, countries in sub-Saharan Africa have stagnated, and remain on very low incomes.
- Economic growth remains important for all countries, at whatever stage of development.
- There may be costs attached to economic growth, particularly in respect of the environment.

part 3

Chapter 15

Policy: supply or demand?

Previous chapters have shown that there may be a range of macroeconomic policy objectives, from economic growth, full employment, the control of inflation and equilibrium on the current account of the balance of payments, to concerns for the environment and for the distribution of income. Attention now turns to the sorts of policy that might be implemented to try to meet these targets. Policies at the macro-economic level are designed either to affect aggregate demand or aggregate supply, and each will be examined in turn.

Learning outcomes

After studying this chapter, you should:

- understand and be able to evaluate policies that affect aggregate demand, including fiscal, monetary and exchange rate policies
- understand and be able to evaluate policies that affect aggregate supply
- be able to appraise the relative merits of policies applied to the demand and supply sides of the macroeconomy
- be familiar with how macroeconomic policy has been conducted in the UK in recent years

Macroeconomic policy objectives revisited

Chapter 13 identified a number of objectives that might be seen as desirable for the macroeconomy. These can be interpreted in terms of Figure 15.1, which shows an economy in macroeconomic equilibrium.

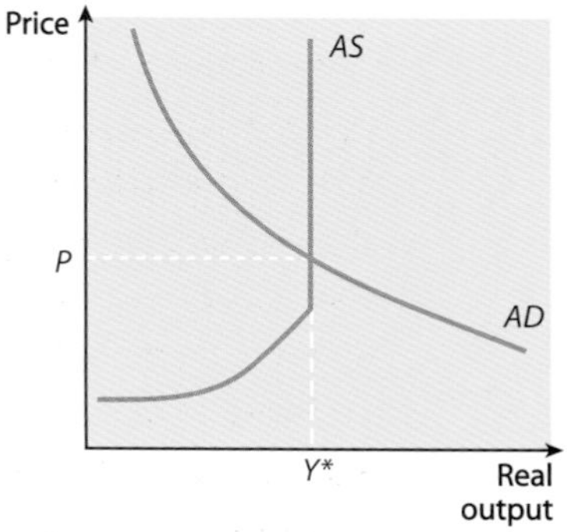

***Figure 15.1** Macroeconomic policy objectives*

Price stability

The first objective discussed related to the control of inflation, and pointed out that prices can increase because of shifts in either aggregate demand or aggregate supply. However, it was also pointed out that *persistent* inflation would arise only in a situation in which money

stock was growing more rapidly than real output. This seems to suggest that one policy response to control persistent inflation would be to control the growth of the money stock.

An increase in money stock affects aggregate demand, shifting the aggregate demand curve to the right and causing prices to rise in an attempt to regain macroeconomic equilibrium. Thus, attempts to control inflation can be interpreted as attempts to create stability in the overall equilibrium price level.

Full employment

A second macroeconomic policy objective is full employment, which occurs at Y^* in Figure 15.1. Such policy will be needed if the aggregate demand curve is positioned well to the left in Figure 15.1, so that macroeconomic equilibrium occurs at less than the full-employment level of real output. This in turn suggests that the policy needed to restore full employment should be aimed at altering the position of the aggregate demand curve in order to bring the economy back to Y^*.

Balance of payments

Policy-makers need to be aware of the dangers of a prolonged and substantial deficit in the balance of payments current account, which can have long-run effects on the ownership pattern of UK assets. If these assets are sold to foreigners, their sale will have a long-run effect on the aggregate supply curve. However, the deficit is caused by an imbalance between the components of aggregate demand, so in a sense the current account objective is related to both aggregate supply and aggregate demand. In effect, the need to achieve current account balance acts as a constraint on attempts to meet other policy objectives, so it is the trade-offs that are of greatest importance in this case.

Economic growth

The achievement of economic growth is a long-term objective, the aim of which is to increase the economy's productive capacity. With respect to Figure 15.1, this can be interpreted in terms of policies affecting the *position* of the aggregate supply curve; in other words, economic growth occurs when the aggregate supply curve moves to the right. Thus, in order to influence the economic growth rate of a country, economists need to look for policies that can affect aggregate supply.

Demand-side policies

Policies that aim to influence an economy's aggregate demand are designed either to stabilise the level of output and employment or to stabilise the price level. The prime focus is thus on the short-run position of the macroeconomy. The two major categories of policy are fiscal policy and monetary policy.

Key term

fiscal policy: decisions made by the government on its expenditure, taxation and borrowing

Fiscal policy

The term fiscal policy covers a range of policy measures that affect government expenditures and revenues.

In Figure 15.2 macroeconomic equilibrium is initially at the intersection of aggregate supply (*AS*) and the initial aggregate demand curve (AD_0), so that real output is at Y_0, which is below the full-employment level of output at Y^*. As government expenditure is one of the components of aggregate demand, an increase in such expenditure moves the aggregate demand curve from AD_0 to AD_1. In response, the economy moves to a new equilibrium, in which the overall price level has risen to P_1 but real output has moved to Y_1, which is closer to the full-employment level Y^*.

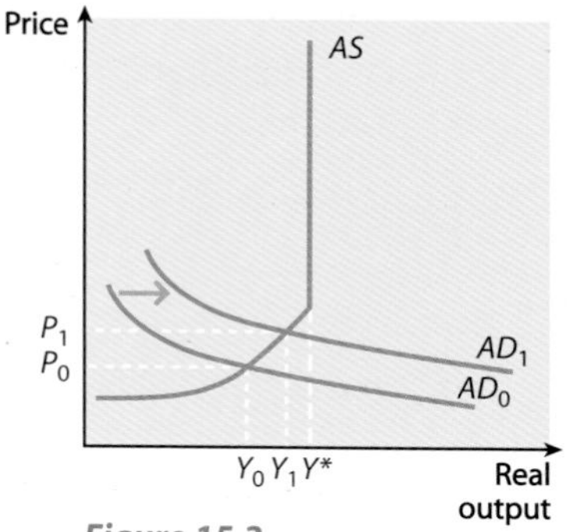

Figure 15.2
The use of fiscal policy

In this scenario government expenditure is treated as an injection into the circular flow, and it will be reinforced by a multiplier effect. In the present context, an increase in government expenditure is effective in raising the level of real output in the economy, although some of the increase is dissipated in the form of an increase in the overall level of prices. Notice that such a move cannot be interpreted as 'economic growth' *per se*, as economists reserve that term for a situation in which there is an increase in the full-employment (potential capacity) level of real output.

This kind of policy is effective only if the aggregate demand curve intersects the aggregate supply curve in the upward-sloping segment of *AS*. If the economy is already at the full-employment level of output, an increase in aggregate demand merely results in a higher overall level of prices. The effective use of such policy thus requires policy-makers to have good information about the current state of the economy; in particular, they need to know whether the economy is at or below full employment. Otherwise, the results could be damaging for the price stability target.

Although the focus of the discussion so far has been on government expenditure, fiscal policy also refers to taxation. In fact, the key issue in considering fiscal policy is the *balance* between government expenditure and government revenue, as it is this balance that affects the position of aggregate demand directly.

An increase in the **government budget deficit** (or a decrease in the **government budget surplus**) thus moves the aggregate demand curve to the right. The budget deficit may arise either from an increase in expenditure or from a decrease in taxation, although the two have some differential effects.

Key term

government budget deficit (surplus): the balance between government expenditure and revenue

To a certain extent, the government budget deficit changes automatically, without active intervention from the government. If the economy goes into a period of recession, unemployment benefit payments will rise, thereby increasing government expenditure. At the same time tax revenues will decrease, partly because people who lose their jobs no longer pay income tax. In addition, people whose income is reduced — perhaps because they no longer work overtime — also pay less tax. This is reinforced by the progressive nature of the income tax system, which means that people pay lower rates of tax at lower levels of income. Furthermore, VAT receipts will fall if people are spending less on goods and services. The opposite effects will be evident in a boom period, preventing the economy from overheating; for example, tax revenues will tend to increase during the boom, and the government will therefore need to make fewer payments of social security benefits. By such **automatic stabilisers,** government expenditure automatically rises during a recession and falls during a boom.

Key term

automatic stabilisers: effects by which government expenditure automatically adjusts to offset the effects of recession and boom without the need for active intervention

In the past there was a tendency for governments to use fiscal policy in a discretionary way in order to influence the path of the economy. Indeed, there have been accusations that governments have sometimes, in some countries, used fiscal policy to create a 'feel-good' factor in the run-up to a general election by allowing the economy to boom as the election approaches, only to impose a clamp-down afterwards.

Such intervention has been shown to be damaging to the long-run path of the economy through its effect on inflation. Furthermore, there are other problems with using fiscal policy in this way. Apart from anything else, it takes time to collect data about the performance of the economy, so its *current* state is never known for certain. Because the economy responds quite sluggishly to policy change, it is often the case that the policy comes into effect just when the economy is already turning around of its own accord. This is potentially destabilising, and can do more harm than good.

Exercise 15.1

Use *AS/AD* analysis to analyse the effect of an expansionary fiscal policy on the equilibrium level of real output and the overall price level. Undertake this exercise with different initial positions along the aggregate supply curve, first analysing an economy that begins at full employment and then one in which aggregate demand creates an equilibrium that is below full employment. Discuss the differences in your results.

Fiscal policy in the UK

If the government spends more than it raises in revenue, the resulting deficit has to be financed in some way. The government deficit is the difference between public sector spending and revenues, and is known as the *Public Sector Net Cash Requirement* (PSNCR), which until 1999 was known as the *Public Sector Borrowing Requirement* (PSBR). Part of the PSNCR is covered by borrowing, and the government closely monitors its *net borrowing.* Over time, such borrowing leads to *net debt,* which is the accumulation of past borrowing. Figure 15.3 shows public sector net debt as a percentage of GDP. The government has aimed to keep this below 40% — and was successful in achieving this for the period shown.

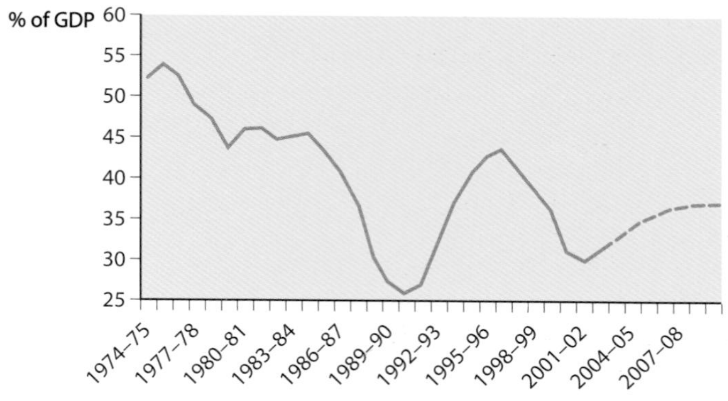

***Figure 15.3** Public sector net debt (% of GDP)*

Source: HM Treasury (projections from 2004/05 onwards).

In 1998 the UK government issued its *Code for Fiscal Stability*, which established its objectives for fiscal policy and the rules under which it would operate. The Treasury set these out in the *Budget 2004* statement as follows:

> The Government's fiscal policy objectives are:
> - over the medium term, to ensure sound public finances and that spending and taxation impact fairly within and between generations; and
> - over the short term, to support monetary policy and, in particular, to allow the automatic stabilisers to help smooth the path of the economy

This highlights two major concerns of the government that represent a change in practice. First, there is a concern for the long-run effects of policy on spending and borrowing. It has come to be recognised that sustainable economic growth has to take into account the needs of future generations. The government therefore has taken the view that its current spending should be met out of current revenues, and that only investment for the future should be met through borrowing.

The second important commitment is to use fiscal policy as a *support* to monetary policy. In other words, monetary policy is seen as the most important way of influencing the macroeconomy, and, although the automatic stabilisers are allowed to cut in, there is no intention of using discretionary policy. This clear statement is intended to increase the credibility of government policy by indicating its refusal to take action that could destabilise the macroeconomy.

This suggests that fiscal policy has two kinds of effect. In the first place, the automatic stabilisers help to regulate the economy over the cycle by allowing aggregate demand to be affected by changes in the government budget deficit during the cycle.

The second one is a supply-side effect. By improving the credibility of government policy, and by ensuring that the macroeconomy is not destabilised by inappropriate interventions, it is hoped that the private sector will have more confidence in the future state of the economy. Such confidence may then affect the amount of investment that firms will be prepared to undertake. This would then shift aggregate supply in the long run.

Summary

- Fiscal policy is concerned with the decisions made by government about its expenditure, taxation and borrowing.
- As government expenditure is an autonomous component of aggregate demand, an increase in expenditure will shift the *AD* curve to the right.
- If *AD* intersects *AS* in the vertical segment of *AS*, the effect of the increase in aggregate demand is felt only in prices.
- However, if the initial equilibrium is below the full-employment level, the shift in *AD* will lead to an increase in both equilibrium real output and the overall price level.
- In fact, it is net spending that it is important, so government decisions on taxation are also significant.
- The government budget deficit (surplus) is the difference between government expenditure and revenue.
- The budget deficit varies automatically through the business cycle because of the action of the automatic stabilisers.
- If the government runs a budget deficit, it may need to undertake net borrowing, which over time affects the net debt position.

Monetary policy

Monetary policy is the approach currently favoured by the UK government to stabilise the macroeconomy. It entails the use of monetary variables such as money supply and interest rates to influence aggregate demand.

> ***Key term***
>
> **monetary policy:** decisions made by government regarding monetary variables such as money supply or the interest rate

The prime instrument of monetary policy in recent years has been the interest rate. Through the interest rate, monetary policy affects aggregate demand. At higher interest rates, firms undertake less investment expenditure and households undertake less consumption expenditure. This is partly because when the interest rate is relatively high the cost of borrowing becomes high, and people are discouraged from borrowing for investment or consumption purposes. There are reinforcing effects that operate through the exchange rate if British interest rates are high relative to elsewhere in the world. If the exchange rate rises because of high interest rates, this will reduce the competitiveness of British goods.

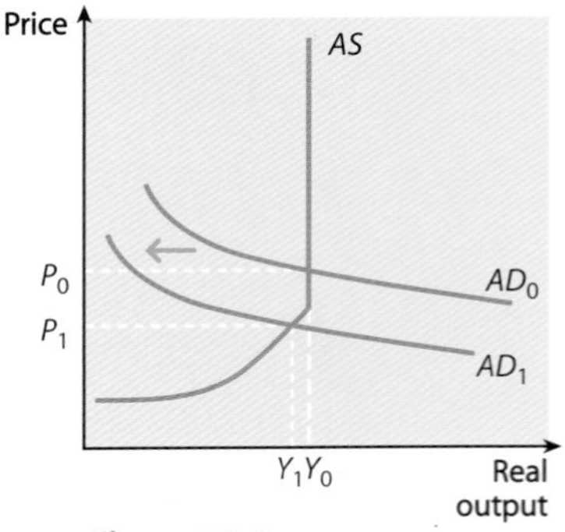

Figure 15.4
The use of monetary policy

Suppose the government believes that the economy is close to full employment and is in danger of overheating. Overheating could push prices up without any resulting benefit in terms of higher real output. An increase in the interest rate will lead to a fall in aggregate demand, thereby relieving the pressure on prices. This is illustrated in Figure 15.4, where the initial position has aggregate demand relatively high at AD_0, real output at the full-employment level Y_0 and the overall price level at P_0. The increase in interest rates shifts aggregate demand to the left, to AD_1. Real output falls slightly to Y_1 and the equilibrium price level falls to P_1.

Monetary policy in the UK

One of the first steps taken by Tony Blair's government after New Labour was first elected in 1997 was to devolve the responsibility for monetary policy to the Bank of England, which was given the task of achieving the government's stated inflation target, initially set at 2.5% for RPIX inflation. As noted in Chapter 11, the target was amended in 2004, when it became 2% p.a. as measured by the CPI.

According to this arrangement, the **Monetary Policy Committee (MPC)** of the Bank of England sets interest rates in such a way as to keep inflation within one percentage point (either way) of the 2% target for CPI inflation. If it fails to achieve this, the Bank has to write an open letter to the chancellor of the exchequer to explain why the target has not been met.

Operationally, the MPC sets the interest rate at which it makes short-term loans to monetary institutions such as banks. This is known as the **repo rate**, which is short for 'sale and repurchase agreement'. The commercial banks tend to use this rate as their own base rate from which they calculate the rates of interest that they charge to their borrowers. Thus, if the MPC changes the repo rate, the commercial banks soon adjust the rates they charge to borrowers. This will vary according to the riskiness of the loans; thus credit cards are charged at a higher rate than mortgages, but all the rates are geared to the base rate set by the commercial banks, and hence indirectly to the repo rate set by the Bank of England.

Key terms

Monetary Policy Committee (MPC): body within the Bank of England responsible for the conduct of monetary policy

repo rate: short for 'sale and repurchase agreement'; the interest rate that is set by the Monetary Policy Committee of the Bank of England in order to influence inflation

Figure 15.5 shows the target rates for RPIX up to December 2003 and for the CPI thereafter, together with the outcomes. Also shown is the repo rate. As you can see,

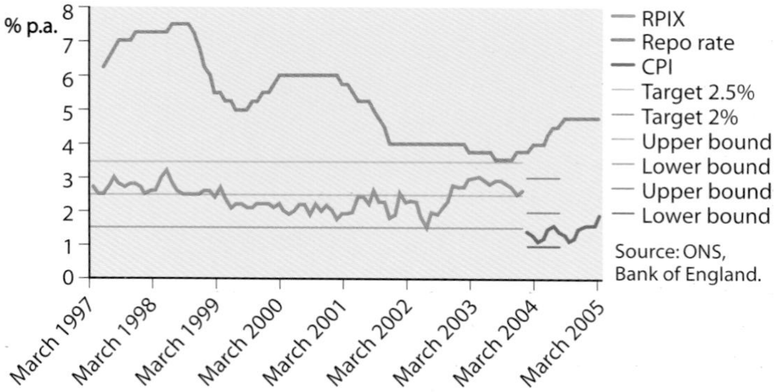

Figure 15.5 UK interest rates and the inflation target, 1997–2005

inflation has remained within the 1% band throughout the period. The association between the repo rate and movements in the inflation rate does not seem very close. This is partly because the relationship between them is obscured to some extent by other influences; it also reflects the fact that the MPC takes into account a wide range of factors when deciding whether to move the repo rate or to leave it as it was in the previous month.

For example, at the October 2004 meeting the MPC discussed developments in:

- financial markets
- the international economy
- money and credit
- demand and output
- the labour market
- costs and prices

All these factors were discussed in some detail before taking a decision on what the repo rate should be. In the interests of transparency, the minutes of the regular MPC meetings are published on the internet — you can see them at **http://www.bankofengland.co.uk/mpc**. By influencing the level of aggregate demand, the MPC can affect the rate of inflation so as to keep it within the target range.

One reason for giving the Bank of England such independence is that it affects the credibility of the policy. If firms and households realise that the government is serious about controlling inflation they will have more confidence in its actions, and will be better able to form expectations about the future path the economy will take. In particular, firms will be encouraged to undertake more investment, and this will have a supply-side effect, shifting the aggregate supply curve to the right in the long run.

Summary

- Monetary policy is concerned with the decisions made by government on monetary variables such as money supply and the interest rate.
- A change in the interest rate influences the level of aggregate demand, through the investment expenditure of firms, the consumption behaviour of households and (indirectly) net exports.
- Since 1997, the Bank of England has been given independent responsibility to set interest rates in order to meet the government's inflation target.
- The Monetary Policy Committee (MPC) of the Bank sets the repo rate, which is then used as a base rate by the commercial banks and other financial institutions.
- Giving independence to the Bank of England in this way increases the credibility of monetary policy.
- If this encourages investment, there may be a long-run impact on aggregate supply.

Policies affecting aggregate supply

Demand-side policies have been aimed primarily at stabilising the macroeconomy in the relatively short run, but with the intention of affecting aggregate supply in the long run, by affecting firms' and households' confidence in the future path of the economy. However, there are also a number of policies that can be used to influence the aggregate supply curve directly.

Chapter 12 indicated that the position of the aggregate supply curve depends primarily on the quantity of factor inputs available in the economy, and on the efficiency with which those factors are utilised. **Supply-side policies** thus focus on affecting these determinants of aggregate supply in order to shift the *AS* curve to the right.

Key term

supply-side policies: a range of measures intended to have a direct impact on aggregate supply — specifically, the potential output capacity of the economy

Investment is one key to this in the long run, and the chapter has already shown how demand-side policies that stabilise the macroeconomy in the short run may also have long-run effects on aggregate supply by encouraging investment.

Education and training

Investment is also needed in human capital, and one form that this can take is education and training. An important supply-side policy therefore takes the form of encouraging workers (and potential workers) to undertake education and training to improve their productivity.

This takes place partly through education in schools and colleges in preparation for work. It is important, therefore, that the curriculum is designed to provide key skills that will be useful in the workplace. However, this does not mean that all education has to be geared directly to providing skills; problem-solving and analytical skills, for example, can be developed through the study of a wide range of disciplines.

Adult education is also important. When the structure of the economy is changing, retraining must be made available to enable workers to move easily between sectors and occupations. This is crucial if structural unemployment is not to become a major problem. For any society – whether industrialised or less-economically developed and needing to reduce its dependence on agriculture – education and skills are necessary to enable workers to switch into new activities in response to structural changes in the economy.

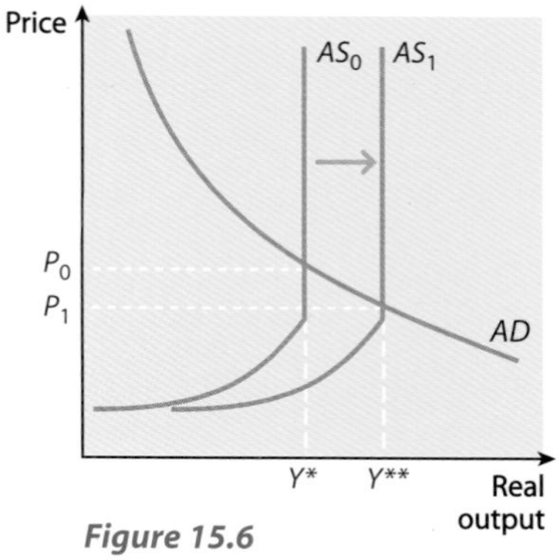

Figure 15.6
A shift in aggregate supply

Figure 15.6 shows how such a policy can affect the aggregate supply curve, moving it from AS_0 to AS_1. This move enables an increase in the potential output capacity of the economy, and it need not be inflationary. Indeed, in the figure the overall price level falls from P_0 to P_1 following the shift in aggregate supply, with real output increasing from Y^* to Y^{**}.

Flexibility of markets

The rationale for including retraining as a supply-side policy rests partly on the argument that this provides for greater flexibility in labour markets, enabling workers to switch between economic activities to improve the overall workings of the economy.

There are other ways of improving market flexibility. One is to limit the power of the trade unions, whose actions can sometimes lead to inflexibility in the labour market, either through resistance to new working practices that could improve productivity or by pushing up wages so that the level of employment is reduced. This issue will be revisited in Chapter 22.

Indeed, maintaining the flexibility of markets is one way in which the macroeconomic stability promoted by disciplined fiscal and monetary policy can improve aggregate supply. Macroeconomic stability enables price signals to work more effectively, as producers are better able to observe changes in relative prices. This can promote allocative efficiency.

The provision of facilities for retraining is an important supply-side policy.

Promotion of competition

Chapter 7 noted that, if firms gain dominance in a market, the pursuit of profits may lead them to use their market position to restrict output and raise prices. Such market dominance arises because of a lack of competition.

In addition, it is possible that in some markets the lack of competition will produce complacency, depriving firms of the incentive to operate at maximum efficiency. This was especially true in the UK for the formerly nationalised industries such as electricity and gas supply, which were widely believed to have operated with widespread productive inefficiency.

Policies that promote competition may thus lead to improvements in both allocative and productive efficiency. This was one of the motivations behind the privatisation drive that began in the 1980s under Margaret Thatcher, and will be explored in Chapter 20. However, it should be noted that there is not wholesale agreement on whether privatisation has invariably led to improvements in efficiency in industries such as the railways or water supply. This too will be examined in Chapter 20.

Unemployment benefits

An important influence on labour supply, particularly for low-income workers, is the level of unemployment benefit. If unemployment benefit is provided at too high a level, it may inhibit labour force participation, in that some workers may opt to live on unemployment benefit rather than take up low-skilled (and low-paid) employment. In such a situation a reduction in unemployment benefit may induce an increase in labour supply, which again will move the aggregate supply curve to the right.

However, such a policy needs to be balanced against the need to provide protection for those who are unable to find employment. It is also important that unemployment benefit is not reduced to such a level that workers are unwilling to leave their jobs to search for better ones, as this may inhibit the flexibility of the labour market.

Incentive effects

Similarly, there are dangers in making the taxation system too progressive. Most people accept that income tax should be progressive — i.e. that those on relatively high incomes should pay a higher rate of tax at than those on low incomes — as a way of redistributing income within society and preventing inequality from becoming extreme. However, there may come a point at which marginal tax rates are so high that a large proportion of additional income is taxed away, reducing incentives for individuals to supply additional effort or labour. This could also have an effect on aggregate supply. Again, however, it is important to balance these incentive effects against the distortion caused by having too much inequality in society.

Exercise 15.2

For each of the following policies, identify whether it is an example of fiscal, monetary or supply-side policy. Discuss how each policy affects either aggregate demand or aggregate supply (or both), and examine its effects on equilibrium real output and the overall price level:

- **a** an increase in government expenditure
- **b** a decrease in the rate of unemployment benefit
- **c** a fall in the rate of interest
- **d** legislation limiting the power wielded by trade unions
- **e** encouragement for more students to attend university
- **f** provision of retraining in the form of adult education
- **g** a reduction in the highest rate of income tax
- **h** measures to break up a concentrated market
- **i** an increase in the repo rate

Relative merits

In the context of the aggregate demand/aggregate supply model, it is clear that demand- and supply-side policies are aimed at achieving rather different objectives.

The primary rationale for monetary and fiscal policies is to stabilise the macroeconomy. In this, fiscal policy has come to take on a subsidiary role, supporting monetary policy. This was not always the case, and there have been periods in which fiscal policy has been used much more actively to try to stimulate the economy. There are still some countries in which such policies are very much the vogue; for example, it has been suggested that much of Latin America's problem with high inflation has stemmed from fiscal indiscipline, although not all Latin American economists accept this argument. The fact that fiscal policy has not always been well implemented does not mean that such policies cannot be valuable tools — but it does warn against misuse.

In the UK, the use of monetary policy with the support of fiscal policy seems to be working reasonably effectively in the early twenty-first century. Furthermore, it seems to be operating in such a way as to complement the supply-side policies. By creating a stable macroeconomic environment, microeconomic markets are able to operate effectively and investment is encouraged, thereby leading to a boost in aggregate supply.

Supply-side policies aim to influence aggregate supply directly, either raising the supply of factor inputs or improving productivity and efficiency.

Summary

- Policies to shift the aggregate supply curve may be used to encourage economic growth.
- Education and training can be viewed as a form of investment in human capital, which is designed to improve the productivity of workers.
- Measures to improve the flexibility of labour and product markets may lead to an overall improvement in productivity and thus may affect aggregate supply.
- Promoting competition can also improve the effectiveness of markets in the economy.
- Incentive effects are an important influence on aggregate supply. For example, if unemployment benefits are set too high this may discourage labour force participation. An over-progressive income taxation structure can also have damaging incentive effects.
- Demand-side and supply-side policies have different objectives. Demand-side policies such as fiscal and monetary policy are aimed primarily at stabilising the economy. Supply-side policies are geared more towards promoting economic growth.
- However, effective stabilisation of the economy may also have long-term effects on aggregate supply.

Review section

In Part 3 attention switched to a consideration of the economy as a whole. This is the part of economics known as *macroeconomics*. The sort of analysis that is employed is similar – similar ways are used of thinking about economic issues. However, the interactions between economic variables at the economy-wide level is rather different than when decisions made by individual economic agents such as households or firms are considered. The following paragraphs review the contents of Chapters 11–15, and highlight some of the key issues. Some sample examination questions are also provided.

Chapter 11 Measuring economic performance

The starting point for the discussion of macroeconomics was an introduction to data on the economic performance of the economy as a whole. The distinction between *real* and *nominal measurements* is very important in this context, as many macroeconomic variables are measured by their money values, so you need to take into account the effects of changing prices. It is especially important to be able to measure the rate of unemployment and the inflation rate, as these are indicators of the buoyancy and stability of the economy. For the long run, it is more important to monitor changes in GDP, and to identify the trend rate of economic growth. The balance of payments, which monitors international transactions, must also be borne in mind when evaluating the performance of the aggregate economy. The circular flow of income, output and expenditure provides a context for the interpretation of GDP, which is also a popular first indicator for comparing living standards between different countries.

Chapter 12 Aggregate demand, aggregate supply and equilibrium output

A key model for analysing the macroeconomy is the *aggregate demand and aggregate supply (AD/AS) model*. In using AD/AS, it is important to remember that the interpretation of the curves is quite different from their microeconomic counterparts, even if superficially they look similar. The shape and position of the aggregate demand curve was seen to depend upon the factors that influence various components of aggregate demand, including households' consumption expenditure and firms' investment, together with government spending and revenue-raising activities, exports and imports. The position of long-run aggregate supply reflects the productive capacity of the economy. Chapter 12 also set out the notion of the *multiplier*, and introduced you to the use of comparative static analysis to investigate changes in aggregate demand and aggregate supply conditions.

Chapter 13 Macroeconomic policy objectives

In evaluating macroeconomic performance, it is natural to think also about the objectives that governments might have for macroeconomic policy. Indeed, the success of macroeconomic policy can be evaluated only if it is known what the government is trying to accomplish. Typical macroeconomic objectives are to achieve:

- *price stability* (a low and stable rate of inflation)
- *full employment* (a low level of unemployment)
- a satisfactory position on the *balance of payments*
- sustainable *economic growth*
- protection of vulnerable groups in society through *income redistribution*

Of these targets, probably the most important in the long run is *economic growth*, which directly affects the standard of living of all people in the country. However, the pursuit of economic growth has to be tempered by a consideration for the *environment*, which is why the target is listed as *sustainable* economic growth. You need to be aware that it may not always be possible to achieve all these targets simultaneously, as they may sometimes conflict with each other.

Chapter 14 Economic growth

As economic growth is seen as such an important target for the long-term wellbeing of the economy, Chapter 14 was devoted entirely to its analysis. This entailed understanding the meaning of economic growth and *productivity*, and an analysis of the factors that can affect the rate of economic growth. Of especial significance in this context is the role of *investment*. Investment is seen as a necessary prerequisite for economic growth, as it is only through investment in capital that the productive capacity of an economy can be raised. It was also pointed out in this chapter that, although economic growth is very important, it does impose some costs on society, and sustainability must be kept in mind.

Chapter 15 Policy: supply or demand?

Having identified the principal objectives of policy, the final chapter in Part 3 considered the policy instruments available for governments trying to meet their targets. *Fiscal*, *monetary* and *exchange rate policies* are used in order to affect aggregate demand, whereas *supply-side policies* tend to operate at the microeconomic level. The chapter appraised the relative merits of demand- and supply-side policies and provided some commentary on how policy has been conducted in the UK in recent years.

Preparing for the examination

Data-response is again crucial for Unit 3 ('Managing the Economy'). It is important to be well familiar with the meanings and importance of the key macroeconomic indicators, as can be seen in the sample questions presented below. It is good to prepare by getting plenty of practice. You do not need to rely only on past questions for this: you can also use the serious newspapers, which often provide commentary on recent announcements of key economic indicators. Alternatively, read *The Economist*, or use the *Data Supplement* of the *Economic Review*; this not only provides some tables of data about the economy, but also gives hints on how to use and interpret the data and some guidance on graphical and arithmetic techniques that you may need to use in tackling the questions.

Although some people are daunted by the sight of data, this is a key skill for understanding the world you live in, and the more you practise, the less daunting it will become.

It is important to use your time wisely. In order to do this effectively, be aware of the relative mark allocations that are given for different parts of the question. In particular, make sure you keep enough time to answer the last question fully. As with Unit 2, only one of the following is to be tackled.

Data-response question P3.1

Unemployment and supply-side policies

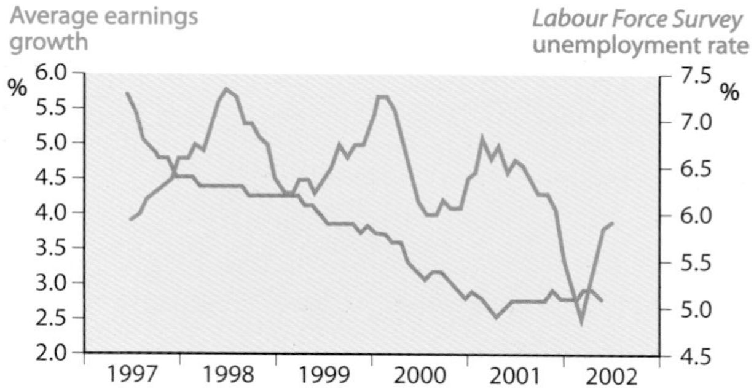

Figure P3.1 Average earnings growth and unemployment, UK, 1997–2002

Source: *Daily Telegraph*, 15 August 2002.

Extract 1

According to the *Labour Force Survey* measure, unemployment was 1.54 million during the three months to June 2002, a rate of 5.1%. The alternative claimant count measure of unemployment fell by 3100 to 949 600 in July 2002, a rate of 3.2%. At the same time, the number of people in work in the UK rose to a record 28.6 million, the highest figure since records began in 1979. The data suggest that the UK may be near to full employment.

However, many of the new jobs created are part-time and are widely believed to have come in the public sector, whereas manufacturing has continued to shed jobs. The number of people employed in the production industries was 174 000 lower than in the same period a year ago.

Why is Britain's manufacturing industry in such a mess? Some continue to blame the high level of the sterling exchange rate. However, part of the explanation may be the low level of British labour productivity. A controversial new study by the consultants McKinsey argues that the reason for this is bad management.

Strikingly, British-based companies with foreign owners manage far higher productivity than those with local bosses. The average foreign-owned company does 60% better; US-owned ones nearly 90%. However, these figures should be viewed with caution: multinationals tend to have higher productivity than domestic firms and this is as likely to be true in the USA as in the UK. Other studies have suggested that the UK is in fact narrowing the productivity gap with its major trading partners.

Source: adapted from *The Economist*, 12 October 2002.

---

a With reference to Figure P3.1,

(i) Explain what is meant by the *Labour Force Survey* measure of unemployment. *(2 marks)*

(ii) Identify the changes in the level of average earnings in 2002. *(3 marks)*

(iii) Using a carefully labelled diagram, explain the likely significance of the average earnings data in 2002 for the level of aggregate demand and the equilibrium level of real output. *(5 marks)*

b Examine how a high sterling exchange rate may lead to unemployment in manufacturing (lines 11–12). *(6 marks)*

c **(i)** Define labour productivity. *(3 marks)*

(ii) Explain the significance to the UK current account of the balance of payments of 'narrowing the productivity gap with its major trading partners' (lines 20–21). *(6 marks)*

d Evaluate the use of supply-side policies in raising the level of real output in an economy which is near to full employment. *(15 marks)*

Data-response question P3.2

UK macroeconomic indicators

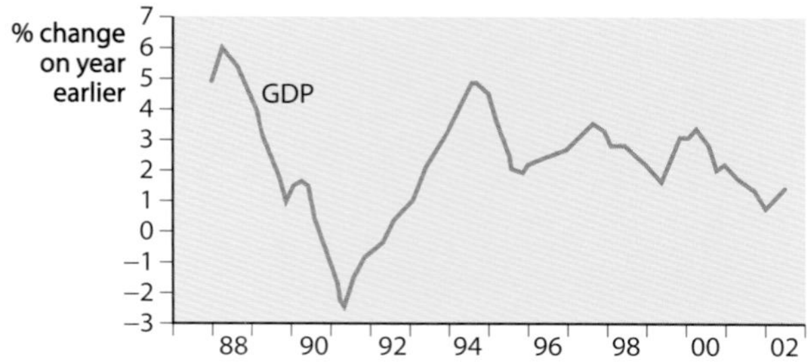

Figure P3.2 *Real GDP growth, UK, 1988–2002*

Source: *The Sunday Times*, 10 November 2002.

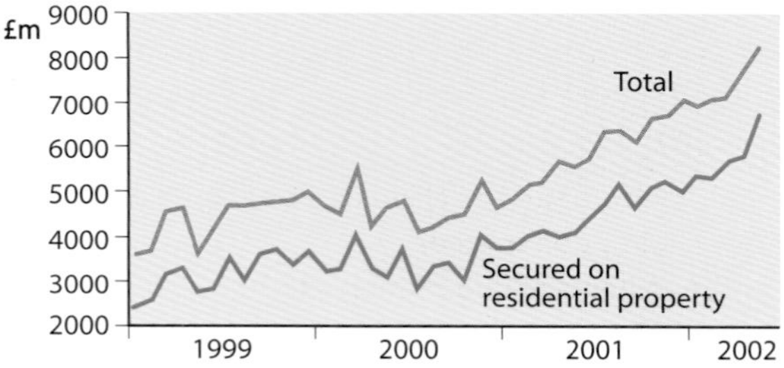

Figure P3.3 *Net lending to individuals, UK, 1999–2002*

Source: *The Financial Times*, 17 July 2002.

Table P3.1 *Some economic indicators for the UK, 1999–2002*

	Average earnings growth (%)	Index of manufacturing output (1995 = 100)	Retail sales growth (%)	Unemployment rate (%, claimant count)
1999	4.8	103.1	3.5	4.2
2000	4.6	105.2	4.5	3.6
2001	4.3	102.8	6.0	3.2
2002	3.0	98.7	6.1	3.2

Extract 2

The house price boom is accelerating, with prices increasing at their fastest rate for two years, according to government figures released this morning. This suggests that the next move in interest rates could be upward.

The news serves as a worrying reminder of the dilemma facing the Bank of England's Monetary Policy Committee, which indicated its confusion yesterday by saying it would be ready to cut interest rates if necessary rather than raise them.

Economists have warned that raising interest rates, while reducing the threat of inflation, would threaten real GDP growth and might raise the level of unemployment.

But they have also warned that reducing interest rates could turn the housing boom into a bubble and then into a crash. House prices rose by 13.5% during the past year – fast enough to be a major cause for concern as far as the Bank's inflation target is concerned.

Management of the economy has become more difficult with imbalances between performances in the manufacturing and services sectors. While manufacturing output is forecast to decline in 2002, the service sector is growing strongly.

Source: adapted from *The Financial Times*, 8 August 2002.

a **(i)** Explain what is meant by 'real GDP growth' (Figure P3.2). *(3 marks)*

(ii) Calculate the percentage change in manufacturing output between 2000 and 2001. *(2 marks)*

(iii) With reference to Table P3.1, explain what happened to average earnings over the period shown. *(3 marks)*

b Using an aggregate demand and supply diagram, examine the likely effect of a sharp rise in house prices on the UK price level. *(6 marks)*

c **(i)** With reference to Table P3.1, why might the claimant unemployment be significant to the Monetary Policy Committee? *(5 marks)*

(ii) Explain the significance of two items of information, other than those shown in the data, that would help the Monetary Policy Committee decide whether to change interest rates. *(6 marks)*

d To what extent is fiscal policy likely to be more effective than monetary policy in dealing with the imbalances in the economy represented by the information provided in the data and extract? *(15 marks)*

These questions were taken from examinations set for the Edexcel AS Economics examination for Unit 3 – Managing the economy. We are grateful to London Qualifications for permission to reproduce them here.

Industrial economics

Part 4

part 4

Chapter 16

Firms and their motivations

In studying AS economics, you will have come to realise the importance of firms in the operation of markets. Industrial economics looks more closely at the decisions made by firms, and the implications of those decisions for the effectiveness of markets in allocating resources within an economy. This chapter examines some of the key concepts that are needed for this important part of economic analysis. In studying this chapter, you may find it helpful to review some of the material that has appeared in earlier chapters.

Learning outcomes

After studying this chapter, you should:

- be aware of the reason for the birth of firms, and the desire for their growth
- be familiar with alternative ways in which firms grow
- be able to distinguish between horizontal, vertical and conglomerate mergers
- be aware of the need for firms to grow if they wish to compete in global markets
- be familiar with short- and long-run cost curves and their characteristics
- understand the significance of economies of scale in the context of the growth of firms
- understand the profit maximisation motive and its implications for firms' behaviour
- be aware of the principal–agent issue, and its influence on the motivations of firms
- be familiar with alternative motivations for firms and how these affect decision-making
- be able to interpret productive and allocative efficiency in terms of a firm's cost curves

What is a firm?

One way of answering this question is to say that **firms** exist in order to organise production: they bring together various factors of production, and organise the production process in order to produce output.

Key term

firm: an organisation that brings together factors of production in order to produce output

There are various forms that the organisation of a firm can take. The simplest is perhaps that of *sole proprietor*, in which the owner of the firm also runs the firm. Examples would be an independent newsagent/corner shop, plumber or hairdresser, where the owner is liable for the debts of the enterprise, but also gets to keep any profits.

In some professions firms are operated on a *partnership* basis. Examples here are doctors, dentists and solicitors. Profits are shared between the partners, as are debts, according to the contract drawn up between them.

Private *joint stock companies* are owned by shareholders, each of whom has contributed funds to the business by buying shares. However, each shareholder's responsibility for the debts of the company is limited to the amount he/she paid for the shares. Profits are distributed to shareholders as dividends. The shares in a private company of this kind are not traded on the stock exchange, and the firms tend to be controlled by the shareholders themselves. Many local businesses are operated on this basis, for example double glazing installation firms or computer consultancies. If you look in your local yellow pages, you will see that some firms indicate that they are this sort of company by the 'Ltd' after their name, which indicates that they have *limited liability*, meaning that the liability of shareholders for the firm's debt is limited to the amount that they paid for their shares.

Firms that are owned by shareholders but are listed on the stock exchange are *public joint stock companies*. Again, the liability of the shareholders is limited to the amount they have paid for their shares. However, such companies are required to publish their annual accounts and also to publish an annual report to their shareholders. Day-to-day decision-making is normally delegated to a board of directors, appointed at the annual general meeting (AGM) of the shareholders. Examples of this sort of company abound – Tesco, HSBC, BP and so on. Again, your local yellow pages will reveal the names of some companies with 'plc' after the name, standing for *public limited company*.

Later in the chapter you will see that the way in which a firm is organised may influence the way in which decisions are taken on key economic issues. However, for now all such forms of organisation will be referred to simply as 'firms'.

The nature of the activity being undertaken by the firm and its scale of operation will help to determine its most efficient form of organisation. For firms to operate successfully, they must minimise the transaction costs of undertaking business.

The growth of firms

A feature of the economic environment in recent years has been the increasing size of firms. Some, e.g. Microsoft, Wal-Mart and Shell, have become giants. Why is this happening?

Firms may wish to increase their size in order to gain market power within the industry in which they are operating. A firm that can gain market share, and perhaps become dominant in the market, may be able to exercise some control

over the price of its product, and thereby influence the market. However, firms may wish to grow for other reasons, which will be explained later in the chapter.

Organic growth

Some firms grow simply by being successful. For example, a successful marketing campaign may increase a firm's market share, and provide it with a flow of profits that can be reinvested to expand the firm even more. Some firms may choose to borrow in order to finance their growth, perhaps by issuing shares (equity).

Such *organic growth* may encounter limits. A firm may find that its product market is saturated, so that it can grow further only at the expense of other firms in the market. If its competitors are able to maintain their own market shares, the firm may need to diversify its production activities by finding new markets for its existing product, or perhaps offering new products.

There are many examples of such activity. Tesco, the leading UK supermarket, has launched itself into new markets by opening branches overseas, and has also introduced a range of new products, including financial services, to its existing customers. Microsoft has famously used this strategy, by selling first its internet browser and later its media player as part of its Windows operating system, in an attempt to persuade existing customers to buy its new products.

Diversification may be a dangerous strategy: moving into a market in which the firm is inexperienced and existing rival firms already know the business may pose quite a challenge. In such circumstances much may depend on the quality of the management team.

Mergers and acquisitions

Instead of growing organically — i.e. based on the firm's own resources — many firms choose to grow by merging with, or acquiring, other firms. The distinction here is that an *acquisition* (or takeover) may be hostile, whereas a *merger* may be the coming together of equals, with each firm committed to forming a single entity.

Growth in this way has a number of advantages; for example, it may overcome the management problem, and allow some rationalisation to take place. On the other hand, firms tend to develop their own culture, or way of doing things, and some mergers have foundered because of an incompatibility of corporate cultures.

Key term

horizontal merger: a merger between two firms at the same stage of production in the same industry

Mergers (or acquisitions) can be of three different types. A **horizontal merger** is a merger between firms operating in the same industry and at the same stage of the production process, for example the merger of two car assembly firms. The car industry has been characterised by such mergers, including the takeover of Rover by BMW in 1994 and the merger of Daimler-Benz with Chrysler in 1998.

A horizontal merger can affect the degree of market concentration, because after the merger takes place there are fewer independent firms operating in the market. This may increase the market power held by the new firm.

A car assembly plant merging with a tyre producer, on the other hand, is an example of a **vertical merger**. A real-life example of this is the brewing company Bass, which has acquired a chain of pubs in the UK.

Vertical mergers may be either upstream or downstream. If a car company merges with a component supplier, that is a backward integration, as it involves merging with a firm that is involved in an earlier part of the production process. Forward integration entails merging in the other direction, as for example if the car assembly plant decided to merge with a large distributor.

The coming together of pharmaceutical giants GlaxoWellcome and SmithKline Beecham is an example of a horizontal merger.

Key terms

vertical merger: a merger between two firms in the same industry, but at different stages of the production process

conglomerate merger: a merger between two firms operating in different markets

Vertical integration may allow rationalisation of the process of production. Car producers often work on a just-in-time basis, ordering components for the production line only as they are required. This creates a potential vulnerability, because if the supply of components fails then production has to stop. If a firm's component supplier is part of the firm rather than an independent operator, this may improve the reliability of, and confidence in, the just-in-time process, and in consequence may make life more difficult for rival firms. However, vertical mergers have different implications for concentration and market power.

The third type of merger involves the merging of two firms that are operating in quite different markets or industries. For example, companies like Unilever or Nestlé operate in a wide range of different markets, partly as a result of acquisitions.

One argument in favour of **conglomerates** is that they reduce the risks faced by firms. Many markets follow fluctuations that are in line with the business cycle but are not always fully synchronised. By operating in a number of markets that are on different cycles, the firm can even out its activity overall. However, it is not necessarily an efficient way of doing business, as the different activities undertaken may require different skills and specialisms. In recent years conglomerate mergers seem to have become less popular.

Exercise 16.1

Categorise each of the following as a horizontal, vertical or conglomerate merger:

a the merger of a firm operating an instant coffee factory with a coffee plantation

b the merger of a brewer and a bakery

c the merger of a brewer and a crisp manufacturer

d the merger of a soft drinks manufacturer with a chain of fast food outlets

e the merger of an internet service provider with a film studio

f a merger between two firms producing tyres for cars

Globalisation

Globalisation, which has been on the increase since the 1980s, has had a significant effect on the growth of firms. In particular, transactions have become quicker and easier with the development of transport and communication technology. The whole process of marketing goods and services has been revolutionised with the spread of the internet and the World Wide Web.

Key term

multinational corporation: a firm that conducts its operations in a number of countries

In some markets this has led to the growth of giant firms operating in global markets. The **multinational corporations** will make a number of appearances in the following chapters of the book, and their increasing role in the global economy will be evaluated. One motive for mergers and acquisitions has been defensive, i.e. to try to compete with other large firms in the global market.

Summary

- A firm is an organisation that exists to bring together factors of production in order to produce goods or services.
- Firms range, in the complexity of their organisation, from sole proprietors to public limited companies.
- Firms may undergo organic growth, building upon their own resources and past profits.
- If limited by the size of their markets, firms may diversify into new markets or products.
- Firms may also grow through horizontal, vertical or conglomerate mergers and acquisitions.
- Globalisation has enabled the growth of giant firms operating on a global scale.

Costs facing firms

To understand why firms wish to grow, you will need to examine the costs of production that they face, as the pursuit of economies of scale (introduced in Chapter 7) provides one of the major motivations for growth — although there are other reasons, as will be explained later in the chapter. This section focuses on the relationship between costs and the level of output produced by a firm. Diagrams will illustrate this relationship using a series of cost curves that apply in various circumstances.

For simplicity, it is assumed that the firm under consideration produces a single product – analysis of conglomerates is a little more complicated. It is also assumed that the firm uses just two factors of production – labour (L) and capital (K). This seems a stronger assumption, but again is made for simplicity. 'Labour' and 'capital' can be thought of as the representative factors of production, although in real life a firm organises a whole range of factors of production – including different types of labour and capital.

These two factors are representative in a particular way. In the short run the firm faces limited flexibility. Varying the quantity of labour input the firm uses may be relatively straightforward – it can increase the use of overtime, or hire more workers, fairly quickly. However, varying the amount of capital the firm has at its disposal may take longer. For example, it takes time to commission a new piece of machinery, or to build a new factory – or a Channel Tunnel! Hence labour is regarded as a flexible factor and capital as a fixed factor. This may not always be correct; for example, it may sometimes be easier to bring in new computers than to train new staff to use them. However, in this chapter 'labour' will be regarded as flexible and 'capital' as inflexible, and the definitions of the **short run** and **long run** are based on this assumption.

The production function

As the firm changes its volume of production, it needs to vary the inputs of its factors of production. Thus, the total amount of output produced in a given period depends upon the inputs of labour and capital used in the production process. Of course, there are many different ways of combining labour and capital inputs, some combinations being more efficient than others. The **production function** summarises the technically most efficient combinations for any given output level.

The nature of technology in an industry will determine the way in which output varies with the quantity of inputs. However, one thing is certain. If the firm increases the amount of inputs of the variable factor (labour) while holding constant the input of the other factor (capital), it will gradually derive less additional output per unit of labour for each further increase. This is known as the **law of diminishing returns**, and is one of the few 'laws' in economics. It is a *short-run* concept, as it relies on the assumption that capital is fixed.

Key terms

short run: the period over which a firm is free to vary the input of one of its factors of production (labour), but faces a fixed input of the other (capital)

long run: the period over which the firm is able to vary the inputs of all its factors of production

production function: function embodying information about technically efficient ways of combining labour and capital to produce output

law of diminishing returns: law stating that if a firm increases its inputs of one factor of production while holding inputs of the other factor fixed, it will eventually derive diminishing marginal returns from the variable factor

It can readily be seen why this should be the case. Suppose a firm has 10 computer programmers working in an office, using 10 computers. The 11th worker may add some extra output, as the workers may be able to 'hot-desk' and take their coffee breaks at different times. The 12th worker may also add some extra output, perhaps by keeping the printers stocked with paper. However, if the firm keeps adding programmers without increasing the number of computers, each extra worker will be adding less additional output to the office. Indeed, the 20th worker may add nothing at all, being unable to get access to a computer.

Figure 16.1 illustrates the short-run relationship between labour input and total physical product (TPP_L), with capital held constant. The curvature of the TPP_L relationship reflects the law of diminishing returns: as labour input increases, the amount of additional output produced gets smaller. An increase in the amount of capital available will raise the amount of output produced for any given labour input, so the TPP_L will shift upwards, as shown in Figure 16.2.

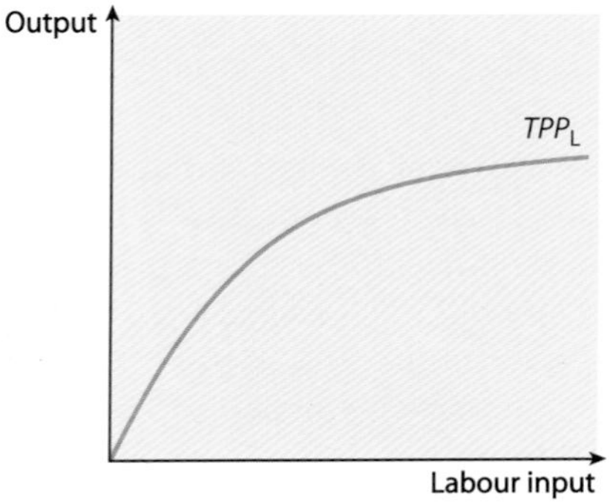

Figure 16.1 A short-run production function

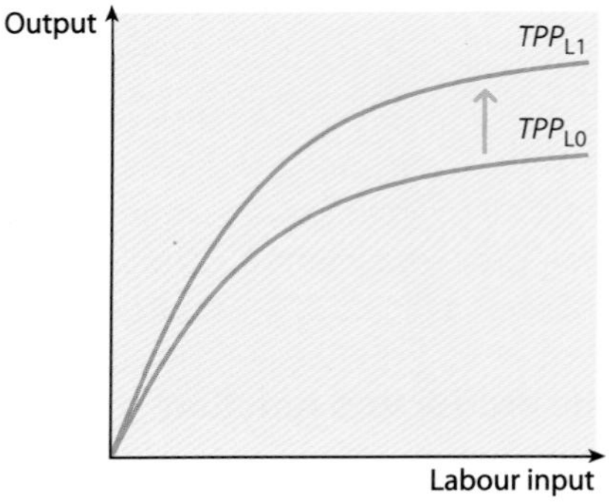

Figure 16.2 The effect of an increase in capital

The production function thus carries information about the physical relationship between the inputs of the factors of production and the physical quantity of output. With this information and a knowledge of the prices the firm must pay for its inputs of the factors of production, it is possible to map out the way in which costs will change with the level of output.

Costs in the short run

Because the firm cannot vary some of its inputs in the short run, some costs may be regarded as fixed, and some as variable. In this short run, some **fixed costs** are **sunk costs**, i.e. costs that the firm cannot avoid paying even if it chooses to produce no output. Total costs are the sum of fixed and **variable costs**:

total costs = total fixed costs + total variable costs

Total costs will increase as the firm increases the volume of production, because more of the variable

Key terms

fixed costs: costs that do not vary with the level of output

sunk costs: short-run costs that cannot be recovered if the firm closes down

variable costs: costs that vary with the level of output

input is needed to increase output. The way in which the costs will vary depends on the nature of the production function, and on whether the prices of labour or capital alter as output increases.

A common assumption made by economists is that in the short run, at very low levels of output, total costs will rise more slowly than output, but that as diminishing returns set in total costs will accelerate, as shown in Figure 16.3.

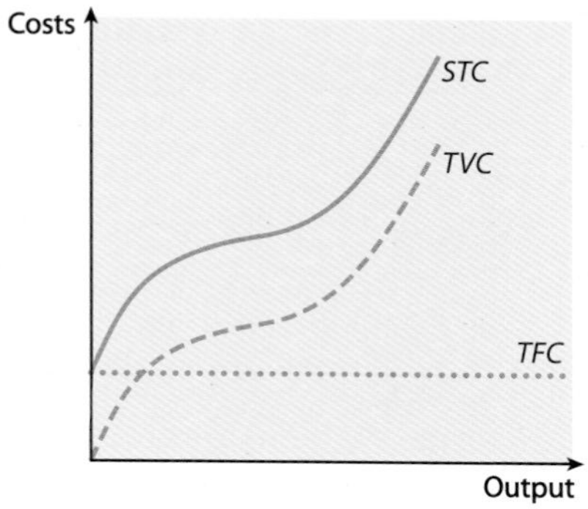

Figure 16.3
Costs in the short run

Total, marginal and average costs

An important relationship exists between total, marginal and **average costs**. Remember from Chapter 6 that **marginal cost** is the additional cost of producing an additional unit of output.

Key terms

average cost: total cost divided by the quantity produced

marginal cost: the cost of producing an additional unit of output

Table 16.1 provides an arithmetic example to illustrate the relationship between these different aspects of costs. The firm represented here faces fixed costs of £225 per week. The table shows the costs of production for up to 6000 units of the firm's product per week. Column (3) shows total variable costs of production: you can see that these rise quite steeply as the volume of production increases. Adding fixed and variable costs gives the short-run total costs (*STC*) at each output level. This is shown in column (4), which is the sum of columns (2) and (3).

(1) Output ('000 units per week)	(2) Fixed costs	(3) Total variable costs	(4) Short-run total costs (2) + (3)	(5) Short-run average total cost (4)/(1)	(6) Short-run marginal cost Δ(4)/Δ(1)	(7) Short-run average variable cost (3)/(1)	(8) Short-run average fixed cost (2)/(1)
1	225	85	310	310		85	225
					65		
2	225	150	375	187.5		75	112.5
					60		
3	225	210	435	145		70	75
					90		
4	225	300	525	131.25		75	56.25
					175		
5	225	475	700	140		95	45
					395		
6	225	870	1095	182.5		145	37.5

Table 16.1 The short-run relationship between output and costs (in £s)

The short-run average cost (*SATC* – column (5)) is calculated as short-run total cost divided by output. To calculate short-run marginal cost, you need to work out the additional cost of producing an extra unit of output at each output level. This is calculated as the change in costs divided by the change in output (Δ column (4) divided by Δ column (1), where Δ means the 'change in').

Finally, average variable costs (*SAVC*, i.e. column (3)/column (1)) and average fixed costs (*SAFC*, i.e. column (2)/column (1)) can be calculated.

These relationships are plotted in Figure 16.4, which shows how they relate to each other. First, notice that short-run average total costs (*SATC*) takes on a U-shape. This is the form often assumed in economic analysis. *SATC* is the sum of average fixed and variable costs (*SAFC* and *SAVC*, respectively). Average fixed costs slope downwards throughout — this is because fixed costs do not vary with the level of output, so as output increases *SAFC* must always get smaller, as the fixed costs are spread over more and more units of output. However, *SAVC* also shows a U-shape, and it is this that gives the U-shape to *SATC*.

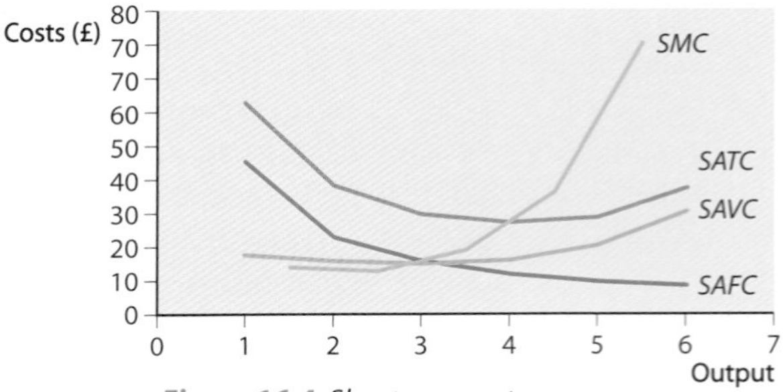

Figure 16.4 *Short-run cost curves*

A very important aspect of Figure 16.4 is that the short-run marginal cost cuts both *SAVC* and *SATC* at their minimum points. This is always the case. If you think about this for a moment, you will realise that it makes good sense. If you are adding on something that is greater than the average, the average must always increase. For a firm, when the marginal cost of producing an additional unit of a good is higher than the average cost of doing so, the average cost must rise. If the marginal is the same as the average, then the average will not change. This is quite simply an arithmetic property of the average and the marginal, and always holds true. So when you draw the average and marginal cost curves for a firm, the marginal cost curve will always cut average cost at the minimum point of average cost. Another way of viewing marginal cost is as the *slope* or gradient of the total cost curve.

Remember that the short-run cost curves show the relationship between the volume of production and costs under the assumption that the quantity of capital is fixed, so that in order to change output the firm has to vary the amount of labour. The *position* of the cost curves thus depends on the quantity of capital. In other words, there is a short-run average total cost curve for each given level of capital.

Costs in the long run

In the long run, a firm is able to vary both capital and labour. It is thus likely to choose the level of capital that is appropriate for the level of output that it expects to produce. Figure 16.5 shows a number of short-run average total cost curves corresponding to different expected output levels.

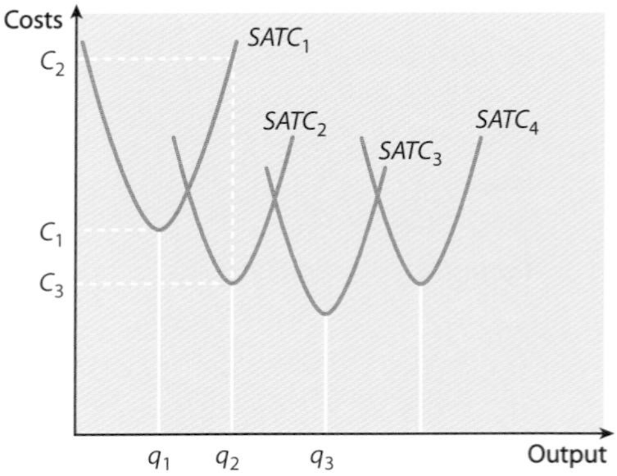

Figure 16.5 *Short-run cost curves with different levels of capital input*

Extension material

For the firm in Figure 16.5, the choice of capital is important. Suppose the firm wants to produce the quantity of output q_1. It would choose to install the amount of capital corresponding to the short-run total cost curve $SATC_1$, and could then produce q_1 at an average cost of C_1 in the short run. However, if the firm finds that demand is more buoyant than expected, and so wants to increase output to q_2, in the short run it has no option but to increase labour input and expand output along $SATC_1$, taking cost per unit to C_2.

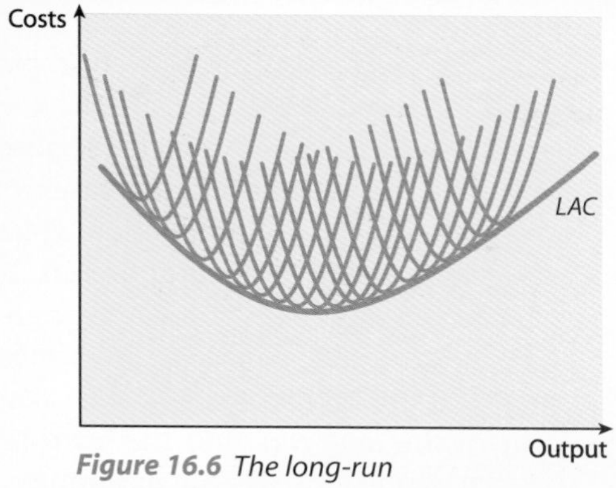

Figure 16.6 The long-run average cost curve

In the longer term, the firm will be able to adjust its capital stock and move on to $SATC_2$, reducing average cost to C_3. Thus, as soon as the firm moves away from the output level for which capital stock is designed, it incurs higher average cost in the short run than is possible in the long run.

In this way a long-run average cost curve can be derived to illustrate how the firm chooses to vary its capital stock for any given level of output. Figure 16.6 shows what such a curve would look like for the firm of the previous figure under the assumption that there is an infinite number of short-run costs curves, each corresponding to a particular desired output level, of which only some are shown! The long-run average cost curve just touches each of the short-run average cost curves, and is known as the 'envelope' of the *SATC* curves.

With the set of *SATC* curves in Figure 16.5, the long-run average cost curve also takes on a U-shape. Chapter 7 introduced the notion of **economies of scale**. It pointed out that there are several reasons why average cost might be expected to fall as a firm expanded its scale of operations. It is now clear that this refers to a situation in which the firm expands its inputs of both fixed and variable factors in order to increase its scale of operation. Economies of scale thus correspond to a situation in which long-run average cost falls as output is increased.

In Figure 16.7, if the firm expands its output up to q^*, long-run average cost falls. Up to q^* of output is the range over which there are economies of scale. To the right of q^*, however, long-run average cost rises as output continues to be increased, and the firm experiences **diseconomies of scale**. The output q^* itself is at the intermediate state of **constant returns to scale**.

Key terms

economies of scale: what happens if an increase in a firm's scale of production leads to production at lower long-run average cost

diseconomies of scale: said to occur when long-run average cost rises as output increases

constant returns to scale: found when long-run average cost remains constant with an increase in output, i.e. when output and costs rise at the same rate

It is important not to confuse the notion of returns to scale with the idea introduced earlier of diminishing marginal returns to a factor. The two concepts arise in different circumstances. The law of diminishing returns to a factor applies in the *short run*, when a firm increases its inputs of one factor of production while facing fixed amounts of other factors. It is thus solely a short-run phenomenon. Diseconomies of scale (sometimes known as *decreasing returns to scale*), can occur in the *long run*, and the term refers to how output changes as a firm varies the quantities of *all* factors.

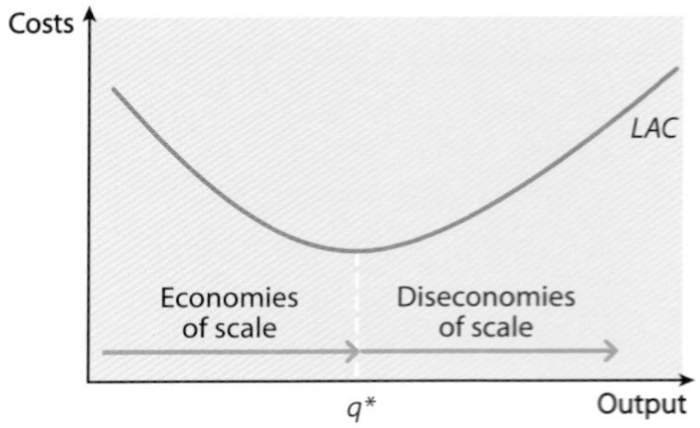

Figure 16.7 The long-run average cost curve

Key term

minimum efficient scale: the level of output at which long-run average cost stops falling as output increases

The point at which long-run average cost stops falling is known as the **minimum efficient scale**. This is the smallest level of output that a firm can produce at the minimum level of long-run average cost.

If the firm is operating at the lowest possible level of long-run average costs it is in a position of *productive efficiency*, which was defined and discussed in Chapter 6. Remember that the long-run average cost curve (*LAC*) is drawn as a U-shape because of the assumptions that were made about the technology of production. The underlying assumption here is that the firm faces economies of scale at relatively low levels of output, so that *LAC* slopes downwards. However, at some point decreasing returns to scale set in, and *LAC* then begins to slope upwards.

This turns out to be a convenient representation, but in practice the *LAC* curve can take on a variety of shapes. Figure 16.8 shows some of these. LAC_1 is the typical U-shape — which you will meet again. LAC_2 is an example of a situation in which there are economies of scale up to a point, after which long-run average cost levels out and there is a long flat range over which the firm faces constant returns to scale. LAC_3 is a bit similar, except that the constant returns to scale (flat) segment eventually runs out and diseconomies of scale set in. In LAC_4 the economies of scale continue over the whole range of output shown. This could occur in a market where the fixed costs are substantial, dominating the influence of variable costs.

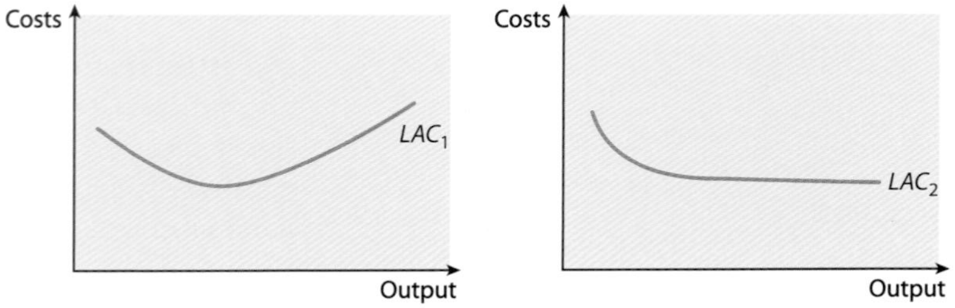

Figure 16.8 Possible shapes of the LAC curve

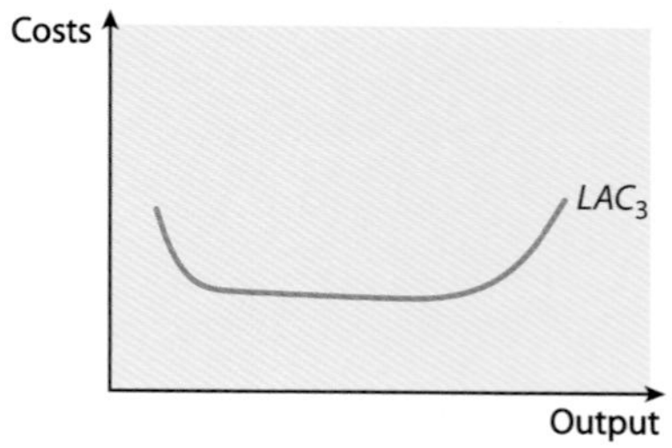

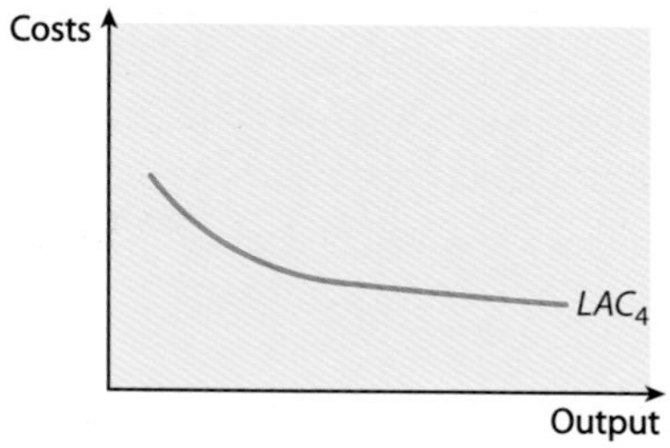

Summary

- A firm may face inflexibility in the short run, with some factors being fixed in quantity and only some being variable.
- The short run is defined in this context as the period over which a firm is free to vary some factors but not others.
- The long run is defined as the period over which the firm is able to vary the input of all of its factors of production.
- The production function shows how output can be efficiently produced through the input of factors of production.
- The law of diminishing returns states that, if a firm increases the input of a variable factor while holding input of the fixed factor constant, eventually the firm will get diminishing marginal returns from the variable factor.
- Short-run costs can be separated into fixed, sunk and variable costs.
- There is a clear and immutable relationship between total, average and marginal costs.
- For a U-shaped average cost curve, marginal cost always cuts the minimum point of average cost.
- The minimum efficient scale is the point at which the long-run average cost curve stops sloping downwards.
- In practice, long-run average cost curves may take on a variety of shapes, according to the technology of the industry concerned.

Exercise 16.2

A firm faces long-run total cost conditions as in Table 16.2:

Table 16.2 Output and long-run costs

Output ('000 units per week)	Total cost (£'000)
0	0
1	32
2	48
3	82
4	140
5	228
6	352

a Calculate long-run average cost and long-run marginal cost for each level of output.

b Plot long-run average cost and long-run marginal cost curves on a graph. (*Hint*: don't forget to plot *LMC* at points that are halfway between the corresponding output levels.)

c Identify the output level at which long-run average cost is at a minimum.

d Identify the output level at which *LAC* = *LMC*.

e Within what range of output does this firm enjoy economies of scale?

f Within what range of output does the firm experience diseconomies of scale?

g If you could measure the nature of returns to scale, what would characterise the point where *LAC* is at a minimum?

Motivations of firms

The opening section of this chapter stated that firms exist to organise production, by bringing together the factors of production in order to produce output. This begs the question of what motivates them to produce particular *levels* of output, and at what price. In the remainder of this chapter consideration will be given to alternative objectives that firms may set out to achieve.

Profit maximisation

Traditional economic analysis has tended to start from the premise that firms set out with the objective of maximising profits. In analysing this, economists define profits as the difference between the total revenue received by a firm and the total costs that it incurs in production:

$$\text{profits} = \text{total revenue} - \text{total cost}$$

Total revenue here is seen in terms of the quantity of the product that is sold multiplied by the price. Total cost includes the fixed and variable costs that have already been discussed. However, one important item of costs should be highlighted before going any further.

Consider the case of a sole proprietor — a small local business. It seems reasonable to assume that such a firm will set out to maximise its profits. However, from the entrepreneur's perspective there is an *opportunity cost* of being in business, which may be seen in terms of the earnings that the proprietor could make in an alternative occupation. This required rate of return is regarded as a fixed cost, and is included in the total cost of production.

Key term

normal profit: the return needed for a firm to stay in a market in the long run

The same procedure applies to cost curves for other sorts of firm. In other words, when economists refer to costs, they include the rate of return that a firm needs to make to stay in a particular market in the long run. Accountants dislike this, as 'opportunity cost' cannot be identified as an explicit item in the accounts. This part of costs is known as **normal profit**.

Profits made by a firm above that level are known as **supernormal profits**, **abnormal profits** or **economic profits**.

In the short run, a firm may choose to remain in a market even if it is not covering its opportunity costs, provided its revenues are covering its variable costs. Since the firm has already incurred fixed costs, if it can cover its variable costs in the short run it will be better off remaining in business and paying off part of the fixed costs than exiting the market and losing all of its fixed costs. Thus, the level of average variable costs represents the shut-down price, below which the firm will exit from the market in the short run.

Key terms

supernormal profits/ abnormal profits/ economic profits: terms referring to profits that exceed normal profits

marginal revenue: the additional revenue gained by the firm from selling an additional unit of output

How does a firm choose its output level if it wishes to maximise profits? Suppose a firm is a relatively small player in a big market, and thus has no influence over the price of its product. Its total revenue is then proportional to the amount of output it sells. If it faces the shape of short-run total cost curve that was introduced earlier in the chapter, its output decision can be analysed by reference to Figure 16.9.

To maximise profits, the firm needs to choose the output level at which the total revenue curve (*TR*) is as far above the total cost curve as possible. This happens at q^*, which is the point at which the slope of *STC* is the same as the slope of *TR*.

Notice that the slope of *STC* is in fact the short-run marginal cost, as noted earlier. Similarly, the slope of *TR* is **marginal revenue**; this is the additional revenue that the firm gains from selling an additional unit of output. Thus it can be seen that profits will be maximised where marginal cost is equal to marginal revenue – with one proviso: total revenue must exceed total cost. After all, the slopes of *STC* and *TR* are also equal at q^-, but at that point total costs are way higher than total revenue, and the firm makes a substantial loss.

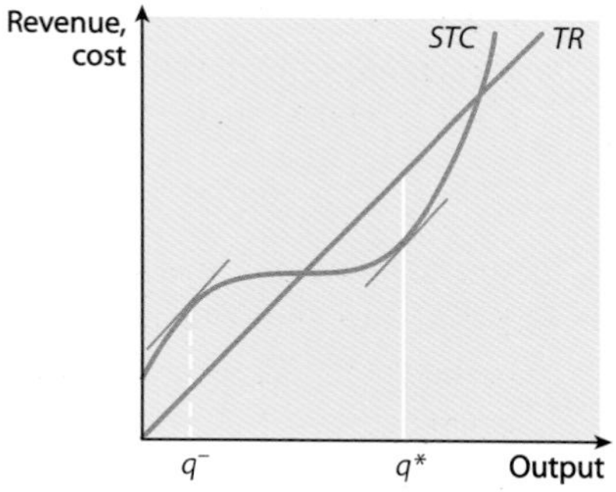

Figure 16.9 Profit maximisation

An alternative way of looking at this decision is to draw the marginal cost and marginal revenue curves as in Figure 16.10. Because it was assumed that the firm could not influence price, the marginal revenue received from selling each additional unit of output is constant, and equal to the price. The marginal cost curve is U-shaped as usual.

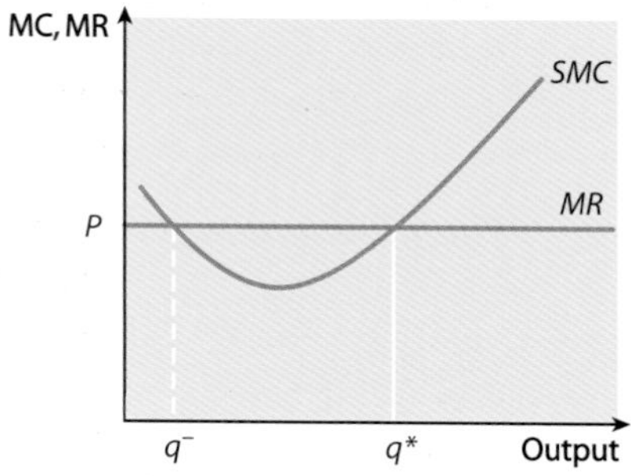

Figure 16.10 Profit maximisation again

Again, you can see that q^* will be the output that maximises profits. If the firm is producing less output than this, it will find that the marginal revenue from selling an additional unit of output is higher than the marginal cost of producing it, so the firm can add to its profits by increasing output. In contrast, if the firm is producing beyond q^*, it will find that the marginal revenue from selling an extra unit fails to cover the cost of producing the unit, so it will not pay the firm to produce beyond q^*. Therefore, q^* can be seen as the level of output that maximises the firm's profits.

The $MC = MR$ rule is a general rule for firms that want to maximise profits, and it holds in all market situations. For example, suppose the firm faces a downward-sloping demand curve for its product, such that it can sell more by reducing the price. In Chapter 3 it was seen that a linear demand curve is associated with a total revenue curve like that shown in Figure 16.11. Assume that the firm faces the usual shape of short-run total cost curve *STC.*

Profits are again maximised where the slopes of *STC* and *TR* are equal, with *TR* exceeding *STC* . This occurs at q_π.

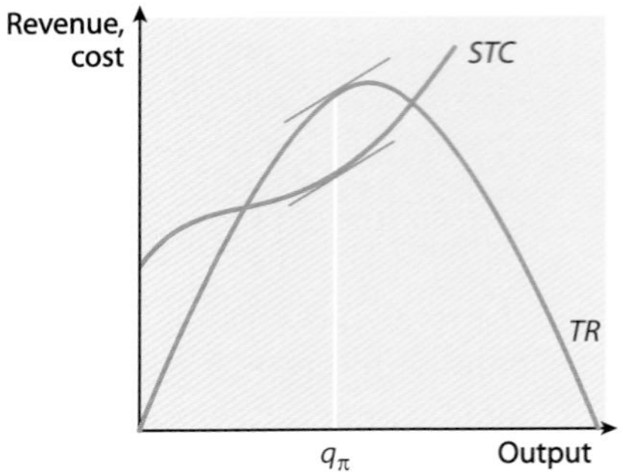

Figure 16.11 Profit maximisation with a downward-sloping demand curve

Exercise 16.3

Figure 16.12 shows a firm in short-run equilibrium. The firm is operating in a market in which it has no influence over price, so it gains the same marginal revenue from the sale of each unit of output. Marginal revenue and average revenue are thus the same. P_1, P_2 and P_3 represent three possible prices that could prevail in the market.

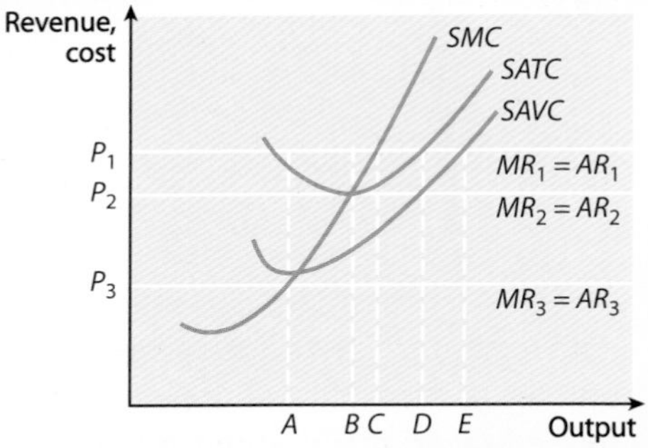

Figure 16.12 Profit maximisation in the short run

a For each price level, identify the output level that the firm would choose in order to maximise profits.

b At each of these output levels, compare the level of average revenue with that of average cost, and consider what this means for the firm's profits.

The principal–agent problem

The discussion so far seems reasonable when considering a relatively small owner-managed firm. In this context, profit maximisation makes good sense as the firm's motivation.

However, for many larger firms — especially public limited companies — the owners may not be involved in running the business. This gives rise to the **principal–agent** (or **agency**) **problem**. In a public limited company, the shareholders delegate the day-to-day decisions concerning the operation of the firm to managers who act on their behalf. In this case the shareholders are the *principals*, and the managers are the *agents* who run things for them.

If the agents are fully in sympathy with the objectives of the owners there is no problem, and the managers will take exactly the decisions that the owners would like. Problems arise when there is conflict between the aims of the owners and those of the managers.

One simple explanation of why this problem arises is that the managers like a quiet life, and therefore do not push for the absolute profit-maximising position, but do just enough to keep the shareholders off their backs. Herbert Simon referred to this as 'satisficing' behaviour, where managers aim to produce satisfactory profits rather than maximum profits.

Key terms

principal–agent (agency) problem: a problem arising from conflict between the objectives of the principals and those of the agents who take decisions on their behalf

X-inefficiency: situation arising when a firm is not operating at minimum cost, perhaps because of organisational slack

Another possibility is that managers become negligent because they are not fully accountable. One manifestation of this may be *organisational slack* in the organisation: costs will not be minimised, as the firm is not operating as efficiently as it could. This is an example of what is called **X-inefficiency**. For example, in Figure 16.13 *LAC* represents the long-run average cost curve showing the most efficient cost positions for the firm at any output level. With X-inefficiency, a firm could end up producing output q_1 at average cost AC_1. Thus, in the presence of X-inefficiency the firm will be operating *above* its long-run average cost curve.

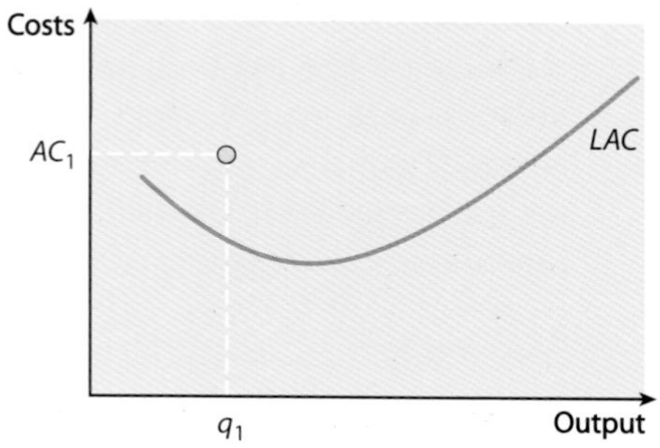

Figure 16.13 X-inefficiency

Some writers have argued that the managers may be pursuing other objectives. For example, some managers may enjoy being involved in the running of a *large* business, and may prefer to see the firm gaining market share — perhaps beyond the profit-maximising level. Others may like to see their status rewarded and so will want to divert part of the profits into managerial perks — large offices, company cars and so on. Or they may feel that having a large staff working for them increases their prestige inside the company. These sorts of activity tend to reduce the profitability of firms.

Revenue maximisation

William Baumol argued that managers may set out with the objective of maximising revenue. The effects of such action can be seen in Figure 16.14. As before, q_π represents the profit-maximising level of output. However, you can see that total revenue is maximised at the peak of the *TR* curve (where *MR* = 0) at q_r. Thus, a revenue-maximising firm will produce more output than a profit-maximising one, and will need to charge a lower price in order to sell the extra output.

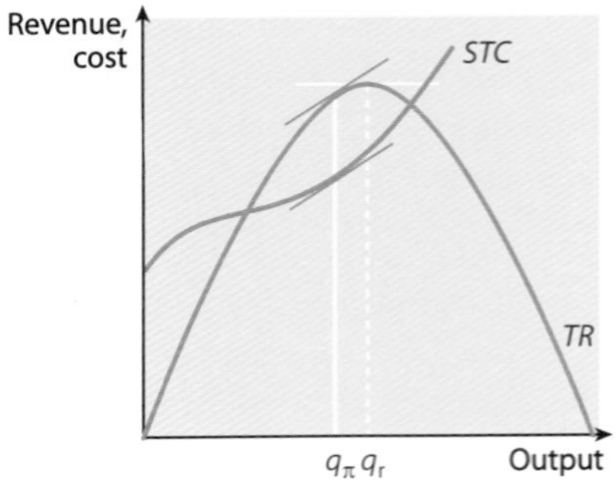

Figure 16.14 Revenue maximisation

Baumol pointed out that the shareholders might not be too pleased about this. The way the firm behaves then depends upon the degree of accountability that the agents (managers) have to the principals (shareholders). For example, the shareholders may have sufficient power over their agents to be able to insist on some minimum level of profits. The result may then be a compromise solution between the principals and the agents, with output being set somewhere between q_π and q_r.

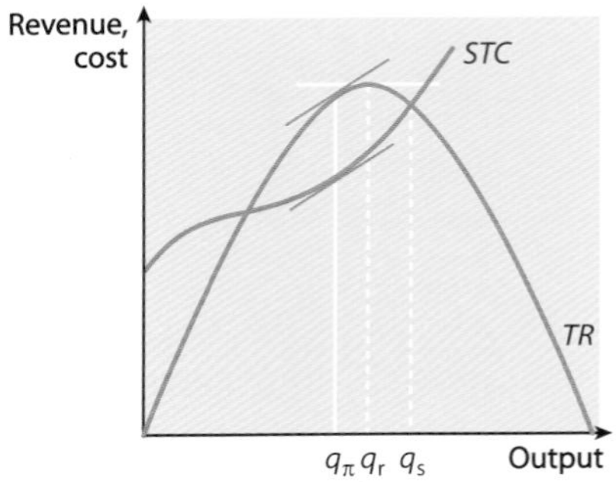

Figure 16.15 Sales maximisation

Sales maximisation

In some cases managers may focus more on the volume of sales than on the resulting revenues. This could lead to output being set even higher, as shown in Figure 16.15. The firm would now push for higher sales up to the point where it just breaks even at q_s. This is the point at which total revenue only just covers total cost. Remember that total cost includes normal profit — the opportunity cost of the resources tied up in the firm. The firm would have to close down if it did not cover this opportunity cost.

Again, the extent to which the managers will be able to pursue this objective without endangering their positions with the shareholders depends on how accountable the managers are to the shareholders. Remember that the managers are likely to have much better information about the market conditions and the internal functioning of the firm than the shareholders, who view the firm only remotely. This may be to the managers' advantage.

Efficiency

An important question is what this analysis implies for the efficiency of markets. How likely are firms to produce in ways that bolster the overall efficiency with which markets work to allocate resources? Chapter 6 introduced two important aspects of efficiency: productive efficiency and allocative efficiency. The conditions necessary for these aspects to be met can be seen in terms of the cost curves.

Productive efficiency itself has two such conditions. First, it requires that firms choose an appropriate set of factor inputs. Second, it requires that those inputs be used in the best possible way in order to minimise costs. These requirements will be met in a market if firms are operating at minimum long-run average cost.

Allocative efficiency in an individual market requires that firms charge a price that is equal to marginal cost. To determine whether this condition will be met, it is necessary to explore how prices are set, which is what the next chapter sets out to do.

Summary

- Traditional economic analysis assumes that firms set out to maximise profits, where profits are defined as the excess of total revenue over total cost.
- This analysis treats the opportunity cost of a firm's resources as a part of fixed costs. The opportunity cost is known as normal profit.
- Profits above this level are known as supernormal profits.
- A firm maximises profits by choosing output such that marginal revenue is equal to marginal cost.
- For many larger firms, where day-to-day control is delegated to managers, a principal–agent problem may arise if there is conflict between the objectives of owners (principals) and those of the managers (agents).
- This may lead to satisficing behaviour and to X-inefficiency.
- William Baumol suggested that managers may set out to maximise revenue rather than profits; others have suggested that sales or the growth of the firm may be the managers' objectives.
- For an individual firm, productive efficiency can be regarded as having been achieved when the firm is operating at minimum long-run average cost.

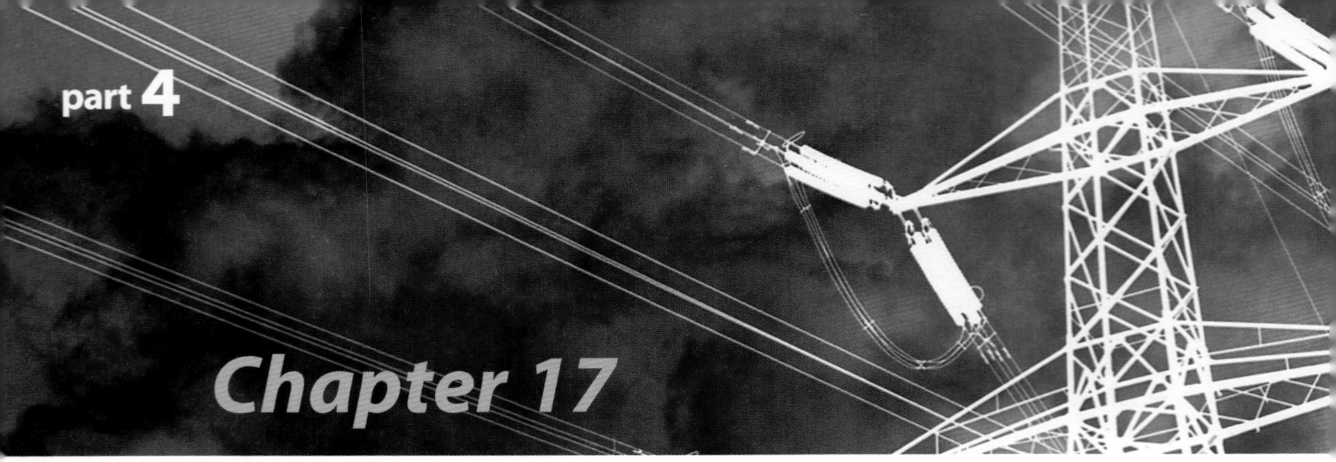

Market structure: perfect competition and monopoly

One of the reasons given for market failure in Part 2 of the book concerned what is termed 'imperfect competition'. It was argued that if firms can achieve market dominance they may distort the pattern of resource allocation. It is now time to look at this more closely. The fact that firms try to maximise profits is not in itself bad for society. However, the structure of a market has a strong influence on how well the market performs. 'Structure' here is seen in relation to a number of dimensions, but in particular to the number of firms operating in a market and the way they interact. The chapter considers two extreme forms of market structure: perfect competition and monopoly.

Learning outcomes

After studying this chapter, you should:

- be familiar with the assumptions of the model of perfect competition
- understand how a firm chooses profit-maximising output under perfect competition
- appreciate how a perfectly competitive market reaches long-run equilibrium
- understand how the characteristics of long-run equilibrium affect the performance of the market in terms of productive and allocative efficiency
- be familiar with the assumptions of the model of monopoly
- understand how the monopoly firm chooses output and sets price
- understand why a monopoly can arise in a market
- understand how the characteristics of the monopoly equilibrium affect the performance of the market in terms of productive and allocative efficiency
- be aware of the relative merits of perfect competition and monopoly in terms of market performance

Perfect competition

Assumptions

At one end of the spectrum of market structures is **perfect competition**. This model has a special place in economic analysis, because if all its assumptions were fulfilled, and if all markets operated according to its precepts, the best allocation of resources would be ensured for society as a whole. Although it may be argued that this ideal is not often achieved, perfect competition nonetheless provides a yardstick by which all other forms of market structure can be evaluated. The assumptions of this model are as follows:

1. Firms aim to maximise profits.
2. There are many participants (both buyers and sellers).
3. The product is homogeneous.
4. There are no barriers to entry to or exit from the market.
5. There is perfect knowledge of market conditions.
6. There are no externalities.

Key term

perfect competition: a form of market structure that produces allocative and productive efficiency in long-run equilibrium

Profit maximisation

The first assumption is that firms act to maximise their profits. You might think that this means that firms, acting in their own self-interest, are unlikely to do consumers any favours. However, it transpires that this does not interfere with the operation of the market. Indeed, it is the pursuit of self-interest by firms and consumers that ensures that the market works effectively.

Many participants

This is an important assumption of the model: that there are so many buyers and so many sellers that no individual trader is able to influence the market price. The market price is thus determined by the operation of the market.

On the sellers' side of the market, this assumption is tantamount to saying that there are limited economies of scale in the industry. If the minimum efficient scale is small relative to market demand, then no firm is likely to become so large that it will gain influence in the market.

A homogeneous product

This assumption means that buyers of the good see all products in the market as being identical, and will not favour one firm's product over another. If there were brand loyalty, such that one firm was more popular than others, then that firm would be able to charge a premium on its price. By ruling out this possibility the previous assumption is reinforced, and no individual seller is able to influence the selling price of the product.

No barriers to entry or exit

By this assumption, firms are able to join the market if they perceive it to be a profitable step, and they can exit from the market without hindrance. This assumption is important when it comes to considering the long-run equilibrium towards which the market will tend.

Perfect knowledge

It is assumed that all participants in the market have perfect information about trading conditions in the market. In particular, buyers always know the prices that firms are charging, and thus can buy the good at the cheapest possible price. Firms that try to charge a price above the market price will get no takers. At the same time, traders are aware of the product quality.

No externalities

Chapter 6 described externalities as a form of market failure that prevents the attainment of allocative efficiency. Here externalities are ruled out in order to explore the characteristics of the perfect competition model.

Perfect competition in the short run

The firm under perfect competition

With the above assumptions, it is possible to analyse how a firm will operate in the market. An important implication of these assumptions is that no individual trader can influence the price of the product. In particular, this means that the firm is a **price taker**, and has to accept whatever price is set in the market as a whole.

> **Key term**
>
> **price taker:** a firm that must accept whatever price is set in the market as a whole

This means that the firm faces a perfectly elastic demand curve for its product, as is shown in Figure 17.1. In this figure P_1 is the price set in the market, and the firm cannot sell at any other price. If it tries to set a price above P_1 it will sell nothing, as buyers are fully aware of the market price and will not buy at a higher price, especially as they know that there is no quality difference between the product as produced by different firms in the market. What this also implies is that the firm can sell as much output as it likes at that going price – which means there is no incentive for any firm to set a price below P_1. Thus, all firms charge the same price, P_1.

The firm's short-run supply decision

If the firm can sell as much as it likes at the market price, how does it decide how much to produce?

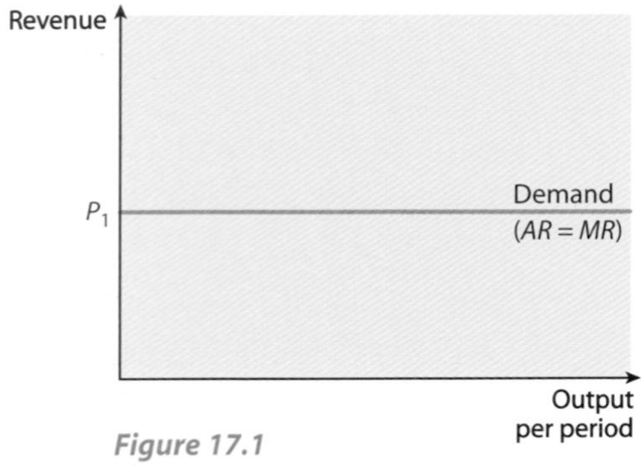

Figure 17.1
The firm's demand curve

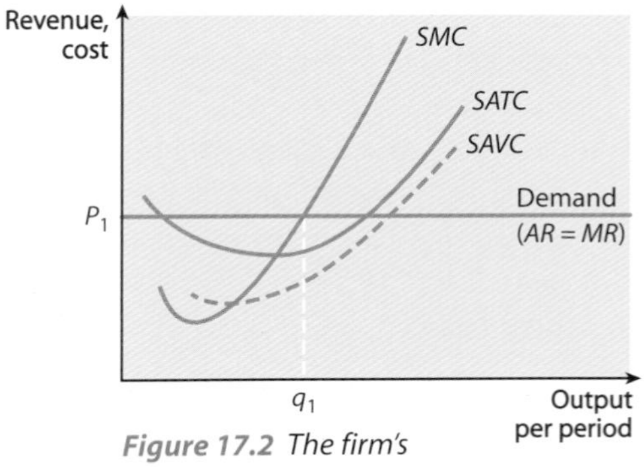

Figure 17.2 The firm's short-run supply decision

Chapter 16 explained that to maximise profits a firm needs to set output at such a level that marginal revenue is equal to marginal cost. Figure 17.2 illustrates this rule by adding the short-run cost curves to the demand curve. (Remember that *SMC* cuts the *SATC* at the minimum point of *SAVC* and *SATC*.) As the demand curve is horizontal, the firm faces constant average and marginal revenue and will choose output at q_1, where *MR* = *MC*.

If the market price were to change, the firm would react by changing output, but always choosing to supply output at the level at which *MR* = *MC*. This suggests that the short-run marginal cost curve represents the firm's short-run supply curve; in other words, it shows the quantity of output that the firm would supply at any given price.

However, there is one important proviso to this statement. If the price falls below short-run average variable cost, the firm's best decision will be to exit from the market, as it will be better off just incurring its fixed costs. So the firm's **short-run supply curve** is the *SMC* curve above the point where it cuts *SAVC* (at its minimum point).

Key term

short-run supply curve: for a firm operating under perfect competition, the curve given by its short-run marginal cost curve above the price at which *MC* = *SAVC*; for the industry, the horizontal sum of the supply curves of the individual firms

Industry equilibrium in the short run

One crucial question not yet examined is how the market price comes to be determined. To answer this, it is necessary to consider the industry as a whole. In this case there is a conventional downward-sloping demand curve, of the sort met in Chapter 3. This is formed according to preferences of consumers in the market and is shown in Figure 17.3.

On the supply side, it has been shown that the individual firm's supply curve is its marginal cost curve above *SAVC*. If you add up the supply curves of each firm operating in the market, the result is the industry supply curve, also shown in Figure 17.3. The price will then adjust to P_1 at the intersection of demand and supply. The firms in the industry between them will supply Q_1 output, and the market will be in equilibrium.

The firm in short-run equilibrium revisited

As this seems to be a well-balanced situation, with price adjusting to equate market demand and supply, the only question is why it is described as just a *short-run equilibrium*. The clue to this is to be found back with the individual firm.

Figure 17.4 returns to the position facing an individual firm in the market. As before, the firm maximises profits by

Note: Σ denotes 'sum of'.

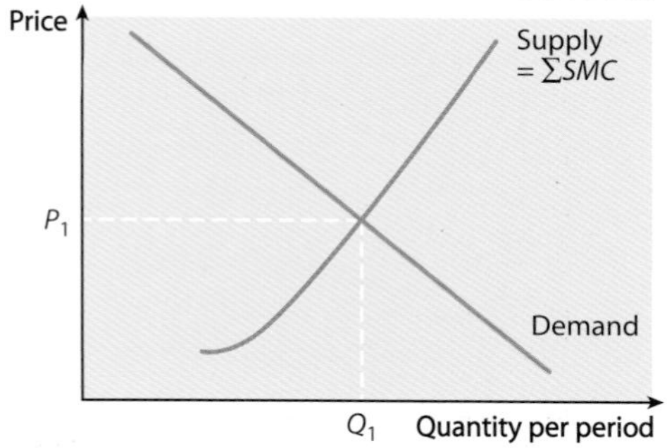

Figure 17.3 A perfectly competitive industry in short-run equilibrium

accepting the price P_1 as set in the market and producing up to the point where $MR = MC$, which is at q_1. However, now the firm's average revenue (which is equal to price) is greater than its average cost (which is given by AC_1 at this level of output). The firm is thus making supernormal profits at this price. (Remember that 'normal profits' are included in average cost.) Indeed, the amount of total profits being made is shown as the shaded area on the graph. Notice that average revenue minus average costs equals profit per unit, so multiplying this by the quantity sold determines total profit.

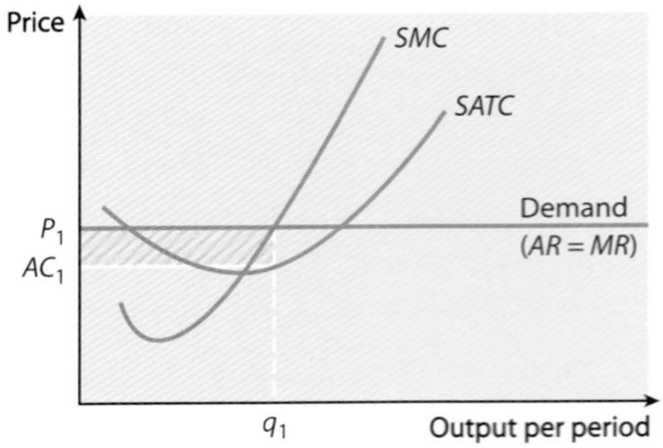

Figure 17.4
The firm in short-run supply equilibrium

This is where the assumption about freedom of entry becomes important. If firms in this market are making profits above opportunity cost, the market is generating more profits than other markets in the economy. This will prove attractive to other firms, which will seek to enter the market – and the assumption is that there are no barriers to prevent them from doing so.

This process of entry will continue for as long as firms are making supernormal profits. However, as more firms join the market, the *position* of the industry supply curve, which is the sum of the supply curves of an ever-larger number of individual firms, will be affected. As the industrial supply curve shifts to the right, the market price will fall. At some point the price will have fallen to such an extent that firms are no longer making supernormal profits, and the market will then stabilise.

If the price were to fall even further, some firms would choose to exit from the market, and the process would go into reverse. Therefore price can be expected to stabilise such that the typical firm in the industry is just making normal profits.

Perfect competition in long-run equilibrium

Figure 17.5 shows the situation for a typical firm and for the industry as a whole once long-run equilibrium has been reached and firms no longer have any incentive to enter or to exit the market. The market is in equilibrium, with demand equal to supply at the going price. The typical firm sets marginal revenue equal to marginal cost to maximise profits, and just makes normal profits.

The long-run supply curve

Comparative static analysis can be used to explore this equilibrium a little more deeply. Suppose there is an increase in the demand for this product. Perhaps, for some reason, everyone becomes convinced that the product is really health-promoting, so demand increases at any given price. This disturbs the market equilibrium, and the question then is whether (and how) equilibrium can be restored.

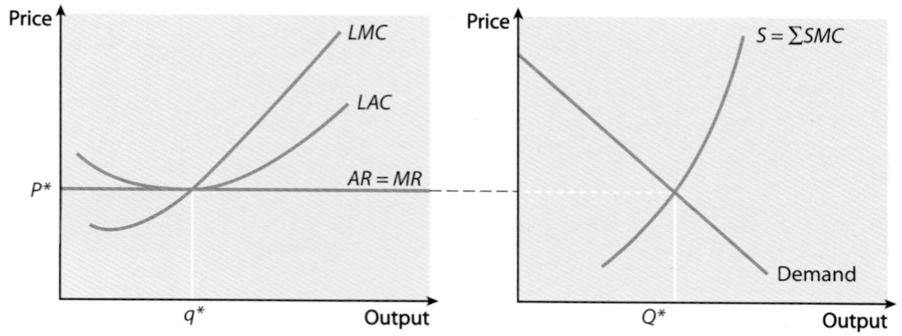

Figure 17.5 Long-run equilibrium under perfect competition

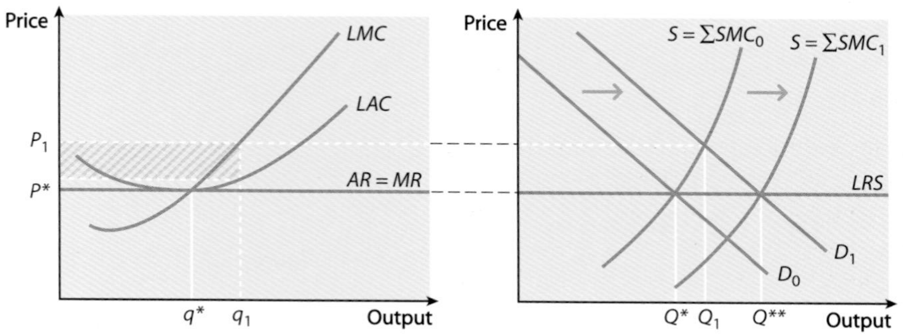

Figure 17.6 Adjusting to an increase in demand under perfect competition

Figure 17.6 reproduces the long-run equilibrium that was shown in Figure 17.5. Thus, in the initial position market price is at P^*, the typical firm is in long-run equilibrium producing q^*, and the industry is producing Q^*. Demand was initially at D_0, but with the increased popularity of the product it has shifted to D_1. In the short run this pushes the market price up to P_1 for the industry, because as market price increases existing firms have the incentive to supply more output; that is, they move along their short-run supply curves. So in the short run a typical firm starts to produce q_1 output. The combined supply of the firms then increases to Q_1.

However, at the higher price the firms start making supernormal profits (shown by the shaded area in Figure 17.6), so in time more firms will be attracted into the market, pushing the short-run industry supply curve to the right. This process will continue until there is no further incentive for new firms to enter the market – which occurs when the price has returned to P^*, but with increased industry output at Q^{**}. In other words, the adjustment in the short run is borne by existing firms, but the long-run equilibrium is reached through the entry of new firms.

This suggests that the **industry long-run supply curve (LRS)** is horizontal at the price P^*, which is the minimum point of the long-run average cost curve for the typical firm in the industry.

Key term

industry long-run supply curve (LRS): under perfect competition, the curve that, for the typical firm in the industry, is horizontal at the minimum point of the long-run average cost curve

Strictly speaking, the LRS is perfectly flat only if all firms face equal cost conditions, and if factor prices remain constant as the industry expands. For example, if there is a labour shortage, then industrial expansion may drive up labour costs, causing firms to face higher costs at any output level. In these sorts of circumstances the LRS is slightly upward sloping.

Exercise 17.1

Figure 17.7 shows the short-run cost curves for a firm that is operating in a perfectly competitive market.

- **a** At what price would the firm just make 'normal' profits?
- **b** What area would represent total fixed cost at this price?
- **c** What is the shut-down price for the firm?
- **d** Within what range of prices would the firm choose to operate at a loss in the short run?
- **e** Identify the firm's short-run supply curve.
- **f** Within what range of prices would the firm be able to make short-run supernormal profits?

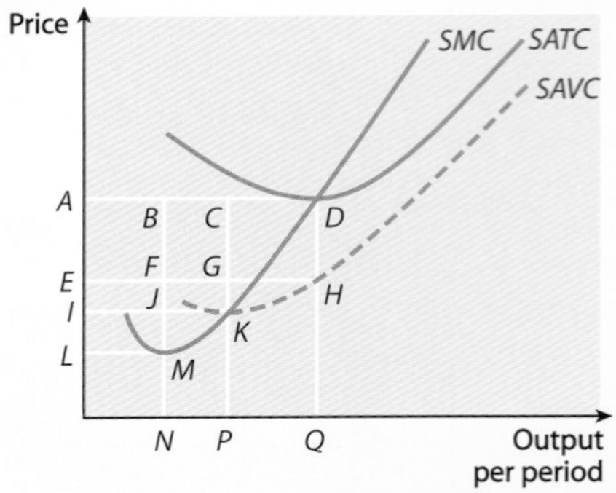

Figure 17.7 A firm operating under short-run perfect competition

Exercise 17.2

Starting from a diagram like Figure 17.5, track the response of a perfectly competitive market to a decrease in market demand for a good — in other words, explain how the market adjusts to a leftward shift of the demand curve.

Efficiency under perfect competition

Having reviewed the characteristics of the long-run equilibrium of a perfectly competitive market, you may wonder what is so good about such a market in terms of productive and allocative efficiency.

Productive efficiency

For an individual market, productive efficiency is reached when a firm operates at the minimum point of its long-run average cost curve. Under perfect competition, this is indeed a feature of the long-run equilibrium position. So productive efficiency is achieved in the long run – but not in the short run, when a firm need not be operating at minimum average cost.

Allocative efficiency

For an individual market, allocative efficiency is achieved when price is set equal to marginal cost. Again, the process by which supernormal profits are competed away through the entry of new firms into the market ensures that price is equal to marginal cost within a perfectly competitive market in long-run equilibrium. So allocative efficiency is also achieved. Indeed, firms set price equal to marginal cost even in the short run, so allocative efficiency is a feature of perfect competition in both the short run and the long run.

Evaluation of perfect competition

A criticism sometimes levelled at the model of perfect competition is that it is merely a theoretical ideal, based on a sequence of assumptions that rarely holds in the real world. Perhaps you have some sympathy with that view.

It could be argued that the model does hold for some agricultural markets. One study in the USA estimated that the elasticity of demand for an individual farmer producing sweetcorn was –31 353, which is pretty close to perfect elasticity.

However, to argue that the model is useless because it is unrealistic is to miss a very important point. By allowing a glimpse of what the ideal market would look like, at least in terms of resource allocation, the model provides a measure against which alternative market structures can be compared. Furthermore, economic analysis can be used to investigate the effects of relaxing the assumptions of the model, which can be another valuable exercise. For example, it is possible to examine how the market is affected if firms can differentiate their products, or if traders in the market are acting with incomplete information. This scenario was in fact explored in Chapter 9, describing the effects of asymmetric information on a market.

So, although there may be relatively few markets that display all the characteristics of perfect competition, that does not destroy the usefulness of the model in economic theory. It will continue to be a reference point when examining alternative models of market structure.

Extension material: a word of warning

Some writers, e.g. Nobel prize winner Friedrich von Hayek, have disputed the idea that perfect competition is the best form of market structure. Hayek argued that supernormal profits can be seen as the basis for investment by firms in new technologies, research and development (R&D) and innovation. If supernormal profits are always competed away, as happens under perfect competition, such activity will not take place. Similarly, Joseph Schumpeter argued that only in monopoly or oligopoly markets can firms afford to undertake R&D. Under this sort of argument, it is not quite so clear that perfect competition is the most desirable market structure.

Summary

- The model of perfect competition describes an extreme form of market structure. It rests on a sequence of assumptions.
- Its key characteristics include the assumption that no individual trader can influence the market price of the good or service being traded, and that there is freedom of entry and exit.

- In such circumstances each firm faces a perfectly elastic demand curve for its product, and can sell as much as it likes at the going market price.
- A profit-maximising firm chooses to produce the level of output at which marginal revenue (*MR*) equals marginal cost (*MC*).
- The firm's short-run marginal cost curve, above its short-run average variable cost curve, represents its short-run supply curve.
- The industry's short-run supply curve is the horizontal summation of the supply curves of all firms in the market.
- Firms may make supernormal profits in the short run, but because there is freedom of entry these profits will be competed away in the long run by new firms joining the market.
- The long-run industry supply curve is horizontal, with price adjusting to the minimum level of the typical firm's long-run average cost curve.
- Under perfect competition in long-run equilibrium, both productive efficiency and allocative efficiency are achieved.

Monopoly

At the opposite end of the spectrum of market structures is monopoly, which is a market with a single seller of a good.

There is a bit more to it than that, and economic analysis of monopoly rests on some important assumptions. In the real world, the Competition Commission, the official body in the UK with the responsibility of monitoring monopoly markets, is empowered to investigate a merger if it results in the combined firm having more than 25% of a market. The operations of the Competition Commission will be discussed in Chapter 20.

Assumptions

The assumptions of the monopoly model are as follows:

1 There is a single seller of a good.
2 There are no substitutes for the good, either actual or potential.
3 There are barriers to entry into the market.

Key term

monopoly: a form of market structure in which there is only one seller of a good or service

It is also assumed that the firm aims to maximise profits. You can see that these assumptions all have their counterparts in the assumptions of perfect competition, and that in one sense this model can be described as being at the opposite end of the market structure spectrum.

If there is a single seller of a good, and if there are no substitutes for the good, the monopoly firm is thereby insulated from competition. Furthermore, any barriers to entry into the market will ensure that the firm can sustain its market position into the future. The assumption that there are no potential substitutes for the good reinforces the situation. (Chapter 19 will explore what happens if this assumption does not hold.)

A monopoly in equilibrium

The first point to note is that a monopoly firm faces the market demand curve directly. Thus, unlike perfect competition, the demand curve slopes downwards. For the monopolist, the demand curve may be regarded as showing average revenue. Unlike a firm under perfect competition, therefore, the monopolist has some influence over price, and can make decisions regarding price as well as output. This is not to say that the monopolist has complete freedom to set the price, as the firm is still constrained by market demand. However, the firm is a *price maker* and can choose a location *along* the demand curve.

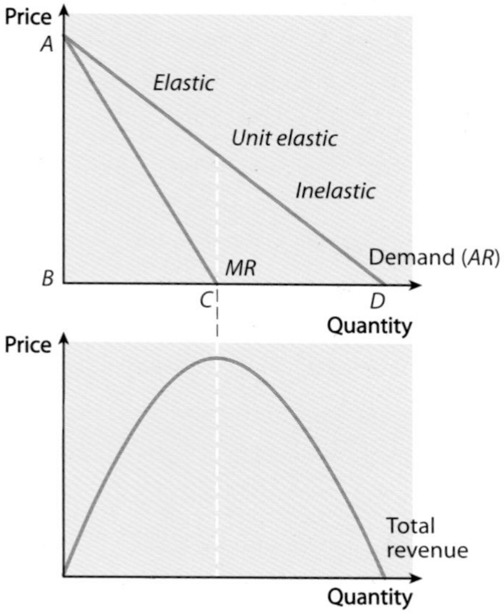

Figure 17.8 Elasticity and total revenue

As a preliminary piece of analysis, recall a piece of analysis in Chapter 3, which looked at the relationship between the own-price elasticity of demand along a straight-line demand curve and total revenue. The key graphs are reproduced here as Figure 17.8. The analysis pointed out that the price elasticity of demand is elastic above the mid-point of the demand curve and inelastic in the lower half, with total revenue increasing with a price fall when demand is elastic and falling when demand is inelastic.

The marginal revenue curve (*MR*) has been added to the figure, and it has a fixed relationship with the average revenue curve (*AR*). This is for similar mathematical reasons as those that explained the relationship between marginal and average costs in the previous chapter. *MR* shares the intercept point on the vertical axis (point *A* in Figure 17.8) and has exactly twice the slope of *AR*. Whenever you have to draw this figure, remember that *MR* and *AR* have this relationship – meeting at *A*, and with the distance *BC* being the same as the distance *CD*. *MR* is zero (meets the horizontal axis) at the maximum point of the total revenue curve.

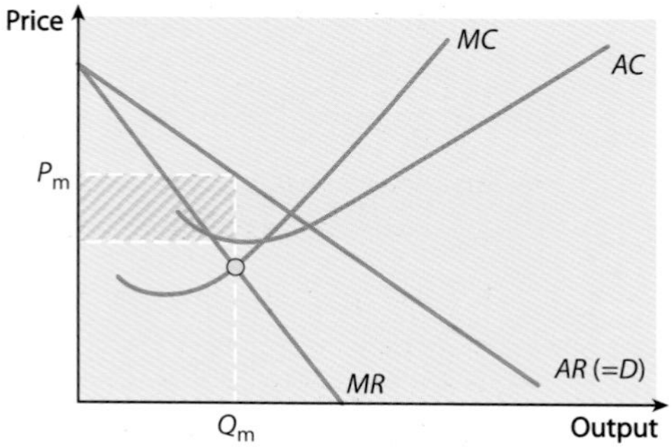

Figure 17.9 Profit maximisation and monopoly

As with the firm under perfect competition, a monopolist aiming to maximise profits will choose to produce at the level of output at which marginal revenue equals marginal cost. This is at Q_m in Figure 17.9. Having selected output, the monopolist then identifies the price that will clear the market for that level of output – in Figure 17.9 this is P_m.

This choice allows the monopolist to make supernormal profits, which can be identified as the shaded area in the figure. As before, this area is average revenue minus average cost, which gives profit per unit, multiplied by the quantity.

It is at this point that barriers to entry become important. Other firms may see that the monopoly firm is making healthy supernormal profits, but the existence of barriers to entry will prevent those profits from being competed away, as would happen in a perfectly competitive market.

It is important to notice that the monopolist cannot be guaranteed always to make such substantial profits as are shown in Figure 17.9. The size of the profits depends upon the relative position of the market demand curve and the position of the cost curves. If the cost curves in the diagram were higher, the monopoly profits would be much smaller, as the distance between average revenue and average costs would be less. It is even possible that the cost curves could be so high as to force the firm to incur losses, in which case it would probably shut down.

Exercise 17.3

Table 17.1 shows the demand curve faced by a monopolist.

Demand (000 per week)	Price (£)
0	80
1	70
2	60
3	50
4	40
5	30
6	20
7	10

***Table 17.1** Demand curve for a monopolist*

a Calculate total revenue and marginal revenue for each level of demand.

b Plot the demand curve (*AR*) and marginal revenue on a graph.

c Plot total revenue on a separate graph.

d Identify the level of demand at which total revenue is at a maximum.

e At what level of demand is marginal revenue equal to zero?

f At what level of demand is there unit own-price elasticity of demand?

g If the monopolist maximises profits, will the chosen level of output be higher or lower than the revenue-maximising level?

h What does this imply for the price elasticity of demand when the monopolist maximises profits?

Exercise 17.4

Draw a diagram to analyse the profit-maximising level of output and price for a monopolist, and analyse the effect of an increase in demand.

How do monopolies arise?

Monopolies may arise in a market for a number of reasons. In a few instances, a monopoly is created by the authorities. For example, for 150 years the UK Post Office held a licence giving it a monopoly on delivering letters. This service is now open to some competition, although any company wanting to deliver packages weighing less than 350 grams and charging less than £1 can do so only by applying for a licence. The Post Office monopoly formerly covered a much wider range of services, but its coverage has been eroded over the years, and competition in delivering larger packages has been permitted for some time. Nonetheless, it remains an example of one way in which a monopoly can be created.

The patent system offers a rather different form of protection for a firm. The patent system was designed to provide an incentive for firms to innovate through the development of new techniques and products. By prohibiting other firms from copying the product for a period of time, a firm is given a temporary monopoly.

In some cases the technology of the industry may create a monopoly situation. In a market characterised by substantial economies of scale, there may not be room for more than one firm in the market. This could happen where there are substantial fixed costs of production but low marginal costs; for example, in establishing an underground railway in a city, a firm faces very high fixed costs in building the network of rails and stations and buying the rolling stock. However, once in operation, the marginal cost of carrying an additional passenger is very low.

Figure 17.10 illustrates this point. The firm in this market enjoys economies of scale right up to the limit of market demand. The largest firm operating in the market can always produce at a lower cost than any potential entrant, so will always be able to price such firms out of the market. Here the economies of scale act as an effective barrier to the entry of new firms and the market is a **natural monopoly**. A profit-maximising monopoly would thus set $MR = MC$, produce at quantity Q_m and charge a price P_m.

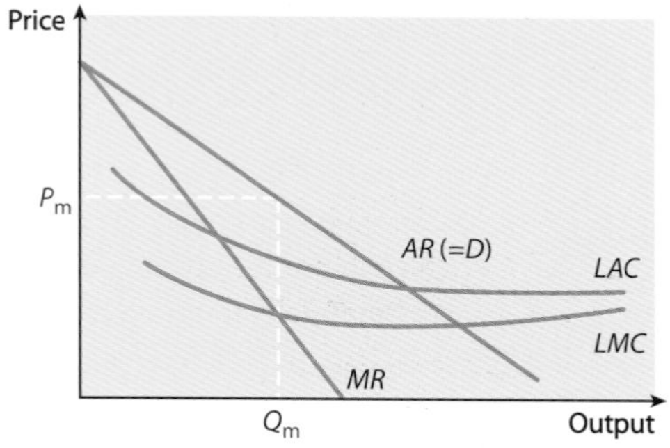

Figure 17.10 *A natural monopoly*

A city underground railway is a good example of a natural monopoly.

Key term

natural monopoly: monopoly that arises in an industry in which there are such substantial economies of scale that only one firm is viable

Such a market poses particular problems regarding allocative efficiency. Notice in the figure that marginal cost is below average cost over the entire range of output. If the firm were to charge a price equal to marginal cost it would inevitably make a loss, so such a pricing rule would not be viable. This problem is analysed in Chapter 20. Notice, however, that it would clearly not make economic sense to have multiple underground railway systems trying to serve the same routes in a city.

There are markets in which firms have risen to become monopolies by their actions in the market. Such a market structure is sometimes known as a *competitive monopoly*. Firms may get into a monopoly position through effective marketing, through a process of merger and acquisition, or by establishing a new product as a widely accepted standard.

In the first Microsoft trial in 1998, it was claimed that Microsoft had gained 95% of the world market for operating systems for PC computers. The firm claimed that this was because it was simply very good at what it does. However, part of the reason why it was on trial was that not everyone agreed with it, and alleged unfair market tactics. This will be examined in Chapter 20.

Exercise 17.5

In 2000, AOL merged with Time Warner, bringing together an internet service provider with an extensive network and a firm in the entertainment business.

One product that such a merged company might produce would be a digitised music performance that could be distributed through the internet. Think about the sorts of cost entailed in producing and delivering such a product, and categorise them as fixed or variable costs. What does this imply for the economies of scale faced by the merged company?

Monopoly and efficiency

The characteristics of the monopoly market can be evaluated in relation to productive and allocative efficiency (see Figure 17.9).

Productive efficiency

A firm is said to be productively efficient if it produces at the minimum point of long-run average cost. It is clear from the figure that this is extremely unlikely for a monopoly. The firm will produce at the minimum point of long-run average cost only if it so happens that the marginal *revenue* curve passes through this exact point – and this would happen only by coincidence.

Allocative efficiency

For an individual firm, allocative efficiency is achieved when price is set equal to marginal cost. It is clear from Figure 17.9 that this will not be the case for a profit-maximising monopoly firm. The firm chooses output where *MR* equals *MC*; however, given that *MR* is below *AR* (i.e. price), price will always be set above marginal cost.

Perfect competition and monopoly compared

It is possible to identify the extent to which a monopoly by its behaviour distorts resource allocation, by comparing the monopoly market with the perfectly competitive market. To do this, the situation can be simplified by setting aside the possibility of economies of scale. This is perhaps an artificial assumption to make, but it can be relaxed later.

Suppose that there is an industry with no economies of scale, which can be operated either as a perfectly competitive market with many small firms, or as a monopoly firm running a large number of small plants.

Figure 17.11 shows the market demand curve ($D = AR$), and the long-run supply curve under perfect competition (LRS). If the market is operating under perfect competition, the long-run equilibrium will produce a price of P_{pc}, and the firms in the industry will together supply Q_{pc} output. Consumer surplus is given by the area $AP_{pc}E$, which represents the surplus that consumers gain from consuming this product. In other words, it is a measure of the welfare that society receives from consuming the good, as was explained in Chapter 5.

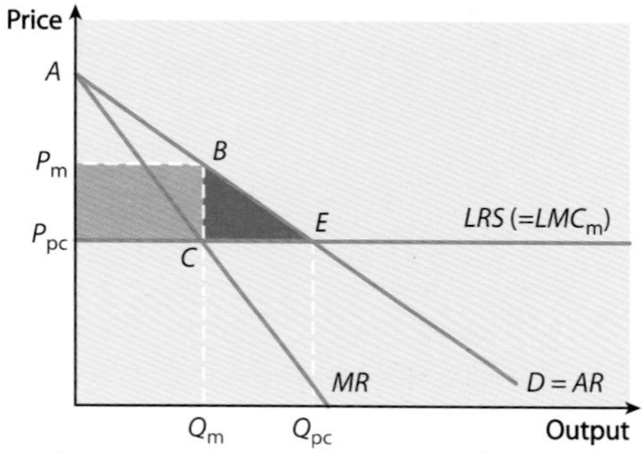

Figure 17.11 Comparing perfect competition and monopoly

Now suppose that the industry is taken over by a profit-maximising monopolist. The firm can close down some of the plants to vary its output over the long run, and the LRS can be regarded as the monopolist's long-run marginal cost curve. As the monopoly firm faces the market demand curve directly, it will also face the MR curve shown, so will maximise profits at quantity Q_m and charge a price P_m.

Thus, the effect of this change in market structure is that the profit-maximising monopolist produces less output than a perfectly competitive industry and charges a higher price.

It is also apparent that consumer surplus is now very different, as in the new situation it is limited to the area AP_mB. Looking more carefully at Figure 17.11, you can see that the loss of consumer surplus has occurred for two reasons. First, the monopoly firm is now making profits shown by the shaded area P_mBCP_{pc}. This is a redistribution of welfare from consumers to the firm, but, as the monopolist is also a member of society, this does not affect overall welfare. However, there is also a deadweight loss, which represents a loss to society resulting from the monopolisation of the industry. This is measured by the area of the triangle BCE. Chapter 20 returns to this issue to examine whether the authorities need to worry about this situation and to explore the sort of policy that could be adopted to tackle the issue.

Summary

- A monopoly market is one in which there is a single seller of a good.
- The model of monopoly used in economic analysis also assumes that there are no substitutes for the goods or services produced by the monopolist, and that there are barriers to the entry of new firms.
- The monopoly firm faces the market demand curve, and is able to choose a point along that demand curve in order to maximise profits.
- Such a firm may be able to make supernormal profits, and sustain them in the long run because of barriers to entry and the lack of substitutes.
- A monopoly may arise because of patent protection or from the nature of economies of scale in the industry (a 'natural monopoly').
- A profit-maximising monopolist does not achieve allocative efficiency, and is unlikely to achieve productive efficiency in the sense of producing at the minimum point of the long-run average cost curve.
- A comparison of perfect competition with monopoly reveals that a profit-maximising monopoly firm operating under the same cost conditions as a perfectly competitive industry will produce less output, charge a higher price and impose a deadweight loss on society.

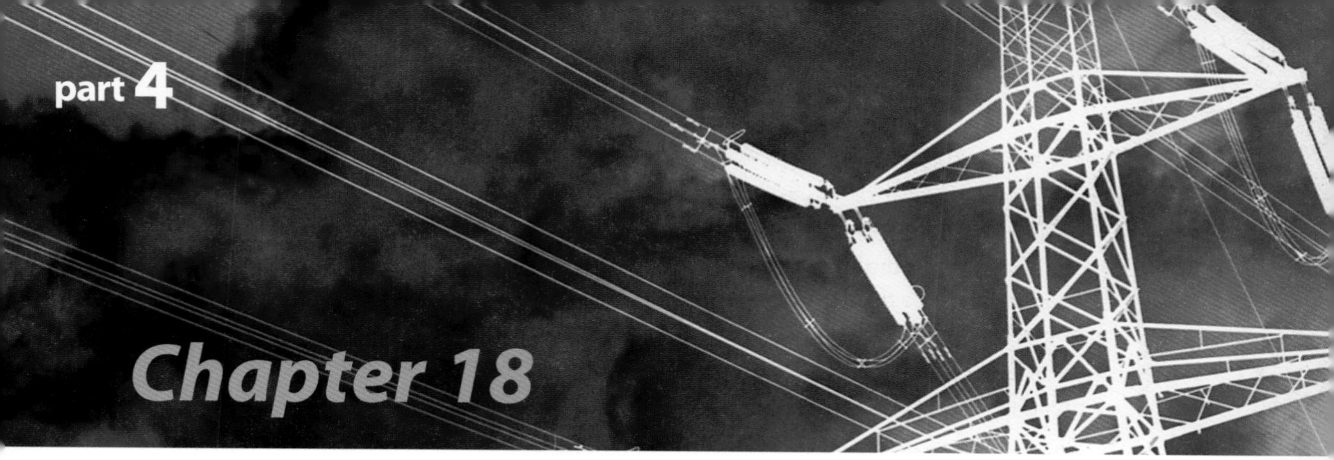

part 4

Chapter 18

Market structure: monopolistic competition and oligopoly

The previous chapter introduced the models of perfect competition and monopoly, and described them as being at the extreme ends of a spectrum of forms of market structure. In between those two extremes are other forms of market structure, which have some but not all of the characteristics of either perfect competition or monopoly. It is in this sense that there is a spectrum of structures. Attention in this chapter is focused on some of these intermediate forms of market structure.

Learning outcomes

After studying this chapter, you should:

- understand the significance of concentration in a market and how to measure it
- be familiar with the range of market situations that exists between the extremes of perfect competition and monopoly
- understand the meaning of product differentiation and its role in the model of monopolistic competition
- understand the conditions under which price discrimination is possible and how this affects consumers and producers
- understand the notion of oligopoly and be familiar with approaches to modelling firm behaviour in an oligopoly market
- understand the benefits that firms may gain from forming a cartel — and the tensions that may result

Market concentration

Chapter 17 pointed out that the models of perfect competition and monopoly produce very different outcomes for productive and allocative efficiency. Perfect competition produces a 'good' allocation of resources, but monopoly results in a deadweight loss. In the real-world economy it is not quite so simple. In particular, not every market is readily classified as following either of these extreme models. Indeed, you might think that the majority of markets do not correspond to either of the models, but instead display a mixture of characteristics.

An important question is whether such markets behave more like a competitive market or more like a monopoly. There are many different ways in which markets with just a few firms operating can be modelled, because there are many ways in which the firms may interact. Some of these models will be explored later in the chapter.

It is helpful to have some way of gauging how close a particular market is to being a monopoly. One way of doing this is to examine the degree of concentration in the market. Later it will be seen that this is not all that is required to determine how efficiently a market will operate; but it is a start.

Concentration is normally measured by reference to the **concentration ratio**, which measures the market share of the largest firms in an industry. For example, the three-firm concentration ratio measures the market share of the largest three firms in the market; the five-firm concentration ratio calculates the share of the top five firms, and so on. Concentration can also be viewed in terms of employment, reflected in the proportion of workers in any industry that are employed in the largest firms.

Key term

***n*-firm concentration ratio:** a measure of the market share of the largest *n* firms in an industry

Consider the following example. Table 18.1 gives average circulation figures for the firms that publish national newspapers in the UK. In the final column these are converted into market shares. Where one firm produces more than one newspaper, their circulations have been combined (e.g. News International publishes both the *Sun* and *The Times*).

Table 18.1 Average daily circulation of UK national newspapers, August 2004

Firm	Average circulation	Market share (%)
News International Newspapers Ltd	3 744 104	34.3
Associated Newspapers Ltd	2 263 414	20.8
Trinity Mirror plc	2 138 901	19.6
Express Newspapers Ltd	1 328 901	12.2
Telegraph Group Ltd	859 258	7.9
Guardian Newspapers Ltd	317 534	2.9
Independent Newspapers (UK) Ltd	225 491	2.1
Financial Times Ltd	27 301	0.3

Source: **www.abc.org.uk**.

The three-firm concentration ratio is calculated as the sum of the market shares of the biggest three firms — that is, 34.3 + 20.8 + 19.6 = 74.7%.

Concentration ratios may be calculated on the basis of either shares in output or shares in employment. In the above example the calculation was on the basis of output (daily circulation). The two measures may give different results, because the largest firms in an industry may be more capital-intensive in their production methods, which means that their share of employment in an industry will be smaller than their share of output. For purposes of examining market structure, however, it is more helpful to base the analysis of market share on output.

This might seem an intuitively simple measure, but it is *too* simple to enable an evaluation of a market. For a start, it is important to define the market appropriately; for instance, in the above example are *The Financial Times* and the *Sun* really part of the same market?

There may be other difficulties too. Table 18.2 gives some hypothetical market shares for two markets. The five-firm concentration ratio is calculated as the sum of the market shares of the largest five firms. For market A this is 68 + 3 + 2 + 1 + 1 = 75; for market B it is 15 + 15 + 15 + 15 + 15 = 75. In each case the market is perceived to be highly concentrated, at 75%. However, the nature of likely interactions between the firms in these two markets is very different, because the large relative size of firm 1 in market A is likely to give it substantially more market power than any of the largest five firms in market B. Nonetheless, the concentration ratio is useful for giving a first impression of how the market is likely to function.

Largest firms in rank order	Market A	Market B
Firm 1	68	15
Firm 2	3	15
Firm 3	2	15
Firm 4	1	15
Firm 5	1	15

Table 18.2 *Market shares (% of output)*

Figure 18.1 shows the five-firm concentration ratio for a number of industrial sectors in the UK. Concentration varies from 14.1% in tools and 15.6% in paper, printing and publishing to 96% in iron and steel and 99.2% in tobacco. In part, the difference between sectors might be expected to reflect the extent of economies of scale, and this makes sense for many of the industries shown.

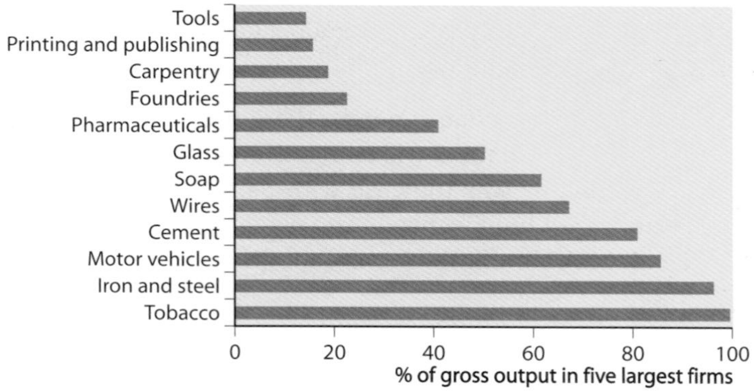

Figure 18.1 *Concentration in UK industry, 1992*

Source: *Census of Production 1992.*

Summary

- Real-world markets do not often conform to the models of perfect competition or monopoly — which are extreme forms of market structure.
- It is important to be able to evaluate the degree of concentration in a market.
- While not a perfect measure, the concentration ratio is one way of doing this, by calculating the market share of the largest firms.

Monopolistic competition

The theory of **monopolistic competition** was devised by Edward Chamberlin, writing in the USA in the 1930s, and his name is often attached to the model, although Joan Robinson published her book on imperfect competition in the UK at the same time. The motivation for the analysis was to explain how markets operated when they were operating neither as monopolies nor under perfect competition.

The model describes a market in which there are many firms producing similar, but not identical, products, e.g. travel agents, hairdressers or fast-food outlets. In the case of fast-food outlets, the high streets of many cities are characterised by large numbers of different types of takeaway – burgers, fish and chips, Indian, Chinese, fried chicken and so on.

> ***Key terms***
>
> **monopolistic competition:** a market that shares some characteristics of monopoly and some of perfect competition
>
> **product differentiation:** a strategy adopted by firms that marks their product as being different from their competitors'

Model characteristics

Three important characteristics of the model of monopolistic competition distinguish this sort of market from others.

Product differentiation

First, firms produce differentiated products, and face downward-sloping demand curves. In other words, each firm competes with the others by making its product slightly different. This allows the firms to build up brand loyalty among their regular customers, which gives them some influence over price. It is likely that firms will engage in advertising in order to maintain such brand loyalty, and heavy advertising is a common characteristic of a market operating under monopolistic competition.

Because other firms are producing similar goods, there are substitutes for each firm's product, which means that demand will be relatively price-elastic. However, it is not perfectly price-elastic, as was the case with perfect competition. These features – that the product is not homogeneous and demand is not perfectly price-elastic – represent significant differences from the model of perfect competition.

Freedom of entry

Second, there are no barriers to entry into the market. Firms are able to join the market if they observe that existing firms are making supernormal profits. New entrants to the market will be looking for some way to differentiate their product slightly from the others – perhaps the next fast-food restaurant will be Nepalese, or Peruvian.

This characteristic distinguishes the market from the monopoly model, as does the existence of fairly close substitutes.

Low concentration

Third, the concentration ratio in the industry tends to be relatively low, as there are many firms operating in the market. For this reason, a price change by one of the firms will have negligible effects on the demand for its rivals' products.

This characteristic means that the market is also different from an oligopoly market, where there are a few firms that interact strategically with each other.

Overview

Taking these three characteristics together, it can be seen that a market of monopolistic competition has some of the characteristics of perfect competition and some features of monopoly; hence its name.

Short-run equilibrium

Figure 18.2 represents short-run equilibrium under monopolistic competition. D_S is the demand curve, and MR_S is the corresponding marginal revenue curve. AC and MC are the average and marginal cost curves for a representative firm in the industry. If the firm is aiming to maximise profits, it will choose the level of output such that $MR_S = MC$. This occurs at output Q_S, and the firm will then choose the price that clears the market at P_S.

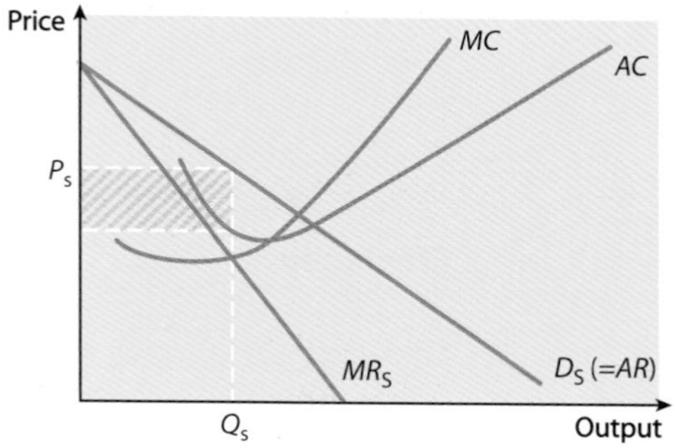

Figure 18.2 Short-run equilibrium under monopolistic competition

This closely resembles the standard monopoly diagram that was introduced in Chapter 17. As with monopoly, a firm under monopolistic competition faces a downward-sloping demand curve, as already noted. The difference is that now it is assumed that there is free entry into the market under monopolistic competition, so that Figure 18.2 represents equilibrium only in the short run. This is because the firm shown in the figure is making supernormal profits, shown by the shaded area (which is $AR - AC$ multiplied by output).

The importance of free entry

This is where the assumption of free entry into the market becomes important. In Figure 18.2 the profits being made by the representative firm will attract new firms into the market. The new firms will produce differentiated products, and this will have two important effects on demand for the representative firm's product. First, the new firms will attract some customers away from this firm, so that its demand curve will tend to shift to the left. Second, as there are now more substitutes for the original product, the demand curve will become more

elastic – remember that the availability of substitutes is an important influence on the own-price elasticity of demand.

Long-run equilibrium

This process will continue as long as firms in the market continue to make profits that attract new firms into the activity. It may be accelerated if firms are persuaded to spend money on advertising in an attempt to defend their market shares. The advertising may help to keep the demand curve downward sloping, but it will also affect the position of the average cost curve, by pushing up average cost at all levels of output.

Figure 18.3 shows the final position for the market. The typical firm is now operating in such a way that it maximises profits (by setting output such that $MR = MC$); at the same time, the average cost curve (AC) at this level of output is at a tangent to the demand curve. This means that $AC = AR$, and the firm is just making normal profit (i.e. is just covering opportunity cost). There is thus no further incentive for more firms to join the market. In Figure 18.3 this occurs when output is at Q_1 and price is set at P_1.

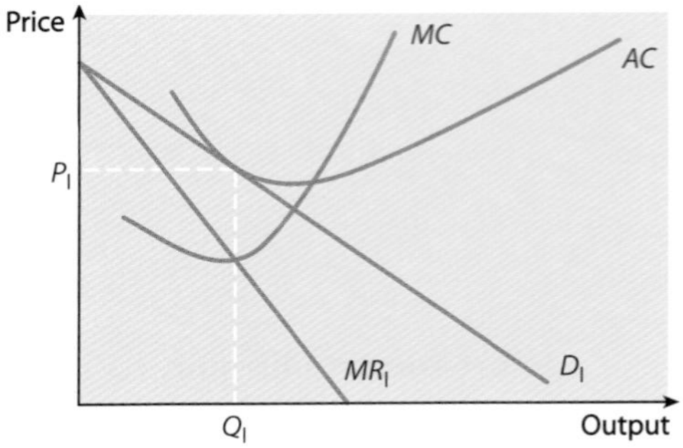

***Figure 18.3** Long-run equilibrium under monopolistic competition*

Efficiency

One way of evaluating the market outcome under this model is to examine the consequences for productive and allocative efficiency. It is clear from Figure 18.3 that neither of these conditions will be met. The representative firm does not reach the minimum point on the long-run average cost curve, and so does not attain productive efficiency; furthermore, the price charged is above marginal cost, so allocative efficiency is not achieved.

Evaluation

If the typical firm in the market is not fully exploiting the possible economies of scale that exist, it could be argued that product differentiation is damaging society's total welfare, in the sense that it is the product differentiation that allows firms to keep their demand curves downward sloping. In other words, too many different products are being produced. However, this argument could be countered by pointing out that consumers may enjoy having more freedom of choice. The very fact that they are prepared to pay a premium price for their chosen brand indicates that they have some preference for it.

Another crucial difference between monopolistic competition and perfect competition is that under monopolistic competition firms would like to sell more of their product at the going price, whereas under perfect competition they can sell as much as they like at the going price. This is because price under monopolistic competition is set above marginal cost. The use of advertising to attract more customers and to maintain consumer perception of product differences may be considered a problem with this market. It could be argued that excessive use of advertising to maintain product differentiation is wasteful, as it leads to higher average cost curves than needed. On the other hand, the need to compete in this way may result in less X-inefficiency than could arise under a complacent monopolist.

Exercise 18.1

Figure 18.4 shows a firm under monopolistic competition.

a Identify the profit-maximising level of output.

b At what price would the firm sell its product?

c What supernormal profits (if any) would be made by the firm?

d Is this a short-run or a long-run equilibrium? Explain your answer.

e Describe any subsequent adjustment that might take place in the market (if any).

f At what level of output would productive efficiency be achieved? (Assume that '*AC*' represents long-run average cost for this part of the question.)

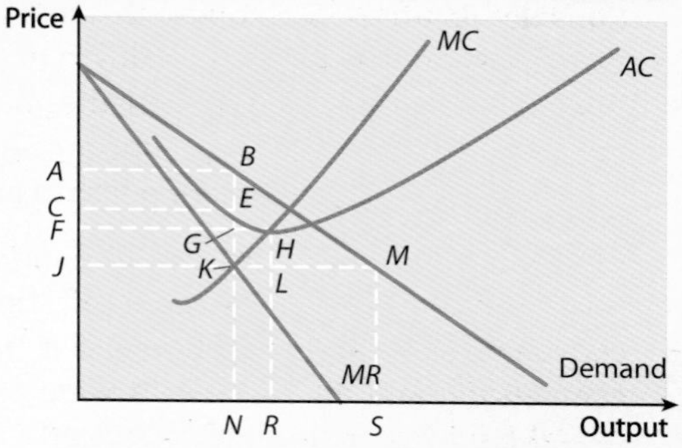

Figure 18.4 *A firm under monopolistic competition*

Summary

- The theory of monopolistic competition has its origins in the 1930s, when economists such as Edward Chamberlin and Joan Robinson were writing about markets that did not conform to the models of perfect competition and monopoly.
- The model describes a market where there are many firms producing similar, but not identical, products.
- By differentiating their product from those of other firms, it is possible for firms to maintain some influence over price.
- To do this, firms engage in advertising to build brand loyalty.
- There are no barriers to entry into the market, and concentration ratios are low.
- Firms in the short run may make supernormal profits.
- In response, new entrants join the market, shifting the demand curves of existing firms and affecting their shape.
- The process continues until supernormal profits have been competed away, and the typical firm has its average cost curve at a tangent to its demand curve.
- Neither productive nor allocative efficiency is achieved in long-run equilibrium.
- Consumers may benefit from the increased range of choice on offer in the market.

Price discrimination

One thing that monopoly and monopolistic competition have in common is that, by setting price above marginal cost, a deadweight loss is imposed on society, with output lower than would be implied by the $P = MC$ outcome. This section examines a special case of monopoly, in which a monopolist will produce the level of output that is allocatively efficient.

Consider Figure 18.5. Suppose this market is operated by a monopolist who faces constant marginal cost *LMC*. (This is to simplify the analysis.) Chapter 17 showed that under perfect competition the market outcome would be a price P^* and quantity Q^*. (See Figure 17.11 for an explanation of this if you need a reminder.) What would induce the monopolist to produce at Q^*?

One of the assumptions made throughout the analysis so far is that all consumers in a market get to pay the same price for the product. This leads to the notion of consumer surplus. In Figure 18.5, if the market were operating under perfect competition and all consumers were paying the same price, consumer surplus would be given by the area AP^*B. If the market were operated by a monopolist, also charging the same price to all buyers, then profits would be maximised where $MC = MR$, i.e. at quantity Q_m and price P_m.

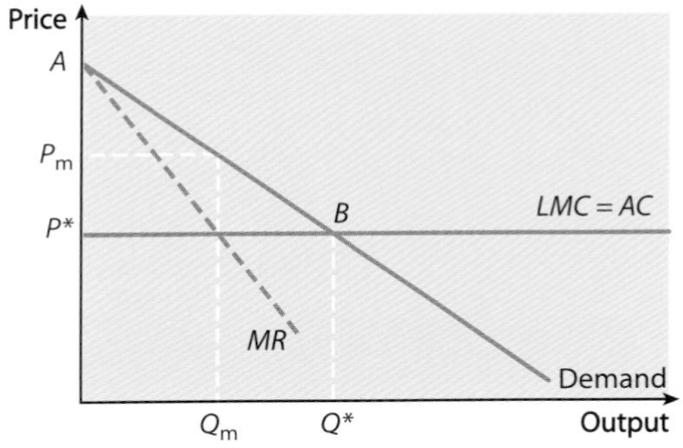

Figure 18.5 *Perfect price discrimination*

But suppose this assumption is now relaxed; suppose that the monopolist is able to charge a different price to each individual consumer. A monopolist is then able to charge each consumer a price that is equal to his/her willingness to pay for the good. In other words, the demand curve effectively becomes the marginal revenue curve, as it represents the amount that the monopolist will receive for each unit of the good. It will then maximise profits at point B in Figure 18.5, where *MR* (i.e. *AR*) is equal to *LMC*. The difference between this situation and that under perfect competition is that the area AP^*B is no longer consumer surplus, but producer surplus, i.e. the monopolist's profits. The monopolist has hijacked the whole of the original consumer surplus as its profits.

From society's point of view, total welfare is the same as it is under perfect competition (but more than under monopoly without discrimination). However, now there has been a redistribution, from consumers to the monopoly — and presumably to the shareholders of the firm. This situation is known as **perfect price discrimination**, or **first-degree price discrimination**.

Key term

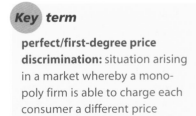

perfect/first-degree price discrimination: situation arising in a market whereby a monopoly firm is able to charge each consumer a different price

Perfect price discrimination is fairly rare in the real world, although it might be said to exist in the world of art or fashion, where customers may commission a painting, sculpture or item of designer jewellery and the price is a matter of negotiation between the buyer and supplier.

However, there are situations in which partial price discrimination is possible. For example, students or old-age pensioners may get discounted bus fares, the young and/or old may get cheaper access to sporting events or theatres etc. In these instances individual consumers are paying different prices for what is in fact the same product.

There are three conditions under which a firm may be able to price discriminate:

1 The firm must have market power.
2 The firm must have information about consumers and their willingness to pay — and there must be identifiable differences between consumers (or groups of consumers).
3 The consumers must have limited ability to resell the product.

Market power

Clearly, price discrimination is not possible in a perfectly competitive market, where no seller has the power to charge other than the going market price. So price discrimination can take place only where firms have some ability to vary the price.

Information

From the firm's point of view, it needs to be able to identify different groups of consumers with different willingness to pay. What makes price discrimination profitable for firms is that different consumers display different sensitivities to price; i.e. they have different price elasticities of demand.

Ability to resell

If consumers could resell the product easily, then price discrimination would not be possible, as consumers would engage in **arbitrage**. In other words, the group of consumers who qualified for the low price could buy up the product and then turn a profit by reselling to consumers in the other segment/s of the market. This would mean that the firm would no longer be able to sell at the high price, and would no longer try to discriminate in pricing.

> ***Key term***
>
> **arbitrage:** a process by which prices in two market segments are equalised by the purchase and resale of products by market participants

In the case of student discounts and OAP concessions, the firm can identify particular groups of consumers; and such 'products' as bus journeys or dental treatment cannot be resold. But why should a firm undertake this practice?

The simple answer is that, by undertaking price discrimination, the firm is able to increase its profits. This is shown in Figure 18.6, which separates two distinct groups of consumers with differing demand curves. Thus, panel (a) shows market A and panel (b) shows market B, with the combined demand curve being shown in panel (c), which also shows the firm's marginal cost curve.

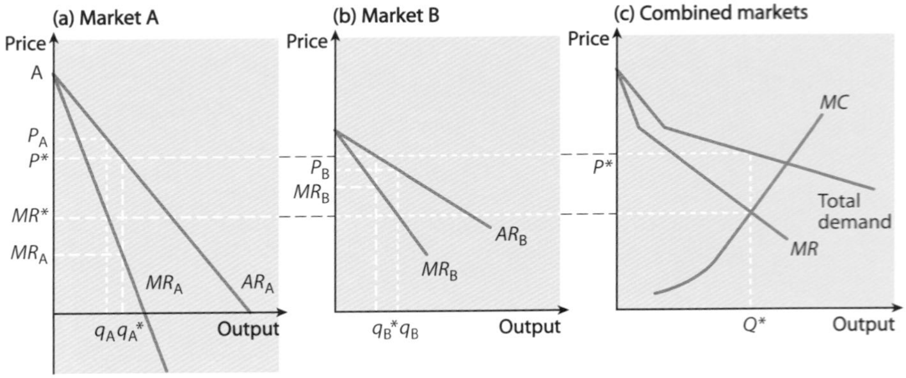

Figure 18.6 A price-discriminating monopolist

If a firm has to charge the same price to all consumers, it sets marginal revenue in the combined market equal to marginal cost, and produces Q^* output, to be sold at a price of P^*. This maximises profits when all consumers pay the same price. The firm sells q_A^* in market A, and q_B^* in market B.

However, if you look at panels (a) and (b), you will see that marginal revenue in market A is much lower (at MR_a) than that in market B (at MR_b). It is this difference in marginal revenue that opens up a profit-increasing opportunity for the firm. By taking sales away from market A and selling more in market B, the firm gains more extra revenue in B than it loses in A. This increases its profit. The optimal position for the firm is where marginal revenue is equalised in the two markets. In Figure 18.6 the firm sells q_A in market A at the higher price of P_A. In market B sales increase to q_B with price falling to P_B. Notice that in both situations the amounts sold in the two sub-markets sum to Q^*.

The consumers in market B seem to do quite well by this practice, as they can now consume more of the good. Indeed, it is possible that with no discrimination the price would be so high that they would not be able to consume the good at all.

An extreme form of price discrimination was used by NAPP Pharmaceutical Holdings, as a result of which the firm was fined £3.2 million by the Office of Fair Trading. NAPP sold sustained-release morphine tablets and capsules in the UK. These are drugs administered to patients with incurable cancer.

NAPP realised that the market was segmented. The drugs were sold partly to the NHS for use in hospitals, but were also prescribed by GPs. As these patients were terminally ill, they tended to spend a relatively short time in hospital before being sent home. NAPP realised that GPs tended to prescribe the same drugs as the patients had received in hospital. It therefore reduced its price to hospitals by 90%, thereby forcing all competitors out of the market and gaining a monopoly in that market segment. It was then able to increase the price of these drugs prescribed through GPs, and so maximise profits. The OFT investigated the firm, fined it and instructed it to stop its actions, thus saving the NHS £2 million per year.

Exercise 18.2

In which of the following products might price discrimination be possible? Explain your answers.

a Hairdressing
b Peak and off-peak rail travel
c Apples
d Air tickets
e Newspapers
f Plastic surgery
g Beer

Summary

- In some markets a monopolist may be able to engage in price discrimination by selling its product at different prices to different consumers or groups of consumers.
- This enables the firm to increase its profits by absorbing some or all of the consumer surplus.
- Under first-degree price discrimination, the firm is able to charge a different price to each customer and absorb all consumer surplus.
- The firm can practise price discrimination only where it has market power, where consumers have differing elasticities of demand for the product, and where consumers have limited ability to resell the product.

Oligopoly

A number of markets seem to be dominated by relatively few firms – think of motor vehicle manufacturing or commercial banking in the UK, or the newspaper industry. A market with just a few sellers is known as an oligopoly market. An important characteristic of such markets is that when making economic decisions each firm must take account of its rivals' behaviour and reactions. The firms are therefore interdependent.

Key term

oligopoly: a market with a few sellers, in which each firm must take account of the behaviour and likely behaviour of rival firms in the industry

An important characteristic of oligopoly is that each firm has to act strategically, both in reacting to rival firms' decisions and in trying to anticipate their future actions.

There are many different ways in which a firm may take such strategic decisions, and this means that there are many ways in which an oligopoly market can be modelled, depending on how the firms are behaving. This chapter reviews just a few such models.

Oligopolies may come about for many reasons, but perhaps the most convincing concerns economies of scale. An oligopoly is likely to develop in a market where there are modest economies of scale – economies that are not substantial enough to require a natural monopoly, but are large enough to make it difficult for too many firms to operate at minimum efficient scale.

Within an oligopoly market, firms may adopt rivalrous behaviour or they may choose to cooperate with each other. The two attitudes have implications for how markets operate. Cooperation will tend to take the market towards the monopoly end of the spectrum, whereas non-cooperation will take it towards the competitive end. In either scenario, it is likely that the market outcome will be somewhere between the two extremes.

The kinked demand curve model

One such model revolves around how a firm *perceives* its demand curve. This is called the kinked demand curve model, and was developed by Paul Sweezy in the USA in the 1930s.

The model relates to an oligopoly in which firms try to anticipate the reactions of rivals to their actions. One problem that arises is that a firm cannot readily observe its demand curve with any degree of certainty, so it must form expectations about how consumers will react to a price change.

Figure 18.7 shows how this works. Suppose the price is currently set at P^*; the firm is selling Q^*, and is trying to decide whether to alter price. The problem is that it knows for sure about only one point on the demand curve: that is, when price is P^*, the firm sells Q^*.

However, the firm is aware that the degree of sensitivity to its price change will depend upon whether or not the other firms in the market will follow its lead. In other words, if its rivals ignore the firm's price change, there will be more sensitivity to this change than if they all follow suit.

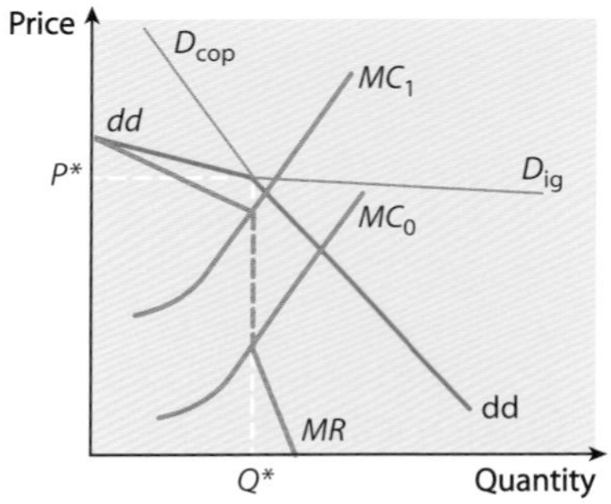

***Figure 18.7** The kinked demand curve*

Figure 18.7 shows the two extreme possibilities for the demand curve the firm perceives that it faces. If other firms ignore its action, D_{ig} will be the relevant demand curve, which is relatively elastic. On the other hand, if the other firms copy the firm's moves, D_{cop} will be the relevant demand curve.

The question then is under what conditions will the other firms copy the price change, and when will they not. The firm may imagine that if it raises price there is little likelihood that its rivals will copy. After all, this is a non-threatening move that gives market share to the other firms. So for a price *increase*, it is D_{ig} that is the relevant section.

On the other hand, a price reduction is likely to be seen by the rivals as a threatening move, and they are likely to copy in order to preserve their market positions. For a price *decrease*, then, it is D_{cop} that is relevant.

Putting these together, the firm perceives that it faces a kinked demand curve (*dd*). Furthermore, if the marginal revenue curve is added to the picture, it is seen to have a discontinuity at the kink. It thus transpires that Q^* is the profit-maximising level of output under a wide range of cost conditions from MC_0 to MC_1; so, even in the face of a change in marginal costs, the firm will not alter its behaviour.

Thus, the model predicts that, if the firm perceives its demand curve to be of this shape, it has a strong incentive to do nothing, even in the face of changes in costs. However, it all depends upon the firm's perceptions. If there is a general increase in costs that affects all producers, this may affect the firm's perception of rival reaction, and thus encourage it to raise price. If other firms are reading the market in the same way, they are likely to follow suit. Notice that this model does not explain how the price reaches P^* in the first place.

Game theory

A more recent development in the economic theory of the firm has been in the application of game theory. This began as a branch of mathematics, but it became apparent that it had wide applications in explaining the behaviour of firms in an oligopoly.

Russell Crowe playing the part of mathematician and game theorist John Nash in A Beautiful Mind.

Key terms

game theory: a method of modelling the strategic interaction between firms in an oligopoly

Prisoners' Dilemma: an example of game theory with a range of applications in oligopoly theory

Game theory itself has a long history, with some writers tracing it back to correspondence between Pascal and Fermat in the mid-seventeenth century. Early applications in economics were by Antoine Augustin Cournot in 1838, Francis Edgeworth in 1881 and J. Bertrand in 1883, but the key publication was the book by John von Neumann and Oskar Morgenstern (*Theory of Games and Economic Behaviour*) in 1944. Other famous names in game theory include John Nash (played by Russell Crowe in the film *A Beautiful Mind*), John Harsanyi and Reinhard Selton, who shared the 1994 Nobel prize for their work in this area.

Almost certainly, the most famous game is the **Prisoners' Dilemma**, introduced in a lecture by Albert Tucker (who taught John Nash at Princeton) in 1950. This simple example of game theory turns out to have a multitude of helpful applications in economics.

Two prisoners, Al Fresco and Des Jardins, are being interrogated about a major crime, and the police know that at least one of the prisoners is guilty. The two are kept in separate cells and cannot communicate with each other. The police have enough evidence to convict them of a minor offence, but not enough to convict them of the major one.

Each prisoner is offered a deal. If he turns state's evidence and provides evidence to convict the other prisoner, he will get off — *unless* the other prisoner also confesses. If both refuse to deal, they will just be charged with the minor offence. Table 18.3 summarises the sentences that each will receive in the various circumstances.

		Des			
		Confess		Refuse	
Al	Confess	10	10	0	15
	Refuse	15	0	5	5

Table 18.3
The Prisoners' Dilemma (years in jail)

In each case, Al's sentence (in years) is shown in orange and Des's in blue. In terms of the entries in the table, if both Al and Des refuse to deal, they will be convicted of the minor offence, and each will go down for 5 years. However, if Al confesses and Des refuses to deal, Al will get off completely free, and Des will take the full rap of 15 years. If Des confesses and Al refuses, the reverse happens. However, if both confess they will each get 10 years.

Think about this situation from Al's point of view, remembering that the prisoners cannot communicate, so Al does not know what Des will choose to do and vice versa. You can see from Table 18.3 that, whatever Des chooses to do, Al will be better off confessing. John Nash referred to such a situation as a **dominant strategy**.

> ***Key term***
>
> **dominant strategy:** a situation in game theory where a player's best strategy is independent of those chosen by others

The dilemma is, of course, symmetric, so for Des too the dominant strategy is to confess. The inevitable result is that if both prisoners are selfish they will both confess — and both will then get 10 years in jail. If they had both refused to deal they would *both* have been better off; but this is too risky a strategy for either of them to adopt. A refusal to deal might have led to 15 years in jail.

What has this to do with economics? Suppose there are two firms (Diamond Tools and Better Spades) operating in a duopoly market (i.e. a market with only two firms). Each firm has a choice of producing 'high' output or 'low' output. The profit made by one firm depends upon two things: its own output, and the output of the other firm.

Table 18.4 shows the range of possible outcomes for a particular time period. Consider Diamond Tools: if it chooses 'low' when Better Spades also chooses 'low', it will make £2 million profit (and so will Better Spades); but if Diamond Tools chooses 'low' when Better Spades chooses 'high', Diamond Tools will make zero profits and Better Spades will make £3 million.

		Better Spades			
		High		Low	
Diamond Tools	High	1	1	3	0
	Low	0	3	2	2

Table 18.4
The Prisoners' Dilemma (profits in £m)

The situation that maximises joint profits is for both firms to produce low; but suppose you were taking decisions for Diamond Tools — what would you choose?

If Better Spades produces 'low' you will maximise profits by producing 'high', whereas if Better Spades produces 'high' you will still maximise profits by producing high! So Diamond Tools has a 'dominant strategy' to produce high — it is the profit-maximising action whatever Better Spades does, even though it means that joint profits will be lower.

Given that the table is symmetric, Better Spades faces the same decision process, and also has a dominant strategy to choose high, so they always end up in the northwest corner of the table, even though southeast would be better for each of them. Furthermore, after they have made their choices and seen what the other has chosen, each firm feels justified by its actions, and thinks that it took the right decision, given the rival's move. This is known as a **Nash equilibrium**, which has the characteristic that neither firm needs to amend its behaviour in any future period. This model can be used to investigate a wide range of decisions that firms need to take strategically.

Key terms

Nash equilibrium: situation occurring within a game when each player's chosen strategy maximises pay-offs given the other player's choice, so that no player has an incentive to alter behaviour

Exercise 18.3

Suppose there are two firms in a market, X and Y; you are taking decisions for firm X. You cannot communicate with the other firm; both firms are considering only the next period. Each firm is choosing whether to set price 'high' or 'low'. Your expectation is that the pay-offs (in terms of profits) to the two firms are as follows (firm X in brown, firm Y in blue):

		Firm Y chooses:			
		High price		Low price	
Firm X chooses:	High price	0	10	1	15
	Low price	15	1	4	4

a If firm Y sets price high, what strategy maximises profits for firm X?

b If firm Y sets price low, what strategy maximises profits for firm X?

c So what strategy will firm X adopt?

d What is the market outcome?

e What outcome would maximise the firms' joint profit?

f How might this outcome be achieved?

g Would the outcome be different if the game were played over repeated periods?

Cooperative games and cartels

Look back at the Prisoners' Dilemma game in Table 18.4. It is clear that the requirement that the firms be unable to communicate with each other is a serious impediment from the firms' point of view. If both firms could agree to produce 'low' they would maximise their joint profits, but they will not risk this strategy if they cannot communicate.

If they could join together in a **cartel**, the two firms could come to an agreement to adopt the low–low strategy.

Key term

cartel: an agreement between firms on price and output with the intention of maximising their joint profits

However, if they were to agree to this each firm would have a strong incentive to cheat, because if each now knew that the other firm was going to produce low, they would also know that they could produce high and dominate the market – at least, given the pay-offs in the table.

This is a common feature of cartels. Collusion can bring high joint profits, but there is always the temptation for each of the member-firms to cheat and try to sneak some additional market share at the expense of the other firm/s in the cartel.

Extension material

You can see how a cartel might operate in Figure 18.8, which shows the situation facing a two-firm cartel (a duopoly). Panels (a) and (b) show the cost conditions for each of the firms, and panel (c) shows the whole market.

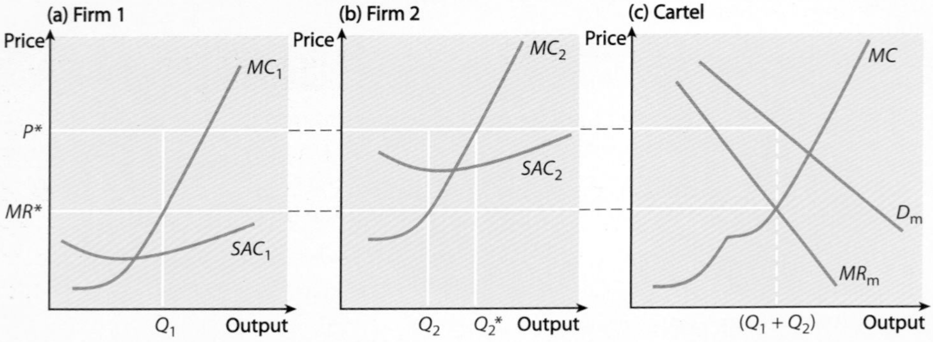

Figure 18.8 Market allocation in a two-firm cartel

If the firms aim to maximise their joint profits, then they set $MR = MC$ at the level of the market (shown in panel (c)). This occurs at the joint level of output $Q_1 + Q_2$, with the price set at P^*. Notice that the joint marginal cost curve is the sum of the two firms' marginal cost curves.

The critical decision is how to divide the market up between the two firms. In the figure, the two firms have different cost conditions, with firm 1 operating at lower short-run average cost than firm 2. If the firms agree to set price at P^*, and each produces up to the point where marginal cost equals the level of (market) marginal revenue at MR^*, then the market should work well. Firm 1 produces Q_1 and firm 2 produces Q_2. Joint profits are maximised, and there is a clear rule enabling the division of the market between the firms.

However, notice that firm 2 is very much the junior partner in this alliance, as it gets a much smaller market share. The temptation to cheat is obvious. If firm 2 accepts price P^*, it sees that its profits will be maximised at Q_2^*, so there is a temptation to try to steal an extra bit of market share.

Of course, the temptation is also there for firm 1, but as soon as either one of the firms begins to increase output the market price will have to fall to maintain equilibrium, and the cartel will be broken: the market will move away from the joint profit-maximising position.

There is another downside to the formation of a cartel. In most countries around the world (with one or two exceptions such as Hong Kong) they are illegal. For example, in the UK the operation of a cartel is illegal under the UK Competition Act, under which the Office of Fair Trading is empowered to fine firms up to 10% of their turnover for each year the cartel is found to have been in operation.

This means that overt collusion is rare. The most famous example is not between firms but between nations, in the form of the Organisation of Petroleum Exporting Countries (OPEC), which over a long period of time has operated a cartel to control the price of oil.

Conditions favouring collusion

Some conditions may favour the formation of cartels – or at least, some form of collusion between firms. The most important of these is the ability of each of the firms involved to monitor the actions of the other firms, and so ensure that they are keeping to the agreement.

In this context, it helps if there is a relatively small number of firms; otherwise it will be difficult to monitor the market. It also helps if they are producing similar goods; otherwise one firm could try to steal an advantage by varying the quality of the product. When the economy is booming it may be more difficult to monitor market shares, because all firms are likely to be expanding. If firms have excess capacity, this may increase the temptation to cheat by increasing output and stealing market share; on the other hand, it also makes it possible for the other firms to retaliate quickly. The degree of secrecy about market shares and market conditions is also important.

Collusion in practice

Although cartels are illegal, the potential gains from collusion may tempt firms to find ways of working together. In some cases firms have joined together in rather loose strategic alliances, in which they may work together on part of their business, perhaps in undertaking joint research and development or technology swaps.

For example, in 2000 General Motors (GM) and Fiat took an equity stake in each other's companies, with GM wanting to expand in Europe and needing to find out more about the technology of making smaller cars. Such alliances have not always been a success, and in the GM–Fiat case GM and Fiat separated in 2005.

The airline market is another sector where strategic alliances have been important, with the Star Alliance and the One World Alliance carving up the long-haul routes between them. Such alliances offer benefits to passengers, who can get access to a wider range of destinations and business class lounges and frequent-flier rewards, and to the airlines, which can economise on airport facilities by pooling their resources. However, the net effect is to reduce competition, and the regulators have interfered with some suggested alliances, such as that between British Airways and American Airlines in 2001, which was investigated by regulators on both sides of the Atlantic. The conditions under which the alliance would have been permitted were such that British Airways withdrew the proposal.

STAR ALLIANCE MEDIA RELATIONS

Strategic alliances in the airline industry are promoted as benefiting customers, but are potentially anti-competitive.

Key term

tacit collusion: situation occurring when firms refrain from competing on price, but without communication or formal agreement between them

Alternatively, firms may look for **tacit collusion**, in which the firms in a market observe each other's behaviour very closely and refrain from competing on price, even if they do not actually communicate with each other. Such collusion may emerge gradually over time in a market, as the firms become accustomed to market conditions and to each other's behaviour.

One way in which this may happen is through some form of *price leadership*. If one firm is a dominant producer in a market, then it may take the lead in setting the price, with the other firms following its example. It has been suggested that the OPEC cartel operated according to this model in some periods, with Saudi Arabia acting as the dominant firm.

An alternative is *barometric price leadership*, in which one firm tries out a price increase and then waits to see whether other firms follow. If they do, a new higher price has been reached without the need for overt discussions between the firms. On the other hand, if the other firms do not feel the time is right for the change they will keep their prices steady, and the first firm will drop back into line or else lose market share. The initiating firm need not be the same one in each round. It has been argued that the domestic air travel market in the USA has operated in this way on some internal routes. The practice is facilitated by the ease with which prices can be checked via the computerised ticketing systems, so that each firm knows what the other firms are doing.

The frequency of anti-cartel cases brought by regulators in recent years suggests that firms continue to be tempted by the gains from collusion. The operation of a cartel is now a criminal act in the UK, as it has been in the USA for some time. This will be discussed in Chapter 20.

Exercise 18.4

For each of the following markets, identify the model that would most closely describe it (i.e. perfect competition, monopoly, monopolistic competition or oligopoly):

a a large number of firms selling branded varieties of toothpaste

b a sole supplier of postal services

c a large number of farmers producing cauliflowers, sold at a common price

d a situation in which a few large banks supply most of the market for retail banking services

e a sole supplier of rail transport

Summary

- An oligopoly is a market with a few sellers, each of which takes strategic decisions based on likely rival actions and reactions.
- Because there are many ways in which firms may interact, there is no single way of modelling an oligopoly market.
- One example is the kinked demand curve model, which argues that firms' perceptions of the demand curve for their products is based on their views about whether or not rival firms will react to their own actions.
- This suggests that price is likely to remain stable over a wide range of market conditions.
- Game theory is a more recent and more flexible way of modelling interactions between firms.
- The Prisoners' Dilemma can demonstrate the potential benefits of collusion, but also shows that in some market situations each firm may have a dominant strategy to move the market away from the joint profit-maximising position.
- If firms could join together in a cartel, they could indeed maximise their joint profits — but there would still be a temptation for firms to cheat, and try to steal market share. Such action would break up the cartel, and move the market away from the joint profit-maximising position.
- However, cartels are illegal in most societies.
- Firms may thus look for covert ways of colluding in a market, for example through some form of price leadership.

Pricing strategies and contestable markets

Having examined a range of models of market structure, it is time to investigate the sorts of pricing strategies that firms may adopt, and how they decide which to go for. This chapter also discusses ways in which firms may try to prevent new firms from joining a market, in terms of both pricing and non-price strategies. The theory of contestable markets is investigated as well.

Learning outcomes

After studying this chapter, you should:

- be aware of the possible pricing rules that can be adopted by firms
- understand the notion of cost-plus pricing, and how this may relate to profit maximisation
- be familiar with the idea of predatory pricing
- be aware of the concept of limit pricing
- understand the notion of contestable markets and its implication for firms' behaviour
- be familiar with other entry deterrence strategies

Pricing rules

In the analysis of market structure, it was assumed that firms set out to maximise profits. However, Chapter 16 pointed out that sometimes they may set out to achieve other objectives. The price of a firm's product is a key strategic variable that must be manipulated in order to attain whatever objective the firm wishes to achieve.

Figure 19.1 illustrates the variety of pricing rules that are possible. The figure shows a firm operating under a form of market structure that is not perfect competition – because the firm faces a downward-sloping demand curve for its product shown by *AR* (= *D*).

Profit maximisation

If the firm chooses to maximise profits, it will choose output such that marginal revenue is equal to marginal cost, and will then set the price to clear the market. In terms of the figure, it will set output at Q_1 and price at P_1.

Revenue maximisation

The economist William Baumol argued that, if there is a divorce of ownership from control in the organisation of a firm, whereby the shareholders have delegated day-to-day decision making to managers (a principal–agent situation), the managers may find themselves with some freedom to pursue other objectives, such as revenue maximisation. A revenue maximiser in Figure 19.1 would choose to produce at the output level at which marginal revenue is zero. This occurs at Q_2 in the figure, with the price set at P_2.

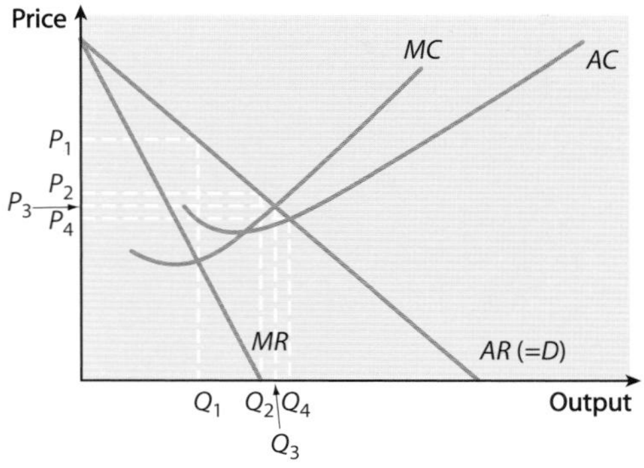

Figure 19.1 *Possible pricing rules*

Sales maximisation

If instead managers set out to maximise the volume of sales subject to covering opportunity cost, they will choose to set output at a level such that price equals average cost, which will clear the market. In Figure 19.1 this happens at Q_4 (with price at P_4).

Allocative efficiency

It has been argued that allocative efficiency in an individual market occurs at the point where price is equal to marginal cost. In Figure 19.1 this is at Q_3 (with price P_3). However, from the firm's perspective there is no obvious reason why this should become an objective of the firm, as it confers no particular advantage.

Exercise 19.1

For each of the following situations, identify the pricing rule most appropriate to achieve the firm's objectives, and comment on the implications that this has for efficiency.

a A firm producing computers tries to achieve as high a market share as possible, measured in value terms.

b A firm producing DVDs tries to make as high a surplus over costs as can be achieved.

c A national newspaper sets out to maximise circulation (subject to covering its costs), knowing that this will affect advertising revenues.

d A farmer producing cabbages finds that she cannot influence the price of her product.

Pricing in practice

It seems clear that in practice most firms do not know the shape of their revenue and cost curves with any great precision. It might thus be argued that they cannot

actually adopt any of these rules, and need to find alternative ways of devising a pricing strategy.

One such approach would be to make a series of small (marginal) changes, and observe the effects each time, thereby moving gradually towards whatever objective the firm wishes to attain. However, if you were to ask managers how they decide on price, many of them would probably say that they use **cost-plus pricing** (sometimes known as mark-up pricing). In other words, they calculate average cost at their chosen output level, and then add on a mark-up to bring them some profit per unit. Indeed, when in 1996 the Bank of England conducted a survey of British companies to see how they set their prices, 37% said that they set prices using a mark-up pricing rule.

> ***Key term***
>
> **cost-plus pricing:** pricing policy whereby firms set their price by adding a mark-up to average cost

Does this nullify the profit-maximising hypothesis? Not necessarily. Saying that a firm sets price as a mark-up on average cost leaves a very important question unanswered: namely, what determines the size of the mark-up that the firm can add to average cost?

The Bank of England survey also discovered that firms in markets in which there were few competitors set higher mark-ups than those in markets in which there were more firms. Mark-ups were also higher in markets where there were differentiated products than in markets producing homogeneous ones.

This pattern of behaviour is entirely compatible with the profit-maximisation hypothesis, where mark-ups are expected to be lower in the presence of a high degree of competition. In other words, mark-up pricing may be a strategy used by firms to find the profit-maximising level of price and output.

Summary

- There are many pricing rules that a firm may choose to adopt, depending on the objectives it wishes to achieve.
- In practice, firms may not know their cost and revenue curves with any accuracy.
- By making marginal changes and observing the effects, they may be able to move towards the price that would achieve their chosen objective.
- Many firms use mark-up pricing, adding a profit margin to average cost.
- The size of the mark-up may depend upon the degree of competition in the market and the extent to which the product is differentiated.
- Mark-up pricing is not inconsistent with profit maximisation.

Price wars

Another finding of the Bank of England's survey was that firms were very strong in saying that they wished to avoid price wars. This could be expected from the kinked demand curve model, where firms in an oligopoly realise that a price reduction is likely to be matched by rivals, leaving all firms with lower profits but having relatively little effect on market shares.

And yet, price wars do break out from time to time. For example, in May 2002 a price war broke out in the UK tabloid newspaper market. It was initiated by the *Express*, but the main protagonists were the *Mirror* and the *Sun*, which joined in after a couple of weeks. The *Mirror* cut its price from 32p to 20p, and the *Sun* from 30p to 20p.

After a week at these lower prices, the editor of the *Sun* was serving champagne in the newsroom in celebration. Their reading of the situation was that the *Mirror* had not expected the *Sun* to follow the price cut. Three weeks after the *Mirror's* price cut, it put its price back up again — followed by the *Sun*. Analysts and observers commented that the only gainers had been the readers, who had enjoyed three weeks of lower prices.

Why should firms act in this way? The *Mirror* argued that it was trying to re-brand itself, and capture new readers who would continue to read the paper even after the price returned to its normal level. This may hint at the reason for a price war — to affect the long-run equilibrium of the market. The *Sun's* retaliation was a natural defensive response to an aggressive move.

In some cases a price war may be initiated as a strategy to drive a weaker competitor out of the market altogether. The motivation then is clear, especially if the initiator of the price war ends up with a monopoly or near-monopoly position in the market. It could be argued that this represents an attempt to maximise profits in the long run by establishing a monopoly position.

Predatory pricing

Perhaps the most common context in which price wars have broken out is where an existing firm or firms have reacted to defend the market against the entry of new firms.

One such example occurred in 1996, in the early years of easyJet, the low-cost air carrier, which was then trying to become established. When easyJet started flying the London–Amsterdam route, charging its now well-known low prices, the incumbent firm (KLM) reacted very aggressively, driving its price down to a level just below that of easyJet's. The response from easyJet was to launch legal action against KLM, claiming it was using unfair market tactics.

Was there a winner in the price war?

> ### Key term
>
> **predatory pricing:** an anti-competitive strategy in which a firm sets price below average variable cost in an attempt to force a rival or rivals out of the market and achieve market dominance

So-called **predatory pricing** is illegal under English, Dutch and EU law. It should be noted that, in order to declare an action illegal, it is necessary to define that action very carefully — otherwise it will not be possible to prove the case in the courts. In the case of predatory pricing, the legal definition is based on economic analysis.

Remember that Chapter 17 defined the shut-down price for the firm, pointing out that if a firm was failing to cover average variable costs its strategy should be to close down immediately, as it would be better off doing so. The courts have backed this theory, and state that a pricing strategy should be interpreted as being predatory if the price is set below average variable costs, as the only motive for remaining in business while making such losses must be to drive competitors out of business and achieve market dominance. This is known as the *Areeda–Turner principle* (after the case in which it was first argued in the USA).

On the face of it, it would seem that consumers have much to gain from such strategies through the resulting lower prices. However, a predator that is successful in driving out the opposition is likely to recoup its losses by putting prices back up to profit-maximising levels thereafter, so the benefit to consumers is short lived.

Having said that, the low-cost airlines survived the attempts of the established airlines to hold on to their market shares. Indeed, in the post-9/11 period, which was a tough one for the airlines for obvious reasons, the low-cost airlines flourished while the more conventional established airlines went through a very difficult period indeed.

In some cases, the very threat of predatory pricing may be sufficient to deter entry by new firms, if the threat is a credible one. In other words, the existing firms need to convince potential entrants that they, the existing firms, will find it in their best interests to fight a price war, otherwise the entrants will not believe the threat. The existing firms could do this by making it known that they had surplus capacity, so that they would be able to increase output very quickly in order to drive down the price.

Whether entry will be deterred by such means may depend in part on the characteristics of the potential entrant. After all, a new firm may reckon that, if the existing firm finds it worth sacrificing profits in the short run, the rewards of dominating the market must be worth fighting for. It may therefore decide to sacrifice short-term profit in order to enter the market — especially if it is diversifying from other markets and has resources at its disposal. The winner will then be the firm that can last the longest; but, clearly, this is potentially very damaging for all concerned.

Exercise 19.2

Discuss the extent to which consumers benefit from a price war.

Limit pricing

An associated but less extreme strategy is limit pricing. This assumes that the incumbent firm has some sort of cost advantage over potential entrants, for example economies of scale.

Key term

limit price: the highest price that an existing firm can set without enabling new firms to enter the market and make a profit

Figure 19.2 shows a firm facing a downward-sloping demand curve, and thus having some influence over the price of its product. If the firm is maximising profits, it is setting output at Q_0 and price at P_0. As average revenue is comfortably above average cost at this price, the firm is making healthy supernormal profits.

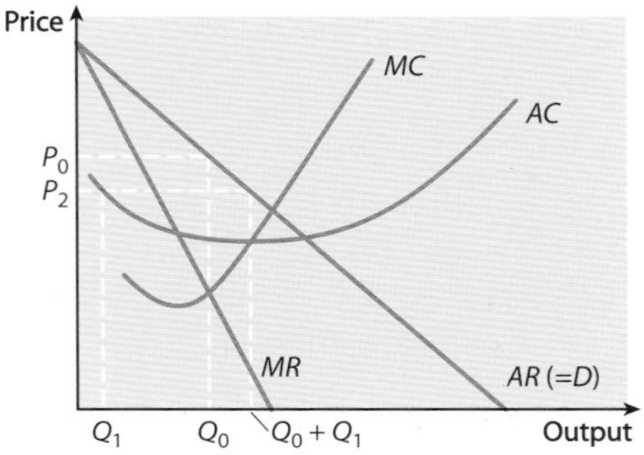

Figure 19.2 Limit pricing

Suppose that the natural barriers to entry in this industry are weak. The supernormal profits will be attractive to potential entrants. Given the cost conditions, the incumbent firm is enjoying the benefit of economies of scale, although producing below the minimum efficient scale.

If a new firm joins the market, producing on a relatively small scale, say at Q_1, the impact on the market can be analysed as follows. The immediate effect is on price, as now the amount $Q_0 + Q_1$ is being produced, pushing price down to P_2. The new firm (producing Q_1) is just covering average cost, so is making normal profits and feeling justified in having joined the market. The original firm is still making supernormal profits, but at a lower level than before. The entry of the new firm has competed away part of the original firm's supernormal profits.

One way in which the firm could have guarded against entry is by charging a lower price than P_0 to begin with. For example, if it had set output at $Q_0 + Q_1$ and price at P_2, then a new entrant joining the market would have pushed the price down to a level below P_2, and without the benefit of economies of scale would make losses and exit the market. In any case, if the existing firm has been in the market for some time it will have gone through a process of learning by doing, and therefore will have a lower average cost curve than the potential entrant. This makes it more likely that limit pricing can be used.

Thus, by setting a price below the profit-maximising level, the original firm is able to maintain its market position in the longer run. This could be a reason for avoiding making too high a level of supernormal profits in the short run, in order to make profits in the longer term.

Notice that such a strategy need not be carried out by a monopolist, but could also occur in an oligopoly, where existing firms may jointly seek to protect their market against potential entry.

Contestable markets

It has been argued that in some markets, in order to prevent the entry of new firms, the existing firm would have to charge such a low price that it would be unable to reap any supernormal profits at all.

This theory was developed by William Baumol, and is known as the theory of contestable markets. It was in recognition of this theory that the monopoly model in Chapter 17 included the assumption that there must be no substitutes for the good, *either actual or potential*.

For a market to be contestable, it must have no barriers to entry or exit and no sunk costs. *Sunk costs* refers to costs that a firm incurs in setting up a business and which cannot be recovered if the firm exits the market. Furthermore, new firms in the market must have no competitive disadvantage compared with the incumbent firm/s; in other words, they must have access to the same technology, and there must be no significant learning-by-doing effects. Entry and exit must be rapid.

Under these conditions, the incumbent firm cannot set a price that is higher than average cost, because as soon as it does it will open up the possibility of *hit-and-run entry* by new firms, which can enter the market and compete away the supernormal profits.

Key term

contestable market: a market in which the existing firm makes only normal profit, as it cannot set a higher price without attracting entry, owing to the absence of barriers to entry and sunk costs

www.econ.nyu.edu/user/baumolw

William Baumol, famous twentieth-century industrial economist who developed the theory of contestable markets.

Consider Figure 19.3, which shows a monopoly firm in a market. The argument is that, if the monopolist charges the profit-maximising price, then if the market is contestable the firm will be vulnerable to hit-and-run entry — a firm could come into the market, take some of the supernormal profits, then exit again. The only way the monopolist can avoid this happening is to set price equal to average cost, so that there are no supernormal profits to act as an incentive for entry.

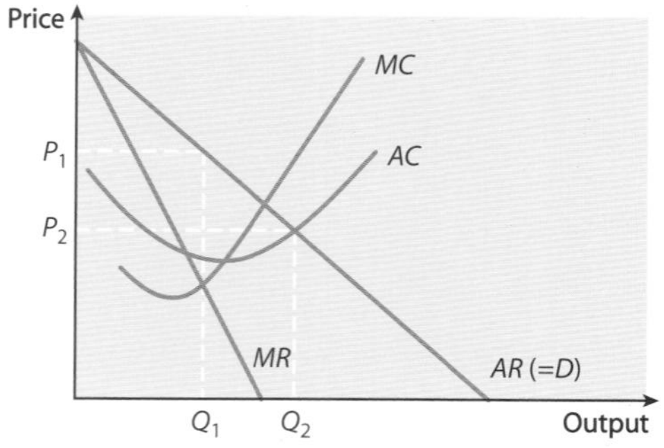

Figure 19.3 *Contestability*

On the face of it, the conditions for contestability sound pretty stringent. In particular, the firm in Figure 19.3 enjoys some economies of scale, so you would think that some sunk costs had been incurred.

However, suppose a firm has a monopoly on a domestic air route between two destinations.

An airline with surplus capacity — i.e. a spare aircraft sitting in a hangar — could enter this route and exit again without incurring sunk costs in response to profits being made by the incumbent firm. This is an example of how contestability may limit the ability of the incumbent firm to use its market power.

Notice in this example that, although the firm only makes normal profits, neither productive nor allocative efficiency is achieved.

A moot point is whether the threat of entry will in fact persuade firms that they cannot set a price above average cost. If entry and exit are so rapid, perhaps the firms can risk making some profit above normal profits and then respond to entry very aggressively if and when it happens. After all, it is difficult to think of an example in which there are absolutely no sunk costs. Almost any business is going to have to advertise in order to find customers, and such advertising expenditure cannot be recovered.

This will be re-examined in the next chapter when discussing competition policy, as it is an important issue in that context, and the degree of contestability may affect the perception of how much market power is in the hands of existing firms.

Other entry deterrence strategies

Pricing is not the only strategy that firms adopt in order to deter entry by new firms. Another approach that has been used over a wide range of economic activities is to raise the fixed costs of being in the industry.

Advertising and publicity

Advertising can be regarded as a component of fixed costs, because expenditure on it does not vary directly with the volume of output. If the firms in an industry typically spend heavily on advertising, it will be more difficult for new firms to become established, as they too will need to advertise widely in order to attract customers.

Similarly, firms may spend heavily on achieving a well-known brand image that will ensure customer loyalty. Hence they may invest a lot in the design and packaging of their merchandise. One such example was the high-profile TV campaign run by Sunny Delight when trying to gain entry into the soft drinks market in the early part of the twenty-first century.

Notice that such costs are also sunk costs, and cannot be recovered if the new firm fails to gain a foothold. It has sometimes been suggested that the cost of excessive advertising should be included in calculations of the social cost of monopoly.

Research and development

A characteristic of some industries is the heavy expenditure undertaken on research and development (R&D). A prominent example is the pharmaceutical industry, which spends large amounts on researching new drugs — and new cosmetics.

This is another component of fixed costs, as it does not vary with the volume of production. Again, new firms wanting to break into the market know that they will need to invest heavily in R&D if they are going to keep up with the new and better drugs and cosmetics always coming on to the market.

Summary

- Although price wars are expected to be damaging for the firms involved, they do break out from time to time.
- This may occur when firms wish to increase their market shares, or when existing firms wish to deter the entry of new firms into the market.
- Predatory pricing is an extreme strategy that forces all firms to endure losses. It is normally invoked in an attempt to eliminate a competitor, and is illegal in many countries.
- Limit pricing occurs when a firm or firms choose to set price below the profit-maximising level in order to prevent entry. The limit price is the highest price that an existing firm can set without allowing entry.
- In some cases the limit price may enable the incumbent firm or firms to make only normal profit. Such a market is said to be contestable.
- Contestability requires that there are no barriers to entry or exit and no sunk costs — and that the incumbent firm/s have no cost advantage over hit-and-run entrants.
- Firms have adopted other strategies designed to deter entry, such as using advertising or R&D spending to raise the cost of entry by adding to required fixed costs.

Exercise 19.3

For each of the following, explain under what circumstances the action of the firm constitutes a barrier to entry and discuss whether there is a strategic element to it, or whether it might be regarded as a 'natural' or 'innocent' barrier.

a A firm takes advantage of economies of scale to reduce its average costs of production.

b A firm holds a patent on the sale of a product.

c A firm engages in widespread advertising of its product.

d A firm installs surplus capacity relative to normal production levels.

e A firm produces a range of very similar products under different brand names.

f A firm chooses not to set price at the profit-maximising level.

g A firm spends extensively on research and development in order to produce a better product.

part 4

Chapter 20

Competition policy and regulation

If resources are going to be allocated efficiently within a society, it is crucial that business organisations make the appropriate economic decisions. Previous chapters have shown that firms may sometimes be able to gain market dominance, giving them sufficient market power to take decisions that cause a distortion in resource allocation. This chapter explores two major policy areas in which authorities attempt to influence firms' economic decision making. It looks first at competition policy, through which the authorities attempt to encourage competition in markets and protect the interests of consumers. It then examines measures introduced to regulate privatised industries, most of which are natural monopolies posing particular problems for resource allocation.

Learning outcomes

After studying this chapter, you should:

- understand the economic underpinnings of competition policy
- appreciate that there may be situations in which unremitting competition may not be in the best interests of society
- be familiar with the roles of the Office of Fair Trading and the Competition Commission
- be aware of the issues that may affect their judgements of a market under investigation
- be familiar with the general institutional background of competition policy in the UK and the EU
- be familiar with some examples of investigations of mergers
- appreciate the arguments for and against privatisation
- understand the need to regulate natural monopolies and some of the problems that may arise in attempting to do so

Competition policy

An awareness of the market failure that can arise from imperfect competition has led governments to introduce measures designed to promote competition and protect consumers. Such measures are known as competition policy.

A key focus of such legislation in the past has been monopoly, as economic analysis highlighted the allocative inefficiency that can arise in a monopoly market if the firm sets out to maximise profit. More recently however, the scope of legislation has widened, and since 1997 competition policy has been toughened significantly.

Key term

competition policy: a set of measures designed to promote competition in markets and protect consumers in order to enhance the efficiency of markets

Before examining competition policy in the context of UK legislation, this chapter describes and evaluates the economic analysis that underpins competition policy measures.

Economic analysis and competition policy

The final section of Chapter 17 undertook a comparison of perfect competition and monopoly, and it is this analysis that lies at the heart of competition policy. Figure 20.1 should remind you of the discussion.

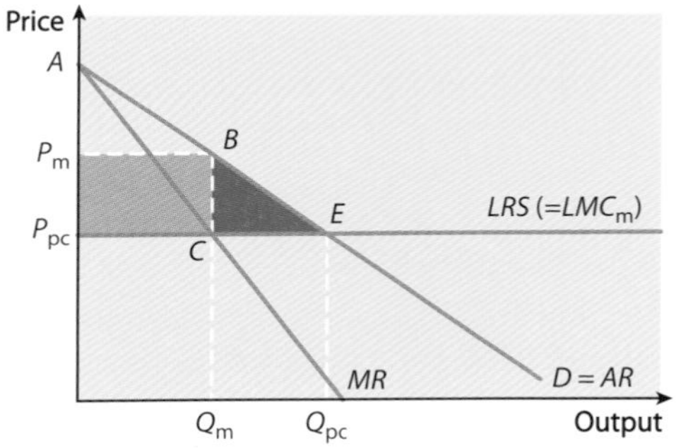

Figure 20.1 Perfect competition and monopoly compared

Here it is assumed there is an industry that can operate either under perfect competition, with a large number of small firms, or as a multi-plant monopolist. For simplicity, it is also assumed that there is no cost difference between the two forms of market structure, so that the long-run supply schedule (LRS) under perfect competition is perceived by the monopolist as its long-run marginal cost curve. In other words, in long-run equilibrium the monopoly varies output by varying the number of plants it is operating.

Under perfect competition, output would be set at Q_{pc} and market price would be P_{pc}. However, a monopolist will choose to restrict output to Q_m and raise price to P_m. Consumer surplus will be reduced by this process, partly by a transfer of the blue rectangle to the monopoly as profits, and partly by the red triangle of deadweight loss. It is this deadweight loss that imposes a cost on society that competition policy is intended to alleviate.

Indeed, this analysis led to a belief in what became known in the economics literature as the *structure–conduct–performance paradigm*. At the core of this belief, illustrated in Figure 20.2, is the simple idea that the structure of a market, in terms of the number of firms, determines how firms in the market conduct themselves, which in turn determines how well the market performs in achieving productive and allocative efficiency.

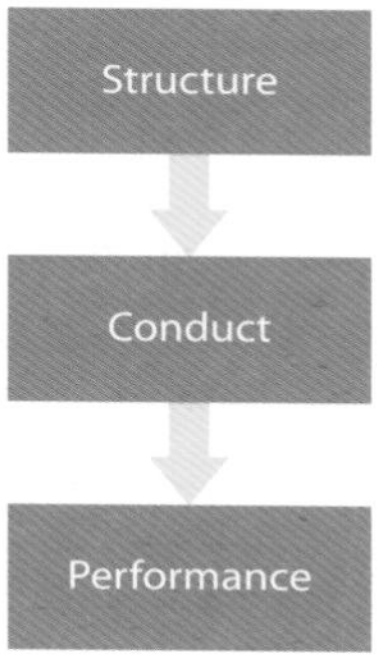

Figure 20.2 *The structure–conduct–performance paradigm*

Thus, under perfect competition firms cannot influence price, and all firms act competitively to maximise profits, thereby producing good overall performance of the market in allocating resources. On the other hand, under monopoly the single firm finds that it can extract consumer surplus by using its market power, and as a result the market performs less well.

This point of view leads to a distrust of monopoly — or, indeed, of any market structure in which firms might be seen to be conducting themselves in an anti-competitive manner. Moreover, it is the structure of the market itself that leads to this anti-competitive behaviour.

If this line of reasoning is accepted, then monopoly is always bad, and mergers that lead to higher concentration in a market will always lead to allocative inefficiency in the market's performance. Thus, legislation in the USA tends to presume that a monopoly will work against the interests of society. However, there are some important issues to consider before pinning too much faith on this assumption.

Cost conditions

The first issue concerns the assumption that cost conditions will be the same under perfect competition as under monopoly. This simplifies the analysis, but there are many reasons to expect economies of scale in a number of economic activities. If this assumption is correct, then a monopoly firm will face lower cost conditions than would apply under perfect competition.

In Figure 20.3, *LRS* represents the long-run supply schedule if an industry is operating under perfect competition. The perfectly competitive equilibrium would be at output level with the price at P_{pc}. However, suppose that a monopolist had a strong cost advantage, and was able to produce at constant long-run marginal cost LMC_m. It would then maximise profit by choosing the output Q_m, where MR_m is equal to LMC_m, and would sell at a price P_m. In this situation the monopolist could actually produce more output at a lower price than a firm operating under perfect competition.

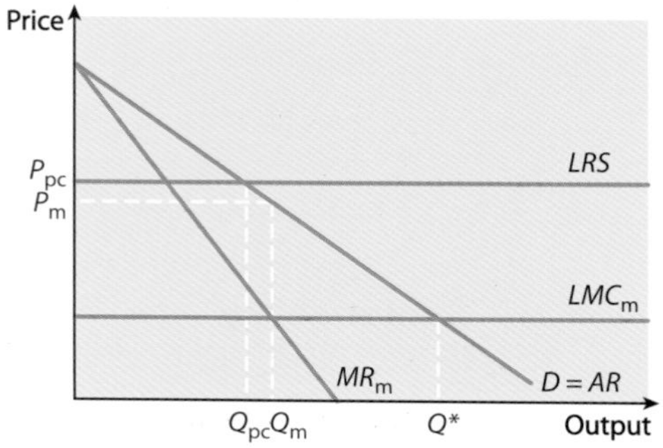

Figure 20.3 *Suppose that monopoly offers much better cost conditions*

Notice that in the monopoly situation the market does not achieve allocative efficiency, because with these cost conditions setting price equal to marginal cost would require the firm to produce Q^* output. However, this loss of allocative efficiency is offset by the improvements in productive efficiency that are achieved by the monopoly firm.

It could be argued that the monopolist should be regulated, and forced to produce at Q^*. However, what incentives would this establish for the firm? If a monopolist knows that whenever it makes supernormal profits the regulator will step in and take them away, it will have no incentive to operate efficiently. Indeed, Joseph Schumpeter argued that monopoly profits were an incentive for innovation, and would benefit society, because only with monopoly profits would firms be able to engage in research and development (R&D). In other words, it is only when firms are relatively large, and when they are able to make supernormal profits, that they are able to devote resources to R&D. Small firms operating in a perfectly competitive market do not have the resources or the incentive to be innovative.

Figure 20.4 illustrates a less extreme case. As before, equilibrium under perfect competition produces output at Q_{pc} and price at P_{pc}. The monopoly alternative faces lower long-run marginal cost, although with a less marked difference than before: here the firm produces Q_m output in order to maximise profits, and sets price at P_m.

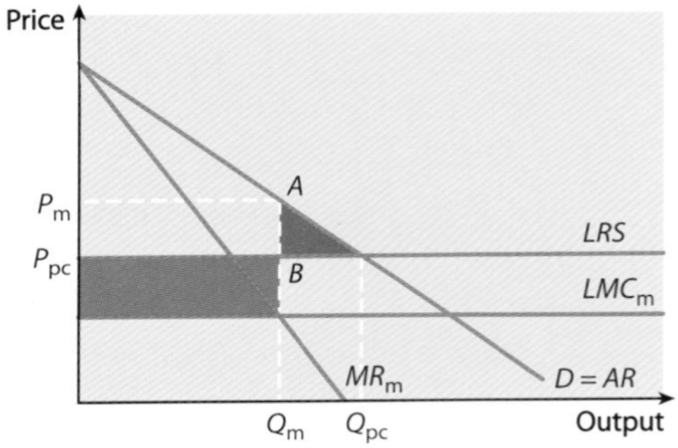

Figure 20.4 Cost conditions again — a less extreme example

Analysis of this situation reveals that there is a deadweight loss given by the red triangle; this reflects the allocative inefficiency of monopoly. However, there is also a gain in productive efficiency represented by the green rectangle. This is part of monopoly profits, but under perfect competition it was part of production costs. In other words, production under the monopoly is less wasteful in its use of resources in the production process.

Is society better off under monopoly or under perfect competition? In order to evaluate the effect on total welfare, it is necessary to balance the loss of allocative efficiency (the red triangle) against the gain in productive efficiency (the green rectangle). In Figure 20.4 it would seem that the rectangle is larger than the triangle, so society overall is better off with the monopoly. Of course, there is also the distribution of income to take into account — the area P_mABP_{pc} would be part of consumer surplus under perfect competition, but under monopoly becomes part of the firm's profits.

Contestability

A second important issue concerns contestability, which was introduced in Chapter 19. If barriers to entry into the market are weak, and if the sunk costs of entry and exit are low, the monopoly firm will need to temper its actions to avoid potential entry.

Thus, in judging a market situation, the degree of contestability is important. If the market is perfectly contestable, then the monopoly firm cannot set a price that is above average cost without allowing hit-and-run entry. In this case, the regulator does not need to intervene. Even without perfect contestability, the firm may need to set a price that is not so high as to induce entry. In other words, it may choose not to produce at the profit-maximising level of output, and to set a price below that level.

Concentration and collusion

The structure–conduct–performance argument suggests that it is not only monopolies that should be the subject of competition policy, but any market in which firms have some influence over price. In other words, oligopolies also need careful attention, because of the danger that they will collude, and act *as if* they were a joint monopoly. After all, it was argued that where a market has just a small number of sellers there may be a temptation to collude, either in a cartel or tacitly. For this reason, government authorities may be wary of markets in which concentration ratios are simply high, even if not 100%.

For this reason, it is important to examine whether a concentrated market is *always* and *necessarily* an anti-competitive market. This is tantamount to asking whether structure necessarily determines conduct. A high concentration ratio may mean that there is a small number of firms of more or less equal size, or it could mean that there is one large firm and a number of smaller competitors. In the latter case you might expect the dominant firm to have sufficient market power to control price.

With a small number of equally sized firms it is by no means certain that they will agree to collude. They may be very conscious of their respective market shares, and so act in an aggressively competitive way in order to defend them. This may be especially true where the market is not expanding, so that a firm can grow only at the expense of the other firms. Such a market could well display intense competition, causing it to drift towards the competitive end of the scale. This would suggest that the authorities should not presume guilt in a merger investigation, since the pattern of market shares may prove significant in determining the firms' conduct, and hence the performance of the market. An example of this appears later in this chapter in the context of the battle for Safeway.

Globalisation

Another significant issue is that a firm that comes to dominate a domestic market may still face competition in the broader global market. This may be especially significant within the European single market.

In this regard, there has been a longstanding debate about how a domestic government should behave towards its large firms. Some economists believe that the government should allow such firms to dominate the domestic market in order that they can become 'national champions' in the global market. This has been especially apparent in the airline industry, where some national airlines are heavily subsidised by their national governments in order to allow them to compete internationally. Others have argued that if a large firm faces competition within the domestic market this should help to encourage its productive efficiency, enabling it to become more capable of coping with international competition.

Summary

- Competition policy refers to a range of measures designed to promote competition in markets and to protect consumers in order to enhance the efficiency of markets in resource allocation.
- One view is that market structure determines the conduct of firms within a market, and this conduct then determines the performance of the market in terms of allocative efficiency.
- A profit-maximising monopolist will produce less output at a higher price than a perfectly competitive market, causing allocative inefficiency.
- However, there may be situations in which the monopolist can enjoy economies of scale, and thereby gain in productive efficiency.
- In the presence of contestability, a monopolist may not be able to charge a price above average cost without encouraging hit-and-run entry.
- In a concentrated market, the pattern of market shares may influence the intensity of competition between firms.
- A firm that is a monopoly in its own country may be exposed to competition in the international markets in which it operates.

Competition policy in the UK

In the UK, competition policy has tended to be less rigid than in the USA, where there seems to be a natural tendency to distrust monopoly. Policy has therefore been conducted in such a way as to take account of the issues discussed above. This has meant that cases of monopoly or concentrated markets have been judged on their individual merits on a case-by-case basis.

This pragmatic approach was embedded in UK legislation from the start — which was the 1948 Monopolies and Restrictive Practices (Inquiry and Control) Act. This Act set up the Monopolies and Restrictive Practices Commission to investigate markets in which a single firm (or a group of firms in collusion) supplied more than one-third of a market. The Commission was asked to decide whether such a market was operating in the public interest, although at that stage the legislation was not very precisely defined.

Since then the legislation has been steadily tightened through a sequence of Acts, the most recent of which are the Competition Act of 1998 and the Enterprise Act of 2002. The Competition Act is in two sections ('chapters'), one dealing with anti-competitive agreements between parties (e.g. firms) and the other dealing with anti-competitive practices by one or more parties — that is, the abuse of a dominant position in a market.

Cartels are covered by Chapter 1 of the 1998 Act, but less formal agreements between firms are also within the scope of the Act, for example price-fixing, agreements to restrict output or agreements to share a market. The Enterprise Act elevated the operation of a cartel to a criminal offence (as opposed to a civil offence).

Sir John Vickers was made Chairman of the Office of Fair Trading in 2003. The OFT has the power to enforce competition and consumer regulation.

The conduct of the policy is entrusted to two agencies: the Office of Fair Trading (OFT) and the Competition Commission. The OFT has the preliminary responsibility for investigating a proposed merger, and then has the power either to impose sanctions directly or to refer the market to the Competition Commission for a full investigation.

A merger is subject to OFT investigation if the firms involved in the proposed merger or acquisition have a combined market share in the UK of more than 25% and if the combined assets of the firms exceed £70 million worldwide. The mission statement of the OFT states:

> The OFT is responsible for making markets work well for consumers. We achieve this by promoting and protecting consumer interests throughout the UK, while ensuring that businesses are fair and competitive. (**http://www.oft.gov.uk/**)

The possible results of an OFT investigation are:

- enforcement action by the OFT's competition and consumer regulation divisions
- referral of the market to the Competition Commission
- recommendations for changes in laws and regulations
- recommendations to regulators, self-regulatory bodies and others to consider changes to their rules
- campaigns to promote consumer education and awareness
- a clean bill of health

The last of these indicates that there is no presumption that the OFT will find anything wrong with a market. Indeed, on a number of occasions the OFT has launched a consumer awareness campaign, having found that the problem with the market lay in the way consumers understood its workings, and not with the market itself.

Probably the best way of understanding how competition policy operates is by exploring some examples of how it has worked in practice. First, however, there is a very important issue to be examined.

Key term

relevant market: a market to be investigated under competition law, defined in such a way that no major substitutes are omitted but no non-substitutes are included

Relevant markets

The first step in any investigation is to identify the relevant market. Until the scope of the market has been defined, it is not possible to calculate market shares or concentration ratios.

How should the market be defined in this context? In other words, which products should be included? Or over which region should the market be defined? Take the market for sugar – is this defined as the market for all sugar, or just for granulated sugar? Is organic sugar a separate product? Or, regarding the market for rail travel in Scotland, do bus services need to be considered as part of the Scottish market for travel?

One way of addressing this question is to apply the *hypothetical monopoly test.* Under this approach, the product market is defined as the smallest set of products and producers in which a hypothetical monopolist controlling all such products could raise profits by a small increase in price above the competitive level.

Extension material

The hypothetical monopoly test is effectively a question about substitution. If in a hypothetical market an increase in price will induce consumers to switch to a substitute product, then the market has not been defined sufficiently widely for it to be regarded as a monopoly. This is demand-side substitutability. One way of evaluating it would be to consult the cross-price elasticity of demand — if it could be measured. This would determine which products were perceived as substitutes for each other by consumers.

For example, in 2003 a number of supermarkets put in bids to take over the Safeway chain. The first step in the investigation was to define the relevant market. One issue that was raised was whether discount stores such as Lidl and Aldi, which sell a limited range of groceries, should be considered part of the same market as supermarkets selling a wide range of grocery products. In the south of the country, the cross-price elasticity of Sainsbury's demand was 0.05 with respect to Lidl's price, but 1.48 with respect to Tesco's price. This suggested that Sainsbury and Tesco were in the same market, but Lidl was not.

It is also important to consider the question of substitutes on the supply side, i.e. whether an increase in price may induce suppliers to join the market. Supply-side substitutability is related to the notion of contestability, in the sense that one way a market can be seen to be contestable is if other firms can switch readily into it, i.e. if there are potential substitutes.

In the following case studies, more detailed material can be gathered from the websites of the OFT (**www.oft.gov.uk**) and the Competition Commission (**www.competition-commission.org.uk**).

Case study 1 Stena and P&O in the Irish Sea

Stena and P&O are two ferry companies providing ferry services across the Irish Sea. In 2003 the OFT reported on an investigation that it had undertaken into a proposed acquisition by Stena of 'certain assets' (five vessels, related staff, port leases and agreements) used by P&O in its ferry operations on the Irish Sea between Liverpool and Dublin and between Fleetwood and Larne.

The OFT began by considering the relevant market; it decided to separate the markets for freight and passengers, and to focus on the ferry services on two of the main routes across the Irish Sea. In terms of the freight market, there were also seen to be two segments, lorry trailers and containers. The OFT chose to focus on the lorry trailer segment.

The OFT found that after such a merger, Stena would have a market share of between 35% and 45%, and that the other three firms operating the route would act as only a weak constraint on Stena's activities. In trying to apply the hypothetical monopoly test, customers were asked whether they would switch their custom to another route if the price were to rise by between 5% and 10%. Many indicated that they would.

The OFT found that in theory there were low barriers to entry into the market, but that in practice the limited availability of berths in the key ports would make entry by a new firm difficult.

In consequence of these investigations, the OFT found that:

> The merger does...appear to result in a substantial lessening of competition within a market or markets in the UK for goods or services.

The merger was thus referred to the Competition Commission for further investigation. The Commission accepted that the merger should be investigated under the share of supply test; in other words, Stena would have more than 25% of the market (as defined) after the merger. The Commission decided that the impact on the tourist market would be small and focused on the market for freight, but it did not accept that the market should be segmented between the lorry trailer and container traffic.

The Commission found that pricing for freight was opaque, and was based on individual negotiations between the ferry company concerned and individual customers. This would allow for price discrimination to take place.

The outcome of the investigation was that the Commission decided that Stena would gain significant market power on the Liverpool–Dublin route, and would have scope to exercise price discrimination on that route, raising prices to some customers in particular. It was felt that the shortage of berths would discourage entry into this market, but that removing that barrier would not be sufficient to attract new firms. The Commission thus prohibited the acquisition by Stena of P&O's assets relating to the Liverpool–Dublin route.

Notice the key steps in the investigation. First, the authorities had to define the market carefully in order to set the context for the investigation. Once that was done, it was not just a question of checking the market shares — although this is important in determining whether the merger qualifies for investigation. The next step was to investigate the extent to which the merged firm would be able to operate without competitive constraint; in other words, how dynamic is the competition from other existing firms, and how likely is it that new firms could gain entry into the market?

Case study 2 Railways in Scotland

The second case study involves FirstGroup plc (First), a UK-based transport company operating a wide range of bus services in Scotland. First put in a bid for the ScotRail franchise, which was due to come into operation in October 2004. The franchise related to the operation of approximately 95% of the passenger rail services in Scotland, together with sleeper services between Scotland and London and through services to Newcastle.

One key issue here is the extent to which bus and rail services were in competition with each other, and the extent to which the combined group would face effective competition.

The OFT collected evidence, some of which suggested that there would be a significant lessening of competition, in particular on 'overlapping routes', i.e. routes in which bus and rail services were both offered. However, First responded that, given that many of its bus

services were already subject to price and frequency regulation, it would have no incentive or ability to give poorer value for money to bus passengers as a result of becoming the rail franchise operator.

The OFT concluded that it could not confidently reject the view that the merger would result in a lessening of competition, and thus referred the proposed acquisition to the Competition Commission.

The Commission's report pointed out that First was the leading supplier of bus travel in the UK, accounting for about 22% of turnover of local bus services in 2003. It was also estimated to operate about 35% of the total route mileage of all bus services in Scotland. As mentioned, the Scottish rail franchise accounts for 95% of railway services in Scotland. So, again, there was no question that the combined group would have a major market share for passenger transport in Scotland were it allowed to go ahead.

In evaluating the likely extent of competition, it was also recognised that the role of private transport could not be ignored in considering the extent of competition.

Of particular concern was the extent to which consumers would be sensitive to changes in the price of bus and rail travel. One source of evidence related to the price elasticities of demand for rail and bus services, and the Commission commissioned a study to collect evidence. The conclusion of this was that the price elasticities of demand for both rail and bus services were significantly inelastic, especially in the short term. In other words, an increase in fares would lead to an increase in revenues of the service operators. This seems to suggest a relatively low degree of competition. However, on overlapping routes bus and rail services were likely to be substitutable.

The Commission then looked in detail at 55 individual routes, focusing on overlapping routes. On 46 of those routes, it concluded that there was a possibility of adverse effects arising from the loss of competition. The expectation was that First would find it profitable to increase fares on the bus services and thus encourage passengers to switch to rail services. This could be reinforced by actions to reduce frequency, re-route services or reconfigure routes. The Commission thus concluded that there would be a substantial lessening of competition on overlapping routes.

There would also be scope for First to introduce multi-modal ticketing, under which passengers could hold tickets that would allow them to use either rail or First bus services. This could be to the detriment of other bus operators.

In this instance, however, the Commission did not prohibit the merger. Instead, it allowed the bid for the franchise to go ahead, on condition that First agree to undertakings related to fares, frequencies and other aspects of services on the affected routes. It was also required to provide information at stations about other operators' bus services.

Thus, a substantial lessening of competition is not always dealt with by prohibiting the merger. After all, if the merger creates economies of scale or economies of scope (as might be available in this instance), then prohibiting the merger prevents those gains in productive efficiency from being achieved.

Case study 3 Biscuits

The third case study involves a proposed acquisition of Jacobs Bakery Ltd (Jacobs) by United Biscuits (UK) Ltd (UB). UB is active mainly in the manufacture and sale of biscuits, cakes and savoury snacks. The OFT investigated the market situation of the firms.

The merger qualified under the turnover test, as the UK turnover of Jacobs alone exceeded £70 million. In addition, the two firms overlapped in the supply of biscuits in the UK, such that the combined firm would together account for a relatively high post-merger share of UK biscuit manufacturing. For these reasons, the merger qualified as a relevant merger situation — hence the OFT involvement.

When the OFT examined the market, it found that there would still be significant competition from other producers across a wide range of biscuit products, from strong retailer own-label products and also from what the OFT referred to as 'non-biscuit snacking products'. In addition, there was evidence of recent new entry from 'non-core' biscuit manufacturers which were successfully gaining market share.

Furthermore, there was some evidence that the manufacturers faced significant buyer power in the form of the supermarkets. Finally, there were a number of alternative biscuit manufacturers that could supply the retailers, not only within the UK but abroad.

Putting all these arguments together, the OFT concluded that the merger would not result in a substantial lessening of competition in the UK biscuit market, and did not refer it for further investigation by the Competition Commission.

Case study 4 The battle for Safeway

In January 2003 the supermarket group Morrison's made an offer for the Safeway group. In the following 3 weeks five other groups expressed an interest in buying Safeway — the rival supermarket groups Sainsbury, Asda and Tesco, plus Philip Green (owner of BHS) and a US venture capital firm Kohlberg Kravis Roberts (KKR).

The Competition Commission had investigated British supermarkets in 1999–2000, and concluded that overall the market was 'generally competitive'. It did however highlight some practices that it considered to be against the public interest; in particular, it investigated the way in which the main supermarkets tended to compete very intensively on a narrow range of products, selling some frequently purchased products below cost, and thereby inhibiting competition in other products. It also investigated the practice of varying prices in different geographic locations in the light of local competitive conditions, i.e. varying prices in ways that did not reflect variations in costs. This implies that the supermarkets were ready to exploit their position in markets where competition was weak. Nonetheless, the Commission concluded that measures to remedy these practices would not be likely to improve overall competitiveness.

So, would changes to the structure of the sector significantly affect these general conclusions in 2003? In other words, would an increase in concentration among British supermarkets be good or bad for consumers?

As usual, any investigation of a market begins by defining the relevant market. In the Competition Commission's earlier investigation, it defined the market as:

> ...the supply in Great Britain of groceries from multiple stores, that is, supermarkets with 600 sq metres or more of grocery sales area, where the space devoted to the retail sale of food and non-alcoholic drinks exceeds 300 sq metres and which are controlled by a person who controls ten or more such stores.

The scope of the inquiry was later extended to the UK (i.e. Northern Ireland was added). 'Groceries' were to include food and drink, cleaning products, toiletries and household goods. This definition then set the context for a discussion of market shares.

Figure 20.5 shows estimated market shares in British supermarkets in January 2003. The issue now begins to become clearer. If Morrison's were to take over Safeway, their combined market share would be 15.9%, which is well below the threshold at which the OFT or Competition Commission would investigate. However, if Tesco, Sainsbury or Asda were to merge with Safeway the combined market share would go through the 25% level, and thus would trigger an investigation.

Figure 20.5 *Market shares among British supermarkets, January 2003*

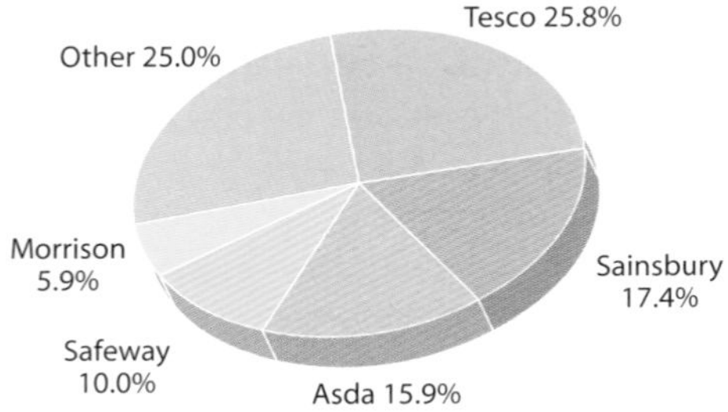

Source: *The Financial Times*, 14 January 2003.

One reason why supermarkets may be looking for merger deals is that planning permission for new stores is increasingly difficult to obtain, so that expansion by buying existing stores is an attractive option.

In analysing this market, a number of issues needed to be weighed carefully before concluding that a merger between Safeway and Morrison's, or Safeway and some other firm, would have costly consequences for consumers or for society as a whole.

It is clear that there are economies of scale in grocery retailing. The corner shop cannot compete on price or on range of produce with the supermarkets, and even specialist quality fishmongers and butchers have a struggle to survive. So perfect competition is not a realistic alternative market structure, and cannot be seen as the reference point for an evaluation of supermarket consolidation.

In any case, in considering a merger involving Safeway, the reference point was the pre-merger market structure. Figure 20.5 shows that the market was already dominated by a few players, so that it was the *marginal* effect on market power that would be important in an investigation.

The relative market shares of firms in the market may be significant. A Morrison's–Safeway merger would create a firm with a 15.9% market share — the same as Asda, and a little smaller than Sainsbury. Morrison's/Safeway might argue that such a merger would enable it to compete more effectively with the other firms in the group, since the result would be to equalise market shares; on the other hand, a move by Tesco for Safeway would create a firm with 35.8% of the market, almost double the size of the second-largest firm. It might be thought that the scope for exploiting market power would be much greater in such a context. Thus, the *pattern* of market shares could be another important consideration.

In its earlier investigation, the Competition Commission was concerned to ensure that consumer choice was protected. In particular, it took steps to guard against the possibility that one of the major players in the market might dominate in particular locations, effectively becoming a local monopoly. It thus recommended that:

> ...if Asda, Morrison, Safeway, Sainsbury or Tesco wish to acquire an existing store, or build a new store, having over 1000 sq metres of grocery retail sales area within a 15-minute drive time of one of its existing stores, or significantly to extend the grocery retailing area of an existing store, it should be required to apply to the Director General of Fair Trading for consent.

In any acquisition of Safeway, analysis would be needed to ensure that such local monopoly situations did not arise. For example, one estimate (*The Financial Times,* 28 January 2003) suggested that Morrison would have to sell 41 stores if it were to acquire Safeway — although the group's own estimate was that it had competition issues in fewer than 10 stores.

Another potentially significant issue arose in the case of Asda, which was bought by the US-based firm Wal-Mart in 1999. Wal-Mart is the world's biggest retailer, and its global *weekly* takings would have sufficed to buy out Safeway. It had expanded at a rapid rate in recent years, with a strong focus on driving down costs to deliver price and value — and to wipe out the competition. Wal-Mart has aspirations to expand in Europe, and thus could be keen to acquire Safeway. However, one stumbling block was that an Asda–Safeway merger would go through the 25% combined market share barrier, and thus threaten to trigger a formal investigation by the OFT/Competition Commission.

Monopsony is a form of market structure that tends to attract less attention than monopoly. Pure monopsony occurs where there is a single *buyer* of a good. The buyer may then be able to exert substantial influence over the suppliers of the good when drawing up contracts on the price and quality of goods. This power may be especially strong when the sellers are relatively small and numerous.

In the context of the supermarkets, it is possible that the sheer buying power of the large chains would leave the relatively fragmented suppliers in a weak bargaining position. The supermarkets would then be able to keep their costs down by using their bargaining strength.

The eventual outcome was that the Commission ruled against all of the bids except that from Morrisons, which was allowed to go ahead — and has indeed now done so.

Key term

monopsony: a market in which there is a single buyer of a good

Competition policy in the European Union

With increasing integration within the European Union, it has become important to be able to investigate possible monopoly situations that arise at an EU level. Accordingly, the EU has a competition policy that enables it to investigate potential abuse of market power when such abuse transcends national borders.

The stance adopted in EU policy has been consistent with that of member countries; indeed, the structure of EU competition policy has informed recent UK legislation. With expanding globalisation, it may be important to coordinate policy still more widely, but this is likely to be problematic. For example, recently Microsoft went on trial in the USA for alleged predatory action in the way that it had launched its internet browser; although initially the judgement went against it, there followed a lengthy appeal. The EU then launched its own court action against Microsoft making similar allegations about the way it marketed its media player.

Summary

- Competition policy in the UK is implemented through the Office of Fair Trading and the Competition Commission.
- The main pillars of policy are legislation dealing with agreements between firms and the abuse of a dominant position.
- A key step in any investigation is to define the relevant market.
- The OFT carries out a preliminary investigation of mergers that meet the criteria in terms of market share and size of assets.
- It then decides whether to refer the merger to the Competition Commission for a thorough investigation.
- Some mergers are allowed to proceed without referral.
- Others are sent to the Commission, which may permit the merger to go ahead, may impose conditions on the firm, or may prohibit it.

Exercise 20.1

The following key facts relate to OFT investigations carried out in recent years. In each case:

- discuss the information provided
- identify actual or potential sources of anti-competitive behaviour
- make a judgement about guilt or innocence
- identify possible remedial action that could be taken (where appropriate)

Case 1 Banking services to small and medium-sized enterprises (SMEs)

There are over 3.5 million SMEs in the UK, accounting for some 55% of employment and 45% of turnover of businesses in the UK; that is, they are crucial to the strength of the economy, especially for their flexibility and adaptability.

There are three separate geographical markets for liquidity management services and general purpose business loans, each highly concentrated, with 90% or more of these services being supplied by four clearing groups.

SMEs are reluctant to switch, and have limited price sensitivity.

A lack of transparency has been observed in the determination of availability and price of overdrafts and general purpose loans.

The main clearing banks show similarities of pricing structure, including in general no payment of interest on current accounts.

There are significant barriers to entry and expansion in the markets for liquidity and general purpose business loans.

Case 2 Veterinary medicines (prescription only medicines (POMs))

Most POMs are supplied by manufacturers to veterinary surgeries via veterinary wholesalers, and are sold by veterinary surgeons to animal owners. Pharmacies also supply to animal owners.

One firm supplies more than a quarter of POMs at the wholesale level.

Veterinary surgeons have been slow to inform animal owners that they can ask for prescriptions; they also tend not to inform clients of the prices prior to dispensing them and not to provide itemised bills. Pricing of POMs does not always reflect the cost of supply, in that prices may not take manufacturers' discounts into account, or may be used to subsidise professional fees.

A group of eight manufacturers has failed to allow pharmacies to obtain supplies of POMs on terms that would enable them to compete with veterinary surgeons. A similar situation exists with all the wholesalers in the market.

Most best-selling POMs in the UK are substantially more expensive in the UK than in Europe, and the price differential is greater for POMs than for other veterinary medicines.

Ex-manufacturer's prices are lowest in countries where pharmacies play a larger role in their supply.

Case 3 Interbrew SA and Bass plc

Interbrew (a quoted Belgian company) acquired Bass plc in May 2000. This merger would have made Interbrew the largest brewer in Great Britain, with an overall market share of between 33% and 38% and a portfolio of leading beer brands. The market would have effectively become a duopoly between Interbrew and Scottish & Newcastle.

The two firms have a common interest in raising operating margins.

Consumers are not price-sensitive in choice of brand.

Interbrew charges different prices according to the type of customer. Discounts are offered to multiple retailers.

It is thought that an increase in non-price competition (advertising and marketing) is likely to follow the merger.

Interbrew argued that the merger would bring synergy benefits and cost savings.

Case 4 Consumer IT goods and services

Around £2 billion is spent on personal computers each year, with the average consumer spending around £1000. In addition, around £250 million is spent by consumers on inkjet printers and £315 million on inkjet cartridges. Over 40% of consumers are first-time buyers.

Overall consumer satisfaction rates are high, and in general consumers can find information enabling them to compare products and prices. However, first-time or inexperienced buyers tend to carry out the least research, placing a premium on point-of-sale information.

Support services are vital for many consumers, but information provided was found to be poor, and the quality of support services often unsatisfactory.

Consumer spending on ink over the lifetime of a printer can amount to more than twice the cost of the inkjet printer, but little information is made available to consumers on the cost per printed page at the point of sale.

Warranty terms tended to be buried in small print.

Regulation of privatised industries

Chapter 17 noted the case of the natural monopoly, and hinted that this poses particular problems with regard to allocative efficiency. Figure 20.6 involves an industry with substantial economies of scale relative to market demand – indeed, the minimum efficient scale is beyond the market demand curve. (In other words, long-run average cost is still falling beyond market demand.)

This market is almost bound to end up as a monopoly, because the largest firm is always able to dominate the market and undercut smaller competitors, as it has a natural cost leadership position. If the monopoly chooses to maximise profits, it will set marginal revenue equal to marginal cost, choose output Q_m and set price at P_m.

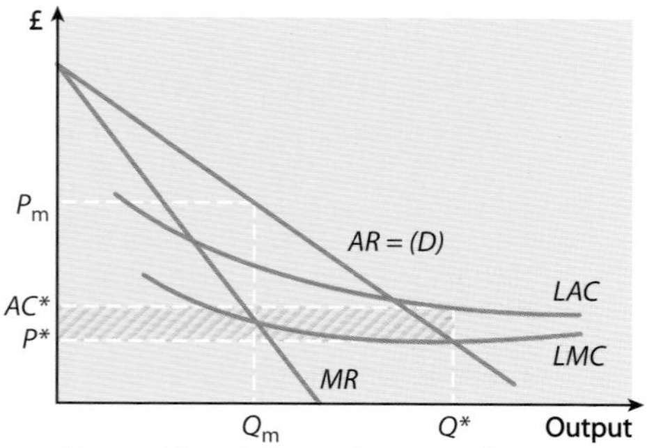

Figure 20.6 *A natural monopoly*

Such industries tend to have large fixed costs relative to marginal costs. Railway systems, water or gas supply and electricity generation are all examples of natural monopolies.

The key problem is that, if such firms were forced to set a price equal to marginal cost, they would make a loss. If the firm in Figure 20.6 were required to set price equal to marginal cost, i.e. at P^*, then it would not be viable: average cost would be AC^*, with losses represented by the shaded area on the diagram.

In the past, one response to this situation would have been to nationalise the industry, i.e. take it into state ownership, since no private-sector firm would be prepared to operate at a loss, and the government would not allow firms running such natural monopolies to act as profit-maximising monopolists making supernormal profits.

In order to prevent the losses from becoming too substantial, many utilities such as gas and electricity supply adopted a pricing system known as a *two-part tariff system*, under which all consumers paid a monthly charge for being connected to the supply, and on top of that a variable amount based on usage. In terms of Figure 20.6, the connection charge would cover the difference between AC^* and P^*, spread across all consumers, and the variable charge would reflect marginal cost.

However, as time went by this sort of system came to be heavily criticised. In particular, it was argued that the managers of the nationalised industries were insufficiently accountable. It could be regarded as an extreme form of the principal–agent problem, in which the consumers (the principals) had very little control over the actions of the managers (their agents), a situation leading to widespread X-inefficiency and waste.

In the 1980s such criticism led to widespread privatisation, i.e. the transfer of nationalised industries into private ownership, one central argument being that now at least the managers would have to be accountable to their shareholders, which would encourage an increase in efficiency.

However, this did not remove the original problem: that they were natural monopolies. So privatisation was accompanied by the imposition of a regulatory system, to ensure that the newly privatised firms did not abuse their monopoly situations.

Wherever possible, privatisation was also accompanied by measures to encourage competition, which was seen as an even better way to ensure efficiency improvements. This proved to be more feasible in some industries than in others, because of the nature of economies of scale – there is little to be gained by requiring that there must be several firms in a market where the economies of scale can be reaped only by one large firm. However, the changing technology in some of the industries did allow some competition to be encouraged, especially in telecommunications.

Where it was not possible, or feasible, to encourage competition, regulation was seen as the solution. Attention of the regulatory bodies focused on price, and the key control method was to allow price increases each year at a rate that was a set amount below changes in the retail price index (RPI). This became known as the (RPI – X) rule, and was widely used, the idea being that it would force companies to look for productivity gains to eliminate the X-inefficiency that had built up. The 'X' refers to the amount of productivity gain that the regulator believes can be achieved, expressed in terms of the change in average costs. For example, if the regulator believed that it was possible to achieve productivity gains of 5% per year, and if the RPI was increasing at a rate of 10% per year, then the maximum price increase that would be allowed in a year would be 10% – 5% = 5%.

There are problems inherent in this approach. For example, how does the regulator set 'X'? This is problematic in a situation where the company has better information about costs than the regulator – another instance of the problems caused by the existence of asymmetric information. There is also the possibility that the firm will achieve its productivity gains by reducing the quality of the product, or by neglecting long-term investment for the future and allowing maintenance standards to lapse.

It is also important to realise that as time goes by, if the (RPI – X) system is effective, the X-inefficiency will be gradually squeezed out, and the 'X' will have to be reduced as it becomes ever more difficult to achieve productivity gains.

In some cases **regulatory capture** is a further problem. This occurs when the regulator becomes so closely involved with the firm it is supposed to be regulating that it begins to champion its cause rather than imposing tough rules where they are needed.

Key term

regulatory capture: a situation in which the regulator of an industry comes to represent its interests rather than regulating it

An alternative method of regulation would be to place a limit on the rate of return the firm is permitted to make, thereby preventing it from making supernormal profits. This too may affect the incentive mechanism: the firm may not feel the need to be as efficient as possible, or may fritter away some of the profits in managerial perks to avoid declaring too high a rate of return.

Case study 5 Gas and electricity supply

British Gas was privatised in 1986, and the electricity sector followed in 1989. These industries have a joint regulator known as Ofgem. They have a joint regulator because together they comprise the energy market.

The energy market in the early twenty-first century is structured as three sub-markets: the wholesale markets, the delivery system and the retail markets.

The delivery sector, which is sometimes referred to as the 'pipes and wires' business, remains a monopoly — or, rather, a sequence of geographical monopolies. These companies run the gas and electricity transportation networks. They are subject to price control using the (RPI – X) rule, and the value of 'X' is reviewed every 5 years.

In the wholesale and retail segments competition has been encouraged. The retail gas market was opened fully to competition in 1998, and the electricity market followed in 1999 — to the extent that price regulation ended in 2002. The wholesale market is now going through a process of reform.

Ofgem claims that the best way to protect customers' interests is through the promotion of competition between suppliers. A review published in 2004 estimated that around 50% of customers had switched their supplier of gas or electricity. The ease of switching supplier is of course crucial if effective competition is to be a way of holding prices at a competitive level. High switching costs are a disincentive to switching.

Research quoted by Ofgem indicates that suppliers lose customers when they increase their prices, and Ofgem claims that this is evidence that competition is working.

A cautionary note is struck by the observation that non-price factors such as brand and marketing methods are increasing in importance, and there have been occasional items on programmes such as BBC's *Watchdog* about high-pressure door-to-door sales methods used to try to get customers to change supplier. Indeed, Ofgem imposed a £2 million penalty on London Electricity (now EDF Energy) for mis-selling, after which complaints about high-pressure sales methods fell by 60%.

Thus, Ofgem's current strategy is to monitor the energy market and find ways of stimulating greater competition among suppliers. The focus is especially on facilitating switching between suppliers and lowering barriers to the entry of new suppliers.

Summary

- Natural monopolies pose particular problems for policy, as setting price equal to marginal cost forces such firms to make a loss.
- In the past, many such industries were run by the state as nationalised industries.
- However, this led to widespread X-inefficiency.
- Many of these industries were privatised after 1979.
- Regulation was put into place to ensure that the newly privatised firms did not abuse their market positions.
- Prices were controlled through the application of the (RPI – X) rule.
- In some cases regulatory capture was a problem, whereby the regulators became too close to their industries.

Review section

Industrial economics is an important branch of economics, dealing with the decisions made by firms and their implications for the allocation of resources. In analysing such decision-making, it soon becomes clear that in some markets there is a danger that the actions taken by firms in pursuit of their objectives may not be the best for society as a whole, so that some form of government intervention may be needed to protect the interests of consumers and of society at large. The chapters in Part 4 examine these issues.

Chapter 16 Firms and their motivations

Given that industrial economics is about the decisions made by firms, the starting point for this part of the book was to identify the key characteristics of firms, why they come into being and why they grow. One way in which firms grow is through *horizontal, vertical* and *conglomerate mergers.* The notions of *short- and long-run cost curves* were introduced as one of the fundamental tools of industrial economics, given the importance of *economies of scale* in the growth of firms. Also fundamental to industrial economics is the identification of the motivations of firms, as it is not possible to analyse the decision-making process without knowing what firms are aiming to achieve by those decisions. *Profit maximisation* is commonly assumed to be an objective of firms, but where shareholders delegate the responsibility for day-to-day decision-making to managers, a *principal–agent problem* may arise which may lead firms to pursue alternative objectives. The concepts of *productive* and *allocative efficiency* were reinterpreted in terms of the cost curves faced by firms.

Chapter 17 Market structure: perfect competition and monopoly

The *market structure* in which a firm operates has a strong influence on its decision-making. *Perfect competition* and *monopoly* may be regarded as two extreme forms of market structure. Make sure you are familiar with the assumptions of both perfect competition and monopoly – they have important implications for how resources are allocated when firms act to maximise profits. You should also be

aware that a monopoly firm is able to choose a combination of price and output, whereas under perfect competition firms have no influence over price. Under perfect competition, a long-run equilibrium is reached that displays both allocative and productive efficiency. Comparing the perfect competition and monopoly outcomes, it can be seen that monopoly with profit maximisation imposes a *deadweight loss* on society – in other words, allocative efficiency is not reached. The conditions under which a monopoly may arise are thus important.

Chapter 18 Market structure: monopolistic competition and oligopoly

The extreme forms of market structure (perfect competition and pure monopoly) are not very common in the real world, so economists need a way of modelling the behaviour of firms in other market environments. Between the extremes is a range of possible market situations with differing degrees of *concentration*. There are markets that have some of the characteristics of monopoly and some features of perfect competition. They tend to be characterised by *product differentiation*, and can be analysed using the model of *monopolistic competition*. Where a market is segmented and different consumers (or groups of consumers) have differing elasticities of demand, a firm may be able to practise *price discrimination*. Markets in which there are just a few sellers are known as *oligopoly* markets. There are many ways of trying to explain firms' behaviour in such markets, where they need to take decisions strategically in anticipation of the actions and reactions of rival firms. By cooperating – for example within a *cartel* – firms may be able to maximise their joint profits, but tensions can arise as each firm may have an incentive to cheat on the cartel agreement.

Chapter 19 Pricing strategies and contestable markets

Firms can use price as a strategic tool in meeting their objectives, whether the objective is profit maximisation or some other goal (such as revenue maximisation) favoured by management. In operational terms, when information about market conditions is incomplete there are a number of rules that a firm may adopt in order to set price, such as *cost-plus pricing*. However, such a pricing rule may take the firm towards profit maximisation, as the size of the markup may depend upon the competitive state of the market in which the firm is operating. In some cases pricing may be used as a strategic tool to deter the entry of new firms, through *predatory* or *limit pricing*. However, where a market is *contestable* a firm may not be able to set price above the competitive price, as hit-and-run entry by competitors might then ensue. Other forms of *barriers to entry* may be used by firms to maintain their market position against new entrants.

Chapter 20 Competition policy and regulation

Competition policy is a set of measures designed to protect consumers and to promote competition in markets. The motivation for such measures arises from the potential deadweight loss that can be imposed on society if firms abuse their market power. Nonetheless, there may be situations in which cost conditions favour the development of large firms that can take advantage of economies of scale, so policy needs to take this into account. Contestability may also provide a natural limit to firms' power. In the UK, competition policy is administered by the *Office of Fair Trading* and the *Competition Commission*, whose role is to monitor firms' behaviour within concentrated markets, considering firms or markets on a case-by-case basis. Competition policy is also in place at the EU level. Chapter 20 also considered the reasons for *privatisation*, and the need to regulate the operation of *natural monopolies*.

Preparing for the examination

For Unit 4 (Industrial Economics) the format is again a combination of supported multiple-choice and data-response questions (one to be chosen). The multiple-choice section requires you to be familiar with the whole range of the topics included in the specification, so do not skip topics during your revision. The data-response section allows you to show the depth of your knowledge and to demonstrate that you can apply the economics that you have learned to particular situations.

Remember that diagrams are an important tool in economics, and you should make use of them wherever appropriate — including in your explanations of the multiple-choice questions. But make sure that you use the diagrams actively. Do not just draw them and hope that the examiner will know why they are there. Explain them, and integrate them into your written response.

Of course, the other thing about diagrams it that it is important to draw them clearly and correctly. Remember to label the axes and curves. Draw your diagrams sufficiently large to be clear — the exam is not the time to save the rainforest by conserving paper. Use a ruler for straight lines — you may think this too obvious a comment, but a sloppily drawn, untidy diagram with the axes drawn freehand creates a poor impression with the examiner. Where there are fixed relationships between curves, remember to draw them carefully — for example, the relationship between *AR* and *MR*, or between *AC* and *MC*. If you do not know what I am talking about here — look it up!

Supported multiple-choice questions

P4.1 Figure P4.1 shows a firm producing at output Q_1.

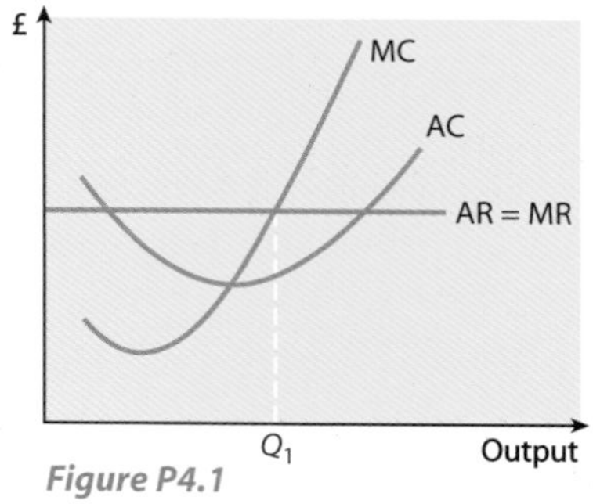

Figure P4.1

Which of the following applies to such a firm?

	Market structure	*Profit*
A	Perfect competition	Normal
B	Perfect competition	Supernormal
C	Monopoly	Normal
D	Monopolistic competition	Normal
E	Monopolistic competition	Supernormal

P4.2 A profit-maximising monopolist experiences an increase in demand. If the firm faces constant average costs, this will lead to:

A lower output and lower supernormal profit
B higher output and lower supernormal profit
C lower output and higher supernormal profit
D higher output and higher supernormal profit
E output and supernormal profit remain unchanged

P4.3 A firm adopting a policy of revenue maximisation will operate at the output level where:

A marginal revenue equals marginal cost
B average costs equal average revenue
C normal profit is zero
D average revenue is zero
E marginal revenue is zero

P4.4 A firm in long-run equilibrium under monopolistic competition will exhibit:

A allocative but not productive efficiency
B productive but not allocative efficiency
C neither productive nor allocative efficiency
D supernormal profits
E both allocative and productive efficiency

P4.5 A profit-maximising monopoly successfully adopts a policy of price discrimination. This policy is likely to result in:

A higher prices to consumers with high price elasticity of demand
B lower prices to consumers with high price elasticity of demand
C an increase in consumer surplus
D differences in marginal revenue in each sub-market
E equality of price elasticity of demand in each sub-market

P4.6 A water supplier finds that it has a natural monopoly, with falling average costs at every level of output. Which of the following statements must be true for such a firm?

A At the profit-maximising level of output the firm will necessarily make a loss.
B The firm will be able to operate in a perfectly contestable market.
C If the firm expands output total costs will necessarily fall.
D The firm's marginal cost will always be below its average costs.
E At the profit-maximising level of output, the firm's marginal revenue will be greater than the marginal cost.

P4.7 The figures in Table P4.1 show national market shares for the UK bus industry.

Company	1994	1997
First Group	12.8	21.6
Stagecoach	13.4	16.0
Arriva	3.5	14.8
Others	70.3	47.6

***Table P4.1** Market shares for the UK bus industry, 1994 and 1997 (%)*

Source: **http://www.competition-commission.org.uk**

From the data it can be deduced that:

- A in 1994 a merger between First Group and Arriva would have been eligible for referral by the Office of Fair Trading
- B in 1997 the bus industry had a three-firm concentration ratio of 47.6%
- C over the period shown the bus industry became more perfectly competitive
- D over the period shown the bus industry became more concentrated
- E over the period shown First Group's sales revenue increased by 8.8%

P4.8 Figure P4.2 shows percentage market shares in the mobile phone market in 2001.

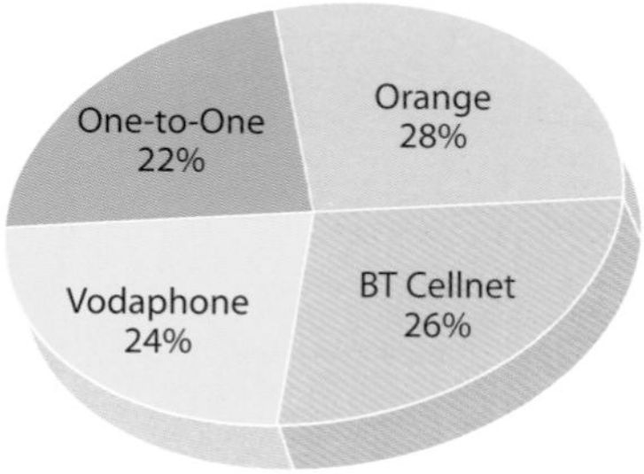

***Figure P4.2** Market shares in the mobile phone market, 2001*

Which of the following statements is true for this market?

- A The market is nearly perfectly competitive because each firm has nearly equal market share.
- B The market is characterised by monopolistic competition because each firm produces mobile phones with different characteristics.
- C The market has a high concentration ratio.
- D The market is perfectly contestable.
- E Tacit collusion is unlikely in this market.

P4.9 In an interview with *The Financial Times* in October 2001, Brian Stewart, chairman of Scottish and Newcastle plc, said he was interested in the potential acquisition of beer distributing companies rather than rival brewers. This suggests that Scottish and Newcastle expect:

- A gains from conglomerate integration
- B gains from vertical integration
- C gains from horizontal integration
- D diseconomies of scale
- E no gains from further growth

P4.10 In 2002, the Competition Commission recommended that the proposed acquisition by Vivendi Water UK plc of another water supplier, Southern Water Services Ltd, be allowed. This recommendation was conditional on Vivendi selling off its holding in another water supplier, South Staffs Group. The basis of such a recommendation would be whether the proposed acquisition was:

- A likely to yield acceptable returns to shareholders
- B politically acceptable to the government
- C likely to cause problems for the UK's trading partners
- D in the interest of Vivendi Water plc
- E in the public interest

Data-response question P4.11

Reuters braced for more cutbacks

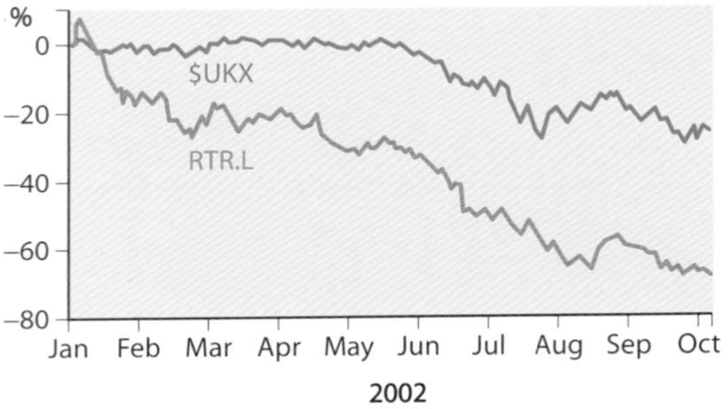

Figure P4.3 *Reuters' share price and the FTSE 100, 2002*

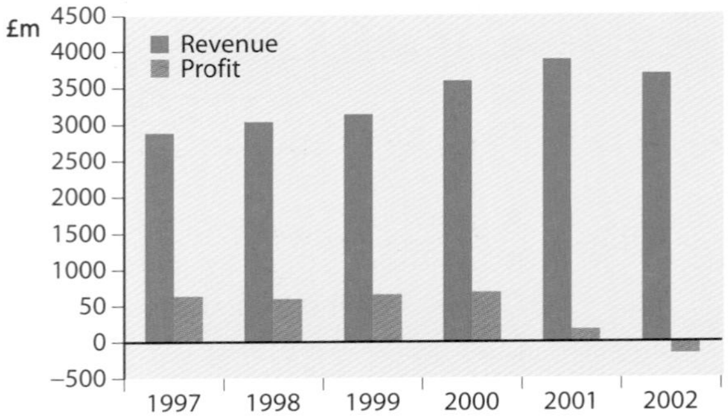

Figure P4.4
Reuters' annual revenue and profit, 1997–2002

Figures for 2002 are annualised half-year results.

Source: **www.reuterssports.org**.

Just a few years ago Reuters, the news organisation, seemed to have everything — a truly global brand, top-notch technology and an internet strategy for the twenty-first century. These days the company is on its knees. The share price has collapsed almost 90% and Tom Glocer, chief executive, is desperately scrambling to cut costs faster than the company loses revenue.

With the downturn in the world economy, Reuters has been revealed to be a bloated organisation that made the greatest error of market leaders: it grew complacent and believed it was safe from competition.

To see just how complacent, look no further than the provision of instant messaging to traders in the City. Bloomberg, Reuters' arch rival, launched its messaging service – a kind of e-mail – in 1992. Traders, analysts and corporate financiers now send 2 million messages a day using Bloomberg's services. Instant messaging is an important reason why so many are reluctant to give up their Bloomberg information terminals. In contrast, Reuters' instant messaging was launched only this year.

Mr Glocer promises that the Reuters' service will prove to be a better product than that of Bloomberg. Reuters' system is designed by Microsoft and, in time, will be capable of carrying voice and pictures. However, Reuters is experiencing a sharp fall in revenue as City workers are laid off in their thousands and companies find that they can obtain information from the internet more cheaply than from dedicated terminals.

The only certainty for Reuters is the need for more cost cutting. Reuters has cut 2400 jobs so far and a full-scale budgetary review is under way. 'We will need to do more cost-cutting and that will, in part, be jobs,' Mr Glocer says. It is difficult to see what other option is open to him. The strategy of slimming the number of product lines while attacking the still-high cost base is supported by major shareholders. Despite the collapse in the share price, it seems that Mr Glocer will be given a chance to revitalise the business.

Adapted from *The Sunday Times*, 20 October 2002

a Using an appropriate diagram, outline how a profit-maximising firm will set the price for its product if it believes that it is 'safe from competition' (line 8). *(4 marks)*

b Analyse the consequences of a fall in demand for such a firm's price, output level and profit. *(6 marks)*

c To what extent do the data suggest that Reuters is a profit-maximising firm? *(8 marks)*

d Explain *two* kinds of economic inefficiency that a firm such as Reuters may exhibit. *(6 marks)*

e To what extent is it likely that new firms will emerge to rival Reuters and Bloomberg? *(8 marks)*

f Evaluate **one** pricing and **one** non-pricing strategy that might be used by Reuters to reverse its decline. *(8 marks)*

Data-response question P4.12

Competition Commission ruling on the provision of food services on trains

In early 2002, Compass Group plc acquired Rail Gourmet UK, a supplier of food services on trains. This was referred to the Competition Commission for investigation.

Food services on trains involve getting food and drink on to trains and then selling it to customers, either as restaurant meals or as buffet and trolley services. Train

operating companies negotiate food contracts with on-train service providers individually. Since the privatisation of the railways, Rail Gourmet UK had attained about 80% of the market. At the time of the acquisition Compass had only 3% of the market, consisting of a small contract with Scotrail and the supply of on-board catering services to Eurostar.

The inquiry focused on whether the acquisition would create any barriers to entry for a competitor wishing to provide on-train food services. It found that there had been a number of new entrants providing trolley services on trains in recent years. This is significant given the potentially adverse consequences for efficiency of the local monopoly enjoyed by on-train food providers. However, the inquiry found less evidence of competition to provide buffet and restaurant-car services.

Compass Group controls about 62% of the supply of food on railway stations under a variety of brand names. However, the product ranges for on-train and on-station food overlap only to a limited extent, and the inquiry considered that this was unlikely to be detrimental to competition.

The Competition Commission concluded that the acquisition by Compass Group of Rail Gourmet does not operate against the public interest.

Source: adapted from **www.competition-commission.org.uk**

---

a **(i)** With reference to the passage, explain why the acquisition of Rail Gourmet UK by Compass Group was eligible for referral to the Competition Commission. *(4 marks)*

(ii) Examine **two** possible motives for Compass Group's acquisition of Gourmet UK. *(8 marks)*

b There have been a number of new entrants to provide trolley services on trains but not to provide restaurant-car and buffet services. Examine **two** possible reasons for this. *(10 marks)*

c Illustrating your answer from the passage or from other material, explain the role of the 'public interest' criterion in UK merger investigations. *(8 marks)*

d Illustrating your answer with a diagram, assess the likely effect on **two** kinds of economic efficiency of the local monopoly enjoyed by on-train food providers (line 14). *(10 marks)*

These questions were taken from examinations set for the Edexcel AS Economics examination for Unit 4 — Industrial economics. We are grateful to London Qualifications for permission to reproduce them here.

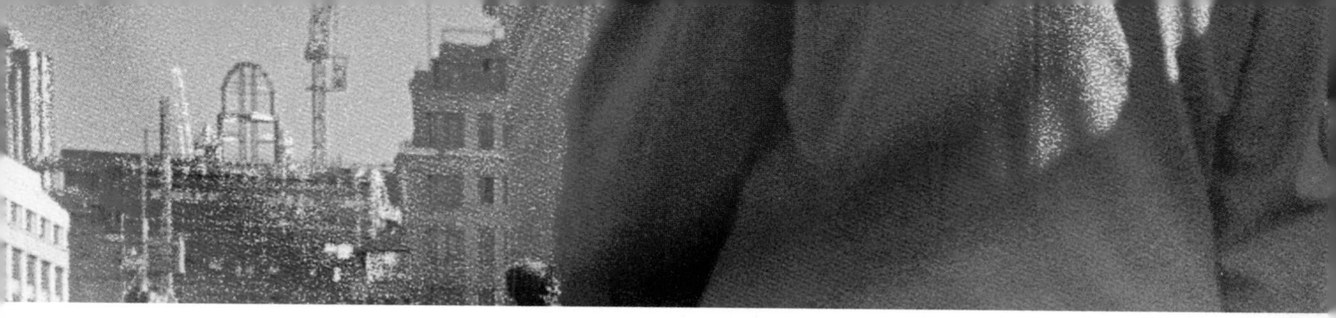

Labour markets

Part 5

part 5

Chapter 21

The demand and supply of labour and market equilibrium

The economic analysis of labour markets sheds light on a range of topical issues. How are wages determined? Why do some people earn far higher wages (or salaries) than others? What is the role of trade unions in the economy? What determines the pattern of unemployment? All these issues and many more will be tackled in this part of the book. The chapter begins by laying the foundations — looking at the labour market as an application of demand and supply analysis.

Learning outcomes

After studying this chapter, you should:

- understand that the demand for labour is a derived demand
- be aware of the relationship between labour input and total and marginal physical product
- understand the concept of marginal revenue product
- be familiar with how a profit-maximising firm chooses the quantity of labour input to use in production
- be aware of the factors that influence the elasticity of demand for labour
- understand the decision of an individual worker as regards labour supply
- be aware of the choice made by the individual worker between work and leisure
- be familiar with the size and structure of the working population in the UK

Demand for labour

Firms are involved in production. They organise the factors of production in order to produce output. Labour is one of the key factors of production used by firms in this process. This means that firms demand labour not for its own sake, but for the sake of the revenue that is obtained from selling the output that labour produces. The demand for labour is thus a **derived demand**, and understanding this is crucial for an analysis of the labour market.

Chapter 16 introduced the notion of the short-run production function, showing the relationship between the quantity of labour input used and the quantity of output produced. Figure 21.1 should remind you of this. Here TPP_L is the **total physical product of labour**. As this is a short-run production function, capital cannot be varied: remember, this is how the short run is defined in this context.

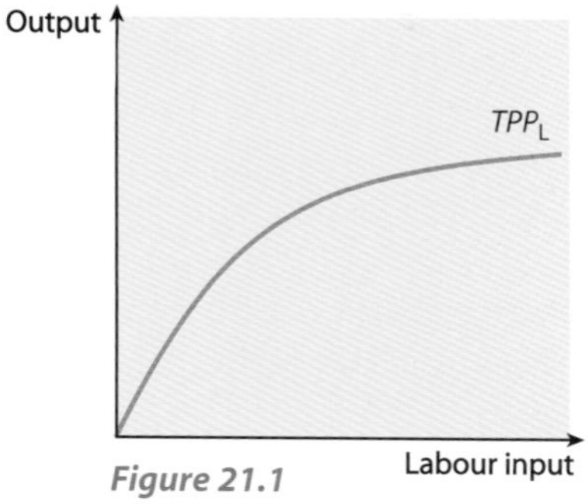

Figure 21.1 A short-run production function

The curve is drawn to show diminishing returns to labour. In other words, as labour input increases, the amount of additional output that is produced diminishes. This is because capital becomes relatively more scarce as the amount of labour increases without a corresponding increase in capital.

In examining the demand for labour, it is helpful to work with the **marginal physical product of labour**, which is the amount of additional output produced if the firm increases its labour input by one unit (e.g. adding one more person-hour), holding capital constant. This is in fact given by the slope of the TPP_L. An example is shown in Figure 21.2. When labour input is relatively low, such as at L_0, the additional output produced by an extra unit of labour is relatively high, at q_0, since the extra unit of labour has plenty of capital with which to work. However, as more labour is added, the marginal physical product falls, so at L_1 labour the marginal physical product is only q_1.

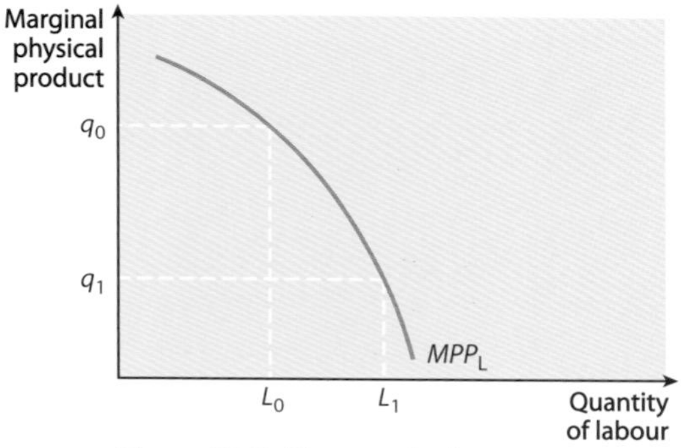

Figure 21.2 The marginal physical product of labour

What matters to the firm is the revenue that it will receive from selling the additional output produced. In considering the profit-maximising amount of labour to employ, therefore, the firm needs to consider the marginal physical product multiplied by the

Key terms

derived demand: demand for a good or service not for its own sake, but for what it produces — for example, labour is demanded for the output that it produces

total physical product of labour (TPP_L): in the short run, the total amount of output produced at different levels of labour input with a fixed amount of capital

marginal physical product of labour (MPP_L): the additional quantity of output produced by an additional unit of labour input

marginal revenue received from selling the extra output, which is known as the **marginal revenue product of labour (MRP_L)**.

If the firm is operating under perfect competition, then marginal revenue and price are the same and MRP_L is MPP_L multiplied by the price. However, if the firm faces a downward-sloping demand curve, it has to reduce the price of its product in order to sell the additional output. Marginal revenue is then lower than price, as the firm must lower the price on *all* of the output that it sells, not just on the last unit sold.

Key term

marginal revenue product of labour (MRP_L): the additional revenue received by a firm as it increases output by using an additional unit of labour input, i.e. the marginal physical product of labour multiplied by the marginal revenue received by the firm

Consider a firm operating under perfect competition, and setting out to maximise profits. Figure 21.3 shows the marginal revenue product curve. The question to consider is how the firm chooses how much labour input to use. This decision is based partly on the knowledge of the MRP_L, but it also depends on the cost of labour.

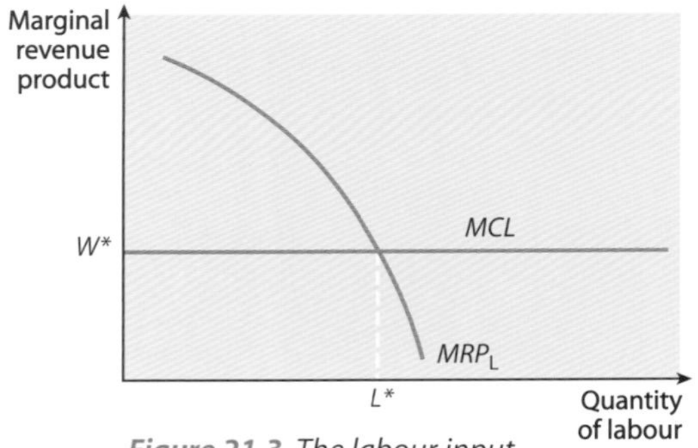

Figure 21.3 The labour input decision of a profit-maximising firm under perfect competition

The main cost of using labour is the wages paid to the workers. There may be other costs — hiring costs and so on — but these can be set aside for the moment. Assuming that the labour market is perfectly competitive, so that the firm cannot influence the market wage and can obtain as much labour as it wants at the going wage rate, the wage can be regarded as the *marginal cost of labour* (*MCL*).

If the marginal revenue received by the firm from selling the extra output produced by extra labour (i.e. the MRP_L) is higher than the wage, then hiring more labour will add to profits. On the other hand, if the MRP_L is lower than the wage, then the firm is already hiring too much labour. Thus, it pays the firm to hire labour up to the point where the MRP_L is just equal to the wage. On Figure 21.3, if the wage is W^*, the firm is maximising profits at L^*. The MRP_L curve thus represents the firm's demand for labour curve. This approach is known as *marginal productivity theory*.

This profit-maximising condition can be written as:

wage = marginal revenue × marginal physical product of labour

which is the same as:

marginal revenue = wage/MPP_L [= marginal cost]

Remember that capital input is fixed for the firm in the short run, so the wage divided by the MPP_L is the firm's cost per unit of output at the margin. This shows that the profit-maximising condition is the same as that derived for a profit-maximising firm in Chapter 16; in other words, profit is maximised where marginal revenue equals marginal cost. This is just another way of looking at the firm's decision.

Exercise 21.1

Table 21.1 shows how the total physical product of labour varies with labour input for a firm operating under perfect competition in both product and labour markets. The price of the product is £5, and the wage rate is £30.

Labour input per period	Output (goods per period)
0	0
1	7
2	15
3	22
4	27
5	29

Table 21.1 A profit-maximising firm

a Calculate the marginal physical product of labour at each level of labour input.

b Calculate the marginal revenue product of labour at each level of labour input.

c Plot the MRP_L on a graph, and identify the profit-maximising level of labour input.

d Suppose that the firm faces fixed costs of £10. Calculate total revenue and total costs at each level of labour input, and check the profit-maximising level.

Factors affecting the position of the demand for labour curve

There are a number of factors that determine the *position* of a firm's labour demand curve. First, anything that affects the marginal physical product of labour will also affect the MRP_L. For example, if a new technological advance raises the productivity of labour, it will also affect the position of the MRP_L. In Figure 21.4 you can see how the demand for labour would change if there were an increase in the marginal productivity of labour as a result of new technology. Initially demand is at MRP_{L0}, but the increased technology pushes the curve to MRP_{L1}. If the wage remains at W^* the quantity of labour hired by the firm increases from L_0 to L_1. Similarly, in the long run, if a firm expands the size of its capital stock, this will also affect the demand for labour.

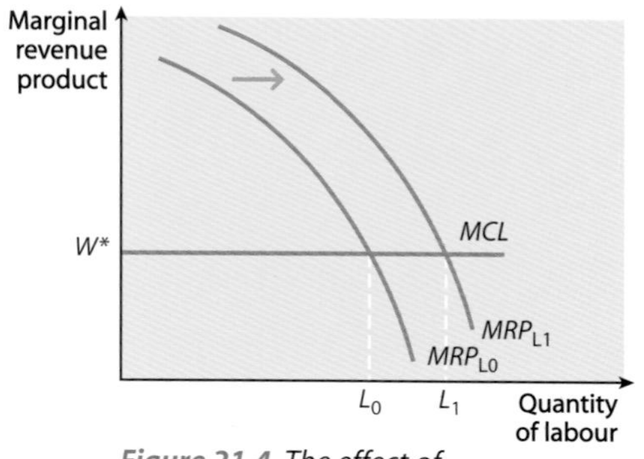

Figure 21.4 The effect of improved technology

Given that the MRP_L is given by MPP_L multiplied by marginal revenue, any change in marginal revenue will also affect labour demand. In a perfectly competitive product market, this means that any change in the price of the product will also affect labour demand. For example, suppose there is a fall in demand for a firm's

product, so that the equilibrium price falls. This will have a knock-on effect on the firm's demand for labour, as illustrated in Figure 21.5. Initially, the firm was demanding L_0 labour at the wage rate W^*, but the fall in demand for the product leads to a fall in marginal revenue product (even though the physical productivity of labour has not changed), from MRP_{L0} to MPR_{L1}. Only L_1 labour is now demanded at the wage rate W^*. This serves as a reminder that the demand for labour is a derived demand that is intimately bound up with the demand for the firm's product.

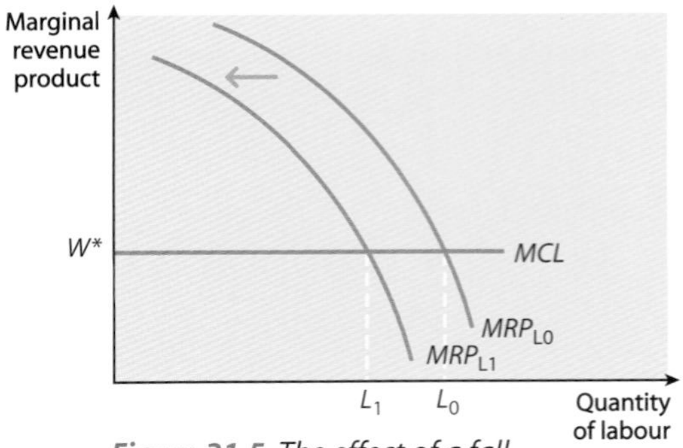

Figure 21.5 The effect of a fall in the demand for a firm's product on the demand for labour

There are a number of possible reasons that could underlie a change in the price of a firm's product — it could reflect changes in the price of other goods, changes in consumer incomes or changes in consumer preferences. All of these indirectly affect the demand for labour.

Summary

- The demand for labour is a derived demand, as the firm wants labour not for its own sake, but for the output that it produces.
- In the short run, a firm faces diminishing returns to increases in labour input if capital is held constant.
- The marginal physical product of labour is the amount of output produced if the firm employs an additional unit of labour, keeping capital input fixed.
- The marginal revenue product of labour is the marginal physical product multiplied by marginal revenue.
- With perfect competition in the product market marginal revenue and price are the same, but if the firm needs to reduce its price in order to sell additional units of output, then marginal revenue is smaller than price.
- A profit-maximising firm chooses labour input such that the marginal cost of labour is equal to the marginal revenue product of labour. This is equivalent to setting marginal revenue equal to marginal cost.
- The firm has a downward-sloping demand curve for labour, given by the marginal revenue product curve.
- The position of the firm's labour demand curve depends on those factors that influence the marginal physical product, such as technology and efficiency, but also on the price of the firm's product.

Elasticity of the demand for labour

In addition to the factors affecting the *position* of the demand for labour curve, it is also important to examine its *shape*. In particular, what factors affect the firm's elasticity of demand for labour with respect to changes in the wage rate? In other words, how sensitive is a firm's demand for labour to a change in the wage rate (the cost of labour)?

Chapter 3 examined the influences on the price elasticity of demand, and identified the most important as being the availability of substitutes, the relative size of expenditure on a good in the overall budget and the time period over which the elasticity is measured. In looking at the elasticity of demand for labour, similar influences can be seen to be at work.

One significant effect on the elasticity of demand for labour is the extent to which other factors of production such as capital can be substituted for labour in the production process. If capital or some other factor can be readily substituted for labour, then an increase in the wage rate (*ceteris paribus*) will induce the firm to reduce its demand for labour by relatively more than if there were no substitute for labour. The extent to which labour and capital are substitutable varies between economic activities, depending on the technology of production, as there may be some sectors in which it is relatively easy for labour and capital to be substituted, and others in which it is quite difficult.

Second, the share of labour costs in the firm's total costs is important in determining the elasticity of demand for labour. In many service activities labour is a highly significant share of total costs, so firms tend to be sensitive to changes in the cost of labour. However, in some capital-intensive manufacturing activity labour may comprise a much smaller share of total production costs.

Third, as was argued above, capital will tend to be inflexible in the short run. Therefore, if a firm faces an increase in wages it may have little flexibility in substituting towards capital in the short run, so the demand for labour may

In many service activities labour is a highly significant share of total costs.

be relatively inelastic. However, in the longer term the firm will be able to adjust the factors of production towards a different overall balance. Therefore, the elasticity of demand for labour is likely to be higher in the long run than in the short run.

These three influences closely parallel the analysis of what affects the price elasticity of demand. However, as the demand for labour is a derived demand, there is an additional influence that must be taken into account: the price elasticity of demand for the product. The more price-elastic is demand for the product, the more sensitive will the firm be to a change in the wage rate, as high elasticity of demand for the product limits the extent to which an increase in wage costs can be passed on to consumers in the form of higher prices.

In order to derive an industry demand curve for labour, it is necessary to add up the quantities of labour that firms in that industry would want to demand at any given wage rate, given the price of the product. As individual firms' demand curves are downward sloping, the industry demand curve will also slope downwards. In other words, more labour will be demanded at a lower wage rate, as shown in Figure 21.6.

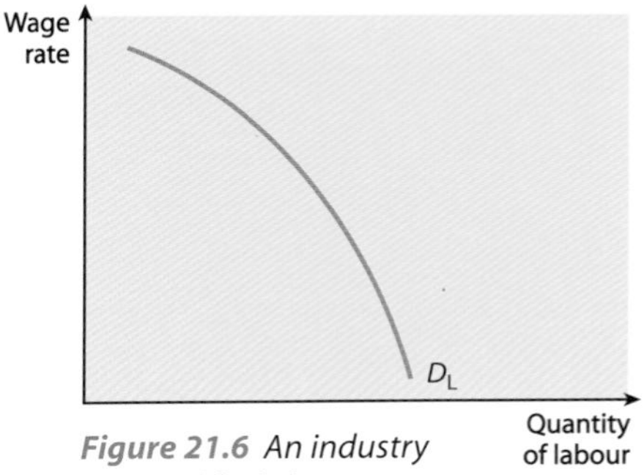

Figure 21.6 *An industry demand for labour curve*

Summary

- The elasticity of demand for labour depends upon the degree to which capital may be substituted for labour in the production process.
- The share of labour in a firm's total costs will also affect the elasticity of demand for labour.
- Labour demand will tend to be more elastic in the long run than in the short run, as the firm needs time to adjust its production process following a change in market conditions.
- As the demand for labour is a derived demand, the elasticity of labour demand will also depend on the price elasticity of demand for the firm's product.

Exercise 21.2

Using diagrams, explain how each of the following will affect a firm's demand for labour:

a a fall in the selling price of the firm's product

b adoption of improved working practices, which improve labour productivity

c an increase in the wage (in a situation where the firm must accept the wage as market determined)

d an increase in the demand for the firm's product

Labour supply

So far, labour supply has been considered only as it is perceived by a firm, and the assumption has been that the firm is in a perfectly competitive market for labour, and therefore cannot influence the 'price' of labour. Hence the firm sees the labour supply curve as being perfectly elastic, as drawn in Figure 21.3, where labour supply was described as *MCL*.

However, for the industry as a whole, labour supply is unlikely to be flat. Intuitively, you might expect to see an upward-sloping labour supply curve (as argued in Chapter 4). The reason given for this was that more people will tend to offer themselves for work when the wage is relatively high. In fact, this is only part of the background to the industry labour supply curve.

An increase in the wage rate paid to workers in an industry will have two effects. On the one hand, it will tend to attract more workers into that industry, thereby increasing labour supply. However, the change may also affect the supply decisions of workers already in that industry, and for existing workers an increase in the wage rate may have ambiguous effects.

Individual labour supply

Consider an individual worker who is deciding how many hours of labour to supply. As with other economic decisions, you need to be aware that every choice comes with an *opportunity cost*. If a worker chooses to take more leisure time, he/she is choosing to forgo income-earning opportunities. In other words, the wage rate can be seen as the opportunity cost of leisure. It is the income that the worker has to sacrifice in order to enjoy leisure time.

Now think about the likely effects of an increase in the wage rate. Such an increase raises the opportunity cost of leisure. This in turn has two effects. First, as leisure time is now more costly, there will be a substitution effect against leisure. In other words, workers will be motivated to work longer hours.

However, as the higher wage brings the worker a higher level of real income, a second effect comes into play, encouraging the consumption of more goods and services — including leisure, if it is assumed that leisure is a *normal good*.

Notice that these two effects work against each other. The substitution effect encourages workers to offer more labour at a higher wage because of the effect of the change in the opportunity cost of leisure. However, the real income effect encourages the worker to demand more leisure as a result of the increase in income. The net effect could go either way.

It might be argued that at relatively low wages the substitution effect will tend to be the stronger. However, as the wage continues to rise, the income effect may gradually become stronger, so that at some wage level the worker will choose to supply less labour and will demand more leisure. The individual labour supply curve will then be backward bending, as shown in Figure 21.7, where an increase in the wage rate above W^* induces the individual to supply fewer hours of work in order to enjoy more leisure time.

Industry labour supply

At industry level, the labour supply curve can be expected to be upward sloping. Although individual workers may display backward-bending supply curves, when workers in a market are aggregated their higher wages will induce people to join the market, either from outside the workforce altogether or from other industries where wages have not risen.

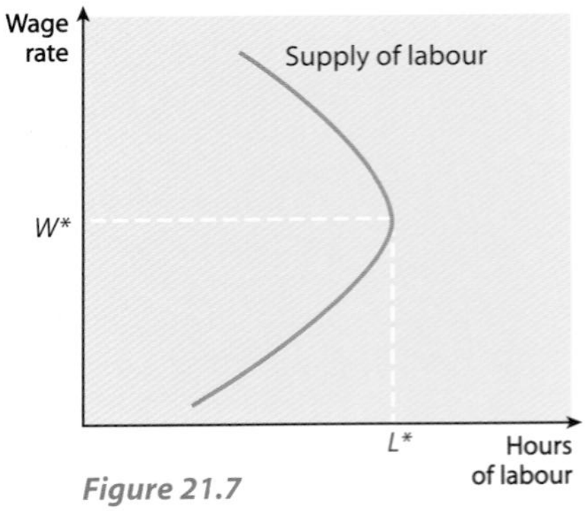

Figure 21.7
A backward-bending individual labour supply curve

Summary

- For an individual worker, a choice needs to be made between income earned from working and leisure.
- The wage rate can be seen as the opportunity cost of leisure.
- An increase in the wage rate will encourage workers to substitute work for leisure through the substitution effect.
- However, there is also an income effect, which may mean that workers will demand more leisure at higher income levels.
- If the income effect dominates the substitution effect, then the individual labour supply curve may become backward bending.
- However, when aggregated to the industry level, higher wages will encourage more people into the industry such that the industry supply curve is not expected to be backward bending.

Labour market equilibrium

Bringing demand and supply curves together for an industry shows how the equilibrium wage is determined. Figure 21.8 shows a downward-sloping demand curve (D_L) based on marginal productivity theory, and an upward-sloping labour supply curve (S_L). Equilibrium is found at the intersection of demand and supply. If the wage is lower than W^* employers will not be able to fill all their vacancies, and will have to offer a higher wage to attract more workers. If the wage is higher than W^* there will be an excess

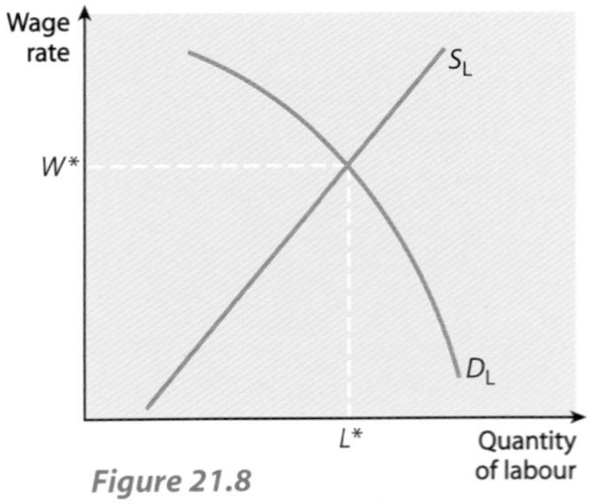

Figure 21.8
Labour market equilibrium

supply of labour, and the wage will drift down until W^* is reached and equilibrium obtains.

Comparative static analysis can be used to examine the effects of changes in market conditions. For instance, a change in the factors that determine the position of the labour demand curve will induce a movement of labour demand and an adjustment in the equilibrium wage. Suppose there is an increase in the demand for the firm's product. This will lead to a rightward shift in the demand for labour, say from D_{L0} to D_{L1} in Figure 21.9. This in turn will lead to a new market equilibrium, with the wage rising from W_0 to W_1.

This may not be the final equilibrium position, however. If the higher wages in this market now encourage workers to switch from other industries in which wages have not risen, this will lead to a longer-term shift to the right of the labour supply curve. In a free market, the shift will continue until wage differentials are no longer sufficient to encourage workers to transfer. The question of wage differentials will be taken up again in the next chapter.

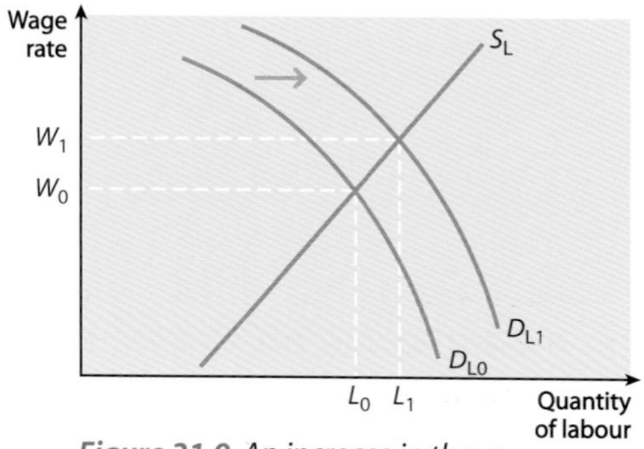

Figure 21.9 An increase in the demand for labour

Summary

- Labour market equilibrium is found at the intersection of labour demand and labour supply.
- This determines the equilibrium wage rate for an industry.
- Comparative static analysis can be used to analyse the effects of changes in market conditions.
- Changes in relative wages between sectors may induce movement of workers between industries.

Labour supply in the UK

For the aggregate situation for labour supply in the UK, in mid-2004 just over 62% of people aged 16 and above were 'economically active'. This means that they were either in employment, were self-employed or were unemployed, i.e. were part of the workforce but could not find jobs.

This overall percentage of the economically active does not vary much from year to year. Since 1992 it has varied between 61.2% and 62.4%. There has been a slight increase in recent years, as the labour market has been relatively healthy, which may have encouraged some people that it is worth their while to join the workforce. Of the 17.5 million people who were economically inactive in mid-2004, 7.9 million (45%) were above the official retirement age.

Focusing on people aged between 16 and 59 (for women) and 64 (for men), 5.9 million (74%) of the economically inactive in this group did not want jobs. Of those who did want jobs, but had not been looking for work in the previous 4 weeks, a number of them were either long-term sick, or looking after family members, or students. There were also small numbers of 'discouraged workers' – that is, people who had withdrawn from the workforce believing that they had no chance of getting a job.

Figure 21.10 shows how the population aged 16 and over have been divided between the various categories in each year since 1992. This shows a gradual rise in the number of employees and a slight fall in the numbers unemployed, although this is easier to see in Figure 21.11, which shows the percentage unemployment rate over this same period.

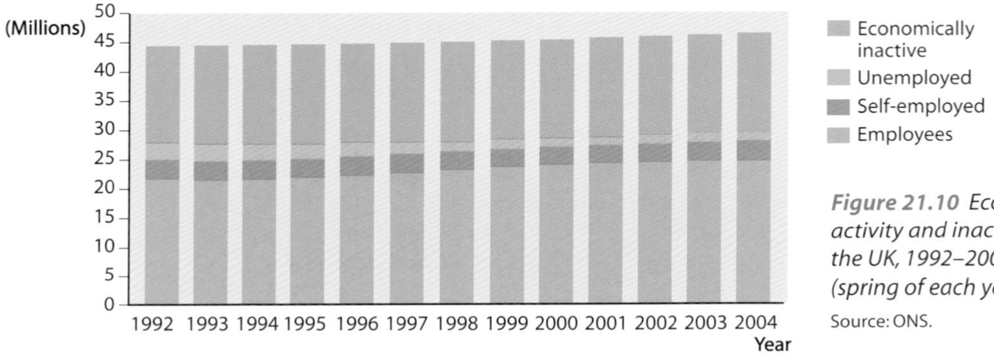

Figure 21.10 Economic activity and inactivity in the UK, 1992–2004 (spring of each year)

Source: ONS.

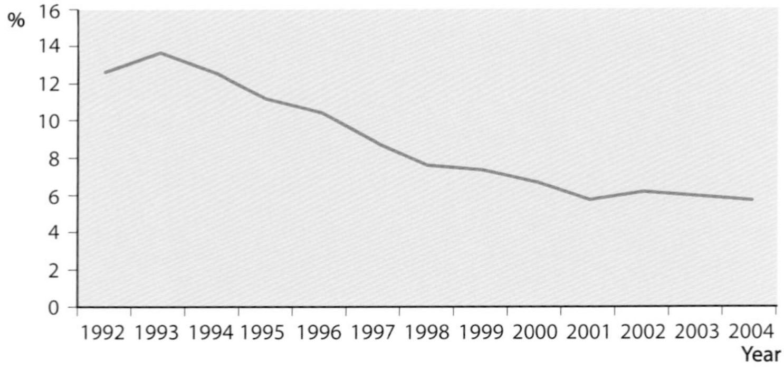

Figure 21.11 Unemployment in the UK, 1992–2004 (spring of each year)

Source: ONS.

Over the past 25 years or so, the UK economy has gone through substantial structural change. You can see something of this in Figure 21.12, which shows the changing pattern of employment in the UK since 1978. One of the key features is the change in the balance of employment between manufacturing activity and services. Back in 1978, 26.7% of workforce jobs were in manufacturing activity, and 61.4% were in services. In 2003 only 12.4% of jobs were in manufacturing, and 78.8% were in services. The finance and business services sector grew especially rapidly during this period, more than doubling the number of jobs between 1978 and 2004. Manufacturing activity virtually halved in the period.

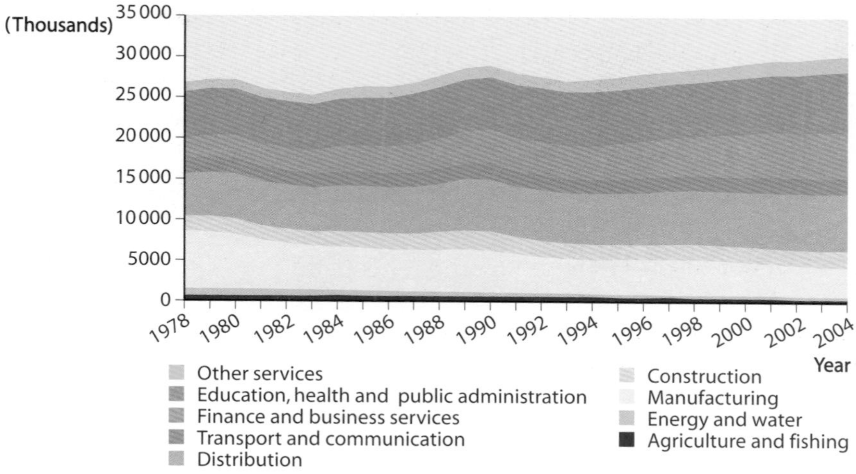

Figure 21.12 *The structure of employee jobs in the UK, 1978–2004*

Source: ONS.

You should not be too surprised at such changes in the pattern of activity over time. In part they may reflect changes in the pattern of consumer demand as incomes have increased over time. In addition, patterns of international trade have also changed over time, especially in the context of closer European integration, which may have affected the pattern of comparative advantage between countries.

Figure 21.13 shows the distribution of workforce jobs in the UK in mid-2004. This underlines the importance of service activity in the UK economy.

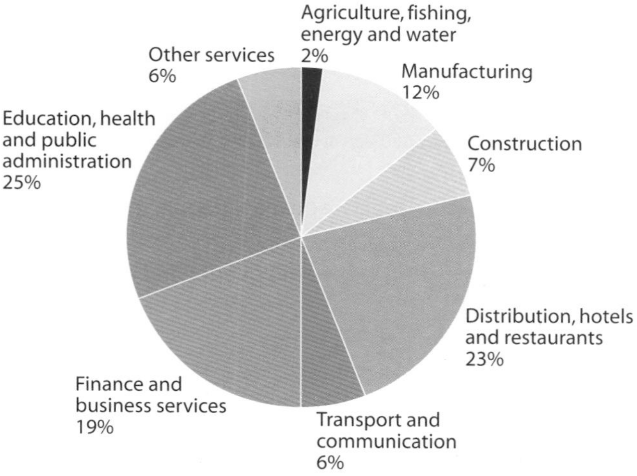

Figure 21.13 *Workforce jobs in the UK, June 2004*

Source: Labour Market Statistics.

Wage differentials, discrimination and the trade unions

Differences in wages between people in different occupations and with different skills can be contentious. For example, why should premiership footballers or pop stars earn such high wages compared with nurses or firefighters? Why do women earn less than men? To what extent has legislation been able to outlaw discrimination on the basis of ethnic origin or gender? And what role do trade unions have in a modern economy? These are some of the issues that will be explored in this chapter.

Learning outcomes

After studying this chapter, you should:

- understand reasons for earnings differentials between people working in different occupations and with different skills
- be aware of some of the issues that arise in explaining gender and ethnic differences in earnings
- be aware of regional differences in wages and earnings
- be familiar with the effect of education on earnings
- understand the role of trade unions in the economy
- understand the effects of trade union activity on the labour market

Labour markets

Chapter 21 examined the demand and supply of labour, sometimes seeing it through the eyes of a firm, sometimes through the eyes of a worker and sometimes looking at an industry labour market. It is important to realise that these are separate levels of analysis. In particular, there is no single labour market in an economy like the UK, any more than there is a single market for goods. In reality, there is a complex network of labour markets for people with different skills and for people in different occupations, and there are overlapping markets for labour corresponding to different product markets.

Thus, when in macroeconomics economists talk about *the* labour market, this is a considerable simplification — helpful in its way, but potentially misleading. This chapter focuses on some microeconomic issues concerning individual labour markets, beginning with an introduction of the important concepts of transfer earnings and economic rent.

Transfer earnings and economic rent

Transfer earnings

Many factors of production have some flexibility about them, in the sense that they can be employed in a variety of alternative uses. A worker may be able to work in different occupations and industries; computers can be put to use in a wide range of activities. The decision to use a factor of production for one particular job rather than another carries an opportunity cost, which can be seen in terms of the next best alternative activity in which that factor could have been employed.

For example, consider a woman who chooses to work as a waitress, because the pay is better than she could obtain as a shop assistant. By making this choice, she forgoes the opportunity to work at, say, John Lewis. The opportunity cost is seen in terms of this forgone alternative. If John Lewis were to raise its rates of pay in order to attract more staff, there would come a point where the waitress might reconsider her decision and decide to be a shop assistant after all, as the opportunity cost of being a waitress has risen.

The threshold at which this decision is taken leads to the definition of transfer earnings. **Transfer earnings** are defined in terms of the minimum payment that is required in order to keep a factor of production in its present use.

Economic rent

In a labour market, transfer earnings can be thought of as the minimum payment that will keep the marginal worker in his or her present occupation or sector. This payment will vary from worker to worker; moreover, where there is a market in which all workers receive the same pay for the same job there will be some workers who receive a wage in excess of their transfer earnings. This excess of payment to a factor over and above what is required to keep it in its present use is known as **economic rent**.

The total payments to a factor can thus be divided between these two — part of the payment is transfer earnings, and the remainder is economic rent.

> ***Key terms***
>
> **transfer earnings:** the minimum payment required to keep a factor of production in its present use
>
> **economic rent:** a payment received by a factor of production over and above what would be needed to keep it in its present use

Probably the best way of explaining the way in which a worker's earnings can be divided between transfer earnings and economic rent is through an appropriate diagram. Figure 22.1 illustrates the two concepts. In the labour market as drawn, firms' demand for labour is a downward-sloping function of the wage rate. Workers' supply of labour also depends on the wage rate, with workers being prepared to supply more labour to the labour market at higher wages. Equilibrium is the point at which demand equals supply, with wage rate W^* and quantity of labour L^*.

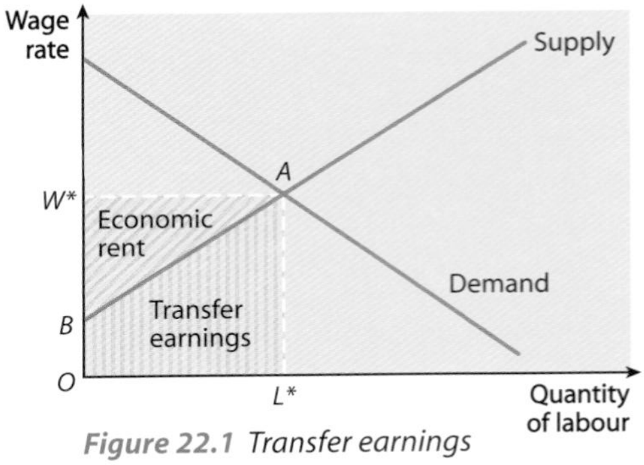

Figure 22.1 Transfer earnings and economic rent

Think about the nature of the labour supply curve. It reveals how much labour the workers are prepared to supply at any given wage rate. At the equilibrium wage rate W^*, there is a worker who is supplying labour at the margin. If the wage rate were to fall even slightly below W^*, the worker would withdraw from this labour market, perhaps to take alternative employment in another sector or occupation. In other words, the wage rate can be regarded as the transfer earnings of the marginal worker. A similar argument can be made about any point along the labour supply curve.

This means that the area under the supply curve up to the equilibrium point can be interpreted as the transfer earnings of workers in this labour market. In Figure 22.1 this is given by the area $OBAL^*$.

Total earnings are given by the wage rate multiplied by the quantity of labour supplied (here, area OW^*AL^*). Economic rent is thus that part of total earnings that is *not* transfer earnings. In Figure 22.1 this is the triangle BW^*A. The rationale is that this area represents the total excess that workers receive by being paid a wage (W^*) that is above the minimum required to keep them employed in this market.

If you think about it, you will see that this is similar to the notion of producer surplus, which is the difference between the price received by firms for a good or service and the price at which the firms would have been prepared to supply that good or service.

The balance between transfer earnings and economic rent

What determines the balance between the two aspects of total earnings? In this connection, the elasticity of supply of labour is of critical importance.

This can be seen by studying diagrams showing varying degrees of elasticity of supply. First, consider two extreme situations. Figure 22.2 shows a labour market in which supply is perfectly elastic. This implies that there is limitless supply of labour at the wage rate W. In this situation there is no economic rent to be gained from labour supply, and all earnings are transfer earnings. Any reduction of the wage below W will mean that all workers leave the market.

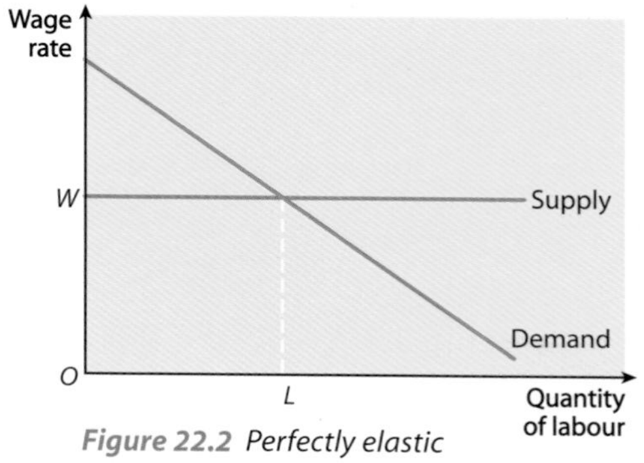

Figure 22.2 Perfectly elastic labour supply

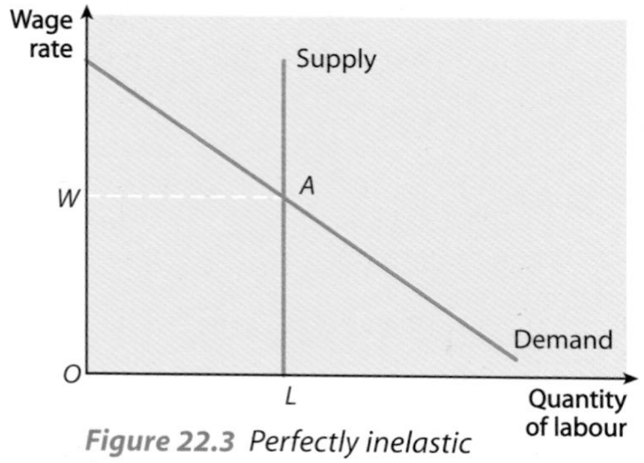

Figure 22.3 Perfectly inelastic labour supply

Now consider Figure 22.3. Here labour supply is perfectly inelastic. There is a fixed amount of labour being supplied to the market, and, whatever the wage rate, that amount of labour remains the same. Another way of looking at this is that there is no minimum payment needed to keep labour in its present use. Now the entire earnings of the factor are made up by economic rent (i.e. the area *OWAL*).

This illustrates how important the elasticity of labour supply is in determining the balance between transfer earnings and economic rent. The more inelastic is supply, the higher the proportion of total earnings that is made up of economic rent.

Surgeons and butchers: the importance of supply

Consider an example of differential earnings — say, surgeons and butchers. First think about the surgeons. Surgeons are in relatively inelastic supply, at least in the short run. The education required to become a surgeon is long and demanding, and is certainly essential for entry into the occupation. Furthermore, not everyone is cut out to become a surgeon, as this is a field that requires certain innate abilities and talents. This implies that the supply of surgeons is limited, and does not vary a great deal with the wage rate. If this is the case, then the total earnings of surgeons is largely made up of economic rent.

The situation may be reinforced by the fact that, once an individual has trained as a surgeon, there may be few alternative occupations to which, if disgruntled, he/she could transfer. There is a natural limit to how many surgeons there are, *and* upon their willingness to exit from the market.

How about butchers? The training programme for butchers is less arduous than for surgeons, and a wider range of people is suitable for employment in this occupation. Labour supply is thus likely to be relatively more elastic than for surgeons, and so economic rent will be relatively less important than in the previous case. If butchers were to receive high enough wages, more people would be attracted to the trade and wage rates would eventually fall.

In addition, there are other occupations into which butchers can transfer when they have had enough of cutting up all that meat; they might look to other sections of the catering sector, for example. This reinforces the relatively high elasticity of supply.

The importance of demand

Economic rent has been seen to be more important for surgeons than for butchers, but is this the whole of the story? The discussion so far has centred entirely on the supply side of the market. But demand is also important.

Indeed, it is the position of the demand curve when interacting with supply that determines the equilibrium wage rate in a labour market. It may well be that the supply of workers skilled in underwater basket weaving is strictly limited; but if there is no demand for underwater basket weavers then there is no scope for that skill to earn high economic rents. In the above example, it is the relatively strong demand for surgeons relative to their limited supply that leads to a relatively high equilibrium wage in the market.

Exercise 22.1

Figure 22.4 shows demand and supply in a labour market.

a Identify the area that represents economic rent.

b Which area shows transfer earnings?

c Sketch some diagrams yourself to see how the balance between economic rent and transfer earnings differs if the supply of labour is more or less elastic.

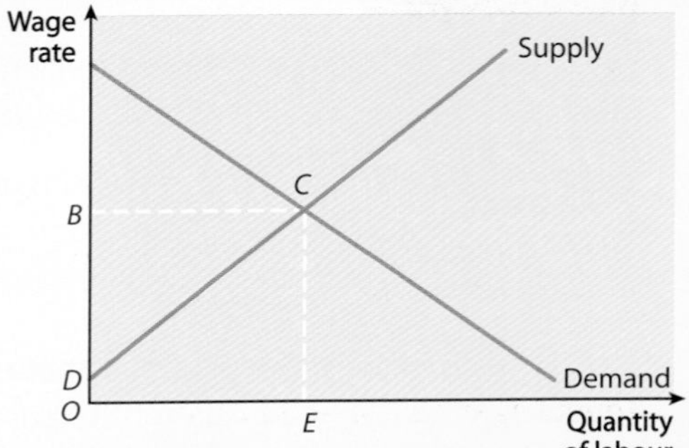

Figure 22.4
Equilibrium in a labour market

Summary

- In a modern economy, there is a complex network of labour markets for workers with different skills and working in different occupations and industries.
- The total payments to a factor of production can be separated into transfer earnings and economic rent.
- Transfer earnings represent the minimum payment needed to keep a factor of production in its present use.
- Economic rent is a payment received by a factor of production over and above what would be needed to keep it in its present use.
- The balance between transfer earnings and economic rent depends critically on the elasticity of supply of a particular kind of labour.

Education and the labour market

The above discussion has highlighted the importance of education and training in influencing wage differentials between occupational groups. Education and training might be regarded as a form of barrier to entry into a labour market affecting the elasticity of supply of labour. Because of differences in innate talents and abilities – not to mention personal inclinations – wage differentials can persist even in the long run in certain occupations. However, economists expect there to be some long-run equilibrium level of differential that reflects the preference and natural talent aspects of various occupations.

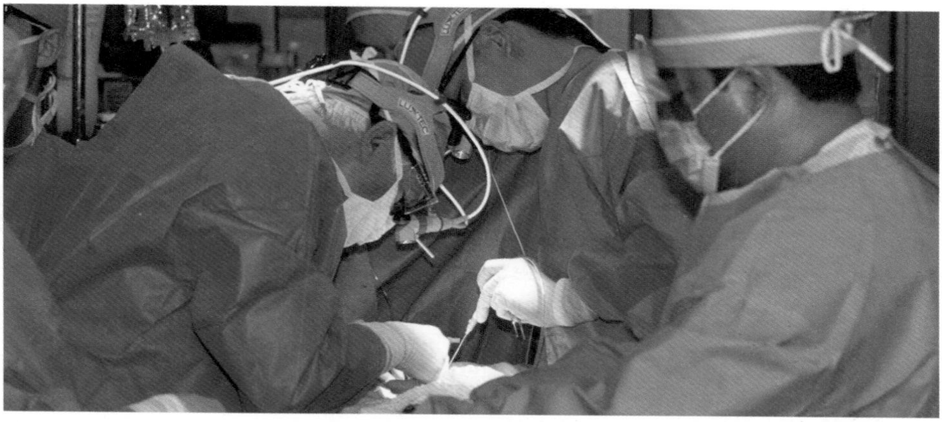

The requirement for high levels of education and training can both restrict labour supply and increase wage differentials.

However, changes in the pattern of consumer demand for goods over time will lead to changes in those equilibrium differentials. For example, during the computer revolution, when firms were increasing their use of computers at work and households were increasing their use of home computers, there was a need for more computer programmers to create the software that people wanted, and a need for more computer engineers to fix the computers when they crashed. This meant that the wage differential for these workers increased. And this in turn led to a proliferation of courses on offer to train or retrain people in these skills. Then, as the supply of such workers began to increase, so the wage differential narrowed.

This is what economists would expect to observe if the labour market is working effectively, with wages acting as signals to workers about what skills are in demand. It is part of the way in which a market system guides the allocation of resources.

Individual educational choices

In specific cases, such as that of the computer programmers, you can see how individuals may respond to market signals. Word gets around that computer programmers are in high demand, and individual workers and job-seekers respond to that. However, not all education is geared so specifically towards such specific gaps in the market. How do individuals take decisions about education?

Such a decision can be regarded as an example of *cost–benefit analysis.* In trying to decide whether or not to undertake further education, an individual needs to balance the costs of such education against its benefits. One important consideration is that the costs tend to come in the short run, but the benefits only in the long run. Much of the discussion of student university tuition fees centres on this issue. Should students incur high debts now in the expectation of future higher earnings? Work through Exercise 22.2 to take this further.

Exercise 22.2

Suppose you are considering undertaking a university education. Compile a list of the benefits and the costs that you expect to encounter if you choose to do so. Discuss how you would go about balancing the benefits and costs, remembering that the timing of these needs to be taken into account.

In Exercise 22.2 you will have identified a range of benefits and costs. On the cost side are the direct costs in terms of the tuition fees and living expenses, but there are also the opportunity costs – the fact that you will have to delay the time when you start earning an income. But there are benefits to set against these costs, which may include the enjoyment you get from undertaking further study and the fact that university can be a great experience – that is, it can be a consumption good as well as an investment good. And, almost certainly, you have considered the fact that you can expect higher future earnings as a university graduate than as a non-graduate.

A recent study by the OECD investigated the relationship between education and earnings in a range of countries. Figure 22.5 presents some of the results, showing the differential in earnings between university graduates and those who left education at the end of secondary schooling. The data are expressed as index numbers, with earnings of secondary school leavers set equal to 100. Thus, for the UK, a male graduate earned 57% more than a secondary school leaver, whereas a female graduate earned 106% more. A study in *Labour Market Trends* of March 2003 also found that those leaving education at age 21 seem to experience around a 50% wage increase compared with those leaving education at 16; however, in that study there was no significant difference between men and women.

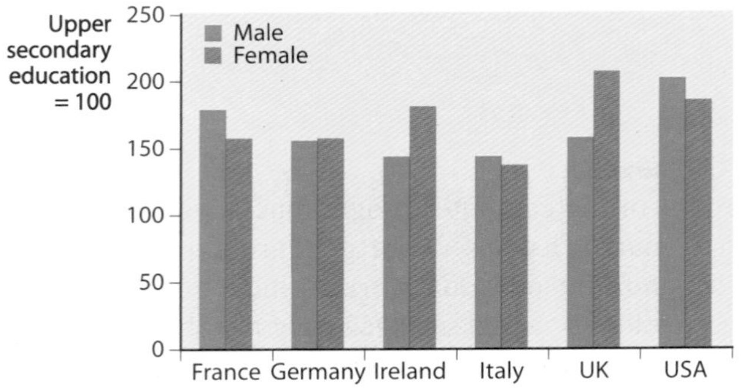

Figure 22.5
Education and earnings

Note: the graph shows the average employment earnings of people with the equivalent of UK university undergraduate degrees relative to people with only secondary education.

Source: OECD.

These data are a little difficult to interpret. They cannot be taken to mean that a university education increases the *productivity* of workers, because it may be that those who chose to undertake university education were naturally more able. This is the so-called 'signalling' view of education, i.e. that the value of the degree is not so much what has been learned during the programme of study as an indication that the person was capable of doing it. However, the fact that the returns to education are seen to vary across degree subjects suggests that employers do look for some value-added to emerge from university education. The evidence suggests that arts degrees have relatively little impact on average wages, whereas degrees in economics, management and law have large effects.

In spite of such evidence that lifetime earnings can be boosted by education, people may still demand too little education for the best interest of society, as was discussed in Chapter 8. This may be because there are *externality effects* associated with education. Although education has been shown to improve productivity, it has also been found that *groups* of educated workers are able to cooperate and work together so that collectively they are even more productive than they are as individuals. From this point of view, an individual worker may not perceive the full social benefit of higher education.

Figure 22.6 is a reminder of this argument. If marginal social benefit (*MSB*) is higher than marginal private benefit (*MPB*), there is a tendency for individuals to demand too little education, choosing to acquire Q_1 education rather than the Q^* that is the best for society. This argument may be used to suggest that government should encourage people to undertake more education.

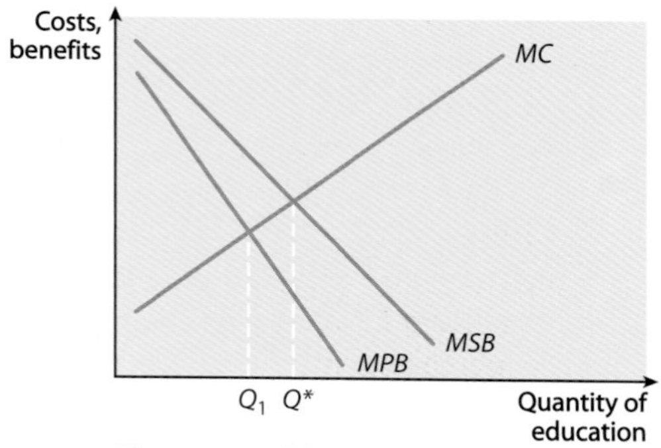

Figure 22.6 Education as a positive consumption externality

Summary

- Wage differentials may act as signals to guide potential workers in their demand for training and retraining.
- People demand education partly for the effect it will have on their future earnings potential.
- Externality effects may mean that people choose to demand less education than is desirable for society as a whole.

Discrimination

Earlier in the chapter, it was explained that you could expect to observe wage differentials across different labour markets within an economy such as the UK. However, the question often arises as to whether such economic analysis can explain all of the differentials in wages that can be observed. For example, consider Table 22.1.

	Female/male pay gap (%)	Female/male part-time pay gap (%)	Ethnic employment gap (% points)
1975	36	34	n/a
1979	37	41	–1
1990	33	41	–7
1997	26	36	–9
2000	25	36	–9
2002	23	36	–9

Table 22.1 Wage differentials in the British economy

Source: Richard Dickens, Paul Gregg and Jonathan Wadsworth, 'The labour market under New Labour', *Economic Review*, September 2003.

These data point to differentials in pay and employment that require some investigation. There would seem to be a noticeable pay gap between women and men. For full-time workers this has narrowed since 1975, but for part-time workers it has not. It also appears that employment opportunities for ethnic minority groups have worsened since 1975 — in spite of legislation that has increasingly tried to ensure equal opportunities for all. It is important to explore the extent to which these differences can be explained by economic analysis, and the extent to which they reflect discrimination in pay or employment opportunities.

The mere fact that there is inequality does not prove that there is discrimination. You have seen the way in which education and training affects earnings, so differentials between different groups of people may reflect the different educational choices made by those different groups. The gender gap may also reflect the fact that childcare responsibilities interrupt the working lives of many women. This is important in terms of human capital, and the build-up of experience and seniority. The increasing introduction of crèche facilities by many firms is reducing the extent of this contribution to the earnings gap, but it has not eliminated it.

Trade unions

Trade unions are associations of workers that negotiate with employers on pay and working conditions. Guilds of craftsmen existed in Europe in the Middle Ages, but the formation of workers' trade unions did not become legal in the UK until 1824. In the period following the Second World War about 40% of the labour force in the UK were members of a trade union. This percentage increased during the 1970s, peaking at about 50%, but since 1980 there has been a steady decline to below 30%.

Trade unions have three major objectives: wage bargaining, the improvement of working conditions, and security of employment for their members. In exploring the effect of the unions on a labour market, it is important to establish whether the unions are in a position to exploit market power and interfere with the proper functioning of the labour market, and also whether they are a necessary balance to the power of employers and thus necessary to protect workers from being exploited.

Key term

trade union: an organisation of workers that negotiates with employers on behalf of its members

There are two ways in which a trade union may seek to affect labour market equilibrium. On the one hand, it may limit the supply of workers into an occupation or industry. On the other hand, it may negotiate successfully for higher wages for its members. It turns out that these two possible strategies have similar effects on market equilibrium.

Union membership peaked at around 50% of the UK labour force in the 1970s, but has since declined to below 30%.

Restricting labour supply

Figure 22.7 shows the situation facing a firm, with a demand curve for labour based on marginal productivity theory. The average going wage in the economy is given by W^*, so if the firm can obtain workers at that wage it is prepared to employ up to L_0 labour.

However, if the firm faces a trade union that is limiting the amount of labour available to just L_1, then the union will be able to push the wage up to W_1. This might happen where there is a *closed shop*, in other words where a firm can employ only those workers who are members of the union. A closed shop allows the union to control how many workers are registered members, and therefore eligible to work in the occupation.

In this situation the union is effectively trading off higher wages for its members against a lower level of employment. The union members who are in work are better off – but those who would have been prepared to work at the lower wage of W^* either are unemployed or have to look elsewhere for jobs. If they are unemployed, this imposes a cost on society. If they are working in a second-choice occupation or industry this may also impose a social cost, in the sense that they may not be working to their full potential.

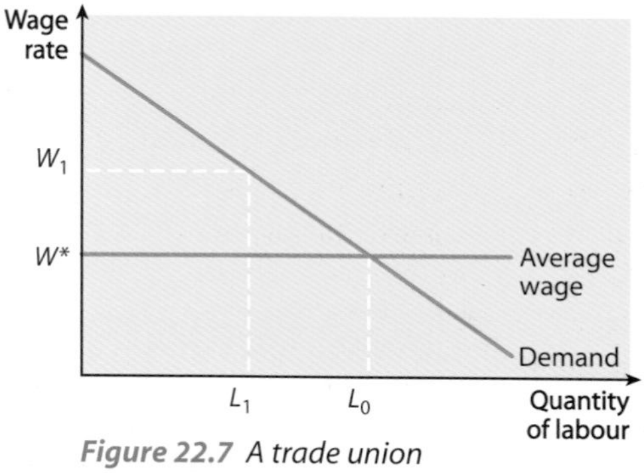

Figure 22.7 A trade union restricts the supply of labour

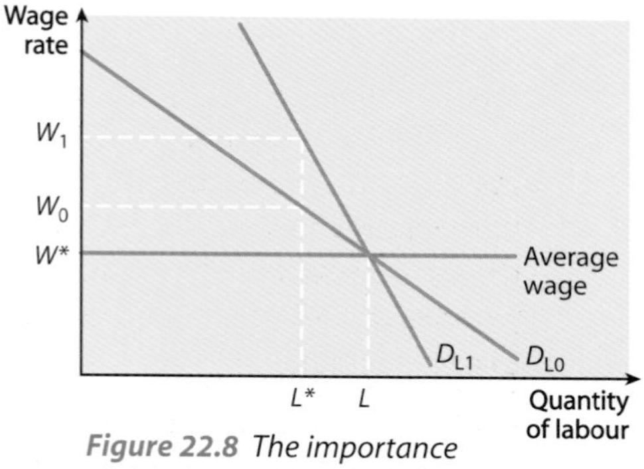

Figure 22.8 The importance of the elasticity of demand for labour

The extent of the trade-off depends crucially on the elasticity of demand for labour, as you can see in Figure 22.8. When the demand for labour is relatively more elastic, as shown by D_{L0}, the wage paid by the firm increases to W_0, whereas with the relatively more inelastic demand for labour D_{L1} the wage increases by much more, to W_1.

This makes good intuitive sense. The previous chapter explained that the elasticity of demand would be low in situations where a firm could not readily substitute

capital for labour, where labour formed a small share of total costs, and where the price elasticity of demand for the firm's product was relatively inelastic. If the firm cannot readily substitute capital for labour, the union has a relatively strong bargaining position. If labour costs are a small part of total costs, the firm may be ready to concede a wage increase, as it will have limited overall impact. If the demand for the product is price-inelastic, the firm may be able to pass the wage increase on in the form of a higher price for the product without losing large volumes of sales. Thus, these factors improve the union's ability to negotiate a good deal with the employer.

Negotiating wages

Alternatively, a trade union's foremost function can be regarded as negotiating higher wages for its members. Figure 22.9 depicts this situation. In the absence of union negotiation, the equilibrium for the firm is where demand and supply intersect, so the firm hires L_e labour at a wage of W_e.

If the trade union negotiates a wage of W^*, such that the firm cannot hire any labour below that level, this alters the labour supply curve, as shown by the kinked red line. The firm now employs only L^* labour at this wage. So, again, the effect is that the union negotiations result in a trade-off between the amount of labour hired and the wage rate. When the wage is at W^*, unemployment is shown on Figure 22.9 as $N^* - L^*$.

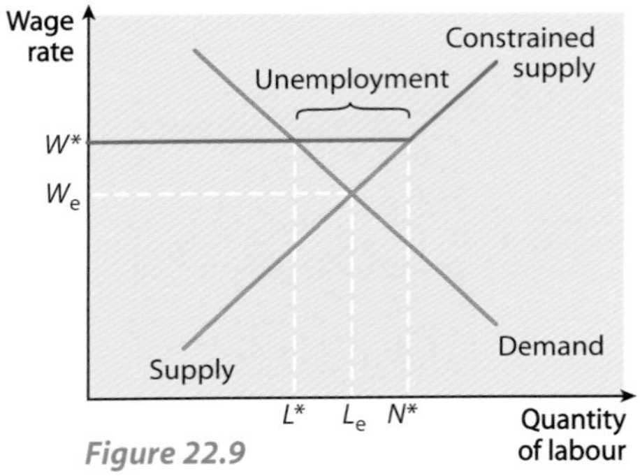

Figure 22.9
A trade union fixes the wage

The elasticity of demand for labour again affects the outcome, as shown in Figure 22.10. This time, with the relatively more inelastic demand curve D_{L1}, the effect on the quantity of labour employed (to L^{**}) is much less than when demand is relatively more elastic (to L^*).

From the point of view of allocative efficiency, the problem is that trade union intervention in the market may prevent wages from acting as reliable signals to workers and firms, and therefore may lead to a sub-optimal allocation of resources.

It is important to notice that this analysis has treated the firm as being very passive in the negotiations. In Chapter 23 you will see that this may change when the firm itself has market power – specifically, when the firm is a monopoly buyer of labour.

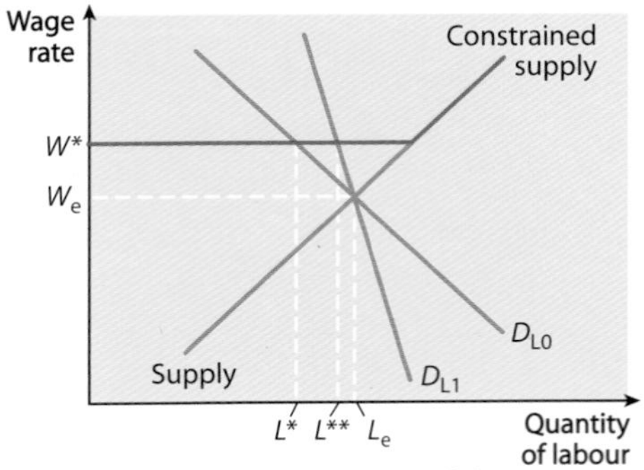

Figure 22.10 The effect of the elasticity of demand for labour when the union fixes the wage

Job security

One possible effect of trade union involvement in a firm is that workers will have more job security; in other words, they may become less likely to lose their jobs with the union there to protect their interests.

From the firm's point of view, there may be a positive side to this. If workers feel secure in their jobs, they may be more productive, or more prepared to accept changes in working practices that enable an improvement in productivity.

For this reason, it can be argued that in some situations the presence of a trade union may be beneficial in terms of a firm's efficiency. Indeed, the union may sometimes take over functions that would otherwise be part of the responsibility of the firm's human resource department.

Labour market flexibility

One of the most telling criticisms of trade unions has been that they have affected the degree of flexibility of the labour market. The most obvious manifestation of this is that their actions limit the entry of workers into a market.

This may happen in any firm, where existing workers have better access to information about how the firm is operating, or about forthcoming job vacancies, and so can make sure that their own positions against newcomers can be safeguarded. This is sometimes known as the *insider–outsider* phenomenon. Its effect is strengthened and institutionalised by the presence of a trade union, or by professional bodies such as the Royal College of Surgeons.

This and other barriers to entry erected by a trade union can limit the effectiveness and flexibility of labour markets by making it more difficult for firms to adapt to changing market conditions.

Summary

- Wage differentials and employment conditions are seen to vary between males and females and between ethnic groups, and only part of the variance can be explained in terms of economic analysis.
- Trade unions exist to negotiate for their members on pay, working conditions and job security.
- If trade unions restrict labour supply, or negotiate wages that are above the market equilibrium, the net effect is a trade-off between wages and employment.
- Those who remain in work receive higher pay, but at the expense of other workers who have either become unemployed or work in second-choice occupations or industries.
- However, by improving job security, unions may make workers more prepared to accept changes in working practices that lead to productivity gains.
- Barriers to the entry and exit of workers may reduce firms' flexibility to adapt to changing market conditions.

Labour market imperfections

Product markets do not always work perfectly. For example, a firm (or small group of firms) may come to dominate a market and use its market power to increase its super-normal profits, to the detriment of the consumer. It has also been shown that some government interventions in product markets do not always have their intended effects. This chapter explores some of the ways in which imperfections can be manifest in labour markets.

Learning outcomes

After studying this chapter, you should:

- understand ways in which labour markets may be imperfect
- be aware of the operation of a labour market in which there is a monopsony buyer of labour
- be familiar with a bilateral monopoly model in which a monopsony buyer of labour faces a trade union
- be aware of ways in which governments may cause imperfections in labour markets through their interventions
- understand how unemployment may arise in a market

Monopsony

One type of market failure in a product market occurs when there is a single *seller* of a good, i.e. a monopoly market. As you may recall, a firm with this sort of market dominance is able to restrict output, and maximise profits by setting a higher price. A similar

> ***Key term***
>
> **monopsony:** a market in which there is a single buyer of a good, service or factor of production

form of market power can occur on the other side of the market if there is a single *buyer* of a good, service or factor of production. Such a market is known as a monopsony.

In previous chapters it was assumed that firms in the labour market face perfect competition, and therefore must accept the market wage. However, suppose that one firm is the sole user of a particular type of labour, or is the dominant firm in a city or region, and thus is in a monopsony situation.

Such a monopsonist faces the market supply curve of labour directly, rather than simply accepting the equilibrium market wage. It views this supply curve as its average cost of labour, because it shows the average wage rate that it would need to offer to obtain any given quantity of labour input.

Figure 23.1 shows a monopsonist's demand curve for labour, which is the marginal revenue product curve (MRP_L), and its supply curve of labour, seen by the firm as its average cost curve of labour (AC_L). If the market were perfectly competitive, equilibrium would be where supply equals demand, which would be with the firm using L^* labour at a wage rate W^*.

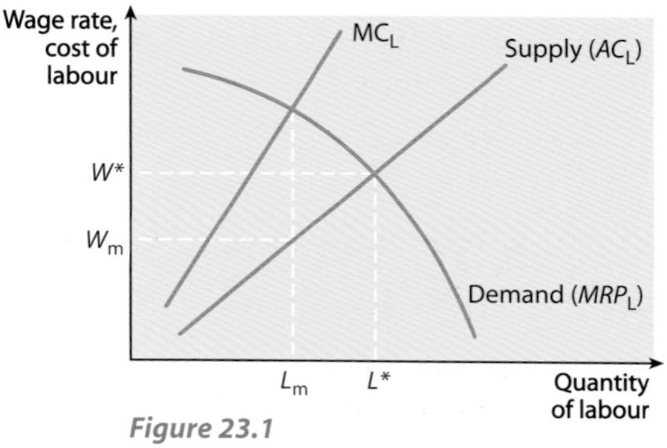

Figure 23.1
A monopsony buyer of labour

However, from the perspective of the monopsonist firm, facing the supply curve directly, if at any point it wants to hire more labour it has to offer a higher wage to encourage more workers to join the market — after all, that is what the AC_L curve tells it. However, the firm would then have to pay that higher wage to *all* its workers, so the *marginal cost* of hiring the extra worker is not just the wage paid to that worker, but the increased wage paid to all the other workers as well. So the marginal cost of labour curve (MC_L) can be added to the diagram.

Remember that, in the diagram for a profit-maximising monopolist in Chapter 17, it was pointed out that there was a fixed relationship between the *AR* and *MR* curves, with the *MR* curve having a slope that was exactly twice as steep as *AR*. This diagram depicts the same sort of relationship, with the MC_L having a slope exactly twice as steep as AC_L. However, this time they are upward sloping.

If the monopsonist firm wants to maximise profit, it will hire labour up to the point where the marginal cost of labour is equal to the marginal revenue product of labour. Therefore it will use labour up to the level L_m, which is where $MC_L = MRP_L$. In order to entice workers to supply this amount of labour, the firm need pay only the wage W_m. (Remember that AC_L is the supply curve of labour.) You can see, therefore, that a profit-maximising monopsonist will use less labour, and pay a lower wage, than a firm operating under perfect competition.

Exercise 23.1

Figure 23.2 shows a firm in a monopsonistic labour market.

a What would the wage rate be if this market were perfectly competitive, and how much labour would be employed?

b As a monopsony, what wage would the firm offer to its workers, and how much labour would it employ?

c Which area represents the employer's wage bill?

d What surplus does this generate for the firm?

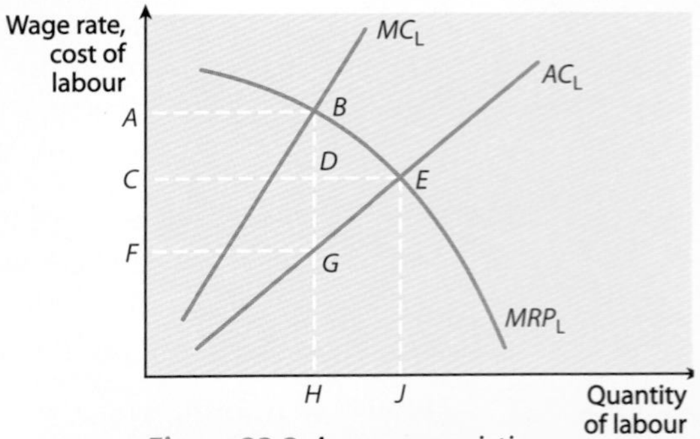

Figure 23.2 *A monopsonistic labour market*

Bilateral monopoly — the trade unions revisited

The previous chapter examined the situation in which a firm in a perfectly competitive market faced a trade union that was a monopoly seller of labour, with the result that the level of employment fell below the free market equilibrium and the firm had to pay an inflated wage. The trade union made use of its market power to exploit the trade-off between employment and the wage rate. Suppose, however, that there is a bilateral monopoly, in which the monopoly trade union seller of labour faces a firm that is a monopsony buyer of labour?

> ***Key term***
>
> **bilateral monopoly:** a market situation in which a monopsony buyer of labour faces a trade union acting as a monopoly provider of labour

The resulting situation is illustrated in Figure 23.1. If unhindered by the trade union, the firm would offer a wage W_m and use L_m labour. However, if the union now negotiates a higher wage rate, what happens is that, as the wage moves upwards from W_m, the firm will take on *more* labour. The market will then move back towards the perfectly competitive level (at wage W^* and quantity L^*).

In this situation, the market power of the two protagonists works against both of them to produce an outcome that is closer to perfect competition. It is not possible to predict where the final resting place for the market will be, but it will lie somewhere between L_m and L^*, depending upon the relative strength and negotiating skills of the firm and the union.

Summary

- A market in which there is a single buyer of a good, service or factor of production is known as a monopsony market.
- A monopsony buyer of labour will employ less labour at a lower wage than if the market is perfectly competitive.

- However, if faced by a trade union acting as a monopoly provider of labour, the monopsony firm's ability to reduce employment and lower wages will be limited.
- The final outcome in such a market will depend upon the relative bargaining power of the employer and the union.

Effects of government intervention

Labour markets can be politically sensitive. Unemployment has been a prominent indicator of the performance of the economy, and there has been an increasing concern in recent years with issues of health and safety and with ensuring that workers are not exploited by their employers. This has induced governments to introduce a number of measures to provide the institutional setting for the operation of labour markets. However, such measures do not always have their intended effects.

Minimum wage

In its manifesto published before the 1997 election, the Labour Party committed itself to the establishment of the National Minimum Wage (NMW). This would be the first time that such a measure had been used in the UK on a nationwide basis, although minimum wages had sometimes been set in particular industries.

Key term

minimum wage: government-set minimum wage rate below which firms are not allowed to pay

After the election, a Low Pay Commission was set up to oversee the implementation of the policy, which came into force in April 1999. Initially the NMW was set at £3.60 per hour for those aged 22 and over and £3 for those aged 18–21. From 1 October 2005 the rates were adjusted to £5.05 for those aged 22 and over and £4.10 for those aged 18–21. A minimum wage of £3.00 per hour was also introduced for 16- and 17-year-olds.

The objectives of the minimum wage policy are threefold. First, it is intended to protect workers against exploitation by the small minority of bad employers. Second, it aims to improve incentives to work by ensuring that 'work pays', thereby tackling the problem of voluntary unemployment. Third, it aims to alleviate poverty by raising the living standards of the poorest groups in society.

The National Minimum Wage was introduced in 1999 in an effort to protect the living standards of low-paid workers.

The policy has been a contentious one, with critics claiming that it meets none of these objectives. It has been argued that the minority of bad employers can still find ways of exploiting their workers, for example by paying them on a piecework rate so that there is no set wage per

hour. Another criticism is that the policy is too indiscriminate to tackle poverty, and that a more sharply focused policy is needed for this purpose; for example, many of the workers receiving the NMW may not in fact belong to poor households, but may be women working part-time whose partners are also in employment. But perhaps most contentious of all is the argument that, far from providing a supply-side solution to some unemployment, a national minimum wage is causing an increase in unemployment because of its effects on the demand for labour.

First, consider a firm operating in a perfectly competitive market, so that it has to accept the wage that is set in the overall market of which it is a part. In Figure 23.3 the firm's demand curve is represented by its marginal revenue product curve (MRP_L), and in a free market it must accept the equilibrium wage W^*. It thus uses labour up to l^*.

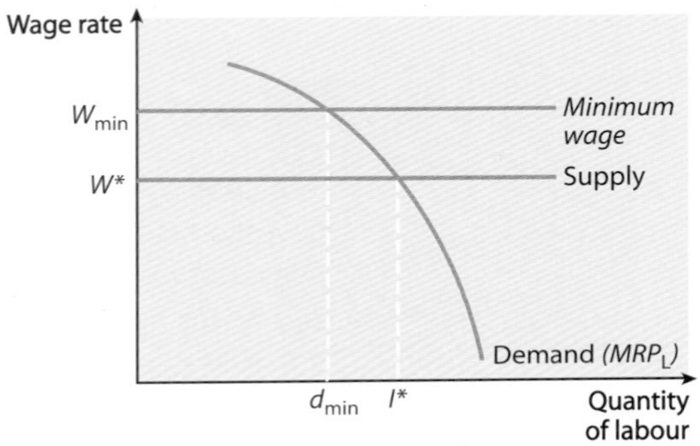

Figure 23.3 The effect of a minimum wage on a firm in a perfectly competitive labour market

If the government now steps in and imposes a minimum wage, so that the firm cannot set a wage below W_{min}, it will reduce its labour usage to d_{min}, since it will not be profitable to employ labour beyond this point.

This effect will be similar for all the other firms in the market, and the results of this can be seen in Figure 23.4. Now the demand curve is the combined demand of all the firms in the market, and the supply curve of labour is shown as upward sloping, as it is the market supply curve. In free market equilibrium the combined demand of firms in the market is L^*, and W^* emerges as the equilibrium wage rate.

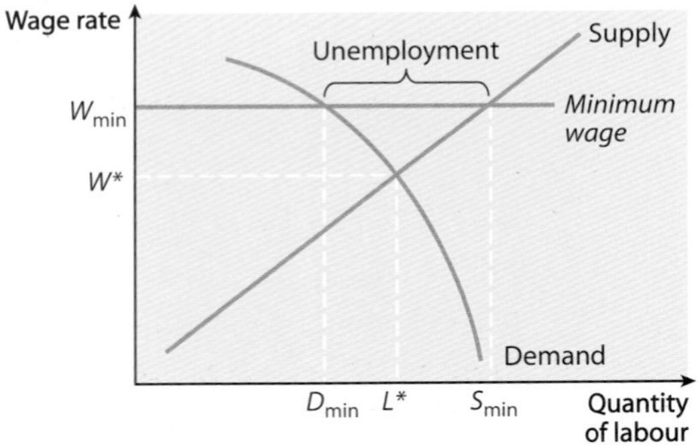

Figure 23.4 The effect of a minimum wage in a perfectly competitive labour market

When the government sets the minimum wage at W_{min}, all firms react by reducing their demand for labour at the higher wage. Their combined demand is now D_{min}, but the supply of labour is S_{min}. The difference between these ($S_{min} - D_{min}$) is unemployment. Furthermore, it is involuntary unemployment — these workers would like to work at the going wage rate, but cannot find a job.

Notice that there are two effects at work. Some workers who were formerly employed have lost their jobs — there are $L^* - D_{min}$ of these. In addition, however, the incentive to work is now improved (this was part of the policy objective, remember?), so there are now an additional $S_{min} - L^*$ workers wanting to take employment at the going wage rate. Thus, unemployment has increased for two reasons.

It is not always the case that the introduction of a minimum wage leads to an increase in unemployment. For example, in the market depicted in Figure 23.5 the minimum wage has been set below the equilibrium level, so will have no effect on firms in the market, who will continue to pay W^* and employ L^* workers. At the time of the introduction of the NMW, MacDonald's argued that it was in fact already paying a wage above the minimum rate set.

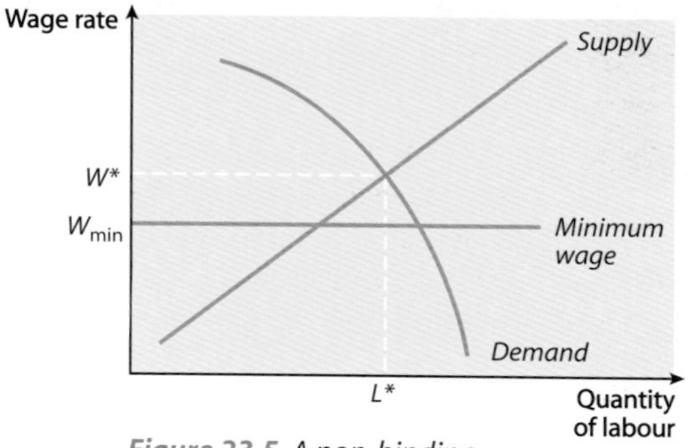

Figure 23.5 A non-binding minimum wage in a perfectly competitive labour market

This is not the only situation in which a minimum wage would *not* lead to unemployment. Suppose that the labour market in question has a monopsony buyer of labour. The firm's situation is shown in Figure 23.6. In the absence of a minimum wage, the firm sets its marginal cost of labour equal to its marginal revenue product, hiring L_0 labour at a wage W_0. A minimum wage introduced at the level W_{min} means that the firm now hires labour up to the point where the wage is equal to the marginal revenue product, and, as drawn in Figure 23.6, this takes the market back to the perfectly competitive outcome.

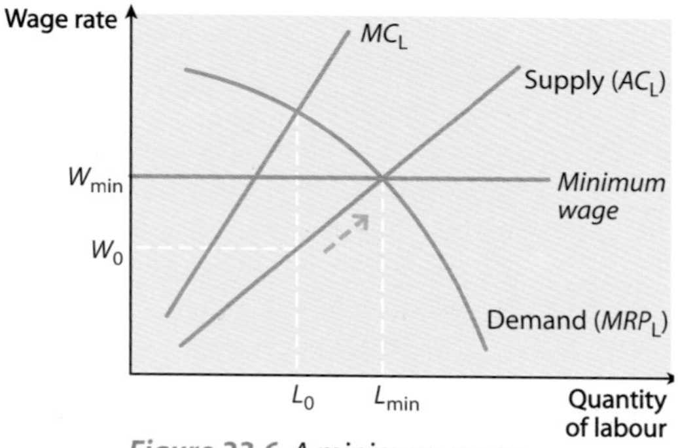

Figure 23.6 A minimum wage with a monopsony buyer of labour

Notice that the authorities would have to be very knowledgeable to set the minimum wage at exactly the right level to produce this outcome. However, any wage between W_0 and W_{min} will encourage the firm to increase its employment to some extent as the policy reduces its market power. Of course, setting the minimum wage above the competitive equilibrium level will again lead to some unemployment. Thus, it is critical to set the wage at the right level if the policy is to succeed in its objectives.

It is also important to realise that there is not just a single labour market in the UK. In fact, it could be questioned whether a single minimum wage set across the whole country could be effective, as it would 'bite' in different ways in different markets. For example, wage levels vary across the regions of the UK, and it must be questioned whether the same minimum wage could be as effective in, say, London as in Northern Ireland or the north of England.

In a government press release in August 2004, it was revealed that the Low Pay Commission had been asked to prepare a report on the operation of the NMW. The Commission was asked to monitor and evaluate the impact of the NMW and to review the levels of the rates. In reviewing the rates, the Commission was further asked to:

> ...have regard to the wider social and economic implications; the likely effect on employment levels, especially within low-paying sectors and amongst disadvantaged people in the labour market; the impact on the costs and competitiveness of business; and the potential costs to industry and the Exchequer.

This seems to indicate that the government is aware of some of the pitfalls of the national minimum wage.

Health and safety regulation

The government intervenes in the labour market through a range of measures designed to improve safety standards in the workplace. These are administered through the Health and Safety Commission and the Health and Safety Executive, whose responsibilities range:

> ...from health and safety in nuclear installations and mines, through to factories, farms, hospitals and schools, offshore gas and oil installations, the safety of the gas grid and the movement of dangerous goods and substances, railway safety, and many other aspects of the protection both of workers and the public.

Health and safety inspectors can enter premises without warning, and can issue improvement notices requiring problems to be put right within a specified time; for the most serious failings, they can prosecute.

Such regulation can impinge quite heavily on labour markets. One example of such regulation is the EU Working Time Directive. This aims to protect the health and safety of workers in the European Union by imposing regulations in relation to working hours, rest periods, annual leave and working arrangements for night workers. The legislation came into effect in the UK in October 1998 (except for junior doctors in training, for whom the directive was to be phased in gradually). The UK implemented the 48-hour week later than countries elsewhere in Europe because of a special dispensation. Countries elsewhere complained about this, arguing that it gave British firms an unfair competitive advantage. This seems to suggest that the Directive does indeed have an effect on the labour market.

The effect of these health and safety measures has been to raise the costs to firms of hiring labour. In the case of the Working Time Directive, firms may have to spread the same amount of work over a greater number of workers, and as there are some fixed hiring costs this raises the cost of labour. Similarly, if the firm has to spend more on ensuring safety, it adds to the firms' costs.

Figure 23.7 illustrates one way of viewing the situation. It shows a perfectly competitive labour market for the market as a whole rather than an individual firm. Without regulation, the market reaches equilibrium with labour employed up to L^* at a wage of W^*. Suppose a health and safety regulation is introduced that adds a constant amount (of £c) to firm's cost per unit of labour employed. Firms then find that the average cost of labour is higher by £c – shown as AC_L in the figure. They will thus employ labour up to the point where the average cost of labour is equal to the marginal revenue product. (Remember that this is a perfectly competitive labour market, so it is the average cost of labour that is significant in the market: each individual firm perceives this as its marginal cost.) This is at the quantity of labour L_1, and wage is given by W_1, which is the wage that attracts L_1 workers into the market.

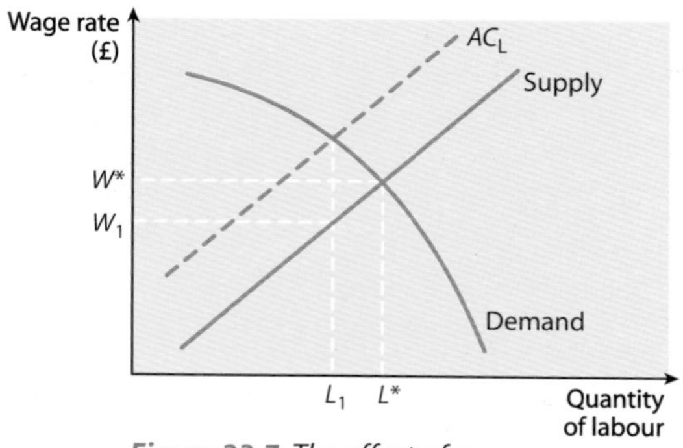

Figure 23.7 The effect of a health and safety regulation in a perfectly competitive labour market

The monopsony market could be analysed in similar fashion, but the effects are comparable — there is a reduction in the amount of labour employed and a fall in the wage rate.

This sort of intervention can be justified by appealing to a merit good argument (which was discussed in Chapter 9), which claims that the government knows better than workers what is good for them. Thus, individual workers' decisions about labour supply do not take health and safety sufficiently into account, and the regulation that adds to firms' costs is a way of protecting the workers, given that firms have an incentive to skimp on health and safety in order to keep costs down.

As with other policies, the judgement of the degree of regulation that is required is a difficult one to get right. If governments misjudge the amount of protection that workers need and set c too high, this could lead to lower employment than is optimal.

Some health and safety issues arise from externality effects. For example, firms transporting toxic or other dangerous substances may not face the full costs of their activities, because they do not have the incentive to control the risks that may affect individuals. Regulation to enforce the appropriate transportation of such substances is a way of internalising such an externality.

Exercise 23.2

Use Figure 23.8 to explain how the externality effect described in the paragraph above comes about.

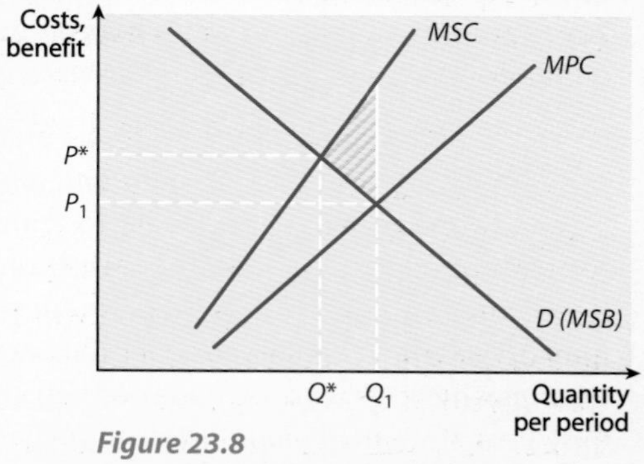

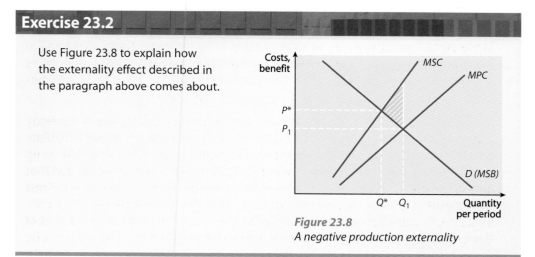

Figure 23.8
A negative production externality

Flexibility

A general issue that arises in respect of government regulation of labour markets is that there is a fine balance to be kept between, on the one hand, providing adequate protection for workers, to ensure that they are given fair opportunities and appropriate working conditions, and on the other hand ensuring that labour markets are flexible. Chapter 24 will return to this when it examines the importance of flexibility in labour markets, and the measures that have been taken in the UK to encourage this.

Summary

- Governments have intervened in labour markets to protect low-paid workers, but policies need to be implemented with care because of possible unintended side effects.
- The Labour government under Tony Blair introduced the National Minimum Wage in 1999.
- In a perfectly competitive labour market, a minimum wage that raises the wage rate above its equilibrium value may lead to an increase in unemployment.
- This is partly because firms reduce their demand for labour, but it also reflects an increased labour supply, as the higher wage is an incentive for more workers to join the market.
- A minimum wage that is set below the equilibrium wage will not be binding.
- A minimum wage established in a monopsony market may have the effect of raising employment.
- Health and safety legislation may help to protect workers, and may be interpreted as an example of a merit good.
- However, it adds to firms' costs, so may reduce employment.
- It is thus important to keep health and safety in perspective, and not over-protect at the expense of lower employment levels.

Unemployment

In Chapter 13 unemployment was discussed at a *macroeconomic* level, as one of the key measures of an economy's overall performance. In that context a number of different causes of unemployment were identified.

Frictional unemployment was seen as arising when workers switch between jobs. This is a purely transitional phenomenon, and is necessary if the labour market is to be flexible in allowing people to transfer between firms or industries. When retraining is needed to ease the transition the unemployment may be longer term; for example, when some sectors are declining and other are expanding, workers may need to be re-skilled in order to make the transfer. This is known as *structural unemployment*. It was also pointed out that in the macroeconomic context there may be a state of *demand-deficient unemployment*, in which aggregate demand in the economy is insufficient for the economy to reach full employment.

In a *microeconomic* context unemployment might be seen from a different angle. While some frictional unemployment cannot be avoided, much of structural unemployment can be regarded as an indicator of some inflexibility in labour markets, slowing the process by which workers can move from one job to another.

One possible cause of structural unemployment may be that firms are not providing sufficient training to ensure a smooth transition. On-the-job training is an important way to enable workers to gain the skills that will make them more productive in the future. When firms are taking employment decisions, they are concerned not only with today's marginal revenue product of workers, but with the longer-term perspective.

Providing training is costly to a firm, however, so it will need some assurance that it will be able to reap the benefits at a later date in the form of higher productivity. It may also be aware that firms choosing not to provide training may be able to poach its newly trained workers without having incurred the costs of the training. In other words, there is a potential *free-rider* problem here.

There may be some skills that are useful only within the firm. Such *firm-specific* skills do not pose quite the same problems. However, for generic transferable skills there is an incentive for firms to under-provide training. Some government intervention may therefore be needed to rectify this situation.

Disequilibrium unemployment

One important potential cause of unemployment is disequilibrium in a labour market. Some examples of this have already been given. A wage set at a level that is above the equilibrium rate can cause unemployment in a labour market.

This is shown in Figure 23.9, where, given the demand curve D^*, the equilibrium wage is at W^*, with labour employed up to L^*. With the wage held above the equilibrium rate, at W_1, the supply of labour (S_1) exceeds the quantity of labour that firms are prepared to hire (D_1), and the difference ($S_1 - D_1$) is unemployment – the number of workers who would like a job at the going wage rate, but are unable to find a job.

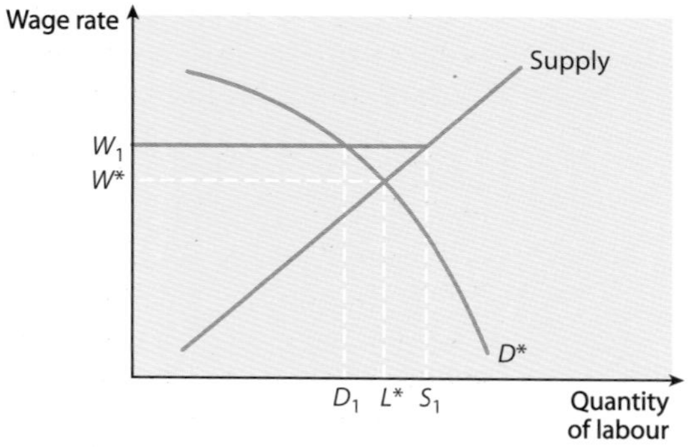

Figure 23.9
Disequilibrium unemployment

This could occur for a number of reasons. In some circumstances the introduction of a minimum wage could have this effect. The previous chapter described the occurrence of a similar situation where a trade union was able to negotiate a wage that was higher than the equilibrium rate.

This could also happen where there is inflexibility in the market. For example, suppose that a firm experiences a fall in the demand for its product. As the price of the product falls, so the marginal revenue

product of labour falls, and the firm would want to move to a lower employment level, and pay lower wages. This is shown in Figure 23.10. If previously the demand for labour was at D_0 then W_0 would have been the equilibrium wage rate, and employment would have been L_0, with no unemployment. When the demand for labour falls to D_1, there would be a new potential equilibrium with the wage at W^* and employment L^*. However, if the market is sluggish to adjust, perhaps because there is resistance to lowering the wages from W_0 to W^*, then this will cause unemployment. In other words, with the wage remaining at W_0, workers continue to try to supply L_0 labour, but firms will only demand L_1, and the difference is unemployment. This situation of sticky wage adjustment is thus another cause of unemployment.

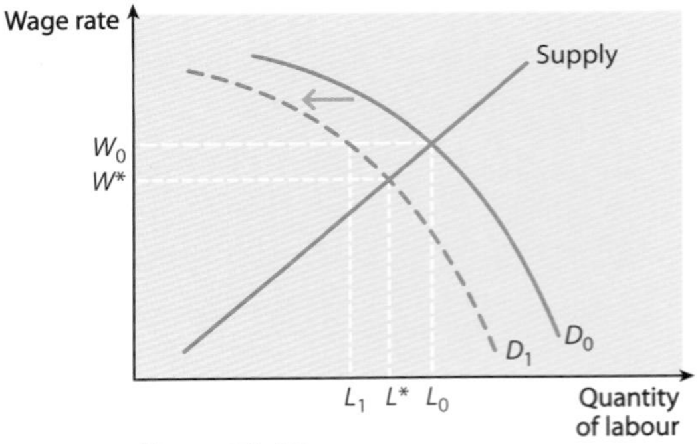

Figure 23.10
Inflexibility in wage adjustment

The efficiency wage

Chapter 9 introduced the problem of *asymmetric information*, where market failure can arise because some traders in a market have better information than others. This can happen in labour markets too.

> ***Key term***
>
> **efficiency wage:** higher-than-average wage paid by a firm in a situation of asymmetric information, in order to keep good-quality workers and provide incentives for workers to work hard

The issue arises from the employer's perspective. When an employer is hiring new workers, a key concern is the quality of the workers applying for jobs. This is partly a question about their innate talents and abilities. It can be overcome to some extent by checking applicants' qualifications; indeed, this is why employers may insist on qualifications, even if they are not directly related to the requirements of the job.

However, there are other differences between workers that are important. Two workers with the same qualifications may show very differing productivity. Some workers are naturally hardworking and conscientious, whereas others are always taking rest breaks and getting away with as little effort as possible. At the hiring stage, the employer may not be able to distinguish between the 'workers' and the 'shirkers'.

Suppose a firm pays a wage that is the average warranted by workers and shirkers combined. As time goes by, some workers are likely to quit and go to higher-paid jobs with other firms. The employees who are most likely to leave are the more productive ones, who realise that, if they are paid the average of what is right for the workers and shirkers taken together, they are being paid less than their own value. In the long run the employer could be left with just the shirkers.

A rational response to this from the employer's perspective is to pay a wage that is higher than the average, in order to encourage the productive workers to stay with the firm. This has the additional benefit of increasing the penalty for being caught shirking (since a worker faces a greater opportunity cost of getting the sack if wages are higher). Thus, paying a higher-than-average wage has an additional incentive effect in that it discourages shirking.

This higher-than-average wage is known as the efficiency wage, and can be seen as a response by firms to the asymmetric information problem. One of the results in the labour market is to raise the level of involuntary unemployment, in the sense that at the higher wage there will be an increase in the number of workers who would be prepared to accept a job but are unable to find employment.

Labour mobility

A further reason for labour market inflexibility is that workers are not perfectly mobile. This means that the available jobs and the available workers may not be located in the same area. The relatively high rate of owner-occupied housing in the UK means that workers who are owner-occupiers may need a strong inducement to move to another part of the country in search of jobs. For council house tenants, too, it may be quite difficult to relocate to a different area for employment purposes, because they will have to return to the bottom of the waiting list for housing. Differences in house prices in different parts of the country further add to the problem of matching workers to jobs.

Summary

- Unemployment arises for a number of reasons at the microeconomic level.
- Structural unemployment, arising from changes in the structure of economic activity within an economy, may reflect inflexibility in a labour market that slow the process by which workers move from declining into expanding sectors.
- Firms may under-provide training in transferable skills because of a possible free-rider effect.
- Unemployment in a market may arise if wages are held above the equilibrium level — because of trade union action, a minimum wage, or sluggish adjustment to a fall in demand.
- In a situation of asymmetric information, firms may pay an efficiency wage, choosing to hire fewer workers but looking to encourage effort and keep good workers with the firm in the longer run.

part 5

Chapter 24

Labour markets in the UK and EU

How well do labour markets work in practice? And how could they be improved? The aim of this chapter is to explore some of these issues, drawing on information about labour markets in the UK and elsewhere in Europe. You will see that flexibility is the key, but that there are some major challenges ahead.

Learning outcomes

After studying this chapter, you should:

- be familiar with the structure and incidence of unemployment in the UK
- understand the importance of labour market flexibility for the smooth operation of markets
- be aware of policies adopted by the UK government to promote flexibility in UK labour markets
- be aware of differences between the UK labour market situation and that in other parts of the European Union
- understand the impact of technology and changing international patterns of comparative advantage on labour markets
- be aware of the importance of demographic change in an economy, and the significance of an ageing population

Causes of unemployment

Earlier in the book some of the causes of unemployment were examined, both from a macroeconomic perspective and in the context of individual markets. Now this analysis is applied in the context of the UK economy.

Measuring unemployment is a key way of trying to evaluate whether labour markets are operating effectively. Large-scale unemployment suggests that a society is failing to use its resources efficiently, and is operating *within* its production possibility frontier; by reallocating resources within the economy, and thus moving to the frontier, society as a whole can be made better off.

Some of the explanations that have been advanced for unemployment suggest that there is a transitional element to unemployment; in other words, that unemployment can occur because the market is sluggish in adjusting to equilibrium, or that workers are unemployed because they do not have the right mix of skills that employers are seeking.

The more flexible labour markets are, the more rapidly such unemployment will subside when equilibrium is reached. Thus, an important set of policies to examine are those that will improve the flexibility with which labour markets can adjust towards equilibrium. It has been claimed that the degree of flexibility of markets is important in explaining differences in observed unemployment rates between countries, which is an issue that will be discussed later in the chapter.

The benefits of flexibility go beyond the labour market itself. If a labour market does not adjust readily, it will slow the whole process of changing resource allocation, and this in turn will slow the process of economic growth, which may be seen as a prime long-term aim of economic policy.

It may not be straightforward to identify when full employment has been reached. Some unemployment cannot be avoided, and will exist even when the labour market is in equilibrium.

The chapter begins by examining some of the facts about unemployment in the UK.

Unemployment in the UK

The overall unemployment rate in the UK since 1971 is presented in Figure 24.1, using the claimant count measurement method. This counts the number of people claiming unemployment benefit each month. It was briefly introduced in Chapter 11, and provides a useful picture of how unemployment has varied through time.

The large swings in unemployment that are visible on the graph are due to a number of causes. The large increase in the early 1980s reflected in part a change

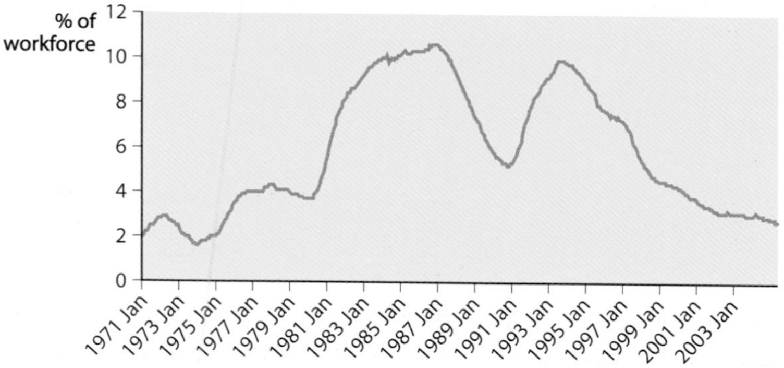

Figure 24.1 *Unemployment in the UK, 1971–2003 (claimant count)*

Source: ONS.

in the emphasis of economic policy. There was a new determination to bring inflation under control using monetary policy whereas in earlier periods the government had been more concerned about achieving full employment. However, other things were happening as well. North Sea Oil came on stream just before the second oil price crisis of 1979–80, a net effect of which was a loss in competitiveness of British goods, which led to a decline in the manufacturing sector in the 1980s. There were also changes to the demographic structure of the population, which will be taken up at the end of the chapter.

The reduction in unemployment in the late 1980s was associated with what has come to be known as the 'Lawson boom', a period of relatively loose monetary policy that was followed by a severe recession in which unemployment rose again. But perhaps the most striking aspect of this graph is the period since 1993, which has seen a steady decline in the unemployment rate and a much steadier pattern.

Figure 24.2 focuses on a different aspect of unemployment. Economists have argued that some unemployment is by its nature transitional, a feature of the adjustment process of the economy. In this context it is useful to examine the extent to which there is long-term unemployment. Figure 24.2 shows the percentage of the unemployed who have been unemployed for more than a year.

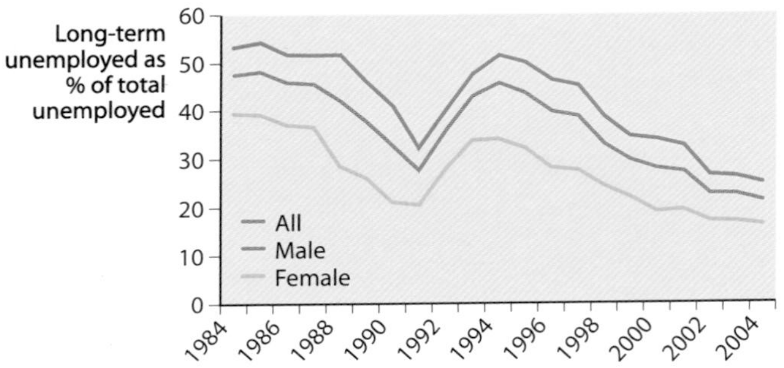

***Figure 24.2** The long-term unemployed in the UK, 1984–2004*

Notes: data relate to the spring of each year. The long-term unemployed are those who have been without work for a year or more.

Source: ONS.

Notice that the data used here are for the spring quarter of each year. One reason for taking a particular quarter rather than looking at the full set of data for the year is that there tend to be seasonal movements in the unemployment rate that can distract from the underlying trend.

The overall picture shows that there has been a large decline in long-term unemployment, from nearly 50% in 1984 to only just over 20% in the spring of 2004. This might be interpreted as an encouraging sign for the economy, indicating that most of the unemployment is relatively short term in nature. Indeed, taking this figure together with the previous one, which showed such a large decline in overall unemployment, it might be concluded that the economy is not far from a full-employment position.

Notice that there is a difference between male and female workers in these data, indicating that the majority of long-term unemployed workers are male. There is also an age effect in the data, which is shown in Figure 24.3. This focuses just on the years 1984 and 2004, and shows that long-term unemployment is more prevalent among older workers. There has clearly been a substantial improvement in all age groups, but the decline has been much more marked for younger workers. This may partly reflect the greater difficulty that older workers find in switching occupations, but it may also be associated with the training schemes for younger workers that have been introduced in recent years and will be discussed shortly.

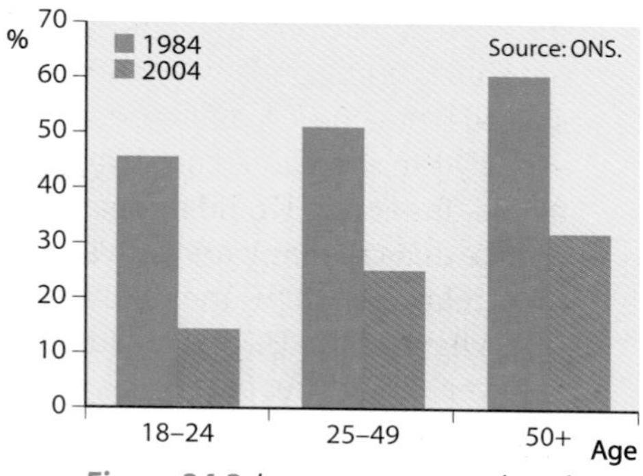

Figure 24.3 *Long-term unemployed as a percentage of all unemployed in the UK by age groups, 1984 and 2004*

The relatively low proportion of long-term unemployed highlights the fact that unemployment is a dynamic variable. It is easy to fall into the trap of thinking of the unemployed as being a pool of people unable to get work. However, in any period there are always people becoming unemployed, and others obtaining jobs. In a typical year more people get jobs, and more become unemployed, than the average number of people who are unemployed at any one time.

It is also important to remember that there are substantial regional variations in unemployment rates across the UK. Figure 24.4 shows the picture in spring 2004. The percentage rate varies from below 4% in the South West, the South East and the East to 6% or more in Scotland and in London. The data for London may be misleading, however, as there is so much commuting into the London area.

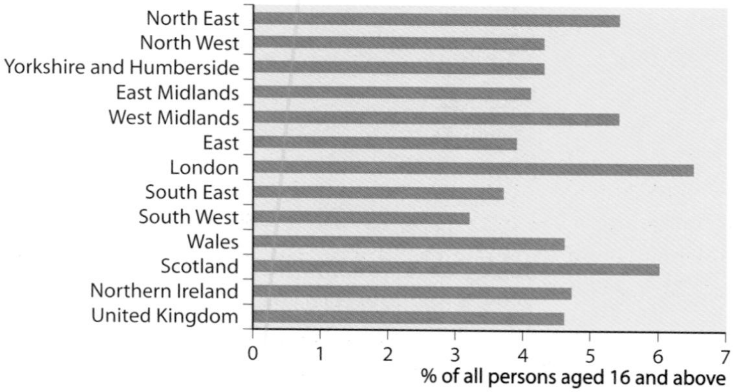

Figure 24.4 *Unemployment in regions of the UK, spring 2004*

Source: ONS.

In part, the variation in unemployment rates between regions reflects the differing pattern of economic activity across the country. If a region happens to have a concentration of employment in a declining industry, it will tend to display higher unemployment rates, because labour is not perfectly mobile, and unemployed workers may find that there are no available jobs in their area but yet may be reluctant to move.

Figure 24.5 compares unemployment in the UK with that of selected other countries. One prominent feature of this graph is that the continuous decline in the

unemployment rate that the UK has enjoyed since 1993 has not been shared by the other countries shown – or by the euro area countries as a whole. Indeed, it would appear that France and Germany are converging on a relatively high unemployment rate, whereas the UK has steadied at a lower rate. The pattern is most striking for Germany, which enjoyed a much lower unemployment rate in the 1980s and early 1990s but has since shown a weaker performance. This may partly reflect the difficulty experienced after the reunification of West and East Germany in the 1990s, beginning with the destruction of the Berlin Wall in 1989. This has undoubtedly affected the unemployment rate.

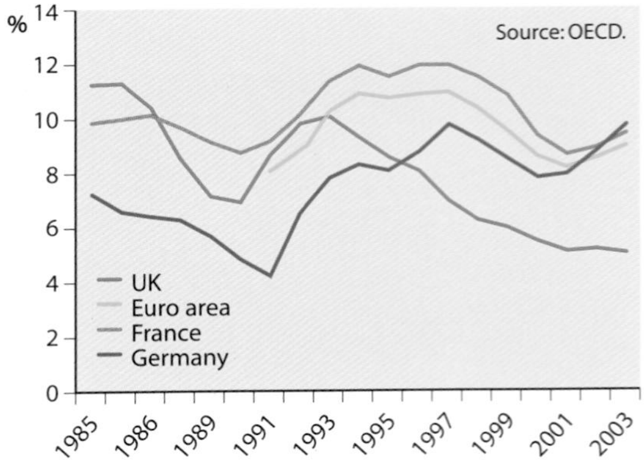

Figure 24.5 Unemployment in selected countries, 1985–2003

Exercise 24.1

Table 24.1 provides data on unemployment in the regions of the UK in 1992 and 2004. For each region and each year, calculate an index number for unemployment in the region based on the UK = 100. (If you need to be reminded about how to calculate index numbers, it was discussed in Chapter 11.) Use your results to identify which regions have experienced the greatest and least changes in the unemployment rate relative to the national average. Discuss reasons for these results.

Region	Spring 1992	Spring 2004
UK	**9.7**	**4.6**
North East	11.8	5.4
North West	10.0	4.3
Yorkshire & Humberside	10.1	4.3
East Midlands	8.8	4.1
West Midlands	10.6	5.4
East	7.7	3.9
London	12.0	6.5
South East	7.8	3.7
South West	9.1	3.2
Wales	8.9	4.6
Scotland	9.5	6.0
Northern Ireland	12.1	4.7

Table 24.1 Unemployment in UK regions, 1992 and 2004, % (spring of each year)

Source: ONS.

Summary

- Unemployment has shown quite wide variations through time in the UK, but declined steadily between 1993 and 2004.
- The proportion of unemployed workers who have been unemployed for more than a year also showed an appreciable decline.
- There are significant variations in unemployment rates across the regions of the UK, but the pattern of the differences altered during the 1990s.

Policies to promote flexibility

What makes for a flexible labour market? At the microeconomic level, where a prime concern is with achieving a good allocation of resources for society, the issue is whether workers can transfer readily between activities to allow resource allocation to change through time. This requires a number of conditions to be met. Workers need to have information about what jobs are available (and, perhaps, where those jobs are available), and what skills are needed for those jobs. Employers need to be able to identify workers with the skills and talents that they need. If workers cannot find the jobs that are available, or do not have the appropriate skills to undertake those jobs, the market will not function smoothly. Similarly, if employers cannot identify the workers with the skills that they need, that too will impede the working of the market.

Arguably, the problem has become acute in recent years, with a change in the balance of jobs between skilled and unskilled workers. As the economy gears up to more hi-tech activities and low-skill jobs are outsourced or relocated to other countries, the need for workers to acquire the right skills becomes ever more pressing.

The New Deal

An important policy launched by the new Labour government in 1997 was a package of policy measures known as the New Deal, which was aimed at reducing long-term unemployment. Figures 24.2 and 24.3 certainly suggest that long-term unemployment has declined, but you cannot assume that this reflects the impact of the New Deal alone. After all, other aspects of the economy have improved in the same period, contributing to an overall fall in the unemployment rate.

Key term

New Deal: a package of measures introduced in 1997 aimed at reducing long-term unemployment

The New Deal measures were aimed at three age groups — the groups shown in Figure 24.3. Young people aged 18–24 years old who had been unemployed for a period of more than 6 months would be assigned a personal adviser to provide them with information about available jobs and contacts with potential employers. If they were still without a job after a further 4 months, they would either enter a year of full-time education or training or take up a job with the voluntary sector for 6 months (or the environmental task force; or they would go into subsidised employment which would include on-the-job-training). Similar targeted programmes were provided for the older age groups.

Notice that such measures are designed to improve the flexibility of the labour market, by providing the unemployed worker with information and skills training. Furthermore, employers receive a subsidy to take on workers, who can then be observed in the workplace, which provides a better insight into their potential than any interview or other screening process.

A survey published in *Labour Market Trends* in 2002 indicated that nine out of ten employers in the survey provided at least some of their employees with job-related

training. Figure 24.6 indicates that a relatively high percentage of employees received such training, especially in the younger age groups.

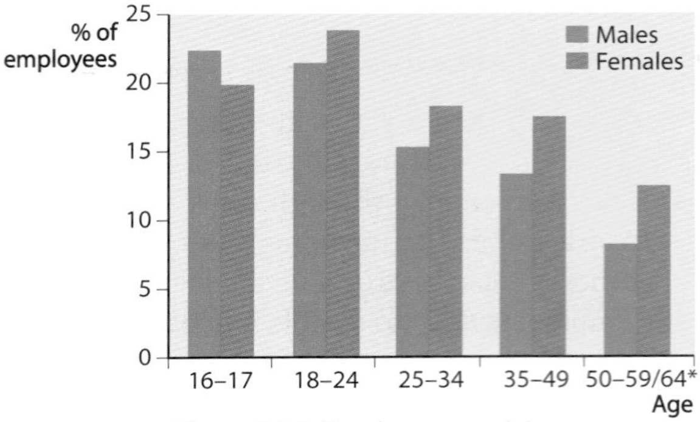

Figure 24.6 Employees receiving job-related training, by age group

*59 for women, 64 for men.

Source: Labour Market Trends.

Trade union reform

Chapter 22 highlighted the effects that trade unions may have on a labour market. By negotiating for a wage that is above the equilibrium level, trade unions may trade off higher wages for lower levels of employment. The potential disruption caused by strike action can also impede the workings of a labour market.

Some indication of this disruption can be seen in Figure 24.7. Clearly, compared with the mid-1980s, the amount of disruption through strikes in recent years has been very low. Even the 1984 figure pales into insignificance besides the 162 million working days lost in the General Strike of 1926; but, in fact, the 1970s and 1980s were a tempestuous period, in which trade union action severely disrupted British industry. So why has life become so much quieter?

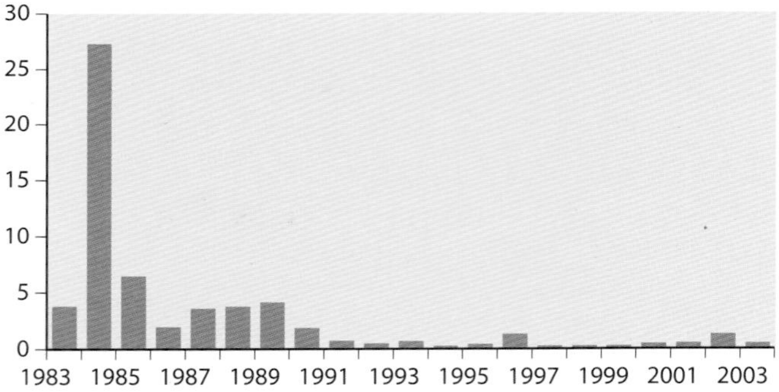

Figure 24.7 Working days lost in the UK through industrial action, 1983–2003 (million)

Source: Labour Market Trends.

It was perhaps no surprise that unions should have worked hard to protect their members during the 1980s, when unemployment was soaring and the Thatcher government was determined to control inflation – including inflation of wages. After the highly disruptive miners' strike ended in 1985, the government introduced a number of reforms designed to curb the power of the trade unions, making it more difficult for them to call rapid strike action. This may help to explain why trade union membership has been in decline since the 1980s. By weakening the power of trade unions in this way, some labour market inflexibility has been removed.

Another factor may have been changes in the structure of economic activity during this period. Manufacturing employment was falling, whereas the service sectors were expanding. Traditionally, union membership has been higher among workers in the manufacturing sector than in services.

Regional policy

There have always been differences in average incomes and in unemployment rates between the various regions of the UK. In broad terms, there are two possible responses to this – either persuade workers to move to regions where there are more jobs, or persuade the firms to move to areas where labour is plentiful. Each of these solutions poses problems. Housing markets limit the mobility of workers, and it is costly for firms to relocate their activities.

Key term

regional policy: policy comprising measures to reduce disparities in the level of economic activity between different regions of a country

The regions most affected in the past have been those that specialised in industries that subsequently went into decline, for example coal mining areas or towns and regions dominated by cotton mills. In a broad context, it is desirable for the economy to undergo structural change as the pattern of international comparative advantage changes, but it is painful during the transition period. Thus, successive governments have implemented regional policies to try to cope with the problems experienced in areas of high unemployment.

At the same time, the booming regions can be affected because of the opposite problem – a shortage of labour. Thus, measures have been taken to encourage firms to consider relocating to regions where labour is available. This included leading by example, with some civil service functions being moved out of London.

EU funding has helped in this regard, with Scotland, Wales and Northern Ireland all qualifying for grants. Since 1999, the Regional Development Agencies set up by the Labour government have been given responsibility for promoting economic development in their regions. There are eight of these agencies covering the country. Although differentials have narrowed in recent years, it is difficult to know how much of this narrowing can be attributed to the success of regional policy.

Regional policies are designed to cope with the problems experienced in areas of high unemployment such as Middlesbrough.

The Social Chapter

In 1991 the UK signed the Maastricht Treaty. Although concerned primarily with moves towards economic integration and monetary union, the treaty also included a Social Chapter, which aimed to harmonise labour market policies across the member countries.

> ***Key term***
>
> **Social Chapter:** part of the Maastricht Treaty, which launched measures designed to harmonise labour market policies across the member states of the European Union

When the UK signed the treaty, the then prime minister, John Major, negotiated an opt-out from the Social Chapter, arguing that it would damage the competitiveness of British firms. This raised complaints from other European countries, who were concerned that Britain would become a magnet for foreign investment from inside and outside Europe. When the Blair government came to power, the decision was taken to sign up to the Social Chapter, arguing that it would benefit British workers.

The treaty does not provide for a specific set of policies, but operates through a series of Directives that member countries are required to implement. One example of such a Directive — the Working Time Directive — was discussed in Chapter 23. Other Directives have covered pregnant worker protection, child labour and redundancy, together with a wide range of health and safety issues. As argued in the previous chapter, the key aim of such Directives is to ensure an appropriate balance between protecting workers (and countering information deficiencies and externalities) and enabling flexibility in the labour market.

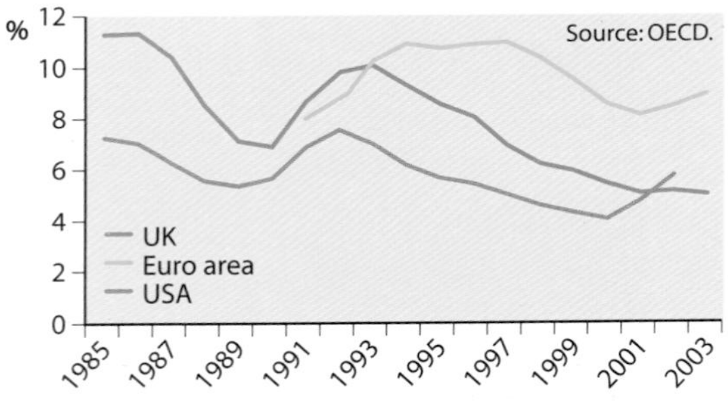

Figure 24.8 Unemployment in selected countries, 1985–2003

It has been widely argued that labour markets are highly flexible in the United States and highly inflexible in Europe, with Britain somewhere in between. To some extent, Figure 24.8 offers some support for this in terms of the general level of unemployment in the USA, the euro area and the UK.

Technology and unemployment

One of the greatest fallacies perpetuated by non-economists is that technology destroy jobs. Bands of labourers known as Luddites rioted between 1811 and 1816, destroying textile machines, which they blamed for high unemployment and low wages. In the twenty-first century there is a strong lobbying group in the USA arguing that outsourcing and cheap labour in China are destroying American jobs.

In fact, new technology and an expansion in the capital stock should have beneficial effects — so long as labour markets are sufficiently flexible. Consider a market in which new technology is introduced. If firms in an industry invest in technology and expand the capital stock, this affects the marginal revenue product of labour and hence the demand for labour, as shown in Figure 24.9, where demand shifts from D_1 to D_2. In this market, the effect is to raise the wage rate from W_1 to W_2 and the employment level from L_1 to L_2.

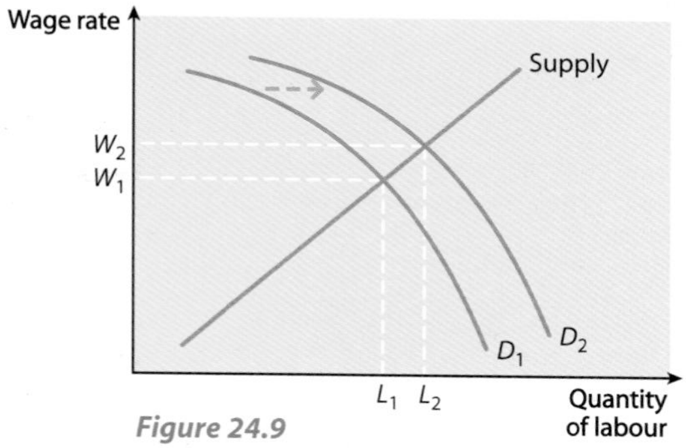

Figure 24.9
An increase in capital

However, it is important to look beyond what happens in a single market, as the argument is that it is all very well expanding employment in the technology sector – but what about the old industries that are in decline? Suppose the new industries absorb less labour than is discarded by the old declining industries? After all, if the effect of technology is to allow call centres to create jobs in India at the expense of the USA or the UK, does this not harm employment in those countries?

The counter to this lies in the law of comparative advantage, which was introduced in Chapter 2. This argues that countries can gain from international trade through specialising in the activities in which they have a comparative advantage. Setting up call centres in India frees British workers to work in sectors in which the UK has a comparative advantage, with the result that Britain can import (and thus consume) more labour-intensive goods than before.

There is one proviso, of course. It is important that the workers released from the declining sectors have (or can obtain) the skills that are needed for them to be absorbed into the expanding sectors. This recalls the question of whether the labour market is sufficiently flexible to allow the structure of economic activity to adapt to changes in the pattern of comparative advantage. However, it also serves as a reminder that policy should be aimed at enabling that flexibility, and not at introducing protectionist measures to reduce trade, which would be damaging overall for the economy. This theme will be discussed further in Chapter 31.

Demographic changes

One of the most significant features of the labour market in many developed countries today concerns the changing age structure of populations. Indeed, some commentators argue that this is *the* most important single issue facing governments.

The fact is that in most developed countries the population is getting older. This can be seen by comparing some population pyramids, which chart the age structure of the population at a given moment in time. Figures 24.10–24.12 show population pyramids for the UK for the years 1971, 2000 and the projected age structure for 2050. The number of males is plotted facing left, and the number of females facing right for each age group. This provides a visual impression of the age structure.

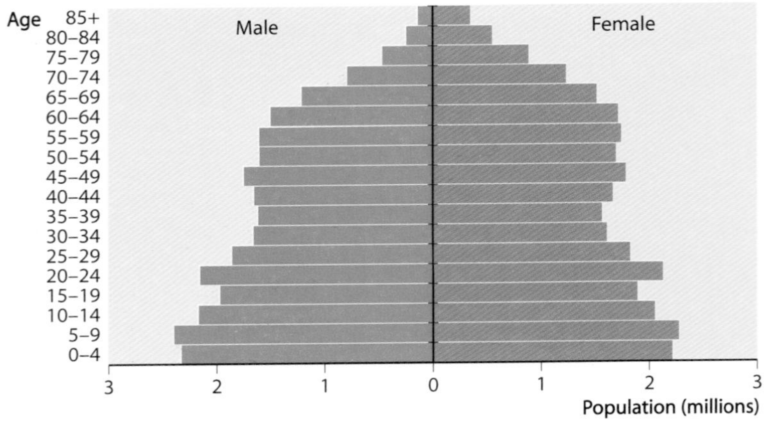

Figure 24.10 *Population pyramid, UK, 1971*

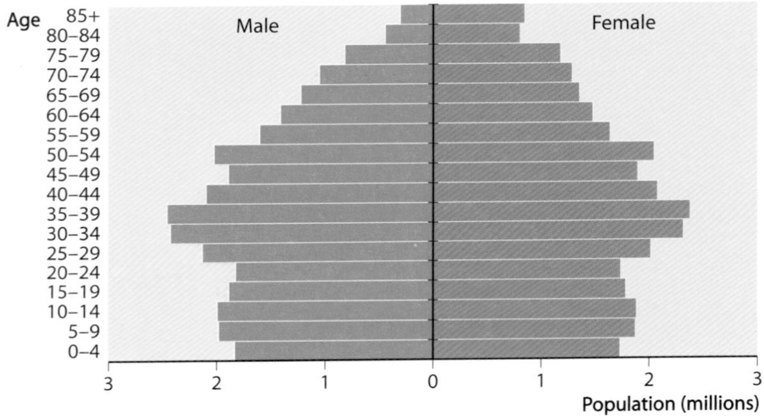

Figure 24.11 *Population pyramid, UK, 2000*

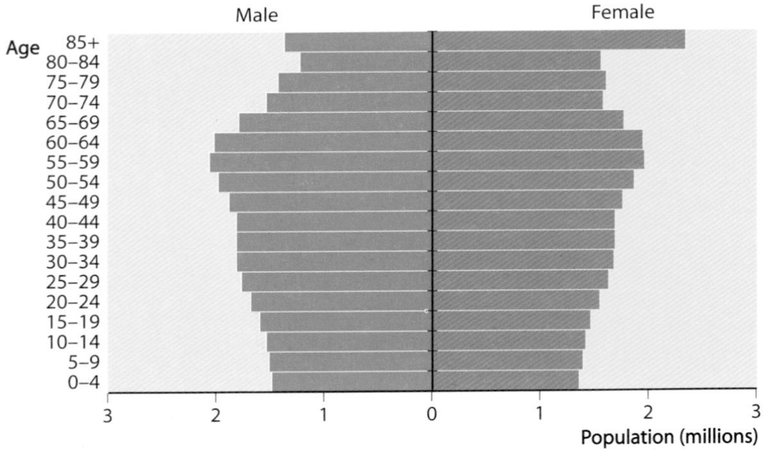

Figure 24.12 *Population pyramid, UK, 2050 (projected)*

Source: US Census Bureau, International Data Base.

If you examine these three figures, you can observe the changing pattern. In 1971 you can see why the graph is called a 'pyramid', as the highest concentration of people is in the lower age groups, and dwindles towards the older groups. In 2000 the pattern begins to thicken out in the middle age groups, and by 2050 the structure is looking much more uniform.

There are two key reasons for the change. One is that the birth rate (the number of live births relative to population size) has been falling steadily over time. People are choosing to have fewer children, and to have them later in life. The second reason is that there has been a big increase in life expectancy. People are simply living for longer because of advances in medicine.

With fewer children, countries are (or will be) seeing a reduction in the size of the working population. For example, in Italy the working population is expected to fall by 20% between 2005 and 2035, and by a further 15% by 2050. With the number of older people increasing, this means that the smaller working population has to support a larger number of older dependants. For the European Union as a whole, it has been estimated that the ratio of people aged 65 and above to those aged 20–64 will increase from less than 30% in 2005 to more than 50% in 2050. In Spain it is estimated that this ratio will be more than 70% by 2050.

A major concern for governments is pensions. If pensions are funded by a 'pay-as-you-go' system, as in the UK, current payments are made from the contributions of those presently in work. If the structure of the population changes so that fewer working people have to fund more pensioners, then problems will arise, and the government will either have to raise taxes on those working, or cut pensions. Neither of these is likely to be a popular measure. The situation has been worsened by the fall in share prices following the terrorist attacks in September 2001, which has affected private pension schemes.

Pensions are a major concern for governments.

There are some steps that can be taken to try to tackle the problem. Since the problem is that there will be fewer workers and more pensioners, approaches must entail either increasing the number of workers in the population, improving their productivity, or reducing the number of pensioners.

Immigration

One possibility might seem to be to increase the rate of immigration in order to boost the size of the working population. The UK government has used this in the past to increase labour supply, in particular during the labour shortages of the 1950s following the Second World War. The expansion of the European market in 2004 to bring in a number of relatively low-income countries, mainly in Eastern Europe and the Baltic, could offer some opportunities for immigration, although this has been politically sensitive. However, it is one possible way of preventing too substantial a fall in labour supply.

It must be remembered that the ageing population phenomenon is widespread across the developed countries, so relying wholly on immigration to boost labour supply is unlikely to be viable.

Increase in birth rate

A second (rather long-term) solution would be to encourage people to have more children. Singapore has tried to do this in the past, by running campaigns lauding the joys of family life and offering financial inducements to parents. A limitation of this approach is that it may affect the timing of families, by encouraging people to have their children earlier in life, but it may not affect the target family size, so that the long-run impact will be negligible.

Labour force participation

Another possible solution is to encourage a higher employment rate. In other words, attempts could be made to increase the proportion of people of working age who choose to join the labour force.

There are several ways in which this might be done. For example, providing improved crèche facilities could allow more parents to return to work more quickly after childbirth; and lowering unemployment benefits might encourage more people to work by raising the opportunity cost of unemployment.

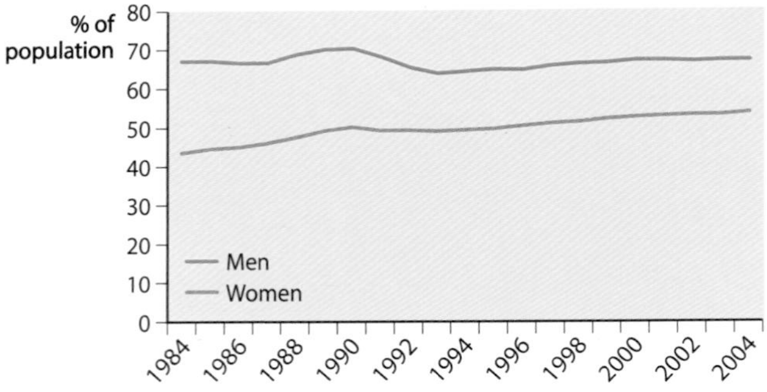

Figure 24.13 Employment rates for men and women in the UK, 1984–2004

Figure 24.13 shows employment rates for men and women in the UK between 1984 and 2004. This measures the number in employment as a percentage of the population. You can see that the employment rate for women has risen relative to that of men during this period, although it is still lower. A major explanation for this is that women continue to bear the main responsibility for child-rearing in society.

Increased productivity

If the numbers of working people cannot be significantly increased, the alternative is to raise the productivity of those who are working. Policies have been introduced to encourage research and development (R&D) activities; for example, in 2000 the UK government launched a system of R&D tax credits for small and medium-sized enterprises, and this was followed by a similar scheme for larger firms in 2002. These credits work by allowing firms to deduct more than 100% of their current expenditure on R&D from their taxable profits, reducing their tax bills.

Such measures may help to stimulate R&D, which may lead to an increase in labour productivity; but it is worth noting that this is now needed simply to halt a *decline* in R&D spending in the UK, which was lower in 2000 (relative to GDP) than it had been 20 years earlier. It has also been suggested that as the population continues to age, R&D and innovation activity will become more difficult, as much of the innovation comes from those in the younger age groups.

Raising the retirement age

Probably the only acceptable way of reducing the number of pensioners — and increasing the labour supply at the same time — is to increase the retirement age, and keep people in work for longer. This is a strategy that is being considered in a number of countries. Again, it is a politically unpopular policy, which has discouraged countries such as Germany from rushing into it. Nonetheless, economic analysis suggests that it may be one way forward.

Summary

- An important factor influencing the rate of unemployment is the degree of flexibility in labour markets.
- The New Deal was a package of measures introduced in 1997 with the objective of reducing long-term unemployment by providing jobseekers with information and training.
- Trade union reforms were introduced during the 1980s, and have contributed to flexibility in labour markets.
- Regional policy has attempted to reduce the differentials in unemployment rates between regions of the UK.
- The Social Chapter has attempted to harmonise labour market policies across the EU. In some cases, this may have reduced flexibility of labour markets in the interests of worker protection.
- Adjustment in labour markets is needed in order to cope with the changing international pattern of comparative advantage.
- The changing demographic structure of the population of many developed countries (including the UK) is posing a major challenge to economic policy for the foreseeable future, making it even more important to ensure that labour markets work effectively.

Exercise 24.2

For each of the following situations, sketch a demand and supply diagram for a labour market and analyse the effects on the wage rate and employment level:

a an increase in the rate of immigration into the country

b a reduction in the rate of the Jobseekers' Allowance

c an improvement in technology that raises labour productivity

d a new health and safety regulation to safeguard workers against industrial injury

e an increase in the percentage of old people in the overall population

part 5

Chapter 25

Poverty and inequality

In all societies there is some inequality in the distribution of income and wealth, although the extent of inequality varies between countries. Indeed, earlier chapters have shown that there is bound to be some inequality, because different people have different innate talents and abilities, and make different choices about education. This chapter explores ways of measuring inequality and poverty, looks at some of the causes of inequality and discusses some of the policies that are used to affect the distribution of income and wealth.

Learning outcomes

After studying this chapter, you should:

- be familiar with ways of identifying and monitoring inequality, including Lorenz curves and the Gini index
- be familiar with ways of measuring relative and absolute poverty
- be aware of the changing pattern of inequality in the UK and elsewhere
- understand the main causes of inequality and poverty
- be familiar with policies designed to affect the distribution of income and wealth

Evaluating inequality

Inequality is present in all societies, and always will be. However, the degree of inequality varies from one country to another; and before exploring the causes of inequality, and the policies that might be used to influence how income and wealth are distributed within society, it is necessary to be able to characterise and measure inequality. This is important in order to be able to judge relative standards of living in different countries or different periods.

One way of presenting data on this topic is to rank households in order of their incomes, and then calculate the share of total household income that goes to the poorest 10%, the poorest 20% and so on. When the groups are divided into tenths they are referred to as *deciles*; thus, the poorest 10% is the first decile, the next 10% is the second decile and so on. Similarly, the poorest 20% is the first *quintile.*

Table 25.1 presents some data for three countries. Notice that the unit of measurement is normally the household rather than the individual, on the presumption that members of a household tend to share their resources — a millionaire's life-partner may not earn any income, but he/she is not usually poor.

	UK, 1991	USA, 1997	Japan, 1993
First decile	*2.6*	*1.8*	*4.8*
First quintile	6.6	5.2	10.6
Second quintile	11.5	10.5	14.2
Third quintile	16.3	15.6	17.6
Fourth quintile	22.7	22.4	22.0
Top quintile	43.0	46.4	35.7
Top decile	*27.3*	*30.5*	*21.7*

Table 25.1 *Distribution of income in the USA, the UK and Japan, by quintiles (%)*

Source: *World Development Report.*

These data are not very easy to assimilate, especially for large numbers of countries, and to explore the question of income inequality some summary measures need to be developed.

By calculating the ratio of the income accruing to the richest decile or quintile to the income of the poorest, some impression can be gained of the gap between the poorest and richest households. Table 25.2 summarises the results of such calculations for the three countries.

Country	Ratio of top decile to poorest decile	Ratio of top quintile to poorest quintile
United States	16.9	8.9
United Kingdom	10.5	6.5
Japan	4.5	3.4

Table 25.2 Ratio of income of richest to poorest households

It can be seen that in the UK households in the top decile receive ten and a half times more income than those in the poorest decile. On the basis of these data, inequality in the UK is lower than that in the USA, but higher than that in Japan.

The Lorenz curve

Although the usual types of graph are not well suited to presenting such data visually, there is a method of presenting the data visually via the Lorenz curve. Some Lorenz curves are shown in Figure 25.1.

Key term

Lorenz curve: a graphical way of depicting the distribution of income within a country

Lorenz curves are constructed as follows. Using the data in Table 25.1, the first step is to convert the numbers in the table into *cumulative* percentages. In other words (using the UK as an example), the data show that the poorest 20% receive 6.6% of total household income, the poorest 40% receive 6.6% + 11.5% = 18.1%, the poorest 60% receive 18.1% + 16.3% = 34.4%, and so on. It is these cumulative percentages that are plotted to produce the Lorenz curve, as in Figure 25.1. (The figure also plots the lowest and highest deciles.)

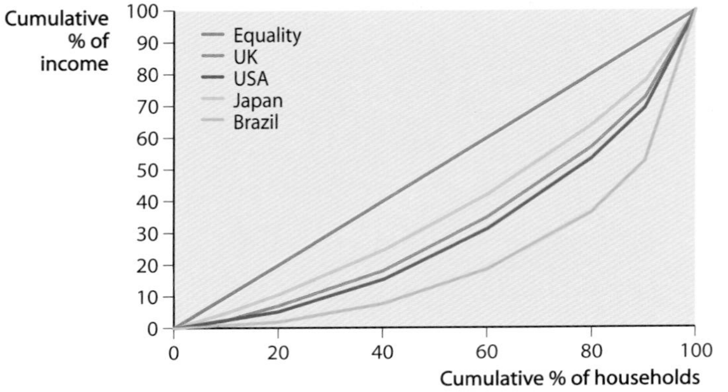

Figure 25.1
Lorenz curves

Source: *WDR 2000/2001.*

Suppose that income were perfectly equally distributed between households. In other words, suppose the poorest 10% of households received exactly 10% of income, the poorest 20% received 20% and so on. The Lorenz curve would then be a straight line going diagonally across the figure.

To interpret the country curves, the closer a country's Lorenz curve is to the diagonal equality line, the more equal is the distribution. You can see from the figure that Japan comes closest to the equality line, bearing out the earlier conclusion that income is more equally distributed in that country. The UK and the US curves are closer together, but there seems to be slightly more inequality in the USA, as its Lorenz curve is further from the equality line. Brazil has also been included on the figure, as an example of a society in which there is substantial inequality.

Exercise 25.1

Use the data provided in Table 25.3 to calculate the ratios of top decile income to bottom decile income, and of top quintile income to bottom quintile income. Then draw Lorenz curves for the two countries, and compare the inequalities shown for Belarus and South Africa with each other and with the countries already discussed.

	Percentage share of income or consumption: South Africa	Belarus
Lowest decile	1.1	5.1
Lowest quintile	2.9	11.4
Second quintile	5.5	15.2
Third quintile	9.2	18.2
Fourth quintile	17.7	21.9
Highest quintile	64.8	33.3
Highest decile	45.9	20.0

Table 25.3
Income distribution in Belarus and South Africa

Source: *World Development Report.*

The Gini index

The Lorenz curve is fine for comparing income distribution in just a few countries. However, it would also be helpful to have an index that could summarise the relationship in a numerical way. The Gini index does just this. It is a way of trying to quantify the equality of income distribution in a country, and is obtained by calculating the ratio of the area between the equality line and the country's Lorenz curve to the whole area under the equality line. This is often expressed as a percentage. The closer the Gini index is to 100, the further the Lorenz curve is from equality, and thus the more unequal is the income distribution. The Gini index values for the countries in Figure 25.1 are shown in Table 25.4.

Key term

Gini index: a measure of the degree of inequality in a society

Country	Gini index
United States	40.8
United Kingdom	36.1
Japan	24.9
Brazil	60.0

Table 25.4 The Gini index

Source: *World Development Report.*

Some measurement issues

When measuring income inequality, some important measurement issues need to be borne in mind. For example, in talking about the 'poorest' and 'richest' households, you need to be aware that absolute income levels per household may be a misleading indicator, given that households are of different sizes and compositions. Thus, when looking at the income distribution in the UK, it is important to make adjustments for this.

The way this is done is by the use of *equivalence scales.* These allow a household to be judged relative to a 'reference household' made up of a childless couple. It can then be decided that a household with a husband, wife and two young children rates as 1.18 relative to the childless couple with a rating of 1. So if the couple with two children had an income of, say, £40 000 per year, this would be the equivalent of 40 000/1.18 = £33 898. In order to examine the inequality of income, it is these equivalised incomes that need to be considered.

A further question is whether income is the most appropriate indicator. People tend to smooth their consumption over their lifetimes (as Chapter 12 explained), and it has been argued that it is more important to look at consumption (expenditure) than income when considering inequality.

Then there is the question of housing costs. In the short run households have no control over their spending on housing. Some measures of inequality therefore choose to exclude housing costs from the calculations in order to focus on the income that households have at their disposal for other expenditures. As housing tends to constitute a higher proportion of the budgets of poor households, measures of inequality that exclude housing costs tend to show greater levels of inequality.

It is also important to bear in mind that the standard of living that households can achieve depends partly on government-provided services, such as health and education. Remember that rich as well as poor households may benefit from these.

Finally, in considering inequality in a society, it may be important to examine inequalities in the distribution of wealth as well as income. Wealth can be regarded as the accumulated stock of assets that households own, and in the UK wealth is more unequally distributed than income.

It is interesting to note that many people remain unaware of where they fit into the income distribution of their country. A survey in the USA in 2000 found that 19% of Americans believed that they were in the top 1% of earners.

Measuring poverty

One aspect of inequality is poverty. If there is a wide gap between the richest and poorest households, it is important to evaluate just how poor those poorest households are, and whether they should be regarded as being 'in poverty'. This requires a definition of poverty.

One way of defining poverty is to specify a basket of goods and services that is regarded as the minimum required to support human life. Households that are seen to have too low an income to allow them to purchase everything in that basic bundle of goods would be regarded as being in **absolute poverty**.

Globally, the UN Development Programme regards households in which income is below $1 per day per person as being in absolute poverty, as this is their declared *poverty line*.

Key terms

absolute poverty: situation of a household whose income is insufficient to allow it to purchase the minimum bundle of goods and services regarded as necessary for survival

relative poverty: situation obtaining if household income falls below 50% of median adjusted household disposable income

For a country like the UK, this absolute poverty line is not helpful, as so few people fall below it. Thus poverty is defined in *relative* terms. If a household has insufficient income for its members to participate in the normal social life of the country, it is said to be in **relative poverty**. This too is defined in terms of a poverty line, set at 50% of the median adjusted household disposable income. (The median is the income of the middle-ranked household.)

Figure 25.2 presents some data for a range of developed countries. The proportion of people below the relative poverty line varies substantially across these countries, from 2.1% in Slovakia to 20.1% in the Russian Federation.

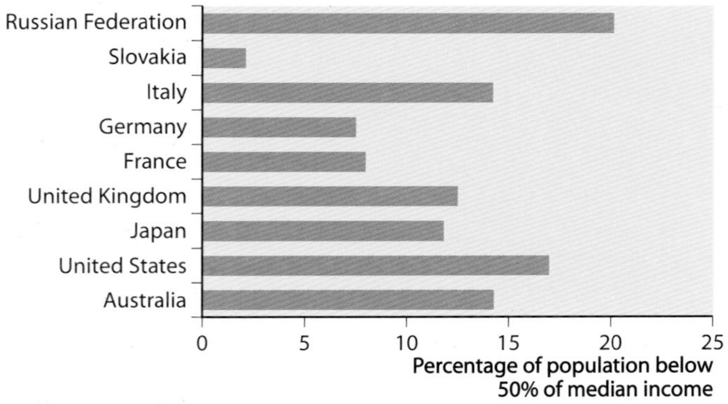

Figure 25.2 *Poverty in some developed countries*

Source: *Human Development Report.*

The percentage falling below the poverty line is not a totally reliable measure on its own: it is also important to know *how far* below the poverty line households are falling. The *income gap* (the distance between household income and the poverty line) is a useful measure of the intensity of poverty as well as of its incidence.

Exercise 25.2

Imagine that you are the Minister for Poverty Alleviation in a country in which the (absolute) poverty line is set at $500. Of the people living below the poverty line, you know that there are two distinct groups, each made up of 50 individuals. The people in group 1 have an income of $450, whereas those in group 2 have only $250. Suppose that your budget for poverty alleviation is $2,500.

a Your prime concern is with the most needy: how would you use your budget?

b Suppose instead that your prime minister instructs you to reduce the percentage of people living below the poverty line: do you adopt the same strategy for using the funds?

c How helpful is the poverty line as a strategic target of policy action?

Changes in inequality and poverty over time

Although the distribution of income does not change rapidly from one year to the next, there have been changes over time. Figure 25.3 graphs the Gini index, calculated for both income and expenditure in the UK over 1974–99.

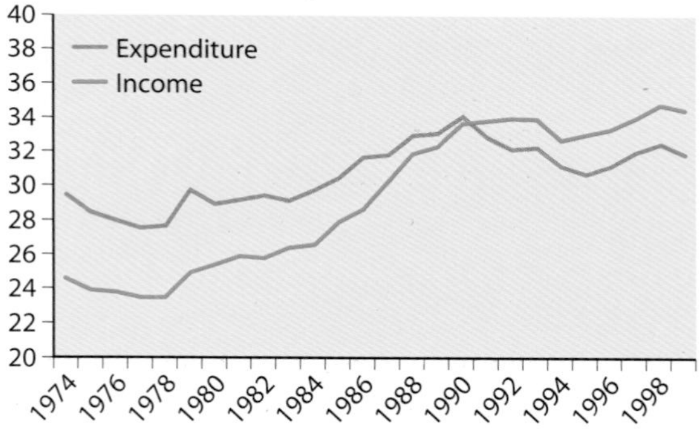

Figure 25.3 The Gini index for income and expenditure in the UK, 1974–99

Source: IFS in *Economic Review*, November 2003.

Because people can be expected to smooth their consumption through time, expenditure inequality is seen to have been a little steadier than income inequality. However, both show a noticeable increase in inequality during the 1980s, since when there seems to have been no discernible trend.

It is worth noting that this has not been a general trend across all of the developed countries. A study by OECD in 2002 found no generalised trend in the distribution of household incomes since the mid-1970s, although about half of the countries studied did show an increase between the mid-1980s and mid-1990s.[1]

Another study, undertaken by the Institute for Fiscal Studies, analysed trends and noted that there were very different trends identifiable over some 'periods of political interest'.[2] In particular, between 1979 and 1990, with Margaret Thatcher as prime minister, income growth was higher for each successive quintile.

[1] Michael Förster and Mark Pearson, 'Income distribution and poverty in the OECD area: trends and driving forces', *OECD Economic Studies* no. 23, 2002.

[2] Alissa Goodman and Andrew Shephard, 'Inequality and living standards in Great Britain: some facts', *IFS Briefing Notes* no. 19, updated December 2002.

The richest quintile saw income growth that was more than eight times that of the poorest. In other words, inequality increased during this period. Under John Major, from 1990 to 1997, growth was sluggish, but the poorest quintile gained relative to higher quintile groups. Under Tony Blair, from 1997 to 2001 income growth was more or less equally divided over the quintile groups.

However, you should not read too much into these differences. The causes of change in income distribution reflect not only the political stance of the government in power, but other changes occurring in society, and in the pattern of employment over time.

Summary

- Some degree of inequality in income and wealth is present in every society.
- Inequality is measured by ranking households in order of income, then comparing the income received by the richest decile (or quintile) with that received by the poorest.
- The Lorenz curve gives a visual impression of the income distribution; this can be quantified into the Gini index as a single statistic representing the degree of income inequality.
- Calculations of the income distribution are normally undertaken using equivalised incomes, taking into account the size and composition of households.
- In some cases consumption (expenditure) provides a more reliable measure of inequality, as people tend to smooth their consumption over time.
- Absolute poverty measures whether individuals or households have sufficient resources to maintain a reasonable life.
- Relative poverty measures whether individuals or households are able to participate in the life of the country in which they live: this is calculated as 50% of median adjusted household disposable income.
- Income distribution and poverty levels change relatively slowly over time.
- In the UK there has been little change since the mid-1990s, following a decade of increasing inequality.

Causes of inequality and poverty

Inequality arises from a variety of factors, some reflecting patterns in the ownership of assets, some relating to the operation of the labour market and some arising from the actions of governments.

Ownership of assets

Perhaps the most obvious way in which the ownership of assets influences inequality and its changes through time is through inheritance. Wealth that accumulates in a family over time and is then passed down to succeeding generations generates a source of inequality that does not arise from the current state of the economy or the operations of markets.

You need to be aware that income and wealth are not the same. Income is a 'flow' of money that households receive each period, whereas wealth is a 'stock', i.e. the accumulation of assets that a household owns. Wealth is considerably less evenly distributed than income. In 2001 the most wealthy 1% of households in the UK owned 23% of the marketable wealth (33% if the value of dwellings is omitted), and the most wealthy 50% of households owned 95% of the country's marketable wealth.

Figure 25.4 charts the percentage of wealth owned by the wealthiest 1% and 5% of the UK population in various years. You can see that there was an increase in the concentration of wealth between 1991 and 1999, and a levelling out since then. The distribution has been strongly influenced by rising house prices in recent years, but was also affected by the fall in share prices following the September 2001 terrorist attacks.

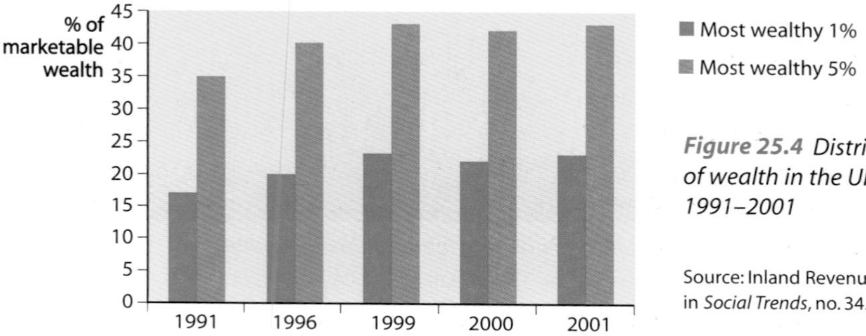

Figure 25.4 *Distribution of wealth in the UK, 1991–2001*

Source: Inland Revenue; cited in *Social Trends*, no. 34.

Notice that, although wealth and income are not the same thing, inequality in wealth can *lead to* inequality in income, as wealth (the ownership of assets) creates an income flow – from rents and profits – which then feeds back into a household's income stream.

A significant change in the pattern of ownership of assets in recent decades has been the increase in home ownership and the rise in house prices. For those who continue to rent their homes, and in particular for those who rent council dwellings, this is a significant source of rising inequality.

Labour market explanations

The previous chapters have set out a number of ways in which the labour market can be expected to give rise to inequalities in earnings. These arise from demand and supply conditions in labour markets, which respond to changes in the pattern of consumer demand for goods and services and changes in international comparative advantage between countries. Differences in the balance between economic rent and transfer earnings between different occupations and economic sectors then reinforce income inequalities.

However, a by-product of changes in the structure of the economy may be an increase in inequality between certain groups in society. For example, a change in the structure of employment, away from unskilled jobs and towards occupations requiring a higher level of skills and qualifications, can lead to an increase in inequality, with those workers who lack the skills to adapt to changing labour market conditions being disadvantaged by the changes. In other words, if the premium that employers are prepared to pay in order to hire skilled or well-qualified workers rises as a result of changing technology in the workplace, then those without such skills are likely to suffer.

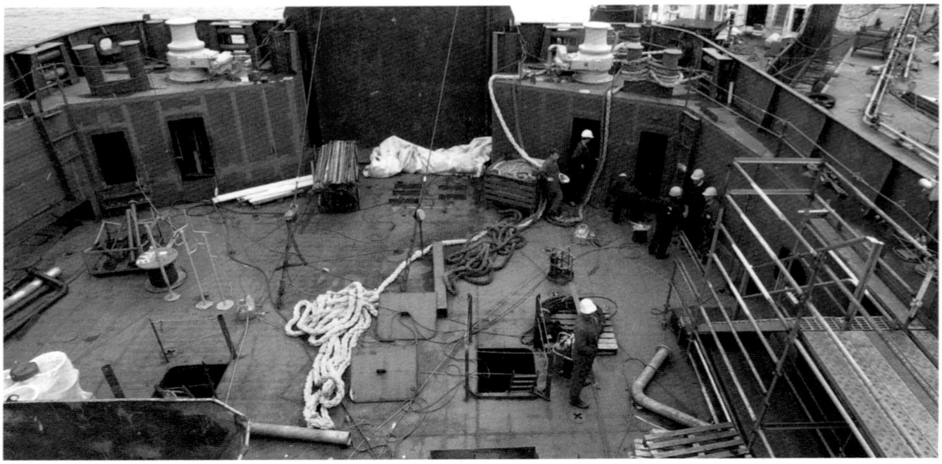

Shipworkers may be vulnerable to changing labour market conditions.

The decline in the power of the trade unions may have contributed to this situation, as low-paid workers may find that their unions are less likely to be able to offer employment protection. It has been argued that this is a *good* thing if it increases the flexibility of the labour market. But again, a balance is needed between worker protection and free and flexible markets.

The difference in earnings between female and male workers was also highlighted. Figure 25.5 provides empirical evidence for some developed countries. In the UK, a female worker with an educational attainment below upper secondary level on average earns 55% of the average male wage. As educational attainment increases, this differential widens somewhat. The pattern varies across this group of countries. For example, in Germany education brings a marked narrowing of the earnings differential between men and women. Overall, the differentials are less for countries like Hungary or Italy than for Germany, the USA or the UK.

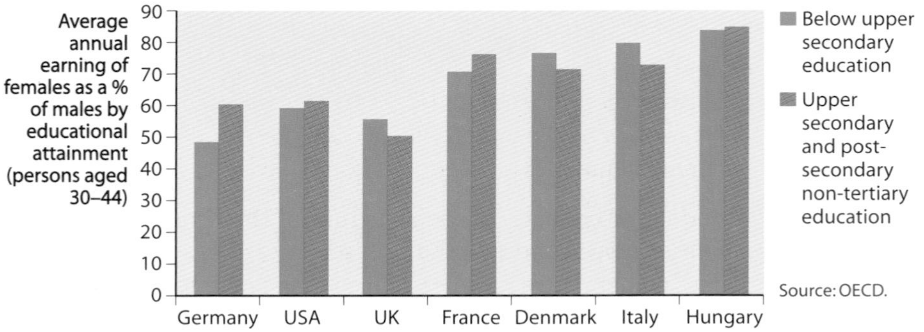

Figure 25.5 Gender inequality in earnings, various countries

In earlier chapters it was pointed out that some of the earnings differences between men and women can be explained on the basis of marginal productivity theory: when women have to take time out from working to look after children, they lose human capital by missing out on work experience. However, such market explanations may not suffice to explain all the differences in earnings that are observed.

Government intervention

There are a number of ways in which government intervention influences the distribution of income in a society, although not all of these interventions are expressly intended to do so. Most prominent is the range of transfer payments and taxation that has been implemented.

The overall effect of these measures has a large effect on income distribution. For example, in 2002/03 the 'original income' of the top quintile of households in the UK was about 15 times greater than that of the bottom quintile. ('Original income' is income before any adjustment is made for the effect of taxation or benefits.) After adjusting for benefits and taxes, the ratio of top to bottom quintile fell to about fourfold. Figure 25.6 shows these data in the form of Lorenz curves. Again, you can see the extent to which tax and benefit measures bring the Lorenz curve closer to the equality line.

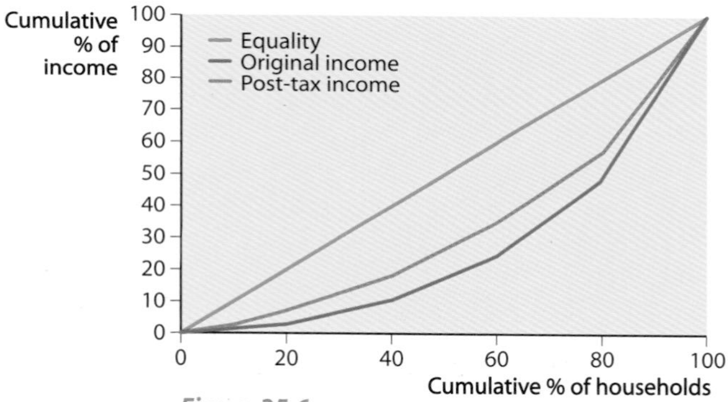

Figure 25.6

Lorenz curves for income in the UK, 2002–03

Source: *Economic Trends*, June 2004.

Benefits

There are two forms of benefit that households can receive to help equalise the income distribution. First, there are various types of cash benefit, such as Income Support, Child Benefit, Incapacity Benefit and Working Families' Tax Credit. These are designed to protect families whose income in certain circumstances would otherwise be very low. Second, there are benefits in kind, such as health and education. These accrue to individual households depending on the number of members of the household and their age and gender.

Of these, the cash benefits are far more important in influencing the distribution of income. For the lowest quintile in 2002/03 such benefits made up about three-fifths of growth in income; they were also significant for the second quintile.

Taxation

Direct taxes (taxes on incomes) tend to be progressive. In other words, higher income groups pay tax at a higher rate. In 2002/03 the top quintile paid 24% of its

gross income in tax, compared with only 9% paid in the bottom quintile.

In the UK the main direct taxes are income tax, corporation tax (paid by firms on profits), capital gains tax (paid by individuals who sell assets at a profit), inheritance tax and petroleum revenue tax (paid by firms operating in the North Sea). There is also the council tax, collected by local authorities.

With a tax such as income tax, its progressive nature is reflected in the way the tax rate increases as an individual moves into a higher income range. In other words, the **marginal tax rate** increases as income increases. The **progressive** nature of the tax ensures that it does indeed help to reduce inequality in income distribution — although its effects are less than the cash benefits discussed earlier.

Key terms

direct tax: a tax levied directly on income

marginal tax rate: tax on additional income, defined as the change in tax payments due divided by the change in taxable income

progressive tax: a tax in which the marginal tax rate rises with income, i.e. a tax bearing most heavily on the relatively well-off members of society

Table 25.5 shows average tax rates for taxpayers in different income bands in 2003/04. Notice that the table shows *average* rather than *marginal* tax rates. When average rates are rising, marginal tax rates are higher than the average. Exercise 25.3 illustrates this.

Income band	Number of taxpayers (m)	Average rate of tax payable (%)	Average amount of tax payable (£)
£4615–£4999	0.5	0.4	20
£5000–£7499	3.3	2.5	160
£7500–£9999	3.8	6.0	520
£10 000–£14 999	6.5	10.3	1 280
£15 000–£19 999	5.1	13.3	2 310
£20 000–£29 999	6.3	15.5	3 780
£30 000–£49 999	3.7	18.3	6 790
£50 000–£99 999	1.3	25.9	17 210
£100 000 and over	0.4	34.0	76 080
All incomes	30.7	18.0	4 040

***Table 25.5** Income tax payable in the UK by annual income 2003/04*

Source: *Social Trends*, no. 34.

Exercise 25.3

Table 25.5 shows the amount of tax paid by an individual as income increases. Calculate the average and marginal tax rates at each of the income levels. (*Remember the definition of the marginal tax rate provided above.*)

Income	Tax paid
£1000	£100
£2000	£300
£3000	£600
£4000	£1000

The effect of **indirect taxes,** on the other hand, can sometimes be **regressive**; in other words, indirect taxes may impinge more heavily on lower-income households. Indirect taxes are taxes that are paid on items of expenditure, rather than on income.

Key terms

indirect tax: a tax on expenditure, e.g. VAT

regressive tax: a tax bearing more heavily on the relatively poorer members of society

Examples of indirect taxes are value added tax (VAT), which is charged on most goods and services sold in the UK at a rate of 17.5%, tobacco taxes, excise duties on alcohol and oil duties. These specific taxes are levied per unit sold. Chapter 10 analysed how the incidence of a tax is related to the price elasticity of demand of a good or service. It explained how, where demand is price-inelastic, producers are able to pass much of an increase in the tax rate on to consumers, whereas if demand is price-elastic they have to absorb most of the increase as part of their costs.

Why should some of these taxes be regressive? Take the tobacco tax. In the first place, the number of smokers is higher among lower-income groups than among the relatively rich — research has shown that only about 10% of people in professional groups now smoke compared with nearly 40% of those in unskilled manual groups. Second, expenditure on tobacco tends to take a lower proportion of income of the rich compared with that of the poor, even for those in the former group who do smoke. Thus, the tobacco tax falls more heavily on lower-income groups than on the better-off.

The balance of taxation

Achieving a balance of taxation between direct and indirect taxes is an important aspect of the government's redistributive policy. A switch in the balance from direct to indirect taxes will tend to increase inequality in a society.

There may be reasons why such a switch is seen as desirable. When Margaret Thatcher came to power in 1979, one of the first actions of her government was to increase indirect taxes and introduce cuts in income tax. An important part of the rationale was that high marginal tax rates on income can have a disincentive effect; if people know that a large proportion of any additional work they undertake will be taxed away, they may be discouraged from providing more work. In other words, cutting income tax can encourage work effort by reducing marginal tax rates.

This is yet another reminder of the need for a balanced policy, one that recognises that, while some income redistribution is needed to protect the vulnerable, disincentive effects may arise if the better-off are over-taxed.

Long-term policy

An economic analysis of the causes of inequality suggests that there are some long-term measures that can be taken to reduce future inequality, although they may take quite a while to become effective. In particular, this Part of the book has

emphasised the importance of education and training. Policies that encourage greater take-up of education, and provide skills retraining, may be important in the long run if the unskilled are not to be excluded from the benefits of economic growth.

Exercise 25.4

Using appropriate economic analysis, discuss the various policy measures available to a government wishing to ensure an equitable distribution of income without damaging incentives to work.

Summary

- Inequality arises from a range of factors.
- The distribution of wealth is strongly influenced by the pattern of inheritance, but in recent years changing patterns of home ownership, coupled with rises in house prices, have also been significant.
- The natural operation of labour markets gives rise to some inequality in income.
- The skills premium resulting from technological change has widened the wage gap between skilled and educated workers on the one hand, and the unskilled on the other.
- Gender differences in pay persist, in spite of successive policies intended to root out discrimination.
- Government action influences the pattern of income distribution, with the net effect being a reduction in inequality.
- Most effective in this is the provision of cash benefits to low-income households.
- Direct taxes tend to be progressive, and help to redistribute income towards poorer households.
- Some indirect taxes, however, can be regressive in their impact.
- It is important to keep a balance between protecting the low-paid and providing incentives for those in work.

Review section

Labour economics is an interesting branch of economics, as it encompasses a wide range of economic issues just asking to be analysed. It also covers issues that will be of direct relevance to you, as at some stage you will join the workforce and become part of the labour market. As in the other review sections, these pages remind you of some key concepts and issues that were raised in the previous five chapters, and provide some recent examination questions for you to try out in preparation for that exam.

Chapter 21 The demand and supply of labour and market equilibrium

In thinking about the market for labour, it is usual to begin with the notions of demand and supply. The demand for labour is a *derived demand*; that is, employers demand labour not for its own sake, but for the revenue they will receive from selling the output that labour produces. The *marginal revenue product* represents the additional revenue that a firm will receive from employing an extra unit of labour, and a profit-maximising employer will hire labour so long as the marginal revenue exceeds the cost of hiring that additional unit of labour. Chapter 21 explained these terms, and also discussed the factors affecting the *elasticity* of demand for labour. On the supply side of the market, the individual worker makes decisions about *labour supply*. The choice made by a worker can be seen as a choice between work and leisure. In addition to analysing these factors and identifying market equilibrium, the chapter provided a brief introduction to the UK labour market.

Chapter 22 Wage differentials, discrimination and the trade unions

It is clear that within the economy there are substantial differences in earnings between people working in different occupations and people having different sorts of skills. This arises partly from differences in the *marginal productivity* of different

workers, but also from a different balance between *economic rent* and *transfer earnings*. Differences can also be seen between male and female workers, among workers from different ethnic groups, and among workers in different regions of the country. These differences can be explained in terms of a number of influences, of which *discrimination* is only one aspect. The role of *education* is seen to be especially important in influencing lifetime earnings. Trade unions can also affect the way the labour markets operate.

Chapter 23 Labour market imperfections

As with product markets, there are influences at work in labour markets that can lead to imperfections in their operation. One example of this is where there is a single *monopsony* buyer of labour, which is able to restrict employment and lower wages. If such a monopsonist is faced with a monopoly trade union in a *bilateral monopoly* market, some of the market imperfections may be cancelled out. Governments also may introduce imperfections into the labour market, for example through the imposition of a *minimum wage*. *Health and safety legislation* may reduce the flexibility of labour markets — but this may be necessary, as health and safety may be regarded as a form of merit good. This chapter also identified various causes of unemployment in a labour market.

Chapter 24 Labour markets in the UK and EU

One reflection of the flexibility of labour markets is the structure and incidence of unemployment. This was explored in the context of the UK economy, with some comparison with other countries in Europe. It was seen that flexibility in labour markets is important if resources are to be allocated efficiently in an economy, especially in the context of improvements in technology and changing patterns of consumer demand and comparative advantage. The UK government has introduced a number of policies intended to improve the flexibility of the UK labour market. These are classified as supply-side policies. A major challenge that many national economies will face in the coming years is the changing demographic structure of their populations, which are ageing in many OECD countries.

Chapter 25 Poverty and inequality

Inequality is a feature of all societies, although the extent of inequality varies between countries. Lorenz curves and the Gini index provide methods of identifying, monitoring and comparing the degree of inequality in income distribution. This chapter examines these measures, and outlines the changing pattern of inequality in the UK and elsewhere. The causes of inequality — and of poverty — were also highlighted, and there was an examination of policies designed to affect the distribution of income and wealth.

Preparing for the examination

Data-response is again the key form of assessment for Unit 5 (Option A: Labour markets). As you tackle the following sample questions, it may be helpful to bear in mind the sorts of skills that the examiners are looking to assess in the examination. For this unit there are four levels of key skill that the mark scheme is designed to examine:

- knowledge (15%)
- application (15%)
- analysis (30%)
- evaluation (40%)

However, the marks are not allocated evenly across these skills. Analysis and evaluation account for 70% of the overall marks. In other words, it is not enough 'just' to know about economics or to be able to apply economic theory to particular situations. You need to be able to demonstrate those higher order skills of analysis and evaluation. Evaluation is especially important, and it is essential to be aware of what this entails. Evaluation involves looking at the strengths and weaknesses of the subject under discussion — its advantages and disadvantages, and plus and minus points. It also requires you to formulate a view about whether the positives or the negatives are stronger. In other words, do not be afraid to express an opinion — but make sure that you can support that opinion by the arguments that you have advanced.

Data-response question P5.1

The German labour market

Extract 1: Germany sinks in a sea of unemployment

The official level of unemployment in Germany now stands at more than 4.3 million (8.3%). The rosy picture presented by the Labour Office of a successful job placement programme is misleading: the unemployed are being trained in professions which offer few job opportunities. The government has strengthened the role of unions in company affairs, increased the tax burden for part-time workers, withdrawn cuts in sick pay and made dismissal more difficult. Greater flexibility in the economy cannot be introduced for fear of a union backlash.

The unemployment is a result of government inaction. It has gambled that population decline would solve the problem, or that GDP growth would reduce the burden of the state deficit. Hans Eichel, the finance minister, has to cut the £34 bn deficit to £6 bn by 2004. The result is that cities are shutting libraries, closing swimming baths and schools, and deferring repairs to housing and the motorway network. Unemployment benefits cost the government close to 2% of GDP: Germany's unemployed get at least £13 200 a year, which is significantly higher than the EU average.

Source: adapted from Michael Woodhead, *The Sunday Times*, 3 March 2002.

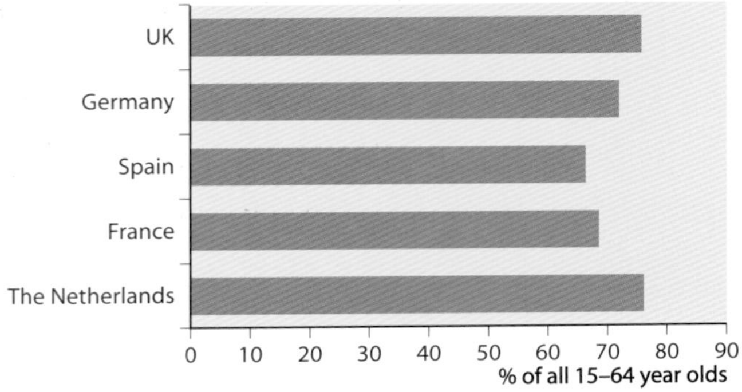

Figure P5.1 Labour participation rates, selected countries, 2001

Percentages of all individuals aged 15–64 who are economically active.

Source: OECD, *Employment Outlook*, 2002.

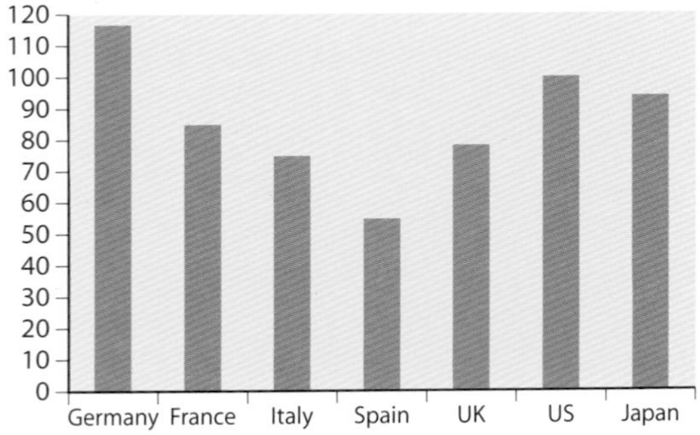

Figure P5.2 Why Germany is 'the sick man of Europe'

Index of hourly labour costs for production workers in manufacturing, including social charges, selected countries (USA = 100).

Source: adapted from Anatole Kaletsky, *The Times*, 14 May 2002.

Extract 2: German unions fail their history lesson

Germany's labour costs are far higher than those of any other country in Europe, or indeed the world as a whole. If we include Germany's huge social charges – payroll taxes, pensions, medical insurance and holiday allowances – an average manufacturing worker costs 40% more to employ than in France, 58% more than in Italy and more than twice as much as in Spain.

German unions seem to have learned nothing from the experiences of reunification and monetary union, which have turned Germany into 'the sick man of Europe'. They haven't understood that Germany's economic decline is connected with grossly uncompetitive labour costs.

First, they seem to believe that they have the right to up to 60% more wages than equally efficient workers just across the border in France, northern Italy and the Netherlands. But German factories are not, in general, more productive than those of their neighbours – French factories now have the world's highest average output per worker hour.

Second, the fairly high productivity levels in existing German factories are of limited relevance in analysing the future economic impact of relative labour costs. When a rational company makes its investment decisions, it will consider the productivity it can achieve at a new factory, not at existing plants. This is just one instance of the principle that economic decisions are made at the margin. A well-managed new factory, equipped with the latest machinery, is likely to achieve much the same productivity whether it is sited in Germany, France, Britain or even Spain.

Finally, German unions seem to have ignored a basic principle of economics: that, in an efficient, competitive labour market, wages are determined not by productivity alone but by the interaction of demand and supply for workers of various skills. Currently there is an excess supply of labour, as illustrated by the high level of unemployment.

Source: adapted from A. Kaletsky, *The Times*, 14 May 2002.

- **a** Discuss **two** factors which might explain differences between the German labour force participation rate and those of the other countries shown. *(10 marks)*
- **b** Using marginal productivity theory, examine the view that 'wages are determined not by productivity alone but by the interaction of demand and supply for workers of various skills' (Extract 2, lines 24–26). *(20 marks)*
- **c** Evaluate the likely effectiveness of **two** policies that the German government could introduce to increase labour market flexibility. *(10 marks)*
- **d** Discuss the likely impact of trade unions on wages and employment levels. *(20 marks)*

Data-response question P5.2

The National Minimum Wage

On 1 April 1999 the first legally binding National Minimum Wage (NMW) was introduced in the UK. Britain had never before had a national wage floor. One might imagine that measuring the number of workers affected by the introduction of the minimum wage would be relatively straightforward. However, the available UK survey data on individuals' hourly earnings are limited. This has led to considerable uncertainty over the likely impact of the minimum wage, both in terms of how many workers will experience a wage increase and the size of that increase. Prior to its introduction, the Low Pay Commission (LPC) estimated that around 2 million workers (or 9%) would receive a wage increase, with the average wage increase being in the region of 30%. However, since then the LPC has revised down its estimates of the number of workers affected to 1.5 million (6.4%) in February 2000 and then to 1.3 million (5.5%) in March 2001. The problem arises because none of the available survey data in the UK provides an accurate measure of individuals' hourly wages.

Trying to estimate the impact of the introduction of the minimum wage on aggregate employment levels is difficult. Perhaps the most detailed sector-specific study of the impact on employment from the introduction of the National Minimum Wage is that by Machin, Manning and Rahman (2001). They conducted a survey of all residential care homes in Britain, collecting information on employment, wages and worker characteristics. They surveyed each firm both before and after the introduction of the minimum wage, enabling them to examine wage and

employment changes over this period. The residential care home sector is possibly the sector with the lowest wage levels in the UK labour market. Their results show that firms affected most by the introduction of the minimum wage are more likely to suffer employment falls. The study reported elasticities of employment change with respect to wage changes which are of the range –0.2 to –0.4. This suggests that a 10% increase in the minimum wage will reduce employment by between 2% and 4%.

The National Minimum Wage was introduced as part of an anti-poverty strategy designed to make work pay. However, many commentators have doubted the effectiveness of the minimum wage as an anti-poverty device. Table P5.1 presents information on the link between low pay and household income, using data from the Family Expenditure Survey 1998/99. The analysis considered the impact of going from a situation with no minimum wage to one of £4.10 for adults and £3.50 for those aged 18–20 (at October 2001 earning levels).

Table P5.1 Household income deciles of individuals in households affected by the National Minimum Wage

Household income decile	Individuals in working age households (% affected)
1st (lowest 10%)	14.2
2nd	21.7
3rd	16.8
4th	18.2
5th	16.8
6th	8.9
7th	9.0
8th	8.9
9th	4.7
10th	4.0

Source: R. Dickens, 'The national minimum wage', in R. Dickens et al., *The State of Working Britain: Update 2001*, Centre for Economic Performance, 2001.

a Discuss the extent to which the introduction of a national minimum wage might have been expected to cause a rise in unemployment. *(20 marks)*

b To what extent might the national minimum wage be an effective way to tackle poverty? *(15 marks)*

c Discuss whether the distribution of income in the UK is likely to have become more equal since 1997. *(10 marks)*

d Assess **three** ways in which the tax and benefit system could be changed in order to reduce income inequalities. *(15 marks)*

These questions are taken from examinations set for the Edexcel GCE Advanced Level Economics Unit 5, Option A – Labour markets. We are grateful to London Qualifications for permission to reproduce them here.

Economic development

Part 6

part 6

Chapter 26

What is development?

One of the gravest economic challenges facing the world today is the global inequity in the distribution of resources. Worldwide, it is estimated that in 1999 more than a billion people were living in what the United Nations regard as absolute poverty. Furthermore, there were 114 million primary-age children who were not enrolled for school, more than a billion people without access to safe water, and 2.4 billion without access to sanitation. Part 6 considers how to come to terms with such facts, and applies economic analysis in an attempt to understand what has gone wrong, and what could be done to improve matters.

Learning outcomes

After studying this chapter, you should:

- understand what is meant by economic and human development
- be familiar with the most important economic and social indicators that can help to evaluate the standard of living in different societies
- be aware of significant differences between regions of the world in terms of their level and pace of development
- recognise the strengths and limitations of such indicators in providing a profile of a country's stage of development
- be familiar with ways of measuring and monitoring inequality and poverty in the context of less-developed countries
- be aware of the importance of political and cultural factors in influencing a country's path of development

Defining development

The first step is to define what is meant by 'development'. You might think that it is about economic growth — if a society can expand its productive capacity, surely that is development? But development means much more than this. Economic growth may well be an *essential* ingredient, since development cannot take place without an expansion of the resources available in a society; however, it is not a *sufficient* ingredient, because those additional resources must be used wisely, and the growth that results must be the 'right' sort of growth.

Wrapped up with development are issues concerning the alleviation of poverty — no country can be considered 'developed' if a substantial portion of its population is living in absolute poverty. Development also requires structural change, and possibly changes in institutions and, in some cases, cultural and political attitudes.

The Millennium Development Goals

In September 2000, the 189 member states of the United Nations met at what became known as the *Millennium Summit.* They agreed the following declaration:

> We will spare no effort to free our fellow men, women and children from the abject and dehumanising conditions of extreme poverty to which more than a billion of them are currently subjected.

This was a global recognition of the extreme inequality that is a feature of the world distribution of resources. Development economics sets out to explain why it is that some countries have gone through a prolonged process of economic growth and development while others have not. It also seeks to propose ways in which less-developed countries can begin to narrow the existing gap in living standards.

Before beginning to analyse these important questions, it is important to identify what is meant by 'development', and to recognise the symptoms of under-development. Once the symptoms have been identified, explanations can be sought.

As part of the Millennium Summit, it was agreed to set quantifiable targets for a number of dimensions of development, in order to monitor progress. These are known as the **Millennium Development Goals (MDGs)**, and will be the starting point for learning to recognise the symptoms of underdevelopment.

There are eight goals, each of which has specific targets associated with it.

Key term

Millennium Development Goals (MDGs): targets set for each less-developed country, reflecting a range of development objectives to be monitored each year to evaluate progress

Goal 1: Eradicate extreme poverty and hunger

The target for goal 1 is to halve the proportion of people whose income is less than $1 per day, and to halve the proportion of people suffering from hunger, between 1990 and 2015. The alleviation of such extreme poverty is essential for development to take place. This will be monitored through the following indicators:

- proportion of population living on less than $1 per day
- poverty gap ratio (incidence × depth of poverty)
- share of poorest quintile in national consumption
- prevalence of underweight children under 5 years of age
- proportion of population below the minimum level of dietary energy consumption

Goal 2: Achieve universal primary education

The target here is to ensure that by 2015 all children everywhere will be able to complete a full course of primary schooling. Education is seen as an essential feature of the process of development, as it provides the knowledge that is needed for people to use resources effectively. The indicators are:

- net enrolment ratio in primary education
- proportion of pupils starting grade 1 who reach grade 5
- literacy rate of 15- to 24-year-olds

Goal 3: Promote gender equality and empower women

This target aims to eliminate gender disparity in primary and secondary education, preferably by 2005, and in all levels of education no later than 2015. Gender inequality is widespread in less-developed countries, and means that large numbers of women are disadvantaged. Indicators are:

- ratio of girls to boys in primary, secondary and tertiary education
- ratio of literate females to males among 15- to 24-year-olds
- share of women in waged employment in the non-agricultural sector
- proportion of seats held by women in national parliament

Goal 4: Reduce child mortality

The target here is to reduce the under-5 mortality rate by two-thirds between 1990 and 2015. The indicators are:

- under-5 mortality rate
- infant mortality rate
- proportion of 1-year-old children immunised against measles

Goal 5: Improve maternal health

The target is to reduce the maternal mortality ratio by three-quarters between 1990 and 2015. The indicators specified to monitor this target are:

- maternal mortality ratio
- proportion of births attended by skilled health personnel

Goal 6: Combat HIV/AIDS, malaria and other diseases

The target is to have halted, and begun to reverse, the spread of HIV/AIDS and the incidence of malaria and other major diseases by 2015. The impact of HIV/AIDS and other diseases has been felt especially in sub-Saharan Africa, and is having adverse effects on the age structure of the population in many less-developed countries. Indicators will cover:

- HIV prevalence among 15- to 24-year-old pregnant women
- contraceptive prevalence rate
- number of children orphaned by HIV/AIDS
- prevalence and death rates associated with malaria
- proportion of population in malaria-risk areas
- prevalence and death rates associated with tuberculosis (TB)
- proportion of TB cases detected and cured under DOTS (directly observed treatment short course)

Goal 7: Ensure environmental sustainability

The targets here are to integrate the principles of sustainable development into country policies and programmes and to reverse the loss of environmental resources, to halve the proportion of people without sustainable access to safe drinking water by 2015, and to have achieved a significant improvement in the lives of at least 100 million slum dwellers by 2020. Development must be *sustainable*, in the sense that the foundations for future development need to be laid in such a way that they do not endanger the resources available for future generations. The indicators are:

- change in land area covered by forest
- extent of land area protected to maintain biological diversity
- GDP per unit of energy use
- carbon dioxide emissions (per capita)
- proportion of population with sustainable access to an improved water source
- proportion of population with access to improved sanitation
- proportion of population with access to secure tenure

Goal 8: Develop a global partnership for development

The target here is to develop further an open, rule-based, predictable, non-discriminatory trading and financial system, including a commitment to good governance, development and poverty reduction, both nationally and internationally. A wide range of indicators will be used to monitor this in relation to *official development assistance* (ODA), *market access*, *debt sustainability* and some other targets. The need for international cooperation in ensuring development is pressing and will be a recurring theme over the following chapters.

This final goal is less focused than the other seven, but no less important. There is a widespread view that less-developed countries have been disadvantaged by the international trading system, and that richer countries have been insufficiently cooperative – partly in terms of the amount of overseas assistance (ODA) that has been provided, but also in terms of a reluctance of some developed countries to open their markets to products from less-developed countries.

A UN summit in the 1970s led to the commitment that 0.7% of developed countries' GDP would be set aside for development aid.

ODA was the subject of an earlier UN summit in the 1970s, at which the more-developed countries promised to provide overseas assistance. Indeed, there was a specific commitment that 0.7% of developed countries' GDP would be devoted to this purpose. But progress towards this goal has fallen well short, as will be seen in Chapter 30.

'Market access' refers to the difficulty experienced by developing countries seeking to increase exports to the developed world in order to earn more foreign exchange. This target is aimed especially at landlocked and small island developing states, but market access is not a problem for these countries alone.

'Debt sustainability' refers to the difficulties that many countries have experienced in paying off their accumulated debt. This has been a major problem in recent years, especially in sub-Saharan Africa, where some countries are devoting more resources to paying off debts than to providing education and healthcare for their people. The issue is being addressed by the HIPC (Heavily Indebted Poor Countries) initiative, but again progress has been relatively slow.

Other targets relate to youth unemployment, access to affordable essential medical drugs and access to new technology, especially in the fields of information and communications.

These eight goals represent the key facets of development that need to be addressed, and they constitute an enormous challenge for the period up to 2015, especially as progress in the early years has been slow and uneven. In thinking about these goals, you can begin to understand the various dimensions of development, and realise that development is about much more than economic growth – although growth may be seen as a prerequisite for the achievement of the goals. At the same time, failure to achieve these goals will retard economic growth.

Summary

- Economic growth is one aspect of economic development, in that it provides an increase in the resources available to members of society in less-developed countries.
- However, in addition, development requires that the resources made available through economic growth are used appropriately to meet development objectives.
- The Millennium Development Goals were set by the Millennium Summit of the United Nations in September 2000.
- These goals comprise a set of targets for each less-developed country, to be achieved by 2015.

Exercise 26.1

Choose two or three less-developed countries in different regions of the world. Visit the Millennium Development Goals website at **http://www.developmentgoals.org**. Discuss the extent to which progress is being made towards the goals for your chosen countries.

Which are the less-developed countries?

In its *Human Development Report 2004*, the United Nations Development Programme (UNDP) identified 137 countries or areas as 'developing'. In addition, there are 27 transition economies in Central and Eastern Europe and the Commonwealth of Independent States (CIS). However, the range of countries that fall in this definition is very wide, including countries such as Singapore and South Korea, which were also classified as being in the 'high-income' bracket. In the discussion that follows this wide range of countries will be referred to as *less-developed countries* (*LDCs*), and the discussion will be illustrated by examples from a selection of countries from different regions of the world.

In broad terms, the countries regarded as LDCs are concentrated in four major regions: sub-Saharan Africa, Latin America, South Asia and South East Asia. This excludes some countries in the 'less-developed' range, but relatively few. For some purposes it may be necessary to treat China separately, rather than including it as part of South East Asia, partly because of its sheer size, and partly because it has followed a rather different development path.

It is very important when discussing economic development to remember that there is wide diversity between the countries that are classified as LDCs, and although it is tempting to generalise, you need to be a little wary of doing so. Different countries have different characteristics, and face different configurations of problems and opportunities. Therefore, a policy that might work for one country may fail totally in a different part of the world.

Indicators of development

GDP per capita

One measure of the level of development is GDP per capita – the average level of income per person in the population. For reasons outlined in Chapter 14, the preferred measure is GDP per capita measured in purchasing power parity dollars (PPP$). This is important, because using official exchange rates to convert from local currency into US dollars can be misleading. The US$ measure understates the *real* purchasing power of income in LDCs, but what is of interest is exactly that, i.e. the relative command over resources that people in different countries have.

Figure 26.1 shows the relative size of GDP per capita in PPP$ for the regional groupings of countries around the world in 2002. The gap in income levels between the LDCs and the high-income OECD countries shows very clearly in the figure; equally, the gap between the countries of sub-Saharan Africa and South Asia and those in East Asia and Latin America is apparent. The figure also puts into context the position of the transition economies of Central and Eastern Europe and the CIS and the Arab states. The Arab states are rather different in character because of the oil resources that have enabled them to increase their average income levels.

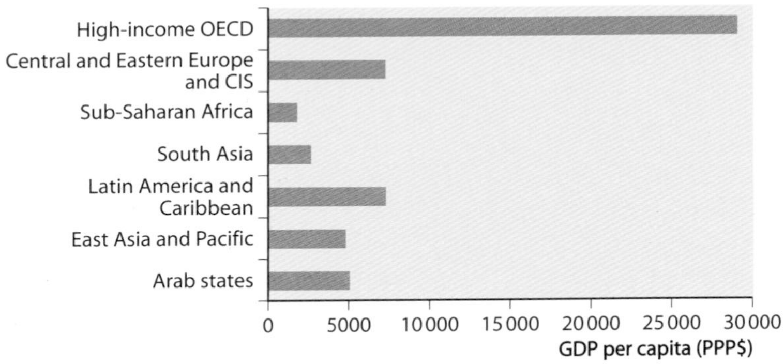

Figure 26.1
GDP per capita, regional groupings, 2002 (PPP$)

Source: *Human Development Report 2004.*

As not all data are available on a regional basis, from here on this chapter will focus on indicators for a selected group of countries, with three countries from each of the major four groupings. The GDP per capita (PPP$) levels in 2002 are shown in Figure 26.2. Because of the diversity of countries in each of the regions, such a selection must be treated with a little caution. Singapore, South Korea and China have been chosen to represent East Asia and the Pacific in order to highlight three of the countries that have achieved rapid economic growth over a sustained period, and the following discussion will highlight some of the factors that have enabled this to take place.

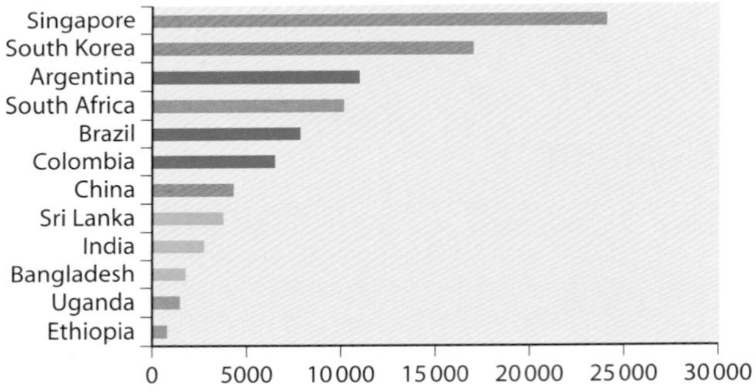

Figure 26.2
GDP per capita, selected countries, 2002 (PPP$)

Source: *Human Development Report 2004.*

As mentioned in Chapter 14 on economic growth, GDP has some limitations as a measure of living standards, even when measured in PPP$. One limitation that is especially important when considering low-income countries is that in many LDCs there is much *informal economic activity*, which may not be captured by a measure like GDP, based on monetary transactions. Such activity includes subsistence agriculture, which remains important in many countries, especially in sub-Saharan Africa. In other words, GDP may not capture production that is directly used for consumption.

However, the informal sector also encompasses many other forms of activity in both rural and urban areas, from petty traders, shoe-shiners and wayside barbers to small-scale enterprises operating in a wide range of activities. In 1999 the ILO estimated that the informal sector accounted for 50.2% of total employment in Ethiopia; in 2000 it was thought to account for 45.8% of total employment in India. This suggests the need for some caution in the use of GDP per capita data.

Income distribution

Another important limitation of GDP per capita as a measure of living standards is that it is an *average* measure, and so does not reveal information about how income is distributed among groups in society.

In Brazil, the poorest 10% of households received less than 1% of total income in the country in 1996, whereas the richest 10% received nearly half. In Belarus, on the other hand, the poorest 10% received 5% of income and the richest 10% received 20%. These are extreme examples of the degree of inequality in the distribution of income within countries. Table 9.1 on page 112 provides similar data for a range of countries around the world.

These data are produced by first ranking the households in order of household income, and then calculating the share of household income going to the poorest 10%, the poorest 20% and so on. The groups of 10% of the population are referred to as *deciles*; thus, the poorest 10% is the first decile, the next 10% is the second decile, and so on. Similarly, the poorest 20% is the first *quintile.*

These data are not very easy to assimilate, especially for a large number of countries, and to explore the question of income inequality, it is important to find a way of summarising the data to make it easier to interpret. Table 26.1 provides some summary data for a range of countries.

Table 26.1 Inequality measures for selected countries

Country	Ratio of top decile to poorest decile	Ratio of top quintile to poorest quintile	Gini index
Ethiopia	59.7	24.8	57.2
Sierra Leone	87.2	57.6	62.9
Uganda	9.9	6.4	37.4
Bangladesh	6.8	4.6	31.8
India	9.5	5.7	37.8
Zimbabwe	22.0	12.0	56.8
Indonesia	7.8	5.2	30.3
China	12.7	8.0	40.3
Belarus	6.9	4.6	30.4
South Africa	65.1	33.6	59.3
Brazil	65.8	29.7	60.7
Malaysia	22.1	12.4	49.2
Hungary	5.0	3.5	24.4
Singapore	17.7	9.7	42.5
United Kingdom	13.4	7.1	36.0
United States	16.6	9.0	40.8
Japan	4.5	3.4	24.9

Source: *Human Development Report 2003.*

By looking at the ratio of the richest decile or quintile to the poorest, it is possible to get some impression of the gap between the poorest and richest households. For example, in Sierra Leone the richest 10% of households receive 87.2 times more income than the poorest 10%, whereas in Hungary the gap is only five-fold.

One thing to notice about this table is that the countries are listed in ascending rank order of average income. If you cast your eye down the columns of the table, you will see that there is no very strong relationship between average income and the decile and quintile ratios. The contrast in the pattern of the income shares between Sierra Leone and Bangladesh is striking, but average income levels are not too different.

The Lorenz curve

It would be useful to have a way of presenting such data visually. Although conventional types of graph are not well suited to this purpose, an alternative graphical technique is the **Lorenz curve**. Some of these are shown in Figure 26.3.

> **Key term**
>
> **Lorenz curve:** a graphical means of depicting the distribution of income within a country

Lorenz curves are constructed as follows. Using data provided in Table 26.2, the first step is to convert the numbers in the table into *cumulative* percentages. In other words (using Brazil as an example), the poorest 20% receives 2.5% of total household income, the poorest 40% receives 2.5% + 5.5% = 8%, the poorest 60% receives 8% + 10% = 18%, and so on. These cumulative percentages are then plotted to produce the Lorenz curve, as in Figure 26.3.

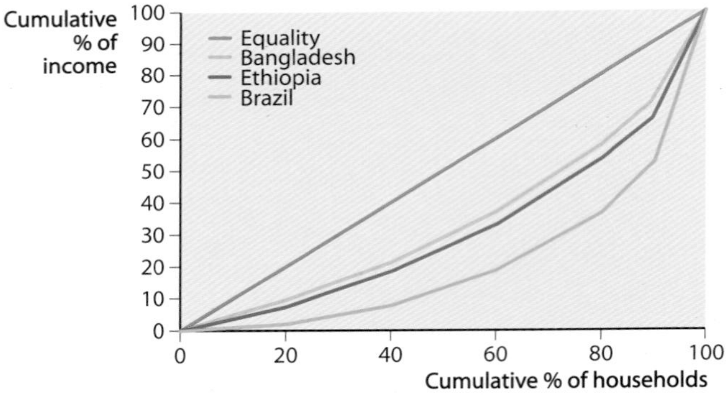

Figure 26.3 *Lorenz curves (various years)*

Source: *World Development Report 2000/2001.*

Country	Lowest 10%	Lowest 20%	Second 20%	Third 20%	Fourth 20%	Highest 20%	Highest 10%
Ethiopia	3.0	7.1	10.9	14.5	19.8	47.7	33.7
Bangladesh	3.9	8.7	12.0	15.7	20.8	42.8	28.6
Brazil	0.9	2.5	5.5	10.0	18.3	63.8	47.6

Table 26.2 *Income distribution in Ethiopia, Bangladesh and Brazil, various years*

Suppose that income is perfectly equally distributed between households — in other words, suppose the poorest 10% of households receive exactly 10% of income, the poorest 20% receive 20% and so on. The Lorenz curve would then be a straight line going diagonally across the figure.

This is a help in interpreting the country curves. The closer a country's Lorenz curve is to the diagonal equality line, the more equal is the distribution. You can see on the figure how unequal the income distribution is in Brazil as compared with that in Bangladesh or Ethiopia.

The Gini index

The Lorenz curve is fine for comparing income distribution in just a few countries. However, it would also be helpful to have an index that can summarise the relationship in a numerical way. The Gini index does just this. It is a way of quantifying the equality of income distribution, and is obtained by calculating the ratio of the area between the equality line and a country's Lorenz curve to the whole area under the equality line. This is normally expressed as a percentage, although sometimes you may find data that treat it as a proportion (i.e. with values between 0 and 1). The closer the Gini index is to 100 (or to 1), the further the Lorenz curve is from equality, and thus the more unequal the income distribution. The values for the Gini index are shown in the final column of Table 26.1.

The Kuznets hypothesis

The economist Simon Kuznets argued that there is expected to be a relationship between the degree of inequality in the income distribution and the level of development that a country has achieved. He claimed that in the early stages of economic development income is fairly equally distributed, with everyone living at a relatively low income level. However, as development begins to take off there will be some individuals at the forefront of enterprise and development, and their incomes will rise more rapidly. So in this middle phase the income distribution will tend to worsen. At a later stage of development, society will eventually be able to afford to redistribute income to protect the poor, and all will begin to share in the benefits of development.

This can be portrayed as the relationship between the Gini index and the level of development. The thrust of the Kuznets hypothesis is that this should reveal an inverted U-shaped relationship, as shown in Figure 26.4. Although the data in Table 26.1 do not strongly support this hypothesis, there is some evidence to suggest that the relationship does hold in some regions of the world.

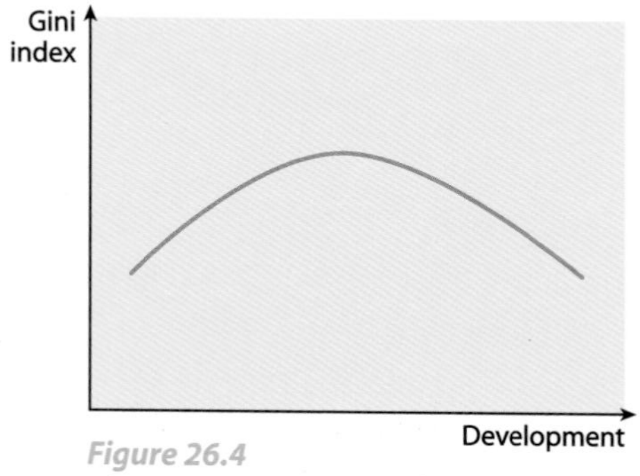

Figure 26.4
The Kuznets curve

The Human Development Index

Another criticism of GDP per capita as a measure of living standards is that it fails to take account of other dimensions of the quality of life. In 1990 the United Nations Development Programme (UNDP) devised an alternative indicator, known as the **Human Development Index** (*HDI*), which was designed to provide a broader measure of the stage of development that a country had reached.

> ***Key term***
>
> **Human Development Index:** a composite indicator of the level of a country's development, varying between 0 and 1

The basis for this measure is that there are three key aspects of human development: resources, knowledge of how to make good use of those resources, and a reasonable life span in which to make use of those resources (see Figure 26.5). The three components are measured by, respectively, GDP per capita in PPP$, indicators of education (adult literacy and school enrolment) and life expectancy. The measurements are then combined to produce a composite index ranging between 0 and 1, with higher values reflecting higher human development.

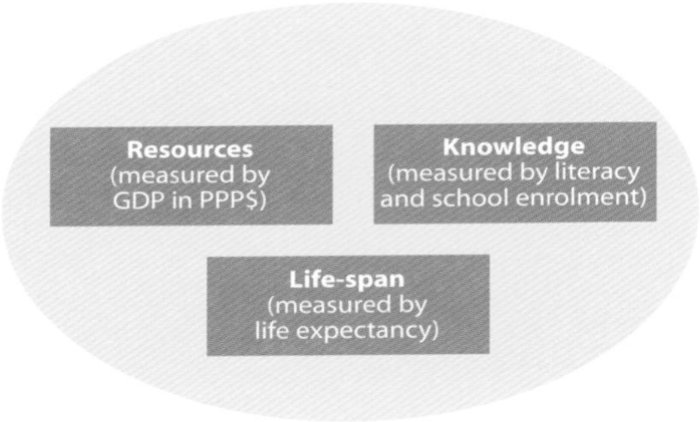

Figure 26.5
Components of the Human Development Index

Values of the HDI for 2002 are charted in Figure 26.6 for the selected countries. You can see that the broad ranking of the countries is preserved, but the gap between low and high human development is less marked. The exception is South Africa, which is ranked much lower on the basis of the HDI than on GDP per capita; in other words, South Africa has achieved relatively high income, but other aspects of human development have not kept pace. There are other countries in the world that share this feature. If you compare the data here with those for Figure 26.2, you will see that there are also countries that seem to perform better on HDI grounds than on GDP per capita – for example China and Sri Lanka.

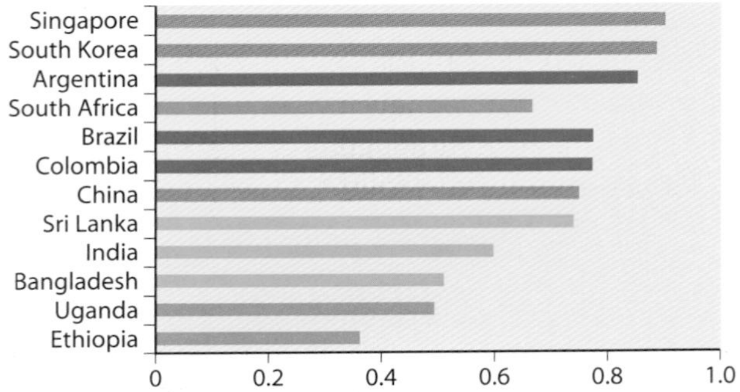

Figure 26.6
The Human Development Index, selected countries

Source: *Human Development Report 2004.*

Figure 26.7 shows the relative contribution of the three components of the HDI for this set of countries, and Figures 26.8 and 26.9 show the actual levels of two of the measures that enter into the HDI, i.e. life expectancy and adult literacy rates. It is clear that it is life expectancy that is primarily responsible for the low ranking of South Africa in the HDI, as its level of life expectancy is not very different from that of the other sub-Saharan African countries in the sample, even though its average income level is much higher. In contrast, Bangladesh performs quite well in terms of lifespan but relatively poorly in terms of education. By comparing these data, you can get some idea of the diversity between countries that was mentioned earlier.

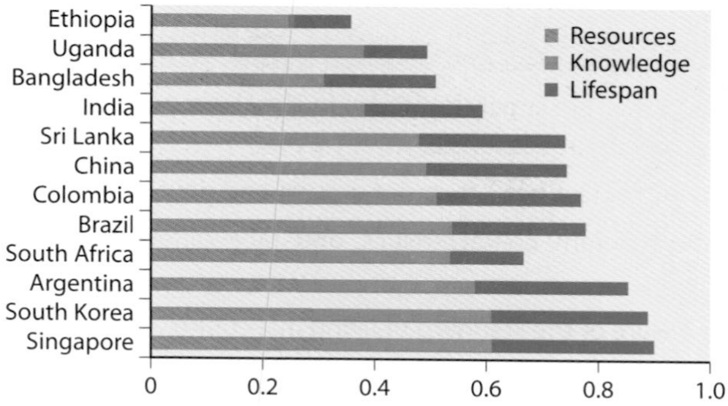

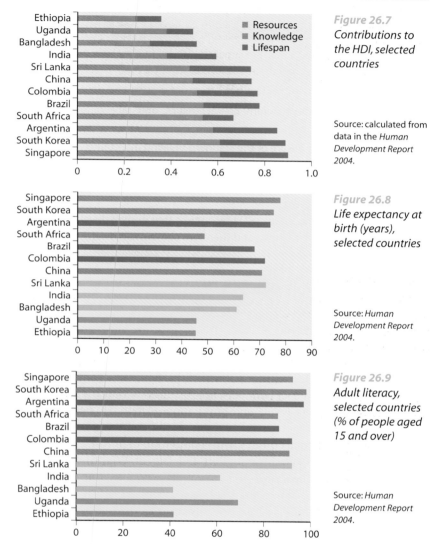

Figure 26.7
Contributions to the HDI, selected countries

Source: calculated from data in the *Human Development Report 2004.*

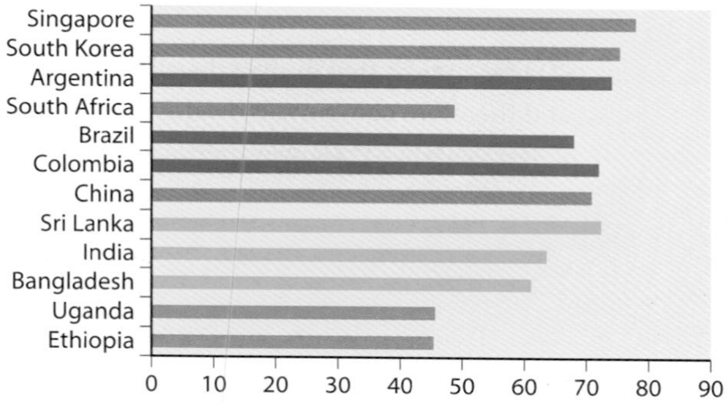

Figure 26.8
Life expectancy at birth (years), selected countries

Source: *Human Development Report 2004.*

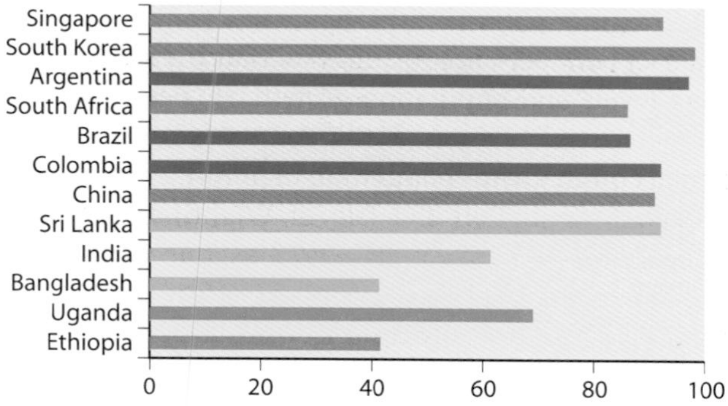

Figure 26.9
Adult literacy, selected countries (% of people aged 15 and over)

Source: *Human Development Report 2004.*

In part, this diversity reflects differing priorities that governments have given to different aspects of development. Countries such as Brazil have aimed primarily at achieving economic growth, while those such as Sri Lanka have given greater priority to promoting education and health care.

There is a view that growth should be the prime objective for development, since by expanding the resources available the benefits can begin to trickle down through the population. An opposing view claims that, by providing first for basic needs, more rapid economic growth can be facilitated. The problem in some cases is that growth has not resulted in the trickle-down effect, and inequality remains. It may be significant that countries such as Brazil and South Africa, where the GDP

per capita ranking is high relative to the HDI ranking, are countries in which there remain high levels of inequality in the distribution of income.

Summary

- Less-developed countries (LDCs) are largely located in four major regions: sub-Saharan Africa, Latin America, South Asia and South East Asia.
- These regions have shown contrasting patterns of growth and development.
- Different countries have different characteristics, and face different configurations of problems and opportunities.
- GDP per capita is one measure of the standard of living in a country, but it has a number of shortcomings for LDCs.
- In particular, it neglects the importance of the informal sector, and fails to take into account inequality in the distribution of income.
- The Human Development Index (HDI) recognises that human development depends upon resources, knowledge and health, and therefore combines indicators of these key aspects.

Other characteristics of LDCs

Demographic issues

Some other characteristics of LDCs are important in setting the scene for analysis of development. It is widely believed that population growth is of especial significance, and Figure 26.10 shows the past experience of population growth in the selected countries. The irregular pattern of this figure (remember that the countries are in descending order of GDP per capita) suggests that there is no strong correlation between income levels and population growth. However, in part this may reflect individual characteristics of some of the countries selected. For example, Singapore is a very small country, with population of only 4.2 million in 2002. (But imagine 4.2 million people living on the Isle of Wight!) Singapore has been concerned that its population is too small, and has put in place policies to encourage people to have more children. This may help to explain its relatively rapid population growth. China, on the other hand, faces the opposite problem, and has imposed policies to discourage large families.

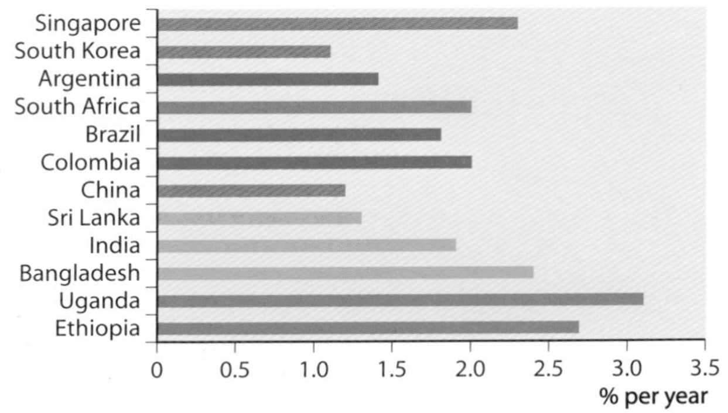

Figure 26.10 Population growth, 1975–2002

Source: *Human Development Report 2004.*

The prime concern about rapid population growth is felt by countries like Ethiopia, Uganda and Bangladesh, where it has been suggested that population has been growing too fast for education and health care services to keep up. Chapter 28 will return to this topic. However, Figure 26.11 shows one aspect of the problem, i.e. the percentage of the population below 15 years of age in selected countries. In Uganda this amounts to more than half of the population, and in Ethiopia it is well over 40%. This reveals the extent of the problem faced by these countries, in so far as they must be supported by the working population. In countries where HIV/AIDS is widespread it is especially difficult, as the disease is especially prevalent amongst those of working age.

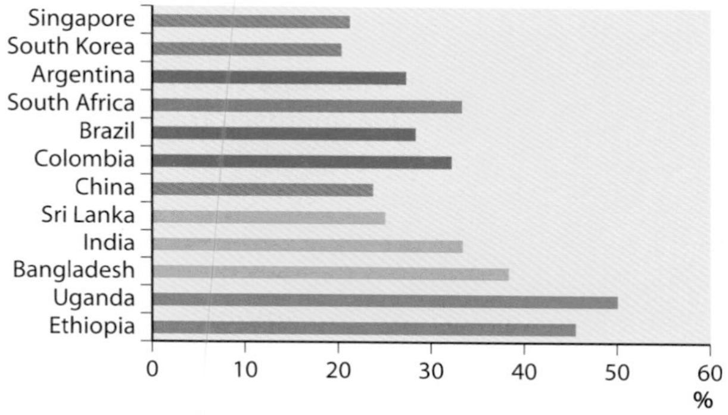

Figure 26.11 *Percentage of population below 15 years of age, selected countries*

Source: *Human Development Report 2004.*

Dependence on agriculture

Many LDCs have an economic structure that is strongly biased towards agriculture. The evidence of this for the selected countries is presented in Figures 26.12 and 26.13. Figure 26.12 shows the percentage of GDP coming from the agricultural sector. Given that labour productivity tends to be lower in agriculture than in other sectors, these data understate the importance of agriculture within the structure, as the percentage of the labour force engaged in agriculture is higher than the agricultural share of output. This is further reinforced by the importance of unrecorded agricultural production in the subsistence sector.

Figure 26.13 underlines the situation by showing the percentage of the population living in urban areas. It would appear that for many of the low-income countries in the group the majority of their people are relying on rural economic activities.

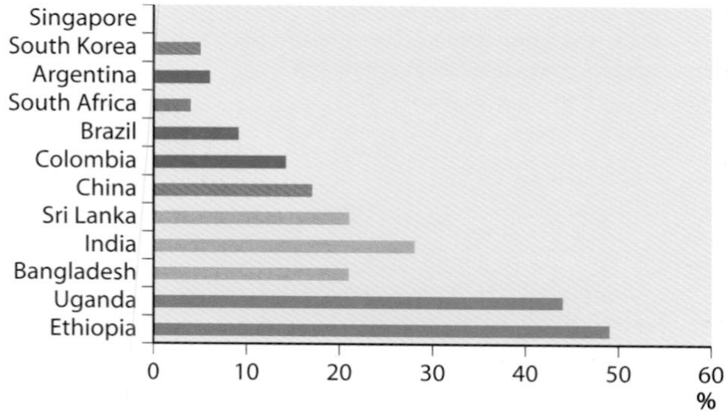

Figure 26.12 *Agriculture as a percentage of GDP, selected countries, 1999*

Source: *World Development Report 2000/2001.*

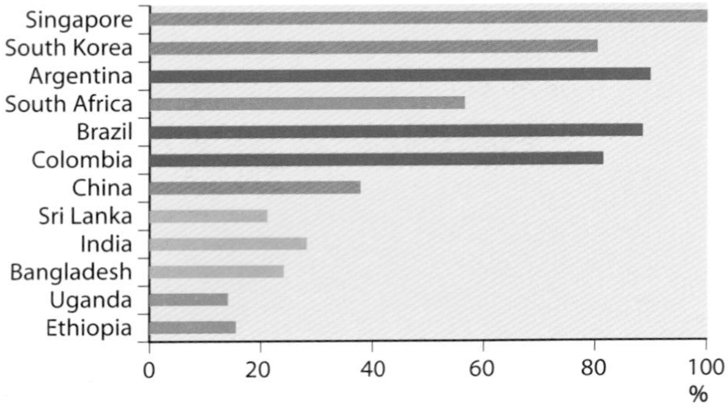

Figure 26.13
Percentage of population living in urban areas, selected countries

Source: *Human Development Report 2004.*

Poverty

A final characteristic of LDCs that should be mentioned at this point is the prevalence of poverty. One approach to measuring poverty is to define a basket of goods and services that is regarded as the minimum required to support human life: households that are seen to have incomes that are too low to allow them to purchase that basic bundle of goods are regarded as being in **absolute poverty**.

> ***Key term***
>
> **absolute poverty:** situation describing a household if its income is insufficient to allow it to purchase the minimum bundle of goods and services needed for survival

The UNDP regards households in which income is below \$1 per day per person as being in absolute poverty, as this is its declared *poverty line*. For a country like the UK the absolute poverty line is not very significant, as so few people fall below it. However, for LDCs absolute poverty is widespread. Figure 26.14 shows the prevalence of absolute poverty in the selected countries. This indicates the extent of the challenge facing some of these countries if they are to meet the Millennium Development Goal of halving the number of people in poverty by 2015.

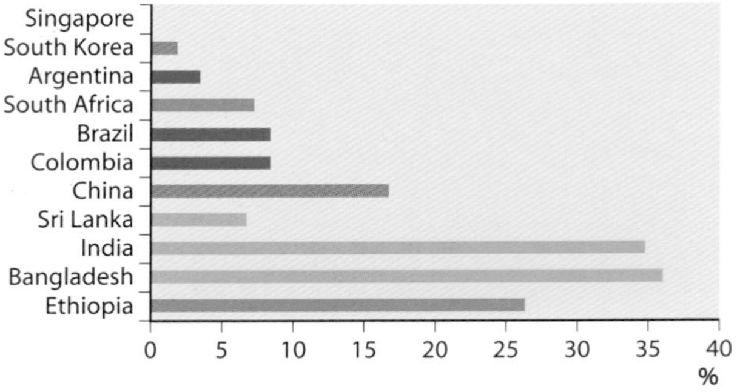

Figure 26.14
Percentage of population living on less than \$1 per day, selected countries

Note: no data are available for Uganda.

Source: *Human Development Report 2004.*

The number of people living below the poverty line is not a perfect measure. In particular, it would also be useful to know how *far* below the poverty line people are living, which would indicate the intensity of poverty. However, this is not easy to measure.

Poverty can also be defined in relative terms. If a household has insufficient income for its members to participate in the normal social life of the country, it is said to be in **relative poverty**. This too is defined in terms of a poverty line, this time defined as 50% of the median-adjusted household disposable income. (The median is income of the middle ranked household.) Relative poverty can occur in any society.

> ***Key term***
>
> **relative poverty:** situation applying to a household whose income falls below 50% of median adjusted household disposable income

The two concepts really reflect different things. Absolute poverty is about whether people have enough to survive, whereas relative poverty is more about inequality than about poverty. This is not to say that relative poverty should not be of concern to policy makers, but people in absolute poverty clearly require urgent action.

One aspect of poverty is seen not in terms of income, but in terms of access to essential services such as healthcare and improved water and sanitation, as illustrated in Figure 26.15. This is another of the Millennium Development Goals that were introduced at the beginning of the chapter (Goal 7).

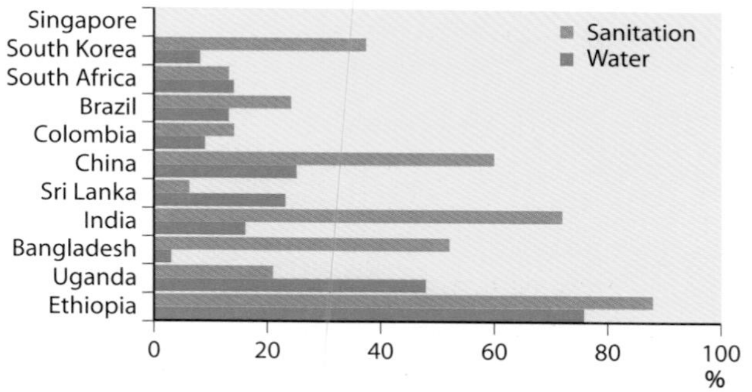

Figure 26.15
Percentage of population with no access to safe water and sanitation, selected countries

Note: there are no data for Argentina; the Singapore entry is 0.

Source: *Human Development Report 2004.*

An important part of development is the provision of *infrastructure*. In part this is necessary to help to alleviate poverty by providing essential services. But there are other vital aspects of infrastructure that are essential for markets to operate effectively. In particular, this can be seen in relation to transport and communications and market facilities. Many areas of infrastructure display characteristics of public goods, so that government intervention is essential to ensure adequate provision. (Public goods were discussed in chapter 9.) A problem for many LDCs, however, is that the government does not have the resources to provide the necessary infrastructure.

Summary

- Demographic factors are important for LDCs, many of which have shown a more rapid rate of population growth than can readily be resourced.
- Many LDCs show a heavy reliance on agriculture or other primary activities to provide employment and incomes.
- Poverty alleviation is a key part of the development process.

Exercise 26.2

Table 26.3 provides a selection of indicators for three countries. One of these is in sub-Saharan Africa, one is in South East Asia and the other is in Latin America. See if you can identify which is which.

Table 26.3 *Indicators for three countries*

	Country A	Country B	Country C
Life expectancy at birth (years)	68.9	73.1	46.4
Adult literacy (%)	95.7	91.4	83.3
Population growth, 1975–2001 (% p.a.)	1.5	2.0	3.2
Urban population (% of total)	20.0	74.6	34.3
% of population under 15 years	25.9	33.3	42.7
% of population with access to safe water, 2000	84	88	57
% of adults aged 15–49 living with HIV/AIDS	1.79	0.28	15.01
Growth of GDP per capita, 1975–2001 (% p.a.)	5.4	0.9	0.3
Gini index (%)	43.2	51.9	44.5
Exports of primary goods (% of all merchandise exports)	22	15	79

Note: data are for 2001 unless otherwise stated.

Source: *Human Development Report 2003*.

part 6

Chapter 27

Economic growth in less-developed countries

Although development is not only about economic growth, growth is of central importance as a prerequisite if progress in development is to be achieved. This chapter examines some models of economic growth that are of special significance for less-developed countries, and highlights some of their limitations. In particular, it evaluates some of the factors that may be thought to contribute to the process of economic growth. This will be illustrated with reference to the experience of the 'tiger economies' of East Asia, which developed rapidly after the 1960s.

Learning outcomes

After studying this chapter, you should:

- understand the importance of economic growth for less-developed countries
- be familiar with the Harrod–Domar model of economic growth, and its relevance for less-developed countries
- understand the importance of factors that can contribute to economic growth, such as capital, technology and human capital
- be aware of the World Bank model of market-friendly economic development and the role of Structural Adjustment Programmes
- realise the importance of sustainability in development

Economic growth

Although development is about more than economic growth, growth is a crucial part of any process of economic and human development. It provides the necessary increase in resources to enable a country to provide for the basic needs of its citizens and to expand its choices in the future, and it lays the foundations for future development.

Key term

economic growth: an increase in the productive capacity of the economy

Chapter 1 interpreted economic growth in terms of a movement of the production possibility frontier (PPF). Figure 27.1 serves as a reminder. Here it is assumed that the country has a choice between producing capital goods (for investment) and producing consumer goods. In the initial period the country begins with the production possibility frontier at PPF_0 and can produce at point A, producing C_1 consumer goods and I_1 capital goods. The increase in capital goods enables an increase in the productive capacity of the economy, so that in the following period the PPF shifts to PPF_1 and the country is able to produce at point B, with C_2 consumer goods and I_2 capital goods. This in turn allows a further shift of the PPF, and so the process of economic growth has begun.

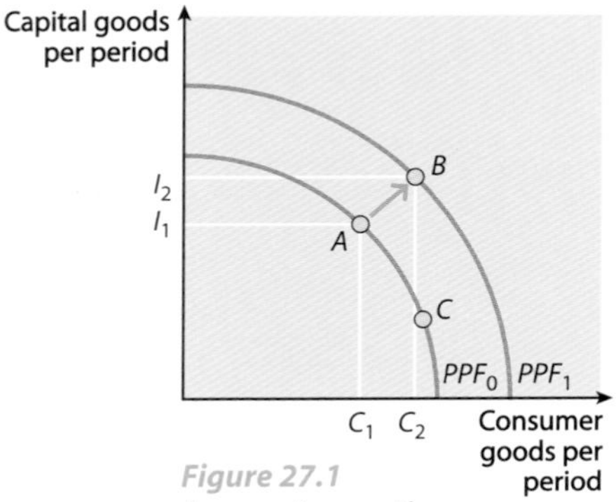

Figure 27.1
Economic growth

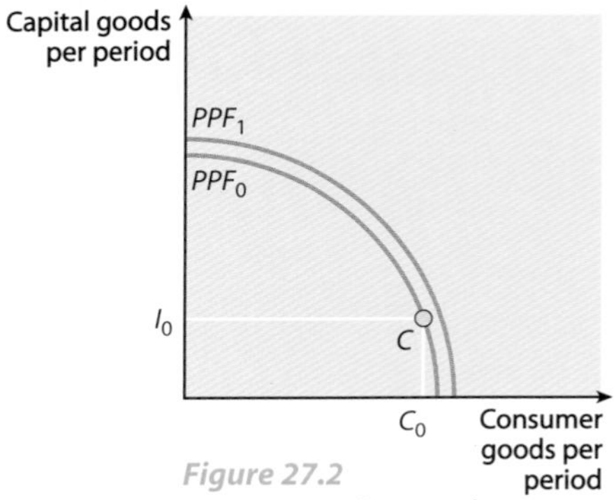

Figure 27.2
Less economic growth

There are some important points to notice about this process. First, in order to produce more consumer goods in the future, current consumption has to be sacrificed. In other words, the country could instead have chosen to be at point C and enjoyed more consumption in the initial period; however, had it done so the opportunity cost would have been less investment, and therefore the PPF would not have moved so far in the second period. This is shown in Figure 27.2, where the choice to be at point C means producing only I_0 capital goods, and the PPF shifts by a very small amount in the following period. Thus, a society that chooses to use its resources for consumption in the present achieves a slower rate of economic growth.

Second, if the country has a limited capacity to produce investment goods the PPF will take on a much flatter shape, as in Figure 27.3. In this case a sacrifice of current consumption will not appreciably increase the amount of capital goods that are produced, and again, the rate of economic growth will tend to be modest.

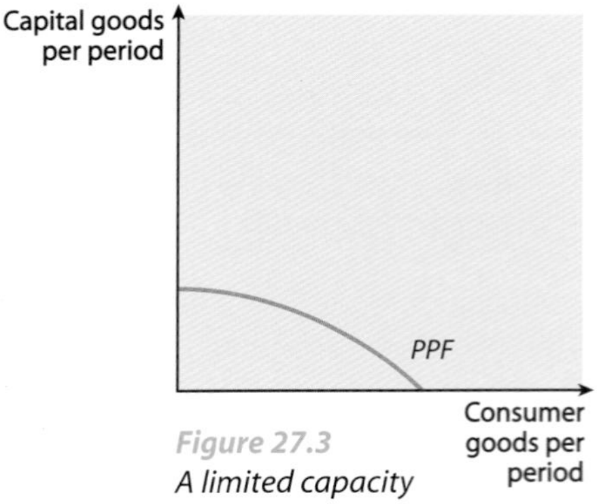

Figure 27.3
A limited capacity to produce capital goods

For a less-developed country (LDC) this may well be the case. In many LDCs the capacity to produce capital goods is limited, because the countries lack the technical knowledge and resources needed to produce capital goods. Furthermore, a country in which there are high levels of poverty, and in which many households face low income-earning opportunities, needs to devote much of its resources to consumption. The question for LDCs is thus how to overcome this problem in order to kick-start a process of economic growth.

Figure 27.4 illustrates the problem. A shortage of capital means low per capita income, which means low savings, which in turn means low investment, limited capital, and hence low per capita incomes. In this way a country can get trapped in a *low-level equilibrium* situation.

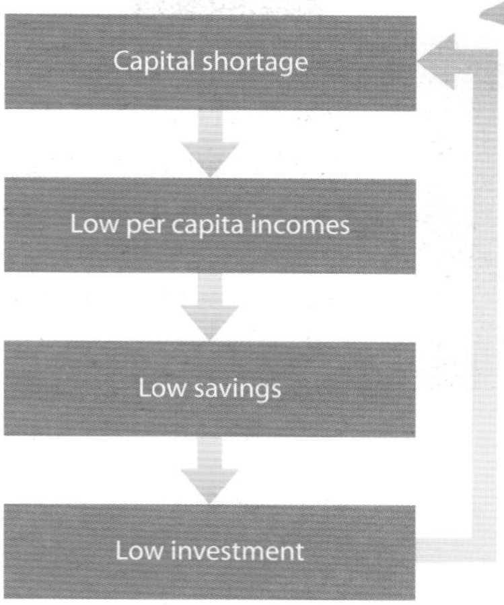

Figure 27.4 A low-level equilibrium trap

Another view of economic growth was presented in Chapter 14, where economic growth was characterised in terms of a shift in the aggregate supply curve. Again, it was argued that investment is critical to the process of expanding the productive capacity of the economy. (This is illustrated in Figure 27.5, where the aggregate supply curve shifts from AS_0 to AS_1.) It was argued that the aggregate supply curve could move to the right either following investment, which would expand the stock of capital, or following an improvement in the effectiveness of markets. All of this suggests that the first focus for LDCs must be on savings and investment.

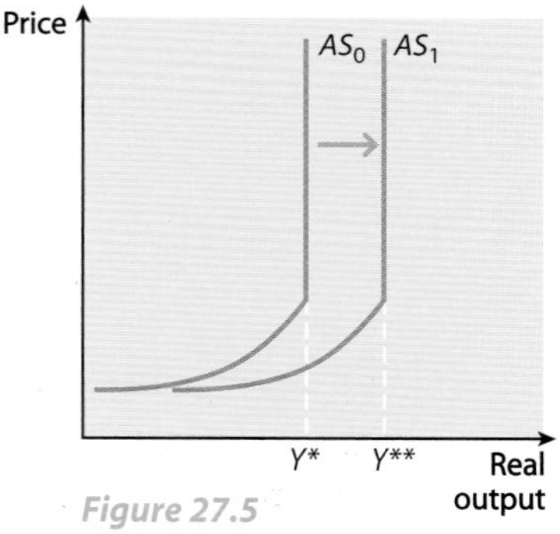

Figure 27.5 Economic growth as a shift in aggregate supply

The Harrod–Domar model

This idea is supported by the **Harrod–Domar model** of economic growth, which first appeared in separate articles by Roy Harrod in the UK and Evsey Domar in the USA in 1939. This model was to become significant in influencing LDCs' attitudes towards the process of economic growth. It was developed in an attempt to determine how equilibrium could be achieved in a growing economy.

Key term

Harrod–Domar model: a model of economic growth that emphasises the importance of savings and investment

The basic finding of this model was that an economy can remain in equilibrium through time only if it grows at a particular rate. This unique stable growth path depends on the savings ratio and the productivity of capital. Any deviation from this path will cause the economy to become unstable. This finding emphasised the importance of savings in the process of economic growth, and led to the conclusion that a country wishing for economic growth must first increase its flow of savings.

Figure 27.6 illustrates the process that leads to growth in a Harrod–Domar world. Savings are crucial in enabling investment to be undertaken — always remembering that some investment will have to be used to replace existing capital that has worn out. Investment then enables capital to accumulate and technology to be improved. The accumulation of capital leads to an increase in output and incomes, which leads to a further flow of savings, and the cycle is back where it started from.

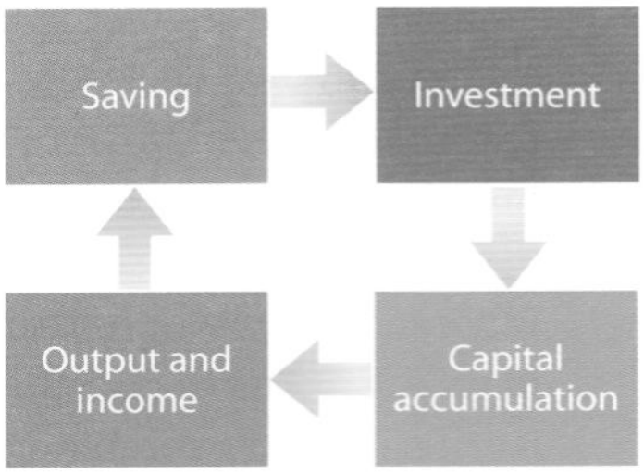

Figure 27.6 The Harrod–Domar process of economic development

The key question is whether this process can allow an LDC to break out of the low-level equilibrium trap. Figure 27.6 can be used to identify a number of problems that may prevent the Harrod–Domar process from being effective for LDCs.

It has already been argued that generating a flow of savings in an LDC may be problematic. When incomes are low households may have to devote most of their resources to consumption, and so there may be a lack of savings. Nonetheless, some savings have proved possible. For example, in the early 1960s South Korea had an average income level that was not too different from that of countries like Sudan or Afghanistan, but it managed to build up the savings rate during that decade.

Setting aside the problem of low savings for the moment, what happens next?

Will savings lead to investment and the accumulation of capital?

If a flow of savings can be generated, the next important step is to transform the savings into investment. This is the process by which the sacrifice of current consumption leads to an increase in productive capacity in the future.

Some important preconditions must be met if savings are to be transformed into investment. If the funds that have been saved are to be mobilised for investment, there must be a way for potential borrowers to get access to the funds. In developed countries this takes place through the medium of financial markets. For example, it may be that households save by putting their money into a savings account at the bank; then with this money the bank can make loans to entrepreneurs, enabling them to undertake investment.

In many LDCs, however, financial markets are undeveloped, so it is much more difficult for funds to be recycled in this way. For example, a study conducted in 1997 by the Bank of Uganda found that almost 30% of households interviewed in rural Ugandan villages had undertaken savings at some time.[1] However, almost none of these had done so through formal financial institutions, which did not reach into the rural areas. Instead, the saving that took place tended to be in the form of fixed assets, or money kept under the bed. Such savings cannot readily be transformed into productive investment.

[1] Polycarp Musinguzi and Peter Smith, 'Structural adjustment and poverty: a study of rural Uganda', *Discussion Papers in Economics and Econometrics*, University of Southampton, 1998.

In addition, governments in some periods have made matters worse by holding down interest rates in the hope of encouraging firms to borrow. The idea here is that a low interest rate means a low cost of borrowing, which should make borrowing more attractive. However, this ignores the fact that if interest rates are very low there is little incentive to save, since the return on saving is so low. In this case, firms may wish to invest but may not be able to obtain the funds to do so.

The other prerequisite for savings to be converted into investment is that there must be entrepreneurs with the ability to identify investment possibilities, the skill to carry them through and the willingness to bear the risk. Such entrepreneurs are in limited supply in many LDCs.

This worked effectively for Hong Kong, one of the so-called *tiger economies.* During its period of rapid development after the 1950s Hong Kong benefited from a wave of immigrant entrepreneurs, especially from Shanghai, who provided the impetus for rapid development. In Singapore the entrepreneurship came primarily from the government, and from multinational corporations who were encouraged to become established in the country. Singapore and South Korea also adopted policies that ensured a steady flow of savings, so that, for example, in Singapore gross domestic savings amounted to 52% of GDP in 1999.

In Hong Kong, entrepreneurs mobilised funds for investment and stimulated development.

Will investment lead to higher output and income?

For investment to be productive in terms of raising output and incomes in the economy, some further conditions need to be met. In particular, it is crucial for firms to have access to physical capital, which will raise production capacity. Given the limited capability of producing capital goods in many LDCs, they have to rely on capital imported from the more-developed countries. This may be beneficial in terms of upgrading home technology, but such equipment can be imported only if the country has earned the foreign exchange to pay for it. A shortage of foreign exchange therefore may make it difficult for the country to accumulate capital.

The tiger economies were all very open to international trade, and focused on promoting exports in order to earn the foreign exchange needed to import capital goods. This strategy worked very effectively, and the economies were able to widen their access to capital and move to higher value-added activities as they developed their capabilities.

The importance of human capital

If the capital *can* be obtained, there is then a need for the skilled labour with which to operate the capital goods. In other words, human capital in the form of skilled, healthy and well-trained workers is as important as physical capital if investment is to be productive.

In principle, it could be thought that today's LDCs have an advantage over the countries that developed in earlier periods. In particular, they can learn from earlier mistakes, and import technology that has already been developed, rather than having to develop it anew. This would suggest that a convergence process should be going on, whereby LDCs are able to adopt technology that has already been produced, and thereby grow more rapidly and begin to close the gap with the more-developed countries.

However, by and large this has not been happening, and a lack of human capital has been suggested as one of the key reasons for the failure. This underlines the importance of education in laying the foundations for economic growth as well as contributing directly to the quality of life.

In the case of the tiger economies, their education systems had been well established, either through the British colonial legacy (in the case of Singapore and Hong Kong) or through past Japanese occupation periods (in Taiwan and South Korea). In all of these countries, education received high priority, and cultural influences encouraged a high demand for education. The tiger economies thus benefited from having highly skilled and well-disciplined labour forces that were able to make effective use of the capital goods that had been acquired.

Harrod–Domar and external resources

Figure 27.7 extends the earlier schematic presentation of the process underlying the Harrod–Domar model of economic growth. This has been amended to underline the importance of access to technology and human capital.

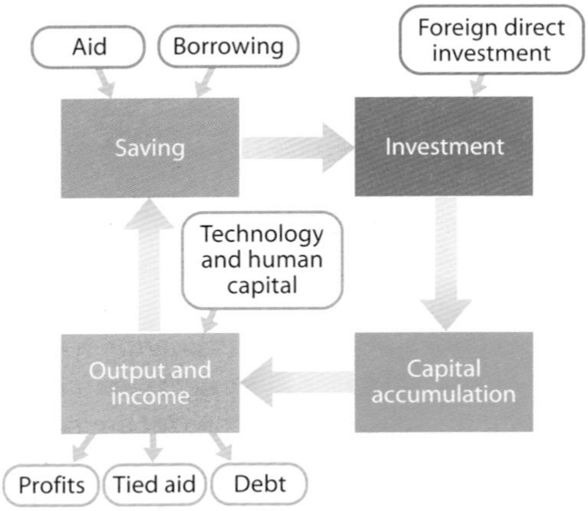

Figure 27.7 The Harrod–Domar process of economic development augmented

The discussion above has emphasised the difficulty of mobilising domestic savings, both in generating a sufficient flow of savings and in translating such savings into productive investment.

The question arises as to whether an LDC could supplement its domestic savings with a flow of funds from abroad. Figure 27.7 identifies three possible injections into the Harrod–Domar process. First, it might be possible to attract flows of overseas assistance from higher-income countries. Second, perhaps the amount of investment could be augmented directly by persuading multinational corporations to engage in foreign direct investment. Third, perhaps the LDC could borrow on international capital markets to finance its domestic investment. It is worth noting that the tiger economies took full advantage of these external sources of funds.

These three possibilities will be explored more fully in Chapter 30. However, it is worth noting that each of these ways of attracting external resources has a downside associated with it. As far as overseas assistance is concerned, in the past such flows have been seen by some donor countries as part of trade policy, and have brought less benefit to LDCs than had been hoped. In the case of the multinational corporations, there is a tendency for the profits to be repatriated out of the LDC, rather than recycled into the economy. Finally, international borrowing has to be repaid at some future date, and many LDCs have found themselves burdened by debt that they can ill afford to repay.

Summary

- Although development is a broader concept than economic growth, growth is a key ingredient of development.
- Economic growth can be seen in terms of a shift in the production possibility frontier, or a shift in long-run aggregate supply.
- The Harrod–Domar model of economic growth highlights the importance of savings, and of transforming savings into productive investment.
- However, where markets are underdeveloped, this transformation may be impeded.
- Human capital is also a critical ingredient of economic growth.
- If resources cannot be generated within the domestic economy, a country may need to have recourse to external sources of funding.

Market-friendly growth

An alternative way of viewing the process of economic growth has been put forward by the World Bank. The core argument here is that markets should be allowed to work without government intervention wherever possible, and that the government should intervene only where markets cannot operate effectively. This is called a market-friendly growth strategy. The World Bank has argued that there are four areas that should be of high priority to LDCs looking to stimulate development; *people*, *microeconomic markets*, *macroeconomic stability*, and *global linkages*.

Key term

market-friendly growth: an approach to economic growth in which governments are recommended to intervene less where markets can operate effectively, but to intervene more strongly where markets are seen to fail

The World Bank has promoted the idea of market-friendly growth.

At the core of this approach is the argument that, if markets can be made to work effectively, this will lead to more efficient resource allocation. Furthermore, governments should intervene only where markets themselves cannot operate effectively because of some sort of market failure. If the four components can be made to work together, it will lay the foundations for economic growth and development.

People

The importance of human capital formation has already been stressed. The need for skilled and disciplined labour to complement capital accumulation is critical for development. However, this is an area in which market failure is widespread.

If people do not fully perceive the future benefits to be gained from educating their children, they will demand less education than is desirable for society. In the rural areas of many LDCs it is common for education to be undervalued in this way, and for drop-out rates from schooling to be high. This may arise both from a failure to perceive the potential future benefits that children will derive from education, and from the high opportunity cost of education in villages where child labour is widespread.

The situation in many LDCs has been worsened in the past by poor curriculum design, whereby the legacy of colonial rule was a school system and curriculum not well directed at providing the sort of education likely to be of most benefit within the context of an LDC. Furthermore, there tended to be a bias towards providing funds to the tertiary sector (which benefits mainly the rich elites within society) rather than trying to ensure that all children received at least primary education.

The benefits from developing people as resources may overflow into other component areas, for example through an increase in labour productivity – if healthy and educated people are able to work better – or by ensuring that products are better able to meet international standards, thereby reinforcing linkages with the rest of the world.

Microeconomic markets

The World Bank has also argued that LDCs need to encourage competitive and effective microeconomic markets in order to ensure that their resources are well allocated.

It is important that prices can act as signals to guide resource allocation. This can then create a climate for enterprise, enabling people to exploit their capabilities. In the past, many governments in LDCs have tended to intervene strongly in markets, distorting prices away from market equilibrium values – especially food prices, which were kept artificially low in urban areas, thus damaging farmers' incentives. In addition, it is important to encourage the development of financial markets that will act to channel savings into productive investment.

Again, there are likely to be overflow effects from this. First, if microeconomic markets can be made to operate effectively, this will ensure that people get a good return on the education that they undertake, which will encourage a greater demand for education in the future. Second, foreign direct investment is more likely to be attracted into a country in which there are effective operational domestic markets. And the existence of effective financial markets creates a financial discipline that encourages stability at the macroeconomic level.

Macroeconomic stability

It is argued that stability in the macroeconomy is important in order to encourage investment. If the macroeconomic environment is unstable, firms will not be sufficiently confident of the future to want to risk investing in projects. In addition, if the government becomes over-active in the economy, this may starve the private sector of resources.

A key aim for an LDC should be to ensure that prices can act as effective signals in guiding resource allocation. If overall inflation is allowed to get out of hand, then clearly allocative efficiency cannot be expected. On the other hand, a stable macroeconomy should serve to improve the operation of microeconomic markets. An economy that is stable should also be better able to withstand external shocks.

Global linkages

The domestic markets of most LDCs are limited in terms of effective demand. For LDC producers to be able to benefit from economies of scale, they need to be exporting in sufficient quantities – which clearly means being involved in and committed to international trade. Global linkages thus become important. Furthermore, LDCs can gain access to technology only from abroad, as they do not have the capacity to produce it themselves.

Again, there are likely to be spillover effects. The availability of physical and financial capital may help the stability of the macroeconomy; participation in world markets may help domestic markets to operate; and global linkages can provide the knowledge and technology that will improve human capital in the domestic economy.

It is important to notice that establishing global links is a two-way process. On the one hand, it is important for an LDC to be in a strong enough position to form links with more-developed countries without creating a vulnerability to outside influence that may damage it, for example in reaching trade agreements. On the other hand, the more-developed countries need to be willing to accept such linkages. This has not always been the case in the past.

So there is an interdependent system in which the four aspects of potential intervention interact. The self-reinforcing aspect of these four components not only provides a focus for analysis, but also highlights the fact that if any one of the elements is lacking, there may be problems.

Whether these aspects are sufficient to encourage development is an important issue. In most LDCs two additional matters will need to be tackled. First, there is the question of infrastructure. The *public good* aspects of some types of infrastructure need to be borne in mind. The provision of transport and communications systems, or the improvement of market facilities to enable trading to take place, may be crucial for the smooth development of an LDC.

Second, it is important that LDC governments maintain an appropriate balance in their spending priorities. Civil and international conflict has all too often diverted resources away from development priorities. Something of this can be seen in Figure 27.8, which shows military expenditure relative to expenditure on health and education.

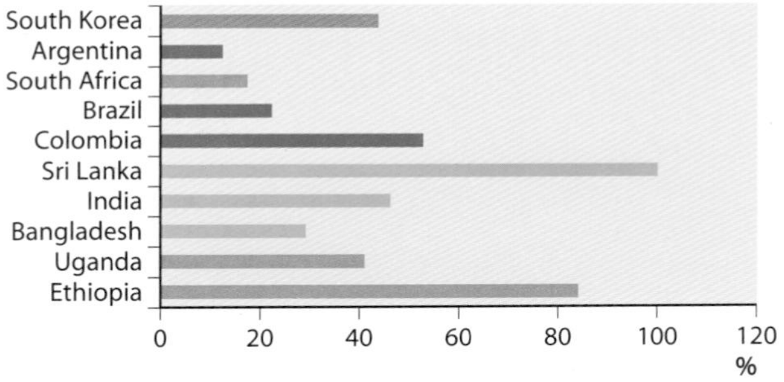

Figure 27.8 *Military expenditure as a percentage of combined public expenditure on education and health, 2001*

Note: data are not available for China and Singapore.

Source: *Human Development Report 2004*.

The tiger economies offer a good illustration of how markets can be enabled to bring about rapid growth and development. Indeed, the World Bank model is based partly on their observation of the experience of these and some other economies. Although in some cases (especially Singapore and South Korea) the governments played an active role in encouraging economic growth and influencing the pattern of economic activity, nonetheless, markets were nurtured and encouraged to play a role in resource allocation.

Structural adjustment programmes (SAPs)

As the World Bank has adopted the market-friendly ideal, it has embedded its central ideas in Structural Adjustment Programmes (SAPs) that LDCs have been encouraged to follow. These will be explored in Chapter 30, where you will see that the central policies to be adopted under SAPs relate to one of the four components outlined above.

Key term

Structural Adjustment Programme: a package of economic policy measures recommended by the World Bank

Summary

- The World Bank has advocated a market-friendly approach to economic growth and development.
- Four key elements are seen as crucial to the process: investment in people, properly functioning microeconomic markets, macroeconomic stability and international linkages.
- These elements reinforce one another.
- These ideas are embedded in the Structural Adjustment Programme approach.

Sustainable development

Chapter 14 discussed economic growth in the context of developed countries. It was pointed out that economic growth may have important effects on the environment, and that care needs to be taken to ensure that, in pursuing growth, countries bear in mind the importance of future generations as well as the needs of the present.

These issues are equally important for LDCs. Deforestation has been a problem for many LDCs with areas of rainforest. In some cases logging for timber has destroyed much valuable land; in other cases land has been cleared for unsuitable agricultural use. This sort of activity creates relatively little present value, and leaves a poorer environment for future generations.

Environmental degradation can have a negative impact on biodiversity.

Another aspect of environmental degradation concerns *biodiversity*. This refers to the way in which misuse of the environment is contributing to the loss of plant species – not to mention those of birds, insects and mammals – which are becoming extinct as their natural habitat is destroyed. In some cases the loss is of species that have not even been discovered yet. Given the natural healing properties of many plants, this could mean the destruction of plants that could provide significant new drugs for use in medicine. But how can something be valued when its very existence is as yet unknown?

One way of viewing the environment is as a factor of production that needs to be used effectively, just like any other factor of production. In other words, each country has a stock of *environmental* capital that needs to be utilised in the best possible way.

However, if the environmental capital is to be used appropriately, it must be given an appropriate value. This can be problematic; if property rights are not firmly established – as they are not in many LDCs – it is difficult to enforce legislation to protect the environment. Furthermore, if the environment (as a factor of production) is underpriced, then 'too much' of it will be used by firms.

There are externality effects at work here too, in the sense that the loss of biodiversity is a global loss, and not just something affecting the local economy. In some cases there have been international externality effects of a more direct kind, such as when forest fires in Indonesia caused the airport in Singapore to close down because of the resulting smoke haze.

China has been one of the fastest growing economies in the world since 1978, as can be seen in Figure 27.9. To have averaged almost 8% growth per annum over such a long period is extraordinary. In 2004 the *Asian Development Bank* reported that China's GDP had grown by 9.1% in 2003, and it predicted that in 2004 the country's growth would account for 15% of the expected expansion in the *world* economy. Exports from the rest of the world to China grew by 34.6% in 2003.

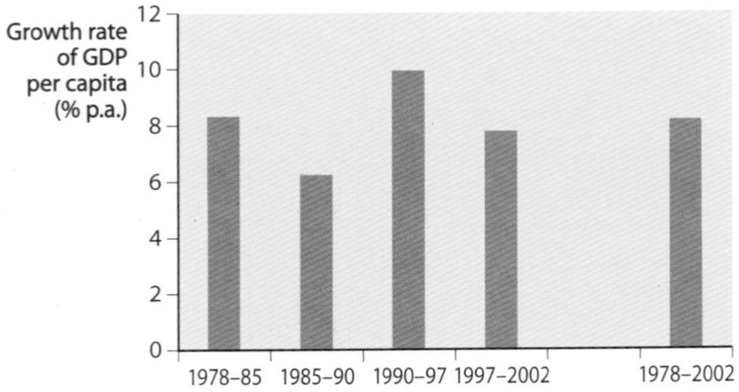

Figure 27.9 *China's economic growth, 1978–2002*

Source: H. Ungang, H. Linlin and C. Zhixiao, 'China's economic growth and poverty reduction, 1978–2002', at **www.imf.org**

In August 2004 *The Economist* reported that 16 of the world's most polluted cities are now located in China, and that around half of China's population (i.e. some 600 million people) have water supplies that are contaminated by animal and human waste. River systems are heavily polluted, and air pollution is becoming a serious issue, partly as a result of the country's heavy reliance on coal-fired electricity generation. Shanghai's environmental protection bureau estimated that 70% of the 1 million cars in Shanghai do not reach even the oldest European emission standard.

This illustrates the trade-off between rapid economic growth and protection of the environment. The other factor in the equation is the desire to alleviate poverty. The World Bank estimated that in 1999, 224 million people in China were living in poverty — defined as people living on less than $1 per day. The need to bring so many people out of extreme poverty lends urgency to the drive for economic growth. However, this needs to be balanced against the need to ensure **sustainable development**. In other words, economic growth must be achieved in such a way that it does not destroy the environment for future generations.

> ***Key term***
>
> **sustainable development:** 'development which meets the needs of the present without compromising the ability of future generations to meet their own needs' (Brundtland Commission, 1987)

There are many aspects to this issue, of which protecting the environment is just one. Sustainable development also entails taking account of the depletion rates of non-renewable resources, and ensuring that renewable resources *are* renewed in the process of economic growth.

So, although economic growth is important to a society, the drive for growth must be tempered by an awareness of the possible trade-offs with other important objectives.

Can the government influence economic growth?

There may be limits to which a government can influence the growth process. Infrastructure can be put in place, and markets encouraged to operate, but nevertheless, there may be limits to what can be done, especially as, with low levels of incomes in the LDC and inefficient tax collection, the government itself may have inadequate resources at its disposal.

In the case of the tiger economies the government did have a strong influence — although less so in the case of Hong Kong. In Singapore the government kept tight reins on the macroeconomy, encouraged savings, nurtured the education system, guided the development of key strategic sectors in the economy and provided good infrastructure for trade and industry, as well as maintaining an open economy. In South Korea the government subsidised the development of large conglomerate firms that provided the foundations for economic growth.

Summary

- In pursuing economic growth, governments must remain aware of the potential costs of such growth.
- These may be seen especially in terms of possible damage to the environment.
- In this connection, deforestation and the loss of biodiversity are critical areas of concern.

- There are many international externality effects at work in the process of economic growth in LDCs.
- The recent rapid economic growth achieved in the Chinese economy has highlighted some of the environmental costs associated with growth.
- Given low per capita incomes and limited resources, LDC governments may not be able to influence growth very readily.

Exercise 27.1

Which of the following can be seen as impediments to growth?

a a lack of savings resulting from low per capita incomes

b underdeveloped financial markets

c lack of confidence in financial assets and institutions

d low real interest rates

e shortage of entrepreneurs

f inadequate infrastructure

g low levels of human capital

h foreign exchange shortage

i limited government resources

Which of these factors are likely to be present in less-developed countries?

part 6

Chapter 28

Obstacles to growth and development

Chapter 26 described how development experiences have varied substantially between different regions of the world. This chapter focuses on some of the obstacles that have hindered development in the less-developed countries, especially sub-Saharan Africa, where very little progress seems to have been made after several decades of development efforts. This is in contrast to some countries in East Asia, which have experienced such rapid growth since the 1960s that they have successfully closed the income gap with countries that developed in earlier periods.

Learning outcomes

After studying this chapter, you should:

- be familiar with the contrasting patterns of development in different regions of the world
- be aware of important obstacles to economic growth and development
- understand the causes and significance of rapid population growth
- understand the dangers of continued dependence on primary production, especially on low productivity agriculture
- appreciate the importance of missing markets, especially financial markets
- be aware of the importance of social capital in promoting long-term development
- appreciate the significance of relationships with more-developed countries

Contrasting patterns of development

The East Asian experience

The rapid growth achieved by the East Asian **tiger economies**, as they came to be known, was undoubtedly impressive, and held out hope that other less-developed countries could begin to close the gap in

Key term

tiger economies: a group of newly industrialised economies in the East Asian region, including Hong Kong, Singapore, South Korea and Taiwan

living standards. Indeed, the term 'East Asian miracle' was coined to describe how quickly these **newly industrialised economies** had been able to develop. At the heart of the success were four countries: Hong Kong, Singapore, South Korea and Taiwan; others, such as Malaysia and Thailand, were not far behind.

How was their success achieved?

None of these countries enjoy a rich supply of natural resources. Indeed, Hong Kong and Singapore are small city-states whose only natural resources are their excellent harbours and good positions — but with small populations.

The tigers soon realised that to develop manufacturing industry it would be crucial to tap into economies of scale. This meant producing on a scale that would far outstrip the size of their domestic markets — which meant that they would have to rely on international trade.

> ***Key terms***
>
> **newly industrialised economies:** economies that experienced rapid economic growth from the 1960s to the present
>
> **export-led growth:** situation in which economic growth is achieved through the exploitation of economies of scale made possible by focusing on exports, and so reaching a wider market than would be available within the domestic economy

By being very open to international trade and focusing on export markets, the tigers were able to sell to a larger market, and thereby improve their efficiency through economies of scale. This enabled them to enjoy a period of **export-led growth**. In other words, the tiger economies expanded by selling their exports to the rest of the world, and building a reputation for high-quality merchandise. This was helped by their judicious choice of markets on which to focus: they chose to move into areas of economic activity that were being vacated by the more-developed nations, which were moving up to new sorts of product.

The export-led growth hypothesis explains part of the success of the tiger economies, but there were other contributing factors. The tiger economies nurtured their human capital and attracted foreign investment. Their governments intervened to influence the direction of the economies but also encouraged markets to operate effectively, fostering macroeconomic and political stability and developing good infrastructure. Moreover, these countries embarked on their growth period at a time when world trade overall was buoyant.

Sub-Saharan Africa

The experience of countries in sub-Saharan Africa is in total contrast to the success story of the tiger economies. Even accepting the limitations of the GDP per capita measure, the fact that GDP per capita was lower in 2000 than it had been in 1975 (or even earlier) paints a depressing picture. Can sub-Saharan Africa learn from the experience of the tiger economies?

Part of the explanation for the failure of growth in this region lies in the fact that sub-Saharan Africa lacks many of the positive features that enabled the tiger economies to grow. Export-led growth is less easy for countries that have specialised in the production of goods for which demand is not buoyant. Furthermore, it is not straightforward to develop new specialisations if human and physical capital levels are low, the skills for new activities are lacking and poverty is rife. Encouraging development when there is political instability, and when markets do not operate effectively, is a major challenge. This chapter considers some of the obstacles to development that are faced by LDCs.

Latin America

Countries in Latin America followed yet another path. There was a period in which the economies of Argentina, Brazil and Mexico, among others, were able to grow rapidly, enabling them to qualify as 'newly industrialised economies'. However, such growth could not be sustained in the face of the high rates of inflation that afflicted many of the countries in this region, especially during the 1980s. Indeed, many of them experienced bouts of hyperinflation, inhibiting economic growth.

The Latin American economies grew strongly in the 1970s, but were hit by high inflation in the 1980s.

In part this reflected fiscal indiscipline, with governments undertaking high levels of expenditure which they financed by printing money. In many cases, countries in this region have tended to be relatively closed to international trade. International debt reached unsustainable levels, and continues to haunt countries such as Argentina which, in 2005, wrote off its debt by offering its creditors about 33% of the value of its outstanding debt. Around three-quarters of the creditors accepted the deal, knowing that otherwise they would probably get nothing at all. However, whether anyone will be prepared to lend to Argentina in the future remains to be seen. Latin American economies also tend to be characterised by high levels of income inequality, and poverty remains a major problem.

Summary

- A small group of countries in South East Asia, known as the East Asian tiger economies, underwent a period of rapid economic growth, closing the gap on the more-developed countries.
- This success arose from a combination of circumstances, including a high degree of openness to international trade, which was seen as crucial if economies of scale are to be reaped.
- However, the tigers are also characterised by high levels of human capital and political and macroeconomic stability.

- In contrast, countries in sub-Saharan Africa have stagnated; in some cases real per capita incomes were lower in 2000 than they had been in 1975.
- Countries in Latin America began well, experiencing growth for a period, but then ran into economic difficulties.

Population growth

Early writers on development were pessimists. For example, Thomas Malthus argued that real wages would never rise above a bare subsistence level. This was based on his ideas about the relationship between population growth and real incomes.

Malthus, having come under the influence of David Ricardo, believed that there would always be *diminishing returns to labour.* This led him to believe that as the population of a country increased the average wage would fall, since a larger labour force would be inherently less productive. Furthermore, Malthus argued that the birth rate would rise with the real wage, because if families had more resources they would have more children; at the same time, the death rate would fall with an increase in the real wage, as people would be better fed and therefore healthier.

Extension material

Figure 28.1 shows one way of looking at the relationship between population growth and real wages. The left-hand panel illustrates the relationship between population size and the real wage rate, reflecting diminishing returns to labour in agriculture. The right-hand panel shows the birth rate (*B*) and death rate (*D*) functions. When the wage is relatively high, say at W_1, the birth rate (B_1) exceeds the death rate (D_1), which in turn means that the population will grow. However, as population grows, the real wage must fall (as shown in the left-hand panel), so eventually the wage converges on W^*, which is an equilibrium situation.

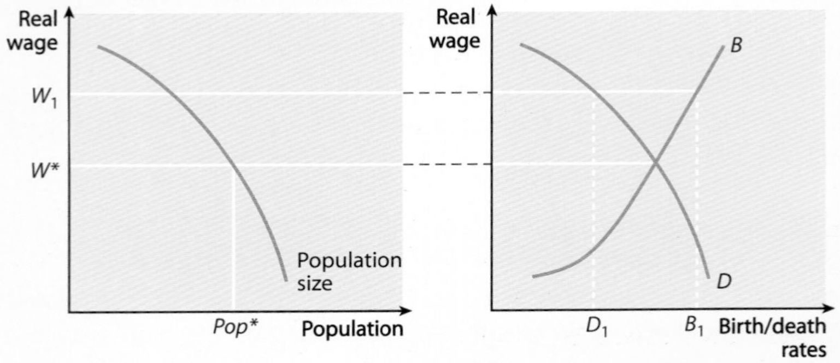

Figure 28.1 *Malthus's theory of population*

For these reasons, Malthus believed that it was not possible for a society to experience sustained increases in real wages, basically because the population was capable of exponential growth, while the food supply was capable of only arithmetic growth, because of diminishing returns.

Although he was proved wrong (he had not anticipated the improvements in agricultural productivity that were to come), the question of whether population growth constitutes an obstacle to growth and development remains. At the heart of this is the debate about whether people should be regarded as key contributors to development, in their role as a factor of production, or as a drain on resources, consuming food, shelter, education and so on. Ultimately, the answer will depend upon the quantity of resources available relative to the population size.

In global terms world population is growing at a rapid rate, by more than 80 million people per year. In November 1999 global population went through the 6 billion mark — that is about six times as many people as in 1800. But the growth is very unevenly distributed: countries like Italy, Spain, Germany and Switzerland are projected to experience declining populations in the 2000–15 period, while sub-Saharan Africa's population continues to grow by 2.4% per annum, and 'low human development' countries (by the UNDP definition) by 2.5%. A country whose population is growing at 2.5% per annum will see a doubling in just 28 years, so the growing pressure on resources to provide education and healthcare is considerable. The proportion of the population aged below 15 is very high for much of sub-Saharan Africa, as was noted in Chapter 26.

It has been observed that developed countries seem to have gone through a common pattern of population growth as their development progressed. This pattern has become known as the **demographic transition**, and is illustrated in Figure 28.2 for England and Wales between 1750 and 2000. This shows the birth rate and death rate for various years over this period. Remember that the natural rate of increase in population is given by the difference between these: the birth rate minus the death rate. (This ignores net migration.)

Key term

demographic transition: a process through which many countries have been observed to pass whereby improved health lowers the death rate, and the birth rate subsequently also falls, leading to a low and stable population growth

Notice that between 1750 and 1820 the death rate fell more steeply than the birth rate, which means that the population growth rate accelerated in this period. This was the time when Britain was embarking on the Industrial Revolution, and corresponds to the early 'take-off' period of economic growth. At this stage the birth rate remains high. However, after 1870 there is a further fall in the death rate, accompanied by an even steeper fall in the birth rate, such that population growth slows down. You can see that by 2000 the natural population growth has shrunk to zero.

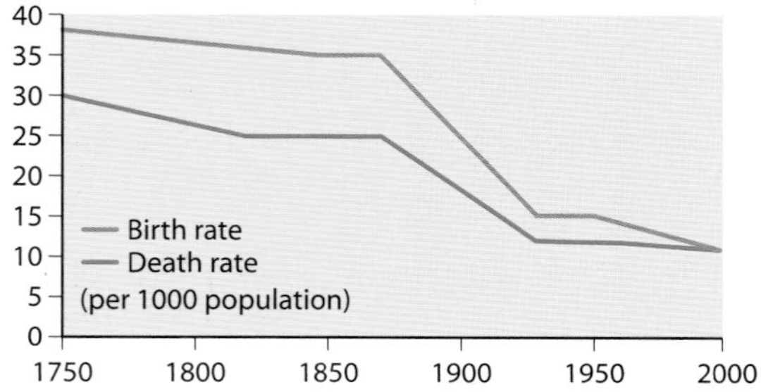

Figure 28.2 The demographic transition in England and Wales, 1750–2000

Source: D. Perkins et al. *The Economics of Development*, Norton/World Bank.

This demographic transition process has been displayed in most of the developed countries. The supporting story is that when the development process begins,

death rates tend to fall as incomes begin to rise. In time families adapt to the change, and new social norms emerge in which the typical family size tends to get smaller. For example, as more women join the workforce, the opportunity cost of having children rises — by taking time out from careers to have children, their forgone earnings are now higher. This process has led to stability in population growth.

However, for countries that have undergone the demographic transition in a later period things have not been so smooth. Figure 28.3 shows the pattern of the demographic transition for Sri Lanka, which is one of the countries that have achieved some stability in the rate of population growth. Here, it is not until after about 1920 that the death rate begins to fall — and it falls more steeply than it did in the early stages of economic growth in England and Wales. After 1950 it falls even more steeply, partly because methods of hygiene and modern medicine were able to bring the death rate down more rapidly.

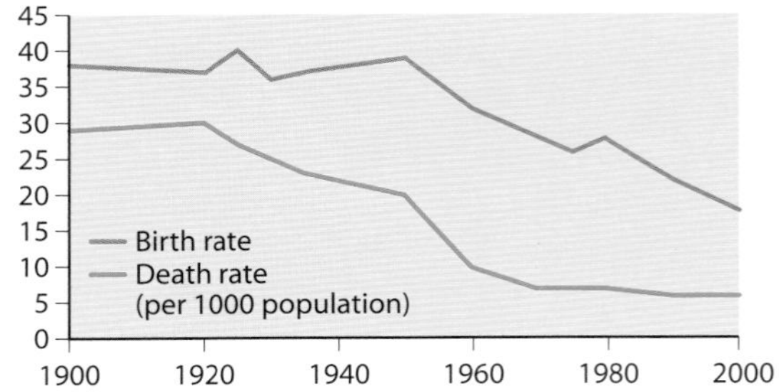

Figure 28.3 The demographic transition in Sri Lanka, 1900–2000

Source: as Figure 28.2.

Perhaps more crucially, the birth rate in Sri Lanka has remained high for much longer — in other words, households' decisions about family size do not seem to have adjusted as rapidly as they did in England and Wales. This has led to a period of relatively rapid population growth.

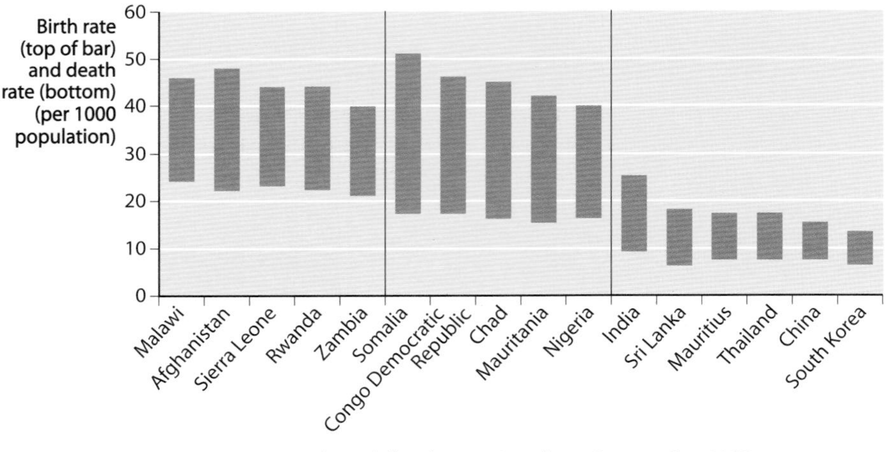

Figure 28.4 Birth and death rates in selected countries, 1999

Source: World Bank.

In Figure 28.4, presenting data for a range of countries around the world, the top point of each bar represents the birth rate and the bottom point the death rate; the length of each bar thus represents the rate of natural population increase. You will see that there are three important groupings. The first is of five countries that do not yet seem to have entered the demographic transition, and for which both birth rates and death rates have remained relatively high. These are mainly low-income countries.

The second group represents countries in which death rates have begun to fall but birth rates have remained high. As a result, these are currently going through a period of rapid population growth.

The final group represents countries that have seen falls in both birth and death rates, so that population growth has now been reduced. Notice that this includes Sri Lanka, which was discussed earlier.

Extension material: the microeconomics of fertility

To some extent, a household's choice of family size might be viewed as an *externality* issue. Figure 28.5 illustrates this. *MPB* (= *MSB*) represents the marginal benefit that the household receives from having different numbers of children (which is assumed to equal the marginal social benefit), and *MPC* represents the marginal private costs that are incurred. If education is subsidised, or if the household does not perceive the costs inflicted on society by having many children, then the marginal social cost of children (*MSC*) is higher than the marginal private cost.

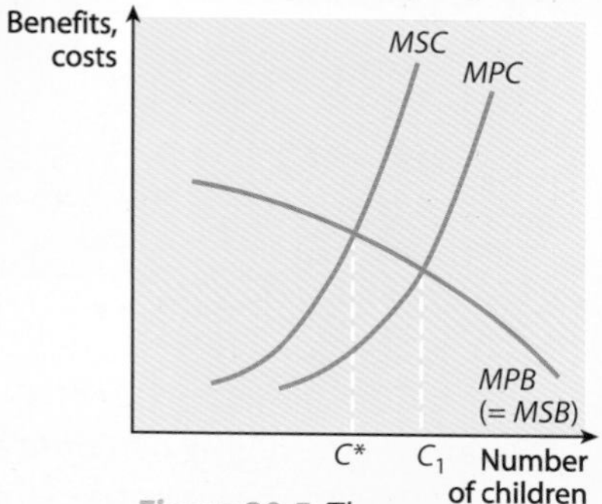

Figure 28.5 The microeconomics of fertility

Households will thus choose to have C_1 children, rather than the C^* that is optimal for society. In other words, a choice of large family size might be interpreted as being a market failure. Note that this discussion assumes that the household has the ability to choose its desired family size by having access to, and knowledge of, methods of contraception.

Figure 28.6 shows fertility rates for the group of countries selected in previous chapters. The fertility rate records the average number of births per woman. Thus, in Uganda the average number of births per woman is more than 7. Of course, this does not mean that the average number of *children* per family is so high, as not all the babies survive.

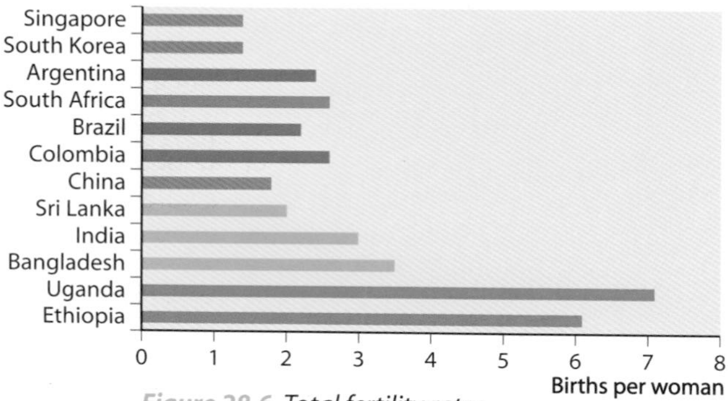

Figure 28.6 Total fertility rates, selected countries, 2000–2005
Source: *Human Development Report 2004.*

This pattern of high fertility has implications for the age structure of the population, leading to a high proportion of young dependants in the population, as is illustrated by the population pyramid for Zimbabwe in Figure 28.7. (*For an explanation of population pyramids, see pages 345–46 in Chapter 24.*) This creates a strain on an LDC's limited resources, because of the need to provide education for so many children, and in this sense high population growth can prove an obstacle to development.

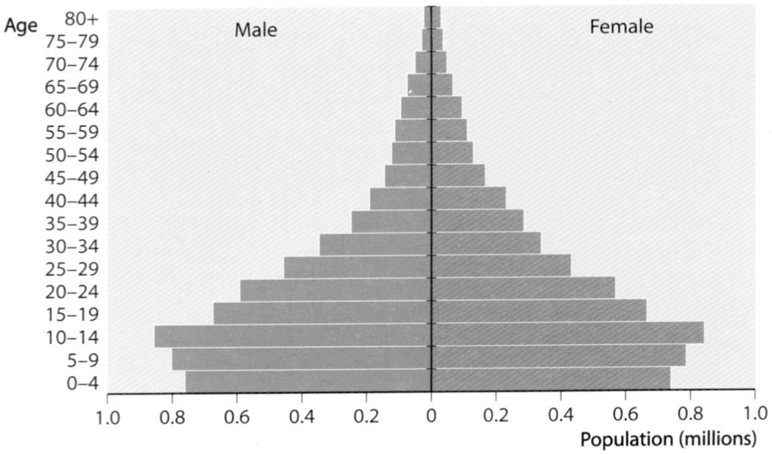

Figure 28.7
A population pyramid for Zimbabwe, 1997

Source: US Census Bureau, International Data Base.

This argument might be countered by pointing out that people themselves are a resource for the country. However, it is a question of the balance between population and the availability of resources.

Summary

- Early writers such as Malthus were pessimistic about the prospects for sustained development, believing that diminishing returns to labour would constrain economic growth.
- Globally, population is growing rapidly, with most of the increase taking place in less-developed countries.
- Developed countries and some LDCs have been seen to have passed through a demographic transition, such that population growth stabilises following decreases in death and birth rates.
- However, many LDCs have not completed the transition, remaining in the rapid population growth phase.
- Coupled with the age structure of the population, rapid population growth can create difficulties for LDCs because of the pressure on resources.

Exercise 28.1

Discuss the way in which the age structure of a population may influence the rate of economic growth and development.

Dependence on primary production

Chapter 26 mentioned that many LDCs, especially in sub-Saharan Africa, continue to rely heavily on the agricultural sector to provide employment and incomes. Because labour productivity in agriculture tends to be relatively low, this may keep rural incomes low.

It is worth remembering that one of the driving forces behind the Industrial Revolution in Britain was an increase in agricultural productivity, enabling more workers to shift into manufacturing activity. In an LDC context, this transition may run into a number of problems. Chapter 29 explores the need and potential for a structural transformation of the economy and the dangers of relying on agriculture in the international trade arena; this chapter focuses on the obstacles to increasing agricultural productivity.

In some LDCs the problem stems from the form of land tenancy agreements, which can lead to inefficiency. In other cases problems arise because of insecure property rights and the inheritance laws that pertain.

Land tenancy

One characteristic of many LDCs is that land is unequally distributed. If a landowner has more land than can be farmed as a single unit, it is likely that he will hire out parcels of land to small farmers. The way in which this is done turns out to be important for productivity and incentives.

One common form of land tenancy agreement in LDCs is that of **sharecropping**. In this system a tenant-farmer and a landlord of a piece of land have an agreement to share the resulting crop. The tenant-farmers in this case act as *agents*, farming the land on behalf of the landlord (the *principal*). The landlord would like the farmers to maximise returns from the land. However, the tenants will set out to balance the return received with the cost of producing the crop in terms of work effort. A *principal–agent problem* arises here, since if tenants receive only a portion of the crop, their incentive will be to supply less effort than is optimal for the landlord. There is also an asymmetric information problem, in the sense that the landlord cannot easily monitor the amount of effort being provided by a tenant. The tenants know how much of the low output results from low effort, and how much from unfavourable weather conditions — but the landlord does not. The problems that can arise from *asymmetric information* are discussed in Chapter 9.

> **Key term**
>
> **sharecropping:** a form of land tenure system in which the landlord and tenant share the crop

Notice that under a sharecropping contract tenants have little incentive to invest in improving the land or the production methods, because part of the reward for innovation goes to the landlord. On the other hand, the risk of the venture is shared between the landlord and the tenant, as well as the returns.

An alternative would be for the landlord to charge the tenants a fixed rent for farming the land. This would provide better incentives for them to work hard, as they now receive all of the returns. However, it would also mean that they carry all the risk involved – if the harvest is poor, it is the tenants who will suffer, having paid a fixed rent for the land.

Yet another possibility would be for the landlord to hire tenants on a wage contract, and pay a fixed wage for their farming the land. This again would provide little incentive for the tenants to supply effort, as the wage would be paid regardless. As the landlord may not be able to monitor the supply of effort, this would create a problem. Furthermore, the landlord would now face all of the risk.

Thus, for these forms of tenancy, careful consideration needs to be given to the incentives for work effort, the incentives for innovation and investment and the sharing of risk.

Land ownership

In other circumstances inheritance laws can damage agricultural productivity, for example where land is divided between sons on the death of the household head, which means that average plot size declines in successive generations. In some societies property rights are inadequate: for example, women may not be permitted to own land, which can bring problems given that much of the agricultural labour is provided by women. Furthermore, in an attempt to make the best of adverse circumstances, over-farming and a lack of crop rotation practices can mean that soil becomes less productive over time. All of this makes it more difficult to achieve improvements in productivity in the agricultural sector.

Poverty is thus perpetuated over time; and with limited resources available for survival, farmers have no chance to adopt new or innovative farming practices. The

Unsuitable land tenure, over-farming and lack of crop rotation can all lead to low agricultural productivity.

very fact that people are struggling to make the best of the resources and arrangements available may make it difficult for them to step back and look for broader improvements that would allow the reform of economic and social institutions.

The previous chapter pointed out that financial markets in many LDCs are relatively underdeveloped. This is especially so in the rural areas, where the lack of formal financial markets makes borrowing to invest in agricultural improvements almost impossible.

One of the problems here is that the cost of establishing rural branches of financial institutions in remote areas is high; the fixed costs of making loans for relatively small-scale projects are similarly high. This is intensified by the difficulty that banks have in obtaining information about the creditworthiness of small borrowers, who typically may have no collateral to offer.

Attempts have been made to remedy this situation through *microfinance* schemes. This approach was pioneered by the Grameen Bank, which was founded in Bangladesh in 1976. The bank made small-scale loans to groups of women who otherwise would have had no access to credit, and each group was made corporately responsible for paying back the loan. The scheme has claimed great success, both in terms of the constructive use of the funds in getting small-scale projects off the ground and in terms of high pay-back rates.

Case study The Grameen Bank

In 1974 a severe famine afflicted Bangladesh, and a flood of starving people converged on the capital city, Dhaka. Muhammad Yunus was an economics professor at Chittagong University. He tells how he was struck by the extreme contrast between the neat and abstract economic theories that he was teaching, and the plight and suffering of those surviving in bare poverty, and suffering and dying in the famine.

He also tells how he decided to study the problem at first hand, taking his students on field trips into villages near to the campus. On one of these visits they interviewed a woman who was struggling to make a living by making bamboo stools. For each stool that she made, she had to borrow the equivalent of 15 pence for the raw materials. Once she had paid back the loan, at interest rates of up to 10% per week, her profit margin was just 1p. The woman was never able to escape from her situation because she was trapped by the need to borrow, and the need to pay back at such punitive rates of interest. Her story was by no means unique, and Yunus was keen to find a way of enabling women like her to have access to credit on conditions that would allow them to escape from poverty. He began experimenting by lending out some of his own money to groups in need.

Muhammad Yunus launched the Grameen Bank experiment in 1976. The idea was to provide credit for small-scale income-generating activities. Loans would be provided without the need for collateral, with borrowers being required to form themselves into groups of five with joint responsibility for the repayments. The acceptance of this joint responsibility and the lack of collateral helped to minimise the transaction costs of making and monitoring the loans.

On any criteria, the project proved an enormous success. The repayment record has been impressive, although the Grameen Bank charges interest rates close to those in the formal commercial sector — which are much lower than the informal money-lenders. After the initial launch of the Bank, lending has been channelled primarily to women borrowers, who are seen to

invest more carefully and to repay more reliably — and to be most in need. Table 28.1 offers some information about the scale and scope of the Grameen Bank by the late 1990s.

By the end of May 1998 more than $2.4 billion had been loaned by Grameen Bank, including more than 2 million loans for milch cows, nearly 100 000 for rickshaws, 57 000 for sewing machines and many more for processing, agriculture, trading, shopkeeping, peddling and other activities. Grameen-type credit programmes are now operating in 59 countries in Africa, Asia, the Americas, Europe and Papua New Guinea.

As for the impact of Grameen loans in economic terms, the loans are seen to have generated new employment, to have reduced the number of days workers are inactive, and to have raised income, food consumption and living conditions of Grameen Bank members — not to mention their social impact on the lives of millions of women.

No. of villages where Grameen operates	38,551
No. of Grameen centres	65,960
No. of branches	1,112
No. of staff	12,589
No. of Grameen members	
Female	2,210,160
Male	124,620
Total	2,334,780
Cumulative no. of houses built with Grameen housing loans	438,764

Table 28.1 *The Grameen Bank as of 31 May 1998*

Source: Muhammad Yunus, Banker to the Poor, Aurum Press, London, 1998.

Other schemes have involved groups of households coming together to pool their savings in order to accumulate enough funds to launch small projects. Members of the group take it in turns to use these joint savings, paying the loan back in order for the next person to have a turn. These are known as *rotating savings and credit schemes (ROSCAS)*, and they have had some success in providing credit for small schemes. In spite of some successful enterprises, however, such schemes have been found to be less sustainable than Grameen-style arrangements, and have tended to be used to obtain consumer durable goods rather than for productive investment and innovation.

Case study Example of a ROSCA

Suppose that 12 individuals are saving for a bicycle (a key form of transport in many developing countries). A bicycle costs $130, and each individual saves $10 per month. Simple arithmetic indicates that it would take 13 months for enough funds to have accumulated for the 12 individuals to buy their bicycles. Suppose that the 12 people agree to work together. First, they explain to the bicycle dealer that there is a guaranteed order for 12 bicycles, and they negotiate a discount of $10 per bicycle. They then meet at the end of each month, and each pays $10 into the fund. At the end of the first month, there are sufficient funds for one person to buy a bicycle — usually chosen by a lottery. As a result, even the last person in turn gets the bicycle earlier because of the discount they negotiated. Of course, without the discount, one unfortunate person would have to wait the full period, but clearly this is a very efficient way of making use of small amounts of savings. With more people, or higher contributions, the funds can be used for more substantial projects. Administration costs are minimal, but the schemes do rely on trust, such that the first person to win the lottery does not then stop making payments.

In the absence of such schemes, households may be forced to borrow from local moneylenders, often at very high rates of interest. For example, the Bank of Uganda survey mentioned earlier found that households were paying rates between 0% (when borrowing from family members) and 500%. In part this may reflect a high risk of the borrower's defaulting, but it may also reflect the ability of local moneylenders to use market power. The absence of insurance markets may also deter borrowing for productive investment, especially in rural areas.

Trade in primary goods

The difficulty of improving agricultural productivity does not make it easy for LDCs to engage in active international trade, but in practice some have little choice but to rely on primary production in their export activity, as shown in Figure 28.8. The figure shows quite a mixed pattern, reflecting the fact that some countries, especially in Asia, have managed to diversify away from primary production, whereas in others, e.g. Ethiopia and Uganda, the share of primary goods in exports remains extremely high.

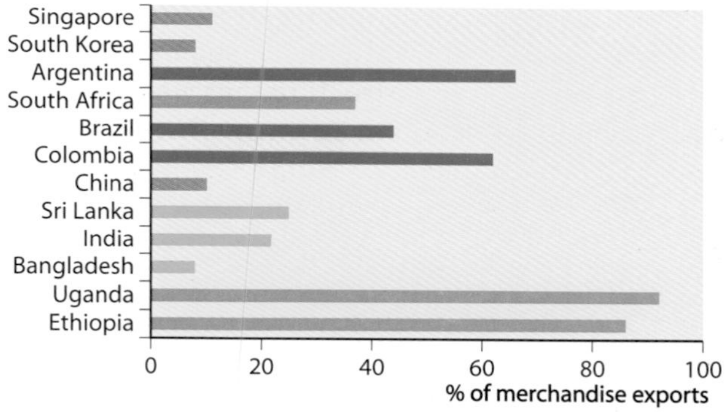

Figure 28.8
Dependence on primary exports, selected countries

Source: *Human Development Report 2004.*

In LDCs, even small enterprises may be involved in exporting activity. For example, many small farmers even in remote villages in Uganda grow some coffee for export. However, they rely on traders travelling around the rural areas to buy the coffee and sell it on to the exporters. This creates difficulties for the farmers, who may not be able to check up readily on the prices being charged in the cities, and who do not have the storage or market facilities to produce on a larger scale. If they do not have the communication links with which to determine what is a good price for their crop, the traders have an information advantage that may be exploited.

The Green Revolution

Given that agricultural productivity is much higher in developed countries than in LDCs, why is it not possible for them to learn from the experience of the more-developed countries, and bring in new technology and farming practices?

Part of the reason why this does not work is that the balance between capital and labour is very different in the two groups of countries. In the more-developed countries, productivity is high because of very intensive cultivation methods and the heavy use of capital and chemical inputs, which are neither available in, nor suitable for, LDCs. For example, given that there is already a surplus of agricultural labour in many LDCs, the introduction of labour-saving machinery would not seem to make sense – especially where running and servicing the machines would be difficult, and where field sizes tend to be too small for effective mechanisation.

In this context, the Green Revolution that began in the 1970s seemed to offer great promise. The Green Revolution was associated with the development of new, improved, *high-yielding varieties* (HYVs) of certain crops. Techniques for using these HYVs tended to be labour-intensive, and they promised greatly improved yields. They also involved food crops such as rice and wheat, which were attractive even to small-scale farmers. In addition they were fast growing, so that in some countries it was possible to increase the number of harvests per year.

These HYVs were widely adopted in Asia, and led to substantial increases in productivity, with some countries switching from being importers to exporters of the crops.

However, there was a downside. In some regions it was the richer farmers who were able to make best use of the new seeds, having had more education and thus understanding better how to grow them. Furthermore, some regions (e.g. Bali in Indonesia) already had the associated infrastructure that was required, such as irrigation systems, and this enabled their quick adoption of the new techniques.

In Africa, however, the Green Revolution had a much lower impact, partly because the main crops for which HYVs were developed (rice and wheat) were not widely grown staple crops in sub-Saharan Africa. So again, Africa seemed left behind. Only relatively recently have HYVs for crops such as maize been developed. Moreover, if the Green Revolution is to be successful in Africa, education levels need to be improved (because farmers need to be able to read and interpret instructions), and the necessary infrastructure provided.

The impact of HIV/AIDS

The HIV/AIDS epidemic has had a major impact on LDCs, especially in sub-Saharan Africa. The relative incidence of the disease across countries is illustrated in Figure 28.9. The high prevalence in sub-Saharan Africa is clearly visible. This

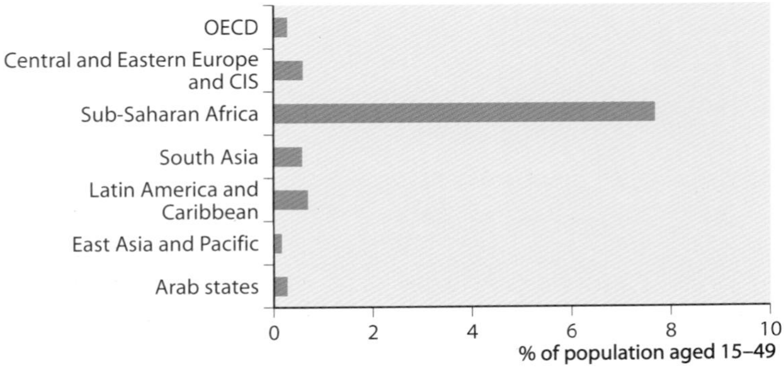

Figure 28.9 *Incidence of HIV/AIDS, selected regions*

Source: *Human Development Report 2004.*

conceals large differences between countries. There are countries in sub-Saharan Africa where the prevalence is unimaginably high; for example, in Botswana it is estimated that in 2003 some 37.3% of the population aged 15–49 were affected; and in Swaziland the prevalence rate was 38.8%.

The repercussions of the disease are especially marked because of its impact on people of working age. This has affected the size of the labour force, and left many orphans with little hope of receiving an education, which in turn has implications for the productivity of future generations.

Governments have reacted to the disease in very different ways. In countries where the government has been open about the onset of the disease and has striven to promote safe sex, the chances of keeping the disease under control are much higher. For example, in 1990 the incidence of HIV/AIDS amongst adults in Thailand and South Africa was similar, at about 1%. Thailand confronted the problem through a widespread public campaign such that, by 2001, the incidence was still about 1%. South Africa did little to stop the spread of the disease, with the President choosing to downplay the problem. In 2001 the incidence of the disease was estimated to be about 25%. Some other governments have also kept silent, perhaps not wanting to admit that it is a problem, and here the disease has run rampant. There may also be problems in measuring the incidence of HIV/AIDS accurately, as individuals may be hesitant to seek treatment or to report that they have the disease for fear of social stigma.

Summary

- Many LDCs continue to rely heavily on primary production as a source of employment, incomes and export revenues.
- The agricultural sector exhibits low productivity, partly arising from inefficiencies in land tenure systems and inequality in land ownership.
- Inadequacies in financial markets, especially in rural areas, make it difficult for farmers to obtain credit for improving productivity.
- The Green Revolution had a large impact on productivity in Asia, but was slow to reach sub-Saharan Africa.
- HIV/AIDS has been a significant obstacle to development in recent years, especially in sub-Saharan Africa, where the prevalence of the disease is higher than in other regions.

Can governments influence growth?

Faced with these and other obstacles to economic growth, how much can LDC governments do to encourage a more rapid rate of growth and development? A major factor to remember is the limitations in terms of resources. Where average incomes are low and tax collection systems are undeveloped, governments have difficulty in generating a flow of revenue domestically, which is needed in order to launch policies encouraging growth and development.

In some cases governments have tended to rely on taxes on international trade, which are relatively easy to administer, rather than on domestic direct or indirect taxes. This has not helped to stimulate international trade, of course.

Some LDC governments have responded to this problem by borrowing funds from abroad. However, in many cases such funds have not been best used. Funds have sometimes been used for prestige projects, which impress lenders (or donors) but do little to further development. Other funds have been diverted into private use by government officials, and there are well documented examples of politicians, officials and civil servants who have accumulated personal fortunes at the expense of the development of their countries. Figure 28.10 presents a Corruption Perception Index, produced regularly by the non-governmental organisation Transparency International. Notice again how Singapore and South Korea, the tiger economies, score as being 'highly clean' – indeed, on this index Singapore was the fifth least corrupt nation in the world.

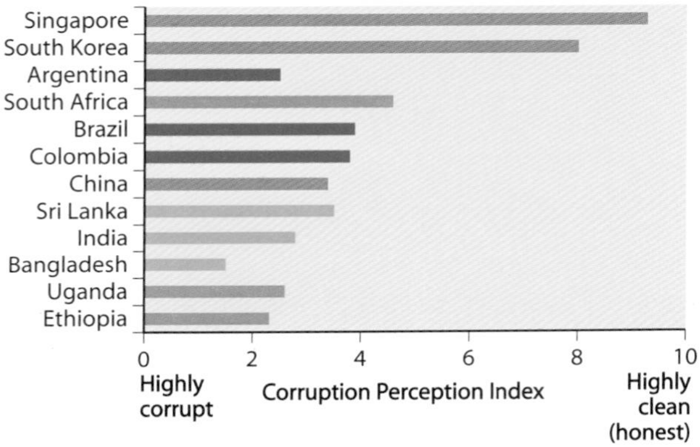

Figure 28.10
Perceptions of corruption, selected countries, 2004

Source: Transparency International (**www.transparency.org**)

There is a need to be careful with such indicators, for by its nature corruption is difficult to identify and to measure. In some countries corruption may be disguised more successfully than in others. Nonetheless, the way in which firms and governments perceive the relative state of corruption in different countries may affect their decisions on where to locate foreign direct investment or provide overseas assistance.

Tendencies towards corruption are likely to be more significant in countries where there is relatively little political stability, so that the government in power knows it will not remain in power for long. Even in the absence of corruption, this discourages such governments from taking a long-term perspective.

Where borrowed funds have not been used wisely, problems inevitably follow when it is time to make repayments on outstanding debt. The debt burden that accumulated for some countries became unsustainable and will be discussed in Chapter 30. Here it suffices to say that the need to repay debt may further limit the resources available for governments to spend on development priorities such as education, health care or infrastructure.

Relationships with more-developed countries

In the past, the now more-developed countries have benefited from the resources of today's LDCs. For example, Britain's early success was built partly on the resources of its colonies, and on protecting its own industry at the expense of those colonies. One of the main dangers for LDCs in the twenty-first century is that the more-developed countries will continue to protect their own industries and will not allow the LDCs to develop theirs. It seems clear that sub-Saharan Africa at least will not be able to promote development without the cooperation of richer countries.

Summary

- Governments in LDCs have limited resources with which to encourage a more rapid rate of economic growth and development.
- Corruption and poor governance has meant that some of the resources that have been available have not been used wisely in some LDCs.
- For LDCs to develop, more cooperation is needed from the more-developed countries.

Exercise 28.2

Looking back over the nature of the economic growth process and the obstacles to growth that have been outlined, discuss the extent to which countries in sub-Saharan Africa may be able to use the pattern of development that was so successful in East Asia to promote growth.

part 6

Chapter 29

Structural change

The previous chapter described how continued dependence on low productivity agriculture can be regarded as an obstacle to development, but explained that the potential for improving productivity in that sector was also fraught with difficulty. This discussion is now extended through an exploration of international trade policy and the possibilities for less-developed countries (LDCs) to develop alternative forms of economic activity.

Learning outcomes

After studying this chapter, you should:

- understand the need for structural transformation in economic activity in less-developed countries
- be aware of the dangers of continued reliance on exporting primary products
- be familiar with alternative approaches to trade policy
- be aware of the significance of and possibilities for industrialisation
- be familiar with the issues surrounding urbanisation in less-developed countries
- understand the potential benefits and costs associated with developing tourism in less-developed countries

The need for structural change

As earlier chapters have described, many LDCs continue to rely heavily on the agricultural sector for employment. However, low productivity in this sector may be an obstacle to improving living conditions and raising average incomes. Given their limited capacity to produce capital goods domestically, it seems vital that LDCs have a way of generating a flow of foreign exchange through exporting activity.

If productivity and real incomes in the agricultural sector cannot be readily improved, this suggests that LDCs should try to transform the structure of their economic activity, and look for new income-earning opportunities. This could entail moving into manufacturing industry, or perhaps developing some service-sector activities such as tourism that could generate a flow of foreign exchange and increase real incomes.

Trade in primary products

Chapter 2 introduced the law of comparative advantage, which argues that countries may gain from trade by specialising in the production of goods and services in which they have a comparative advantage. For LDCs such comparative advantage almost inevitably lies in the production of labour- and/or land-intensive goods. LDCs tend to have relatively abundant natural resources and labour, but scarce capital. This pattern determines the nature of their comparative advantage.

However, it is now being argued that LDCs should try to reduce their reliance on primary production and develop new activities. It is clearly important to investigate how these two different arguments can be reconciled — in other words, to explore why it is that LDCs cannot continue to rely on their existing comparative advantage.

It is worth noting that some countries are heavily dependent not just on primary products in general, but on a very narrow range of primary products — in some cases a single commodity. Figure 29.1 shows the extent to which some countries rely on a narrow range of commodities. This dependence creates a situation of great vulnerability if the markets for those commodities are not stable. It must be remembered that most LDCs are relatively small players in international markets, so may have little or no influence over price.

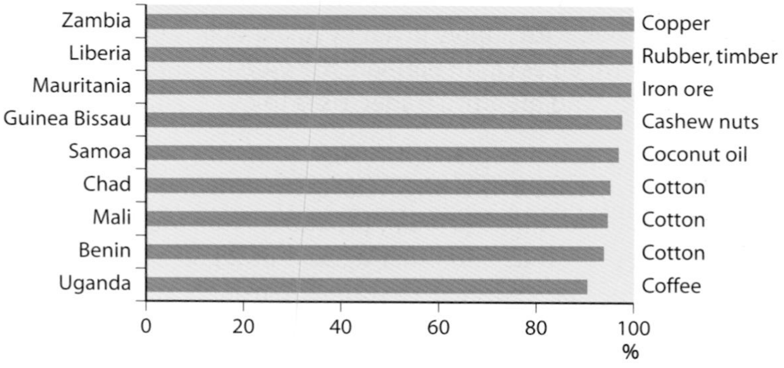

Figure 29.1 *Dependence on non-fuel primary commodity exports (as a percentage of total merchandise exports)*

Source: WTO, *World Trade Report 2003*.

There are two ways in which LDCs have been affected by the pattern of their comparative advantage in the conduct of international trade. These relate to the short-run and long-run movements in relative prices — the **terms of trade**.

Suppose that both export and import prices are rising through time, but import prices are rising more rapidly than export prices. This means that the ratio of export to import prices will fall — which in turn means that a country must export a greater volume of its goods in order to acquire the same volume of imports. In other words, a fall in the terms of trade makes a country worse off.

Key term

terms of trade: the ratio of export prices to import prices

Example

Consider a simple example of how a deterioration in the terms of trade may affect a country. Suppose a country imports 100 000 units of a manufactured good each year and that the price in year 1 is £1. In order to pay for these imported goods, the country exports 100 000 units of agricultural goods, which are also priced at £1 per unit in year 1. In year 2 the country still wants to buy 100 000 units of imported manufactures, but finds that the price has risen to £1.08 per unit. Furthermore, the price of its exported agricultural goods has fallen to 90p.

The terms of trade are calculated as the ratio of export prices to import prices. In year 1 this is $100 \times 1/1 = 100$. However, in year 2 the calculation is $100 \times 0.90/1.08 = 75$. There has thus been an appreciable deterioration in the terms of trade.

The effects of this can be seen in the volume of exports that are now needed for the country to maintain its volume of imports. In order to buy its 100 000 units of imports, the country now needs to export $100\,000 \times 1.08/0.9 = 120\,000$ units of exports.

One problem faced by LDCs that export primary products is that they are each too small as individual exporters to be able to influence the world price of their products. They must accept the prices that are set in world commodity markets.

Short-run volatility

In the case of agricultural goods, demand tends to be relatively stable over time but supply can be volatile, varying with weather and climatic conditions from season to season. Figure 29.2 shows a typical market in two periods. In period 1 the global harvest of this commodity is poor, with supply given by S_1: equilibrium is achieved with price at P_1 and quantity traded at Q_1. In period 2 the global harvest is high at S_2, so that prices plummet to P_2 and quantity traded rises to Q_2.

Notice that in this case the movement of prices is relatively strong compared with the variation in quantity. This reflects the price elasticity of demand, which is expected to be relatively inelastic for many primary products. From the consumers' point of view, the demand for foodstuffs and other agricultural goods will tend to be inelastic, as demand will not be expected to respond strongly to changes in prices.

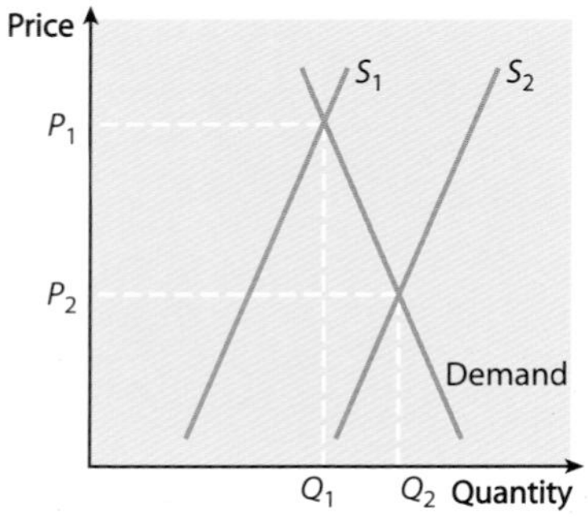

Figure 29.2 Volatility in supply

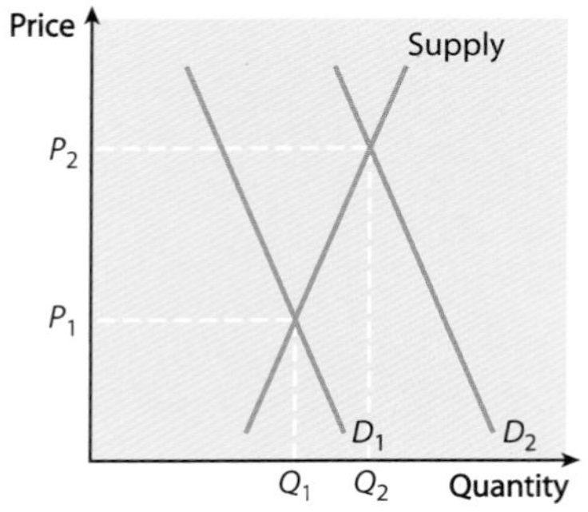

Figure 29.3 Volatility in demand

For many minerals and raw materials, however, the picture is different. For such commodities supply tends to be stable over time, but demand fluctuates with the business cycle in developed countries, which are the importers of raw materials. Figure 29.3 illustrates this. At the trough of the business cycle demand is low, at D_1, and so the equilibrium price will also be low, at P_1. At the peak of the cycle demand is more buoyant, at D_2, and price is relatively high at P_2.

From an individual LDC's point of view, the result is the same: the country faces volatility in the prices of its exports. From this perspective it does not matter whether the instability arises from the supply side of the market or from the demand side. The problem is that prices can rise and fall quite independently of conditions within the domestic economy.

Instability of prices also means instability of export revenues, so if the country is relying on export earnings to fund its development path, import capital equipment or meet its debt repayments, such volatility in earnings can constitute a severe problem.

Long-run deterioration

The nature of the demand for primary products may be expected to influence the long-run path of relative prices. In particular, the income elasticity of demand is an important consideration. As real incomes rise in the developed countries, the demand for agricultural goods can be expected to rise relatively slowly. Ernst Engel pointed out that at relatively high income levels the proportion of expenditure devoted to foodstuffs tends to fall and the demand for luxury goods rises. This would suggest that the demand for agricultural goods shifts relatively slowly through time.

In the case of raw materials, there have been advances in the development of artificial substitutes for many commodities used in manufacturing. Furthermore, technology has changed over time, improving the efficiency with which inputs can be converted into outputs. This has weakened the demand for raw materials produced by LDCs.

Furthermore, if some LDCs are successful in boosting output of these goods, there will be an increase in supply over time. Figure 29.4 shows the result of such an increase. Suppose that the market begins with demand at D_0 and supply at S_0. Market equilibrium results in a price of P_0 and quantity of Q_0. As time goes by, demand moves to the right a little to D_1, and supply shifts to S_1. The result is a fall in the price of the commodity to P_1.

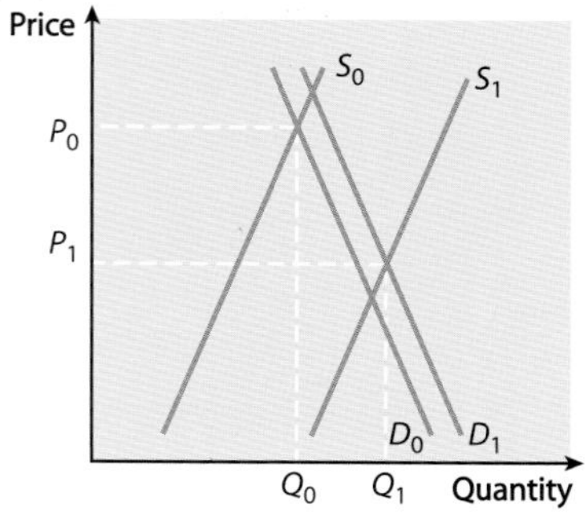

Figure 29.4 Long-term movements of demand and supply

It is thus clear that, not only may LDCs experience short-run volatility in prices, but the terms of trade may also deteriorate in the long run. Indeed, some of these arguments were advanced by Raul Prebisch and Hans Singer in the early 1950s. These economists produced

some empirical evidence to support their arguments, suggesting that the terms of trade had moved in favour of manufactured goods over a long period of time. Figure 29.5 provides some more recent evidence on this situation, showing the relative price of non-fuel primary commodities (compared with manufactured goods) during the twentieth century. You can see that the long-run trend is downwards.

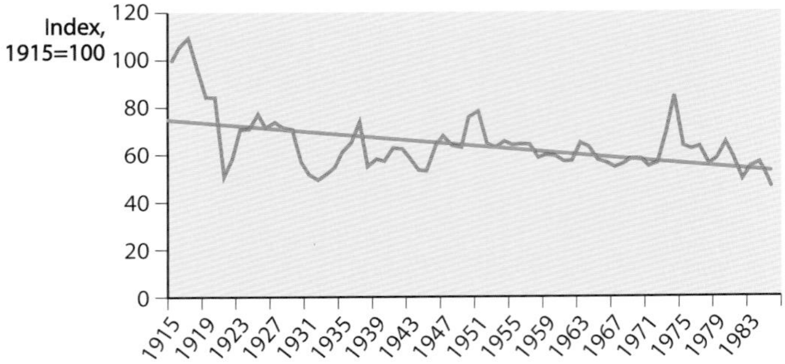

Figure 29.5 Index of the price of non-fuel primary commodities relative to manufactured goods, 1915–85

Source: Enzo Grilli and Maw Cheng Yang, *World Bank Economic Review*, January 1988.

Summary

- The pattern of existing comparative advantage suggests that LDCs should specialise in the production of primary commodities such as agricultural goods, minerals or other raw materials.
- However, the prices of such goods tend to be volatile in the short run, varying from year to year as a result of instability arising from either the supply side or from the demand side.
- Furthermore, the nature of demand for such products and the development of artificial substitutes for some raw materials may be expected to lead to a long-run deterioration in the terms of trade for primary producers.
- These factors will limit the extent to which LDCs benefit from international trade in primary commodities.

Trade policy

If a country is short of foreign exchange, there are two broad approaches that it can take in drawing up its trade policy to deal with the problem. One is to reduce its reliance on imports in order to economise on the need for foreign currency — in other words, to produce goods at home that it previously imported. This is known as an **import substitution** policy.

An alternative possibility is to try to earn more foreign exchange through **export promotion**.

Key terms

import substitution: policy entailing the encouragement of domestic production of goods previously imported in order to reduce the need for foreign exchange

export promotion: policy entailing the encouragement of domestic firms to export more goods in order to earn foreign exchange

Import substitution

The import substitution strategy has had some

appeal for a number of countries. The idea is to boost domestic production of goods that were previously imported, thereby saving foreign exchange. A typical policy instrument used to achieve this is the imposition of a **tariff**.

Key term

tariff: a tax imposed on imported goods

Figure 29.6 shows how a tariff is expected to operate. D represents the domestic demand for a commodity, and S_{dom} shows how much domestic producers are prepared to supply at any given price. The price at which the good can be imported from world markets is given by P_w. So in the absence of a tariff domestic demand is given by D_0, of which S_0 is supplied within the domestic economy and the remainder ($D_0 - S_0$) is imported. If domestic producers can be encouraged to produce more of this good, then the country may be able to save foreign exchange, as less will need to be imported.

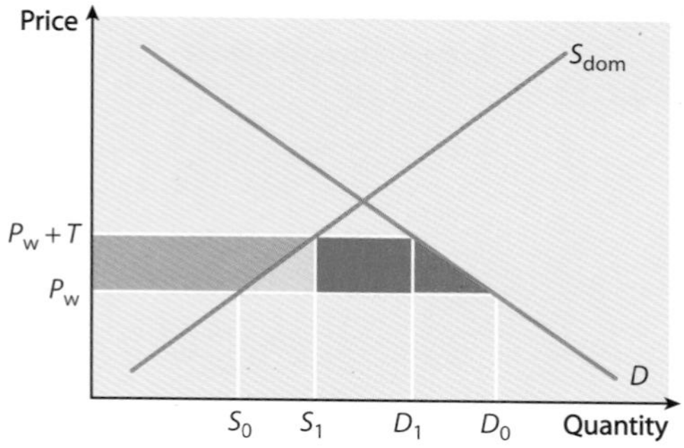

Figure 29.6
The effects of a tariff

If the government imposes a tariff, the domestic price rises to $P_w + T$, where T is the amount of the tariff. This has two key effects. One is to reduce the demand for the good from D_0 to D_1. The second is to encourage domestic producers to expand their output of this good, from S_0 to S_1. As a consequence imports fall substantially, to $D_1 - S_1$. On the face of it, the policy has achieved its objective of encouraging domestic producers to produce goods that were previously imported, so that the need for foreign exchange is reduced. Furthermore, the government has been able to raise some tax revenue (shown by the green rectangle).

However, not all the effects of the tariff are favourable for the economy. Consumers are certainly worse off, as they have to pay a higher price for the good. They will therefore consume less, so there will be a loss of consumer surplus. Some of what was formerly consumer surplus will now be redistributed to others in society. The government gains the tariff revenue, as mentioned. In addition, producers gain economic rent, given by the dark blue area in the figure. There is also a deadweight loss to society, represented by the red and pale blue triangles. In other words, overall, society is worse off as a result of the tariff.

Effectively, the government is subsidising inefficient local producers, and forcing domestic consumers to pay a price that is above that of the good if imported from abroad.

Some would defend this policy on the grounds that it allows the LDC to protect an infant industry. In other words, through such encouragement and protection, the new industry will eventually become sufficiently efficient to compete in world markets.

There are two key problems with this argument. First, unless the domestic market is sufficiently large for the industry to reap economies of scale, local producers will never be in a position to compete globally. Second, because of such protection domestic firms are never exposed to international competition, and so will not have an incentive to improve their efficiency. In other words, tariff protection fosters an inward-looking attitude among local producers that discourages them from trying to compete in world markets. They remain happy with the protection that provides them with economic rent.

Export promotion

Export promotion requires a more dynamic and outward-looking approach, as domestic producers need to be able to compete with producers already established in world markets. The choice of which products to promote is critical, as it is important that the LDC develops a new pattern of comparative advantage if it is to benefit from an export promotion strategy.

For primary producers, a tempting strategy is one that begins with existing products and tries to move along the production chain. For example, in 1997 (under encouragement from the World Bank) Mozambique launched a project whereby, instead of exporting raw cashew nuts, it would establish processing plants that would then allow it to export roasted cashew nuts. In the early 1970s Mozambique was the largest producer of cashew nuts in the world, but by the late 1990s the activity had stagnated, and the country had been overtaken by producers in Brazil and India.

By the late 1990s Mozambique had been overtaken by cashew nut producers in Brazil and India.

This would seem to have been a good idea, because it makes use of existing products and moves the industry into higher value-added activity. However, the project ran into a series of problems. On the one hand, there were internal constraints: processing the nuts requires capital equipment and skilled labour, neither of which was in plentiful supply in Mozambique. In addition, tariff rates on processed commodities are higher than on raw materials, so the producers faced more barriers to trade. In addition, they found that they were trying to break into a market that was dominated by a few large existing producers which were reluctant to share the market. Furthermore, the technical standards required to sell processed cashew nuts were beyond the capability of the newly established local firms.

These are just some of the difficulties that face new producers from LDCs wanting to compete in world markets. Indeed, the setting of high technical specifications for imported products is one way in which countries have tried to protect their own domestic producers — it is an example of a **non-tariff barrier**.

Key term

non-tariff barrier: an obstacle to free trade other than a tariff, e.g. quality standards imposed on imported products

The East Asian tiger economies pursued export promotion strategies, making sure that their exchange rates supported the competitiveness of their products and that their labour was appropriately priced. However, it must be remembered that the tiger economies expanded into export-led growth at a time when world trade itself was booming, and when the developed countries were beginning to move out of labour-intensive activities, thereby creating a niche to be filled by the tigers. If many other countries had expanded their exports at the same time, it is not at all certain that they could all have been successful.

As time goes by, it becomes more difficult for other countries to follow this policy. It is particularly difficult for countries that originally chose import substitution, because the inward-looking attitudes fostered by such policies become so deeply entrenched.

It should also be remembered that there will always be dangers in trying to develop new kinds of economic activity that may entail sacrificing comparative advantage. This is not to say that LDCs should remain primary producers for ever, but it does suggest that it is important to select the new forms of activity with care in order to exploit a *potential* comparative advantage.

Summary

- In designing a trade policy, an LDC may choose to go for import substitution, nurturing infant industries behind protectionist barriers in order to allow them to produce domestically goods that were formerly imported.
- However, such infant industries rarely seem to grow up, leaving the LDC with inefficient producers which are unable to compete effectively with world producers.
- Export promotion requires a more dynamic and outward-looking approach, and a careful choice of new activities.

Exercise 29.1

Discuss the relative merits of import substitution and export promotion as a trade strategy. Under what conditions might import substitution have a chance of success?

Industrialisation

So what are the prospects for a country wanting to move towards **industrialisation**, and to reduce its reliance on primary production?

> **Key term**
>
> **industrialisation:** a process of transforming an economy by expanding manufacturing and other industrial activity

In an influential paper in 1954, Sir Arthur Lewis argued that agriculture in many LDCs was characterised by surplus labour. Perhaps farms were operated on a household basis, with the work, and the crop, being shared out between members of the household. If there was not enough work to

be done by all the members of the household, then, although all seemed to be employed, there would in fact be hidden unemployment, or underemployment. Given the size of the rural population and its rapid growth, there could be almost unlimited surplus labour existing in this way.

Lewis then pointed out that it would be possible to transfer such surplus labour into the industrial sector without a loss of agricultural output, as the remaining labour would be able to take up the slack. All that would be necessary would be for the industrial sector to set a wage sufficiently higher than the rural wage to persuade workers to transfer. Industry could then reap profits that could be re-invested to allow industry to expand, without any need for the industrial wage to be pulled upwards to cause inflation.

Unfortunately, the process did not prove to be as smooth as Lewis suggested. One reason relates to human capital levels. Agricultural workers do not have the skills or training that prepare them for employment in the industrial sector, so it is not so straightforward to transfer them from agricultural to industrial work.

Furthermore, to the extent that they were able to transfer, the expanding industry did not always reinvest the surplus in order to enable continuous expansion of the industrial sector. Foreign firms tended to repatriate the profits (as will be seen in Chapter 30), and in any case tended to use modern, relatively capital-intensive technology that did not require a large pool of unskilled labour.

Perhaps more seriously, Lewis's model encouraged governments to think in terms of industry-led growth, and to neglect the rural sector. This meant that agricultural productivity often remained low, and inequality between urban and rural areas grew.

Urbanisation

A natural result of the perceived disparity in living conditions between urban and rural areas was to encourage migration from the villages to the towns, a process known as **urbanisation**.

Migration occurs in response to a number of factors. One is the attraction of the 'bright lights' of the cities — people in rural areas perceive urban areas as offering better access to education and healthcare facilities, and better recreational opportunities. Perhaps more important are the economic gains to be made from migrating to the cities, in terms of the wage differential between urban and rural areas.

Key term

urbanisation: process whereby an increasing proportion of the population comes to live in cities

Urban wages tend to be higher for a number of reasons. Employment in the manufacturing or service sectors typically offers higher wages, in contrast to the low productivity and wages in the agricultural sector. Furthermore, labour in the urban areas tends to be better organised, and governments have often introduced minimum wage legislation and social protection for workers in the urban areas — especially where they rely on them for electoral support.

A township on the outskirts of Cape Town — urbanisation results when rural populations are lured to cities in search of work.

Such wage differentials attract a flow of migrants to the cities. However, in practice there may not be sufficient jobs available, as the new and growing sectors typically do not expand sufficiently quickly to absorb all the migrating workers. The net result of this is that rural workers exchange poor living conditions in the rural areas for unemployment in the urban environment.

This can be partly regarded as an *externality* effect. Consider Figure 29.7. Here *MPB* represents the marginal private benefit that migrants expect to gain from moving to the cities. *MPC* represents the marginal private costs that migrants face in relocating. Thus, people will migrate up to the point Q_0. However, migrants impose costs on other urban dwellers, in terms of congestion, pollution, noise and perhaps in the rise of shanty towns that allow disease to spread. In other words, there are externality effects on other urban residents, and marginal social costs (*MSC*) are higher than the private costs perceived by migrants. As a result, society would prefer to be at Q^* in terms of city size.

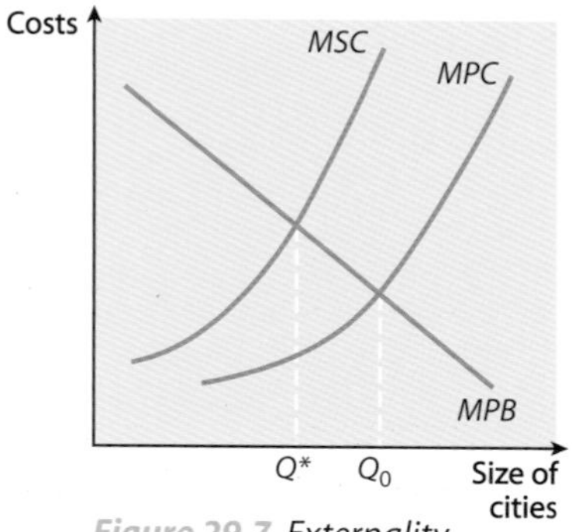

Figure 29.7 Externality effect of migration

Figure 29.8 shows the rate of migration since 1975, and projected to 2015, in a range of countries.

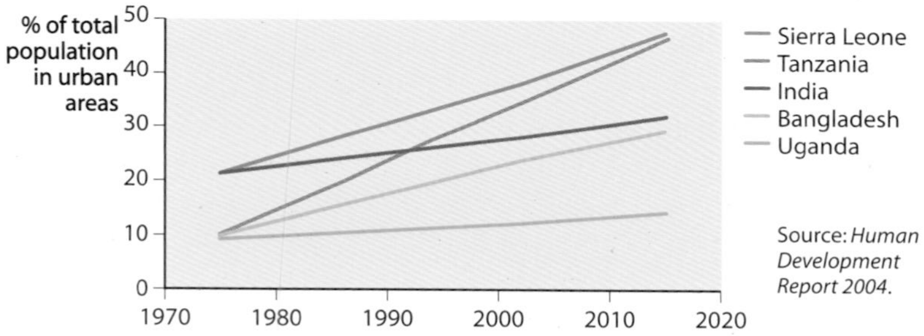

Figure 29.8 Urbanisation in LDCs, selected countries, 1975–2015 (projected)

For example, in Tanzania the percentage of the population living in the urban areas was just 10.1% in 1975, but is projected to rise to 46.8% in 2015. The pressure on urban infrastructure from such a change is substantial.

Furthermore, as employment in the newer sectors cannot expand at such a rate, the result is an expansion of the *informal sector*. Migrants to the city who cannot find work are forced to find other forms of employment, as most LDCs do not have well-developed social security protection. The cities of many LDCs are therefore characterised by substantial amounts of informal activity, as was explained in Chapter 26. The scale of the informal sector can be seen in Figure 29.9 – you can see that in Ghana more than 80% of employment in the urban areas is made up of informal activity.

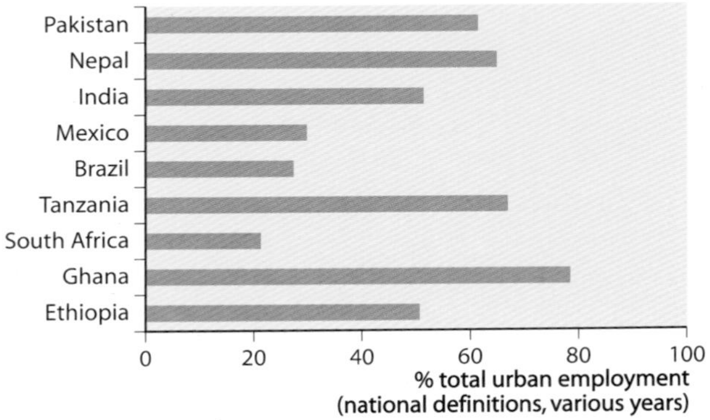

Figure 29.9 The urban informal sector, selected countries

Source: International Labour Office.

Tourism

The analysis so far suggests that LDCs need to diversify away from primary production and into new activities that do not require large amounts of capital, preferably involving the production of goods or services that can earn foreign exchange and that have a high income elasticity of demand. On the face of it, tourism would seem to fit the bill.

In the first place, the income elasticity of demand for tourism is strongly positive. This means that, as real incomes rise in the more-developed countries, there will be an increase in the demand for tourism. Within the domestic economy in the LDC, the development of the tourist sector will have an impact on employment. In the early stages there will be a demand for construction workers, and later there will be jobs in hotels and in transport and other services. Tourism is also the sort of activity that is likely to have large multiplier effects on the domestic economy. The World Bank has reported that visitor expenditures outside the hotel sector can range from half to nearly double the in-hotel spending. In addition, there is likely to be scope for small labour-intensive craft-based activities to sell goods to foreigners without actually having to go into the export business – because the tourists come to the producers. Tourism may also attract foreign direct investment if international hotel chains move in to cater for the visiting tourists.

Tourism will require an improvement in the country's infrastructure. For example, it may require road improvements, and upgraded transport and communications facilities. However, such facilities not only help the tourist sector, but also generate externality effects, in the sense that local businesses (and residents) benefit from the improvements as well.

Another potentially important aspect of tourism from the government's perspective is that it may generate a flow of tax revenue. This may come partly from taxes on goods and services, but also from airport taxes and landing fees.

As usual, however, there is a potential downside as well. Tourists will also demand goods that cannot be produced locally, so there may be a need to increase imports, adding to the current account deficit on the balance of payments. This may be reinforced by the outflow of profits from the foreign direct investment. In addition, there may be negative externality effects arising from the erosion of the environment. And tourists exhibit different lifestyles, which may alter the aspirations of the local population, and encourage the consumption of inappropriate (and perhaps imported) products.

It is also important to keep opportunity costs in mind. The development of any new activity entails the sacrifice of some alternative. In deciding to develop tourism, some other option will have to be forgone. For example, resources that are used to improve the transport and communications infrastructure cannot be used to improve education or healthcare. Of course, tourism may prove to be so successful that it will generate resources that can be devoted to education or healthcare, but it is not an issue that can be ignored in the present.

Case study Tanzania

Tanzania is among the lowest-income countries in the world. It is located in sub-Saharan Africa, and relies heavily on agriculture for employment, income and export earnings. In 2001, 84% of its merchandise exports consisted of primary goods, and the terms of trade had declined to 44 based on 1980 = 100. Could Tanzania benefit from tourism?

In its favour, Tanzania has a rich wildlife and the potential to offer safari holidays, so there are resources that could attract foreign visitors. However, how widespread would the benefits from tourism be in the society?

Traditionally, the farmers that work the fields on the outskirts of Tanzania's capital city, Dar es Salaam, sold their produce in the outdoor markets in the city. This entailed an early start to the day, and a trek to the city over poor paths and roads, with the farm produce loaded on to bicycles. In 2001 the Royal Palm Hotel in Dar es Salaam was taken over by new management, which needed a regular supply of fresh vegetables and flowers to serve its guests. It was decided to obtain these by sending a truck into the villages to buy produce directly from the farmers. This meant that the hotel got its produce fresh from the fields, and that the farmers had a new and more convenient market in which to sell their produce. This is one example of how the multiplier effect can extend the benefits from tourism beyond those directly affected.

The story about the farmers was taken from a World Bank website, **www.miga.org**.

Summary

- Sir Arthur Lewis argued that the agricultural sectors in many LDCs are characterised by surplus labour, which could be transferred into the manufacturing and service sectors and thus generate structural change and economic growth.
- However, this process has not been as smooth as Lewis predicted, and in some cases has led to rural neglect and a bias of resources towards the urban areas.
- Migration to the cities has been a feature of many LDCs in recent years, bringing negative externality effects.
- Tourism has been recommended as a potentially profitable area for LDCs to develop, but here again there may be costs as well as benefits.

Exercise 29.2

Identify the factors that an LDC should take into account if planning to change its pattern of comparative advantage by developing new economic activities.

part 6

Chapter 30

Mobilising external resources for development

The previous chapters dealing with economic development have frequently referred to the limited resources that are available within less-developed countries (LDCs), which has constrained attempts to stimulate economic growth and development. If domestic resources are lacking, it is important to consider the alternative possibility of mobilising resources from outside the country. This can be done by attracting foreign direct investment, accepting overseas assistance or borrowing on international capital markets. This chapter reviews these possibilities, and also considers the role of the World Bank, the International Monetary Fund (IMF) and the World Trade Organisation (WTO).

Learning outcomes

After studying this chapter, you should:

- be aware of the need for less-developed countries to mobilise external resources for development
- understand the benefits and costs associated with foreign direct investment
- be familiar with the potential use of overseas assistance for promoting development, and the effectiveness of such flows of funds in the past
- be aware of the possible use of borrowing to obtain funds for development and its dangers
- understand the role of the Bretton Woods institutions in international development
- be familiar with Structural Adjustment Programmes and the HIPC initiative

The role of external resources in development

The shortage of resources in many LDCs has been a severe obstacle to their economic growth and development. This was emphasised by the Harrod–Domar model of economic growth which was introduced in Chapter 27. Figure 30.1 offers a reminder.

The underlying process by which growth can take place requires the generation of a flow of savings that can be transformed into investment in order to generate an increase in capital, which in turn enlarges the productive capacity of the economy. This then enables output and incomes to grow, which in turn feeds back into savings and allows the process to become self-sustaining.

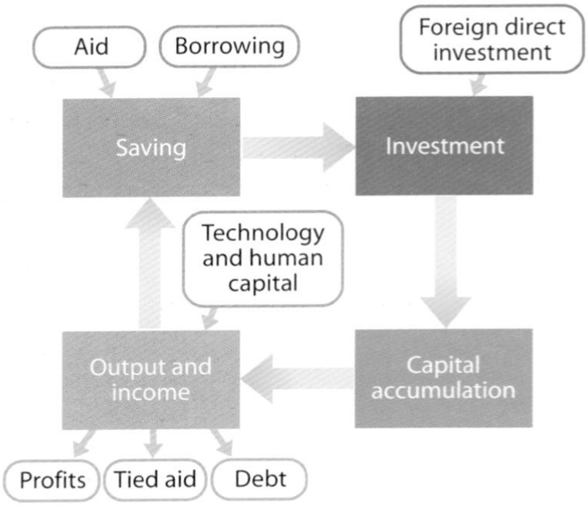

Figure 30.1 The Harrod–Domar process of economic development

However, the process will break down if savings are inadequate, or if markets do not operate sufficiently well to maintain the chain. This chapter considers the possibility that the process could be initiated by an inflow of resources from outside the economy. There are three possible routes to be examined: foreign direct investment, overseas aid and international borrowing. As Figure 30.1 indicates, associated with each of these inflows there are likely to be some costs, and potential leakages from the system.

Foreign direct investment

One possible source of external funding that has been attractive to many LDCs is **foreign direct investment (FDI)**. This entails encouraging foreign **multinational corporations (MNCs)** to set up part of their production in an LDC.

In evaluating the potential impact of MNCs operating in LDCs, it is important to consider the characteristics of such companies. Many operate on a large scale, often having an annual turnover that exceeds the less-developed country's GDP. They tend to have their origins in the developed countries, although some LDCs are now beginning to develop their own MNCs.

> **Key terms**
>
> **foreign direct investment (FDI):** investment undertaken by foreign companies
>
> **multinational corporation (MNC):** a company whose production activities are carried out in a number of different countries

MNCs are in business to make profits, and it can be assumed that their motivation is to maximise global after-tax profits. While they may operate in globally oligopolistic markets, they may have monopoly power within the LDCs in which they locate. They operate in a wide variety of different product markets — some are in primary production (Geest, Del Monte, BP), some are in manufacturing (General Motors, Mitsubishi) and some are in tertiary activity (McDonald's). These characteristics are important in shaping the analysis of the likely benefits and costs of attracting FDI into an LDC.

MNCs have three basic motivations for locating in another country:

1. market-seeking
2. resource-seeking
3. efficiency-seeking

Some MNCs may engage in FDI because they want to sell their products in a particular market, and find it preferable to produce within the market rather than elsewhere: such FDI is *market seeking*. Other MNCs may undertake investment in a country in order to take advantage of some key resource – say, a natural resource such as oil or natural gas, or a labour force with certain skills, or simply cheap unskilled labour: such FDI is *resource seeking*. Still other MNCs may simply review their options globally and decide that they can produce most efficiently in a particular location, which might entail locating a part of their production chain in a certain country. Such FDI is *efficiency seeking*.

To set a context for the discussion, Figure 30.2 shows the relative size of net FDI inflows for the set of countries selected previously. This reveals a very uneven pattern, with Bangladesh receiving only 0.1% of GDP as inflows of FDI and Singapore receiving 7%.

In some ways this chart is misleading, as it conceals the true size of FDI inflows into China. Remember that China's GDP is very large, so almost 4% of China's GDP represents a very substantial flow of investment. Some of this is market-seeking, as the opening up of China's market of 1.3 billion people is a major attraction. However, it may also be partly resource seeking, with MNCs wanting to take advantage of China's resource of labour.

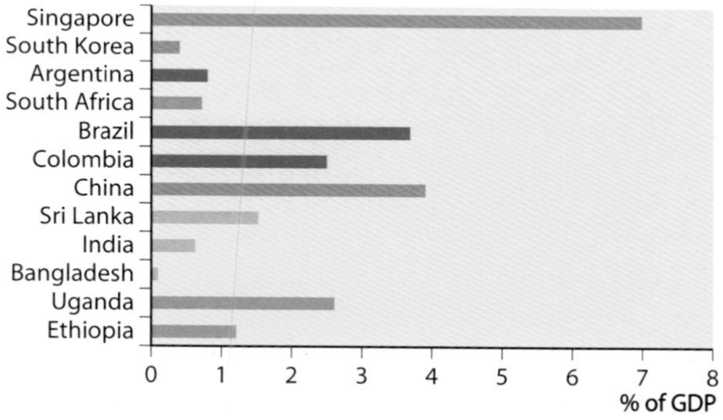

Figure 30.2
Net foreign direct investment inflows, selected countries, 2002

Source: *Human Development Report 2004.*

Potential benefits

Perhaps the prime motivation for attracting FDI inflows for LDCs is the injection they provide into the Harrod–Domar chain of development. In addition to providing investment, MNCs are likely to supply capital and technology, thereby helping to remedy the LDC's limited capacity to produce capital goods. They may also assist with the development of the country's human capital, by providing training and skills development for the workers they employ, together with management expertise and entrepreneurial skills, all of which may be lacking in the LDC.

LDCs may also hope that the MNC will provide much needed modern-sector jobs by employing local workers. Given the rate of migration to the urban areas discussed in Chapter 29, such employment could be invaluable to the LDC, where employment cannot keep up with the rapid growth of the labour force.

The LDC government may also expect to be able to collect tax revenues, both directly from the MNC in the form of a tax on profits and indirectly from taxes on the workers' employment incomes. Moreover, the MNC will export its products, and thus generate a flow of foreign exchange for the LDC.

In time, there may also be spillover effects. As local workers learn new skills and gain management expertise and knowledge about technology, they may be able to benefit local firms if at some stage they leave the MNC and take up jobs with local companies – or use their new-found knowledge to start their own businesses. These externality effects can be significant in some cases.

Potential costs

In evaluating the potential benefits of FDI, however, LDCs may need to temper their enthusiasm a little, as there may be some costs associated with attracting MNCs to locate within their borders. This would certainly be the case if the anti-globalisation protesters are to be believed, as they have accused the MNCs of exploiting their strength and market power in order to damage the LDCs in various ways.

LDCs entice multinational companies to their shores, in the hope of promoting development — a hope not always fulfilled.

In examining such costs, it is important to be objective and to try to reach a balanced view of the matter, and to be aware that some of the accusations made by the critics of globalisation may have been overstated. On the other hand, it is also important to remember that MNCs are profit-making firms, and not humanitarian organisations seeking to promote justice and equality.

A first point to note is that, because most MNCs originate in more-developed countries, they tend to use technology that suits the conditions with which they are familiar. In many cases these will tend to be relatively capital-intensive, which may not be wholly appropriate for LDC factor endowments. One upshot of this is that the employment effects may not be substantial, or may be limited to relatively low-skilled jobs.

It is dangerous to generalise here. The sort of technology that MNCs tend to use may be entirely suitable for a country like Singapore, which has progressed to the stage where it needs hi-tech capital-intensive activity to match its well-trained and disciplined workforce. However, such technology would not be appropriate in much of sub-Saharan Africa. But MNCs are surely aware of such considerations when taking decisions about where to locate. A decision to set up production in China may be partly market oriented, but efficiency considerations will also affect the choice of technology.

An important consideration is whether the MNC will make use of local labour. It might hire local unskilled labour, but use expatriate skilled workers and managers. This would tend to reduce the employment and spillover effects of the MNC presence. Another possibility is that the MNC may pay wages that are higher than necessary in order to maintain a good public image, and to attract the best local workers. (You might like to read the section of Chapter 23 on the *efficiency wage* on pages 334–35. The argument for firms paying a higher wage than needed is an efficiency wage argument.) This is fine for the workers lucky enough to be employed at a high wage, but it can make life difficult for local firms if they cannot hold on to their best workers.

In addition, the LDC government's desire for tax revenue may not be fully met. In seeking to attract MNCs to locate within their borders, LDCs may find that they need to offer tax holidays or concessions as a 'carrot'. This will clearly limit the tax revenue benefits that the LDC will receive. It is also possible that MNCs can manipulate their balance sheets in order to minimise their tax liability. A high proportion of the transactions undertaken by an MNC are internal to the firm. Thus, it may be possible to set prices for internal transactions that ensure that profits are taken in the lowest tax locations. This process is known as *transfer pricing*. It is not strictly legal, but is difficult to monitor.

As far as the foreign exchange earnings are concerned, a key issue is whether the MNC will recycle its surplus within the LDC or repatriate its profits to its shareholders elsewhere in the world. If the latter is the case, this will limit the extent to which the LDC will benefit from the increase in exports. However, at least the MNC will be able to market its products internationally, and if the country becomes better known as a result then, again, there may be spillovers for local firms. Gaining credibility and the knowledge to sell in the global market is problematic for LDCs, and this is one area in which there may be definite benefits from the MNC presence.

The LDC should also be aware that the MNC may use its market power within the country to maximise profits. Local competitors will find it difficult to compete, and the MNC may be able to restrict output and raise price. In addition, MNCs have been accused of taking advantage of more lax environmental regulations, polluting the environment to keep their costs low. The actions of the anti-globalisation protesters in this area may have influenced MNCs to clean up their act somewhat.

Finally, MNCs tend to locate in urban areas in LDCs — unless they are purely resource seeking, in which case they may be forced to locate near the supply of whatever natural resource they are seeking. Locating in the urban areas may increase the rural–urban inequality discussed in Chapter 29, and encourage an even greater rate of migration.

Exercise 30.1

Draw up a list of the benefits and costs of MNC involvement in an LDC, and evaluate the benefits relative to the costs. Remember that many LDCs are enthusiastic about attracting MNCs to locate in their countries. Try to identify which are the most important benefits that they are looking for.

Given the need to evaluate the benefits and costs of FDI flows, it is important that LDC governments can negotiate good deals with the MNCs. For example, countries such as Indonesia have negotiated conditions on the share of local workers that

will be employed by the MNC after a period of, say, 5 years. This helps to ensure that the benefits are not entirely dissipated. Of course, it helps if the LDC has some key resource that the MNC cannot readily acquire elsewhere. There is some recent evidence that high levels of human capital help to attract FDI flows, which may help to explain why East Asia and China have been recipients of more FDI inflows than countries in sub-Saharan Africa.

Summary

- Multinational corporations (MNCs) are companies whose production activities are carried out in more than one country.
- Foreign direct investment (FDI) by MNCs is one way in which an LDC may be able to attract external resources.
- MNCs may be motivated by markets, resources or cost effectiveness.
- LDCs hope to benefit from FDI in a wide range of ways, including capital, technology, employment, human capital, tax revenues and foreign exchange. There may also be spillover effects.
- However, MNCs may operate in ways that do not maximise these benefits.

Overseas assistance

If LDCs could enter a phase of economic growth and rising incomes, one result would be an increase in world trade. This would benefit nations around the world, and the more-developed industrial countries would be likely to see an increase in the market for their products. This might be a reason for the governments of more-developed countries to help LDCs with the growth and development of their economies. Of course, there may also be a humanitarian motive for providing assistance, i.e. to reduce global inequality.

Indeed, there may be market failure arguments for providing aid. For example, it may be that governments have better information about the riskiness of projects in LDCs than private firms have. In relation to the provision of education and healthcare, it was argued earlier that there may be externality effects involved. However, LDC governments may not have the resources needed to provide sufficient education for their citizens. Similarly, it was argued that some infrastructure may have public good characteristics that require intervention.

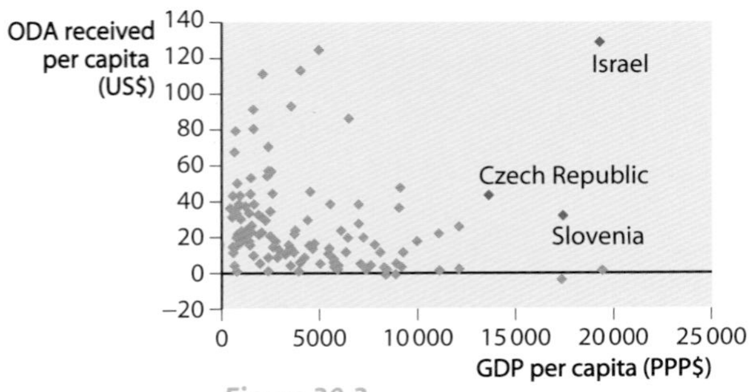

Figure 30.3
ODA and GDP per capita, 2000

Official aid is known as **overseas development assistance (ODA)**, and is provided through the Development Assistance Committee of the OECD. Figure 30.3 shows the relationship between the amount of ODA received per capita and GDP per capita in 2000. It suggests that humanitarian motives are not always paramount in

Key term

overseas development assistance: aid provided to LDCs by countries in the OECD

determining the recipients of aid. In particular, the fact that Israel receives more ODA per person than any other country, in spite of being a high-income country, suggests a political motivation. Israel actually receives more ODA as a percentage of GDP than India. Indeed, there has been much criticism of the USA over many years for the way in which aid has been used to favour countries that have been important in US foreign policy.

A contentious issue is whether ODA should be channelled to those countries most in need of it, or focused on those countries best equipped to make good use of the funding. If humanitarian motives are uppermost, then you would expect there to be a strong relationship between flows of overseas assistance and average income levels. However, if other motives are important, this relationship might be less apparent.

Figure 30.4 shows the top ten recipients of aid in terms of US dollars. Countries in the UNDP's 'low human development' category are coloured green in this figure. You need to be careful in interpreting these data, as measuring in US$ terms does not take account of differing country sizes. For this reason Figure 30.5 may be more useful. This chart shows the extent to which countries are dependent on overseas assistance by expressing receipts of ODA relative to the country's investment. Again, 'low human development' countries are coloured green. This gives a different picture, and emphasises the extent to which low human development countries rely on flows of overseas assistance.

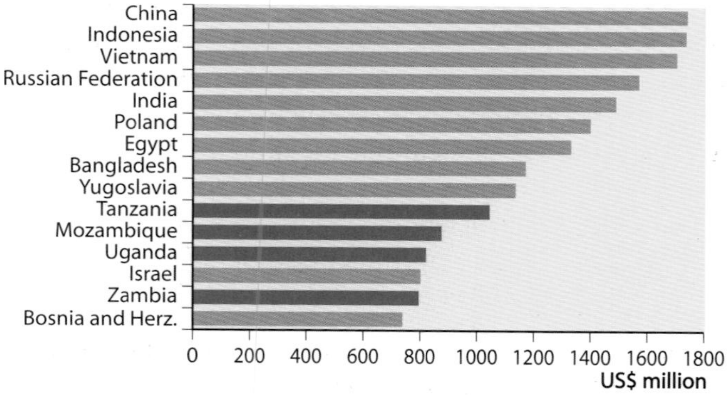

Figure 30.4
Top ten recipients of aid, 2000

Source: OECD.

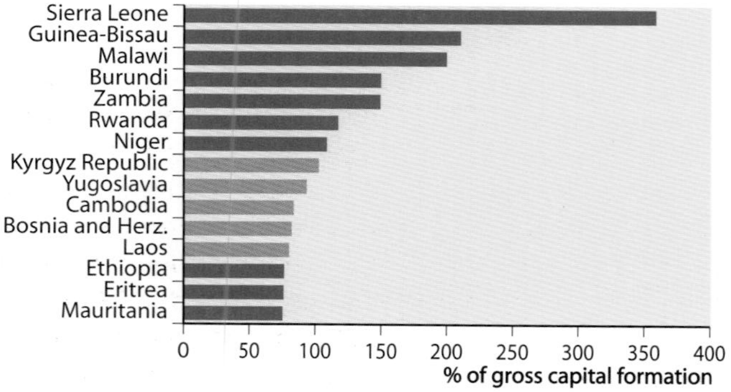

Figure 30.5
Top ten recipients of aid, 2000 (% of investment)

Source: OECD.

At a meeting of the United Nations in 1974, the industrial countries agreed that they would each devote 0.7% of their GNP to ODA. This goal was reiterated at the Millennium Summit as part of the commitment to achieving the Millennium Development Goals. Progress towards this target has been unimpressive. In 2002 only five countries (Denmark, Norway, Sweden, the Netherlands and Luxembourg) achieved the target. Figure 30.6 shows the performance of selected donor countries relative to this target. In fact, the UK figure has improved since 1997, but the US contribution has declined.

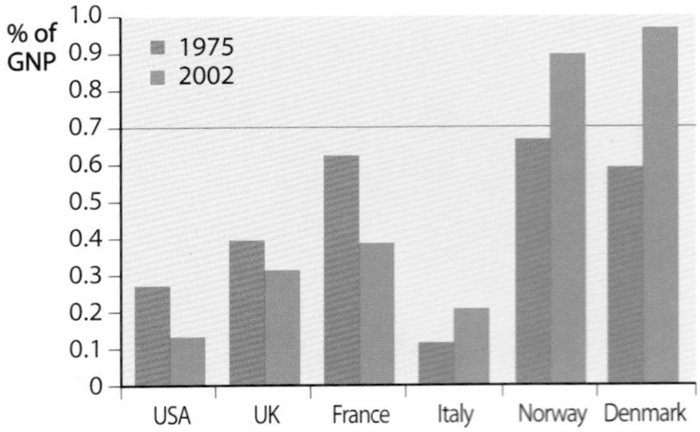

Figure 30.6 Overseas Development Assistance, 1975 and 2002

Source: World Bank, *UNDP*.

A World Bank study of the effectiveness of aid, published in 1997, reported that 'foreign aid to developing countries since 1970 has had no net impact on either the recipients' growth rate or the quality of their economic policies...'. Some evidence was found to suggest that aid was more effective in countries where 'sound economic management' was being practised. In other words, it was argued that aid might prove effective in stimulating growth only if the country were also implementing 'good' economic policies – particularly in terms of openness to trade, low inflation and disciplined fiscal policy.

There may be many reasons for the ineffectiveness of aid. It may simply be that providing aid to the poorest countries reduces its effectiveness, in the sense that the resources of such countries are so limited that the funding cannot be efficiently utilised. In some cases it may be related to the fact that aid flows are received by LDC governments, which can be inefficient or corrupt, so there are no guarantees that the funds are used wisely by these governments. Or it might simply be that the flows of aid have not been substantial enough to have made a difference.

Large amounts of foreign aid have been supplied to LDCs, but it has not always helped.

There are other explanations, however. For example, some donor countries in the past have regarded aid as part of their own trade policy. By tying aid to trade deals, the net value of the aid to the country is much reduced; for instance, offering aid in this way may commit the recipient country to buying goods from the donor country at inflated prices.

In other cases aid has been tied to use in specific projects. This may help to assure the donor that the funds are being used for the purpose for which they were intended. However, it is helpful only if appropriate projects were selected in the first place. There may be a temptation for donors to select prestige projects that will be favourably regarded by others, rather than going for the LDC's top-priority development projects.

Such deals are becoming less common, as now more ODA is being channelled through multilateral organisations than bilaterally between donor and recipient directly. This may mean that aid flows will be more effective in the future. In 1994, 66.1% of total aid was untied (45.8% from the UK), but by 1999 the proportion had increased to 83.8% (91.8% from the UK).

Notice that the aid under discussion here has been in terms of long-term development assistance, rather than the emergency aid that is required after specific events such as droughts or earthquakes. An important issue for all sorts of aid is that it should be provided in a way that does not damage incentives for local producers. For example, dumping cheap grain into LDC markets on a regular basis would be likely to damage the incentives for local farmers by depressing prices.

Summary

- Overseas development assistance (ODA) comprises grants and concessional funding provided from the OECD countries to LDCs.
- The countries most in need of ODA may not be in a position to use it effectively.
- In some cases the direction of ODA flows is influenced by the political interests of the donor countries.
- The more-developed countries have pledged to devote 0.7% of their GNPs to ODA, but few have reached this target.
- Some evidence suggests that aid has been ineffective except in countries that have pursued 'good' economic policies.
- The tying of aid to trade deals or to specific projects can limit the aid's benefits to recipient LDCs.

Exercise 30.2

Examine the arguments for and against providing assistance to those countries in most need of it, as opposed to those best equipped to make good use of it.

International borrowing

The final option for LDCs is to borrow the funds needed for development. This may be on concessional terms from the World Bank or the IMF, or on a commercial basis from international financial markets.

It is important to notice that, when countries borrow from the World Bank or the IMF, the loans come with strings attached. In other words, these bodies impose conditions on countries wanting to borrow, typically in relation to the sorts of economic policy that should be adopted. Such policy programmes will be considered below.

As with other forms of external finance, problems have arisen for some LDCs that have tried to borrow internationally. These problems first became apparent in the early 1980s, when Mexico announced that it could not meet its debt repayment commitments. The stock of outstanding debt has been a major issue for many LDCs, especially in sub-Saharan Africa.

Figure 30.7 presents some data about this. It can be seen that in 1990 the debt position for many of these countries was serious indeed. In the case of Uganda, in 1990 more than 80% of the value of exports of goods and services was needed just to service the outstanding debt. For a country with limited resources, this leaves little surplus to use for promoting development. The encouraging aspect of Figure 30.7 is that for most of these countries the situation was much improved in 2002.

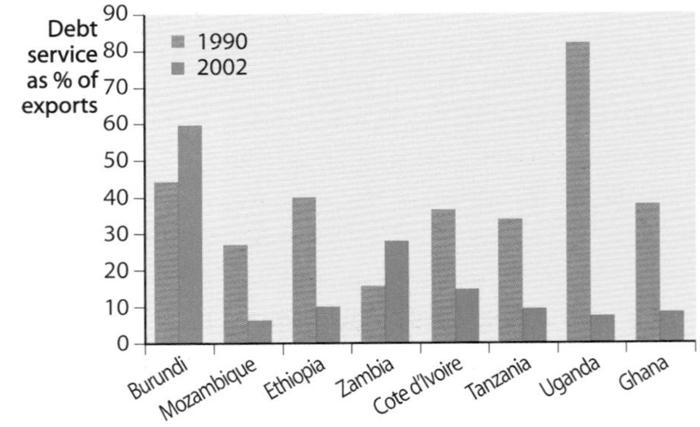

Figure 30.7 *Debt servicing in sub-Saharan Africa, 1990 and 2002*

Source: *Human Development Report 2004.*

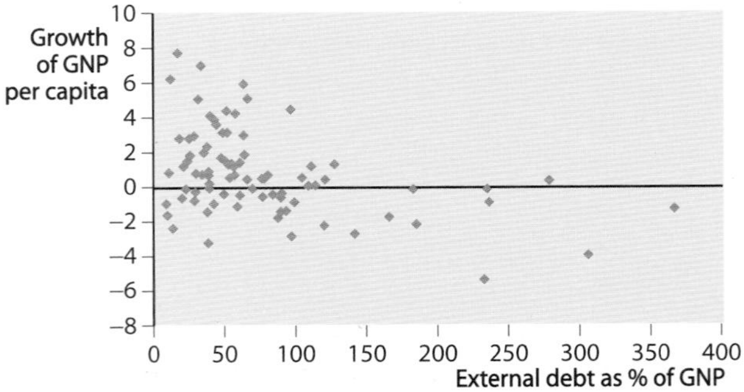

Figure 30.8 *Debt and growth*

Source: *Human Development Report 1999.*

Figure 30.8 shows the relationship between stocks of external debt and the growth of GNP per capita in the late 1990s. Nicaragua is excluded because its debt level at that time was way off the scale. The striking aspect of this figure is that the countries with the highest levels of debt experienced low or negative growth, supporting the contention that debt is a constraint on growth.

But how did this situation arise? The story begins in the mid-1970s with the first oil price crisis. In 1973–74 oil prices quadrupled. Countries that were not oil producers were suddenly faced with a deficit on the current account of the balance of payments, as the demand for oil in the short run was highly inelastic.

For LDCs, this was a major problem. They knew that if they went to the IMF for a loan they would be forced to accept onerous conditions, so they were reluctant to do this. On the other hand, the oil producers were enjoying windfall gains, and their surpluses were lodged with the banks, which were thus keen to lend. LDCs were therefore encouraged to borrow from the banks rather than the IMF, and they took out loans at variable interest rates.

The second oil price crisis came in 1979–80, when prices tripled. Many LDCs were now in deep trouble, carrying a legacy of past debts and now needing to borrow still more. Furthermore, countries like the USA and the UK were adopting macroeconomic policies that were pushing interest rates to high levels, making it more difficult for LDCs to meet their existing commitments.

This resulted in the debt crisis of the 1980s, when a number of countries were threatening to default on their debts. A number of plans (including the Baker and Brady Plans) were introduced to safeguard the international financial system, but from the LDC viewpoint these entailed mainly a rescheduling of existing debt; in other words, they were given longer to pay. A consequence was that debt levels continued to grow.

The problems were made worse because in some countries the borrowed funds were not used wisely. Development through borrowing is sustainable only if the funds are used to enable exports to grow, so that the funds can be repaid. When they do not lead to increased export earnings, repayment problems will inevitably result.

Before looking at more recent events, this chapter examines the role of the so-called Bretton Woods institutions — the World Bank, the IMF and the World Trade Organisation.

Summary

- A third way for LDCs to obtain external funds is through borrowing.
- Loans provided by the World Bank and the IMF have conditions attached that are not always palatable for LDCs.
- Many LDCs have borrowed in the past, but have then been unable to meet the repayments.
- In some cases this was because the funds were not well used.

Exercise 30.3

Discuss the extent to which good government within a developing country is a necessary condition for the successful mobilisation of internal and external resources.

The Bretton Woods institutions

At the end of the Second World War in 1945, a conference was held at Bretton Woods, New Hampshire, USA, to establish a system of fixed exchange rates. This became known as the dollar standard, as countries agreed to fix their currencies relative to the US dollar. John Maynard Keynes was an influential delegate at the conference. In addition to establishing the exchange rate system (which operated until the early 1970s), the conference set up three key institutions with prescribed roles, in support of the international financial system.

International Monetary Fund

The **International Monetary Fund (IMF)** was set up with a specific brief to offer short-term assistance to countries experiencing balance of payments problems. Thus, if a country were running a deficit on the current account, it could borrow from the IMF in order to finance the deficit. However, the IMF would insist that, as a condition of granting the loan, the country put in place policies to deal with the deficit — typically, restrictive monetary and fiscal policies.

World Bank

The International Bank for Reconstruction and Development was the second institution established under the Bretton Woods agreement. It soon became known as the **World Bank**. The role of the World Bank is to provide longer-term funding for projects that will promote development. Much of this funding is provided at commercial interest rates, as the role of the Bank was seen to be the channelling of finance to projects that normal commercial banks would perceive as being too risky. However, some concessional lending is also made through the International Development Association (IDA), which is part of the World Bank.

World Trade Organisation

Initially, Bretton Woods set up the **General Agreement on Tariffs and Trade (GATT)**, with a brief to oversee international trade. This entailed encouraging countries to reduce tariffs, but the GATT also provided a forum for trade negotiations and for settling disputes between countries.

The GATT was replaced by the **World Trade Organisation (WTO)** in 1995. Between them, these organisations have presided over a significant reduction in the barriers to trade between countries — not only tariffs, but other forms of protection too.

Key terms

International Monetary Fund (IMF): a multilateral institution that provides short-term financing for countries experiencing balance of payments problems

World Bank: multilateral organisation that provides financing for long-term development projects

General Agreement on Tariffs and Trade (GATT): precursor of the WTO, GATT organised a series of 'Rounds' of tariff reductions

World Trade Organisation (WTO): multilateral body responsible for overseeing the conduct of international trade

Heavily Indebted Poor Countries (HIPC) Initiative

In the run-up to the Millennium it was clear that many countries' international debt burdens had become unsustainable. Pressure was put on the World Bank and the UN to offer debt forgiveness to LDCs to herald the Millennium.

The World Bank was reluctant to consider this route. One of the reasons for its reluctance concerns *moral hazard.* It is argued that if a country expects to be forgiven its debt it will have no incentive to behave responsibly. Furthermore, a country that has been forgiven its debt may have no incentive to be more responsible in the future — and other countries too will have less of an incentive to pay off their debts.

Key terms

HIPC Initiative: initiative launched in 1995 to provide debt relief for heavily indebted poor countries

Structural Adjustment Programme (SAP): package of policy measures recommended by the World Bank to LDCs

The response was the **HIPC Initiative**, which allows for debt forgiveness on condition that the country demonstrates a commitment to 'good' policies over a period of time. The HIPC Initiative was first launched in 1995, but the conditions were so restrictive that few countries were able to benefit. Thus, a number of pressure groups, including Jubilee 2000, lobbied the World Bank to allow the initiative to be more accessible. The original HIPC measures required countries to follow the policy package for a period of 6 years before they would qualify for any debt relief.

The policies concerned overlap with a previous package of measures, which came to be known as a **Structural Adjustment Programme (SAP)**. SAPs have been on the World Bank agenda for many years, and comprise a package of policies designed to help a country initiate a process of growth and development. Under the HIPC Initiative, a new set of measures was added to encourage countries to devote funds to poverty alleviation programmes.

The HIPC policy package incorporates four main steps:

1. successful implementation of policies to enhance economic growth (the World Bank's model of market-friendly growth was discussed in Chapter 27)
2. development of a Poverty Reduction Strategy Paper (PRSP)
3. encouragement of private enterprise
4. diversification of the export base

Uganda was the first country to qualify for debt relief under HIPC, and Figure 30.7 seems to suggest that this has had an effect, with debt service having been reduced substantially. Indeed, there is some evidence that debt levels for low-income countries are coming under control, as can be seen in Figure 30.9, showing that the ratio of total debt service to exports has fallen for all low-income countries from 27% in 1990 to 15% in 2002. Indeed, for the least-developed countries the ratio is down to 7.7% in 2002, from 16.2% in 1990. However, the regional pattern shown in Figure 30.9 indicates that debt levels continue to grow in Latin America and the Caribbean and in Central and Eastern Europe and the CIS.

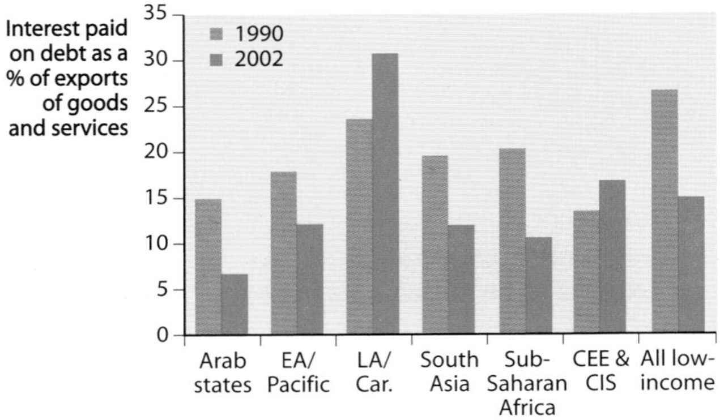

Figure 30.9 *Debt service, selected regions, 1990 and 2002*

Source: *Human Development Report 2004.*

Case study Uganda

Uganda was the first country to qualify for debt relief under the HIPC Initiative and illustrates some of the key issues.

Uganda is a landlocked country in East Africa, bordering a range of countries and with ongoing civil conflict in the north.

The country gained independence from Britain in 1962, and was governed initially by Milton Obote. There was some political instability in this period, although GDP per capita remained fairly constant. Obote stayed in power partly by using the army to carry out a coup against his own government. Then in 1971 he was overthrown by Idi Amin, who ruled through military power. During this period the Ugandan economy essentially collapsed, as you can see in Figure 30.10, which shows the time-path of Uganda's real GDP per capita. This was partly through Amin's expulsion of all Asian Ugandans, who had run the country's limited manufacturing industry and distribution sector. He also killed an estimated 300 000 people during his regime.

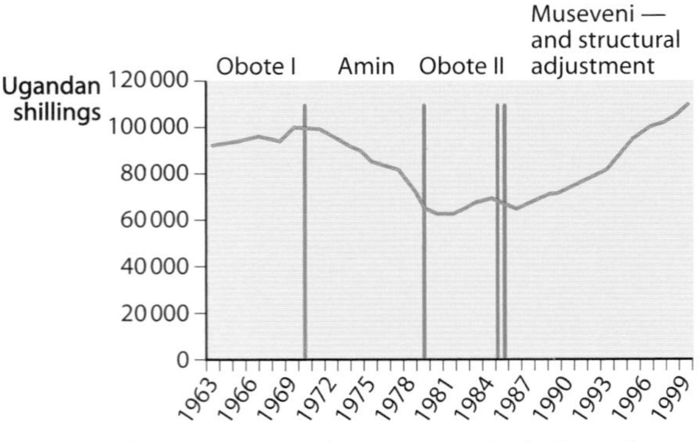

Figure 30.10 *Real GDP per capita in Uganda*

Amin was illiterate, and allowed no written instructions, which impeded the bureaucracy. In 1978 he invaded Tanzania, but the Tanzanian army, with the help of exiled Ugandans, fought back and took Kampala in 1979. Elections were held in 1980, and Milton Obote came back to power, albeit under allegations of election fixing. Obote's second period was characterised by civil war, and lasted until the next coup in 1985 (Okello). The Okello regime lasted only until 1986, when the present President Museveni took over, bringing some stability and economic recovery. Indeed, the introduction of an SAP followed soon after Museveni came to power.

In terms of the HIPC requirements, Uganda has done everything expected of it. It has established a strong record of sound macroeconomic policies and structural adjustment reforms. It has produced its Poverty Reduction Strategy Paper (PRSP) and tried to implement it. The Plan included a drive for universal primary education initiated in 1997, supported by $75 million from the World Bank.

I visited Uganda in November 1997 to undertake a survey in the rural areas. Even at this early stage in the new policy, some of the effects of the HIPC Initiative were evident. In some cases children had been held back from attending school in anticipation of the new measures. In other cases, some older children had returned to school — there were several 13-year-olds in the first year of primary education, and ' children' of up to 19 years old enrolled in primary education.

However, although the debt burden has lessened (see Figure 30.7), and in spite of rapid growth during the 1990s (Uganda was one of the fastest-growing economies in the world in this period), the country remains poor. In terms of the HDI, Uganda remains in the 'low human development' group of countries.

There seem to be a number of factors that have affected Uganda's situation. First, the international price of coffee has fallen to unanticipated low levels. With Uganda continuing to rely heavily on coffee for export earnings, this is a major setback. Efforts have been made to bring about greater diversification, and this is beginning to show results. However, the IMF also concedes that 'further cooperation of the international community is needed to help remove the barriers to trade'. There is a major issue lurking here: it is all very well persuading LDCs to stimulate and diversify their exports, but if they cannot find buyers the impact will be limited.

In addition, some countries have not conceded the debt relief that is due under the agreements, another indication that international cooperation is crucial in enabling the HIPC measures to become effective.

There is some further evidence that one of the reasons for the persistence of poverty in the rural areas, in spite of the macroeconomic success, was the lack of integration of these rural areas into national markets. In part this is a result of poor infrastructure — poor roads, lack of market facilities and poor information about national trading conditions.

THE AUTHOR

Summary

- The Bretton Woods conference in 1945 set up three major multilateral organisations: the IMF, the World Bank and the GATT (which later became the WTO).
- The IMF has the role of providing short-term finance for countries experiencing balance of payments problems.
- The World Bank provides longer-term financing for development projects.
- The WTO oversees the conduct of international trade.
- The HIPC Initiative was designed to address the problems of debt in the poorest countries.
- Under the HIPC Initiative, debt relief is provided to countries that have shown a commitment to World Bank-approved policies and have implemented a Poverty Reduction Strategy Paper (PRSP).

Review section

The problems facing less-developed countries are daunting. The gap in living standards between developed countries such as those in North America, Western Europe and Japan on the one hand, and the less-developed countries of sub-Saharan Africa, parts of Asia and Latin America on the other is simply enormous. There are millions of people around the world who live in conditions of absolute poverty. Part 6 has asked what economic analysis can say about why some countries have remained undeveloped while others have enjoyed rapid economic growth over long periods of time. Economists are beginning to understand why this situation has evolved, but the question of what to do about it is much more challenging.

Chapter 26 What is development?

The starting point of development economics is to define what is meant by 'development', and to devise indicators that will enable development to be recognised when it happens. Development is a broader concept than just economic growth, although economic growth is a vital prerequisite for development to take place. Economic growth provides the resources needed to tackle the provision of the other ingredients of development — adequate education and healthcare, good sanitation, clean water supply, the alleviation of poverty and so on. The *gross domestic product (GDP)* is one indicator, but it suffers from some limitations; for example, it disguises the state of inequality in a society and focuses on the material provision of goods and services, to the exclusion of other dimensions of development. The *Human Development Index (HDI)* is one indicator that attempts to provide a broader measure to enable international comparisons of living standards. The economic analysis of underdevelopment cannot be completely divorced from political and cultural factors which can also shape the development path that an economy follows.

Chapter 27 Economic growth in less-developed countries

The importance of economic growth for less-developed countries lies increasingly in the provision of resources with which they can address the range of problems that they face. The *Harrod–Domar model* provides some insight into the process of economic growth, and highlights some of the factors that may impede growth. The model stresses the importance of *savings*, and the need to be able to channel savings into productive *investment* in order to raise output and incomes – and so generate more savings to maintain the process. However, physical investment is not sufficient of itself: technology and human capital are also vital to promote economic growth. There is no point in installing a lot of new capital goods if the skilled labour needed to operate them is not available. The *World Bank* has promoted a market-based model of development that underlies the *Structural Adjustment Programmes* that less-developed countries have been encouraged to adopt. As with developed countries, it is also important to ensure that development is *sustainable* in the long run.

Chapter 28 Obstacles to growth and development

In exploring why some countries have not been able to stimulate a process of development, a number of obstacles can be identified. Rapid population growth can constitute an obstacle if the country does not have the resources to support its rapidly growing population. Over-dependence on low productivity or other primary production activities has been a problem for some countries. Also significant is the situation where markets are insufficiently developed to operate effectively. This is especially important in the case of financial markets, where inadequacies can seriously impede the translation of savings into investment and from there into higher productive capacity. Social capital is important too, as is the nature of a country's relationships with the more-developed countries; some policy actions taken by the richer countries have made it difficult for less-developed countries to become fully involved in international trade.

Chapter 29 Structural change

In order to achieve economic development, a process of structural transformation of economic activity is required. Many less-developed countries continue to rely on exporting primary commodities. This has created problems of price volatility in the short run, and a deterioration in the terms of trade in the long run. In devising policy for international trade, two basic approaches have been adopted. *Import substitution* encourages the domestic production of goods previously imported, whereas *export promotion* depends on expanding exports – perhaps of new sorts of products – in order to earn foreign exchange. This chapter also examined the significance of industrialisation for less-developed countries, and the possibilities of pursuing it. The problem of *urbanisation* is important for some countries, in which a rapidly growing urban population has put pressure on infrastructure, created a large informal sector and exaggerated the inequities between rural and urban areas, further stimulating internal migration. The possibilities for developing *tourism* as a route to development were also investigated.

Chapter 30 Mobilising external resources for development

Many less-developed countries face the problem that they have inadequate domestic resources to enable them to initiate the process of development. The

question then arises as to whether it is possible for less-developed countries to draw in resources from abroad. Possibilities include *foreign direct investment (FDI)* by multinational corporations, *overseas assistance* from the more-developed countries and *international borrowing.* Each of these routes to development has benefits but also costs, which need to be carefully evaluated. The *World Bank* and *International Monetary Fund* are institutions established at the Bretton Woods conference at the end of the Second World War, which (together with the *World Trade Organisation*) have played a significant role in setting the international framework for development. An important aspect of this has been the *Structural Adjustment Programme* approach, and more recently the *Heavily Indebted Poor Countries (HIPC)* Initiative which sets out to assist countries facing unsustainable levels of international debt.

Preparing for the examination

In any examination it is important not to panic, although there may be times when it is tempting. Unit 5, Option B (Economic Development) is based on data-response. For this style of question the danger of panic may be especially present, as you need to spend time at the beginning assimilating the contents of the data provided — which of course includes text as well as statistics and graphs. You will need to be disciplined about time, allowing enough (but not too much) time to read the passage(s) provided and think about the questions that you need to address. Some of this time should be spent in planning your response, so that you do not forget anything. Success in the exam is all about making the best of what you know, and presenting yourself as well as you possibly can. It is not about how much you can write: it is about the *quality* of what you write. When you practise tackling past questions, try to do it within the time frame permitted in the exam, so that you can judge how quickly you can think and write — although the adrenalin rush in the exam room should help on the day.

Data-response question P6.1

AIDS in Africa

Extract 1

Time is supposed to be a great healer. Not for AIDS. For AIDS, time is simply the great killer as far as most people are concerned. It need not be so.

In the developed world, the availability of modern drugs means that most people infected by HIV can lead more or less normal lives, for years if not decades. But developing countries cannot afford these drugs. In due course, those of their citizens that are infected will develop AIDS and die. In Africa – the continent with the greatest number of sufferers, with over 70% of the total – an unimaginable human tragedy is now unfolding. It is a tragedy that affects many more than the 28 million Africans or so living with the virus. AIDS blights almost every activity of government, every aspect of the economy. Unchecked, it will wipe out the progress of decades of development.

A few examples from Botswana illustrate the devastation. Twenty years ago the life expectancy of a Botswanan was well over 60 years; now it is below 40. Projections – guesses may be a better word – suggest that by 2010 Botswana will have 32% less output than it would have had without AIDS. Because of greater spending on the disease and reduced revenues resulting from this, other government expenditure will be cut by a fifth. Within families, each main breadwinner is expected to carry four extra dependants. Botswana will probably have 214 000 orphans by 2010. Some will have been infected at birth. Many may be lucky enough to be looked after by grandparents or other relations. But who will pay the school fees? Who, indeed, will teach in the schools when 39% of adults are HIV positive? The outlook is just as serious in at least a dozen other countries. In mines in Zambia, four people have to be trained for every skilled job, in the knowledge that three will die.

Yet all is not hopeless. Uganda has shown how a concerted campaign against AIDS can bring dramatic results. It cut its adult infection rate from 30% in 1992 to 11% in 2000. Modern drugs not only alleviate suffering, but also reduce transmission rates from mother to child. The Bill and Melinda Gates Foundation and other private donors are contributing $50 million in cash and medication. The US government has sent four professionals to help fight the southern African drug abuse problem. Harvard University is providing assistance in research, together with other hospitals and universities in Europe.

	Aid per head $		**Aid as % of gross national income**		**Aid as % of imports of goods and services**	
	1995	**2000**	**1995**	**2000**	**1995**	**2000**
Botswana	62	19	1.9	0.6	3.5	0.9
South Africa	43	37	0.3	0.4	1.0	1.3
Uganda	43	37	14.7	13.3	57.3	40.0
Zambia	226	79	63.0	28.5	103.7	48.7
Zimbabwe	43	14	7.2	2.5	14.9	7.9
Sub-Saharan Africa	33	20	5.8	4.0	15.3	9.5

Table P6.1 Aid dependency in Africa, 1995 and 2000

Source: **www.OECD.org**

	Gross domestic product average annual % growth	**Agriculture average annual % growth**	**Manufacturing average annual % growth**	**Services average annual % growth**
Botswana	4.3	0.3	3.9	6.3
South Africa	1.9	1.0	1.1	2.4
Uganda	7.2	3.7	14.2	8.1
Zambia	0.2	9.4	0.7	0.3
Zimbabwe	2.8	4.6	0.7	3.5
Sub-Saharan Africa	2.2	2.7	1.6	2.4

Table P6.2 Growth rates in Africa, 1990–99

Source: **www.OECD.org**

A vast amount remains to be done in Africa. The demands of living with AIDS are where the developed world can help the most. Sufferers need drugs, not just because they are human beings who deserve treatment for reasons of humanity, but because their early deaths bring huge costs to society and are avoidable. In 2001 the UN set up a global fund to fight AIDS, and some of its money could go towards buying drugs for use in developing countries. Both a vaccine and better drugs are desperately needed. Too many people are dying needlessly, taking too much with them.

Source: adapted from *The Economist*, 11 May 2002.

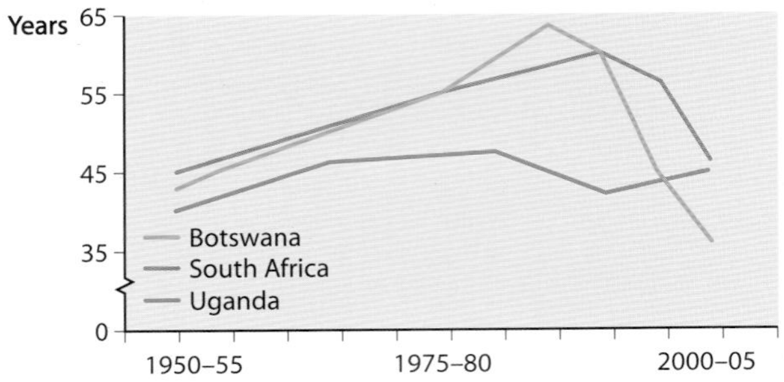

Figure P6.1
Life expectancy

Source: adapted from *The Economist*, 11 May 2002.

a With reference to Extract 1, to what extent might AIDS act as a constraint upon economic development in Africa? *(15 marks)*

b With reference to Table P6.2, examine the implications for a developing economy of different growth rates between the three sectors of the economy shown. *(15 marks)*

c To what extent can international aid assist economic growth? *(20 marks)*

d Discuss **two** reasons, apart from official aid, for differing rates of economic growth between developing countries within the same continent. *(10 marks)*

Data-response question P6.2

Tourism

Extract 1

It boasts 76 luxury beachfront apartments and the longest swimming pool in the South Pacific. But Trendwest's new resort on Denarua Island, Fiji, had the misfortune to open on 8 May 2000, just 11 days before a coup (an illegal takeover of government) sent the Pacific nation's tourism industry reeling. It was the former British colony's third coup in 13 years, and the impact on tourism, the country's most important industry, was devastating.

One year on, however, Trendwest is close to completing an A$15 million (£5.5 million) expansion of the resort, and tourism is recovering more strongly than expected. Fiji experienced its best year for tourism in 1999, when the number of overseas visitors reached 410 000 and the sector accounted for 17% of the economy. Back in 1986, sugar cane was Fiji's biggest industry and fewer than 260 000 foreign visitors made it to the island state. But for the 55 days that followed 19 May 2000 Fiji was front-page news in Australia and New Zealand, its two most important tourist markets, as gunmen held the Fijian prime minister and his cabinet hostage.

A main plank in the recovery plan has been reduced air fares. Return air fares from Australia and New Zealand on Air Pacific were cut to A$499, down from A$800. At the same time, however, Fiji's tourism sector – long constrained by the limited number of international flights coming into the island – has also been hit by Air New Zealand's decision to reduce its flights to and from Japan. These had stopped in Nadi, the main airport serving Fiji's tourism trade.

As the first anniversary of the coup passes, recovery remains patchy. At Trendwest occupancy levels are at more than 70%. But, while the short-haul market has bounced back, new bookings are much slower for meetings, conferences and conventions. And attempts to win back the lucrative Japanese market are being hindered by government travel warnings and the lower number of direct flights.

Source: V. Marsh, 'Fiji's Year to Clear Away the Clouds', *The Financial Times*, 28 May 2001.

Extract 2

The day after being sworn in as Peru's new president in Lima, the capital, on 28 July 2001, Alejandro Toledo plans to repeat the ceremony among the mighty terraces and temples of the Inca citadel of Machu Picchu. For Mr Toledo that is a way of celebrating his achievement in becoming Peru's first elected president of indigenous descent. He also says it will boost the country's $1 billion-a-year tourist industry, which he sees as a good bet for much-needed jobs.

But can the fragile ruins of Machu Picchu stand so much attention? Sheltered by clouds on an Andean ridge in the high rainforests of Cusco, Machu Picchu was 'discovered' only in 1911. Now it is Peru's most famous attraction, and is increasingly besieged.

The biggest long-term threat is Machu Picchu's fast-growing popularity with tourists. Each year some 300 000 visit the site, which is surrounded by a large nature reserve sheltering more than 400 species of birds and dozens of rare orchids. In the dry season (May to September) up to 2200 people tramp around the ruins each day. With them come problems: the gradual erosion of the Inca roads to the site; the chaotic growth of Aguas Calientes, a nearby village that has become an ugly town; and rubbish and other pollution at the ruins.

The underlying trend for Peru's tourist industry remains one of steady growth. Managing the growth so that the increase in jobs does not come at the expense of the sites the tourists wish to visit will be the next task for Mr Toledo.

Source: 'Tourism in Peru', *The Economist*, 21 July 2001.

a Examine **three** factors affecting the number of tourists to a developing country. *(15 marks)*

b Evaluate the case for the development of tourism in a developing country such as Fiji. *(15 marks)*

c Assess **two** methods by which a developing country could minimise the adverse effects of tourism on sites that are popular to visit. *(10 marks)*

d To what extent is it necessary for the government in a developing country over-reliant on tourism to consider the expansion of agriculture and manufacturing? *(20 marks)*

These questions were taken from examinations set for the Edexcel Advanced Economics examination for Unit 5 – Option B: Economic development. We are grateful to London Qualifications for permission to reproduce them here.

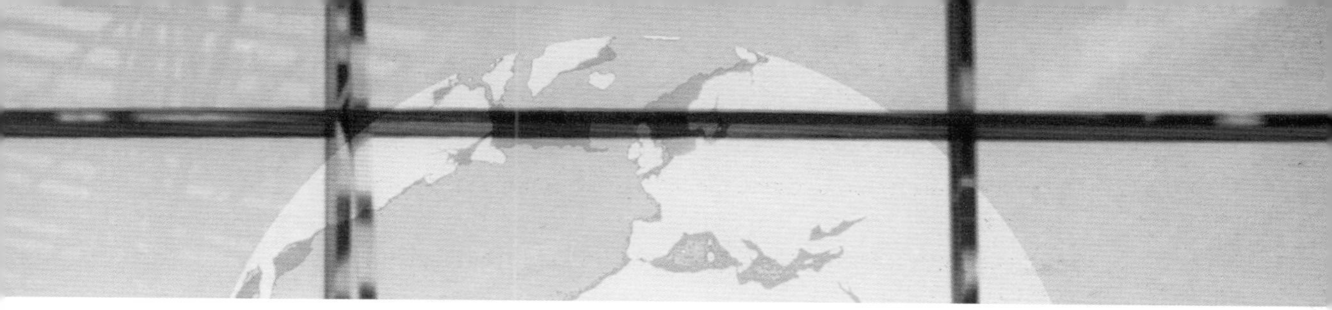

The UK in the global economy

Part 7

part 7

Chapter 31

Globalisation and the world economy

The world economy is becoming increasingly integrated, and it is no longer possible to think of any single economy in isolation. The UK economy is no exception. It relies on international trade, engaging in exporting and importing activity, and many UK firms are increasingly active in global markets. This situation has created opportunities for British firms to expand and become global players, and for British consumers to have access to a wider range of goods and services. However, there is also a downside: global shocks, whether caused by oil prices, financial crises or the emergence of China as a world economic force, can reverberate throughout economies in all parts of the world. These are some of the issues that will be explored in this chapter.

Learning outcomes

After studying this chapter, you should:

- understand what is meant by globalisation, and be aware of the factors that have given rise to this phenomenon
- appreciate the importance of trade and exchange between nations
- be familiar with the arguments for trade liberalisation as opposed to protectionism
- be aware of the role and workings of the World Trade Organisation
- understand the importance of foreign direct investment and the role of multinational corporations
- be aware of the impact that external shocks can have within the global economy

Causes of globalisation

The term 'globalisation' has been much used in recent years, especially by the protest groups that have demonstrated against it. It is therefore important to be clear about what

Key term

globalisation: a process by which the world's economies are becoming more closely integrated

the term means before seeking to evaluate the strengths and weaknesses of the phenomenon.

Ann Krueger, the first deputy managing director of the IMF, defined globalisation as 'a phenomenon by which economic agents in any given part of the world are much more affected by events elsewhere in the world' than before. Joseph Stiglitz, the Nobel Laureate and former Chief Economist at the World Bank, defined it as follows:

> Fundamentally, [globalisation] is the closer integration of countries and peoples of the world which has been brought about by the enormous reduction of costs of transportation and communication, and the breaking down of artificial barriers to the flows of goods, services, capital, knowledge, and (to a lesser extent) people across borders.
>
> (*Globalization and its Discontents*, Penguin, 2004)

On this basis, globalisation is crucially about the closer integration of the world's economies. Critics have focused partly on the environmental effects of rapid global economic growth, and partly on the opportunities that powerful nations and large corporations have for exploiting the weak. Some of these arguments will be evaluated after a more careful exploration of the topic.

The quotation from the book by Joseph Stiglitz not only defines what is meant by globalisation, but also offers some reasons for its occurrence.

Transportation costs

One of the contributory factors to the spread of globalisation has undoubtedly been the rapid advances in the technology of transportation and communications.

Improvements in transportation have enabled firms to fragment their production process to take advantage of varying cost conditions in different parts of the world. For example, it is now possible to site labour-intensive parts of a production process in parts of the world where labour is relatively plentiful, and thus relatively cheap. This is one way in which **multinational corporations** arise, in some cases operating across a wide range of countries.

Furthermore, communications technology has developed rapidly with the growth of the worldwide web and e-commerce, enabling firms to compete more easily in global markets.

These technological changes have augmented the existing economies of scale and scope,

Improvements in transport have been partly responsible for increasing international trade and globalisation.

Key term

multinational corporation (MNC): a company whose production activities are carried out in a number of countries

enabling firms to grow. If the size of firms were measured by their gross turnover, many of them would be found to be larger in size than a lot of the countries in which they operate (when size is measured by GDP), e.g. on this basis General Motors is bigger than Hong Kong or Norway.

Reduction of trade barriers

A second factor that has contributed to globalisation has been the successive reduction in trade barriers during the period since the Second World War, first under the auspices of the **General Agreement on Tariffs and Trade (GATT)**, and later under the **World Trade Organisation (WTO)** which replaced it.

In addition to these trade-liberalising measures, there has been a trend towards the establishment of free trade areas and customs unions in various parts of the world, with the European Union being just one example.

Key terms

General Agreement on Tariffs and Trade (GATT): the precursor of the WTO, which organised a series of 'Rounds' of tariff reductions

World Trade Organisation (WTO): a multilateral body responsible for overseeing the conduct of international trade

By facilitating the process of international trade, such developments have encouraged firms to become more active in trade, and thus have added to the impetus towards globalisation.

Deregulation of financial markets

Hand in hand with these developments, there have been moves towards removing restrictions on the movement of financial capital between countries. Many countries have removed capital controls, thereby making it much easier for firms to operate globally. This has been reinforced by developments in technology that enable financial transactions to be undertaken more quickly and efficiently.

The pattern of world trade

In order to provide the context for a discussion of the place of the UK economy in the global economy, it is helpful to examine the pattern of world trade.

	Destination							
Origin	**North America**	**Latin America**	**Western Europe**	**C/E Europe/ Baltic/CIS**	**Africa**	**Middle East**	**Asia**	**World**
North America	**382**	152	170	7	12	20	204	947
Latin America	215	**54**	44	3	4	5	23	348
Western Europe	270	55	**1787**	168	66	68	208	2622
C/E Europe, etc.	14	6	176	**80**	4	7	24	311
Africa	24	5	71	1	**11**	3	24	139
Middle East	38	3	40	2	9	**17**	116	225
Asia	394	39	260	21	26	48	**792**	1580
World	1337	314	2548	282	132	168	1391	6172

*Table 31.1 Intra- and interregional merchandise trade, 2002 (US$bn)**

*World totals have been calculated from the table.

Source: World Trade Organisation.

Table 31.1 presents some data on this pattern. It shows the size of trade flows between regions. The rows of the table show the exports from each of the regions to each other region, while the columns show the pattern of imports from each region. The numbers on the 'diagonal' of the table (in bold type) show the trade flows *within* regions. One remarkable feature of the table is the high involvement of Western Europe in world trade, accounting for 40.6% of imports and 42.4% of the exports. Of course, this includes substantial flows within Europe. In contrast, Africa shows very little involvement in world trade, in spite of the fact that, in population terms, it is far larger.

Indeed, trade flows between the developed countries – and with the more advanced developing countries – have tended to dominate world trade, with the flows between developing countries being relatively minor. This is not surprising, given that by definition the richer countries have greater purchasing power. However, the degree of openness to trade of economies around the world varies also as a result of conscious policy decisions. Some countries, especially in East Asia, have adopted very open policies towards trade, promoting exports in order to achieve export-led growth. In contrast, countries such as India and a number of Latin American countries have been much more reluctant to become dependent on international trade, and have adopted a more closed attitude towards trade.

The pattern of UK trade

Figures 31.1(a) and (b) show the destination of UK exports of goods and services to major regional groupings in the world. The most striking feature of this graph is the extent to which the UK relies on Europe and the USA for more than three-quarters

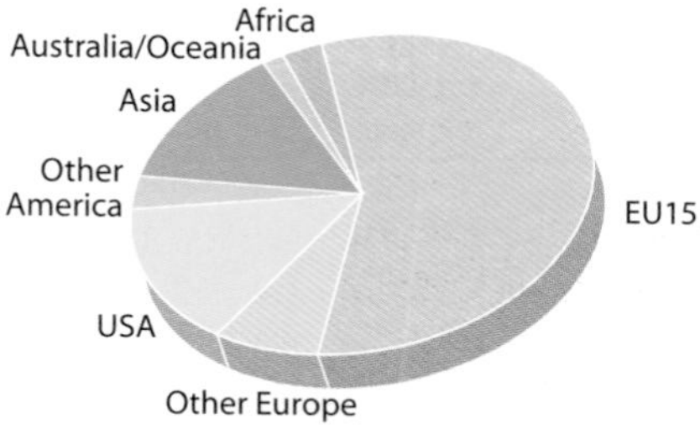

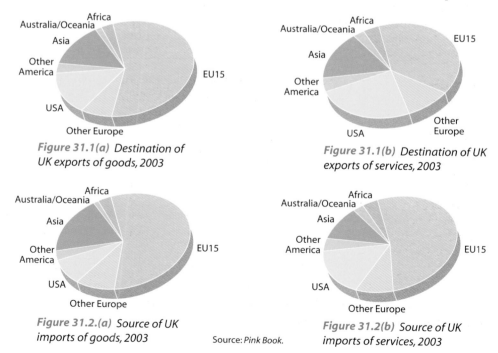

Figure 31.1(a) *Destination of UK exports of goods, 2003*

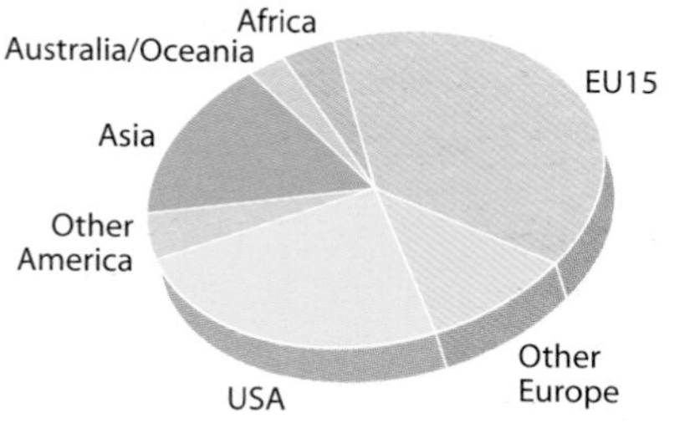

Figure 31.1(b) *Destination of UK exports of services, 2003*

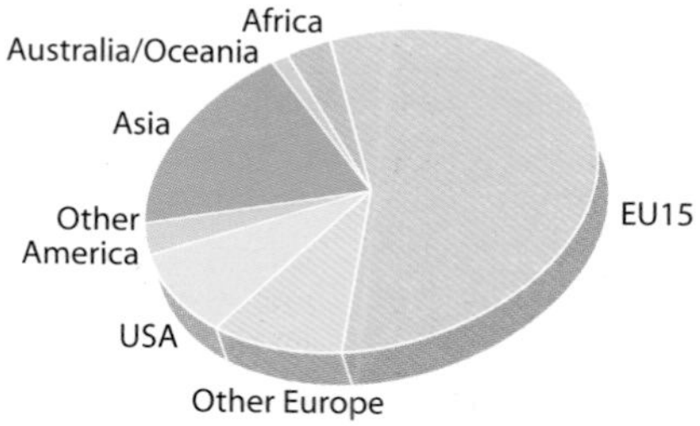

Figure 31.2.(a) *Source of UK imports of goods, 2003*

Source: *Pink Book.*

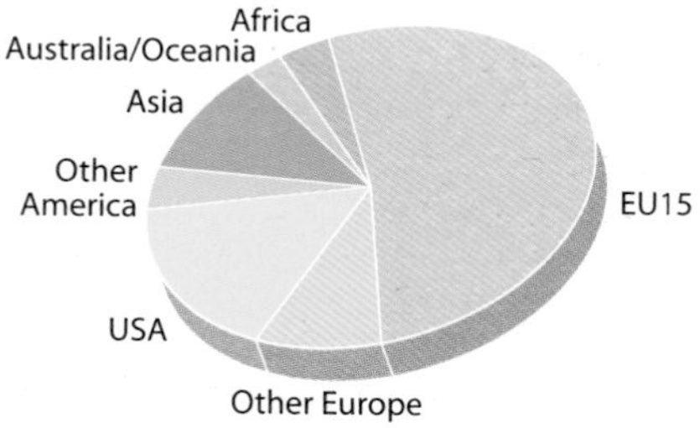

Figure 31.2(b) *Source of UK imports of services, 2003*

of its exports. Figures 31.2(a) and (b) reveal a similar pattern for the UK's imports of goods and services.

The proportion of UK trade (both exports and imports) that is with Europe has undergone substantial change over the past 40 years. This can be seen in Figure 31.3. In 1960, when the Commonwealth was still thriving and the UK was ambivalent about the idea of European integration, less than a quarter of UK exports went to other European countries. However, this has changed as the UK has grown closer to Europe, and now more than half of the UK's exports go to other members of the European Union.

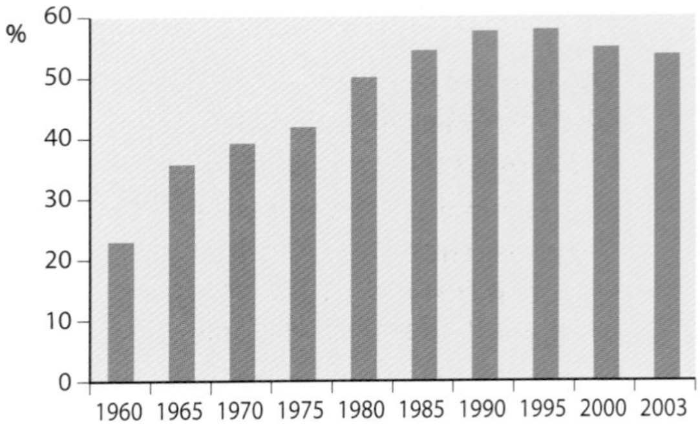

Figure 31.3 UK exports of goods to EU15 (%)

Note: 'EU15' refers to the 15 countries that were members of the European Union prior to the most recent expansion in May 2004.

Source: calculated from data in Europa: *EU Economy Annual Review 2004.*

Table 31.2 shows the top 10 countries that make up the UK's export markets and import sources, and the top 10 export and import commodities in 2003. This again shows the importance of UK trade with European countries in the twenty-first century, although the USA remains an important trading partner, ranked first among the UK's export markets, and the second largest source of imports into the UK.

	Export markets		**Import sources**		**Exports**		**Imports**	
	Country	**% of total UK exports**	**Country**	**% of total UK imports**	**Commodity**	**% of total UK exports**	**Commodity**	**% of total UK imports**
1	USA	15.4	Germany	14.2	Road vehicles	9.3	Road vehicles	12.7
2	Germany	11.0	USA	9.7	Oil	7.8	Office machines	6.7
3	France	10.0	France	8.6	Pharmaceuticals	6.3	Electrical machinery	6.3
4	Netherlands	7.2	Netherlands	7.0	Power-generating equipment	6.2	Misc. manufactures	5.5
5	Irish Republic	6.5	Belgium–Lux.	5.6	Electrical machinery	5.7	Telecomms. equipment	5.2
6	Belgium–Lux.	6.0	Italy	4.8	Misc. manufactures	5.7	Oil	4.5
7	Spain	4.7	Irish Republic	4.2	Office machines	5.1	Clothing	4.4
8	Italy	4.5	Spain	3.9	Telecomms. equipment	4.9	Other transport equipment	3.7
9	Sweden	2.0	China	3.5	General industrial machinery	3.9	General industrial machinery	3.6
10	Japan	2.0	Japan	3.4	Other transport equipment	3.9	Pharmaceuticals	3.5

Table 31.2 The UK's top 10 export markets, import sources and export and import commodities, 2003

A substantial share of exports consists of road vehicles together with machinery and equipment of various types and pharmaceuticals – and oil, of course. In terms of these commodities, it is noticeable how many commodity groups appear in both top ten lists, i.e. as both exports and imports – most obviously road vehicles, which tops both lists. In part, this reflects the fact that the commodity groups are quite widely defined. In other words, there are many different types of road vehicle or pharmaceutical product, and specialisation may mean that firms in particular countries focus on particular types of vehicle or drug. The only item that appears in the top ten list of imports that does not also appear in exports is clothing.

Exercise 31.1

a Using the data provided in Table 31.1, calculate the share of each region of world exports and imports. Think about the factors that might influence the contrasting performance of Western Europe and Africa. Also, for each region calculate the share of exports and imports that are within the region and comment on any significant differences that you find.

b Using Table 31.2, calculate the cumulative percentage of exports and imports in the UK's top 10 export markets and import sources. Discuss the extent to which this suggests that the UK concentrates on trading with a relatively small number of partners.

c Why should the list of top 10 export commodities contain so many common items with the list of top 10 imports?

d Are there any aspects of the pattern of world trade that took you by surprise? Can you find reasons for these?

Summary

- Globalisation has taken place as countries and peoples of the world have become more closely integrated.
- Factors contributing to this process have been the rapid advances in the technology of transportation and communications, the reduction of trade barriers and the deregulation of financial markets.
- There are substantial differences in the degree to which countries trade: trade with and within western Europe accounts for an appreciable proportion of world trade, whereas Africa shows very little involvement.
- More than three-quarters of UK exports go to Europe and the USA.
- The share of UK trade with the rest of Europe has increased substantially over the past 40 years.

Comparative advantage revisited

Chapter 2 introduced the law of comparative advantage, under which countries can gain from engaging in international trade by specialising in the production of goods and services in which they have a lower opportunity cost of production. This helps to explain some of the patterns in world trade that are shown in the data.

When you think about the global economy, it should be clear that comparative advantage will vary according to the very different balance of conditions around the world, not only in terms of climate (which may be important in agricultural production), but also in terms of the relative balance of factors of production (labour, capital, land, entrepreneurship etc.) and the skills of the workforce. This helps to explain why MNCs may choose to locate capital-intensive parts of their production process in one location and labour-intensive activities elsewhere, reflecting different relative prices in different countries.

It may also help to explain some of the patterns of trade. At first glance, it may seem curious that the UK both exports and imports cars, as initially this may seem to contradict comparative advantage. However, if British and (say) German cars have different characteristics, then each country may choose to specialise in certain segments of the market, taking advantage of the economies of scale that are so crucial in car production. Consumers benefit from this, as they then have a wider range of products to choose from.

Trade liberalisation or protectionism?

In spite of the well-known gains from trade, countries often seem reluctant to open their economies fully to international trade, and tend to intervene in various ways to protect their domestic producers.

Tariffs

A policy instrument commonly used in the past to give protection to domestic producers is the imposition of a tariff. Tariff rates in the developed countries have been considerably reduced in the period since the Second World War, but nonetheless are still in place.

Key term

tariff: a tax imposed on imported goods

Figure 31.4 shows how a tariff is expected to operate. *D* represents the domestic demand for a commodity, and S_{dom} shows how much domestic producers are prepared to supply at any given price. The price at which the good can be imported from world markets is given by P_w. If dealing with a global market, it is reasonable to assume that the supply at the world price is perfectly elastic. So in the absence of a tariff domestic demand is given by D_0, of which S_0 is supplied within the domestic economy and the remainder ($D_0 - S_0$) is imported. If the government wishes to protect this industry within the domestic economy, it needs to find a way of restricting imports and encouraging home producers to expand their capacity.

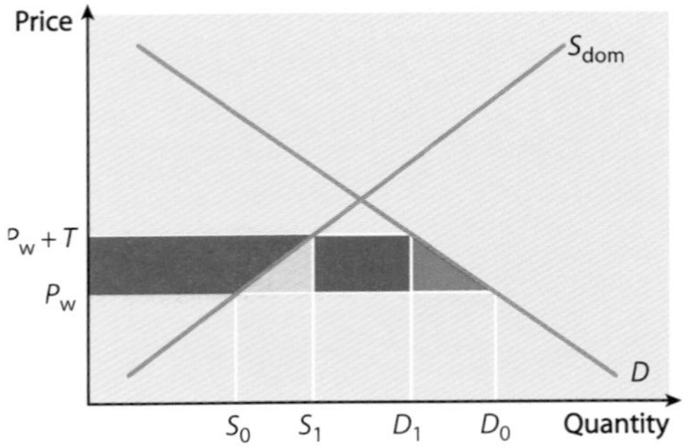

Figure 31.4 The effects of a tariff

By imposing a tariff, the domestic price rises to $P_w + T$, where T is the amount of the tariff. This has two key effects. One is to reduce the demand for the good from D_0 to D_1; the second is to encourage domestic producers to expand their output of this good from S_0 to S_1. As a consequence imports fall substantially, to $(D_1 - S_1)$. On the face of it, the policy has achieved its objective. Furthermore, the government has been able to raise some tax revenue (given by the green rectangle).

However, not all the effects of the tariff are favourable for the economy. Consumers are certainly worse off, as they have to pay a higher price for the good; they therefore consume less, and there is a loss of consumer surplus. Some of what was formerly consumer surplus has been redistributed to others in society. The government has gained the tariff revenue, as mentioned. In addition, producers gain economic rent, shown by the dark blue coloured area. There is also a deadweight loss to society, represented by the red and pale blue triangles. In other words, overall the society is worse off as a result of the imposition of the tariff.

Effectively, the government is subsidising inefficient local producers, and forcing domestic consumers to pay a price that is above that of similar goods imported from abroad.

Some would try to defend this policy on the grounds that it allows the country to protect an industry, thus saving jobs that would otherwise be lost. However, this goes against comparative advantage, and forces society to incur the deadweight loss. In the longer term it may delay structural change. For an economy to develop new specialisations and new sources of comparative advantage, there needs to be a transitional process in which old industries contract and new ones emerge. Although this process may be painful, it is necessary in the long run if the economy is to remain competitive. Furthermore, the protection that firms enjoy that allows them to reap economic rents from the tariff may foster complacency and an inward-looking attitude. This is likely to lead to X-inefficiency, and an inability to compete in the global market.

Even worse is the situation that develops where nations respond to tariffs raised by competitors by putting up tariffs of their own. This has the effect of further reducing the trade between countries, and everyone ends up worse off, as the gains from trade are sacrificed.

Quotas

An alternative policy that a country may adopt is to limit the imports of a commodity to a given volume. For example, a country may come to an agreement with another country that only a certain quantity of imports will be accepted by the importing country. Such arrangements are sometimes known as **voluntary export restraints (VERs)**.

Figure 31.5 illustrates the effects of a quota. D represents the domestic demand for this commodity, and S_{dom} is the quantity that domestic producers are prepared to supply at any given price.

Key term

voluntary export restraint (VER): an agreement by a country to limit its exports to another country to a given quantity

Suppose that without any agreement producers from country A would be prepared to supply any amount of the product at a price P_a. If the product is sold at this price, D_0 represents domestic demand, of which S_0 is supplied by domestic producers and the remainder $(D_0 - S_0)$ is imported from country A.

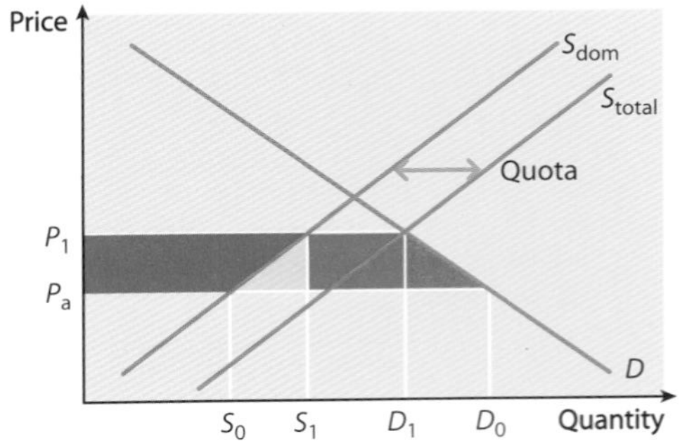

Figure 31.5 The effects of a quota

By imposing a quota, total supply is now given by S_{total}, which is domestic supply plus the quota of imports allowed into the economy from country A. The market equilibrium price rises to P_1 and demand falls to D_1, of which S_1 is supplied by domestic producers and the remainder is the agreed quota of imports.

Figure 31.5 shows who gains and who loses by this policy. Domestic producers gain by being able to sell at the higher price, so (as in the case of the tariff) they receive additional economic rent given by the dark blue area. Furthermore, the producers exporting from country A also gain, receiving the green rectangle (which, in the case of the tariff, was tax revenue received by the government). As in the case of the tariff, the two triangles (red and pale blue) represent the deadweight loss of welfare suffered by the importing country. Such an arrangement effectively subsidises the foreign producers by allowing them to charge a higher price than they would have been prepared to accept. Furthermore, although domestic producers are encouraged to produce more, the protection offered to them is likely to lead to X-inefficiency and weak attitudes towards competition.

There are a number of examples of such agreements, especially in the textile industry. For example, the USA and China have long-standing agreements on quotas for a range of textile products. Ninety-one such quotas expired at the end of 2004 as part of China's accession to the World Trade Organisation (WTO). As you might expect, this led to extensive lobbying by producers in the USA, especially during the run-up to the 2004 presidential election. Trade unions in the USA supported the producers, arguing that 350 000 jobs had been lost since the expiry of earlier quota agreements in 2002. In the case of three of these earlier agreements, some restraint had been reinstated for bras, dressing gowns and knitted fabrics. Producers in other countries, such as Sri Lanka, Bangladesh, Nepal, Indonesia, Morocco, Tunisia and Turkey, were lobbying for the quotas to remain, regarding China as a

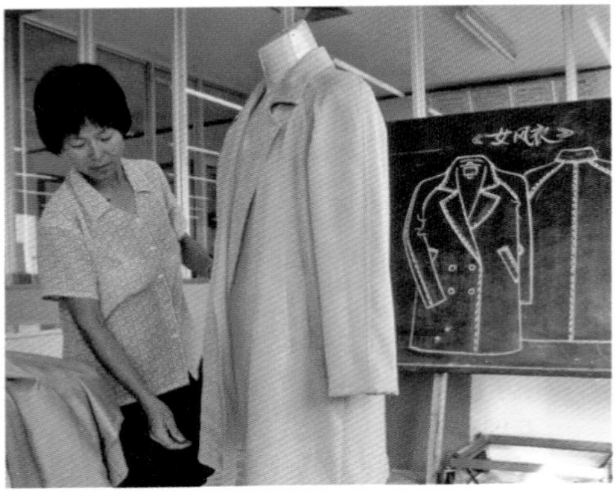
The USA has tried to curtail growth of the highly-competitive Chinese textile industry through the use of import quotas.

major potential competitor. However, for the USA at least, it can be argued that the removal of the quotas would allow domestic consumers to benefit from lower prices, and would allow American textile workers to be released for employment in higher-productivity sectors, where the USA maintains a competitive advantage.

Non-tariff barriers

There are other ways in which trade can be hampered, one example being the use of what are known as non-tariff barriers. These often comprise rules and regulations that control the standard of products that can be sold in a country.

Key term

non-tariff barriers: measures imposed by a government that have the effect of inhibiting international trade

This is a grey area, as some of the rules and regulations may seem entirely sensible and apply equally to domestic and foreign producers. For example, laws that prohibit the sale of refrigerators that contain CFCs are designed to protect the ozone layer, and may be seen to be wholly appropriate. In this case, the regulation is for purposes other than trade restriction.

However, there may be other situations in which a regulation is more clearly designed to limit trade. For example, the USA specifies a larger minimum size for vine-ripened tomatoes than for green tomatoes, thereby raising costs for the former. This has to do with trade, because vine-ripened tomatoes are mainly imported from Mexico, but green tomatoes are mainly grown in Florida. Thus, the regulation gives Florida producers an advantage.

Such rules and regulations may operate especially against producers in less-developed countries, who may find it especially difficult to meet demanding standards of production. This applies in particular where such countries are trying to develop new skills and specialisations to enable them to diversify their exports and engage more actively in international trade.

The European Common Agricultural Policy

Another source of contention in the trade arena has been the operation of the EU's Common Agricultural Policy (CAP). This has been in operation since the creation of the European Union (initially known as the European Economic Community) in 1957. The policy is a set of measures that guarantees farmers a price for their products that is set above the market equilibrium rate.

For example, Figure 31.6 shows the demand and supply for a particular crop within the CAP. If the market were allowed to be in equilibrium, the price would be P_e and quantity traded would be Q_e. If, however, farmers are guaranteed a price of at least P_1, then they will plant more of the crop in order to supply the quantity S_1. However, consumers will then demand only

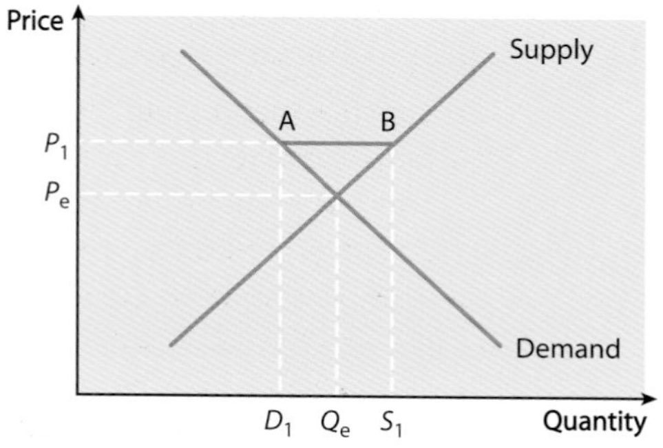

Figure 31.6 The CAP

D_1 of this product, and the remainder ($S_1 - D_1$: the distance AB) will need to be bought up by the authorities in order to maintain the price. If the guaranteed price is consistently above the equilibrium, the result is a build-up of surplus production – hence the notorious wine 'lakes' and butter 'mountains'.

Furthermore, consumers must pay the higher price for the product, and there is a deadweight loss imposed on society – not to mention the cost to the taxpayer of purchasing and storing the surplus. Farmers in the EU are then protected from external competition by the Common External Tariff.

The strategic arguments for protecting agriculture (that food supplies need to be assured in case of war) are less telling now than they were in 1957, and there have been many complaints from countries outside Europe that the CAP represents unfair subsidisation of EU farmers that inhibits trade and competition.

Exercise 31.2

Figure 31.7 illustrates the impact of a tariff. S_{dom} represents the quantity supplied by domestic producers, and D_{dom} shows the demand curve of domestic consumers. The world price is OE, and the country can import as much of the good at that price as it wishes.

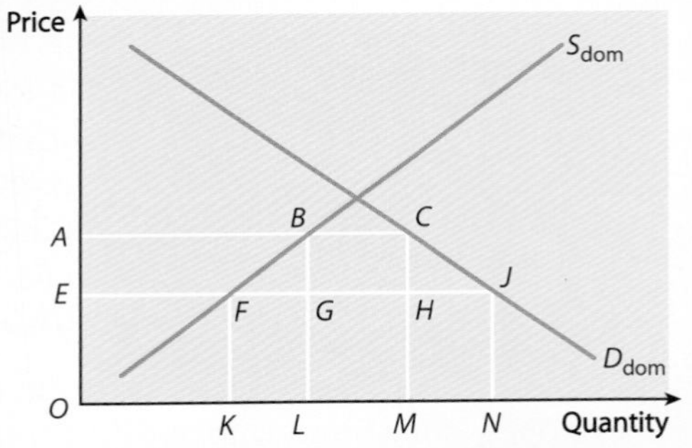

Figure 31.7 *A tariff*

a In the absence of government intervention, identify domestic demand and supply, and the quantity of imports.

b Suppose now that a tariff is imposed on imports of this product. Identify the price that will be charged in the domestic market.

c What will be the quantity demanded, the quantity supplied by home producers, and the quantity imported?

d Which area represents government revenue from the tariff?

e Identify the additional economic rent received by domestic producers.

f Identify and explain the deadweight loss of the tariff.

g Discuss whether a tariff can be beneficial for society.

h Suppose that a tariff has been in place on this commodity, but that the government proposes to remove it. Discuss the effects that the removal of the tariff will have, and the difficulties a government might face in removing it.

Summary

- The law of comparative advantage shows that countries can gain from international trade by specialising in the production of goods or services in which they have a lower opportunity cost of production.

- In spite of these possible gains, countries have often introduced protectionist measures to restrict trade, including tariffs, quotas and non-tariff barriers.
- The price guarantee system of the EU's Common Agricultural Policy has been much criticised as inhibiting trade, and reforms have been introduced.

Trade groupings

Despite the tendency towards protectionism, there are also trends in the opposite direction, with countries in various parts of the world coming together to form trade groupings of varying degrees of formality. These are intended to encourage trade among a group of nations, normally on a regional basis, in order to tap the gains from trade. Examples are ASEAN (an organisation of 10 countries in South East Asia), MERCOSUR (four countries in Latin America), NAFTA (Canada, the USA and Mexico) and of course the European Union. These groupings are at very different stages of integration and cooperation.

Free trade areas

A free trade area is a group of countries that agree to trade without barriers between themselves, but maintain their own individual barriers with countries outside the area. The North American Free Trade Area (NAFTA) is one such grouping. The Association of South East Asian Nations (ASEAN) has the aim of establishing a free trade area by the year 2020.

Customs unions

A customs union goes further than a free trade area, not only eliminating barriers to trade between the member countries, but also having a common tariff barrier against the rest of the world. The European Single Market is such an agreement. A customs union does not need to have a common currency, so that the UK is a member of the Single Market even though it has not yet adopted the euro. European integration will be the topic of Chapter 34.

Key terms

free trade area: a group of countries that agree to trade without barriers between themselves, but having their own individual barriers with countries outside the area

customs union: a group of countries that agree to trade without barriers between them, and with a common tariff barrier against the rest of the world

Evaluation

An important question in evaluating both free trade areas and customs unions is the extent to which they are able to generate increased trade and improved efficiency in production.

By creating a free trade area or customs union (i.e. without or with common barriers against the rest of the world), it is possible that the member nations will trade with each other instead of with the rest of the world; in other words, it is possible that trade will simply be diverted from the rest of the world to the partners in the agreement. Such trade diversion does not necessarily mean that gains from trade are being fully exploited, as ideally there should be *trade creation* as well as trade diversion.

However, it is to be hoped that a trading agreement such as a free trade area or customs union would generate efficiency gains. If firms are able to service a larger overall market, it should be possible to exploit economies of scale and scope, which would reduce average production costs. This may require countries to alter their pattern of specialisation to take full advantage of the enlarged market. For example, within the European Union there is a wide range of countries having different patterns of comparative advantage, ranging from countries like the UK, France or Germany to the new members from Eastern Europe and the Baltic. The relative endowment of labour and capital among the member states can be expected to be very different.

This diversity is important for the success of a trade grouping. Remember that it is the *difference* in relative opportunity costs of production that drives the comparative advantage process and creates the potential gains from trade. However, it is clear that there also tends to be a strong political dimension affecting the outcome of such trade agreements.

The World Trade Organisation

A famous conference was held at Bretton Woods in the USA at the end of the Second World War to agree on a set of rules under which international trade would be conducted. This conference established an exchange rate system under which countries agreed to set the price of their currencies relative to the US dollar (see Chapter 32). In addition, the conference set up three institutions to oversee matters. The International Monetary Fund (IMF) would provide assistance (and advice) to countries experiencing balance of payments difficulties and the World Bank would provide assistance (and advice) on long-term development issues. However, it was also recognised that the conduct of trade would need some oversight. Initially, this role was fulfilled by the General Agreement on Tariffs and Trade (GATT), under the auspices of which there was a sequence of 'Rounds' of reductions in tariffs, together with a significant reduction in quotas and voluntary export restraints. The last of these was the Uruguay Round, which covered the period 1986–94 and led to the formation of the World Trade Organisation (WTO), which replaced the GATT in 1995.

While continuing to pursue reductions in barriers to trade, the WTO has also taken on the role of providing a framework for the settlement of trade disputes. You will appreciate that, with all the moves towards regional integration and protectionism, such a role is very important. Indeed, the WTO reports that around 300 cases for settlement of disputes were brought to the WTO in its first 8 years – about the same number that were dealt with over the entire life of the GATT, i.e. 1947–94.

In 2000 new talks started covering agriculture and services. The fourth WTO Ministerial Conference in Doha in November 2001 incorporated these discussions into a broader work programme, the Doha Development Agenda. According to the WTO website, this agenda includes:

> ...work on non-agricultural tariffs, trade and environment, WTO rules such as anti-dumping and subsidies, investment, competition policy, trade facilitation,

transparency in government procurement, intellectual property, and a range of issues raised by developing countries.

Progress on the Doha agenda has not been smooth. This is partly because agriculture is an especially contentious area, with the USA, the EU and Japan having large-scale policies in place to support their agricultural sectors. In the case of the EU's Single Market, some moves have been made towards reforming the Common Agricultural Policy, but progress has not been as rapid as developing countries would like – remembering that agriculture is especially important for many of the less-developed countries. *The Economist* in 2003 drew attention to the fact that 'the rich world spends over $300 billion a year supporting its farmers, more than six times the amount it spends on foreign aid.'

Summary

- Regional groupings of countries have been formed to promote trade between neighbours; examples include ASEAN, MERCOSUR, NAFTA and the EU's Single Market.
- A free trade area is a group of countries that agree to trade between themselves without barriers.
- A customs union not only eliminates barriers to trade between member countries, but also imposes a common tariff against the rest of the world.
- A key factor influencing the success of such arrangements is the degree to which there is trade creation as well as trade diversion.
- The World Trade Organisation (WTO) has a responsibility to promote trade by pursuing reductions in tariffs and other barriers to trade, and also discharges a role in dispute settlement between nations.

Foreign direct investment

An important aspect of globalisation has been the spread of foreign direct investment (FDI) by MNCs. UNCTAD has identified three main reasons for such activity:

1 market-seeking
2 resource-seeking
3 efficiency-seeking

Key term

foreign direct investment (FDI): investment undertaken in one country by companies based in other countries

Some MNCs may engage in FDI because they want to sell their products within a particular market, and find it preferable to produce within the market rather than elsewhere: such FDI is *market seeking*. Second, MNCs may undertake investment in a country in order to take advantage of some key resource. This might be a natural resource such as oil or natural gas, or a labour force with certain skills, or simply be cheap unskilled labour: such FDI is *resource seeking*. Third, MNCs may simply review their options globally, and decide that they can produce most efficiently in a particular location. This might entail locating just part of their production chain in a certain country. Such FDI is *efficiency seeking*.

Market-seeking FDI has been important in some regions in particular. The opening up of China to foreign investment has proved a magnet for MNCs wanting to gain access to this large and growing market. In addition, non-European firms have been keen to gain entry to the EU's Single Market, which has encouraged substantial flows of FDI into Europe.

For the UK, there has been a two-way flow of direct investment. In other words, foreign investors have invested in the UK, and UK investors have invested abroad. Figure 31.8 shows the inward and outward flows, expressed as a percentage of GDP. Both inward and outward flows peaked in 2000, a year in which outward direct investment reached more than 16% of GDP. This reflected intense merger and acquisition activity at that time. The largest outward acquisitions were by Vodafone Airtouch, which invested in Mannesmann AG to the tune of £100 billion, and BP Amoco plc, which purchased Atlantic Richfield Company for a reported £18 billion. After 2000 merger and acquisition activity slowed down, partly following the terrorist attacks in September 2001.

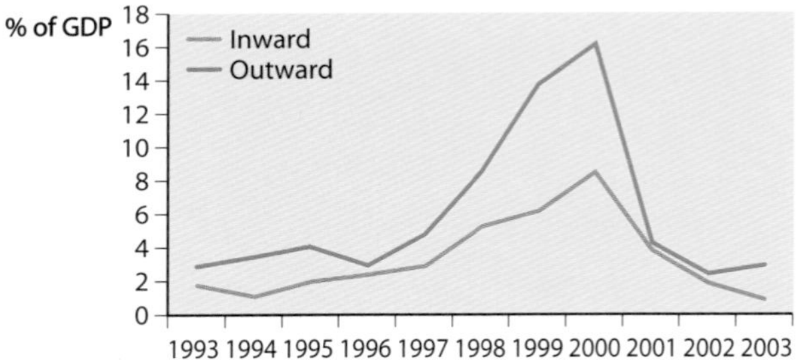

Figure 31.8 *UK foreign direct investment, 1993–2003*

Source: *Pink Book*.

Summary

- An important part of globalisation has been the spread of foreign direct investment (FDI) by multinational corporations.
- Motivations for FDI include market-seeking, resource-seeking and efficiency-seeking reasons.
- Cross-border mergers and acquisitions have tended to follow a cyclical pattern over time, with a peak in 2000.

External shocks

One of the issues concerning a more closely integrated global economy is the question of how robust the global economy will be to shocks. In other words, globalisation may be fine when the world economy is booming, as all nations may be able to share in the success. But if the global economy goes into recession, will all nations suffer the consequences? There are a number of situations that might cause the global economy to take a downturn.

Oil prices

Oil prices seem to provide one possible threat. In the past, sudden changes in oil prices have caused widespread disruption — for example, in 1973–74 and in 1979–80.

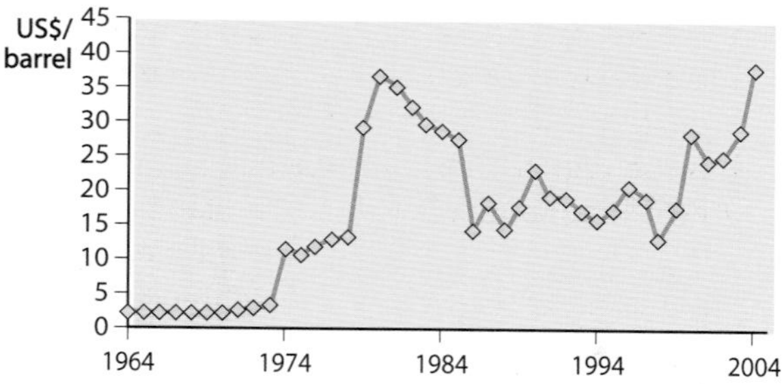

Figure 31.9 The price of oil, 1964–2004

Source: IMF.

Figure 31.9 shows the historical time path of the price of oil, measured in US dollars. In 1973–74 the sudden increase in the price of oil took most people by surprise. Oil prices had been steady for several years, and many economies had become dependent upon oil as an energy source, not only for running cars but for other uses such as domestic central heating. The sudden increases in the price in 1973–74 and again in 1979–80 caused widespread problems, because demand in the short run was highly inelastic, and oil-importing countries faced sudden deficits on their balance of payments current accounts. However, in time people switched away from oil for heating, firms developed more energy-efficient cars, and demand was able to adjust. Arguably, national economies in the 2000s are less vulnerable to changes in the price of oil than they were in 1973. This is not to say that the rise in oil prices to over $40 a barrel in 2004 did not cause problems, but economies were better equipped to withstand the increase. The UK was partly able to weather the storm because of its position as an oil producer.

Another difference was that the price rises in 1973–74 and 1979–80 had been primarily supply-side changes, caused by disruptions to supply following the actions of the OPEC cartel. In the 2000s part of the upward pressure on price is coming from demand, with China's demand for oil being especially strong.

Financial crises

Given the increasing integration of financial markets, a further concern is whether globalisation increases the chances that a financial crisis will spread rapidly between countries, rather than being contained within a country or region. The 1997 Asian financial crisis provides some evidence on this issue.

This crisis began in Thailand and South Korea. Both countries had been the recipients of large flows of FDI. In the case of Thailand, a significant part of this had been investment in property, rather than in productive investment. The Thai currency (the baht) came under speculative pressure early in 1997, and eventually the authorities had to allow a devaluation. This sparked a crisis of confidence in the region, and foreign investors began to withdraw funds, not only from Thailand but from other countries too. As far as globalisation was concerned, the key questions were how far the crisis would spread, and how long it would last.

In the event, five countries bore the main burden of the crisis: Indonesia, Malaysia, the Philippines, South Korea and Thailand. Beyond this grouping there were some knock-on effects because of the trade linkages, but arguably these were not too severe, and were probably dominated by other events taking place in the period.

At the time of the crisis, Indonesia and the Philippines had been at a somewhat lower stage of development than the other countries involved, and thus suffered more deeply in terms of recession. However, with the benefit of hindsight, it seems that the region showed resilience in recovering from the crisis. Indeed, it can be argued that South Korea and Thailand especially emerged as stronger economies after the crisis, through the weeding out of some relatively inefficient firms and institutions and through a heightened awareness of the importance of sound financial regulation.

China and the USA

An important question in the early to mid-2000s was how the global economy would cope with two seemingly distant but related phenomena: the rapid growth of the Chinese economy, and the deficit on the US current account of the balance of payments. The US current account deficit arose partly from the heavy public expenditure programme of the Bush Administration. However, the deficit grew to unprecedented levels partly through the actions of China and other East Asian economies that had chosen to peg their currencies to the US dollar. Effectively, this meant that those economies were buying US government securities as a way of maintaining their currencies against the dollar, thereby keeping US interest rates relatively low and allowing the American public to borrow to finance high consumer spending.

Who gains from this situation? The USA is able to spend, and China is able to sell, fuelling its rapid rate of economic growth. For how long the situation can be sustained remains to be seen.

Globalisation evaluated

The economic arguments in favour of allowing freer trade are strong, in the sense that there are potential gains to be made from countries specialising in the production of goods and services in which they have a comparative advantage. Globalisation facilitates and accelerates this process. And yet, there have sometimes been violent protests against globalisation, directed in particular at the WTO, whose meeting at Seattle in 1999 ended in chaos following demonstrations in the streets.

Tension has always been present during moves towards freer trade. Even if the economic arguments appear to be compelling, nations are cautious about opening up to free trade. In particular, there has been concern about jobs in the domestic economy. This is partly because there are transitional costs involved in liberalising trade, as some economic activities must contract to allow others to expand. Vested interests can then lead to lobbying and political pressure, as was apparent in the USA in the early part of the twenty-first century. There is also the question of whether globalisation will allow recession to spread more quickly between countries — but this is not proven.

In many ways, the WTO gets caught in the middle. The WTO has the responsibility of encouraging moves towards free trade, and thus comes under pressure from nations that want to keep some degree of protection because they are unwilling to undergo the transitional costs of structural change. The WTO thus has the unpalatable job of protecting countries from themselves, enforcing short-term costs in the interests of long-term gains.

However, the anti-globalisation protests are based on rather different arguments. One concern is that economic growth can proceed only at some cost to the environment. It has been argued that, by fragmenting the production process, the cost to the environment is high. This is partly because the need to transport goods around the world uses up valuable resources. It is also argued that nations have an incentive to lower their environmental standards in order to attract MNCs by enabling low-cost production. This is not so much an argument against globalisation as an argument that an international agency is required to monitor global environmental standards.

It has also been suggested that it is the rich countries of the world that stand to gain most from increasing global trade, as they have the market power to ensure that trading conditions work in their favour. Again, the WTO may have a role here in monitoring the conditions under which trade takes place. At the end of the day, trade allows an overall increase in global production and more choice for consumers. The challenge is to ensure that these gains are equitably distributed, and that the environment can be conserved.

Summary

- Although closer integration may bring benefits in terms of increased global production and trade, it may also create a vulnerability by allowing adverse shocks to spread more rapidly between countries.
- Such shocks would include oil price changes or financial crises. However, the integrated global economy may turn out to be more resilient in reacting to adverse circumstances.
- Globalisation facilitates and accelerates the process by which gains from trade may be tapped.
- However, the transitional costs for individual economies in terms of the need for structural change have encouraged politicians to turn to protectionist measures.
- Critics of globalisation have pointed to the environmental costs of rapid global economic growth and the expansion of trade, and have argued that it is the rich countries and the multinational corporations that gain the most, rather than the less-developed countries.

Exercise 31.3

Examine the economic arguments for and against globalisation.

part 7

Chapter 32

The balance of payments and competitiveness

For an individual economy, the potential gains from international trade in a globalised economy depend on the pattern of comparative advantage and on the competitiveness of domestic economic activity compared with the rest of the world. The ultimate health of the economy also requires long-term external balance. This chapter explores these issues.

Learning outcomes

After studying this chapter, you should:

- understand the role and significance of the balance of payments and the need to maintain external balance in the long run
- be familiar with the factors that influence international competitiveness
- be aware of the relative competitiveness of the UK in the world economy, and the changing importance of the manufacturing and service sectors
- appreciate the degree of openness of the UK economy
- understand ways in which government intervention has influenced the competitiveness of UK economic activity
- be familiar with the use of alternative policy measures to manage the balance of payments

The balance of payments

Chapter 11 introduced the balance of payments, a set of accounts that monitors the transactions that take place between UK residents and the rest of the world. For an individual household it is important to monitor incomings and outgoings, as items purchased must be paid for in some way — either by using income or savings, or by borrowing. In a similar way, a country has to pay for goods, services or assets that are bought from other countries. The balance of payments accounts enable the analysis of such international transactions.

As with the household, transactions can be categorised as being either incoming or outgoing items. For example, if a car made in the UK is exported (i.e. purchased by a non-resident of the UK), this is an 'incoming' item, as the payment for the car is a credit to the UK. On the other hand, the purchase of a bottle of Italian wine (an import) is a debit item.

Similarly, all other transactions entered into the balance of payments accounts can be identified as credit or debit items, depending upon the direction of the payment. In other words, when money flows into the country as the result of a transaction, that is a credit; if money flows out, it is a debit. As all items have to be paid for in some way, the overall balance of payments when everything is added together must be zero. However, individual components can be positive or negative.

In line with international standards, the accounts are divided into three categories. The **current account** identifies transactions in goods and services, together with income payments and international transfers. Income payments here include the earnings of UK nationals from employment abroad and payments of investment income. Transfers are mainly transactions between governments, for example between the British government and EU institutions, which makes up the largest component. Also included here are flows of bilateral aid and social security payments abroad.

The **financial account** measures transactions in financial assets, including investment flows and central government transactions in foreign exchange reserves.

The **capital account** is relatively small. It contains capital transfers, the largest item of which is associated with migrants. When a person changes status from non-resident to resident of the UK, then any assets owned by that person are transferred to being British-owned.

Figure 32.1 shows the relative size of the main accounts since 1970. Notice that these data are in current prices, so

Key terms

current account of the balance of payments: account identifying transactions in goods and services between the residents of a country and the rest of the world

financial account of the balance of payments: account identifying transactions in financial assets between the residents of a country and the rest of the world

capital account of the balance of payments: account identifying transactions in (physical) capital between the residents of a country and the rest of the world

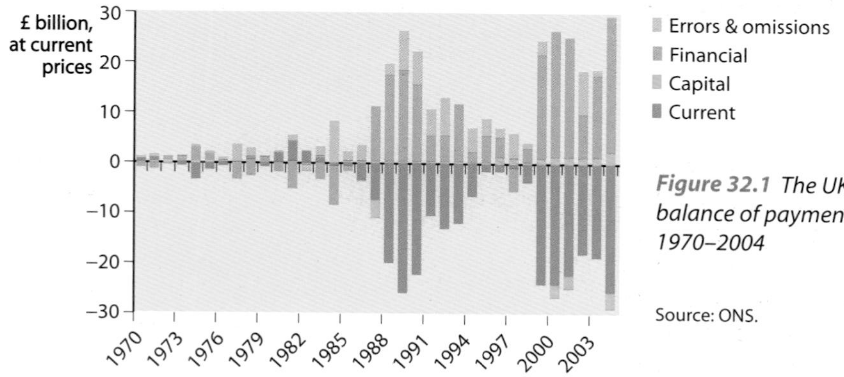

Figure 32.1 The UK balance of payments, 1970–2004

Source: ONS.

no account has been taken of changing prices during the period. This has the effect of compressing the apparent magnitude of the variables in the early part of the period (when prices were relatively low), and exaggerating the size towards the end of the period. Expressing these nominal values as a percentage of nominal GDP (as in Figure 32.2 for a longer period) provides a less misleading picture.

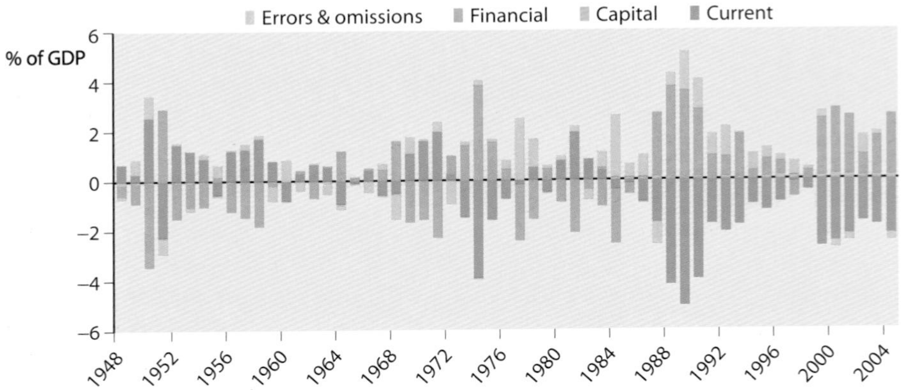

Figure 32.2 The UK balance of payments, 1948–2004
Source: ONS.

As the total balance of payments must always be zero, the surplus (positive) components above the line must always exactly match the deficit (negative) items below the line. However, both figures indicate that the magnitudes of the three major accounts varies through time.

The current account

The current account has been in deficit every year since 1984. The recorded current account surpluses in 1980–83 were associated with North Sea oil, which was then just coming on stream. There followed a phase in which the deficit grew to record levels, peaking in 1989. During the 1990s, the deficit fell until 1999, at which time the UK economy entered into a period in which the current account has been consistently in substantial deficit, and the financial account in surplus.

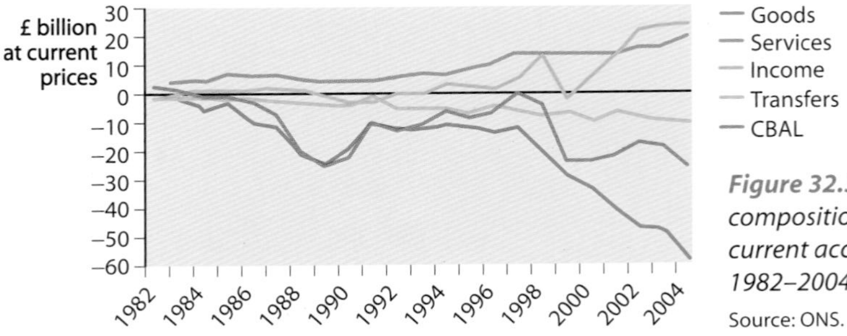

Figure 32.3 The composition of the current account, 1982–2004 (balances)
Source: ONS.

Figure 32.3 shows the components of the current account. You can see that until the early 1990s the overall balance on the current account (CBAL) tracked closely the trade in goods. More recently, however, the trade in goods has moved further into deficit, although this has been partially offset by a gradual increase in the trade in services and (except in 1999) by an increase in income – which is made up mainly of investment income.

Key terms

visible trade: trade in goods

invisible trade: trade in services

Trade in goods (sometimes known as **visible trade**) has traditionally shown a deficit for the UK – it has shown a surplus in only 6 years since 1900. As reserves of oil in the North Sea run down, the UK is likely to become a net importer of oil, but up to 2003 the UK continued to be a net exporter of oil; in other words, the oil part of the trade in goods is in surplus. However, imports of cars and other consumer goods have persistently exceeded exports. A summary for 2003 is presented in Table 32.1. You should be aware that these data are in current prices, so you need to focus on the relative sizes rather than the absolute values.

Item	1993	2003
Food, beverages and tobacco	–4127	–10 259
Basic materials	–2801	–2806
Oil	2612	4110
Coal, gas and electricity	–1010	940
Semi-manufactured goods:		
Chemicals	4762	5222
Precious stones and silver	367	769
Other	–4304	–7557
Finished manufactured goods		
Motor cars	–3583	7167
Other consumer goods	–6073	–18 453
Intermediate goods	–997	–3397
Capital goods	643	–6794
Ships and aircraft	1212	–1156
Commodities not classified	233	–742
Total	**–13 066**	**–47 290**

Table 32.1 UK trade in goods (balances), 1993 and 2003 (£m in current prices)

Source: *Pink Book.*

In contrast, trade in services has recorded a surplus in every year since 1966. This is sometimes referred to as **invisible trade**. Table 32.2 shows the component items in 1993 and 2003 – again, measured in current prices, so that no allowance has been made for the effects of inflation.

As you can see, the largest deficit items in trade in services are transportation (especially air transport services, which has shown a deficit every year since the mid-1980s) and travel, where again the deficit has grown significantly since the late 1980s. The main reason for this is the increasing number of UK residents travelling aboard. However, these negative items are more than compensated by the surplus components, especially financial services, which has grown steadily, as have computer and information services. You can see that 'Other business' also makes a significant contribution. This category includes trade-related services such as merchanting, consultancy services such as advertising, engineering and legal services, and operational leasing.

Item	1993	2003
Transportation	–628	–4236
Travel	–2810	–15 812
Communications	–204	59
Construction	20	29
Insurance	1427	5630
Financial	4014	9936
Computer and information	352	2489
Royalties and licence fees	503	1539
Other business	4000	15 112
Personal, cultural and recreational	264	609
Government	–357	–738
Total	**6581**	**14 617**

Table 32.2 UK trade in services (balances), 1993 and 2003 (£m in current prices)

Source: *Pink Book.*

An important item on the current account is investment income, which represents earnings on past investment abroad. This item has shown strong growth since 1999 (when there was a deficit). The largest item in this part of the account is earnings from direct investment, although there is also an element of portfolio investment – earnings from holdings of bonds and other securities. The final category is current transfers. This includes taxes and social contributions received from non-resident workers and businesses, bilateral aid flows and military grants. However, the largest item is transfers with EU institutions, which has been in persistent deficit.

The financial account

The trend towards globalisation means that both inward and outward investment increased substantially during the 1990s, although there was a dip after 2000. However, Figure 32.1 shows that the financial account has been in strong surplus in the early part of the twenty-first century. This is in part forced by the deficit on the current account. In other words, if an economy runs a current account deficit, it can do so only by running a surplus on the financial account. Effectively, what is happening is that, in order to fund the current account deficit, the UK is selling assets to foreign investors and borrowing abroad.

An important question is whether this practice is sustainable in the long run. Selling assets or borrowing abroad has future implications for the current account, as there will be outflows of investment income, and debt repayments in the future following today's financial surplus. It also has implications for interest rate policy. If the authorities hold interest rates high relative to the rest of the world, this will tend to attract inflows of investment, again with future implications for the current account.

The capital account

The capital account is relatively small. The largest item relates to the flows of capital associated with migration. If someone migrates to the UK, that person's status changes from being a non-resident to being a resident. His or her property then becomes part of the UK's assets, and a transaction has to be entered in the balance of payments accounts. There are also some items relating to various EU transactions. This account has been in surplus for 20 years.

Summary

- The balance of payments is a set of accounts that contains details of the transactions that take place between the residents of an economy and the rest of the world.
- The accounts are divided into three sections: the current, financial and capital accounts.
- The current account identifies transactions in goods and services, together with some income payments and international transfers.
- The financial account measures transactions in financial assets, including investment flows and central government transactions in foreign reserves.
- The capital account, which is relatively small, contains capital transfers.
- The overall balance of payments must always be zero.

- The current account has been in persistent deficit since 1984, reflecting a deficit in trade in goods that is partly offset by a surplus in invisible trade.
- The financial account has been in strong surplus — as is required to balance the current account deficit.

Exercise 32.1

Allocate each of the following items to either the current, financial or capital accounts, and calculate the balances for each account. Check that (together with errors and omissions) the total is zero. All data refer to 2002, at current prices in £ billion.

a	Trade in goods	−46.68	**g**	Trade in services	+15.58
b	Migrants' transfers	+1.28	**h**	Other capital transfers	−0.41
c	Total net direct investment	−5.11	**i**	Compensation of employees	+0.07
d	Investment income	+21.41	**j**	Total net portfolio investment	+50.09
e	Current transfers	−8.60	**k**	Other transactions in financial assets	−36.59
f	Transactions in reserve assets	+0.46	**l**	Errors and omissions	+8.50

International competitiveness

In analysing the balance of payments, the relative competitiveness of British goods and services is an important issue. If the UK persistently shows a deficit on the current account, does that imply that UK goods are uncompetitive in international markets?

The demand for UK exports in world markets depends upon a number of factors. In some ways, it is similar to the demand for a good. In general, the demand for a good will depend on its price, on the prices of other goods, and on consumer incomes and preferences. In a similar way, you can think of the demand for UK exports as depending on the price of UK goods, on the price of other countries' goods, and on incomes in the rest of the world and foreigners' preferences for British goods over those produced elsewhere. However, in the case of international transactions the exchange rate will also be relevant, as this determines the purchasing power of UK incomes in the rest of the world. Similarly, the demand for imports into the UK will depend upon the relative price of domestic and foreign goods, incomes in the UK, preferences for foreign and domestically produced goods and the exchange rate. These factors will all come together to determine the balance of demand for exports and imports.

The exchange rate plays a key role in influencing the levels of both imports and exports, and Chapter 33 is devoted to analysing how exchange rates are determined. Figure 32.4 shows the time path of the US$/£ exchange rate since 1971. It shows some fluctuations between 1971 and the late 1980s, although around a declining trend. However, since then the exchange rate seems to have remained fairly steady.

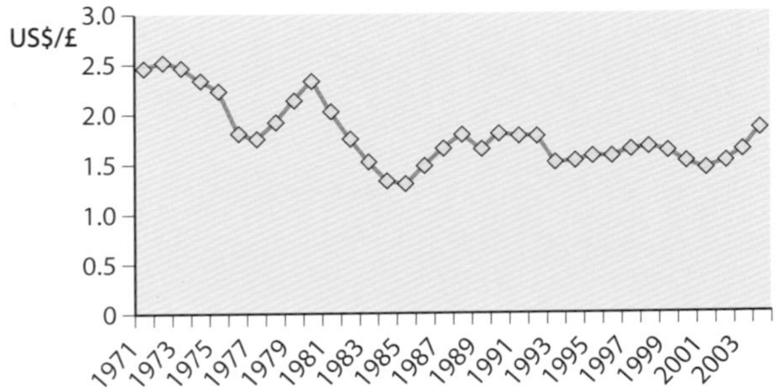

Figure 32.4 The nominal exchange rate, US$/£, 1971–2003

Source: ONS.

Nonetheless, there was a fall from a peak of $2.50 to the pound in 1972 to $1.50 some 30 years later. Other things being equal, this would suggest an improvement in the competitiveness of UK products. In other words, Americans wanting to buy UK goods got more pounds for their dollars in 2002 than in 1972, and thus would tend to find UK goods more attractive.

However, some care is needed, because other things do not remain equal. In particular, remember that the competitiveness of British goods in the US market depends not only on the exchange rate, but also on movements in the prices of goods over time, so this needs to be taken into account – which is why Figure 32.4 refers to the *nominal exchange rate*. In other words, if the prices of UK goods have risen more rapidly than prices in the USA, this will partly offset the downward movement in the exchange rate.

Figure 32.5 shows the nominal exchange rate again, but also the ratio of UK/US consumer prices. This reveals that between 1971 and 1977 UK prices rose much more steeply than those in the USA, and continued to rise relative to the USA until the 1990s. Thus, the early decline in the nominal exchange rate was offset by the movement in relative prices.

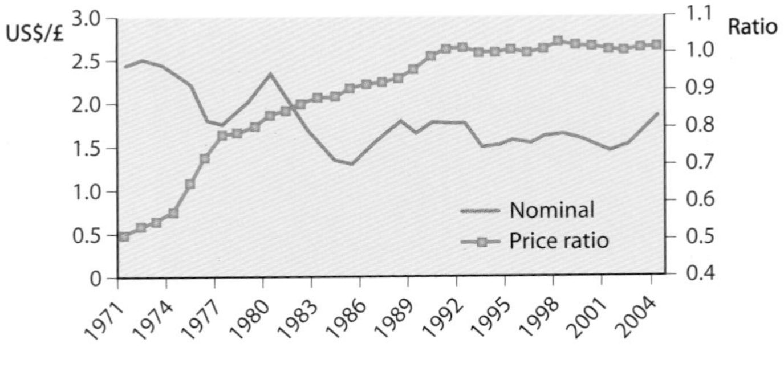

Figure 32.5 The real exchange rate, US$/£, and the ratio of UK/US prices, 1971–2004

Source: ONS, IMF.

In order to assess the overall competitiveness of UK goods compared with the USA, it is necessary to calculate the **real exchange rate**, which is defined as the nominal exchange rate multiplied by the ratio of relative prices.

Key term

real exchange rate: the nominal exchange rate adjusted for differences in relative inflation rates between countries

The real exchange rate is shown in Figure 32.6. The real exchange rate also shows some fluctuations, especially between about 1977 and 1989. However, there does not seem to be any strong trend to the series, although the real rate was higher at the end of the period than at the beginning.

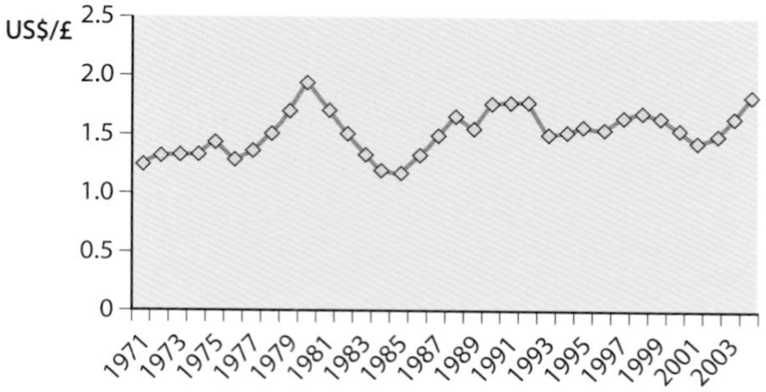

Figure 32.6 *The real exchange rate, US$/£, 1971–2003*

Notice that this series relates only to competitiveness relative to the USA, as it is the real US$/£ exchange rate. An alternative measure is the *sterling effective exchange rate*, shown in Figure 32.7. This shows the strength of sterling relative to a weighted average of exchange rates of the UK's trading partners.

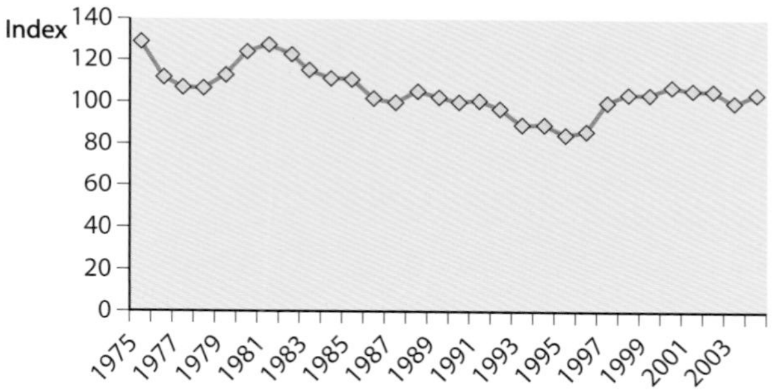

Figure 32.7 *The sterling effective exchange rate, 1975–2004 (1990 = 100)*

Source: ONS.

Exercise 32.2

Table 32.3 provides data for the €/£ exchange rate, together with the consumer price index for the euro area and for the UK. Use these data to calculate the real exchange rate for the period, and comment on the effect that any movement will have had on the competitiveness of British goods and services relative to the euro area.

	Nominal exchange rate (€/£)	Consumer price index (2000 = 100)	
		UK	Euro area
1998	1.4796	97.9	96.6
1999	1.5189	99.2	97.7
2000	1.6456	100.0	100.0
2001	1.6092	101.2	102.1
2002	1.5952	102.5	104.4
2003	1.4481	103.9	106.6
2004	1.4753	105.3	108.9

Table 32.3 *Competitiveness of the UK compared to the euro area*

Source: OECD, IMF.

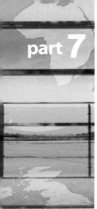

The terms of trade

A final indicator to consider is the **terms of trade**. This is defined as the ratio of export prices to import prices, and provides information about the purchasing power of exports in terms of imports.

Key term

terms of trade: the ratio of export prices to import prices

A fall in the terms of trade indicates that the same volume of exports will purchase a smaller volume of imports than before. A downward movement in the terms of trade is thus unfavourable for an economy. Figure 32.8 shows the terms of trade for the UK economy since 1970. The substantial fall that is seen in 1973 and 1974 is due to the adverse oil price shock that occurred at that time. However, it would seem from this figure that the terms of trade have remained fairly constant since the early 1980s.

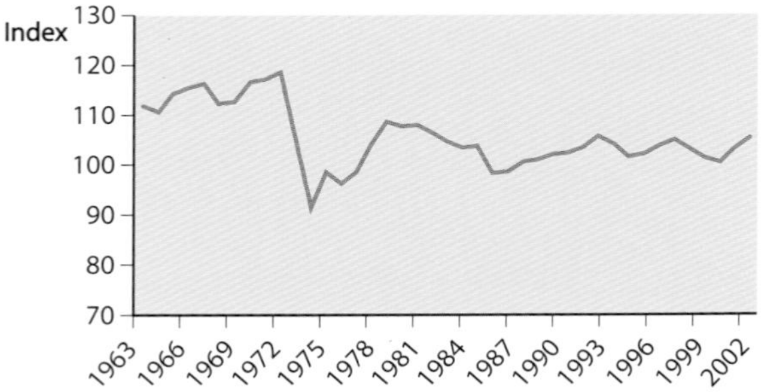

Figure 32.8
The UK terms of trade, 1963–2002 (2001 = 100)

Source: ONS.

The terms of trade are calculated purely with respect to prices, and take no account of changing volumes of trade. In other words, a deterioration in the terms of trade does not necessarily mean that an economy is worse off, so long as the volume of trade is increasing sufficiently rapidly.

Summary

- Relative prices and the exchange rate are an important influence on the competitiveness of goods and services in the international market.
- The real exchange rate adjusts the nominal exchange rate to allow for differing inflation rates between countries.
- The terms of trade are measured by the ratio of export prices to import prices.

International differences in productivity

From a different angle, competitiveness also depends upon relative costs of production in different countries, which influences the prices that firms can charge. This in turn partly reflects different levels of productivity across countries. Remember that productivity is a measure of productive efficiency; for example, labour productivity is output per unit of labour input. Different countries show appreciable differences in efficiency by this measure.

However, international comparisons of productivity are not straightforward, as measurements are subject to differences in data collection and differences in work practices. Figure 32.9 presents data for 2003 on GDP per head of population, expressed as index numbers with the USA being the reference country, and thus set to 100. On this measure, the UK performs rather better than Japan, France, Germany and Italy. As a measure of productivity levels, however, this is a misleading indicator. In particular, working hours are longer in the UK than in many other countries (especially within Europe), so in part GDP per head reflects differences in the quantity of labour input. For this reason, GDP per hour worked is often seen as a more reliable indicator of relative productivity levels. This measure is graphed in Figure 32.10, and shows quite a different pattern. Indeed, on this basis both Ireland and France show higher productivity than the USA, and the UK's performance is much more modest.

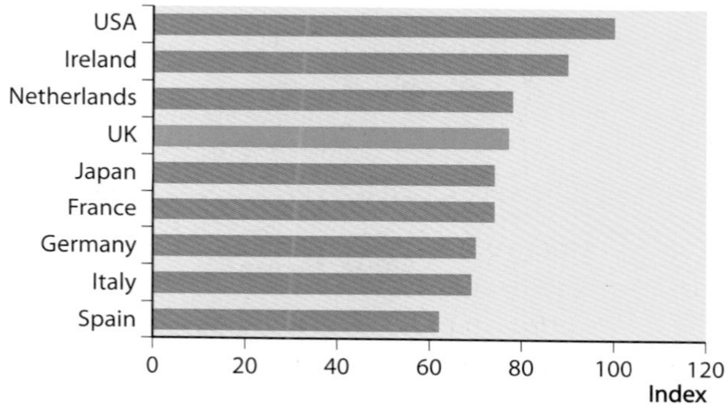

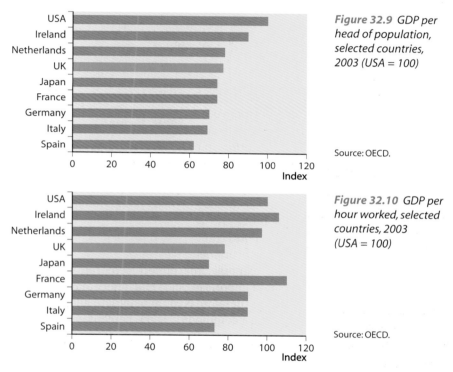

Figure 32.9 *GDP per head of population, selected countries, 2003 (USA = 100)*

Source: OECD.

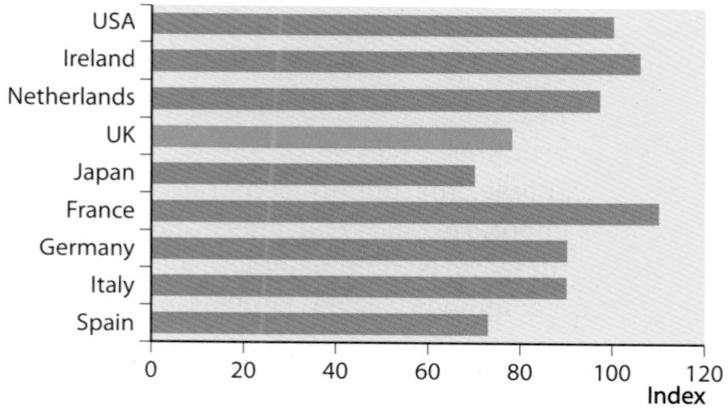

Figure 32.10 *GDP per hour worked, selected countries, 2003 (USA = 100)*

Source: OECD.

Figure 32.11 gives the time path for an index of GDP per hour worked, based this time on 1970 = 100. It shows that European countries have been experiencing stronger productivity growth than the USA over this period.

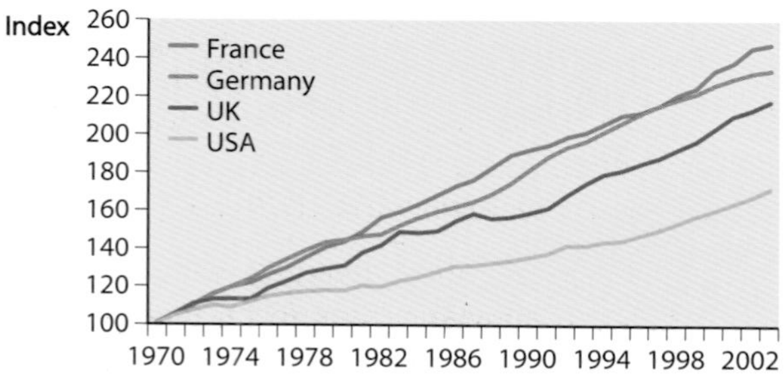

Figure 32.11 *Index of GDP per hour worked, selected countries, 1970–2002 (1970 = 100)*

Source: OECD.

It is also important to realise that labour productivity is not the only relevant measure, as countries may also differ in their use of capital. Total factor productivity is more difficult to measure, as the measurement of capital stock is especially prone to error and misinterpretation. However, some estimates of multifactor productivity growth are shown in Figure 32.12.

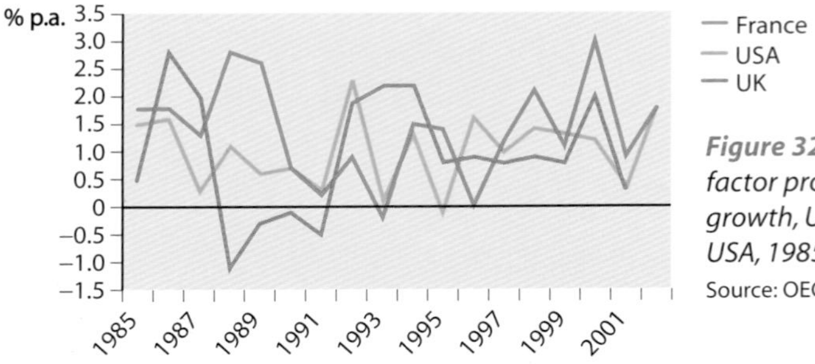

Figure 32.12 *Multi-factor productivity growth, UK, France and USA, 1985–2001*

Source: OECD.

The trade performance of the UK economy

One way of exploring the performance of the British economy in international trade is to look at **import penetration ratios** and **export sales ratios**.

> **Key terms**
>
> **import penetration ratio:** ratio of the percentage of imports of a product to home demand
>
> **export sales ratio:** ratio of the percentage of exports of a product to total manufacturers' sales

The import penetration ratio measures the portion of home demand that is met by imports of particular commodities. As a measure, this is a little difficult to interpret where a sector is engaged in exporting as well as importing activity; for example, the import penetration ratio (without allowing for exporting) shows that imports of office machinery and computers were 122% of home demand in 2001. It therefore is more helpful to allow for exports by measuring import penetration for a commodity as the percentage ratio of imports to (home demand + exports). Some examples for 2001 are shown in Figure 32.13.

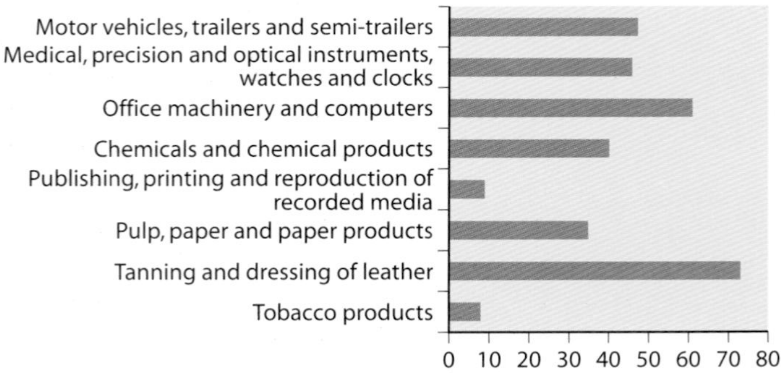

Figure 32.13 *Import penetration ratio*, selected commodities, 2001*

*Ratio of imports to [home demand + exports].

Source: ONS: *Annual Abstract of Statistics*.

Similarly, Figure 32.14 shows export sales ratios, again allowing for the fact that trade is often two way, so that some allowance has to be made for importing activity, rather than just considering the ratio of exports to total sales.

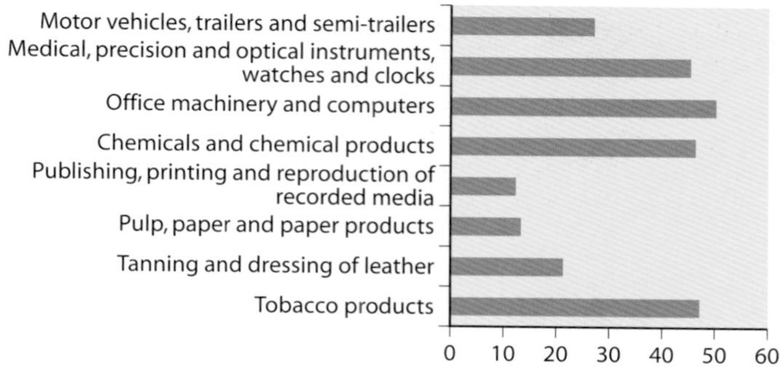

***Figure 32.14** Export sales ratio*, selected commodities, 2001*

*Ratio of exports to [total sales + imports].

Source: ONS: *Annual Abstract of Statistics.*

These data provide some information about the extent to which British firms are active in international trade. For example, the commodity group of office machinery and computers shows an import penetration ratio of 61%: in other words, imports make up 61% of home demand plus exports. However, you can also see that export sales constitute 50% of total sales plus imports. In contrast, both import penetration and export sales ratios for publishing, printing and reproduction of recorded media are relatively low, suggesting much less engagement in international trade in this activity. In the case of the tanning and dressing of leather, import penetration is relatively high but the export sales ratio is relatively low, suggesting that this is a product in which the UK does not have a comparative advantage, relying on imports and not engaging in much exporting activity.

There have been some significant changes in these ratios since 1992. Sectors in which import penetration has risen include pharmaceuticals; TV, radio and phone transmitters; jewellery and related products; coal extraction; and tobacco products. Import penetration has fallen for sports goods and toys; oil and gas extraction, 'other textiles'; and special purpose machinery. The rapid growth of output (and exports) by the UK service industries between 1992 and 2002 has meant that very few service products have high import penetration ratios.

Openness to international trade

The extent to which economies are open to international trade varies substantially. One way of measuring this is to calculate the ratio of exports plus imports to GDP, as has been done for selected countries in Figure 32.15. Countries like Hong Kong, Malaysia and South Korea have deliberately encouraged international trade as a route to economic growth, hoping that trade will give rise to economies of scale. Indeed, Hong Kong is an extreme example of this, with both exports and imports exceeding the value of GDP. This is possible because the data include re-exports – where products are imported and then exported again. For countries like Hong Kong and Singapore, where trading activity itself is part of their comparative advantage, such transactions are important. At the other extreme, Japan and the USA show a low dependence on international trade. In the case of Brazil, India, Argentina and China, trade dependence is relatively low because of a deliberate policy to limit their dependence on trade. In all of these cases, the ratio of trade to GDP has increased noticeably since 1990 – especially in the case of China, which has opened up rapidly, and is expanding both imports and exports.

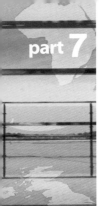

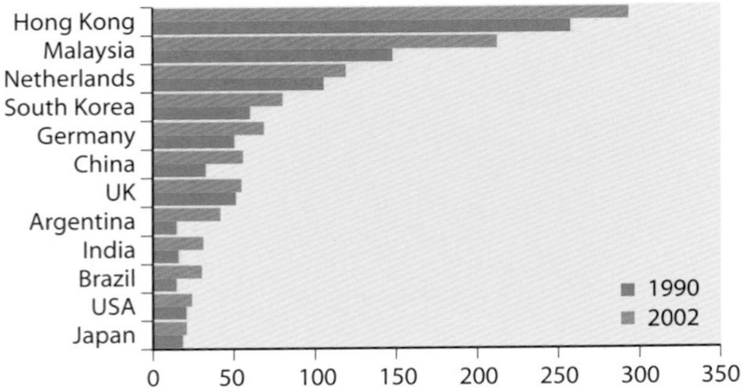

*Figure 32.15 Openness to trade, selected countries, 1990 and 2002**

*[Exports + imports] as % of GDP.

Source: World Bank.

Figure 32.16 presents the share of UK exports and UK imports in GDP since 1950. This shows a gradual increase in the UK's openness to trade, but conceals substantial changes in the direction of trade; these were discussed in Chapter 31, which highlighted the increasing importance of the EU as a trading partner.

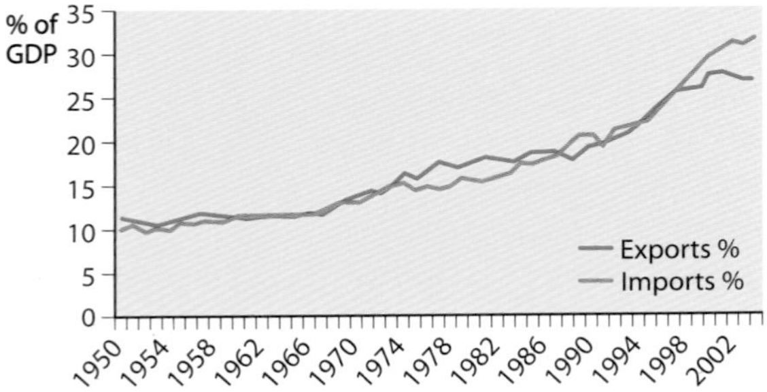

Figure 32.16 UK exports and imports in GDP, 1950–2004

Source: ETAS.

Summary

- Competitiveness also depends upon the relative costs of production in different countries, which in turn partly reflects differences in productivity.
- Data for international comparison of productivity differences need to be treated with some care, but GDP per hour worked is a helpful indicator.
- Labour productivity is not a sufficient measure, given that countries differ in their relative endowments of labour, capital and other factors of production.
- Information about the pattern of trade is provided by import penetration and export sales ratios.
- Import penetration ratios have been relatively low for UK service industries, which have expanded rapidly.
- The extent to which countries are open to international trade varies substantially around the world.
- In the UK exports and imports have increased as a share of GDP, but at a relatively slow pace.

Trade and the UK government

There are a number of ways in which policies adopted by governments have affected UK trade and competitiveness. Some of these policies were deliberately targeted at trade or competitiveness; others may have had different objectives.

Deregulation and privatisation

The British economy has gone through a process of deregulation and privatisation since 1980 that has had a major impact on many parts of the economy. One of the main aims of the privatisation drive that began in the 1980s was to reduce X-inefficiency by making the managers of formerly state-run enterprises more accountable. As efficiency improved, British firms experienced an improvement in their cost structures that should have improved competitiveness. For example, if the privatisation of power generation leads to productivity gains that allow electricity to be supplied at a lower price, this reduces costs for firms throughout the economy.

However, deregulation also entailed changes in many other sectors. Of particular relevance for trade and competitiveness is the liberalisation of financial markets that also took place. Such measures as the removal of restrictions on capital movements encourage trade. The advances in the technology of communications have reinforced this by enabling rapid, reliable and efficient financial transactions.

Foreign direct investment

The UK government has introduced policies to attract foreign direct investment (FDI). These may encourage trade directly. For example, if a Japanese car manufacturer chooses to build a factory in the UK in order to supply the European market, this will have an effect on UK exports. However, it will also mean an outflow of dividend payments to Japanese shareholders at a later date, so the effects on the balance of payments may not be as great as they first appear.

However, there may also be indirect effects. If a Japanese firm becomes successful operating in the UK, it is possible that working practices used by the firm may spread to other UK firms, which in turn may improve their efficiency and thereby make them more competitive internationally. Indeed, the very presence of foreign firms competing in the domestic market may be a spur for domestic firms to become more efficient.

The British government has introduced policies to attract FDI.

Labour market flexibility

One of the most important policy areas as far as trade and competitiveness is concerned has been the increased flexibility in labour markets that has been encouraged by successive governments. For example, the trade union reforms that were introduced by the Thatcher government during the 1980s enabled firms to adopt more flexible working practices, and enabled labour markets to adjust more easily to changes in the pattern of consumer demand and in the UK's comparative advantage.

Furthermore, improvements in education and training have increased the skill levels of the labour force, improving productivity directly and also encouraging the growth of economic activities requiring higher skills levels. This flexibility in adjusting to a changing market environment has improved British industry and service activity and enabled firms to take advantage of new trading opportunities. In particular, the EU Single Market has encouraged British firms to compete within Europe, where labour markets tend to be less flexible. In this way, the UK has been able to maintain a competitive edge.

Moreover, these policies, which have produced a flexible labour market and a skilled workforce, have increased the attractiveness of the UK as a destination for foreign direct investment, since foreign multinationals value these characteristics.

Managing the balance of payments

It was argued earlier that, although in the short run it may be possible to balance a deficit on the current account of the balance of payments by a surplus on the financial account, in the long run this might not be sustainable. The main reason for this is that there may be a limit on foreign exchange reserves and on the extent to which it is desirable to fund the current account by borrowing or by selling UK assets.

The question then is how the government could manage the balance of payments; in other words, how is it possible to alter the structure of transactions by reducing the size of the current account deficit? There are three basic routes that could contribute to this if the government decided that it needed to do so: demand management, supply-side policies or exchange rate adjustments.

Demand management

One reason for a current account deficit is that, as real incomes rise in the economy, there is a tendency for UK residents to buy more imported goods or services, because the income elasticity of demand for imports tends to be relatively high. One possibility therefore would be to control the level of aggregate demand in order to limit the demand for imports; for example, the government could raise taxes, or reduce government expenditure. Whether the government would want to do this may depend upon whether such a policy would damage other aspects of the economy. For example, a reduction in aggregate demand might cause an increase in unemployment, and if the government gave a higher priority to achieving full employment it might prefer to live with the current account deficit. It is also possible that long-run economic growth could be inhibited. (The question of conflict between government policy objectives will be discussed in Chapter 35.)

The alternative would be to introduce a policy that was targeted more towards reducing the demand for imports. For example, the use of tariffs or quotas would raise the price of imports, and so reduce demand for them, and at the same time encourage domestic producers to increase their production. However, within the context of the EU it is not realistic to imagine that the UK could set its own independent tariff rates, even if it wanted to do so. In any case, it has already been explained that the use of tariffs entails a misallocation of resources in society, and a deadweight loss.

Supply-side policies

An alternative approach would be to make use of supply-side policies to influence the deficit. Many of the policies discussed earlier in this chapter that have affected trade and competitiveness fall into this category; for example, policies to improve the flexibility of the labour market would be classified as supply-side policies. If these can improve the competitiveness of British firms, they should stimulate trade.

In addition, it might be argued that steps taken to increase the productive capacity of the economy would allow an increase in exports that would (*ceteris paribus*) reduce the current account deficit.

Notice that the extent of the gain depends in part upon the import content of UK exports. Remember, from the discussion of penetration ratios and export sales ratios, that many exporting sectors also import from abroad. For example, component parts might be imported into the country, assembled and then re-exported. This may limit the gain from increasing exports.

Nonetheless, supply-side policies are an effective way of improving the competitiveness of the British economy, thereby reducing a current account deficit.

Exchange rate adjustment

The competitiveness of British exports and of domestic goods and services relative to imports both depend crucially on the exchange rate, as was mentioned early in this chapter. The role of the exchange rate and how it is determined is the subject of the next chapter. However, for now it is important to note that the exchange rate will influence the size of the current account deficit. Under current policy procedures, the prime target of macroeconomic policy is to keep inflation at a low level. This is achieved by the Bank of England setting interest rates at the level needed to hit the inflation target. If the interest rate required for this purpose is high relative to elsewhere in the world, there will tend to be flows of financial capital into the UK. In turn, this suggests that the equilibrium for the exchange rate will be relatively high, which limits the competitiveness of British goods and services and results in a balance of payments that is achieved through a current account deficit and a financial account surplus. In this way, the government may be restricted in the extent to which it can manipulate the exchange rate to reduce the current account deficit, unless it is prepared to give a higher priority to this than to other targets of macroeconomic policy. This helps to explain why it is supply-side policies that have been at the forefront in ensuring the competitiveness of British firms in international markets.

Summary

- Trade and competitiveness have been affected by government policy, both directly and indirectly.
- Privatisation has led to productivity improvements by reducing X-inefficiency.
- Deregulation of financial markets, coupled with improved technology for undertaking financial transactions, has encouraged international trade.
- Policy measures were introduced to encourage foreign direct investment, which may have had beneficial spillover effects on domestic firms.
- Measures to improve the flexibility of labour markets have helped to make British firms competitive internationally.
- Improved education and skills training have also contributed to the competitiveness of British firms.
- Demand management could be used to reduce a deficit on the current account of the balance of payments, but governments may be reluctant to use this approach if it damages targets for full employment or economic growth.
- Supply-side policies have encouraged trade by improving the efficiency of UK industry.
- In principle, exchange rate adjustments could be used to influence the balance of payments, but careful attention needs to be given to the effects on other targets of macro-economic policy.

Exercise 32.3

Figure 32.17 shows the current account deficits of the UK and the USA, expressed as a percentage of GDP. Discuss the extent to which this represents a potential problem for the two countries. Does it make a difference that the US dollar plays a role as a reserve currency?

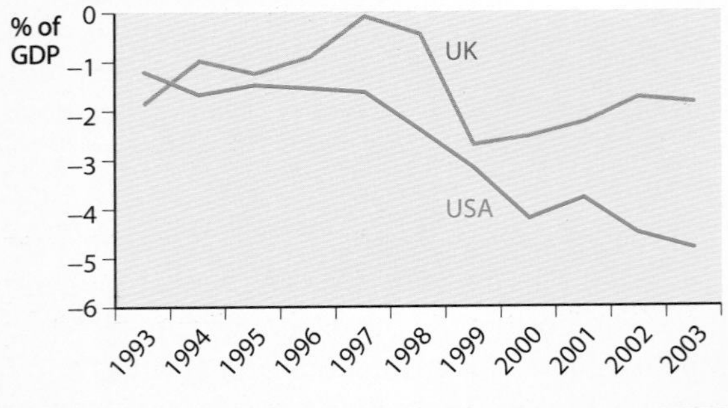

Figure 32.17 *Current account deficits, UK and USA, 1993–2003*

part 7

Chapter 33

Exchange rate systems

For any economy that is open to international trade, the exchange rate is a crucial variable, as it influences the competitiveness of domestic firms in international markets. The way in which the exchange rate is determined has wide-reaching effects on the conduct and effectiveness of macroeconomic policy. From the end of the Second World War until the early 1970s, a system of fixed exchange rates was in operation, whereby economies set the value of their currency relative to the US dollar. After this system broke down, most developed countries allowed their currencies to 'float', finding their own market levels, although at times governments have been tempted to intervene in this market. Some countries continue to peg their exchange rates to the US dollar. This chapter investigates why the exchange rate is so important, and how the various systems for determining its value work.

Learning outcomes

After studying this chapter, you should:

- understand what is meant by the market for foreign exchange
- understand the operation of a fixed exchange rate system
- be familiar with a floating exchange rate system
- be aware of the major determinants of exchange rates within a floating exchange rate system
- understand the way in which macroeconomic policy influences the exchange rate, and vice versa
- understand how changes in exchange rates can affect the level of economic activity in a country

The foreign exchange market

Chapter 4 introduced the foreign exchange market, and argued that it could be regarded as involving demand and supply, just like any normal market. A foreign exchange transaction is needed whenever trade takes place. If, as a UK resident, you buy goods from abroad, you need to purchase foreign exchange – say, euros

– and you will have to supply pounds in order to buy euros. Similarly, if a French tourist in the UK buys UK goods or services, the transaction needs to be carried out in pounds, so there is a demand for pounds.

This market is shown in Figure 33.1. The demand curve is downward sloping because when the €/£ rate is low British goods, services and assets are relatively cheap in terms of euros, so demand is relatively high. On the other hand, when the €/£ rate is relatively high, Europeans receive fewer euros for their pounds, so the demand will be relatively low.

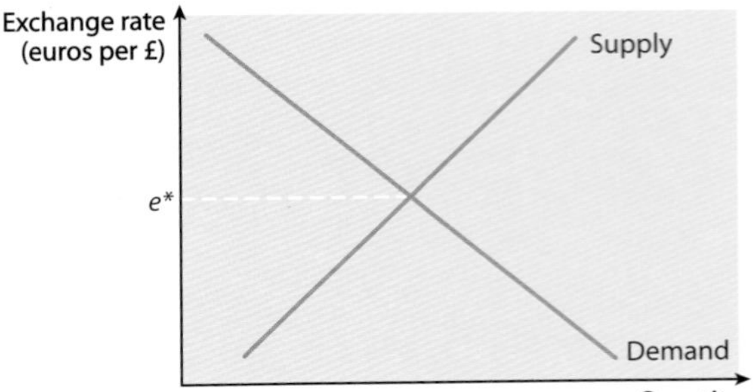

Figure 33.1 The market for pounds

The supply curve of pounds is upward sloping. When the €/£ rate is relatively high, the supply of pounds will be relatively strong, as UK residents will get plenty of euros for their pounds and thus will demand European goods, services and assets, supplying pounds in order to buy the foreign exchange needed for the transactions. When the €/£ rate is low, European goods, services and assets will be relatively expensive for UK residents, so fewer pounds will be supplied.

The market is in equilibrium at e^*, where the demand for pounds is just matched by the supply of pounds. This position has a direct connection with the balance of payments. If the demand for pounds exactly matches the supply of pounds, this implies that there is a balance between the demand from Europeans for UK goods, services and assets and the demand by UK residents for European goods, services and assets. In other words, the balance of payments is in overall balance. The key question for consideration is how the market reaches e^* – in particular, do the authorities allow the exchange rate to find its own way to e^*, or do they intervene to ensure that it gets there?

Summary

- The foreign exchange market can be seen as operating according to the laws of demand and supply.
- The demand for pounds arises when non-residents want to buy British goods, services or assets.
- The supply of pounds arises when UK residents wish to buy foreign goods, services or assets.
- When the exchange rate is at its equilibrium level, this automatically ensures that the overall balance of payments is zero.

A fixed exchange rate system

In the Bretton Woods conference at the end of the Second World War, it was agreed to establish a fixed exchange rate system, under which countries would commit to maintaining the price of their currencies in terms of the US dollar. This system remained in place until the early 1970s. For example, from 1950 until 1967 the sterling exchange rate was set at \$2.80, and the British government was committed to making sure that it stayed at this rate. This system became known as the Dollar Standard. Occasional changes in exchange rates were permitted after consultation if a currency was seen to be substantially out of line — as happened for the UK in 1967.

Figure 33.2 illustrates how this works. Suppose the authorities announce that the exchange rate will be set at e_f. Given that this level is set independently by the government, it cannot be guaranteed to correspond to the market equilibrium, and in Figure 33.2 it is set above the equilibrium level. At this exchange rate the supply of pounds exceeds the demand for pounds. This can be interpreted in terms of the overall balance of payments. If there is an excess supply of pounds, the implication is that UK residents are trying to buy more American goods, services and assets than Americans are trying to buy British; in other words, there is an overall deficit on the balance of payments.

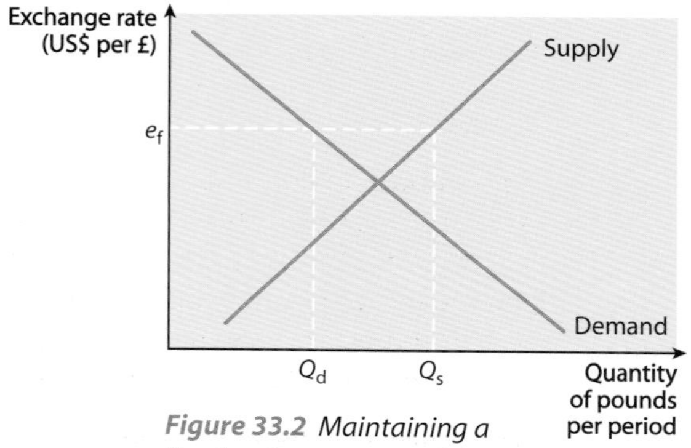

Figure 33.2 Maintaining a fixed exchange rate

In a free market, you would expect the exchange rate to adjust until the demand and supply of pounds came back into equilibrium. However, with the authorities committed to maintaining the exchange rate at e_f, such adjustment cannot take place. However, the UK owes the USA for the excess goods, services and assets that its residents have purchased, so the authorities then have to sell **foreign exchange reserves** in order to make the books balance.

Key term

foreign exchange reserves: stocks of foreign currency and gold owned by the central bank of a country to enable it to meet any mismatch between the demand and supply of the country's currency

In terms of Figure 33.2, Q_d represents the demand for pounds at e_f and Q_s represents the supply. The difference represents the amount of foreign exchange reserves that the authorities have to sell to preserve the balance of payments. Such transactions were known as 'official financing', and are now incorporated into the financial account of the balance of payments.

Notice that the *position* of the demand and supply curves depends on factors other than the exchange rate that can affect the demand for British and American goods, services and assets in the respective countries. It is likely that through time these will shift in position. For example, if the preference of Americans for British goods changes through time, this would affect the demand for pounds.

Consider Figure 33.3. For simplicity, suppose that the supply curve remains fixed but demand shifts through time. Let e_f be the value of the exchange rate that the UK monetary authorities have undertaken to maintain. If the demand for pounds is at D_1, the chosen exchange rate corresponds to the market equilibrium, and no action by the authorities is needed. If demand is at D_0, then with the exchange rate at e_f there is an excess supply of pounds (as shown in Figure 33.2). The monetary authorities in the UK need to buy up the excess supply by selling foreign exchange reserves. Conversely, if the demand for pounds is strong, say because Americans have developed a preference for Scotch whisky, then demand could be at D_2. There is now excess demand for pounds, and the British monetary authorities supply additional pounds in return for US dollars. Foreign exchange reserves thus accumulate.

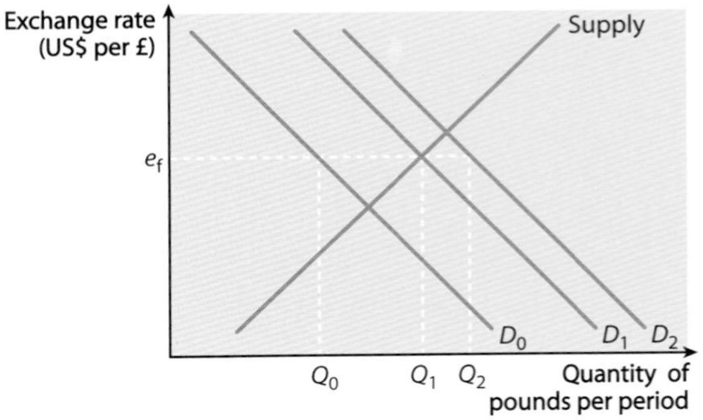

Figure 33.3 Maintaining a fixed exchange rate in the face of changing demand for pounds

In the long term, the system will operate successfully for the country so long as the chosen exchange rate is close to the average equilibrium value over time, so that the central bank is neither running down its foreign exchange reserves nor accumulating them.

A country that tries to hold its currency away from equilibrium indefinitely will find this problematic in the long run. For example, in the early years of the twenty-first century China and some other Asian economies were pegging their currencies against the US dollar at such a low level that they were accumulating foreign exchange. In the case of China, it was accumulating substantial amounts of US government stock. The low exchange rate had the effect of keeping the exports of these countries highly competitive in world markets. However, such a strategy relies on being able to continue to expand domestic production to meet the high demand; otherwise inflationary pressure will begin to build.

During the period of the Dollar Standard, the pound was probably set at too high a level, which meant that British exports were relatively uncompetitive, and in 1967 the British government announced a **devaluation** of the pound from $2.80 to $2.40.

During the Dollar Standard period, the British economy went through what became known as a 'stop–go' cycle of growth. When the government tried to stimulate economic growth, the effect was to suck in imports, as the marginal propensity to import was high. The effect of

Key terms

devaluation: process whereby a government reduces the price of its currency relative to an agreed rate in terms of foreign currency

revaluation: process whereby a government raises the price of domestic currency in terms of foreign currency

this was to generate a deficit on the current account of the balance of payments, which then needed to be financed by selling foreign exchange reserves.

This process has two effects. First of all, in selling foreign exchange reserves, domestic money supply increases, which then puts upward pressure on prices, threatening inflation. In addition, the Bank of England has finite foreign exchange reserves, and cannot allow them to be run down indefinitely. This meant that the government had to rein in the economy, thereby slowing the rate of growth again. Hence the label 'stop–go'.

An important point emerges from this discussion. The fact that intervention to maintain the exchange rate affects domestic money supply means that under a fixed exchange rate regime the monetary authorities are unable to pursue an independent monetary policy. In other words, money supply and the exchange rate cannot be controlled independently of one another. Effectively, the money supply has to be targeted to maintain the value of the currency. Governments may be tempted to use tariffs or non-tariff barriers to reduce a current account deficit, but this has been shown to be distortionary.

The effects of devaluation

During the stop–go period there were many debates about whether there should be a devaluation. The effect of devaluation is to improve competitiveness. At a lower value of the pound, you would expect an increase in the demand for exports and a fall in the demand for imports, *ceteris paribus*.

However, this does not necessarily mean that there will be an improvement in the current account. One reason for this concerns the elasticity of supply of exports and import substitutes. If domestic producers do not have spare capacity, or if there are time lags before production for export can be increased, then exports will not expand quickly in the short run, and so the impact of this action on exports will be limited. Furthermore, similar arguments apply to producers of goods that are potential substitutes for imported products, which reinforces the sluggishness of adjustment. In the short run, therefore, it may be that the current account will worsen rather than improve, in spite of the change in the competitiveness of domestic firms.

This is known as the *J-curve effect*, and is shown in Figure 33.4. Time is measured on the horizontal axis, and the current account is initially in deficit. A devaluation at time *A* initially pushes the current account further into deficit, because of the inelasticity of domestic supply. Only after time *B*, when domestic firms have had time to expand their output to meet the demand for exports, does the current account move into surplus.

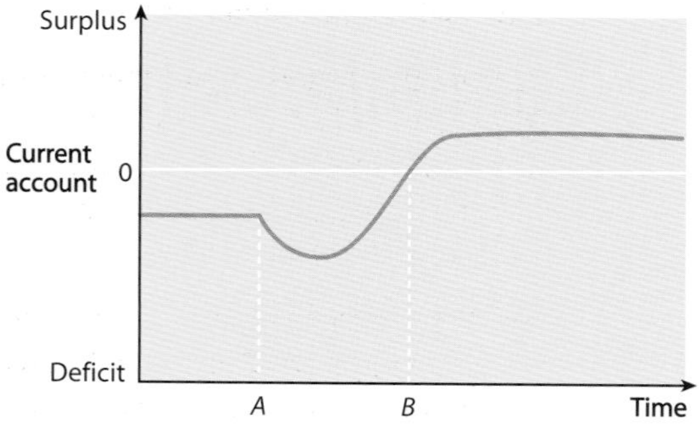

Figure 33.4 The J-curve effect of a devaluation

A second consideration relates to the elasticity of demand for exports and imports. Again, if competitiveness improves but demand does not respond strongly, there may be a negative impact on the current account. If the demand for exports is price-inelastic, a fall in price will lead to a fall in revenue. Indeed, the *Marshall–Lerner condition* states that a devaluation will have a positive effect on the current account only if the sum of the elasticities of demand for exports and imports is negative and numerically greater than 1.

The Bretton Woods Dollar Standard broke down in the early 1970s. Part of the reason for this was that such a system depends critically on the stability of the base currency (i.e. the US dollar). During the 1960s the US need to finance the Vietnam war meant that the supply of dollar currency began to expand, one result of which was accelerating inflation in the countries that were fixing their currency in terms of the US dollar. It then became increasingly difficult to sustain exchange rates at fixed levels. Britain withdrew from the dollar standard in June 1972. Following this, the pound fell steadily for the next 5 years or so, as was shown in Figure 32.4.

Summary

- After the Bretton Woods conference at the end of the Second World War, the Dollar Standard was established, under which countries agreed to maintain the value of their currencies in terms of US dollars.
- In order to achieve this, the monetary authorities engaged in foreign currency transactions to ensure that the exchange rate was maintained at the agreed level, accumulating foreign exchange reserves to accommodate a balance of payments surplus and running down the reserves to fund a deficit.
- Occasional realignments were permitted, such as the devaluation of sterling in 1967.
- Under a fixed exchange rate system, monetary policy can only be used to achieve the exchange rate target.
- A devaluation has the effect of improving international competitiveness, but the effect on the current account depends upon the elasticity of demand for exports and imports.
- The current account may deteriorate in the short run if the supply response is sluggish.
- The Bretton Woods system broke down in the early 1970s.

Exercise 33.1

A firm wants to purchase a machine tool which is obtainable in the UK for a price of £125 000, or from a US supplier for $300 000. Suppose that the exchange rate is fixed at £1 = $3.

a What is the sterling price of the machine tool if the firm chooses to buy in the USA?

b From which supplier would the firm be likely to purchase?

c Suppose that between ordering the machine tool and its delivery the UK government announces a devaluation of sterling, so that when the time comes for the firm to pay up the exchange rate is £1 = $2. What is the sterling price of the machine tool bought from the USA?

d Comment on how the competitiveness of British goods has been affected.

e Discuss the effects that the devaluation is likely to have on the economy as a whole.

Floating exchange rates

Under a floating exchange rate system, the value of the currency is allowed to find its own way to equilibrium. This means that the overall balance of payments is automatically assured, and the monetary authorities do not need to intervene to make sure it happens. In practice, however, governments have tended to be wary of leaving the exchange rate entirely to market forces, and there have been occasional periods in which intervention has been used to affect the market rate.

An example of this was the **Exchange Rate Mechanism (ERM)**, which was set up by a group of European countries in 1979 with the objective of keeping member countries' currencies relatively stable against each other. This was part of the EMS (European Monetary System). Each member nation agreed to keep its currency within 2.25% of a weighted average of the members' currencies (known as the European Currency Unit (ECU). This was an *adjustable peg* system. Eleven realignments were permitted between 1979 and 1987.

> ***Key term***
>
> **Exchange Rate Mechanism (ERM):** a system that was set up by a group of European countries in 1979 with the objective of keeping member countries' currencies relatively stable against each other

The UK opted not to join the ERM when it was first set up, but started shadowing the Deutschmark in the mid-1980s, aiming to keep the rate at around DM3 to the pound, as you can see in Figure 33.5. Britain finally decided to become a full member of the ERM in September 1990. However, the rate at which sterling had been set against the Deutschmark was relatively high, and the situation was worsened by the effects of German reunification, which led to substantial capital flows into Germany, reinforcing the overvaluation of sterling. Once it became apparent that sterling was overvalued, speculative attacks began, and the Bank of England's foreign exchange reserves were depleted; in 1992 the pound left the ERM. You can see in Figure 33.5 that the value of the pound fell rapidly after exit.

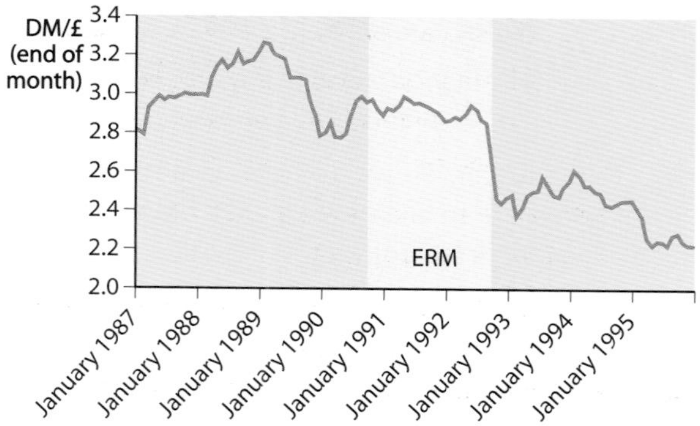

***Figure 33.5** The nominal DM/£ exchange rate, 1987–1995*

Source: Bank of England.

What determines exchange rates?

If the foreign exchange market is left free to find its own way to equilibrium, it becomes important to consider what factors will influence the level of the exchange rate. In particular, will the exchange rate resulting from market equilibrium be consistent with the government's domestic policy objectives?

Exchange rate equilibrium also implies a zero overall balance of payments. If the exchange rate always adjusts to the level that ensures this, it might be argued that the long-run state of the economy is one in which the competitiveness of domestic firms remains constant over time. In other words, you would expect the exchange rate to adjust through time to offset any differences in inflation rates between countries. The **purchasing power parity theory of exchange rates** argues that this is exactly what should be expected in the long run. If you look back at Figure 32.6, you will see that, aside from some fluctuations, the real exchange rate has remained fairly constant through time and shows no underlying trend. This is what would be expected if the nominal exchange rate was adjusting to offset changes in relative prices between countries.

Key terms

purchasing power parity theory of exchange rates: theory stating that in the long run exchange rates (in a floating rate system) are determined by relative inflation rates in different countries

hot money: stocks of funds that are moved around the world from country to country in search of the best return

However, in the short run the exchange rate may diverge from its long-run equilibrium. An important influence on the exchange rate in the short run is speculation. So far, the discussion of the exchange rate has stressed mainly the current account of the balance of payments. However, the financial account is also significant, especially since regulation of the movement of financial capital was removed. Some of these capital movements are associated with direct investment, which was discussed in the last chapter. However, sometimes there are also substantial movements of what has come to be known as **hot money**, i.e. stocks of funds that are moved around the globe from country to country in search of the best return. The size of the stocks of hot money is enormous, and can significantly affect exchange rates in the short run.

'Hot money' moves swiftly around the world in search of the best rate of interest.

Such movements can influence the exchange rate in the short run. The returns to be gained from such capital flows depend on the relative interest rate in the country targeted, and on the expected exchange rate in the future, which in turn may depend on expectations about inflation.

Suppose you are an investor holding assets denominated in US dollars, and the UK interest rate is 2% higher than that in the USA. You may be tempted to shift the funds into the UK in order to take advantage of the higher interest rate. However, if you believe that the exchange rate is above its long-run equilibrium, and therefore is likely to fall, this will affect your expected return on holding a British asset. Indeed, if investors holding British assets expect the exchange rate to fall, they are likely to shift their funds out of the country as soon as possible — which may then have the effect of pushing down the exchange rate. In other words, this may be a self-fulfilling prophecy. However, speculators may also react to news in an unpredictable way, so not all speculative capital movements act to influence the exchange rate towards its long-run equilibrium value.

Speculation was a key contributing factor in the unfolding of the Asian financial crisis of 1997. Substantial flows of capital had moved into Thailand in search of high returns, and speculators came to believe that the Thai currency (the baht) was overvalued. Outward capital flows put pressure on the exchange rate, and although the Thai central bank tried to resist, it eventually ran down its reserves to the point where it had to devalue. This then sparked off capital flows from other countries in the region, including South Korea.

Summary

- Under a floating exchange rate system, the value of a currency is allowed to find its own way to equilibrium without government intervention.
- This means that an overall balance of payments of zero is automatically achieved.
- The purchasing power parity theory argues that the exchange rate will adjust in the long run to maintain international competitiveness, by offsetting differences in inflation rates between countries.
- In the short run, the exchange rate may diverge from this long-run level, in particular because of speculation.
- The exchange rate is thus influenced by relative interest rates and expected inflation, as well as by news about the economic environment.

Fixed or floating?

In evaluating whether a fixed or a floating regime is to be preferred, there are many factors to be taken into account; this section will consider three of them. First, it is important to examine the extent to which the respective systems can accommodate and adjust to external shocks that push the economy out of equilibrium. Second, it is important to consider the stability of each of the systems. Finally, there is the question of which system best encourages governments to adopt sound macroeconomic policies.

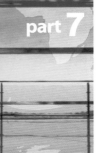

Adjustment to shocks

Every economy has to cope with external shocks that occur for reasons outside the control of the country. A key question in evaluating exchange rate systems is whether there is an effective mechanism that allows the economy to return to equilibrium after an external shock.

Under a **floating exchange rate** system, much of the burden of adjustment is taken up by changes in the exchange rate. For example, if an economy finds itself experiencing faster inflation than other countries, perhaps because those other countries have introduced policies to reduce inflation, then the exchange rate will adjust automatically to restore competitiveness.

> ***Key terms***
>
> **floating exchange rate:** a system in which the exchange rate is permitted to find its own level in the market
>
> **fixed exchange rate:** a system in which the government of a country agrees to fix the value of its currency in terms of that of another country

However, if the country is operating a **fixed exchange rate** system, the authorities are committed to maintaining the exchange rate, and this has to take precedence. Thus, the only way to restore competitiveness is by deflating the economy in order to bring inflation into line with other countries. This is likely to bring with it a transitional cost in terms of higher unemployment and slower economic growth. In other words, the burden of adjustment is on the real economy, rather than on allowing the exchange rate to adjust.

The Bretton Woods system operated for more than 20 years in a period in which many economies enjoyed steady economic growth. However, in the UK the system brought about a stop–go cycle, in which the need to maintain the exchange rate hampered economic growth, because of the tendency for growth to lead to an increase in imports and thus to a current account deficit. The increasing differences between inflation rates in different countries led to the final collapse of the system, suggesting that it was unable to cope with such variation.

Furthermore, a flexible exchange rate system allows the authorities to utilise monetary policy in order to stabilise the economy — remember that under a fixed exchange rate system monetary policy has to be devoted to the exchange rate target.

Stability

When it comes to stability, a fixed exchange rate system has much to commend it. After all, if firms know that the government is committed to maintaining the exchange rate at a given level, they can agree future contracts with some confidence. Under a floating exchange rate system, trading takes place in an environment in which the future exchange rate has to be predicted. If the exchange rate moves adversely, firms then face potential losses from trading. This foreign exchange risk is reduced under a fixed rate regime.

In a climate where speculative activity creates volatility in exchange rates, international trade may be discouraged because of the exchange rate risk. The effects of such volatility can be mitigated to some extent by the existence of **futures markets**. In such a market, it is possible to buy foreign exchange at a fixed price for delivery at a specified future date.

For example, suppose a firm is negotiating a deal to buy component parts for a manufacturing process that will be delivered in 3 months' time. The firm can buy the foreign exchange needed to close the deal in the futures market, and then knows that the contract will be viable, having negotiated a price for the components based on the known exchange rate, rather than on the unpredictable rate that will apply at that future date. The firm may of course have to pay a price for the foreign currency that is below the current (*spot*) exchange rate, but, as the future rate has been built into the terms of the contract, that will not affect the viability of the deal. The process by which a firm avoids losses by buying forward is known as *hedging*.

Key term

futures market: a market in which it is possible to buy a commodity at a fixed price for delivery at a specified future date; such a market exists for foreign exchange

However, even with the use of hedging to reduce the risk, it is costly to engage in international trade when exchange rates are potentially volatile, so world trade is unlikely to be encouraged under such a system. Of course, it might be argued that the risk to firms under a fixed exchange rate system is still present, in the sense that a government may choose to realign its currency, with even greater costs to firms that are tied into contracts. However, such realignments were rare under Bretton Woods, and are more predictable than the volatility that can occur on a day-to-day basis in the foreign exchange market.

Macroeconomic policy

Critics of the flexible exchange rate system argue that it is too flexible for its own good. If governments know that the exchange rate will always adjust to maintain international competitiveness, they may have no incentive to behave responsibly in designing macroeconomic policy. Thus, they may be tempted to adopt an inflationary domestic policy, secure in the knowledge that the exchange rate will bear the burden of adjustment. In other words, a flexible exchange rate system does not impose financial discipline on individual countries.

An example of this was seen in the UK in the early 1970s when Britain first moved to a floating exchange rate regime. Money supply was allowed to expand rapidly, and inflation increased to almost 25%, aided by the oil price shock. Other examples are evident in Latin America, where hyperinflation affected many countries during the 1980s and early 1990s. For the country itself, such policies are costly in the long run, as reducing inflation under flexible exchange rates is costly. If interest rates are increased in order to reduce domestic aggregate demand and thus reduce inflationary pressure, the high return on domestic assets encourages an inflow of hot money, thereby putting upward pressure on the exchange rate. This reduces the international competitiveness of domestic goods and services, and deepens the recession.

There may also be spillover effects on other countries. Suppose that two countries have been experiencing rapid inflation, and one of them decides to tackle the problem. It raises interest rates to dampen domestic aggregate demand, which leads to an **appreciation** of its currency. For the other country, the effect is a **depreciation** of the currency. (If one currency appreciates, the other must depreciate.) The other country thus finds that its competitive position has improved, and it faces inflationary pressure in the short run. It may then also choose to tackle inflation, which in turn will affect the other country. These spillover effects could be minimised if the countries were to harmonise their policy action.

Key terms

appreciation: a rise in the exchange rate within a floating exchange rate system

depreciation: a fall in the exchange rate within a floating exchange rate system

The exchange rate and macroeconomic policy

The discussion above has shown that the relationship between the exchange rate and macroeconomic policy is an important one. Under a fixed exchange rate system, the need to maintain the value of the currency is a constraint on macroeconomic policy, and forces the economy to adjust to disequilibrium through the real economy. On the other hand, it does have the benefit of imposing financial discipline on governments.

Under floating exchange rates the relationship with policy is less obvious. With a flexible exchange rate, the authorities can use monetary policy to stabilise the economy, knowing that there will be overall balance on the balance of payments. Nonetheless, the government needs to monitor the structure of the balance of payments. When interest rates are set at a relatively high level compared with other countries, the financial account will tend to be in surplus because of capital inflows, with a corresponding deficit on the current account. This may not be sustainable in the long run.

Summary

- There are strengths and weaknesses with both fixed and floating exchange rate systems. A floating exchange rate system is more robust in enabling economies to adjust following external shocks, but it can lead to volatility and thus discourage international trade. A fixed rate system has the added advantage of imposing financial discipline on governments, and may allow policy harmonisation.
- The move towards a fixed exchange rate system within the European Union is partly in recognition that international trade is encouraged by stability in trading arrangements, and is discussed in the next chapter.
- Under a floating exchange rate system, much of the burden of adjustment to external shocks is borne by changes in the exchange rate, rather than by variations in the level of economic activity, which may be affected more under a fixed exchange rate system.

- A fixed exchange rate system offers stability, in the sense that firms know the future value of the currency, whereas under a floating rate regime there is more volatility.
- A fixed exchange rate system imposes discipline upon governments, and may facilitate international policy harmonisation.

Exercise 33.2

Critically evaluate the following statements, and discuss whether you regard fixed or floating exchange rates as the better system.

a A flexible exchange rate regime is better able to cope with external shocks.

b A fixed exchange rate system provides a more stable trading environment and minimises risk.

c Floating exchange rates enable individual countries to follow independent policies.

d A fixed exchange rate system may encourage governments to adopt distortionary policies such as tariffs and non-tariff barriers in order to control imports.

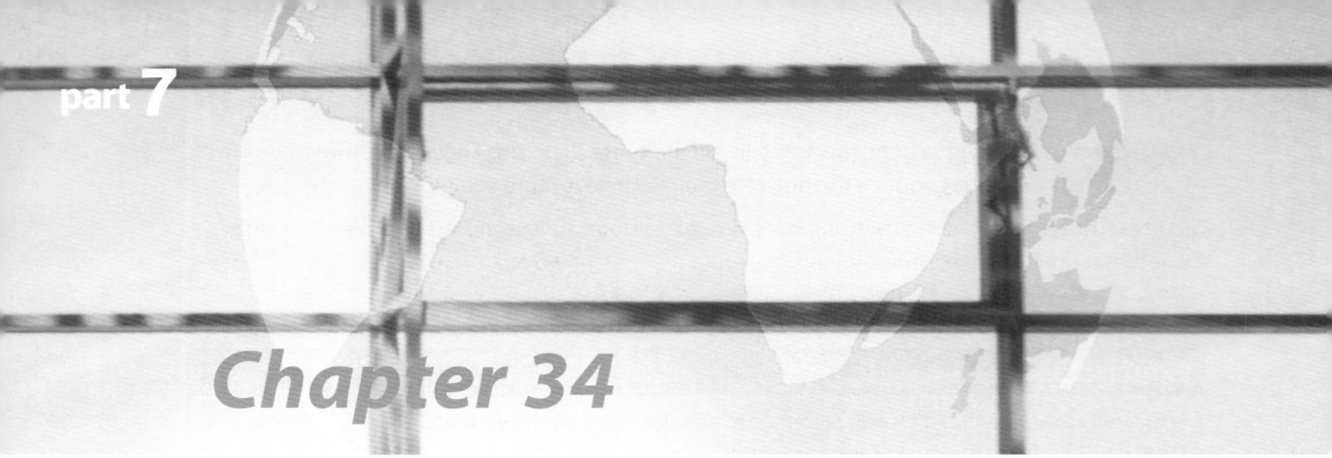

part 7

Chapter 34

European monetary union

No economic topic has raised more controversy and discussion in recent years than the question of whether Britain should join the euro single currency area. In this chapter the history of European integration will be examined, and the arguments for and against the Single Market and the euro currency area will be investigated.

Learning outcomes

After studying this chapter, you should:

- be familiar with the chronology of moves towards closer European integration
- understand the significance of the Single Market
- be able to evaluate the costs and benefits of membership of a single currency area
- be aware of the role and effectiveness of monetary and fiscal policy in a single currency area
- be able to evaluate the arguments for and against Britain joining the euro zone

Evolution of the European Union

More than 50 years ago, Robert Schuman (the then French Foreign Minister) proposed that France and West Germany should pool their coal and steel resources. That was the beginning of the long road towards European integration. Although integration has been primarily a question of economics, the political background cannot be ignored. To some people integration of the countries within Europe was seen as an attempt to avoid the conflict and wars that had afflicted Europe in the past.

The European Coal and Steel Community was established in 1951, with six participating countries: Belgium, France, West Germany, Italy, Luxembourg and the Netherlands. These same countries then formed the European Economic Community (EEC) in 1957. This became known as the *Common Market*. Since then the Community has evolved, drawing in more countries and expanding the scope of its operations. Table 34.1 sets out a chronology of the key events in the development of the present European Union (EU).

9 May 1950	Robert Schuman proposes that France and West Germany pool their coal and steel resources
1951	Treaty of Paris: European Coal and Steel Community (ECSC) is established by Belgium, France, West Germany, Italy, Luxembourg and the Netherlands
1957	Treaties of Rome: European Economic Community (EEC/'Common Market') and European Atomic Energy Community (EURATOM) are established by the six ECSC countries.
1967	Institutions of the EEC merge: a single Commission, a single Council of Ministers and a European Parliament; now known as the European Community (EC)
1970	Werner Plan proposes European monetary unity.
1973	Denmark, Ireland and the UK join the EC
1979	The European Monetary System (EMS) is launched, including the Exchange Rate Mechanism (ERM), a precursor of the single currency.
1981	Greece joins the EC
1985	Single European Market Act contains plans for completing the internal market within Europe
1986	Spain and Portugal join the EC
1989	The Delors Plan sets out proposal for creating European Economic and Monetary Union (EMU), including a single currency and European Central Bank
September 1990	The UK joins the ERM
September 1992	The UK leaves the ERM
1 January 1993	The Single Market comes into effect
November 1993	Treaty of Maastricht comes into force, creating the European Union (EU)
1995	Austria, Finland and Sweden join the EU
1 January 2002	12 EU countries adopt the euro as their currency; Denmark, Sweden and the UK are not part of this group
2004	Cyprus, the Czech Republic, Estonia, Hungary, Latvia, Lithuania, Malta, Poland, Slovakia and Slovenia join the EU

Table 34.1 *Chronology of European integration*

The 10 countries that joined in May 2004 brought the membership of the EU to 25 countries in all (the 'EU25'). Figure 34.1 shows the population size of these 25 countries in 2002, and the years in which they joined. Bulgaria and Romania were judged not to be ready to join in 2004, but were in the queue; discussions with Turkey were due to begin in 2005. If Turkey were to join, this would add a massive 70 million more citizens to the EU.

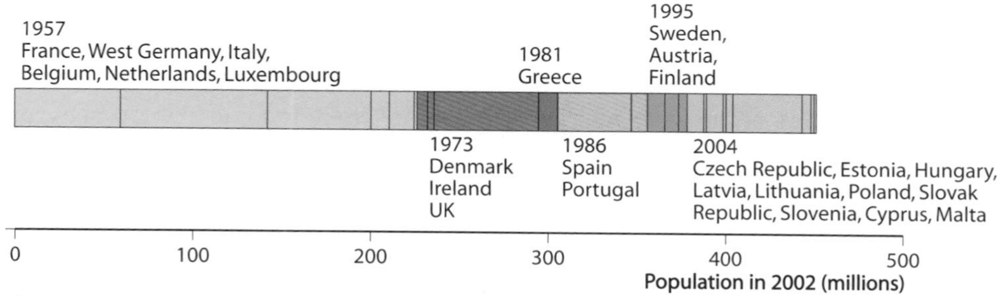

Figure 34.1 *Population of EU countries, 1957–2004*

Source: data from the *World Development Report* 2004.

Figure 34.2 shows how the enlarged EU would stand in the world rankings of big countries. This underlines the fact that the 15 pre-2004 member countries of the EU (the 'EU15') already contained more people than the USA; the combined population of the EU25 member states is 473 million, compared with 288 million in the USA.

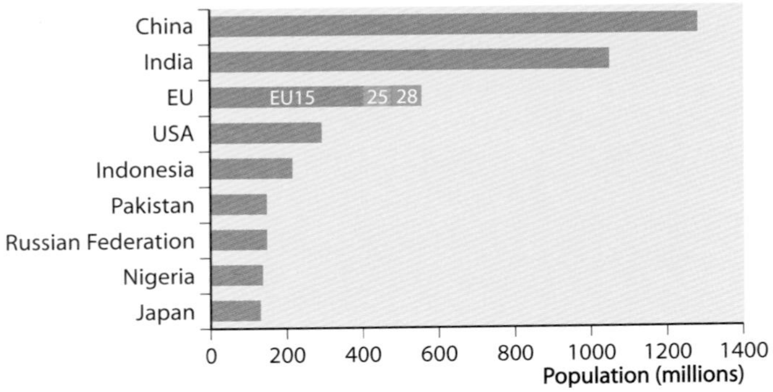

Figure 34.2
Population of selected countries, 2002 (millions)

Source: World Bank.

But how important is sheer size of population? After all, what matters in a market is the *effective* demand for goods and services — in other words, demand backed up by real purchasing power. So it is important to look not only at population size, but at purchasing power. For example, average levels of gross national income (GNI) per capita in US dollars could be a way of trying to judge purchasing power. There will be substantial variation here, with the poorest EU acceding country, Latvia, having a GNI per capita of US$3480 in 2002, compared with an estimated US$12 320 for Cyprus.

However, comparisons of GNI in US dollars can be quite misleading, as such measurements do not necessarily reflect local purchasing power because they are based on a conversion from local currency into US dollars using official exchange rates. This can give a distorted view of the comparison of income between countries, especially if the US dollar itself is away from its equilibrium level.

Figure 34.3 presents an alternative way of looking at the relative average income levels of the new member countries. The data here relate to GDP per capita measured in purchasing power parity dollars (PPP$), which helps to avoid the distortionary effects of official exchange rates. The data have then been converted into index number form, so that for each country the index shows GDP per capita relative to the EU15 average. For example, the index for the UK is 108.7, showing that the UK enjoys GDP per capita that is 8.7% higher than the average level in the first 15 EU member countries. For Latvia the index is 36.6, meaning that average income is 36.6% of the EU15 average. Notice that there is some overlap between the average income levels of the countries that joined in 2004 and some of the lower-income previous members: Cyprus has higher average income than Greece, whereas Slovenia and Malta have about the same level as Portugal.

Another way of comparing living standards across countries is by using the Human Development Index (HDI), which was introduced in Chapter 26. This takes into account not only GDP per capita, but also education and life expectancy. It takes on values between 0 and 1, with the higher values indicating higher human development. Figure 34.4 shows the values for 2002. All except Romania, Bulgaria and Turkey have reached the 'high human development' category.

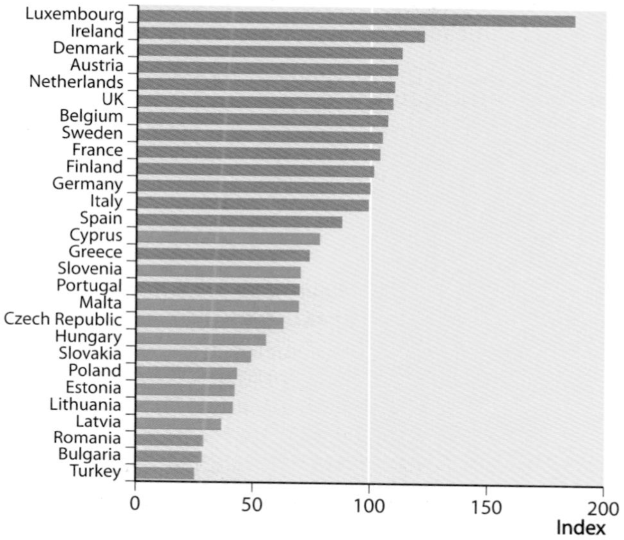

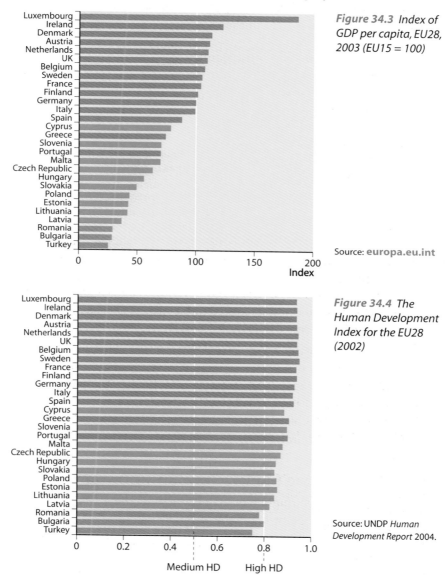

Figure 34.3 *Index of GDP per capita, EU28, 2003 (EU15 = 100)*

Source: **europa.eu.int**

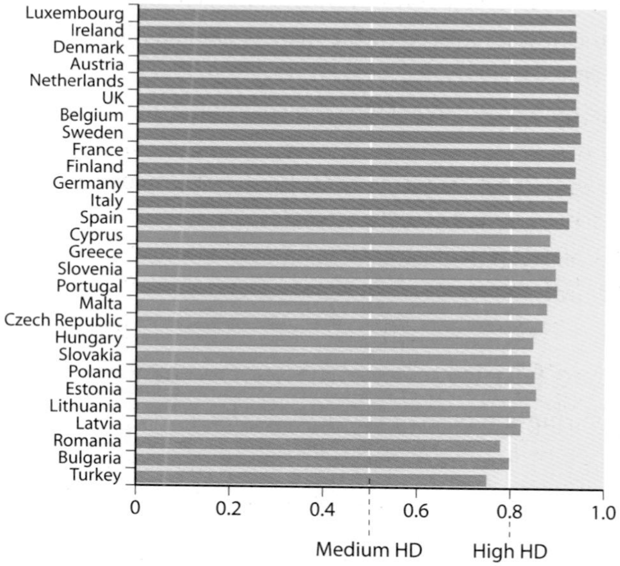

Figure 34.4 *The Human Development Index for the EU28 (2002)*

Source: UNDP *Human Development Report* 2004.

Nonetheless, it is clear that average income levels are lower in the member nations that joined in 2004 than in the incumbent members. This has implications for the size of effective demand coming from the additional consumers within the Single Market, and also implications for the *pattern* of consumer demand in terms of the sorts of goods and services that are in demand.

Figure 34.5 compares the overall structure of economic activity in the EU15 and EU28 in 2001, as measured by the contribution of the major sectors to gross value added. The left-hand column shows how important the service sector has become in the structure of economic activity, contributing some 71% of GDP of the EU15 on the value-added measure in 2001. In the acceding countries agriculture, industry and construction are relatively more important than in the EU15. Thus there may be scope for gains from trade.

In analysing European integration, there are two tiers to be considered: the evolution of the Single Market, and the development of the euro single currency area. Each will be considered in turn.

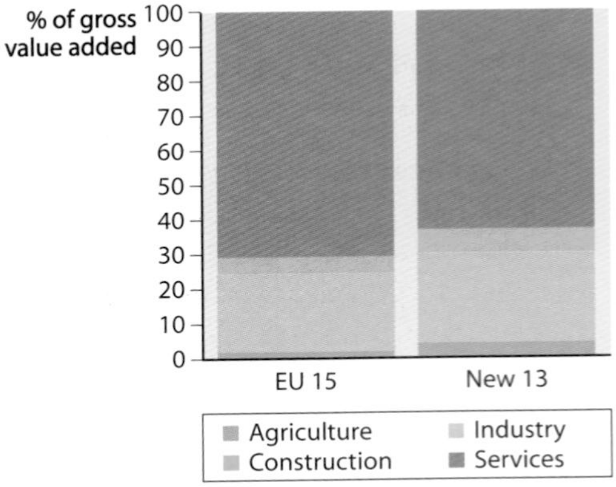

Figure 34.5 The structure of economic activity in the EU, 2001

Note: data include Bulgaria, Romania and Turkey as well as those that joined the EU in May 2004.

Source: Eurostat.

Summary

- Practical steps towards economic integration in Europe began with the European Coal and Steel Community in 1951, whereby six countries agreed to pool their coal and steel resources.
- This was so successful that it was replaced by the more wide-ranging European Economic Community (EEC), established in 1957.
- Over the following years, the EEC expanded the scope of its operations and the number of participating nations.
- By 2004, when ten more countries were granted membership, the combined membership in population terms represented some 473 million people.
- There was substantial diversity in the member countries in both living standards and the structure of economic activity.

The European Single Market

From the moment of formation of the EEC in 1957, the member countries began working towards the creation of a single market, in which there would be free movement of goods, services, people and capital. In other words, the idea was to create a common market in which there would be no barriers to trade.

The EEC was a **customs union**, in which internal tariffs and non-tariff barriers were to be removed and a common tariff was to be set against the rest of the world.

Key term

customs union: a protected free trade area, in which there are no internal barriers to trade between member nations, and a common tariff is imposed against imports from outside the union

The EEC also established the Common Agricultural Policy (CAP), which was discussed in Chapter 31. Indeed, the main focus in the early years of the EEC was on coal and steel plus the CAP. Initially, the objective of the CAP was to produce as much food as cheaply as possible, but the focus has changed in more recent years, especially since the 2003 reforms.

The Single Market package of measures came into effect in January 1993, and might be seen as the final stages of the evolution of the Single Market. The key measures in the 1992 package related to the removal (or reduction) of border controls and the winding down of non-tariff barriers to trade within the EU. Associated with these measures were a number of expected benefits. In time, it has become increasingly easy for people to move around within the EU, with passport and customs checks being abolished at most internal borders.

Transaction costs

Although tariff barriers were substantially reduced under the auspices of the GATT Rounds, a range of non-tariff barriers had built up over the years as countries sought to protect domestic employment. It was expected that the removal of these obstacles to trade, combined with the removal of border controls, would reduce the costs of trade within the EU. However, it is difficult to gauge the significance of these transaction cost savings, as it is not easy to quantify them.

Economies of scale

As trade increases, firms will find that they are operating in a larger market. This should allow them to exploit more fully the economies of large-scale production. From society's point of view, this should lead to a more efficient use of resources. These issues were discussed in Chapter 31 in the context of globalisation.

Intensified competition

Firms will find that they are facing more intense competition within that larger market from firms in other parts of the EU. This then brings up the same arguments that are used to justify privatisation — that intensified competition will cause firms or their managers to seek more efficient production techniques, perhaps through the elimination of X-inefficiencies. This again is beneficial for society as a whole.

Who gains most from this?

As trade within Europe becomes freer, there are two groups of countries which stand to gain the most. First, the pattern of comparative advantage between countries will be important. Many EU countries are advanced industrial nations, where labour is expensive relative to capital. These countries tend to specialise in manufacturing or capital-intensive service activities, and already have fairly similar structures. It is thus possible that the relatively labour-abundant countries of southern Europe may gain more from closer integration and an expansion of trade. This diversity was reinforced by the new entrants who joined in May 2004.

Second, if the main effect of integration is to remove barriers to trade, then the countries with the most to gain may be those that begin with relatively high barriers.

Figure 34.6 shows growth rates in all of the countries in 2001–02, just before the enlargement of 2004. This shows that the joining members were, on the whole, enjoying more rapid economic growth than the EU15 countries. The enlargement thus may have the effect of introducing new *dynamic economies*, and this may have spillover effects for the rest of the member nations.

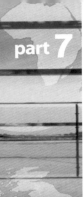

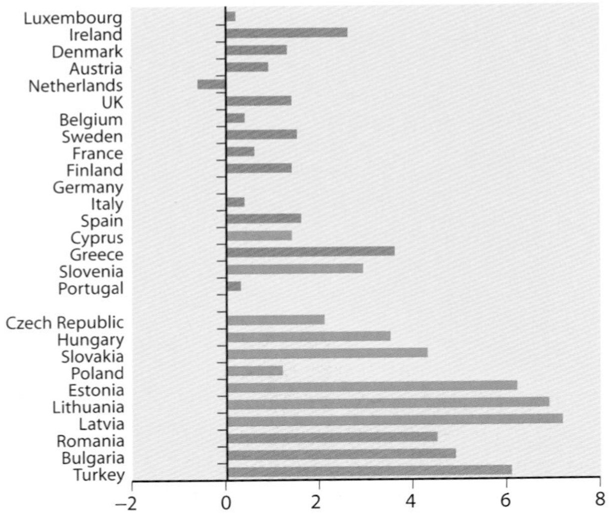

***Figure 34.6** Growth of GDP per capita, EU28, 2001–2002*

Note: no data available for Malta.

Source: *World Development Report* 2003.

How important is this to the UK?

An important piece of background information here is that over the years UK trade has become increasingly focused on Europe. This was seen in Figure 31.3, which showed the percentage of UK exports going to the EU15 countries: you can see that this has increased steadily, from about 23% in 1960 to about 53% in 2003.

Summary

- The prime objective of the EEC was to create a single market in Europe, in which there would be free movement of goods, services, people and capital.
- The EEC was a customs union, in which internal tariffs and non-tariff barriers were to be removed and a common tariff was set against the rest of the world.
- The EEC also established the Common Agricultural Policy to protect agriculture and to produce as much food as cheaply as possible.
- The Single Market package came into effect at the beginning of 1993, freeing up trade between participating countries and winding down non-tariff barriers.
- This was expected to encourage trade by lowering transaction costs, enabling firms to reap economies of scale, and enhancing efficiency by stimulating competition between European firms.

Exercise 34.1

Explain why it might be the relatively labour-intensive countries of southern Europe — and the countries of eastern Europe and the Baltic that joined in 2004 — that stand to gain most from the Single Market.

The single currency

The establishment of the Single Market was seen by some as an end in itself, but others regarded it as a step towards full monetary integration, in which all member states would adopt a single currency, thereby reducing the transaction costs of international trade even more. However, full monetary union and the adoption of a common currency is about much more than transaction costs and has raised much debate, not least because of the political dimension. Critics of closer integration are concerned about the loss of sovereignty of individual countries. This concern is partly an economic one, focusing on the loss of separate currencies and (perhaps more significantly) the loss of control over national economic policy.

European Monetary System

The foundations for monetary union began to be laid down in 1979, with the launch of the European Monetary System (EMS). One aspect of the EMS was the Exchange Rate Mechanism, which can be seen as a precursor of the single currency. As was discussed in Chapter 33, those countries that chose to opt into the ERM agreed to maintain their exchange rates within a band of plus or minus 2.25% against the average of their currencies – known as the European Currency Unit (ECU). The UK remained outside the ERM except for a brief flirtation between September 1990 and September 1992 (as was discussed in Chapter 33).

During the period of the EMS/ERM, it was recognised that occasional realignment of currencies might be needed, and in fact there were 11 realignments between 1979 and 1987. However, the conditions under which such realignments were permitted were gradually tightened, so that they became less frequent as time went by.

Another key feature of the EMS period was the removal of capital controls. During the early part of this period, most of the member nations restricted the movement of financial capital across borders. This gave them some scope for using monetary policy independently of other countries. However, it was agreed that such capital controls would be phased out.

The Delors Plan, issued in 1989, set out proposals for creating European Economic and Monetary Union (EMU), together with plans for a single currency and a European central bank. It was crucial to establish a European central bank, because with a single currency a central bank is needed to administer monetary policy throughout the EU.

Treaty of Maastricht

The next major step was the Maastricht Treaty, which created the European Union (EU). This Treaty encompassed not only economic issues, such as the introduction of the single currency, but also aspects of social policy (the Social Chapter, which was discussed in Chapter 24), steps towards creating a common foreign, security and defence policy, and the development of a notion of European 'citizenship'.

It was considered vital that, if a single currency was to be established, the participating nations would need to have converged in their economic characteristics.

In other words, if the countries were too diverse in their economic conditions the transition to a single currency would be costly. For example, if they had very different inflation rates, interest rates or greatly differing levels of outstanding government debt, the tensions of union might be too great to sustain. Strong countries would be dragged down, and weak countries would be unable to cope. The Maastricht Treaty therefore set out the *convergence criteria* by which countries would be eligible to join the single currency area. These criteria covered aspects of both monetary and fiscal policy.

Monetary policy

This is obviously important, as monetary union entails the centralisation of monetary policy within the EU. If there is to be a single currency and a single central bank to control interest rates or money supply, the monetary conditions of the economies concerned need to be reasonably close before union takes place. It was thus important to evaluate whether countries were sufficiently close to be able to join with minimal tension.

The European Central Bank was established to oversee the euro currency.

Inflation

Could countries with widely different inflation rates successfully join in a monetary union? One view is that it would be unreasonable to expect a country with 10% or 20% inflation to join a monetary union along with a country experiencing inflation at just 1%. However, an alternative view is that it is equally unreasonable to ask that a country cure its inflation before joining a union when one of the alleged benefits of joining is that it will cure inflation by forcing financial discipline, by removing discretion over monetary policy from individual states. However, the first criterion specified by the Treaty was that countries joining the union should be experiencing low and similar inflation rates — defined as inflation no more than 1.5% above the average of the lowest three countries in the EMS.

Interest and exchange rates

Given that financial capital tends to follow high interest rates, it is argued that diversity of interest rates before union may be undesirable, as this would imply instability of capital movements. Similarly, it has been argued that a period of exchange rate stability before union would be some indication that countries have been following mutually consistent policies, and would indicate that union is plausible.

The criteria set out in the Treaty required that long-term interest rates be no more than 2% above the average of the lowest three EMS countries, and that each joining country should have been in the narrow band of the ERM for a period of 2 years without the need for a realignment.

Fiscal policy

Should there also be conformity in fiscal stance between countries? Would there be severe problems if countries embarked upon union and policy coordination in conditions in which unemployment rates differed markedly? These are separate but related questions. If unemployment is high, this will be connected (via social security payments) with the fiscal stance adopted by the government – as judged in terms of the government budget deficit.

The reason why unemployment rates may be relevant is that there may need to be fiscal transfers between member states in order to reduce the differentials. This will clearly be politically significant within the context of a monetary union, and is an issue that will affect the long-term viability of the union.

Two areas are critical in judging the distance between countries in terms of fiscal policy. First, there is the question of the short-term fiscal stance, which can be measured by the budget deficit. Second, it is important to consider some indication of a longer-term commitment to stability in fiscal policy, in terms of achieving sustainable levels of outstanding government debt. Thus, the Treaty required that the budget deficit be no larger than 3% of GDP, and that the national debt be no more than 60% of GDP.

Economic and Monetary Union

The final stage of the transition towards the single currency was European Economic and Monetary Union (EMU). Under EMU, exchange rates between participating countries were permanently fixed, i.e. no further realignments were allowed. Furthermore, the financial markets of the countries were integrated, with the European Central Bank setting a common interest rate across the union. This was achieved in 1999.

Formation of the euro area

In the event, 11 countries were judged to have met the Maastricht criteria (Belgium, Germany, Spain, France, Ireland, Italy, Luxembourg, the Netherlands, Austria, Portugal and Finland). Together with Greece, these countries formed the single currency area, which came into operation on 1 January 2002.

Figure 34.7 shows how interest rates in some of the euro zone countries moved from 1977 (2 years before the formation of the EMS) until the first year of the euro. The figure shows interest rates in each country as an index based on the average of the euro zone countries as 100. You can see that, although there is some evidence that some of the countries were converging in the run-up to monetary union, there seems to have been little historical tendency for interest rates to move together. This is especially the case for Italy, which at times seemed to have followed opposite paths to the others. Germany showed consistently lower interest rates than most other countries. From 1999, convergence was forced under EMU, which meant an especially rapid adjustment for Italy. The figure also reveals how a different time path of interest rates was followed by the UK.

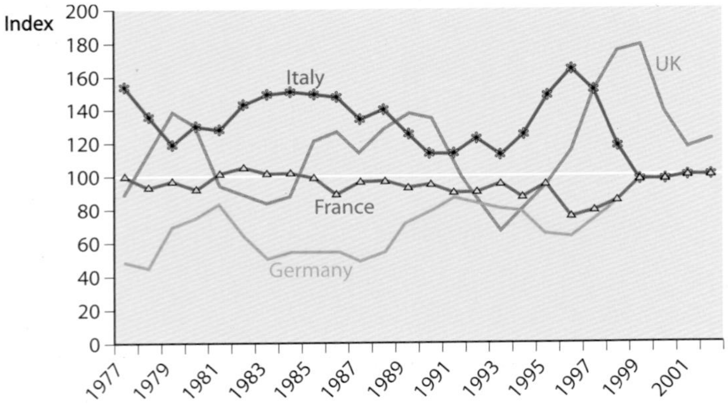

Figure 34.7 *Interest rates in Europe, 1977–2001 (EU12 = 100)*

Source: European Commission.

Costs and benefits of a single currency

Chapter 33 discussed alternative exchange rate regimes and evaluated the relative merits of fixed and floating exchange rate systems. Some of the arguments for and against a single currency area such as the euro zone are similar, since a common currency is effectively creating an area in which exchange rates between member nations are fixed for ever, even if that common currency varies relative to the rest of the world. The question of whether such an arrangement is beneficial overall for the member states rests on an evaluation of the benefits and costs of joining together. An *optimal currency area* occurs when a group of countries are better off with a single currency.

Benefits

The main benefits of a single currency area come in the form of a *monetary efficiency gain*, which will have the effect of encouraging more trade between member countries. The hope is that this will bring further gains from exploiting comparative advantage between countries and enabling firms to reap the benefits of economies of scale.

The efficiency gain comes from two main sources. First, there are gains from reducing *transaction costs*, if there is no longer the need to convert from one currency into another. Second, there are the gains from the *reduction in uncertainty*, in the sense that there is no longer a need to forecast future movements in exchange rates — at least between participating countries. This is similar to the gains from a fixed exchange rate system, but it goes further, as there is no longer a risk of occasional devaluation or revaluation of currencies.

The extent to which these gains will be significant will depend upon the degree of integration between the participating nations. If most of the trade that takes place is between the participants, then the gains will clearly be much more significant than if member nations are also trading extensively with countries outside the single currency area.

Costs

The costs come in the conduct and effectiveness of policy. Within the single currency area individual countries can no longer have recourse to monetary policy in order to stabilise the macroeconomy. As with the fixed exchange rate system, one key question then is how well individual economies are able to adjust to external shocks. Thus, it is important for each economy to have flexibility. In addition, individual countries have to be aware that, once in the single currency area, it is impossible to use monetary policy to smooth out fluctuations in output and employment.

In this context, it is very important that the business cycles of participating economies are well synchronised. If one economy is out of phase with the rest, it may find itself facing an inappropriate policy situation. For example, suppose that most of the countries within the euro zone are in the boom phase of the business cycle, and are wanting to raise the interest rate in order to control aggregate demand: if one country within the zone is in recession, then the last thing it will want is rising interest rates, as this will deepen the recession and delay recovery.

The UK and the euro

The British government's policy stance was set out by the chancellor of the exchequer in October 1997 after only a few months of the new Labour government. This stance was essentially that, while in principle the government was in favour of UK membership, it would be prepared to enter only at a time when the economic conditions were right. Table 34.2 sets out the five economic tests that the chancellor specified as his conditions for deciding whether a case can be made for entry.

	Test	Explanation
1	Convergence	Are business cycles and economic structures compatible so that UK citizens and others could live comfortably with euro interest rates on a permanent basis?
2	Flexibility	If problems emerge is there sufficient flexibility to deal with them?
3	Investment	Would joining EMU create better conditions for firms making long-term decisions to invest in Britain?
4	Financial services	What impact would entry into EMU have on the competitive position of the UK's financial services industry, particularly the City's wholesale markets?
5	Employment	Will joining EMU promote higher growth, stability and a lasting increase in jobs?

***Table 34.2** The chancellor's five tests*

Source: H. M. Treasury.

Convergence

Sustainable convergence is seen to be crucial if the UK is to be successful within the euro area. What sort of evidence should be looked for in order to judge whether the UK's business cycle is converging on Europe? The chancellor could look at fluctuations in GDP, to see whether the phase of GDP growth in the UK is in tune with the rest of Europe. However, if the concern is with interest rates because of their importance with respect to policy, it may make sense to look at interest rates directly. Figure 34.7 showed that towards the end of the period 1977–2001 UK rates had converged to some extent, while still remaining a little higher than in member countries.

Another aspect of this issue that makes the convergence test especially important for the UK is the nature of the British housing market. A larger proportion of home owners in the UK hold mortgages on a variable interest rate basis compared to their counterparts elsewhere in Europe, where fixed-rate mortgages are more common. This makes interest rates a particularly sensitive issue.

It is also argued that in any approach to entry the exchange rate is critical. The brief experience of the UK trying to tie its currency to the Exchange Rate Mechanism in the early 1990s illustrates the dangers of joining with the exchange rate at too high a level, and this is a mistake that the Treasury does not want to repeat.

Flexibility

The convergence test is concerned with whether the UK's business cycle is sufficiently synchronised with the euro zone. The flexibility test is about what would happen if this were not the case, or if the UK fell out of line. In other words, if the UK were to be out of phase, would the economy be sufficiently flexible to be able to get back into line in the absence of an independent monetary policy? It is about resilience.

It is quite difficult to measure flexibility in this sense, and there is no simple indicator that gives a ready judgement about whether an economy is sufficiently flexible to deal with situations which may or may not occur.

The key issues here concern the flexibility of markets, and the extent to which fiscal policy can be activated in order to help stabilise the economy should that be deemed necessary. One danger is that inflation could become more variable if the UK joins the euro, as happened to Ireland. This is because at present the exchange rate is able to fluctuate in order to accommodate differences between national economies.

In the Treasury's assessment of the tests published in June 2003, the flexibility test was said to have been failed. Although the UK labour market was found to be relatively flexible, the Treasury identified a number of areas needing improvement. In particular, it argued that regional pay differentials were insufficient to reflect differences between the regions in the demand and supply of labour, and that there was a significant skills gap between the UK and the euro zone members. It was also difficult to judge whether the UK tax system could be sufficiently flexible to allow rapid stabilisation. In these circumstances, it is hard to say whether or not any convergence would be sustainable.

Investment

The issue for investment revolves around the incentives for firms to invest in the UK. There are two aspects to this. First, there is the question of UK-based firms, and whether they would find membership of the euro zone conducive to investment. Second, there is the question of overseas firms, and the conditions under which they would be prepared to invest in the UK.

The question of whether firms would be prepared to invest more if the UK were part of the euro zone depends in part on the success of the economy in meeting the convergence and flexibility tests. If firms have good expectations about the future they will be more prepared to invest, so if they see Britain as thriving within the euro area this will be beneficial.

However, an additional consideration concerns the reduction in foreign exchange risk within the single currency area. This may encourage investment by reducing the risk premium required by firms considering investment.

Inward foreign direct investment (FDI) may depend on a number of factors. In particular, there may be US or Japanese firms looking to gain a foothold in Europe – will they choose Britain? Figure 34.8 shows annual FDI into the UK since 1965, expressed as a percentage of GDP. An interesting feature of this time path is the way FDI boomed towards the end of the 1990s, but seems to have languished in 2001 and 2002, since the euro area came into operation.

You need to be a little careful in interpreting this, however, as there was a fall in FDI at the global level in 2001, following the events of 11 September. The fact that there are often multiple factors influencing economic decisions is seen to be a common problem in economics.

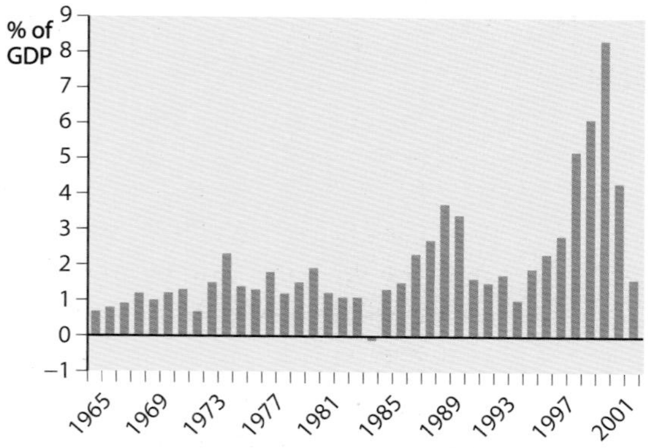

Figure 34.8 Foreign direct investment in the UK (inward), 1965–2001

Source: ONS.

Financial services

The fourth test concerns financial services. In the June 2003 Treasury analysis this was the only test that the UK economy was judged to have passed. The financial services sector was singled out for a special mention because of its importance in the structure of the UK economy. The UK is seen to have a significant comparative advantage in wholesale financial services, and it was accepted that the City is the pre-eminent financial centre in Europe. There was thus a concern that becoming part of the single currency area would damage the competitiveness of this sector. The evidence here seems to suggest that the UK financial sector benefits from EMU even with the UK being outside the euro area, but that it would gain even more if the UK were to join. Financial services have become a significant item in the balance of payments, with a positive balance of almost £10 billion in 2003. This is a substantial share of the overall surplus in trade in services, which was about £14.6 billion. If the UK were a full member of the single currency area, it is likely that this balance would be even more positive.

Growth, stability and employment

The final test relates to whether becoming part of the euro zone would promote higher growth, stability and a lasting increase in jobs in the UK. This might be interpreted as an overall assessment of the potential success of the single currency in the long run. However, this test cannot be divorced from the others. In particular, sustainable convergence (i.e. convergence plus flexibility) would be expected to influence firms' expectations about the future and could affect their willingness to invest, which in turn would contribute to the rate of economic growth.

Figure 34.9 provides some context, showing rates of unemployment in 1990 and 2002 in a range of European countries. The countries are ranked in descending order of their unemployment rates in 2002. It is evident that the UK in 1990 experienced an unemployment rate that was below, but close to, the average of the euro area countries. However, since then the UK rate has fallen appreciably while the euro average rate has increased. The relativities between countries seem to have altered quite a lot over this period, with Germany showing a substantial increase and Ireland a dramatic decrease.

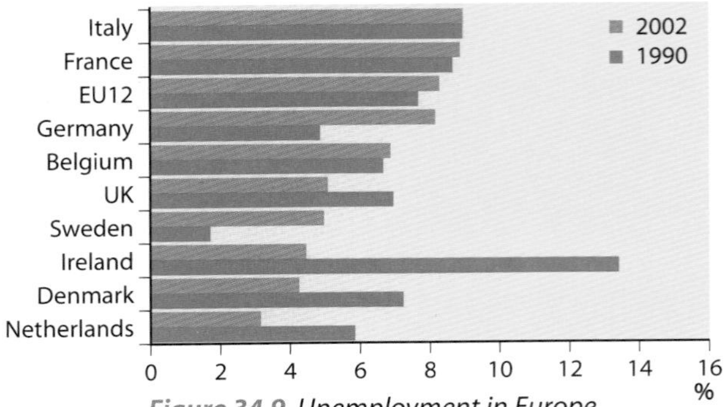

Figure 34.9 Unemployment in Europe, 1990 and 2002

Source: European Commission.

Summary

- The first step towards monetary union was the launch of the European Monetary System (EMS) in 1979.
- An important part of this was the Exchange Rate Mechanism (ERM), under which participating countries (which did not include the UK) agreed to keep their currencies within a narrow band (2.25%) against the average of their currencies.
- The Maastricht Treaty created the European Union (EU), and set out the route towards closer integration.
- The Treaty also set out the convergence criteria, to be used to judge which countries were ready to join in monetary union. These criteria covered financial and fiscal aspects.
- Twelve countries adopted the euro as their common currency in January 2002.
- The main benefits of a common currency area are that it encourages trade by further reducing transaction costs and reducing foreign exchange risk.
- However, the downside is that individual countries have less autonomy in controlling their macroeconomies. Adjusting to external shocks and smoothing short-term fluctuations in output and employment becomes more difficult with a common monetary policy that may not always be set in ways that are appropriate for all participating countries.
- From the UK's point of view, the government stated in 1997 that it intended to join the euro area, but only when the economy had passed five economic tests set by the chancellor: on convergence, flexibility, investment, financial services and employment.

Exercise 34.2

Identify the costs and benefits that would be associated with Britain's entry into the euro single currency group of countries, and discuss whether you believe that Britain should join when the time is right.

part 7

Chapter 35

Economic policy

Governments have a range of economic policy instruments with which to meet their stated objectives. However, their targets may sometimes conflict with one another, and the policy tools can have unintended consequences, so policy coordination and careful design are crucial. This chapter explores these issues and draws together analysis of the various areas of, and approaches to, economic policy.

Learning outcomes

After studying this chapter, you should:

- be familiar with the objectives of economic policy
- appreciate the role and limitations of fiscal policy in influencing the course of the economy
- understand the role and operation of monetary policy in influencing the course of the economy
- be aware of the role and significance of supply-side policies
- be familiar with the conflicts that can arise between policy objectives
- be familiar with the Phillips curve and the notion of the natural rate of unemployment
- be in a position to appraise the relative merits of alternative policy approaches

Objectives of economic policy

Chapter 13 identified a range of policy objectives that governments seek to pursue. Here is a brief reminder.

Price stability

The control of inflation has been a prime target of macroeconomic policy in the UK since the mid-1970s. Figure 35.1 shows inflation (as measured by the annual rate of change of the consumer price index in the UK since 1997). The present target for the CPI inflation rate is 2% per annum. You can see from the figure that inflation has been consistently below the target rate.

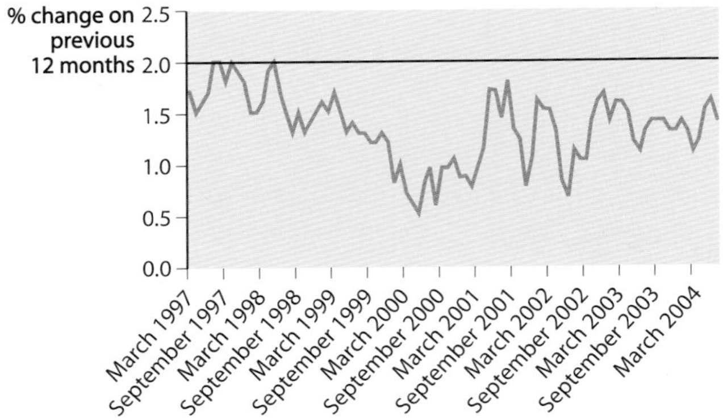

Figure 35.1 Inflation in the UK, 1997–2004

Source: ONS.

Prices play a key role in an economy, acting as signals that guide the allocation of resources. When prices are unstable firms may find it difficult to interpret these price signals, and this may lead to a misallocation of resources. Furthermore, instability of prices creates difficulties for firms trying to forecast future expected demand for their products, which may discourage them from undertaking investment. This in turn means that the economy's capacity to produce may expand by less than it could otherwise have done – in other words, high or unstable inflation may dampen economic growth through its effect on investment. (Chapter 13 identified some other costs of inflation, and you may wish to look back to remind yourself of them. However, the effects on resource allocation and investment are widely accepted to be the most important damaging effects of inflation.)

Full employment

A second key policy objective is that of full employment. Unemployment imposes costs on society and on the individuals who are unemployed. From society's point of view, the existence of substantial unemployment represents a waste of resources and indicates that the economy is working below full capacity. Unemployment in the UK in the early part of the twenty-first century is at a relatively low level, having fallen from the peak reached in the mid-1980s. This is shown in Figure 35.2.

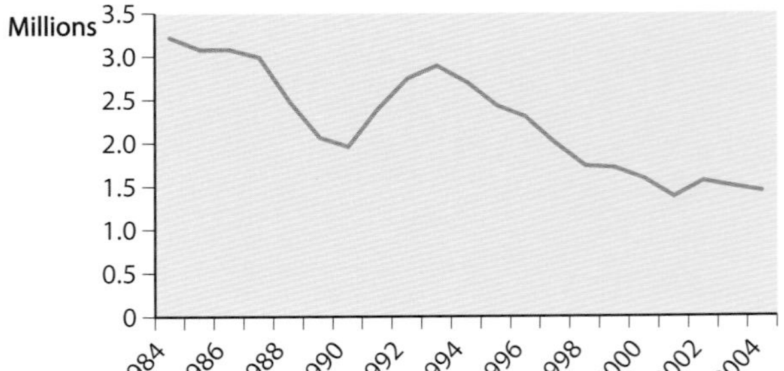

Figure 35.2 ILO unemployment in the UK, 1984–2004

Note: numbers unemployed in March–May each year (average).

Source: ONS.

Balance of payments

Earlier chapters have shown that under a flexible exchange rate system the overall balance of payments will always be zero, because the exchange rate adjusts to ensure that this is so. Nevertheless, the balance of payments remains an objective, not so much to ensure overall balance as to maintain a reasonable balance between the current account and the financial account. If the current account is in persistent deficit, this could cause problems in the long run, as the implication is that the country is selling off its assets in order to obtain goods for present consumption. Under a fixed exchange rate system, the need to maintain the exchange rate acts as a constraint upon economic growth, which tends to lead to an increase in imports, creating a current account deficit.

Economic growth

It is through economic growth that the productive capacity of the economy is raised, and this in turn allows the living standards of the country's citizens to be progressively improved over time. In a sense, therefore, this is the most fundamental of the policy objectives. However, attaining other policy objectives may be a prerequisite for success with growth.

Environmental considerations

It must be recognised that it is not only resources that contribute to living standards: conserving a good environment is also important. Sustainable growth and development means growth that does not prejudice the consumption possibilities of future generations, and this consideration may act as a constraint on the rate of economic growth.

Income redistribution

The final macroeconomic policy objective considered in Chapter 13 concerned attempts to influence the distribution of income within a society. This may entail transfers of income between groups — that is, from the rich to the poor — in order to protect the vulnerable. Such transfers may take place through progressive taxation (whereby those on higher incomes pay a greater proportion of their income in tax) or through a system of social security benefits such as the Jobseekers' Allowance or Income Support.

Correcting market failure

At the *microeconomic* level there are policy measures designed to deal with various forms of market failure. Competition policy is one example of this; it is designed to prevent firms from abusing monopoly power, and to improve the allocation of resources. Although such policies operate at the microeconomic level, they have consequences for macroeconomic objectives such as economic growth.

Policy instruments

The government has three main types of policy instrument with which to attempt to meet these objectives. These were introduced in Chapter 15:

1 *Fiscal policy*: the term 'fiscal policy' covers a range of policy measures that affect government expenditures and revenues through the decisions made by the government on its expenditure, taxation and borrowing. Fiscal policy is used to

influence the level and structure of aggregate demand in an economy. As this chapter unfolds, you will see that the effectiveness of fiscal policy depends crucially on the whole policy environment in which it is utilised.

2 *Monetary policy*: this entails the use of monetary variables such as money supply and interest rates to influence aggregate demand. Remember that under a fixed exchange rate system monetary policy becomes wholly impotent, as it has to be devoted to maintaining the exchange rate. So here again, the effectiveness of monetary policy will depend upon the policy environment in which it is used.

3 *Supply-side policies*: such policies comprise a range of measures intended to have a direct impact on aggregate supply — specifically, on the potential capacity output of the economy. These measures are often microeconomic in character and are designed to increase output and hence economic growth.

Aggregate supply revisited

To analyse policy options, return to the model of aggregate supply and aggregate demand (AS/AD), first introduced in Chapter 12. Notice that it is important to be aware of a debate that developed over the shape of the aggregate supply curve: this is important because it has implications for the conduct and effectiveness of policy options.

During the 1970s, an influential school of macroeconomists, which became known as the **Monetarist School**, argued that the economy would always converge on an equilibrium level of output that they referred to as the **natural rate of output**. Associated with this long-run equilibrium was a **natural rate of unemployment**. If this were the case, then the long-run relationship between aggregate supply and the price level would be vertical, as shown in Figure 35.3. Here Y^* is the natural rate of output, i.e. the full-employment level of aggregate output. In other words, a change in the overall price level does not affect aggregate output, because the economy always readjusts rapidly back to full employment.

An opposing school of thought (often known as the **Keynesian School**) held that the macroeconomy was not sufficiently flexible to enable continuous full employment. They argued that the economy could settle at an equilibrium position below full employment, at least in the medium term. In particular, inflexibilities in

Key terms

Monetarist School: a group of economists who believed that the macroeconomy always adjusts rapidly to the full-employment level of output, and that monetary policy should be the prime instrument for stabilising the economy

natural rate of output: the long-run equilibrium level of output to which Monetarists believe the macroeconomy will always tend

natural rate of unemployment: the unemployment rate that would exist when the economy is in long-run equilibrium

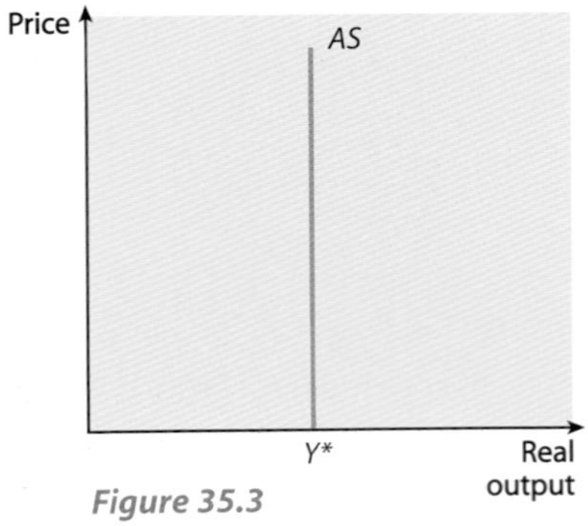

Figure 35.3
Aggregate supply in the long run (the 'monetarist' view)

labour markets would prevent adjustment. For example, if firms had pessimistic expectations about aggregate demand, and thus reduced their supply of output, this would lead to lower incomes because of the workers being laid off. This would then mean that aggregate demand was indeed deficient, so firms' pessimism was self-fulfilling.

Key term

Keynesian School: a group of economists who believed that the macroeconomy could settle in an equilibrium that was below full employment

These sorts of argument led to a belief that there would be a range of output over which aggregate supply would be upward sloping. Figure 35.4 illustrates such an aggregate supply curve, and will be familiar from Chapter 12 (see Figure 12.10). In this diagram Y^* still represents full employment; however, when the economy is operating below this level of output, aggregate supply is somewhat sensitive to the price level, becoming steeper as full employment is approached.

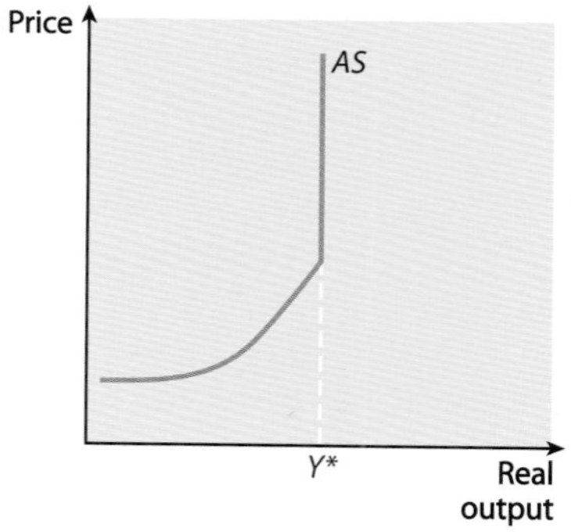

Figure 35.4 Aggregate supply in the long run (the 'Keynesian' view)

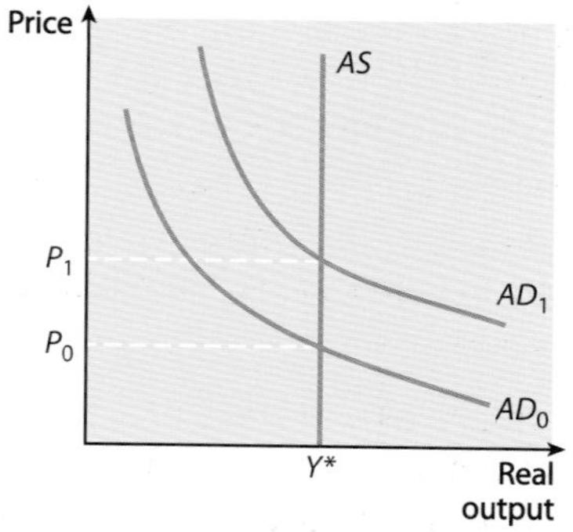

Figure 35.5 Demand-side policy with a vertical AS curve

The policy implications of the monetarist *AS* curve are strong. If the economy always converges rapidly on the full-employment level of output, no manipulation of aggregate demand can have any effect except on the price level. This is readily seen in Figure 35.5, where, regardless of the position of the aggregate demand curve, the level of real output remains at Y^*. If aggregate demand is low at AD_0, then the price level is also relatively low, at P_0. An increase in aggregate demand to AD_1 raises the price level to P_1 but leaves real output at Y^*. In such a world, only supply-side policy (which affects the position of the aggregate supply curve) has any effect on real output.

Summary

- Governments pursue a range of policy objectives, including low inflation and low unemployment, a favourable balance of payments position, economic growth, maintenance of a good environment, income redistribution and the correction of market failure.
- In order to pursue these objectives, governments have recourse to fiscal, monetary and supply-side policies.

- In using the AD/AS model to analyse policy options, it is useful to distinguish between monetarist and Keynesian views about the shape of aggregate supply.
- Monetarist economists have argued that the economy always converges rapidly on equilibrium at the natural rate of output, implying that policies affecting aggregate demand have an impact only on prices, leaving real output unaffected. Aggregate supply in this world is vertical.
- The Keynesian view is that the economy may settle in an equilibrium that is below full employment, and that there is a range over which aggregate supply slopes upwards.

Fiscal policy

What is the role of fiscal policy in a modern economy? The traditional aim of fiscal policy was to affect the level of aggregate demand in the economy. In other words, the overall balance between government receipts and outlays affects the position of the aggregate demand curve, which is reinforced by multiplier effects. When government outlays exceed government receipts, the result is a *fiscal deficit*. This occurs when the revenues raised through taxation are not sufficient to cover the government's various types of expenditure.

Figure 35.5 shows that shifting the aggregate demand curve affects only the overall price level in the economy when the aggregate supply curve is vertical — and the Monetarist School of thought argued that it would always be vertical. Hence a key issue for a government considering the use of fiscal policy is knowing whether there is spare capacity in the economy, because otherwise an expansion in aggregate demand from increased government spending will push up prices but leave real output unchanged.

Looking more closely at what is happening, you can see that there are some forces at work that are acting to weaken the multiplier effect of an increase in government expenditure. One way in which this happens is through interest rates. If the government finances its deficit through borrowing, a side-effect is to put upward pressure on interest rates, which then may cause private-sector spending — by households on consumption and by firms on investment — to decline, as the cost of borrowing has been increased. This process is known as the **crowding out** of private-sector activity by the public sector. It limits the extent to which a government budget deficit can shift the aggregate demand curve, especially if the public-sector activity is less productive than the private-sector activity that it replaces.

> **Key term**
>
> **crowding out:** a process by which an increase in government expenditure crowds out private-sector activity by raising the cost of borrowing

Automatic and discretionary fiscal policies

It is important to distinguish between automatic and discretionary changes in government expenditure. Some items of government expenditure and receipts vary automatically with the business cycle. They are known as **automatic stabilisers**. For example, if the economy enters a period of recession, government expenditure will rise because of the increased payments of unemployment and other social security benefits, and revenues will fall because fewer people are paying income tax, and because receipts from VAT are falling. This helps to offset the recession without any active intervention from the government.

Key term

automatic stabilisers: a process by which government expenditure and revenue varies with the business cycle, thereby helping to stabilise the economy without any conscious intervention from government

More important, however, is the question of whether the government can or should make use of discretionary fiscal policy in a deliberate attempt to influence the course of the economy. As already mentioned, the key issue is whether or not the economy has spare capacity, because attempts to stimulate an economy that is already at full employment will merely push up the price level.

Balance between the public and private sectors

Even if the overall size of the budget deficit limits the government's actions in terms of fiscal policy, there are still decisions to be made about the overall balance of activity in the economy. A neutral government budget can be attained either with high expenditure and high revenues, or with relatively small expenditure and revenues. Such decisions affect the overall size of the public sector relative to the private sector. Over the years, different governments in the UK have taken different decisions on this issue — and different countries throughout the world have certainly adopted different approaches.

In part, such issues are determined through the ballot box. In the run-up to an election, each political party presents its overall plans for taxation and spending, and typically they adopt different positions as to the overall balance. It is then up to those voting to give a mandate to whichever party offers a package that most closely resembles their preferences.

Figure 35.6 shows the time path of government consumption as a share of GDP from 1949 to 2003; it shows fluctuations around a downward trend, suggesting that the public sector has been gradually reducing its share of the economy. Notice that this does not give the full picture, as public-sector investment is not taken into account in these data. There are one or two periods in the figure where the decline seems to have been especially rapid. In the early 1950s this partly reflects the wind-down of government activity in the aftermath of rebuilding following the Second World War. The steep section in the 1980s reflects

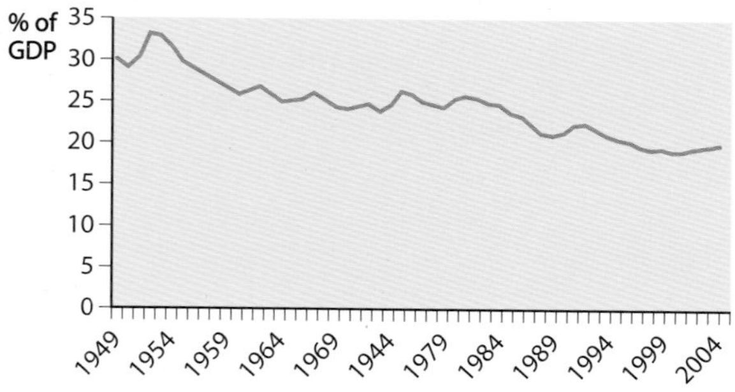

Figure 35.6 Government final consumption, 1949–2004

Source: ONS.

the privatisation drive of that period, when the government was withdrawing from some parts of the economy.

Figure 35.7 provides an international perspective, showing the share of current and capital expenditure by governments in a range of countries. This reveals something of a contrast between on the one hand North America, Australia and Japan, and on the other many European countries, where government has been more active in the economy. In part this reflects the greater role that government plays in some countries in providing services such as education and healthcare, whereas in other countries the private sector takes a greater role, often through the insurance market.

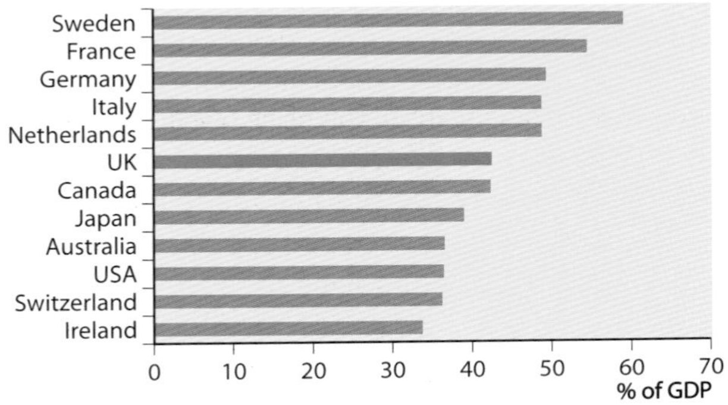

Figure 35.7 *Total government expenditure as a percentage of GDP, selected countries, 2002*

Source: OECD.

Direct and indirect taxes

Fiscal policy, and taxation in particular, has not only been used to establish a balance between the public and private sectors of an economy. In addition, taxation remains an important weapon against some forms of market failure, and it also influences the distribution of income. In this context, the choice between using direct and indirect taxes is important.

Remember that direct taxes are taxes levied on income of various kinds, such as personal income tax. Such taxes are designed to be progressive and so can be effective in redistributing income; for example, a higher income tax rate can be charged to those earning high incomes. In contrast, indirect taxes — taxes on expenditure, such as VAT and excise duties — tend to be regressive. As poorer households tend to spend a higher proportion of their income on items that are subject to excise duties, a greater share of their income is taken up by indirect taxes. Even VAT can be regressive if higher-income households save a greater proportion of their incomes.

When she became prime minister, Margaret Thatcher moved quickly to switch the emphasis from direct to indirect taxation.

When Margaret Thatcher came to power in 1979, one of her first actions was to introduce a switch away from direct taxation towards indirect taxes. VAT was increased, and the rate of personal income tax was reduced. In support of this move, it was pointed out that if an income tax scheme becomes too progressive it can provide a disincentive towards effort. If people feel that a high proportion of their income is being taken in tax, their incentives to provide work effort are weak. Indeed, a switch from direct to indirect taxation might be regarded as a sort of supply-side policy intended to influence the position of aggregate supply.

Indirect taxes can be targeted at specific instances of market failure; hence the high excise duties on such goods as tobacco (seen as a demerit good), and petrol (seen as damaging to the environment because of the externality of greenhouse gas emissions).

Sustainability of fiscal policy

Another important issue that came to the fore during the 1990s concerned the sustainability of fiscal policy. This is wrapped up with the notion that current taxpayers should have to fund only expenditure that benefits their own generation, and that the taxpayers of the future should make their own decisions, and not have to pay for past government expenditure that has been incurred for the benefit of earlier generations.

Key term

Golden Rule of fiscal policy: rule stating that over the economic cycle net government borrowing will be for investment only, and not for current spending

In this context, what is significant is the overall balance between receipts and outlays through time. If outlays were always larger than receipts, the spending programme could be sustained only through government borrowing, thereby shifting the burden of funding the deficit to future generations. This could also be a problem if it made it more difficult for the private sector to obtain funds for investment, or if it added to the national debt. The chancellor of the exchequer is committed to following a **Golden Rule of fiscal policy**, which states that, on average over the economic cycle, the government should borrow only to invest and not to fund current expenditure. This is intended to help achieve equity between present and future generations.

Figure 35.8 shows total public-sector receipts and outlays since 1986. Outlays here include investment, but you can see how the two series tend to move in opposite directions over the cycle. To some extent this is to be expected, because of the operation of the automatic stabilisers.

If receipts and outlays more or less balance over the economic cycle, the economy is not in a position whereby the current generation is forcing future generations to pay for its consumption. However, as the economy does go through a business cycle, it is not practical to impose this rule at every part of the cycle, so the so-called Golden Rule is to apply over the economic cycle as a whole.

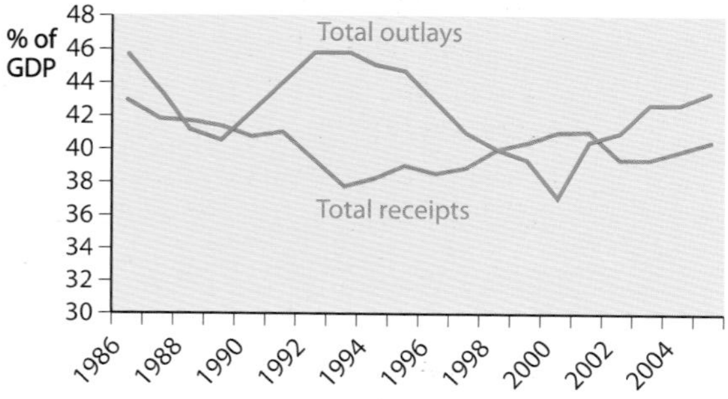

Figure 35.8 UK public-sector receipts and outlays, 1986–2005

Source: OECD.

There is also a commitment to keep public-sector net debt below 40% of GDP — again, on average over the economic cycle. Figure 15.3 shows data for this on a quarterly basis since 1997.

Summary

- Fiscal policy concerns the use of government expenditure and taxation to influence aggregate demand in the economy.
- If the economy is in a state in which the aggregate demand curve cuts the vertical segment of aggregate supply, demand-side policy affects only the overall price level, and not real output.
- If the government funds its expenditure by borrowing, higher interest rates may crowd out private-sector activity.
- The stance of the government budget varies with the business cycle, as a result of the operation of automatic stabilisers.
- The overall balance between private and public sectors varies through time and across countries.
- Direct taxes help to redistribute income between groups in society, but if too progressive they may dampen incentives to provide effort.
- The Golden Rule for fiscal policy is that the government should aim to borrow only for investment, and not for current expenditure (averaged over the economic cycle).
- There is also a commitment to keep the national debt below 40% of GDP.

Exercise 35.1

Discuss the extent to which the major British political parties adopt differing stances towards establishing a balance between the private and public sectors, i.e. the extent to which each is 'high tax/high public spending' or 'low tax/low public spending'. Analyse the economic arguments favouring each of the approaches.

Monetary policy

Monetary policy has become the prime instrument of government macroeconomic policy, with the interest rate acting as the key control variable. In principle, monetary policy involves the manipulation of monetary variables in order to influence aggregate demand in the economy.

It is important at the outset to realise that it is not possible to control money supply and interest rates simultaneously and independently. Firms and households choose to hold some money. They may do this in order to undertake transactions, or as a precaution against the possible need to undertake transactions at short notice. In other words there is a *demand for money.* However, in choosing to hold money they incur an opportunity cost, in the sense that they forego the possibility of earning interest by purchasing some form of financial asset.

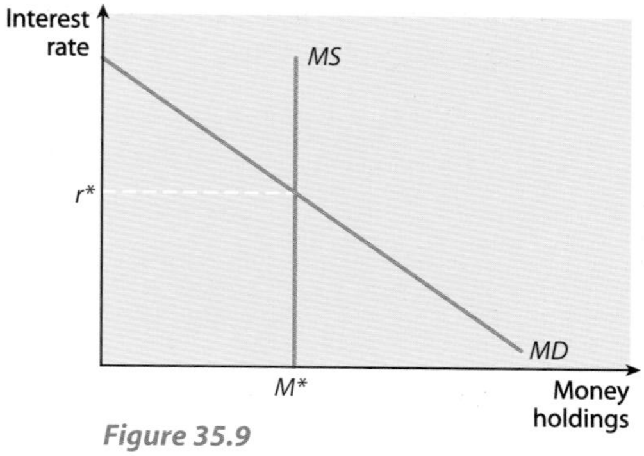

Figure 35.9
The demand for money

This means that the interest rate can be regarded as the opportunity cost of holding money; put another way, it is the price of holding money. At high rates of interest, people can be expected to choose to hold less money, as the opportunity cost of holding money is high. *MD* in Figure 35.9 represents such a money demand curve. It is downward sloping.

Suppose the government wants to set the money supply (*MS*) at *M** in Figure 35.9. This can be achieved in two ways. If the government controls the supply of money at *M**, then equilibrium will be achieved only if the interest rate is allowed to adjust to *r**. An alternative way of reaching the same point is to set the interest rate at *r** and then allow the money supply to adjust to *M**. The government can do one or the other — but it cannot set money supply at *M** and hold the interest rate at any value *other than r** without causing disequilibrium.

A problem with attempting to control the money supply directly is that the complexity of the modern financial system makes it quite difficult to pin down a precise definition or measurement of money. For this and other reasons, the chosen instrument of monetary policy is the interest rate. By setting the interest rate, monetary policy affects aggregate demand through the so-called **monetary transmission mechanism**.

Key term

monetary transmission mechanism: channel through which changes in the interest rate feed through into the real economy

Extension material: money supply and inflation

One way of measuring the money stock is from the *monetary base*, which comprises all notes and coins in circulation and the commercial banks' deposits at the Bank of England, and is known as *M0*.

However, there are many assets that are 'near-money', such as interest-bearing current account deposits at banks. These are highly liquid, and can readily be converted into cash for transactions. *M4* is a wide measure of the money stock, and includes M0 together with sterling wholesale and retail deposits with monetary financial institutions such as banks. In other words, it includes all bank deposits that can be used for transactions, even though some of these deposits may require a period of notice for withdrawal.

Figure 35.10 presents the annual percentage rate of change of M0 and M4 since 1990, together with the annual inflation rate (measured by RPI). This shows the extent to which it is possible for M0 and M4 to follow different paths through time — in 1999, for instance, M4 accelerated while M0 decelerated (and inflation fell). Over the years, the Bank of England has introduced various changes in the way the money definitions are measured, and there have been changes in the categories of institutions that are recognised for purposes of calculating M4.

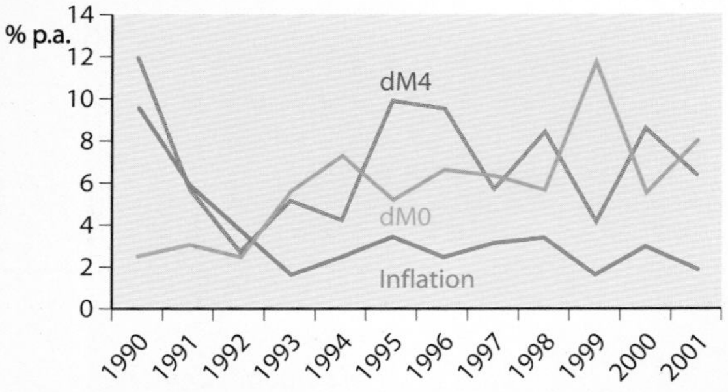

Figure 35.10 Money supply and inflation in the UK, 1990–2001

Note: d = annualised change in (M0 or M4).

Source: ETAS.

At a higher interest rate, firms undertake less investment expenditure and households undertake less consumption expenditure. Furthermore, if UK interest rates are high relative to elsewhere in the world, they will attract overseas investors, increasing the demand for pounds. This will tend to lead to an appreciation in the exchange rate — which in turn will reduce the competitiveness of British goods and services, reducing the foreign demand for UK exports and encouraging UK residents to reduce their demand for domestic goods and buy imports instead. All these factors lower the level of aggregate demand, shifting the *AD* curve to the left. Such a policy stance may be needed in order to maintain control of inflation. A reduction in interest rates would of course have the reverse effect. However, notice that the interaction of the money supply, interest rates and the exchange rate makes policy design a complicated business.

Indeed, as has been explained, under a fixed exchange rate regime monetary policy is powerless to influence the real economy, as it must be devoted to maintaining the exchange rate. Under a floating exchange rate system monetary policy is freed from this role, but even so it must be used in such a way that the current account deficit of the balance of payments does not become unsustainable in the long run. In other words, the use of interest rates to target inflation has implications for the magnitude of the current and financial accounts of the balance of payments.

As was pointed out in Chapter 15, an important aspect of monetary policy since 1997 has been the delegation of responsibility for it to the Bank of England's Monetary Policy Committee (MPC). The rationale for this is based on the observation that the effectiveness of monetary policy depends quite heavily on people's expectations. It operates much more effectively if people believe it is going to work, because then they will amend their behaviour more quickly, speeding up the process of adjustment to equilibrium. By delegating responsibility for monetary policy to the Bank of England, the credibility of policy is enhanced and it thereby becomes more effective, and the government cannot be tempted to buy election success by increasing spending financed through inflationary printing of money.

In creating a stable macroeconomic environment, the ultimate aim of monetary policy is not simply to keep inflation low, but to improve the confidence of decision-makers, and thereby encourage firms to invest in order to generate an increase in production capacity — which will stimulate economic growth and create an opportunity to improve living standards.

The Monetary Policy Committee is responsible for setting monetary policy in the UK.

Summary

- Monetary policy entails the manipulation of monetary variables in order to influence aggregate demand in the economy.
- The prime instrument of monetary policy is the interest rate.
- People hold money in order to undertake transactions (among other reasons), and the interest rate can be regarded as the opportunity cost of holding money.
- The monetary authorities can control either the money supply or interest rates, but not both independently.
- In the UK, monetary policy is conducted by the Bank of England, which has had independent responsibility for meeting the inflation target since 1997.
- It is hoped that, by keeping inflation low, firms will be confident about the future, will invest more, and thereby increase the productive capacity of the economy.

Exercise 35.2

Use *AS/AD* to analyse the effect of an expansionary monetary policy on the equilibrium level of real output and the overall price level. Undertake this exercise with a monetarist vertical aggregate supply curve and with a Keynesian aggregate supply curve in which aggregate demand creates an equilibrium that is below full employment. Discuss the differences in your results.

Supply-side policies

Supply-side policies are directed at influencing the position of the aggregate supply curve. In Figure 35.11, Y^* represents full-employment output before the policy, with the equilibrium overall price level at P_0. Supply-side policies that lead to an increase in the economy's productive capacity shift equilibrium output to Y^{**} and the overall price level to P_1.

Notice that the effect on real output is achieved from supply-side policies whether the equilibrium is in the vertical segment of the *AS* curve (or with a monetarist *AS* curve) or in the upward-sloping segment of a Keynesian *AS* curve, as you can see in Figure 35.12, where the shift in aggregate supply raises equilibrium real output from Y_0 to Y_1.

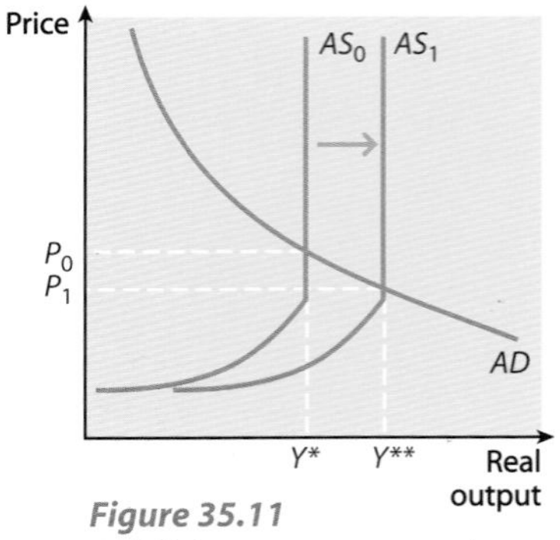

Figure 35.11
A shift in aggregate supply (with a monetarist effect)

Such policies include measures like encouraging education and training, improving the flexibility with which markets operate and promoting competition. These policies were discussed in Chapter 15, so you might want to remind yourself of how they operate.

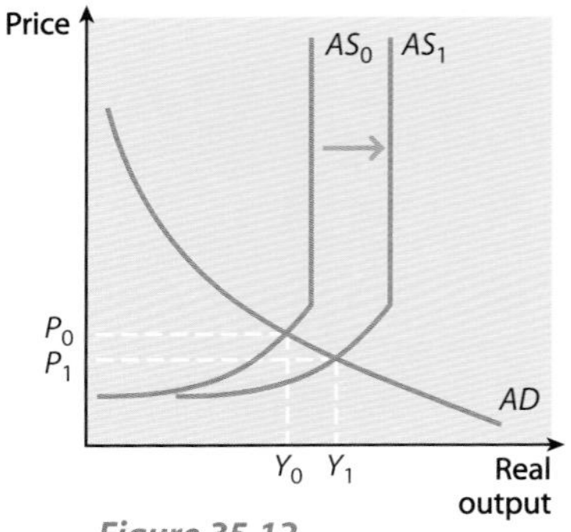

Figure 35.12
A shift in aggregate supply (with a Keynesian effect)

Notice that it is quite difficult to quantify the effects of these supply-side policies. In the case of education and training, some of the effects of increased spending become evident only after very long time lags. In the case of competition policy, again, it is not easy to identify the effects on productive capacity. It is particularly difficult to isolate the impact of these policies when so much else in the economy is changing through time. Nonetheless, these policies do have the effect of stimulating economic growth without inflationary pressure.

Conflicts between policy objectives

Having reviewed the main macroeconomic policy objectives, it should be clear that the designing of economic policy is likely to be something of a juggling act. This is especially so because there may be conflict between some of the targets of policy.

For example, there may be a conflict between economic growth and the environment, so that the pursuit of economic growth may need to be tempered by concern for the environment. Policy must therefore be designed bearing in mind that there may be a trade-off between these two objectives — at some point, it could be that more economic growth is possible only by sacrificing environmental objectives.

Unemployment and inflation

This notion of trade-off between conflicting objectives applies in other areas too. One important trade-off was discovered by the Australian economist Bill Phillips. In 1958 Phillips claimed that he had found an 'empirical regularity' that had existed for almost a century and that traced out a relationship between the rate of unemployment, and the rate of change of money wages. This was rapidly generalised into a relationship between unemployment and inflation (by arguing that firms pass on increased wages in the form of higher prices).

Figure 35.13 shows what became known as the **Phillips curve**. Although Phillips began with data, he also came up with an explanation of why such a relationship should exist. At the heart of his argument was the idea that when the demand for labour is high firms will be prepared to bid up wages in order to attract labour. To the extent that higher wages are then passed on in the form of higher prices, this would imply a relationship between unemployment and inflation: when unemployment is low inflation will tend to be higher, and vice versa.

Key term

Phillips curve: a curve illustrating the trade-off relationship between unemployment and inflation

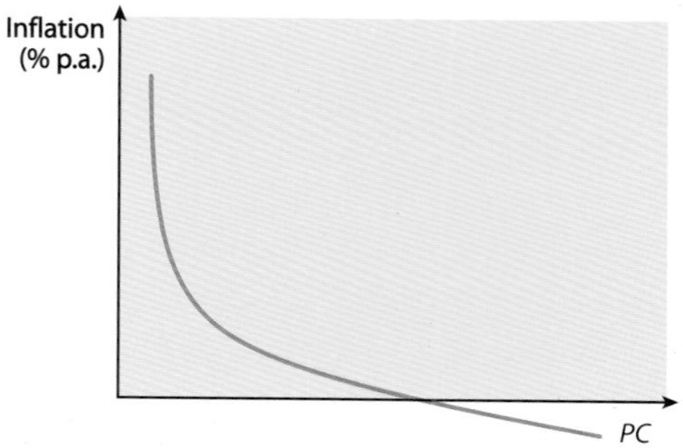

Figure 35.13
The Phillips curve

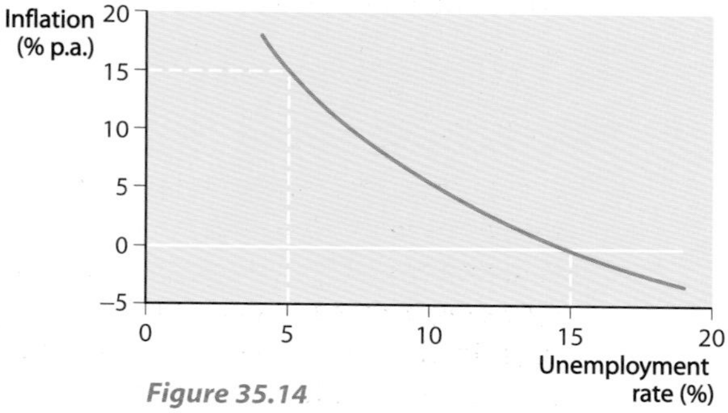

Figure 35.14
The Phillips curve inflation–unemployment trade-off

From a policy perspective – at least within the Keynesian tradition – this suggests a trade-off between unemployment and inflation objectives. If the Phillips curve relationship holds, attempts to reduce the rate of unemployment are likely to raise inflation. On the other hand, a reduction in inflation is likely to result in higher unemployment. This suggests that it might be difficult to maintain full employment and low inflation at the same time. For example, Figure 35.14 shows a Phillips curve that is drawn such that to achieve an unemployment rate of 5%, inflation would need to rise to 15% per annum; this would not be acceptable these days, when people have become accustomed to much lower inflation rates. Furthermore, to bring inflation down to zero would require an unemployment rate of 15%. Having said that, as recently as 1990 the UK economy was experiencing inflation of nearly 10% and unemployment of 7%, which is not far from this example.

Nonetheless, the Phillips curve trade-off offers a tempting prospect to policy-makers. For example, if an election is imminent it should be possible to reduce unemployment by allowing a bit more inflation, thereby creating a feel-good factor. After the election the process can be reversed. This suggests that there could be a political business cycle induced by governments seeking re-election. In other words, the conflict between policy objectives could be exploited by politicians who see that in the short run an electorate is concerned more about unemployment than inflation.

The 1970s provided something of a setback to this theory, when suddenly the UK economy started to experience both high unemployment and high inflation simultaneously, suggesting that the Phillips curve had disappeared. This combination of stagnation and inflation became known as **stagflation**.

> **Key term**
>
> **stagflation:** situation in which an economy simultaneously experiences stagnation (high unemployment) and high inflation

One possibility is that the Phillips curve had not in fact disappeared, but had moved. Suppose that wage bargaining takes place on the basis of *expectations* about future rises in retail prices. As inflation becomes embedded in an economy, and people come to expect it to continue, those expectations will be built into wage negotiations. Another way of viewing this is that expectations about price inflation will influence the *position* of the Phillips curve.

Figure 35.15 shows how this might work. PC_0 represents the initial Phillips curve. Suppose we start with the economy at the *natural rate of unemployment* U_{nat}. (Remember this was defined earlier in the chapter.) If the economy is at point *A*, with inflation at π_0 and unemployment at U_{nat}, the economy is in equilibrium. If the government then tries to exploit the Phillips curve by allowing inflation to rise to π_1, the economy moves in the short run to point *B*. However, as people realise that inflation is now higher, they adjust their expectations. This eventually begins to affect wage negotiations; the Phillips curve then moves to PC_1, and unemployment returns to the natural rate. The economy settles at *C* and is again in equilibrium, but now with higher inflation than before — and the same initial rate of unemployment. For this reason, the natural rate of unemployment is sometimes known as the **non-accelerating inflation rate of unemployment (NAIRU)**.

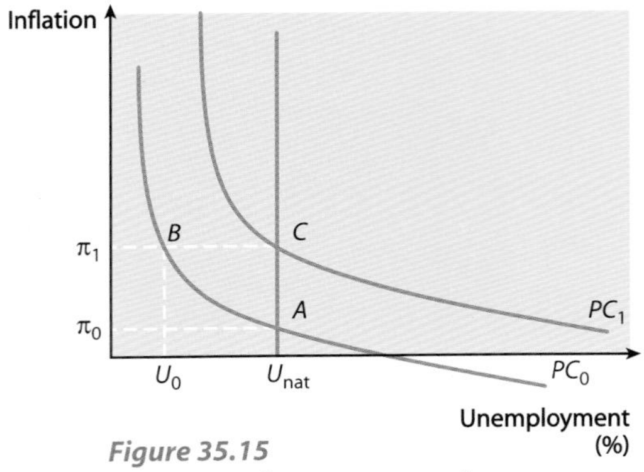

Figure 35.15
An expectations-augmented Phillips curve

> **Key term**
>
> **non-accelerating inflation rate of unemployment (NAIRU):** the rate of unemployment in an economy that is consistent with a constant rate of inflation; equivalent to the natural rate of unemployment

The problem that arises with this is of how to get back to the original position with a lower inflation rate. This can happen only if people's expectations adjust so that lower inflation is expected. This means that the economy has to move down along PC_1, pushing up unemployment in order to reduce inflation. Then, once expectations adjust, the Phillips curve will move back again until the natural rate of unemployment is restored. If this takes a long time, then the cost in terms of unemployment will be high.

Figure 35.16 shows some empirical data for the UK since 1986. From 1986 until 1993 (or even until 1995), the pattern seems consistent with a Phillips curve relationship. However, after that time inflation seems to have stabilised, and unemployment is gradually falling – as if, with stable inflation, people's expectations have kept adjusting and allowed unemployment to fall.

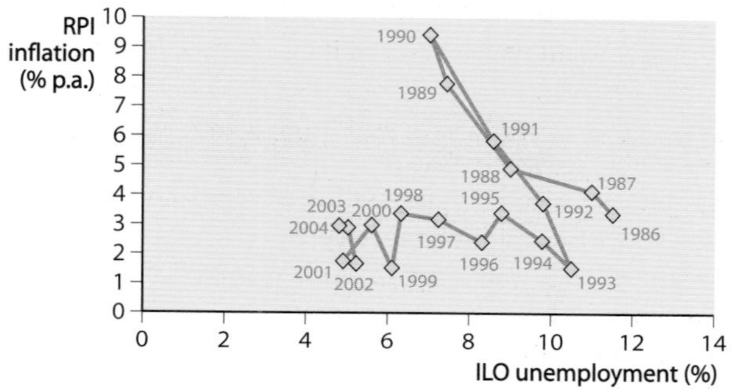

Figure 35.16 *Unemployment and inflation in the UK, 1986–2004*

Source: ONS.

Figures 35.17 and 35.18 show the pattern of the relationship between unemployment and inflation for two other countries, Sweden and France. Sweden shows a classic Phillips curve pattern; France has experienced less variation in the unemployment rate.

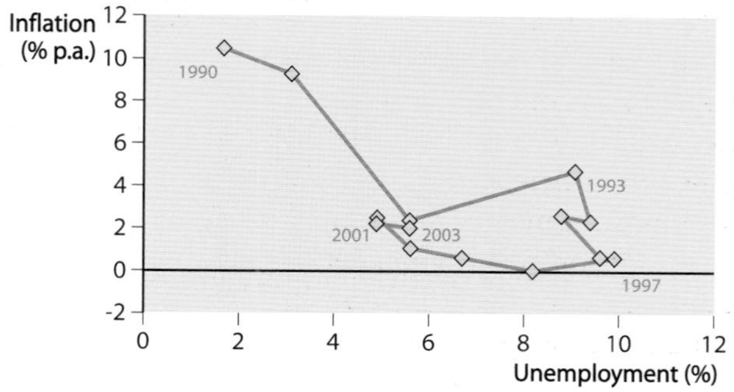

Figure 35.17 *Unemployment and inflation in Sweden, 1990–2003*

Source: OECD.

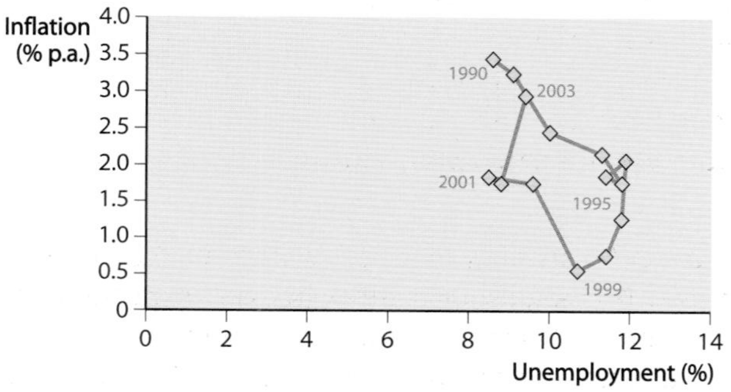

Figure 35.18 *Unemployment and inflation in France, 1990–2003*

Source: OECD.

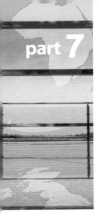

Economic growth and the current account

In some circumstances, conflict can also arise between achieving economic growth and attaining equilibrium on the current account of the balance of payments. An increase in economic growth resulting in higher real incomes could lead to an increase in imports of goods and services, if UK residents spent a high proportion of their additional income abroad. This was seen as a major problem during the fixed exchange rate era of the 1950s and 1960s, when any deficit on the current account had to be met by running down foreign exchange reserves. This led to a 'stop–go' cycle of macroeconomic policy, where every time growth began to accelerate the current account went into deficit, and policy then had to be adjusted to slow down the growth rate to deal with the deficit.

Exercise 35.3

Given the following list of policy objectives, discuss the possible conflicts that may arise between them, and discuss how these might be resolved:

- low inflation
- low unemployment
- high economic growth
- a low deficit on the current account of the balance of payments
- maintenance of a high environmental quality
- equity in the distribution of income

Designing the policy mix

The design and conduct of economic policy may be seen as an elaborate balancing act. Differing policy objectives need to be prioritised, as in many cases there may be conflict between them. Choices have to be made about the balance to be achieved between fiscal, monetary and supply-side policies.

The consensus view in the early part of the twenty-first century is that fiscal policy should be used to achieve the desired balance between the public and private sectors. Monetary policy should be devoted to meeting the inflation target in order to create a stable macroeconomic environment; this will then encourage growth and enable improvements in the standard of living. Supply-side policies are perhaps the most important, as these contribute to a raising of efficiency and an increase in the productive capacity of the economy.

The keynote in policy design lies in enabling markets to operate as effectively as possible.

If the UK were to join the single currency area, this would create a new policy environment, in which responsibility for monetary policy would be delegated to the European Central Bank. This would leave fiscal policy and supply-side policies as the sole instruments available to a UK government.

Summary

- Supply-side policies aim to influence the position of the aggregate supply curve and to raise the productive capacity of the economy, primarily by helping markets to work more effectively.
- The achievement of the various policy objectives is complicated by the fact that some are in conflict with one another, so that the achievement of one target may endanger another.
- The Phillips curve claims a trade-off relationship between unemployment and inflation, although the appearance of stagflation in the 1970s cast doubt on the hypothesis.
- The position of the Phillips curve may be seen to depend on people's expectations about future inflation, so that in the long run the Phillips curve may be vertical at the natural rate of unemployment (or the non-accelerating inflation rate of unemployment — the NAIRU).
- Fiscal policy in a modern economy tends to be confined to determining the balance between the public and private sectors.
- Monetary policy tends to be devoted to meeting the inflation target in order to encourage economic growth.
- Supply-side policies are of greatest importance, influencing the efficiency with which markets work, and thus affecting the long-run capacity of the economy to produce.

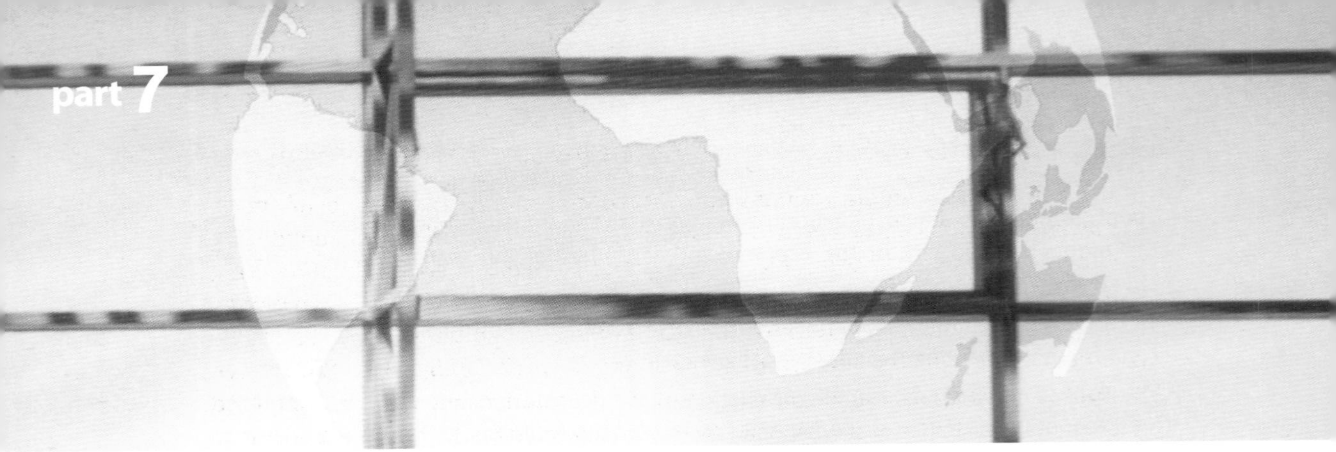

Review section

Although the prime focus of this final part of the book is on the UK in the global economy, the topic draws on economic ideas and theories from the whole course in order to explain economic aspects of the real world. When looking at the UK economy in an international perspective, both microeconomics and macroeconomics need to be drawn upon, although the natural focus is perhaps more macroeconomic in nature. One reason for this is that ultimately the success of an economy depends not only on macroeconomic factors such as inflation or unemployment, but also on how well microeconomic markets are operating in order to allocate resources. For this reason, the two strands of economic thinking cannot be divorced. In approaching this final unit, therefore, you need to be aware of the need to use all the economic tools and theories at your disposal.

Chapter 31 Globalisation and the world economy

Advances in technology, especially in the realms of transport and communications, have presented the world with great opportunities. This has been seen in the drive towards *globalisation*, the increasingly close integration of countries and peoples (and economies) of the world. The process has also attracted its critics, and a key question is how best to make use of the opportunities on offer. As globalisation escalates, trade and exchange between nations are becoming ever more important, and there have been moves towards the *liberalisation of trade*. However, although governments in many countries may pay lip service to the benefits of such liberalisation, there is often a reluctance to abandon the *protectionism* that has been a feature of many economies in the past. The *World Trade Organisation (WTO)* has played a significant role in encouraging trade liberalisation, and has also acted as mediator in trade disputes between nations. An important feature of globalisation has been the role of *multinational corporations* in carrying out *foreign direct investment (FDI)*. A downside of globalisation is that *external shocks* may spread more rapidly from one economy to another, and it is important that economies are sufficiently robust to be able to absorb such shocks.

Chapter 32 The balance of payments and competitiveness

In a world in which international trade is becoming central to many economies, the *balance of payments* has become increasingly important as a way of monitoring trading activity and ensuring that the external balance is sustainable in the long run. This chapter examined the role and significance of the balance of payments, and also the factors that determine the *international competitiveness* of a country's products. In the UK the pattern of activity has been changing, with the service sectors (especially financial services) growing in relative importance compared with manufacturing activity. As the UK is an *open economy*, it is also important to monitor the effects of government policy on the competitiveness of UK economic activity. Alternative policy measures for the management of the balance of payments were also examined.

Chapter 33 Exchange rate systems

A crucial backdrop to the way an economy operates is the way in which the *exchange rate* is determined, as this strongly influences the competitiveness of domestic firms in international markets, and also has far-reaching implications for the conduct and effectiveness of macroeconomic policy. Under a *fixed exchange rate system* monetary policy has to be devoted to maintaining the value of the currency. Under a *floating exchange rate system* monetary policy can help to stabilise the domestic economy, but it needs to be carefully managed if an overall balance is to be maintained between the exchange rate, interest rates and inflation. In other words, it is important to be aware of the way in which macroeconomic policy influences the exchange rate and vice versa, and also to be aware that changes in exchange rates can affect the level of economic activity within a country.

Chapter 34 European monetary union

Another aspect of globalisation has been the growing importance of regional groupings of countries. The moves towards growing *European integration* have naturally been prominent in media discussions about the British economy. This chapter examines the chronology of moves towards integration within Europe, examining the significance of the *Single Market* measures and evaluating the costs and benefits of membership of a *single currency area.* This requires an examination of the role and effectiveness of monetary and fiscal policy within a single currency area. The potential for British membership of the euro zone is evaluated, and the chancellor's five tests explained.

Chapter 35 Economic policy

As was set out in Part 3 of the book, typical macroeconomic objectives are to achieve:

- *price stability* (a low and stable rate of inflation)
- *full employment* (a low level of unemployment)

‰ a satisfactory position on the balance of payments
- *sustainable economic growth*
- the protection of vulnerable groups in society through *income redistribution*

In addition, policy has a role to play at the microeconomic level in attempting to correct *market failure*. This may be seen as a step towards improving the allocation of resources within society in order to optimise the productive capacity of the economy. To meet these objectives, the government can use a combination of *fiscal policy, monetary policy* and *supply-side policies*. Attaining all policy objectives simultaneously may not be feasible, as there are trade-offs between some of the targets. This requires the government to be careful to ensure an appropriate balance of policy reflecting its priorities among the objectives. One particular aspect of this is the potential trade-off between unemployment and inflation, as reflected in the *Phillips curve*. However, if the economy moves towards the *natural rate of unemployment*, this question resolves into one of how to stabilise the economy in such a way that the adjustment is as smooth as possible. The chapter concludes with an appraisal of the relative merits of the three core strands of policy.

Preparing for the examination

Unit 6 (The UK in the global economy) is designated as a 'synoptic' unit. The idea behind this is that you will be required to draw together what you have learned across the other five units, to show that you have an overview of the subject and can think like an economist. For example, in the Edexcel specification this synoptic unit is designed to test your ability to:

- understand the inter-relatedness of many economic issues, problems and institutions
- understand how certain economic concepts, theories and techniques may be relevant to a range of different contexts
- apply such concepts, theories and techniques in analysing economic issues and problems and in evaluating arguments and evidence

From your point of view, it helps to be aware that this synoptic assessment is happening, but there is no need to worry about it. Unit 6 is designed to rest on these sorts of skill, and the chance to show what you can do is built into it. All you have to do is to take advantage of the opportunities presented by being aware that you may need to draw on material from anywhere in the specification.

In order to enable you to show the full range of your skills and knowledge (and ability to be evaluative), the examination comprises a combination of essay questions and an extended data-response question. *One* essay is to be tackled, and *one* data-response.

Essay questions

P7.1

a Examine possible factors that might have led to changes in the value of the pound sterling against the euro in recent years. *(40 marks)*

b Evaluate the likely economic effects of a significant fall in the value of sterling against the euro. *(60 marks)*

P7.2

a Examine the impact of the European Union's Common Agricultural Policy on the world trade in agricultural goods. *(40 marks)*

b Evaluate the implications of a significant reduction in barriers to the trade in goods and services for the global economy. *(60 marks)*

P7.3

Since the early 1990s, the UK rate of inflation has been less than 5% in every year while unemployment has fallen from over 2.7 million to less than 1 million in 2002.

a To what extent do these data contradict the Phillips curve analysis? *(40 marks)*

b Examine the factors that might explain why the UK has experienced low inflation rates and low unemployment in recent years. *(60 marks)*

Data-response question P7.4

US steel tariffs

Extract 1

A bitter trade battle between the United States and its commercial rivals intensified as controversial US tariffs on imported steel came into effect. The USA has unilaterally imposed tariffs of up to 30% on imported steel for 3 years, claiming that other countries are 'dumping' steel at below the cost of production and damaging its domestic industry. However, the claim is bitterly disputed by the European Union, Japan and other steel producers, who say that their firms are more efficient than American producers. As a result, the EU is likely to impose quotas on steel imports to prevent its own industry from being damaged by steel redirected from US markets.

Table P7.1 Steel jobs

Country	No. of employees	Job losses in last 4 years
USA	175,000	20,000
UK	26,500	10,000
Germany	85,200	7,900

The USA claimed that its move was prompted by 'unfair' government support for steelmakers in other countries, and is supported by WTO rules. EU steelmakers say that they stand to lose $2 billion a year as a result of the US tariffs. Last week the OECD said that steel producers need to cut more than 100 million tonnes of capacity worldwide to restore the industry to profitability.

Source: **http://news.bbc.co.uk/hi/English/business/newsid**, 20 March 2002.

Extract 2

The retaliatory tariffs and quotas surrounding two of the world's largest steel markets (the USA and the EU) will badly disrupt a global commodity business. It will leave producers in developing countries cut off from the main sources of demand and could create a sizeable black market in steel. Further, steelmakers in emerging markets are likely to suffer most. The former Soviet Republic countries produce 85 million tonnes of steel annually but consume only 32 million, leaving 53 million looking for a buyer.

The USA imports some 23 million tonnes every year and the Anglo-Dutch firm Corus is the biggest European exporter. The company reckons that some 740 000 tonnes of steel would be affected, about 5% of the group's output.

Source: adapted from *The Times*, 6 March 2002.

Extract 3

This is the worst decision George W. Bush has made. The move will prove futile in helping steelworkers and will be positively damaging to other American jobs. Start with the futility. When the 175 000 steelworkers called for 40% tariffs, they were basing [their demand] on what they thought they could get away with, rather than on fine economic models. Well, they got three-quarters of their demand. But industry analysts say the effect may be to raise prices of imported steel by a few percentage points. That is not enough to save the 31 steel mills that have filed for bankruptcy in the past 4 years (with the loss of 20 000 jobs). They have lost out to sharper competition from 'mini-mills' at home – about half of the industry's jobs – as well as abroad.

In fact, the move is likely to cost many more jobs in steel-consuming industries than it saves for those in steel mills. And that is considering only the effect of higher import prices before taking account of any retaliation by furious trading partners. Russia has already banned imports of poultry products.

Source: *The Times*, 6 March 2002.

---

a Distinguish between tariffs and quotas. *(4 marks)*

b With the aid of a diagram, examine the impact of US tariffs on the US price of steel and on its domestic steel production. *(10 marks)*

c With reference to Extract 3, to what extent do you agree that steel tariffs 'will prove futile in helping steel workers and will be positively damaging to other American jobs'? (lines 1–2) *(10 marks)*

d From the information provided, assess the strength of the case for European retaliation against steel tariffs imposed by the USA. *(10 marks)*

e With reference to Extract 2, explain why 'steelmakers in emerging markets are likely to suffer most' (lines 4–5). *(6 marks)*

f Assess the basis for trade liberalisation as promoted by the World Trade Organisation. *(10 marks)*

Data-response question P7.5

Public finance

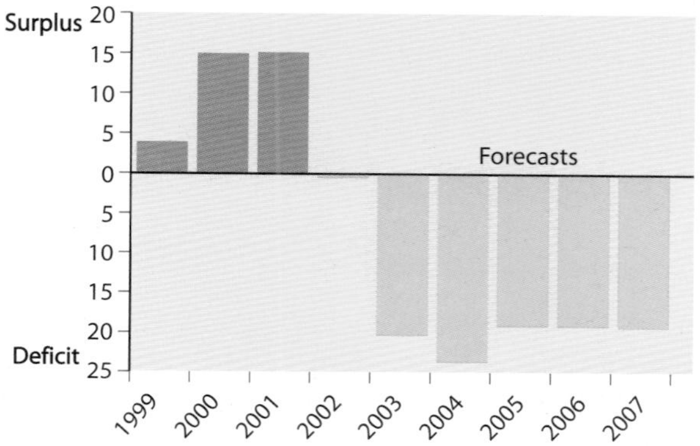

Figure P7.1 The UK's fiscal position

Public sector net borrowing, 1999–2007 (forecast) (£bn).

Source: *The Financial Times*, 28 November 2002.

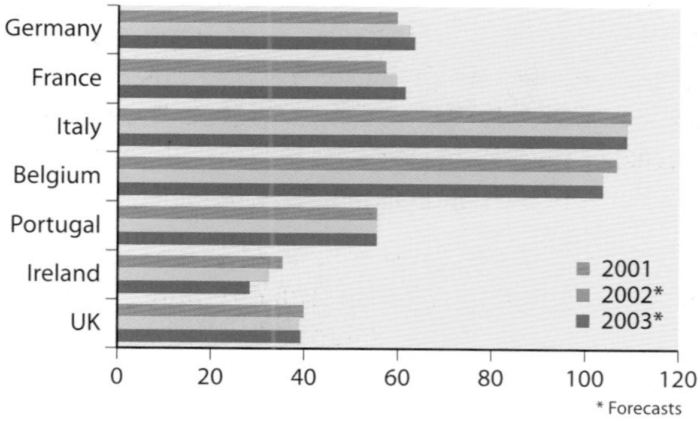

Figure P7.2 The national debt of selected EU countries as a percentage of GDP

Source: *The Financial Times*, 28 November 2002.

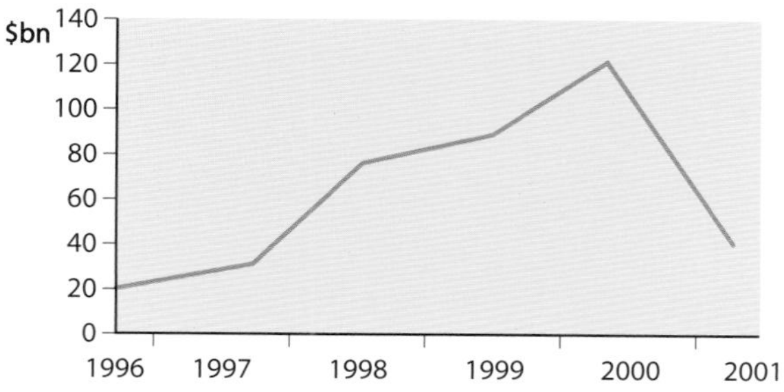

Figure P7.3 Inward investment into the UK, 1996–2001

Source: *The Times*, 2 December 2002.

UK	£9.70
Slovenia	£2.89
Turkey	£2.21
Hungary	£1.36
Czech Republic	£1.32
Slovak Republic	£0.90
Estonia	£0.89

***Table P7.2** Hourly pay of manufacturing workers, selected countries*

Source: *The Times*, 2 December 2002.

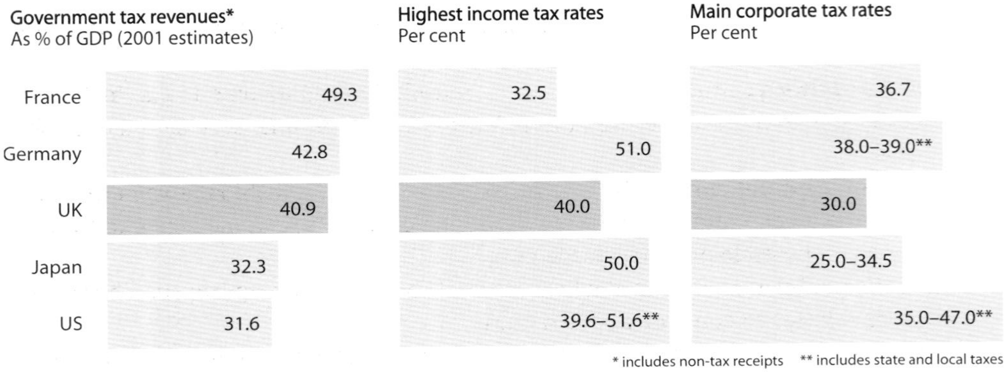

***Figure P7.4** Taxes around the world*

Source: *The Financial Times*, 8 March 2001.

---

a With reference to Figure P7.1,

(i) What is a 'fiscal deficit'? *(2 marks)*

(ii) Examine **two** factors that might explain the forecast changes in the UK's fiscal position over the period shown. *(8 marks)*

b With reference to Figure P7.2,

(i) How might the differences in the national debt–GDP ratio between the UK and Italy have arisen? *(4 marks)*

(ii) To what extent might a high national debt–GDP ratio be a cause for concern? *(10 marks)*

c **(i)** With reference to Figure P7.3, how might the UK's non-membership of the euro explain the trend in inward investment? *(6 marks)*

(ii) With reference to the data, examine **two** other economic factors that might influence the level of foreign direct investment into the UK. *(8 marks)*

(iii) Evaluate the likely economic implications of a fall in foreign direct investment for the UK economy. *(12 marks)*

These questions were taken from examinations set for the Edexcel Advanced Economics examination for Unit 6 – The UK in the global economy (synoptic unit). We are grateful to London Qualifications for permission to reproduce them here.

Glossary of key terms

absolute advantage: the ability to produce a good more efficiently (e.g. with less labour)

absolute poverty: situation describing a household if its income is insufficient to allow it to purchase the minimum bundle of goods and services needed for survival

aggregate demand curve (AD): a curve showing the relationship between the level of aggregate demand and the overall price level; it shows planned expenditure, at any given possible overall price level

allocative efficiency: achieved when society is producing an appropriate bundle of goods relative to consumer preferences

appreciation: a rise in the exchange rate within a floating exchange rate system

arbitrage: a process by which prices in two market segments are equalised by the purchase and resale of products by market participants

asymmetric information: a situation in which some participants in a market have better information about market conditions than others

automatic stabilisers: a process by which government expenditure and revenue varies with the business cycle, thereby helping to stabilise the economy without any conscious intervention from government

average cost: total cost divided by the quantity produced

balance of payments: a set of accounts showing the transactions conducted between residents of a country and the rest of the world

barrier to entry: a characteristic of a market that prevents new firms from readily joining the market

bilateral monopoly: a market situation in which a monopsony buyer of labour faces a trade union acting as a monopoly provider of labour

buffer stock: surplus stock that is bought up when the harvest is good with a view to selling when it is poor, in an attempt to stabilise commodity prices

business cycle: a phenomenon whereby GDP fluctuates around its underlying trend, following a regular pattern

capital account of the balance of payments: account identifying transactions in (physical) capital between the residents of a country and the rest of the world

capitalism: a system of production in which there is private ownership of productive resources, and individuals are free to pursue their objectives with minimal interference from government

capital productivity: measure of output per unit of capital

cartel: an agreement between firms on price and output with the intention of maximising their joint profits

centrally planned economy: one in which decisions on resource allocation are guided by the state

claimant count of unemployment: measure by which the number of people claiming the Jobseeker's Allowance is calculated

comparative advantage: the ability to produce a good *relatively* more efficiently, i.e. at a lower opportunity cost

comparative static analysis: examines the effect on equilibrium of a change in the external conditions affecting a market

competition policy: an area of economic policy designed to promote competition within markets to encourage efficiency and safeguard consumer interests

complements: goods for which the demand is likely to fall if the price of a related good rises

conglomerate merger: a merger between two firms operating in different markets

constant returns to scale: found when long-run average cost remains constant with an increase in output, i.e. when output and costs rise at the same rate

consumer price index (CPI): a measure of the average level of prices in the UK

consumer surplus: the value that consumers gain from consuming a good or service over and above the price paid; represented by the area under the demand curve above the market price

consumption externality: an externality that impacts on the consumption side of a market, which may be either positive or negative

consumption function: shows the relationship between consumption and disposable income, which also depends upon the other factors that affect how much households spend on consumption

contestable market: a market in which the existing firm makes only normal profit, as it cannot set a higher price without attracting entry, owing to the absence of barriers to entry and sunk costs

cost efficiency: the appropriate combination of inputs of factors of production, given the relative price of those factors

cost-plus pricing: pricing policy whereby firms set their price by adding a mark-up to average cost

cost-push inflation: inflation initiated by an increase in the costs faced by firms, arising on the supply side of the economy

cross-price elasticity of demand: a measure of the sensitivity of quantity demanded of one good or service to a change in the price of some other good or service, measured as:

$$\frac{\text{\% change in quantity demanded of good X}}{\text{\% change in price of good Y}}$$

crowding out: a process by which an increase in government expenditure crowds out private-sector activity by raising the cost of borrowing

current account of the balance of payments: account identifying transactions in goods and services between the residents of a country and the rest of the world

customs union: a protected free trade area, in which there are no internal barriers to trade between member nations, and a common tariff is imposed against imports from outside the union

deadweight loss: the social cost arising from market failure; for example, the loss of consumer surplus that arises when a monopoly raises price and restricts output

demand: the quantity of a good or service that a consumer would choose to buy at any possible price in a given period

demand curve: a curve showing how much of a good will be demanded by consumers at any given price

demand-deficient unemployment: unemployment that arises because of a deficiency of aggregate demand in the economy, so that the equilibrium level of output is below full employment

demand-pull inflation: inflation initiated by an increase in aggregate demand

demerit good: a good that society believes will bring lower-than-expected benefits to consumers

demographic transition: a process through which many countries have been observed to pass whereby improved health lowers the death rate, and the birth rate subsequently also falls, leading to a low and stable population growth

depreciation (of capital): the fall in value of physical capital equipment over time as it is subject to wear and tear

depreciation (of currency): a fall in the exchange rate within a floating exchange rate system

derived demand: demand for a good or service not for its own sake, but for what it produces, e.g. labour is demanded for the output that it produces

devaluation: process whereby a government reduces the price of its currency relative to an agreed rate in terms of foreign currency

direct tax: a tax levied directly on income

diseconomies of scale: a situation in which an increase in the scale of production leads to production at higher average cost for a firm

disposable income: the income that households have to devote to consumption and saving, taking into account payments of direct taxes and transfer payments such as social security benefits

division of labour: a process whereby the production procedure is broken down into a sequence of stages, and workers are assigned to particular stages

dominant strategy: a situation in game theory where a player's best strategy is independent of those chosen by others

economic growth: an increase in the productive capacity of the economy

economic rent: a payment received by a factor of production over and above what would be needed to keep it in its present use

economies of scale: economies arising if an increase in the scale of production leads to production at a lower long-run average cost

economies of scope: economies arising when average cost falls as a firm increases output across a range of different products

efficiency wage: higher-than-average wage paid by a firm in a situation of asymmetric information, in order to keep good-quality workers and provide incentives for workers to work hard

elasticity: a measure of the sensitivity of one variable to changes in another variable

excess burden of a sales tax: the deadweight loss suffered by society following the imposition of a sales tax

exchange rate: the price of one currency in the terms of another

Exchange Rate Mechanism (ERM): a system that was set up by a group of European countries in 1979 with the objective of keeping member countries' currencies relatively stable against each other

export-led growth: situation in which economic growth is achieved through the exploitation of economies of scale made possible by focusing on exports, and so reaching a wider market than would be available within the domestic economy

export promotion: policy entailing the encouragement of domestic firms to export more goods in order to earn foreign exchange

export sales ratio: ratio of the percentage of exports of a product to total manufacturers' sales

externality: a cost or a benefit arising from an economic activity or transaction that is not reflected in market prices

external economies of scale: cost savings arising if average costs for a firm fall as the output of its industry as a whole expands

factors of production: resources used in the production process; inputs into production, in particular including labour, capital, land and entrepreneurship

financial account of the balance of payments: account identifying transactions in financial assets between the residents of a country and the rest of the world

firm: an organisation that brings together factors of production in order to produce output

fiscal policy: decisions made by the government on its expenditure, taxation and borrowing

fixed cost: a component of a firm's costs that does not vary with the quantity of output produced

fixed exchange rate: a system in which the government of a country agrees to fix the value of its currency in terms of that of another country

floating exchange rate: a system in which the exchange rate is permitted to find its own level in the market

foreign direct investment: investment undertaken in one country by companies based in other countries

foreign exchange reserves: stocks of foreign currency and gold owned by the central bank of a country to enable it to meet any mismatch between the demand and supply of the country's currency imported goods

free market economy: one in which resource allocation is guided by market forces without intervention by the state

free-rider problem: when an individual cannot be excluded from consuming a good, and thus has no incentive to pay for its provision

free trade area: a group of countries that agree to trade without barriers between themselves, but having their own individual barriers with countries outside the area

frictional unemployment: unemployment associated with job search, i.e. with people who are between jobs

futures market: a market in which it is possible to buy a commodity at a fixed price for delivery at a specified future date; such a market exists for foreign exchange

game theory: a method of modelling the strategic interaction between firms in an oligopoly

GDP deflator: an implicit price index showing the relationship between real and nominal measures of GDP, providing an alternative measure of the general level of prices in the economy

General Agreement on Tariffs and Trade (GATT): the precursor of the WTO, which organised a series of 'Rounds' of tariff reductions

Gini index: a measure of the degree of inequality in a society

globalisation: a process by which the world's economies are becoming more closely integrated

Golden Rule of fiscal policy: rule stating that over the economic cycle net government borrowing will be for investment only, and not for current spending

government budget deficit (surplus): the balance between government expenditure and revenue

government failure: a misallocation of resources arising from government intervention

gross domestic product (GDP): a measure of the total amount of goods and services produced in an economy over a period by residents living on its territory

Harrod–Domar model: a model of economic growth that emphasises the importance of savings and investment

HIPC Initiative: initiative launched in 1995 to provide debt relief for heavily indebted poor countries

horizontal merger: a merger between two firms at the same stage of production in the same industry

hot money: stocks of funds that are moved around the world from country to country in search of the best return

human capital: the stock of skills and expertise that contribute to a worker's productivity; can be increased through education and training

Human Development Index: a composite indicator of the level of a country's development, varying between 0 and 1

ILO unemployment rate: measure of the percentage of the workforce who are without jobs but are available for work, willing to work and looking for work

import penetration ratio: ratio of the percentage of imports of a product to home demand

import substitution: policy entailing the encouragement of domestic production of goods previously imported in order to reduce the need for foreign exchange

incidence of a tax: the way in which the burden of paying a sales tax is divided between buyers and sellers

income elasticity of demand: a measure of the sensitivity of the quantity demanded of a good or service to a change in consumer income, measured as:

$$\frac{\%\text{ change in quantity demanded}}{\%\text{ change in consumer income}}$$

index number: a device for comparing the value of a variable with a base point

indirect tax: a tax levied on expenditure on goods or services (as opposed to a direct tax, which is a tax charged directly to an individual based on a component of income)

industrialisation: a process of transforming an economy by expanding manufacturing and other industrial activity

industry long-run supply curve: under perfect competition, the curve that, for the typical firm in the industry, is horizontal at the minimum point of the long-run average cost curve

inferior good: one for which the quantity demanded decreases in response to an increase in consumer incomes

inflation: a rise in the overall price level

internal economies of scale: cost savings arising if average costs fall as a firm increases its scale of production as a result of advantages internal to the firm

internalising the externality: an attempt to deal with an externality by bringing an external cost or benefit into the price system

International Monetary Fund (IMF): a multilateral institution that provides short-term financing for countries experiencing balance of payments problems

investment: expenditure undertaken by firms to add to the capital stock

invisible hand: term used by Adam Smith to describe the way in which resources are allocated in a market economy

invisible trade: trade in services

involuntary unemployment: situation arising when an individual who would like to accept a job at the going wage rate is unable to find employment

Keynesian School: a group of economists who believed that the macroeconomy could settle in an equilibrium that was below full employment

labour productivity: measure of output per worker, or output per hour worked

law of comparative advantage: a theory arguing that there may be gains from trade arising when countries (or individuals) specialise in the production of goods or services in which they have a comparative advantage

law of demand: a law that states that there is an inverse relationship between quantity demanded and the price of a good or service, *ceteris paribus*

law of diminishing returns: law stating that, if a firm increases its inputs of one factor of production while holding inputs of the other factor fixed, it will eventually derive diminishing marginal returns from the variable factor

limit price: the highest price that an existing firm can set without enabling new firms to enter the market and make a profit

long run: the period over which the firm is able to vary the inputs of all its factors of production

Lorenz curve: a graphical way of depicting the distribution of income within a country

luxury good: one for which the income elasticity of demand is positive and greater than 1, so that as income rises consumers spend proportionally more on the good

macroeconomics: the study of the interrelationships between economic variables at an aggregate (economy-wide) level

marginal cost: the cost of producing an additional unit of output

marginal physical product of labour (MPPL): the additional quantity of output produced by an additional unit of labour input

marginal revenue: the additional revenue gained by the firm from selling an additional unit of output

marginal revenue product of labour (MRPL): the additional revenue received by a firm as it increases output by using an additional unit of labour input, i.e. the marginal physical product of labour multiplied by the marginal revenue received by the firm

marginal social benefit: the additional benefit from a good that society gains from consuming an additional unit of a good or service

marginal tax rate: tax on additional income, defined as the change in tax payments due divided by the change in taxable income

market: a set of arrangements that allows transactions to take place

market failure: a situation in which the free market mechanism does not lead to an optimal allocation of resources, e.g. where there is a divergence between marginal social benefit and marginal social cost

market-friendly growth: an approach to economic growth in which governments are recommended to intervene less where markets can operate effectively, but to intervene more strongly where markets are seen to fail

merit good: a good that society believes brings unanticipated benefits to the individual consumer

microeconomics: the study of economic decisions taken by individual economic agents, including households and firms

Millennium Development Goals (MDGs): targets set for each less-developed country, reflecting a range of development objectives to be monitored each year to evaluate progress

minimum efficient scale: the level of output at which long-run average cost stops falling as output increases

minimum wage: a system designed to protect the low paid by setting a minimum on the wage rate that employers are permitted to offer workers

mixed economy: one in which resources are allocated partly through price signals and partly on the basis of direction by government

model: a simplified representation of reality used to provide insight into economic decisions and events

Monetarist School: a group of economists who believed that the macroeconomy always adjusts rapidly to the full-employment level of output, and that monetary policy should be the prime instrument for stabilising the economy

monetary policy: decisions made by government regarding monetary variables such as money supply or the interest rate

Monetary Policy Committee: body within the Bank of England responsible for the conduct of monetary policy

monetary transmission mechanism: channel by which changes in the interest rate feed through into the real economy

money stock: the quantity of money in circulation in the economy

monopolistic competition: a market that shares some characteristics of monopoly, and some of perfect competition

monopoly: a form of market structure in which there is only one seller of a good or service

monopsony: a market in which there is a single buyer of a good, service or factor of production

multinational corporation (MNC): a company whose production activities are carried out in a number of different countries

multiplier: the ratio of a change in equilibrium real income to the autonomous change that brought it about

Nash equilibrium: situation occurring within a game when each player's chosen strategy maximises pay-offs given the other player's choice, so that no player has an incentive to alter behaviour

natural monopoly: monopoly that arises in an industry in which there are such substantial economies of scale that only one firm is viable

natural rate of output: the long-run equilibrium level of output to which monetarists believe the macroeconomy will always tend

natural rate of unemployment: the unemployment rate that would exist when the economy is in long-run equilibrium

net investment: gross investment *minus* depreciation

New Deal: a package of measures introduced in 1997 aimed at reducing long-term unemployment

newly industrialised economies: economies that have experienced rapid economic growth from the 1960s to the present

***n*-firm concentration ratio:** a measure of the market share of the largest *n* firms in an industry

NIMBY: a syndrome under which people are happy to support the construction of an unsightly or unsocial facility, so long as it is 'Not In My Back Yard'

nominal value: value of an economic variable based on current prices

non-accelerating inflation rate of unemployment (NAIRU): the rate of unemployment in an economy that is consistent with a constant rate of inflation; equivalent to the natural rate of unemployment

non-tariff barrier: an obstacle to free trade other than a tariff, e.g. quality standards imposed on imported products

normal good: one for which the quantity demanded increases in response to an increase in consumer incomes

normal profit: the return needed for a firm to stay in a market in the long run

normative statement: a statement about what ought to be

oligopoly: a market with a few sellers, in which each firm must take account of the behaviour and likely behaviour of rival firms in the industry

opportunity cost: in decision-making, the value of the next best alternative that could have been chosen

overseas development assistance: aid provided to LDCs by countries in the OECD

Pareto optimum: an allocation of resources such that no reallocation of them can make any individual better off without making some other individual worse off

perfect competition: a form of market structure that produces allocative and productive efficiency in long-run equilibrium

perfect/first-degree price discrimination: situation arising in a market whereby a monopoly firm is able to charge each consumer a different price

Phillips curve: a curve illustrating the trade-off relationship between unemployment and inflation

positive statement: a statement about what *is*, i.e. about facts

predatory pricing: an anti-competitive strategy in which a firm sets price below average variable cost in an attempt to force a rival or rivals out of the market and achieve market dominance

price elasticity of demand: a measure of the sensitivity of quantity demanded to a change in the price of a good or service, measured as:

$$\frac{\text{\% change in quantity demanded}}{\text{\% change in price}}$$

price elasticity of supply: a measure of the sensitivity of quantity supplied to a change in the price of a good or service, measured as:

$$\frac{\text{\% change in quantity supplied}}{\text{\% change in price}}$$

price taker: a firm that must accept whatever price is set in the market as a whole

principal–agent (agency) problem: a problem arising from conflict between the objectives of the principals and those of the agents who take decisions on their behalf

Prisoners' Dilemma: an example of game theory with a range of applications in oligopoly theory

private good: a good that, once consumed by one person, cannot be consumed by somebody else

producer surplus: the difference between the price received by firms for a good or service and the price at which they would have been prepared to supply that good or service

product differentiation: a strategy adopted by firms that marks their product as being different from their competitors'

production externality: an externality that impacts on the production side of a market, which may be either positive or negative

production function: function embodying information about technically efficient ways of combining labour and capital to produce output

production possibility frontier (PPF): diagram showing the maximum combinations of goods or services that can be produced in a given period with available resources

productive efficiency: attained when a firm is operating at minimum average total cost

productivity: measure of the efficiency of a factor of production

progressive tax: a tax in which the marginal tax rate rises with income, i.e. a tax bearing most heavily on the relatively well-off members of society

prohibition: an attempt to prevent the consumption of a demerit good by declaring it illegal

public good: a good that is non-exclusive and non-rivalrous; consumers cannot be excluded from consuming such a good, and consumption by one person does not affect the amount of the good available for others to consume

purchasing power parity theory of exchange rates: theory stating that in the long run exchange rates (in a floating rate system) are determined by relative inflation rates in different countries

real exchange rate: the nominal exchange rate adjusted for differences in relative inflation rates between countries

real value: value of an economic variable taking account of changing prices over time

regional policy: policy comprising measures to reduce disparities in the level of economic activity between different regions of a country

regressive tax: a tax bearing more heavily on the relatively poorer members of society

regulatory capture: a situation in which the regulator of an industry comes to represent its interests rather than regulating it

relative poverty: situation applying to a household whose income falls below 50% of median adjusted household disposable income

relevant market: a market to be investigated under competition law, defined in such a way that no major substitutes are omitted but no non-substitutes are included

repo rate: short for 'sale and repurchase agreement'; the interest rate that is set by the Monetary Policy Committee of the Bank of England in order to influence inflation

retail price index (RPI): a measure of the average level of prices in the UK

revaluation: process whereby a government raises the price of domestic currency in terms of foreign currency

revealed preference: an approach to valuing an environmental good that entails surveying people who visit an environmental facility to see how much they spent to get there

scarcity: a situation that arises when people have unlimited wants in the face of limited resources

sharecropping: a form of land tenure system in which the landlord and tenant share the crop

short run: the period over which a firm is free to vary the input of one of its factors of production (labour), but faces a fixed input of the other (capital)

short-run aggregate supply curve: a curve showing how much output firms are prepared to supply in the short run at any given overall price level

short-run supply curve: for a firm operating under perfect competition, the curve given by its short-run marginal cost curve above the price at which $MC = SAVC$; for the industry, the horizontal sum of the supply curves of the individual firms

Social Chapter: part of the Maastricht Treaty, which launched measures designed to harmonise labour market policies across the member states of the European Union

social cost–benefit analysis: a process of evaluating the worth of a project by comparing both direct and social costs and benefits, including externality effects

stagflation: situation in which an economy simultaneously experiences stagnation (high unemployment) and high inflation

Structural Adjustment Programme (SAP): package of policy measures recommended by the World Bank to LDCs

structural unemployment: unemployment arising because of changes in the pattern of economic activity within an economy

subsidy: a grant given by the government to producers to encourage production of a good or service

substitutes: goods for which the demand is likely to rise if the price of a similar good increases

sunk costs: short-run costs that cannot be recovered if the firm closes down

super-normal profits/abnormal profits/economic profits: terms referring to profits that exceed normal profits

supply curve: a curve showing the quantity supplied at any given price

supply-side policies: a range of measures intended to have a direct impact on aggregate supply – specifically, the potential output capacity of the economy

sustainable development: 'development which meets the needs of the present without compromising the ability of future generations to meet their own needs' (Brundtland Commission, 1987)

tacit collusion: situation occurring when firms refrain from competing on price, but without communication or formal agreement between them

tariff: a tax imposed on imported goods

technical efficiency: attaining the maximum possible output from a given set of inputs

terms of trade: the ratio of export prices to import prices

tiger economies: a group of newly industrialised economies in the East Asian region, including Hong Kong, Singapore, South Korea and Taiwan

total factor productivity: the average productivity of all factors, measured as the total output divided by the total amount of inputs used

total physical product of labour (TPPL): in the short run, the total amount of output produced at different levels of labour input with a fixed amount of capital

trade union: an organisation of workers that negotiates with employers on behalf of its members

transfer earnings: the minimum payment required to keep a factor of production in its present use

transition economies: a set of economies that are in the process of transition from central planning to being mixed economies

unemployment: results when people seeking work at the going wage cannot find a job

urbanisation: process whereby an increasing proportion of the population come to live in cities

variable cost: a component of a firm's costs that varies with the level of output

vertical merger: a merger between two firms in the same industry, but at different stages of the production process

visible trade: trade in goods

voluntary export restraint (VER): an agreement by a country to limit its exports to another country to a given quantity

voluntary unemployment: situation arising when an individual chooses not to accept a job at the going wage rate

World Bank: multilateral organisation that provides financing for long-term development projects

World Trade Organisation (WTO): a multilateral body responsible for overseeing the conduct of international trade

X-inefficiency: situation arising when a firm is not operating at minimum cost, perhaps because of organisational slack

Index

A

absolute advantage 14
absolute poverty 354, 384
aggregate demand 155, 161, 165
aggregate supply 162, 166, 181, 520
agricultural markets 43, 113, 418
agriculture 383, 409
Akerlof, George 109
allocative efficiency 71, 73, 236, 242, 250, 322
arbitrage 253
Areeda–Turner principle 268
assistance 436
asymmetric information 289, 334, 409
automatic stabilisers 150, 196, 522
average cost 72

B

balance of payments 151–154, 175, 472, 486, 518
balance of payments current account 194
barriers to entry 87, 118, 238, 248
Baumol, William 265, 270
bilateral monopoly 326
biodiversity 397
Bretton Woods 442, 490
buffer stock 114

C

CAP see Common Agricultural Policy
capital 4, 183, 389
capital account 473, 476
capitalism 56
capital productivity 182
cartel 259
centrally planned economy 4, 57
ceteris paribus 21
China 57, 62, 183, 184, 398
circular flow of income, expenditure and output 147
claimant count of unemployment 145
closed shop 321
Coase, Ronald 125
cobweb model 114
coincident indicators 150
collusion 261, 277
commodity markets 43, 420
Common Agricultural Policy (CAP) 116, 463
comparative advantage 13, 345, 419, 459
comparative static analysis 39, 51, 165, 309
competition 202
Competition Commission 75, 86, 119, 279
competition policy 119, Chapter 20
competitiveness 477
complements 24
concentration 245, 277
concentration ratio 246
congestion charge 97
conspicuous consumption 23
constant returns to scale 83
consumer price index 142
consumer surplus 52, 88, 128, 243
consumption 156, 158
consumption externality 92
contestability 276
contestable markets 270
Corruption Perception Index 416
cost–benefit analysis 100, 317
cost efficiency 72
cost of living 142
cost-plus pricing 266
cost-push inflation 169
costs of inflation 170
Cournot, Antoine Augustin 257
cross-price elasticity of demand 36
crowding out 522
current account of the balance of payments 151, 175, 473, 474
customs union 465

D

deadweight loss 88, 92, 129, 243
demand 20
demand curve 22, 51
demand-deficient unemployment 173, 332
demand for labour 301
demand for money 526
demand-pull inflation 170
demerit good 124, 129
demographics 345
demographic transition 405
depreciation 183
derived demand 45, 301
devaluation 492-493
differential earnings 315
diminishing returns to labour 301
direct taxes 359, 524
discrimination 320
diseconomies of scale 80
disposable income 157
division of labour 13, 79
Doha Development Agenda 466
Domar, Evsey 389
dominant strategy 258

E

economic cycle 525
economic growth 9, 177, Chapter 14, 194, 387, 519
economic policy 517
economic rent 313
economies of scale 78, 81, 87, 119, 241, 402
economies of scope 82
education 98, 201, 316, 372, 394
efficiency 70
efficiency wage 334, 435
elasticity of demand for labour 305
entrepreneurship 4
entry deterrence 271
environment 95, 99, 177, 189, 373, 397, 519
equity 76, 110
European Monetary System (EMS) 495, 509
European Single Market 506
European Union Chapter 34
euro single currency area 509
excess burden 129
exchange rate 46, 154, 175, 187, 477, 487, 489, 496
Exchange Rate Mechanism (ERM) 495
expenditure 156
export-led growth 402
export promotion 422
exports 159, 458, 482
external economies of scale 81
externality 75, Chapter 8, 119, 177, 185, 398, 427

F

factors of production 4, 182
financial account 151, 473, 476
firm 212
fiscal deficit 522
fiscal policy 194, 196, 519, 522
fixed costs 79
fixed exchange rate system 490
floating exchange rate system 495
foreign direct investment (FDI) 393, 432, 467, 485, 515
foreign exchange market 46
free market economy 51
free-rider problem 104
free trade area 465
frictional unemployment 173, 332
Friedman, Milton 157
full employment 164, 172, 181, 194, 518
futures market 499

G

game theory 257
GDP 9, 147, 148, 156, 181, 185, 375
GDP deflator 148
General Agreement on Tariffs and Trade (GATT) 456
Giffen good 24
Giffen, Sir Robert 24
Gini index 353, 379
globalisation 62, 216, 454
global market 277
global warming 122
Golden Rule of fiscal policy 525
government budget 195
government expenditure 156, 159, 195, 522
government failure 126
Grameen Bank 411
Green Revolution 413

H

Harrod, Roy 389
Harrod–Domar model 389, 431, 433
Harsanyi, John 257
Health and Safety 330
healthcare 97
HIPC Initiative 443
HIV/AIDS 184, 372, 383, 414
housing market 44, 127
human capital 184, 201, 392, 394
Human Development Index 379
hyperinflation 171
hypothetical monopoly test 280

I

ILO unemployment rate 146
imperfect competition 75
imports 159, 458, 482
import substitution 422
incidence of a tax 48
income elasticity of demand 36
index numbers 141
indirect taxes 47, 361, 524
industrialisation 425
inequality 178, 186, 350, 377, 379
inferior goods 23
inflation 142-143, 169, 517, 530
inflation target 171, 199, 487
influences on the price elasticity of demand 34
informal sector 186
information failure 76
infrastructure 396
insider–outsider 323
internal economies of scale 81
international debt 393, 440
International Monetary Fund 442
international trade 15, 413, 483
investment 156, 159, 183, 201, 390
invisible hand 56
involuntary unemployment 174

J

J-curve effect 493

K

Keynes, John Maynard 156, 160, 442
Keynesian School 520
kinked demand curve 256, 266
Kuznets, Simon 379
Kuznets hypothesis 379

L

labour 4, 184
labour markets 45, 126, 202, Part 5
labour productivity 182
labour supply 307
labour supply in the UK 309
land 4, 409
law of comparative advantage 14
law of demand 21
leading indicators 150
learning by doing 84
Lewis, Sir Arthur 425
life-cycle hypothesis 157
limit pricing 269
long run 82
long-run average cost 82
long-run supply curve 235
Lorenz curve 351, 378
luxury goods 36

M

M0 527
M4 527
Maastricht Treaty 344, 509
macroeconomic equilibrium 164
macroeconomic policy Chapter 13
macroeconomics 10, 139
Malthus, Thomas 404
management 4
marginal consumer 52
marginal cost 72
marginal cost of labour 302
marginal physical product of labour 301
marginal productivity theory 302
marginal revenue product of labour 302
marginal social benefit 52
marginal tax rate 360
market dominance 86
market economy 4, 55
market failure 74, 519
market-friendly growth 393
markets 21
market structure Chapter 17, Chapter 18
Marshall–Lerner condition 494

Marx, Karl 57
mergers 118
merit goods 185
microeconomics 10
microfinance 411
Microsoft 75, 242
migration 426
Millennium Development Goals 371
minimum efficient scale 83
minimum wage 126, 174, 327
mixed economy 4, 58-59
models 6
Modigliani, Ando 157
Monetarist School 520
monetary base 527
monetary policy 198, 520, 526
Monetary Policy Committee (MPC) 199, 528
monetary transmission mechanism 527
money stock 170, 194
monopolistic competition 248
monopoly 86, 118, 238, 274
monopsony 285, 325
moral hazard 443
Morgenstern, Oskar 257
multinational corporations (MNCs) 216, 393, 432, 455, 467
multiplier 160, 195

N

NAPP 254
Nash, John 257
Nash equilibrium 259
natural monopoly 80, 85, 287
natural rate of unemployment 520, 532
negative production externality 91
New Deal 341
newly industrialised economies 402
NIMBY 124
nominal values 141
non-accelerating inflation rate of unemployment (NAIRU) 532
non-tariff barriers 424, 463
normal good 23

O

Office of Fair Trading 75, 86, 119, 254, 279
Ofgem 289
oligopoly 85, 255
opportunity cost 3, 6, 14, 56, 159, 224
overseas assistance 373, 393, 436

P

P&O 280
Pareto optimum 71
Pareto, Vilfredo 71
patent system 87, 241
pensions 347
perfect competition 231, 274, 302
permanent income hypothesis 157
Phillips, Bill 530
Phillips curve 531
polluter pays principle 119
pollution permit system 121
population growth 382, 404
population pyramid 345, 408
positive and normative analysis 10, 93
poverty 354, 371, 384
poverty line 354
Prebisch, Raul 421
predatory pricing 268
price discrimination 252
price elasticity of demand 48
price elasticity of supply 37
price leadership 262
price wars 266
pricing rules 264
principal–agent problem 226–227, 265, 288, 291, 409
Prisoners' Dilemma 257
privatised industries 287, 485
producer surplus 53, 88, 128
product differentiation 248
production possibility frontier 6, 14, 70, 180, 388
productive efficiency 71, 236, 242, 250
productivity 182, 480
progressive tax 360
prohibition 129
propensity to consume 157
property rights 96, 125
protectionism 460
public goods 76, 396
Public Sector Borrowing Requirement 196
public sector in the UK economy 59
public-sector net debt 526
purchasing power parity 496

Q

quota 461

R

real values 141
recession 149
regional policies 343
regressive tax 361
regulation 287
regulatory capture 289
relative poverty 354, 385
relevant market 279
rent controls 127
repo rate 199
research and development (R&D) 237, 276
retail price index 143
revaluation 492
Ricardo, David 12, 404
road pricing 123
RPI 144
RPIX 143

S

Safeway 283
sales tax 128
Samuelson, Paul 5
savings 389
Schumpeter, Joseph 237, 276
Selton, Reinhard 257
sharecropping 409
short run 82
short-run supply curve 233
Singer, Hans 421
single currency 509
Smith, Adam 12, 56
snob effect 23
Social Chapter 344
specialisation 13, 79
stagflation 532
standard of living 186
Stena 280
Structural Adjustment Programme (SAP) 397, 443
structural change 418
structural unemployment 173, 201, 332
structure–conduct–performance paradigm 274
subsidies 47-48, 117
substitutes 24
supply curve 26
supply-side policies 201, 520, 529
sustainable development 373, 399
Sweezy, Paul 256

T

tacit collusion 262
target 143
tariff 423, 460
technical efficiency 72
technology 79
terms of trade 419, 480
tiger economies 391, 396, 399, 401, 425
total factor productivity 182
tourism 99, 428
trade 419, 456
trade unions 320, 326, 342
transfer earnings 313
transition economies 61
transport 97

U

Uganda 443-444
unemployment 145, 172, 322, 332, 336, 518, 530
unemployment benefit 174, 203
urbanisation 426

V

value added tax 361
variable costs 79
Veblen, Thorstein 23
voluntary export restraints 461
voluntary unemployment 174
von Hayek, Friedrich 237
von Neumann, John 257

W

Working Time Directive 330
World Bank 442
World Trade Organisation (WTO) 442, 456, 466

X

X-inefficiency 251, 485